GREEK COINS
AND THEIR VALUES

By

DAVID R. SEAR

Volume I

EUROPE

Coins of Spain, Gaul, Italy, Sicily, the Balkan lands, Greece, the Cyclades and Crete; also the Celtic issues of Western and Central Europe.

London

A CATALOGUE OF GREEK COINS by G. ASKEW, 1951
GREEK COINS AND THEIR VALUES by H. A. SEABY and J. KOZOLUBSKI
First Edition 1959
Second Edition (by H. A. SEABY) 1966
Second Edition (*revised prices*) 1975

GREEK COINS AND THEIR VALUES (Volume I: Europe) by David R. Sear, 1978
Volume II: Asia and North Africa (in preparation)

Photographs by P. Frank Purvey

© SEABY PUBLICATIONS LTD., 1978

Distributed by B. A. Seaby Ltd.,
11 Margaret St., London, W1N 8AT

ISBN 0 900652 46 2

Printed in England by ROBERT STOCKWELL LTD., LONDON, SE1 1YP

CONTENTS

PREFACE

Nearly two decades have elapsed since the last major revision of Seaby's Greek coin catalogue was undertaken by H. A. Seaby and J. Kozolubski in 1959. This work, which I myself assisted in compiling, proved immensely popular with collectors in the U.K. and overseas, and went through several editions. I am glad to have had the opportunity of preparing the successor to this catalogue and hope that it will be equally well received by classical numismatists everywhere.

The precise chronology of much of the ancient Greek coinage remains controversial, even after a century of intense study. Recently, argument has centred on the date of the famous "Demareteion" dekadrachm of Syracuse, with all its implications for the subsequent chronology of the 5th Century Sicilian coinage. Similarly, there is dispute over the Athens dekadrachm. Even in the late Hellenistic period there are problems with the exact dating of the vast "new style" issues of the Athenian mint, despite the masterly treatment of the subject by Miss Margaret Thompson.

The evidence of coin hoards, which is now being interpreted with great skill by the leading scholars of Greek numismatics, is forcing us to make many adjustments to the traditionally accepted dates for the introduction and spread of coinage in the ancient world. The message of every archaic hoard analysed would seem to be the same—the first Greek coins are not as early as we used to think. Little, if any, coinage was produced before the last quarter of the 7th Century B.C.; and the first European issues—those of Aigina—are probably no earlier than *circa* 550 B.C., a century and a half later than the traditional date for their introduction. This down-dating has had a significant effect on our view of the archaic period of Greek coinage. We now see it as little more than a century of exciting expansion and development, most of it, indeed, compressed into just seven decades (550-480 B.C.). This is very different from the view held by previous generations of numismatists, who saw the archaic Greek coinage as something which evolved quite gradually over more than two hundred years.

In preparing this new catalogue I have tried to incorporate most of the current views on chronology, attribution, and interpretation of types which are the result of the immense amount of research undertaken over the past few decades by scholars in Europe and America. The scope of the listing has also been enlarged to include representative examples of each period of issue for every mint. Bronze coins have received particular attention, as so many collectors these days have to specialize in coins at the lower end of the price scale. For this reason, and also because they are generally more difficult to date with precision than the silver issues, I have listed the bronze coins separately under each mint heading. In the cases of Italy and Sicily the lists of bronzes are entirely separate from the precious-metal issues. Once again this is for the convenience of collectors, many of whom specialize in the bronze coins of the western mints, where token money originated.

Another new feature of this work is the incorporation of photographs in the text. The advantages of having description and illustration printed together on the same page are obvious, and the popularity of *Byzantine Coins and Their Values*, published three years ago, has encouraged us to adopt the same arrangement in the case of the present catalogue. The illustrations are exceedingly numerous and should add greatly to the value of the book as an aid to identifying Greek coins.

In order to carry out these improvements the size of the work has had to be increased to the point where it is no longer feasible to publish it in a single volume. Accordingly, the decision has been taken to divide it into two parts—EUROPE, and ASIA & NORTH AFRICA. Volume I includes Greek coins of Spain and Gaul, Italy, Sicily, the Balkans, Greece, the Cyclades and Crete, together with Celtic issues of western Europe (including Britain) and the Danubian area. Volume II, to be published later, will deal with the coins of the Asiatic Greeks (the earliest coin-issuing states), the Persian Empire, the Hellenistic Kingdoms and subsequent autonomous issues, Palestine, North Africa and Carthage. When complete, this two-volume work should prove to be an invaluable aid to the collector, in identifying and valuing the coins in his collection, and to the student of Greek art and coinage, to whom it will present a fully illustrated documentation of the development of numismatic art in every state of the Greek world.

The various forms of spelling for many ancient place names have occasioned a certain amount of confusion amongst collectors. The standard practice in the past, for most popular publications, has been the adoption of the later, Roman, form rather than the original Greek name. Thus, Thourioi is more often referred to as Thurium, Akragas as Agrigentum and Taras as Tarentum. Recently, the trend has been to revert to the original spellings in books dealing specifically with Greek coins, and collectors who have read G. K. Jenkins' excellent

Ancient Greek Coins, published in 1972, will already be aware of this.   I have followed this practice in the present publication and feel sure that collectors will soon familiarize themselves with the different spellings and forms of place names.   In many cases I have also given the later form, in parentheses, following the mint-heading.   Inevitably, of course, I have not been able to achieve total uniformity in this.   Athens, for example, is so well known to English-speaking people under this modern version of its name that it would have been foolish to start calling it "Athenai" in this catalogue.   And there are other lesser known instances where the precise original form of the name would be unacceptable for one reason or another.   Nevertheless, I feel that I have followed the right path in endeavouring to get back to the original Greek names in a catalogue which is devoted to Greek coinage.

A considerable amount of research has gone into the estimation of values as quoted in this catalogue.   However, in the present situation of uncertain currencies and considerable market fluctuations it must be borne in mind that the valuations here expressed can only be taken as an approximate guide, especially those quoted for rarities, in which the Greek series abounds. The prices given are for specimens in an average state of preservation—*VF* in the case of gold, electrum and silver, *F* in the case of billon and bronze.   Poorly preserved examples are, of course, worth much less than the values quoted; unusually well-preserved coins and those of better than average style are worth substantially more.

Almost all the coins illustrated in this catalogue are from the National Collection, and I should like to express my deep gratitude to G. K. Jenkins, Keeper, and M. J. Price, Assistant Keeper, of the Department of Coins and Medals, British Museum, for the facilities which they so readily granted to Frank Purvey and myself.   With one of the finest collections of Greek coins in the world at our disposal we were able, with the minimum of difficulty, to assemble and photograph a superb selection of pieces, adding immeasurably to the value of the catalogue as a work of reference.   Frank Purvey's photographs are of his usual matchless standard, and I should also like to thank him for all the help and encouragement which he has given me in the preparation of this work.

Little Melton, Norfolk.   DAVID R. SEAR
April, 1978

ON COLLECTING GREEK COINS

Many potential collectors of this series might hesitate these days to embark on a hobby which, on the face of it, appears to be beyond their financial resources. Greek coins have so much to offer the collector that I feel it would be a pity for him to dismiss them, in favour of something less interesting but less costly, without going a little further into the subject.

Greek numismatics spans a period of no less than nine centuries, though for the last three hundred years Greek coins were merely a secondary 'local currency' in the eastern half of the Roman Empire. And for several centuries before this Rome had exerted a strong political influence over most of the Greek world. From their origins, then, shortly before 600 B.C. to the time of the establishment of the Roman Empire, Greek coins underwent six centuries of development and change, and this is the period covered by *Greek Coins and Their Values*. These six centuries have bequeathed to us a truly remarkable array of coins, issues of a multitude of independent city-states as well as of the great kingdoms of the Hellenistic age. The rise and fall of tyrants and of whole communities are faithfully chronicled in the numismatic record which has come down to us, providing fertile ground for the growth of a collection which can be a source of endless interest and satisfaction to its owner. Such a collection need not be large, as long as the coins are carefully selected, and need not be very costly; though, of course, those fortunate few with large sums to invest will, by specializing in Greek coins, have the opportunity of possessing some of the most beautiful numismatic creations which mankind has ever produced.

It must be stated that many of the silver issues will be beyond the price range of the majority of collectors. The products of tiny city states of limited resources, and only circulating within a small area, these coins are often of great beauty and command prices commensurate with their rarity. Of course there are many exceptions to this—cities like Athens and powerful kingdoms such as Macedon, Syria and Egypt—which were prosperous enough to issue vast quantities of silver money. Examples of these, even the collector of quite modest means should be able to acquire. But a really exciting field is opened up by the masses of token bronze currency put into circulation by the Greeks. Originating in Sicily in the mid-5th Century B.C., bronze coins were not widely adopted until the first half of the 4th Century, but thereafter quickly replaced the inconveniently small fractional denominations in silver. Greek bronze coins can be costly in the highest grades of preservation, but they are seldom seen in this state and if the collector does not set himself an unrealistically high standard he should be able to assemble a really worthwhile collection at quite modest cost. The problem of counterfeit coins is also largely avoided by the collector who specializes in bronzes, which brings us to another important topic.

Forgery of Greek coins, particularly of the most spectacular types in gold and silver, has been going on for hundreds of years, but the most dangerous copies have been produced in the 19th and 20th Centuries. It is not possible, in a brief introduction such as this, to go deeply into the question of recognition of forgeries. The most obvious things to look for are indications of casting (air-bubbles on the surface, filing on the edge) and signs that the piece may be a modern electrotype copy (traces of the joining together of the two halves of the coin round the edge). The exact weight is also of importance, as Greek gold and silver coins conform to quite strict standards and many forgeries do not fall within the correct range of weights. The recognition of die-struck forgeries, however, requires a degree of experience and expertise which few collectors possess, and for this reason it cannot be too strongly emphasized that one should never purchase expensive Greek gold and silver coins from a dubious source. Some forgeries are so good that they have been known to pass undetected through the hands even of experienced numismatists. But if coins are purchased from a reputable dealer one will always have the assurance that if a piece is proved to be false it will be taken back and your money refunded without question.

Before commencing the formation of a collection one would be well advised to read an authoritative book covering all aspects of ancient Greek coinage. Having obtained a good grounding in the subject it will be easier to plan the development of a collection, and one may be saved the costly error of purchasing pieces not really required. The books recommended in the previous *Greek Coins and Their Values* have been somewhat outdated by recent developments in the study of Greek coins, so works published within the past decade are to be preferred. My recommendation would be G. K. Jenkins' *Ancient Greek Coins* published in 1972 by Barrie and Jenkins in the series *The World of Numismatics*. Scholarship of the highest calibre combined with superb illustrations, many in full colour, make this an invaluable volume to anyone with an interest in Greek numismatics, and the beginner will find the text easy to follow.

A BRIEF ACCOUNT OF GREEK HISTORY AND THE DEVELOPMENT OF COINAGE

For several centuries prior to the invention of coined money the Greeks, then emerging from the dark ages following the destruction of Mycenaean civilization, had been engaged in colonization. The pressures created by an expanding population, together with the desire to foster trade led to the establishment of settlements far from the mother cities. Southern Italy and Sicily, and the northern coastline of the Aegean were areas particularly popular with the settlers, but colonies were also established in Spain, southern Gaul, north Africa and along the Black Sea coastline.

Prior to the advent of coinage, then, the Greeks were already widely scattered throughout much of the Mediterranean world, so it is hardly surprising that the new invention, once established, spread so rapidly over a large area. It is doubtful if we shall ever know the precise origin of the first coins but we can feel reasonably sure that this remarkable development occurred in the latter part of the 7th Century B.C., in western Asia Minor (modern Turkey). Whether it was the Ionian Greeks or their eastern neighbours, the Lydians, who made the first crude attempts at coinage it is impossible to say. But examples of these primitive pieces—globules of electrum without obverse or reverse design—have been found at the Ionian city of Ephesos; whilst the metal of which they are composed occurs as a natural alloy in the silt of the river which passes through the Lydian capital of Sardis.

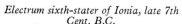

Electrum sixth-stater of Ionia, late 7th Cent. B.C.   *Silver stater of Aigina, circa 530 B.C.*

In 560 B.C. Kroisos (Croesus) came to the Lydian throne. His reign was significant for the development of coinage, as he was responsible for the introduction of the first bimetallic currency—coins struck in both gold and silver, instead of the alloy electrum alone. This provided a much greater range of denominations and is evidence of the important part coinage was already playing in the economic life of the Lydian kingdom. In 546 B.C. Kroisos was defeated by Cyrus, King of the Medes and Persians. The Lydian kingdom ceased to exist and the Greek cities of Asia Minor were obliged to acknowledge Persian suzerainty. This was the beginning of the long struggle between Greeks and Persians which culminated in Alexander's epic eastern campaign more than two centuries later.

The second half of the 6th Century witnessed the westward expansion of coinage from its origins in Asia Minor. Probably the first European city to issue coins was Aigina, situated on an island between Attica and eastern Peloponnese. Soon after followed the earliest coins of mints such as Athens, Corinth and the Euboian cities of Chalkis and Eretria. All of these mints were active from the middle of the century, or within the following decade. From these beginnings originated two of the important weight-standards to which many later Greek coinages adhered. The Aiginetic standard, based on a silver didrachm-stater of about 12 grams, became very widespread in central Greece, Peloponnesos and the Aegean islands, including Crete. The Attic weight, with a didrachm of about 8.5 grams and, later, a tetradrachm of 17 grams, was to become the principal standard of a later period, following Athens' domination of the Aegean world throughout the latter part of the 5th Century. In the west the closing decades of the 6th Century also saw much activity in coin production at the colonies in southern Italy and in Sicily. A unique type of coin production was used at some of the Italian mints, in which the obverse type was 'mirrored' on the reverse, though incuse instead of in relief. This peculiar technique was abandoned in the early part of the 5th Century.

Silver stater of Poseidonia in Italy,
circa 530 B.C.

Silver siglos of Darius I of Persia,
circa 500 B.C.

The conflict between Greeks and Persians which had been threatening in the closing decades of the 6th Century, suddenly erupted in 499 B.C. with the revolt of the Ionian cities of Asia Minor against Persian domination. Despite Athenian help the rebellion collapsed in 494 B.C., but there was only a short respite before hostilities recommenced. This time (490 B.C.) Darius of Persia sent a naval expedition against Athens, but after initial successes the Persian forces were decisively beaten at the battle of Marathon and were later obliged to return home. Darius died five years later and his son and successor, Xerxes, resolved to avenge the Persian humiliation by a full-scale invasion of Greece. This eventually took place in 480 B.C., after much preparation, when an immense Persian army crossed the Hellespont and advanced through Thrace and Macedon into Greece, supported by a large fleet. Against all the odds the Greeks first checked the enemy at Thermopylai, then destroyed the Persian fleet at the battle of Salamis and, finally (in 479 B.C.), defeated the invading army at Plataia. This brought the conflict to an end and the Persians never again intervened directly in the affairs of mainland Greece.

These momentous events were to have far-reaching effects on the subsequent history of Greece. Athens emerged as the 'saviour of the Greeks' and capitalized on this to extend her influence throughout the Aegean world. The Confederacy of Delos, constituted soon after the victory over the Persians, was ostensibly an Athenian-led alliance of independent maritime states, dedicated to freeing the Ionian cities of Asia Minor from the Persian yoke. In reality, it quickly developed into an Athenian maritime empire, the annual contributions of the member-states being paid to Athens, making her the richest and most powerful state in mainland Greece.

Silver tetradrachm of Athens,
circa 485 B.C.

Electrum stater of Kyzikos,
circa 430 B.C.

In the decades following the Persian wars Greek coinage was entering a transitional stage which was to see the stiff and unrealistic style of the early (archaic) period gradually give way to the more elegant representations of the classical era. Proper reverse types were now being employed by most mints in preference to the simple incuse squares which had typified most archaic issues. Silver was the primary metal used for coin production, right down to the tiniest denominations which were inconveniently small to use. These were not generally replaced by token bronze coinage until the first half of the following century (after 400 B.C.). In Asia Minor, however, electrum—the metal of the earliest coins—was still extensively employed by important mints such as Kyzikos, Phokaia and Mytilene (the chief city of the island of Lesbos). As the power of Athens grew she attempted to place restrictions on the freedom of other states to issue silver coins, culminating in the enigmatic 'Coinage Decree' of *circa* 449 B.C. promulgated by Perikles, the author of Athenian imperialism. This measure brought about the severe curtailment of issues from many mints during the sixth and seventh decades of the century. But with the outbreak of the Peloponnesian War, in 431 B.C., Athens' iron grip was relaxed.

Silver tetradrachm of Syracuse by the artist Kimon, circa 410 B.C.

The West (south Italy and Sicily) was relatively unaffected by these events and developments in Greece.   Here, at about the same time as the Persian defeat, another great enemy of the Greeks—the Carthaginians—suffered humiliation at the hands of Gelon, tyrant of Syracuse, when they attacked the Sicilian colonies.   Thereafter Syracuse became the dominant Greek state in the West, and the artists producing the dies for her coinage were in the forefront of a remarkable advance in numismatic art.   The Greek coinage of Sicily in the closing decades of the 5th Century was to reach heights of artistic brilliance which were unmatched elsewhere and which served as an inspiration to the die-engravers of later periods.   Notable amongst the beautiful creations of this period are the noble dekadrachms by the engravers Euainetos and Kimon, and also the latter's superb rendering of the facing female head in his masterpiece—the Arethusa head—on a Syracusan tetradrachm.   Many of the Greek mints in Sicily participated in this blossoming of numismatic art, but the whole movement was brought to an abrupt end by the Carthaginian invasions at the end of the century (commencing 409 B.C.).

Silver tetradrachm of Athens,
circa 430 B.C.

Athenian domination of the Aegean world was not destined to last beyond the closing years of this century.   The Athenian mint, with its plentiful supplies of silver from the mines of Laurion, had produced prodigious quantities of tetradrachms from *circa* 449 B.C.   Much of this wealth was used to finance grandiose building schemes in the city, such as the Parthenon, but after 431 B.C. ever-increasing sums were required to defray the costs of war.   The great Peloponnesian War was sparked-off by an incident at the Boeotian city of Plataia.   It dragged on, intermittently, for the next twenty-seven years and was, in essence, a struggle for supremacy between the old arch-enemies, Athens and Sparta.   Finally, in 404 B.C., Athens capitulated. She was financially and politically ruined, and although she made a remarkable recovery from this disaster in the first half of the following century, she never again achieved the pre-eminence which she had enjoyed during the age of Perikles.   Her mantle now passed to the Spartans who soon showed themselves to be too insular to establish and maintain a position of leadership amongst the Greek states.   The first half of the 4th Century was a period of seemingly interminable strife, but despite the political confusion, these years saw the production of some of the most beautiful coins in the Greek series.   Classical art had now reached a peak from which it was gradually to decline.

Silver tetradrachm of the Chalkidian League,
circa 385 B.C.

These were also troubled years in the West. The Carthaginians had invaded Sicily and attacked many of the Greek cities at the end of the 5th Century. Dionysios, the powerful ruler of Syracuse, conducted a long and inconclusive war against the invaders which resulted in a division of the island between Greeks and Carthaginians. Dionysios also adopted an aggressive policy in southern Italy in order to extend the influence of Syracuse. But two great powers were beginning to arise on the fringes of the Greek world. In the north, the Kingdom of Macedon was emerging from a period of confusion, led by its brilliant young ruler Philip II (359-336 B.C.). Philip's ambitions knew no bounds, and he and his son, Alexander the Great, transformed the political face of the ancient world in less than three decades. In the west, however, another power was stirring; one which was destined, ultimately, to engulf the whole of the Mediterranean basin and reduce all the Greek lands to provincial status. That power was Rome.

Gold stater of Philip II of Macedon
(359-336 B.C.)

Silver tetradrachm of Amphipolis,
circa 380 B.C.

In 357 B.C. Philip captured Amphipolis, an Athenian colony near the rich silver-mining area of Mt. Pangaion in eastern Macedon. Nine years later he destroyed Olynthos, the capital city of the Greek colonies forming the Chalkidian League. In 338 B.C., at the battle of Chaeronea, the combined forces of Athens and Thebes were defeated by Philip, who was now acknowledged as the master of Greece. At a congress of Greek states, held at Corinth, Philip was chosen to lead an attack on the Persian Empire, in order to liberate the Greek cities of Asia Minor. Preparations for this expedition were already far advanced when, in 336 B.C., Philip was assassinated and was succeeded on the Macedonian throne by his son, Alexander, known to posterity as 'the Great.' The remarkable series of military campaigns, by which Alexander destroyed the Persian power and established a Greek empire in its place, need not be described in detail here. Suffice it to say that his thirteen-year reign was a turning-point in Greek history. The age of the city-states was over; its place being taken by an era marked by the dominance of great Kingdoms, such as the Ptolemaic in Egypt and the Seleukid in Syria and the east. With the eventual weakening and disintegration of these kingdoms came the spread of Roman power in the eastern Mediterranean.

Silver stater of Olympia, circa 360 B.C.

These great political changes were reflected in the coinage. As already mentioned, the first half of the 4th Century B.C., during which many of the city-states enjoyed their final period of autonomy, produced some of the artistic masterpieces of the Greek coinage. Noteworthy are the magnificent tetradrachms of Amphipolis with facing head of Apollo; those of Olynthos, in the name of the Chalkidians, with reverse type lyre; some of the staters issued at Olympia by the Eleans, with noble heads of Zeus and his consort Hera; and the fine staters of the Arkadians depicting, on the reverse, Pan seated upon a rock. Some of the earlier issues of Philip II of Macedon are also of a high artistic standard; but as the territorial extent of Philip's realm was extended and the coinage was produced in ever-increasing quantities, so the quality of the workmanship declined. This is particularly noticeable in the coins issued after his death, though still in the name of Philip. Alexander's money was an imperial coinage in every sense, unlike anything which the Greek world had seen before, with the possible exception of the Athenian tetradrachms of the Periklean age. But it set the pattern for centuries to come—mass produced regal issues largely replacing autonomous coins of individual cities. Inevitably this brought about a decline in artistic standards. When many of the cities regained a degree of independence, in the 2nd Century B.C., the process had gone too far to be reversed. Some individual pieces amongst the autonomous coins of the late Hellenistic age might be called attractive rather than beautiful.

Silver tetradrachm of Alexander the Great
(336-323 B.C.)

Gold stater of Philip III Arrhidaeus
(323-317 B.C.)

On the death of Alexander at Babylon (June, 323 B.C.) his vast realm, stretching from Macedon to India, became the object of endless disputes between his generals. These 'wars of the Diadochi' ultimately led to the formation of a number of independent kingdoms, though in the early years the appearance of unity was maintained. Officially, Alexander was succeeded by his infant son, Alexander IV, and by an idiot-brother of the great king, called Arrhidaeus, now named Philip (III). During the minority of the boy-kings the responsibility for administering the huge empire rested with men such as Perdikkas, Antipater, Antigonos the One-eyed, Ptolemy, Seleukos and Lysimachos. These were the true successors of Alexander and some of them went on to found dynasties which endured for many generations. The unfortunate Alexander IV and Philip III met violent ends; both were dead within twelve years of Alexander the Great's decease.

Silver tetradrachm of Ptolemy I of Egypt, circa 310-305 B.C.

Other than the original Kingdom of Macedon, the two great realms to emerge from these struggles were the Kingdom of Egypt, founded by Ptolemy, and the dominions of Seleukos, commonly known as the Seleukid Empire, comprising the greater part of Alexander's conquests. About the middle of the 3rd Century B.C. the Seleukid Empire was further divided when the eastern provinces of Baktria and Parthia each achieved independence; the latter destined to survive for nearly five centuries and to become the troublesome eastern neighbour of the Roman Empire. Meanwhile, in the west the power of Rome was rapidly growing. Following her victory over Carthage in the First Punic War (241 B.C.) Rome acquired her first province—Sicily—and to this was added Spain in the closing years of the century. At about the same time came the first conflict with the Macedonian Kingdom, now ruled by the energetic Philip V

Silver tetradrachm of Philip V of Macedon (221-179 B.C.)

221-179 B.C.). In 197 B.C., at the battle of Kynoskephalai, the Romans inflicted a heavy defeat on Philip. The following year the Roman general Flamininus made his celebrated proclamation of the 'Freedom of Greece' at the Isthmian Games. But in reality Greece had merely become subject to a new and more powerful master. The once proud Macedonian Kingdom lingered on for three decades more, under Philip V and his son Perseus, but was finally destroyed by the Romans in 168 B.C. Macedonia was divided into four republics and in 146 B.C. was reduced to provincial status.

Silver tetradrachm of Antiochos the Great (223-187 B.C.)

Roman conflict with another of the great Hellenistic monarchies, the Seleukid, came soon after the Macedonian defeat at Kynoskephalai. Antiochos III, the Great (223-187 B.C.), a bitter opponent of Rome, invaded Greece in 192 B.C. at the invitation of the Aitolians. Defeated at Thermopylai, Antiochos fled back to Asia Minor. The Romans relentlessly followed him there and in 190 B.C., at the battle of Magnesia (Caria), the power of the Seleukids was broken. Most of their possessions in Asia Minor were given to King Eumenes of Pergamon, Rome's ally during the campaign. The Seleukid Kingdom, now restricted to Syria and the surrounding area, maintained a precarious existence for more than a century. It finally succumbed to Pompey the Great in 64 B.C. The other great Hellenistic Kingdom, that of Egypt, was the furthest removed, geographically, from Rome's eastward advance. But Roman supremacy in the eastern Mediterranean from the early part of the 2nd Century necessitated the maintenance of friendly relations on the part of the Greek rulers of Egypt. This policy succeeded in maintaining the existence of the Ptolemaic Kingdom longer than that of any of the other

Silver tetradrachm of Cleopatra VII of Egypt, Askalon mint, 30 B.C.

Hellenistic states. Rome did not intervene directly in Egyptian affairs until 48 B.C., when Caesar, in pursuit of Pompey, came to Alexandria and found himself involved in a dynastic squabble between Queen Cleopatra and her brother Ptolemy. The story of Cleopatra, Caesar and Mark Antony is well known, and need not be recounted here. The upshot of the whole affair was the termination of the three hundred year-old Greek dynasty in Egypt. Henceforth the country became part of the Roman Empire and was administered as a private estate of the emperor.

"New style" silver tetradrachm of Athens, circa 157/6 B.C.

The coinage in this final phase of Greek history is varied, interesting, but mostly lacking in artistic merit. The Kingdoms of Macedon, Pergamon, Syria and Egypt produced a considerable volume of currency, mostly silver tetradrachms, in continuation of the traditions established by Alexander the Great and his successors. Side by side with these, and in ever increasing numbers as the power of the Kingdoms declined, came the autonomous issues of individual city-states and groups of cities which banded together for reasons of trade and defence. The large, spread flans, which had typified the tetradrachm coinage of the later Macedonian Kings, were adopted as the norm by many of the newly-liberated states in the 2nd Century B.C. Athens led the way with her vast and complex 'new style' coinage; whilst in Asia Minor mints such as Kyzikos, Lampsakos, Tenedos, Kyme, Myrina, Kolophon, Herakleia, Magnesia and Smyrna produced extensive issues of large and impressive tetra-drachms.   Also much in evidence were the coinages of the various confederacies and leagues, notably that of Thessaly in the north, with its handsome double victoriati, and the Achaean League in Peloponnesos, with its prodigious output of little hemidrachms issued by more than twenty mints.   As Rome's grip on Greece and the eastern Mediterranean area gradually tightened, so this last flowering of Greek coinage withered.   In the final stages of this process most of the Greek cities were deprived of the right to issue silver coinage and many ceased issuing altogether.

Silver double victoriatus of the Thessalian   Silver hemidrachm of the Achaean League,
League, 196-146 B.C.   Patrai mint, 196-146 B.C.

However, under the Roman Empire there was a revival of coinage at many of the Greek mints in the East, particularly in Asia Minor.   This 'Greek Imperial' coinage survived well into the 3rd Century A.D. until the political and economic collapse of the Roman Empire put an end to it.   Most, though not all, Greek Imperial issues bore an imperial portrait as the obverse type, whilst the reverse often featured an inscription or type of purely local interest— names of games and festivals, names of magistrates and provincial administrators, types picturing local architecture and statuary.   This final phase of Greek coinage, providing a wealth of detailed information on the eastern provinces of the Roman Empire, is not included in this present work.   Chronologically, the Greek Imperial series belongs to Roman times and will be given full treatment in a new catalogue to be published at some future date.

GREEK COIN TYPES

The designs appearing on ancient Greek coins are remarkably varied. Even the issues of one mint can exhibit a surprising diversity of types, but the underlying theme is nearly always religious.

Silver tetradrachm of Athens,
circa 510-505 B.C.

In the archaic period a design is normally found only on the obverse of the coin, produced by the lower (anvil) die. The reverse die, consisting merely of a square or oblong punch, was employed simply to hold the blank firmly in position during striking and to ensure that sufficient pressure was exerted to obtain a clear impression of the obverse die. Towards the end of the archaic period, as minting techniques improved, designs began appearing on the reverse dies too, though still within the incuse square, which now formed a frame for the type. Good examples of early 'double-sided' types are to be found at Athens (head of Athena/owl) and at Corinth (Pegasos/head of Athena), both types introduced at the end of the 6th Century.

Silver stater of Corinth, circa
500 B.C.

The choice of types in this formative period of Greek numismatics is of special interest. Traditions were being established which were to have a lasting influence on all subsequent coinage, right down to the present day. It was recognized, almost from the start, that here was a completely new medium for artistic expression, whilst the issuing authorities saw the opportunity of advertising the special characteristics of their states. The great diversity of deities in the Greek pantheon and the different interpretations of the roles played by each god and goddess provided scope for much local variation in religious beliefs. It is hardly surprising, therefore, that religious subjects were dominant in the earliest phases of coinage. In this way the individuality of each city could be proclaimed whilst the artist was given the greatest scope for his talents in representing the grandeur and mystery of the Olympians and their minions.

Gold third-stater of Metapontion,
late 4th Cent. B.C.

Silver tetradrachm of Ephesos,
mid-4th Cent. B.C.

Although religious types dominated the obverses and reverses of the Greek coinage down to the age of Alexander the Great, nevertheless there are many issues which do not fall within this category. The corn-ear of Metapontion, the crab of Akragas, the shield of Boeotia, the bee of Ephesos and the silphium plant of Kyrene are all emblematic types, being the official 'badges' of their states. Even here, however, there are religious connotations: the ear of corn is associated with Demeter and Persephone, whilst the bee was sacred to Artemis who was especially revered by the Ephesians. Other 'badges', such as the amphora, triskelis, knuckle-bone, wheel, etc., found on the 'Wappenmunzen' coinage of Athens, could be heraldic devices associated with the Athenian nobility of the 6th Century B.C. But, here again, a religious interpretation of the types seems more likely, with the various aspects of the cult of Athena providing the inspiration. Punning allusions to the names of cities are also not infrequently encountered. At Selinus, in Sicily, the leaf of the wild celery plant (*selinon*) is the constant obverse type of the city's archaic coinage, whilst the Aegean island of Melos similarly features the apple (*melon*). There are many such examples from mints in all parts of the Greek world.

Silver didrachm of Selinus, late 6th Cent. B.C.

With the establishment of the great Hellenistic Kingdoms in the period following the death of Alexander came a most important development in the evolution of Greek coin types—the beginnings of royal portraiture. The names of the Macedonian Kings had appeared regularly on the coinage from the first half of the 5th Century B.C., but no effigy had ever been produced by the die-engravers, not even of the great Alexander himself. Several of Alexander's successors, however, placed their portraits on their coins and once the tradition was established

Silver tetradrachm of Antiochos I of Syria (280-261 B.C.)

the heads of kings and queens became a regular feature of much of the Greek coinage from the 3rd to the 1st Century B.C.   Why it was that none of the powerful tyrants of the 5th and 4th Centuries ever seized this opportunity to proclaim their position and immortalize their features must remain something of a mystery.

The main series of portrait coins were produced by the Ptolemaic dynasty in Egypt, the Seleukids of Syria and the Antigonids of Macedon.   The Ptolemies, unfortunately, adopted the practice of reproducing the head of their founder, Ptolemy Soter, on most of their regular silver issues right down to the end of the dynasty.   This detracts greatly from the interest of the series (and also complicates the attributions of coins to particular reigns).   The Seleukid coinage, on the other hand, presents us with a portrait gallery of kings and queens spanning

Silver tetradrachm of Antimachos of Baktria (circa 171-160 B.C.)

more than two centuries.   Mention should also be made here of the splendid coinage produced by the Greek rulers of Baktria and India—once the easternmost part of the Seleukid realm, but independent from the mid-3rd Century B.C.   The remarkable series of portraits featured on these coins have the additional interest of being, in many cases, the only evidence for the very existence of these rulers.   The Antigonids of Macedon produced some fine portrait coins in

Silver tetradrachm of Demetrios Poliorketes of Macedon (294-287 B.C.)

the 3rd and 2nd Centuries, notably tetradrachms of Demetrios Poliorketes, Philip V and Perseus; whilst the Kingdoms of Pergamon, Bithynia and Pontus all made notable contributions to numismatic portraiture in the Hellenistic age.   On these regal issues religious symbolism was now mostly relegated to the reverses of the coins and each dynasty tended to adopt a tutelary deity.   The earlier Seleukids favoured Apollo, who is depicted seated on the omphalos of Delphi on many of the 3rd Century silver and bronze coins.   An eagle standing upon a thunderbolt, both symbolic of Zeus, is the constant reverse design for the Ptolemaic coinage in Egypt, and the bearded head of the god himself regularly occupies the obverse of the bronze denominations.

Silver tetradrachm of Mithradates III of Pontos (circa 220-185 B.C.)

In conclusion, there follows a list of some of the principal deities appearing as Greek coin types, with explanatory notes relating to their origins and functions. This list is largely the work of Lieut.-Col. J. Kozolubski and first appeared in the 1959 edition of this catalogue. The names in parentheses are the equivalent Roman deities.

Zeus Ammon on a silver tetradrachm of Kyrene, circa 360 B.C.

Ammon. Originally a Libyan divinity, probably protecting and leading the flocks, Ammon was later introduced into Egypt and Greece, where he was identified with Zeus. The head of Zeus Ammon is represented on Egyptian coins as a bearded man, diademed and with a ram's horn at the temple (Ammon's horn), the ram being sacred to him.

Aphrodite on a silver stater of Aphrodisias, circa 380 B.C.

Aphrodite (Venus). One of the twelve great Olympian divinities, Aphrodite was goddess of love and beauty. She was believed to have been created from the foam of the sea, hence she sometimes appears on coins with a sea-horse or dolphin. Others of her attributes are the myrtle, rose, apple, poppy; and doves, swans and sparrows were sacred to her. She is represented on coins nude, semi-nude or dressed and crowned, often accompanied by Eros, her child attendant. The apple she sometimes holds in her hand is the prize awarded her by Paris in the contest with Hera and Athena on Mount Ida.

Apollo with tripod on a silver tetradrachm of Seleukos II (246-226 B.C.)

Apollo. He was the sun-god, one of the great gods of the Greeks, and was the son of
Zeus and Leto; he was also the god of prophecy, of song, music and the arts, and protector of
flocks and herds. He punished and destroyed the wicked and overbearing, but afforded help
to men in distress by warding off evil. He exercised his power of prophecy through various
oracles, of which that at Delphi was the most important. The head of Apollo and his attribute
the lyre are common types on early Greek coinage.

Ares (Mars). God of war and another of the great Olympian deities, Ares was the son
of Zeus and Hera. He loved war for its own sake and often changed sides in assisting one or
the other combatant parties, but he could be worsted in battle and even be wounded by mortals.
His helmeted head, beardless or bearded, appears on many coins and his full-length figure is
sometimes depicted helmeted but naked, or wearing a cuirass, and holding shield, spear or
trophy. He is sometimes shown in the company of Aphrodite, whose lover he was.

Artemis and stag on a silver octobol of Ephesos, circa 270 B.C.

Artemis (Diana). One of the great divinities and sister of Apollo, Artemis was the
deity of the chase, goddess of the Moon, and protectress of the young. In Ionia, and in
particular as goddess of the famous temple of Ephesos, she took over the fructifying and
all-nourishing powers of nature from an older Asiatic divinity whom the Greeks, who settled
in that area, renamed Artemis. The coin types representing Artemis are very varied for she is
represented as a huntress with bow and arrow, running with a hound or killing a stag. As
Artemis Tauropolos she is portrayed riding a bull holding a veil over her head. Yet another
type is the cultus-statue of the Ephesian Artemis, standing facing, and she is also shown
carrying one or two torches.

Asklepios (Aesculapius). God of medicine and healing, he is shown as a man of mature
years, leaning on a staff about which a serpent is entwined. Sometimes the boy Telesphoros,
the personification of the genius of recovery, stands by his side. Serpents, symbols of prudence
and renovation, were sacred to Asklepios for they were believed to have the power of guarding
wells and discovering healing herbs.

Athena with Nike on a silver stater of Aphrodisias, circa 380 B.C.

Athena (Minerva). Surnamed Pallas, and sometimes known by this name alone, Athena was goddess of wisdom, patroness of agriculture, industry and the arts. She guided men through the dangers of war, where victory was gained by prudence, courage and perseverance. Her full-length image, or bust or head only, are amongst the commonest of Greek coin types. She is usually wearing the Spartan sleeveless chiton, peplos, and helmet, and holds spear and shield. She is sometimes shown hurling a thunderbolt, covering her left arm with an aegis, or holding Nike. Sacred to her were the owl, serpent, cock and olive, and these attributes often appear with her on coins. She had many additional titles, such as Areia (at Pergamon), Ilia (at Ilion), Argeia (at Alexandria), Itonia (in Thessaly), etc.

Baal. A Semitic god, lord (deity) of a locality, Baal was usually identified by the Greeks with Zeus.

Bakchos. *See* Dionysos.

Head of Demeter on a silver stater of Delphi, 336 B.C.

Demeter (Ceres). Goddess of fertility, agriculture and marriage, Demeter was sister to Zeus. When her daughter Persephone was carried off to the underworld by Hades, Demeter, by her mourning, withheld fertility from the earth until, through the mediation of Zeus, it was arranged that Persephone should spend half the year (winter) with Hades and the other half with her mother. The myth of Demeter and her daughter embodies the idea that the productive powers of nature are rested and concealed during the winter season. The head of Demeter on coins is wreathed with corn or veiled. She sometimes carries a sceptre or ears of corn, or searches for her daughter with a torch. She is also represented holding two torches and standing in a chariot drawn by two winged and crested serpents.

Dione. The consort of Zeus at Dodona, Dione was probably a sky-goddess. She appears on coins of Epeiros together with Zeus, with a laureate stephanos and veil, or alone, laureate and veiled.

Dionysos on a silver tetradrachm of Maroneia, circa 145 B.C.

Dionysos (Liber). Sometimes known as Bakchos (Bacchus), Dionysos was god of vegetation and the fruits of the trees, particularly the vine. Represented on coins as a youth holding a bunch of grapes, or with his head crowned with ivy or vine leaves, or riding or accompanied by a panther. Vine branches, kantharos and thyrsos are symbols of Dionysos.

The Dioskouroi on horseback: gold stater of Taras, circa 315 B.C.

Dioskouroi (Dioscuri). Kastor (Castor) and Polydeukes (Pollux), sons of Zeus and Leda and brothers of Helen of Troy, were protectors of travellers, particularly sailors, and helpers of those in distress. They received divine honours at Sparta and their worship spread from the Peloponnesos over the whole of Greece, Sicily and Italy. On coins the two brothers are represented on horseback or standing by their horses, carrying lances and wearing egg-shaped helmets surmounted by stars. They are sometimes confused with the Kabeiroi.

Eros (Cupid). The god of love, and later connected with Aphrodite, Eros is represented as a youth or boy, naked, winged, and holding a bow and arrows or a torch. Sometimes he is depicted riding on a dolphin (coins of Carteia) or driving the chariot of Hades who is carrying off Persephone. Occasionally, two Erotes are shown.

Head of Gorgo on a silver stater of Neapolis, circa 500 B.C.

Gorgo or **Medusa.** A monster with a round, ugly face, snakes instead of hair, teeth of a boar and huge wings, Gorgo was said to have eyes that could transform people into stone. Killed by the hero Perseus, she gave birth to Pegasos and Chrysaor in the moment of her death. Her head is shown as a main type on some coins and also as an adornment of shields.

Helios (Sol).   The sun-god, who crosses the sky from east to west in his chariot each day, sees and hears everything.   He was later identified with Apollo.   He is usually depicted nude or with chlamys, with radiate head and holding a globe, whip or torch.   On some coins he rides in a quadriga of horses.

Hera (Juno).   The sister and consort of Zeus, and the queen of heaven, Hera was the great goddess of nature, worshipped from the earliest times.   She was considered to be the mother of many other gods and goddesses, and is usually represented as a majestic woman of mature age, her hair adorned with a crown or diadem, often with a veil hanging down her back. One of her chief attributes was the peacock, her favourite bird.

Herakles fighting the Hydra: silver stater of Phaistos, circa 300 B.C.

Herakles (Hercules).   The son of Zeus and Alkmene, Herakles was the most famous of all the heroes of antiquity; his strength, courage and wonderful exploits being the subject of numerous stories and poems all over the ancient world.   His head, bust or full-length figure are amongst the most common of Greek coin types.   He is often represented as a young beardless man with his head covered by the skin of the Nemean lion whom he strangled with his hands. He is also shown as a bearded, bull-necked man, usually naked, holding his club, lion's skin or bow.   A club, bow, and also a bow-case, are also types referring to Herakles.

Head of Hermes on a silver stater of Lycia, late 5th Cent. B.C.

Hermes (Mercury).   A son of Zeus and Maia, Hermes was the messenger of the gods, hence his herald's staff, the ribbons of which were later changed into the serpents of the caduceus.   Other attributes of Hermes are the broad-brimmed travelling hat (petasos) adorned with wings, the golden sandals, the winged ankles, and a purse, for Hermes was patron not only of merchants but also of thieves, as well as artists, orators and travellers.   He was regarded as the inventor of the lyre and plectrum, and of the syrinx.   The palm-tree and tortoise were sacred to Hermes, so too were the number 4 and several kinds of fish.   The caduceus adorned with a pair of wings to indicate the speed of the messenger is occasionally used as a coin type.

Isis.   The wife of Osiris and mother of Horus, Isis was a national deity in Egypt, and during Hellenistic times became a leading goddess in the Mediterranean lands.   She is portrayed on coins in a long garment with a characteristic knot of drapery on the breast (the *nodus Isiacus*) and with the ancient Egyptian head-dress which is one of her symbols.   The sistrum, a musical instrument, is another attribute.

Kabeiroi. These non-Hellenic, probably Phrygian deities—from four to eight in number—promoted fertility and protected sailors. On coins they are represented with hammer and snake (coins of the Balearic Islands) or with rhyton (drinking horn ending in animal's head). Often confused with the Dioskouroi.

Kore. *See* Persephone.

Medusa. *See* Gorgo.

Melqarth riding hippocamp: silver double shekel of Tyre, circa 360 B.C.

Melqarth or **Melkart.** "Lord" of Tyre (Baal-Tsur), worshipped in Phoenicia, seems to have been originally a marine deity, as he is represented riding a sea-horse. Later he was identified with Herakles.

Nike with wreath and trophy: gold stater of Pyrrhos, 278-276 B.C.

Nike (Victoria). Greek goddess of victory, Nike was depicted as a woman in a long chiton, sometimes wingless (as on the coins of Terina) but more usually winged, holding wreath and palm and crowning the horses of a victorious charioteer or decorating a trophy.

Pan (Faunus). God of shepherds and flocks, Pan had horns, beard, puck nose, tail, goat's feet, was covered with hair and dwelt in grottoes. He is said to have had a terrific voice that struck terror into those who heard it. He was fond of music and is regarded, besides Hermes, as inventor of the syrinx or shepherd's pipes with which he is sometimes represented on coins (of Arkadia).

Persephone or **Kore.** Daughter of Demeter and wife of Hades (Plouton), Persephone is associated with the cult of her mother. She is usually represented with a wreath of corn on her head. *See* Demeter.

Poseidon brandishing trident: silver tetradrachm of Demetrios Poliorketes.

Poseidon (Neptune). A brother of Zeus, Poseidon was god of earthquakes and ruler of the sea. He is usually represented holding a dolphin and a trident, or the prow ornament of a galley, and standing with one foot on a rock. A trident ornamented or entwined with dolphins appears on coins as the symbol of Poseidon.

Sarapis. The name is derived from the Egyptian *Hesar-Hapi*, the deified sacred bull Apis. The cult of Sarapis arose at Memphis under the Ptolemies and the deity combined the attributes of many Hellenic gods with some characteristics of Osiris. He was represented bearded with a modius on his head. Sarapis was a healer of the sick, worker of miracles, superior to fate, ruler of the visible world and underworld, and god of the sun.

Head of Zeus on a silver tetradrachm of Philip II.

Zeus (Jupiter). The greatest of the Olympian gods, Zeus was considered to be the father of both gods and men. He was a son of Kronos and Rhea and brother of Poseidon, Hades, Hestia, Demeter, and Hera; and he was also married to his sister Hera. He was worshipped throughout the Greek world, and in the later Hellenic age was frequently identified with local supreme gods like Ammon, Sarapis, etc. He had an immense number of epithets and surnames which were derived partly from the localities where he was worshipped and partly from his functions and powers. The eagle and oak-tree were sacred to him. His usual attributes are the sceptre, eagle, thunderbolt, and also a small figure of Nike which he holds in his hand. The Olympian Zeus sometimes wears a wreath of olive and the Dodonaean Zeus a wreath of oak leaves. He is usually represented bearded, nude or semi-nude, hurling a thunderbolt or sitting on a throne.

WEIGHT STANDARDS AND DENOMINATIONS

The earliest coins, issued by the Ionians or the Lydians in western Asia Minor in the latter part of the 7th Century B.C., were produced in only one metal, electrum, a naturally-occurring alloy of gold and silver. They were based on a stater weighing a little over 14 grammes, and although various fractional denominations were struck from an early date (half, third, sixth, etc.) the relatively high intrinsic value of the metal precludes the possibility that these coins enjoyed a wide everyday circulation. The truth of the matter would seem to be that the earliest coins provided a convenient means of paying quite large sums (possibly to mercenary soldiers) rather than to facilitate the day-to-day commerce of the ordinary citizens. The electrum stater, in fact, probably represented a month's pay for a soldier.

Silver half-stater of Kroisos of Lydia
(561-546 B.C.)

Gold daric of the Persian Empire,
5th-4th Cent. B.C.

This state of affairs continued until the Lydian King Kroisos (Croesus), who reigned 561-546 B.C., introduced a new monetary system based on coins of gold and silver instead of electrum. The gold stater, although still of the same value as its electrum predecessor was necessarily of lighter weight (a little over 8 grammes) and fractional denominations down to one-twelfth (hemihekton) were produced in the same metal. Silver denominations, now issued for the first time, bore the same design as the gold and provided a much greater range of values at the lower end of the scale. In these times the ratio of silver to gold was $13\frac{1}{3}$:1 and the weight of the silver stater was fixed so as to make it the equivalent of one-tenth of the gold stater (almost 11 grammes). The smallest coin in this series, the silver hemihekton, was 1/120th of the gold stater, which gives some idea of the wide range of values obtainable under this new bimetallic system. The main disadvantage was the inconvenience of handling such tiny coins in everyday transactions—the silver hemihekton was less than half the diameter of our modern ½ New Penny. This was a problem which was not finally solved until the 4th Century B.C., when token bronze coinage largely replaced the smallest silver denominations. The Lydian Kingdom ceased to exist in 546 B.C. when Kroisos was defeated by the Persians under King Cyrus. But coinage, on the same standard and with the same types, continued to be issued from Sardis under the new regime. Towards the end of the 6th Century the old Lydian type (foreparts of lion and bull) was replaced by a Persian type showing an archer (sometimes described as the King) in a kneeling-running pose. The gold stater, now called a 'daric' (after Darius), was initially the same weight as Kroisos' coin, whilst the silver 'siglos' was the equivalent of the old half-stater and worth one-twentieth of the 'daric'. Subsequently, slight adjustments had to be made in their weights to maintain the correct ratio when there were changes in the relative values of the precious metals. These coins continued in issue, with only minor modifications, for almost two centuries, until the Persian Empire was overthrown by Alexander.

Electrum stater of Chios, circa 550 B.C.

When the Lydian Kingdom fell in 546 B.C. the Greek cities of Ionia were obliged to acknowledge Persian overlordship, though this seems to have had no effect on their output of coinage. Unlike the Lydians, the Greeks had continued using electrum for the majority of their coins, issued as staters and fractions right down to ninety-sixths. Silver was introduced in the closing decades of the 6th Century, though it seems to have played only a subsidiary role to the more important electrum issues. Quite a large number of mints would seem to have been at work—Ephesos, Phokaia, Miletos, and others—though it is difficult for us now to attribute most types to their cities of origin. The picture is further complicated by the existence of several different weight-standards for the electrum coinage, and we find staters weighing 17.2 grammes ('Euboic' standard), 16.1 gm. (Phokaic) and 14.1 gm. (Milesian). Of these, the Phokaic standard was ultimately adopted for the extensive electrum coinages which the Asiatic Greeks produced in the 5th and 4th Centuries B.C., down to the time of Alexander. Three mints were principally involved in the production of this fascinating and beautiful coinage. Kyzikos, a Milesian colony on the sea of Marmara, issued a series of staters (weight 16.1 gm.) of which more than two hundred different types are known. The Ionian mint of Phokaia, and Mytilene, the chief city of the island of Lesbos, produced long series of hektai (sixth-staters, 2.6 gm.), possibly striking in alternate years. The products of the two mints are easily distinguished—those of Phokaia are without reverse type, whilst the examples from Lesbos always have a reverse design, sometimes in intaglio.

Electrum sixth-stater of Phokaia,   *Electrum sixth-stater of Lesbos,*
4th Cent. B.C.   *4th Cent. B.C.*

Around the middle of the 6th Century the practice of issuing coined money spread to Greece itself and a number of mints commenced operations in the decade following 550 B.C. Electrum was foreign to the European Greeks who never adopted this metal for their coinage. In its place silver was employed right from the start. The first issues of Aigina, Athens, Corinth, and the Euboian cities of Chalkis, Eretria and Karystos all belong to this time. Important weight standards, which were destined to play a leading role in the development of Greek coinage, now appeared for the first time. The Attic standard, based initially on a didrachm of 8.6 gm. but later on a tetradrachm of 17.2 gm., was adopted at Athens and later spread to Sicily and the northern Aegean area. The great prosperity and political importance of Athens in the 5th Century contributed to the widespread popularity of this weight standard and it was later adopted by Alexander the Great for his vast imperial coinage.

Silver stater of Corinth, circa 525 B.C.

The Corinthian standard was closely linked to the Attic in that it was based on a stater of 8.6 gm., the same weight as the Attic didrachm. However, the Corinthian stater was divided into *three* drachms of 2.9 gm. Coins on this standard were produced over a long period at Corinth, with smaller and mostly late issues coming from her numerous colonies in north-west Greece, Italy and Sicily.

Silver Aiginetic stater of Naxos, late
6th Cent. B.C.

The Aiginetic standard received its name from the maritime state, situated between the coastlines of Attica and Argolis, which was in all probability the earliest mint in European Greece.   The Aiginetic stater, normally weighing about 12.3 gm., was widely adopted in the Peloponnese, in Central Greece, and especially in the southern Aegean area (the Cyclades group of islands, Crete and south-west Asia Minor).   Politically and economically Aigina was eclipsed by Athens in the mid-5th Century B.C. though her weight standard remained in use in many places.

Other important standards in use from early times include the Achaean (silver stater of 8 gm.), used by the Greek colonies in southern Italy; and the Euboic (stater of 17.2 gm.), employed by colonies from Euboia situated in the northern Aegean area and in Sicily.   In the East, the Persian standard, derived from the bimetallic coinage of Kroisos, was adhered to by many of the mints of Asia Minor under Achaemenid domination, including those of Cyprus. After *circa* 400 B.C. the Chian (or Rhodian) standard achieved considerable popularity in Asia Minor, and was also adopted at Ainos in Thrace.   It was based on a tetradrachm of 15.6 gm.

Phoenician 4-shekel piece of Sidon, circa 375 B.C.

In the Levant, the Phoenician standard (silver shekel of 7 gm.) was used by Sidon, Tyre and Byblos.   A not dissimilar standard is found in parts of northern Greece, though there can hardly have been any connection between the two.   In fact, the whole question of weight standards in northern Greece is fraught with difficulties.   Different standards appear to have been in use contemporaneously, sometimes at the same mint, and there were certainly three series of weights with no simple inter-relationship.   The whole group is termed "Thraco-Macedonian".

Within each weight standard there was normally a wide range of denominations, serving the requirements of major transactions down to everyday purchases in the market-place. Some denominations were struck more regularly than others, such as the tetradrachm at Athens, the tridrachm-stater at Corinth and the didrachm-stater at Aigina.   Some areas had a preference for small denominations: most Peloponnesian mints, for example, seldom issued anything larger than a triobol (hemidrachm) during the 5th Century B.C.   Other areas preferred larger coins: the Thraco-Macedonian tribes of the north regularly produced silver octadrachms (c. 29 gm.), dodekadrachms (c. 40.5 gm.) and even a double octadrachm, the heaviest of all Greek silver coins.

Thraco-Macedonian dodekadrachm of the Derrones, circa 475 B.C.

The table below shows the large number of denominations which were produced under the Attic weight system. Not all of these denominations would have been in regular issue—the dekadrachm, for example, was only struck on special occasions—and some mints never produced the tiny fractions of the obol. The weights given are approximate, and reflect the figures actually achieved rather than the ideal.

Dekadrachm	=	10	drachms	:	43 gm.
Tetradrachm	=	4	drachms	:	17.2 gm.
Didrachm	=	2	drachms	:	8.6 gm.
Drachm	=	6	obols	:	4.3 gm.
Tetrobol	=	4	obols	:	2.85 gm.
Triobol (hemidrachm)	=	3	obols	:	2.15 gm.
Diobol	=	2	obols	:	1.43 gm.
Trihemiobol	=	$1\frac{1}{2}$	obols	:	1.07 gm.
Obol				:	0.72 gm.
Tritartemorion	=	$\frac{3}{4}$	obol	:	0.54 gm.
Hemiobol	=	$\frac{1}{2}$	obol	:	0.36 gm.
Trihemitartemorion	=	$\frac{3}{8}$	obol	:	0.27 gm.
Tetartemorion	=	$\frac{1}{4}$	obol	:	0.18 gm.
Hemitartemorion	=	$\frac{1}{8}$	obol	:	0.09 gm.

The smallest coin in this system, the hemitartemorion represents 1/480th of the largest piece, the dekadrachm. Similar tables can be constructed for other weight standards, but it should be borne in mind that in some systems the stater is divided into thirds, sixths, twelfths, etc., instead of halves and quarters.

Silver litra of Kamarina, circa 460 B.C.

Bronze hemilitron of Himera, circa 450 B.C.

One weight standard which we have not so far mentioned is that based on the Sicilian *bronze* litra. Indigenous to the island, the litra was at first represented by a small silver coin (wt. 0.86 gm.) which was only slightly heavier than the obol and had to be distinguished by the use of different types. The Sicilian Greeks must have found this a troublesome arrangement, for as early as the mid-5th Century B.C. they hit on the idea of producing a bronze litra. Such a coin would not be so inconveniently small to handle and there would no longer be any danger of confusing it with the silver obol. Which city was the first to take this step we cannot be certain but Himera, on the north coast of the island, was certainly amongst the earliest of the bronze-issuing mints. Although some of the original bronze litrai were somewhat cumbersome, the weight was soon reduced to a more acceptable level for everyday circulation. So from their earliest stages bronze coins came to be accepted as a token currency, the intrinsic value of which was considerably below the circulating value which had been placed upon them by the issuing authority. By the latter part of the 5th Century many of the Greek cities in Sicily had adopted this base-metal currency and were finding it very useful indeed for the small daily transactions of urban life—the purchase of food and drink, clothing, etc. In fact the modern concept of currency, as a convenient means of payment for all goods and services from the largest transactions down to the most trifling, is a direct result of this important development in Greek Sicily 2,400 years ago.

Bronze litra of Syracuse, circa 340 B.C.

The bronze litra was divided into twelve onkiai—hence the Roman uncia (1/12th of a pound), the troy ounce (1/12th of a pound) and the inch (1/12th of a linear foot). The hemilitron (=6 onkiai, mark of value six pellets) was also struck, together with the pentonkion (5 onkiai, five pellets), the tetras (4 onkiai, four pellets), the trias (3 onkiai, three pellets), the hexas (2 onkiai, two pellets), and the onkia itself (mark of value one pellet). In the earliest stages of bronze coinage in Sicily the denomination produced in greatest quantities was the trias or quarter-litra.

Bronze trias of Syracuse, early 4th Cent. B.C.

From its beginnings in Sicily the idea of base-metal token coinage eventually spread to all parts of the Greek world. In the half century after *circa* 400 B.C. most mints produced their first issues of bronze though some, such as Athens, seemed reluctant to adopt the innovation. Athens, from the early years of the 5th Century, had possessed plentiful supplies of silver from her rich mines at Laurion, and well on into the 4th Century was still producing quantities of the absurdly small fractions of the obol. Eventually she, too, acknowledged the obvious advantages of having token bronze denominations to represent the lowest values, and the Athenian mint began striking them in the latter part of the 4th Century.

One of the problems of Greek bronze coins is trying to relate them to the silver denominations is the absence, in most cases, of marks of value. Unfortunately, few Greek mints followed the practice of the Sicilian innovators of bronze coinage by clearly marking the denomination in terms of some basic unit representing a known fraction of the smallest silver coin in common

Bronze obol of Metapontion, inscribed "ΟΒΟΛΟΣ".

use. A remarkable late 4th Century bronze of the south Italian mint of Metapontion bears the inscription 'ΟΒΟΛΟΣ' clearly proclaiming its value as the equivalent of one obol, and it would seem a fair surmise that the majority of Greek bronzes represent fractions or, in rarer cases, multiples of the silver obol. It is known that at Athens the obol was divided into eight chalkoi, and in all probability the tiniest Athenian bronze piece represents the chalkos. Larger pieces would be multiples, such as the dichalkon (two chalkoi), tetrachalkon (four chalkoi = hemiobol), etc. It may be hoped that one day we shall have acquired sufficient knowledge of the Greek bronze coinage to give precise names to most pieces. The present system of merely measuring the diameter in millimetres or inches is most unsatisfactory.

THE DATING OF GREEK COINS

Tetradrachm of Alexander I of Syria: Seleukid date 162 = 151/150 B.C.

In general, Greek coins were not marked with their year of issue until a very late period (2nd Century B.C.), when the Hellenistic Kingdoms of Syria and Egypt commenced the practice. The Seleukids dated their coins according to an era commencing in 312 B.C., when Seleukos I regained possession of Babylon. The Ptolemies, on the other hand, used the less satisfactory method of indicating only the regnal year; and as every Greek King of Egypt bore the name 'Ptolemy' the dates appearing on their coins provide only limited assistance in our efforts to establish the precise chronology of the Ptolemaic series. But even in the case of these late regal issues many of the coins are not dated and the practice only spread to a limited number of autonomous city mints. In attempting to establish the approximate period of issue for the majority of Greek coins, then, the numismatist must have recourse to other criteria, such as style and fabric.

Archaic winged figure on a tetradrachm of   Archaic eagle on a stater of Elis,
Peparethos, circa 500 B.C.   early 5th Cent. B.C.

Broadly speaking, the six centuries of Greek coinage, prior to the establishment of the Roman Empire, divide up into three periods, each characterized by artistic style and, to a lesser extent, by the method of production. In the Archaic period (from the invention of coinage down to the time of the Persian defeat in 479 B.C.) representations of the human form have a stiff, almost stylized look. In profile heads the eye tends to be represented full face, whilst in showing the full-length figure to left or to right there is a tendency to depict the head and legs correctly in profile, whilst the torso has a more frontal aspect. Similarly, with flying birds the body is in profile whilst the wings are depicted as if viewed from below. Although lacking the artistic finesse and sculptural qualities of later periods much of the work produced by the early die-engravers is pleasing to the eye and fascinating in its symbolization of a most exciting period in the history of civilization. To begin with, coins bore no reverse types and simply had an incuse square sometimes roughly divided into segments. In the later archaic period the divisions of the incuse square became more formalized and finally, in the closing years of the 6th Century, the first true reverse types began to appear. However, some mints, such as Aigina, never abandoned the use of the incuse square reverse. In the Aegean area the flans of the earliest coins are often very thick, almost globular, whilst subsequent issues gradually become thinner and larger. In the West the opposite is often the case; the very thin, spread flans of the earliest issues giving way to thicker, more compact coins. A curious feature of the first issues of many of the Magna Graecian mints was the mirroring of the obverse type on the reverse, in incuse form.

Tetradrachm of Segesta in Sicily, circa 410 B.C.

The period 479-336 B.C., from the Persian Wars to the time of Alexander, is termed the Classical period of Greek coinage.   Its first few decades witness a progressive transition from the unlifelike representations of archaic art to a more natural style, though still retaining something of the old severity in the earlier phases.   Towards the latter part of the 5th Century, and especially in Sicily, numismatic art reaches a level of realism combined with nobility of style which makes many of the coins masterpieces in miniature.   Nothing comparable has been produced in the twenty-four centuries which have since elapsed.   Although the Sicilian coinage was cut short by the Carthaginian invasions at the end of the century, mints in other parts of the Greek world were also producing coins of fine style, and these issues continued until the beginning of the Macedonian domination of Greece.   This despite the political turmoil which the Greek world found itself in as the aftermath of the great Peloponnesian War.

Hellenistic tetradrachm of Myrina, circa 150 B.C.

The eastern conquests of Alexander and the subsequent establishment of great kingdoms brought about fundamental changes in the coinage.   The Hellenistic period, which lasted three centuries until the suicide of Cleopatra of Egypt (30 B.C.), saw the first mass-production of Greek coinage, with the possible exception of the Athenian 'owls' produced in the age of Perikles.   The vast realms over which the Hellenistic monarchs ruled required coinage on a scale unknown in the days of the city-states.   Working under such pressure even experienced die-engravers could hardly be expected to produce notable work, and as time went by there was a steady decline in the artistic standard of the coinage.   Although there was something of a revival in the 2nd Century B.C., when many cities were temporarily liberated from regal control by Rome's intervention in eastern affairs, still the general impression conveyed by most of the later Hellenistic coins is one of artistic decadence and hurried, careless production.

In the foregoing notes I have tried to make clear the principal characteristics of each major period—Archaic, Classical and Hellenistic.   In order to arrive at a more precise dating for an individual piece a close study of the history of the mint can sometimes provide valuable clues. Many Greek cities were destroyed by their neighbours, or by foreign invaders, to be rebuilt at a later date and sometimes even to suffer a second destruction.   The names of cities could be changed, sometimes more than once: the Italian city of Sybaris was renamed Thourioi in

425 B.C., the name which it bore until the Romans changed it to Copia in 194 B.C. Such events enable us to construct a chronological framework for the coinages of certain cities; and as the majority of mints were active only sporadically we are able, sometimes, to fix the precise occasion for some special issue. This knowledge can then be used to date the coins of other mints in the same vicinity, and so the picture is gradually built up like a giant jigsaw puzzle.

There is much still to be learnt about the chronology of Greek coins, and our views often have to be modified in the light of evidence provided by hoards. But in this brief survey of a most complex and controversial subject I hope I have not only made the reader aware of the difficulties involved in the dating of Greek coins but also have conveyed something of the fascination and the challenge which this subject affords.

The table below explains the Greek letter-numerals by which dates are expressed on certain issues of the 2nd and 1st Centuries B.C.

1 A	9 Θ	80 Π
2 B	10 I	90 Ϙ
3 Γ	20 K	100 P
4 Δ	30 Λ	200 Σ
5 Є	40 M	300 T
6 S	50 N	400 Y
7 Z	60 Ξ	500 Φ
8 H	70 O	600 X

BOOKS OF REFERENCE AND OTHER SOURCES QUOTED IN THIS CATALOGUE

Babelon, E.   Traité des monnaies grecques et romaines.   Paris, 1901-1933.

Berlin Museum Catalogue = Beschreibung der antiken Münzen.   Berlin, 1888-1894.

Boehringer, E.   Die Münzen von Syrakus.   Berlin, 1929.

Boston Museum Catalogue = Museum of Fine Arts: Catalogue of Greek Coins, by A. Baldwin Brett.   Boston, 1955.

British Museum Catalogue of Greek Coins, various authors, London, 1873-1927.   Ten out of the twenty-nine volumes are quoted in this catalogue, numbered as follows:

    B.M.C. 1.   Italy: published 1873.
    B.M.C. 2.   Sicily: published 1876.
    B.M.C. 3.   Thrace, etc.: published 1877.
    B.M.C. 5.   Macedonia, etc.: published 1879.
    B.M.C. 7.   Thessaly to Aetolia: published 1883.
    B.M.C. 8.   Central Greece: published 1884.
    B.M.C. 9.   Crete and Aegean Islands: published 1886.
    B.M.C. 10.   Peloponnesus: published 1887.
    B.M.C. 11.   Attica, Megaris, Aegina: published 1888.
    B.M.C. 12.   Corinth and Colonies: published 1889.

(*B.M.C.* references in this catalogue provide the volume number and the listing number for each mint.   The reference *B.M.C. 8.* 135, for a coin of Thebes, is to no. 135 in the listing of Theban issues in the volume "Central Greece".)

Clerk, M. G.   Catalogue of the coins of the Achaean League.   London, 1895.

De la Tour, H.   Atlas de Monnaies Gauloises.   Paris, 1892.

Desneux, J.   Les tetradrachmes d'Akanthos (in Revue Belge de Numismatique, vol. 95, 1949).

Evans, Sir A.   The "Horsemen" of Tarentum (in Numismatic Chronicle, 1889).

Forrer, R.   Keltische Numismatik der Rhein- und Donaulande.   Strassburg, 1908.

Gabrici, E.   La monetazione del bronzo nella Sicilia antica.   Palermo, 1927.

Garrucci, R.   Le monete dell' Italia antica.   Rome, 1885.

Grose, S. W.   Catalogue of the McClean collection of Greek coins.   Cambridge, 1923-9.

Head, B. V.   Historia Numorum.   Oxford, 1911.   *Hist. Num.*

Head, B. V.   A guide to the principal coins of the Greeks.   Revised edition, London, 1959.   *Principal Coins.*

Head, B. V.   On the chronological sequence of the coins of Boeotia.   London, 1881.

Heiss, A.   Description générale des monnaies antiques de l'Espagne.   Paris, 1870.

Hill, G. F.   Coins of ancient Sicily.   London, 1903.

Holm, A.   Geschichte des sicilischen Münzwesens.   Leipzig, 1898.

Hunterian Catalogue = Catalogue of Greek coins in the Hunterian collection, by G. Macdonald.   Glasgow, 1899-1905.

Jenkins, G. K.   The coinage of Gela.   Berlin, 1970.

Jenkins, G. K.   Coins of Punic Sicily (in Swiss Numismatic Review, vol. 50, 1971).

Jenkins, G. K.   Ancient Greek coins.   London, 1972.

Jenkins, G. K., and Lewis, R. B.   Carthaginian gold and electrum coins.   London, 1963.

Kraay, C. M.   Coins of ancient Athens.   Newcastle upon Tyne, 1968.

Kraay, C. M.   Archaic and Classical Greek coins.   London, 1976.

Le Rider, G.   Monnaies Crétoises du Vᵉ au Iᵉʳ siècle av J.-C.   Paris, 1966.

Mack, R. P.   The coinage of Ancient Britain.   London, 1975.
May, J. M. F.   The coinage of Damastion.   Oxford, 1939.
May, J. M. F.   The coinage of Abdera.   London, 1966.
Müller, L.   Die Münzen des thrakischen König Lysimachos.   Copenhagen, 1858.

Newell, E. T.   A hoard from Siphnos.   New York, 1934.
Noe, S. P.   The Mende (Kaliandra) hoard.   New York, 1926.
Noe, S. P.   The coinage of Metapontum.   New York, 1927.
Noe, S. P.   The Thurian di-staters.   New York, 1935.
Noe, S. P.   The coinage of Caulonia.   New York, 1958.
Numismatic Chronicle = the annual publication of the Royal Numismatic Society, London.

Pick, B.   Die antiken Münzen Nord-Griechenlands, Vol. I.   Berlin, 1898.
Price, M.   Coins of the Macedonians.   London, 1974.
Price, M. and Waggoner, N.   Archaic Greek silver coinage: the "Asyut" hoard.   London, 1975.

Ravel, O.   The "colts" of Ambracia.   New York, 1928.
Ravel, O.   Les "poulains" de Corinthe: part I, Basel, 1936; part II, London, 1948.
Raymond, D.   Macedonian regal coinage to 413 B.C.   New York, 1953
Robinson, D. M. and Clement, P. A.   Excavations at Olynthus IX: the Chalcidic mint and the excavation coins found in 1928-34.   Baltimore, 1938.

Sambon, A.   Les monnaies antiques de l'Italie, Vol. I.   Paris, 1903.
Schwabacher, W.   Ein fund archaischen Münzen von Samothrake (in Transactions of the International Numismatic Congress, London, 1936).
Seaby.   Standard Catalogue of British coins.   London, 1978.
Seltman, C. T.   The temple coins of Olympia.   Cambridge, 1921.
Seltman, C. T.   Athens: its history and coinage before the Persian invasion.   Cambridge, 1924.
Starr, C. G.   Athenian coinage 480-449 B.C.   Oxford, 1970.
Svoronos, J. N.   Numismatique de la Crète Ancienne.   Macon, 1890.
Sylloge Nummorum Graecorum, American Numismatic Society, 1969, 1972.
Sylloge Nummorum Graecorum, Copenhagen, 1942- .
Sylloge Nummorum Graecorum, Lloyd collection, 1933-7.

Thompson, M.   The New Style silver coinage of Athens.   New York, 1961.
Tudeer, L. O. Th.   Die tetradrachmenprägung von Syrakus in der Periode der signierenden Künstler.   Berlin, 1913.

Wallace, W. P.   The Euboian League and its coinage.   New York, 1956.
Weber = Descriptive catalogue of the collection of Greek coins formed by Sir Hermann Weber, by L. Forrer.   London, 1922-9.
Williams, R. T.   The confederate coinage of the Arcadians in the fifth century B.C.   New York, 1965.

Semitic	Phoenician and Punic	Israelite	Aramaic	Greek early	Greek late	North Italian	Early Latin and Roman	English
⋈	✶✦✦	F ᛕ	ᛆ†	⊿⋀A	A A	ᛘᛘN	⋀⋀A	A
ᕾ	ᕾ⟆ᕾ	ᕾᕾ	ᵞᵞ	ᥰᒹB	B B	8B	B	B
⅂	≻⟩∧	∧⌐	∧⋋	‹⋀Γ	Γ	⟩⟩⊂	‹CG	CG
⊿	⊿⋖	ᖰ⅃	⋔⋔	▷▷△	Я	ᴚ	D	D
∃	⋨⋨∃	⪯	⋔⊓	ᵹ⪽E	Є E	⅋ᴢE	E E	Ě
ᵞ	ᵞᵞ	ᵞᵗ	ᒣ	‹ᖴᖴ		⅂ᒣᛏ	F F	F
‡	Ⲓᘔ	⅄	Ι	‡Ι	Z Ι	Ⲓ‡Ⲓ	Z	Z
ᗺ	ᕼᕼ	ᗺᗺ	H	ᕼᕼᗺ	H	ᗺᗱH	H	H (Ē)
	⊕⊖⊝			⊞⊕◇	ᗺ⊙⊖	⊗⊙◇		Th
ᛁ	ᘔᛖᛘᛃ	ᛉᛉ	ᛱ	ᘰ⪽Ɩ	Ι	Ι	Ι	Ι
ᵞ	ᵞᖴᵞ	ᵞᘰ	ᕼᵞ	K	K	ᛕK	K	K
ᒺ	ᖽᒺᒷ	ᒺ	⌐⌐	ᒺᒣ∧	∧	ᥝᒺ	L	L
ᛘ	ᛘᵞ✕	ᵞᵞ	ᵞ	ᛜᛜM	M M	ᛜᛜᛞ	ᛜM	M
ᒿ	ᵞᵞᛁ	ᵞᵞ	ᵞ	ᛜN	N	ᛞᛜᛞ	N	N
‡	‡ᛉ		ᛉ	‡ᚻ‡	Ξ Ξ Ξ		✕	X
ᴏ	ᴏᵕ	ᕼᵕ	ᵕ	◻◇Ο	Ο	Ο	◇ᴏᴏ	Ŏ
ᒣ	ᒣᒷᒷ		ᒣᒣ	ᒥᒣᒺ	ᒥᴨᴨ	ᒣᒣᒥ	ᵖᵖ	P
	ᛙᵕᒣ	ᛉᛛ		ᛙᵀ				(san)
φ	φφᵠ	ᵖᵠ	ᵠ	ᵠᵠᵞ	Q		ᵠQ	Q
◁	◁ᵞᵞ	ᵞᵞ	ᕼᕼ	R ▷ᵖ	P	◁ᵞR	DR	R
ᴟ	ᴟᵞᵞ	ᵞᵞ		ᵞᵞS	⊏⊏Σ	ᵞᵞᵞ	ᵞ S	S
†	✕ᵞᕼ	✕†	ᕼᕼ	ᵞᵀ	ᵀ	ᵞᵞᵞ	ᵀ	T
				ᵞᵛᵞ	Υ	Υᵛᵛ	ᵛ	U. V. W. Y.
				⊞⊘⊘	ᵠᵠφ	⊕⅏		Ph
				↓ᵞ✕	✕	↓ᵞ		Kh
				ᵛᵞ	Ψ			Ps
				ᴏΩ	ᛜΩ			Ō

ANCIENT ALPHABETS

ABBREVIATIONS

A′	gold	r.	right	rad.	radiate
R	silver	l.	left	diad.	diademed
Æ	copper or bronze	hd.	head	dr.	draped
obv.	obverse	var.	variety	cuir.	cuirassed
R or *rev.*	reverse	laur.	laureate	stg.	standing

STATES OF PRESERVATION IN ORDER OF MERIT

Abbreviation	*English*	*French.*	*German.*	*Italian.*
FDC	mint state.	fleur-de-coin.	Stempelglanz.	fior di conio
EF	extremely fine.	superbe.	vorzüglich.	splendido.
VF	very fine.	très beau.	sehr schön.	bellisimo.
F	fine.	beau.	schön.	multo bello.
Fair	fair.	très bien conservé.	sehr gut erhalten.	bello.
M	mediocre.	bien conservé.	gut erhalten.	discreto.
P	poor.			

VALUES

The prices given are for specimens in an average state of preservation—'VF' in the case of gold, electrum and silver, 'F' in the case of billon and bronze. Poorly preserved examples are, of course, worth *much* less than the values quoted; unusually well-preserved coins and those of better than average style are worth substantially more.

KEY TO MAPS

Mints which commenced issuing coins during the archaic period are denoted by a dot surrounded by a circle and other mints by a plain dot.

SPAIN

Phoenician and Greek contact with Spain stretched back to the Seventh Century B.C. at least; possibly several centuries earlier in the case of the Phoenicians. A lively trade was carried on with the rich mining culture based on the city of Tartessos, but about 500 B.C. the Carthaginians destroyed Tartessos having already taken control of the Phoenician settlements in Spain. Carthaginian pre-eminence in southern and eastern Spain lasted until the time of the Punic Wars between Carthage and Rome. It was from Spain that Hannibal launched his famous invasion of Italy which came so close to destroying the Roman Republic in the infancy of its power. But Hannibal was defeated and Spain became a Roman province (206 B.C.). During the Second Century B.C. Rome gradually extended her influence into the interior of the country and permitted the Iberian tribes to issue a native currency bearing Iberian legends. This coinage ceased with the provincial reforms carried out in 133 B.C. The various civil wars in Spain in the First Century B.C. saw the temporary revival of bronze issues from certain mints. It was not until 19 B.C., in the reign of Augustus, that the whole of the peninsula came under Roman control with the conquest of northwestern Spain. For table of Iberian letters, see page 9.

Early Coinage

1 **Emporiai** (founded by the Phokaians of Massalia between 400 and 350 B.C.). Mid-4th-mid-3rd Cent. B.C. Æ *trihemiobol*. Female hd. facing between E and M. ℞. Naked rider on horse prancing l. *Heiss* (*Description Générale des Monnaies Antiques de L'Espagne*) 16 .. .. £175

    2   5   7

2 — Æ *obol*. Helmeted hd. of Athena r. ℞. Goat stg. l., E above. *Heiss* 15 .. £125

3 — — Hd. of Persephone r., wreathed with corn; E behind neck, M beneath chin. ℞. Pegasos flying r. *Heiss* 11 .. .. £125

4 Before *c.* 250 B.C. Æ *drachm*. Hd. of Persephone l., wreathed with corn; around, three dolphins. ℞. Pegasos flying r., ΕΝΠΟΡΙΤΩΝ beneath. *Heiss* 2 .. .. £300

5 — — *Obv.* Similar, but hd. r. ℞. Pegasos flying r., his hd. in the form of a seated genius; beneath, ΕΜΠΟΡΙΤΩΝ. *Heiss* 3 .. .. £250

6 *Circa* 250-206 B.C. Æ *drachm*. Similar, but with Iberian instead of Greek legend beneath Pegasos on *rev*. *Heiss* 28 .. .. £275
    See also nos. 15, 16, 54, 55.

7 **Rhoda** (founded by the Rhodians in the 6th Cent. B.C.). Before *c.* 250 B.C. Æ *drachm*. Hd. of Persephone l., wreathed with corn; before, ΡΟΔΗΤΩΝ. ℞. Rose in full bloom viewed from beneath. *Heiss* 1-2 .. .. £450

    8   10   11

8 **Gades** (founded by the Phoenicians at a very early date, perhaps in the first century of the last millennium B.C.). *Circa* 250-206 B.C. Æ *hemidrachm*. Hd. of Herakles (Melkart) r., wearing lion's skin. ℞. Tunny fish r., Phoenician legends above and beneath. *Heiss* 1 .. .. £300

9 — Æ ½ *drachm*. *Obv.* Similar, but hd. l. ℞. Tunny fish r.; no legend. *Heiss* 3 £120

10 Æ 17. Hd. of Herakles (Melkart) facing, wearing lion's skin. ℞. Two tunny fish r., Phoenician legends above and beneath. *Heiss* 14, *variety* £10

11 — Æ 10. Dolphin r. ℞. Two tunny fish r. *Heiss* 18 .. .. .. £8
    See also nos. 46-48.

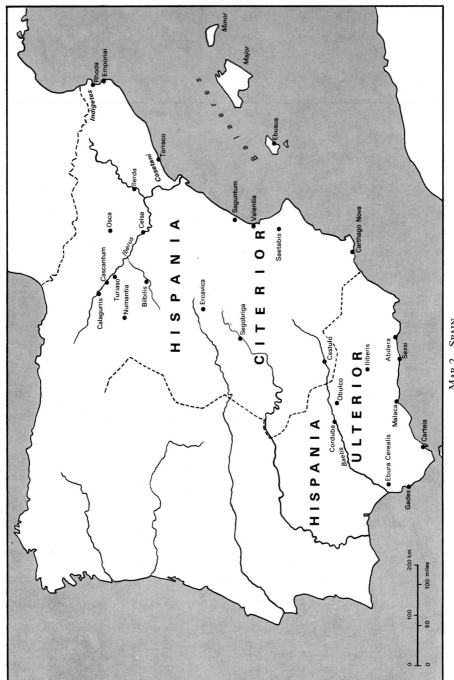

MAP 2 SPAIN

12 **BALEARIC ISLANDS, Ebusus** (a Phoenician colony dating perhaps from the late-Eighth Century B.C.). Mid-3rd–early 2nd Cent. B.C. Æ *hemidrachm.* Squatting Kabeiros facing, holding hammer and serpent. R. Bull walking l. *Heiss (Minorca)*
2   ..   ..   £250

13 — Æ 21.   *Obv.*   Similar, but with palm in field to l.   R. Phoenician legend in two lines. *Heiss* 3   ..   ..   £24

14 — Æ 11.   Squatting Kabeiros facing, holding hammer and serpent, sometimes with pellets in field to l. R. Same as *obv. Heiss* 21-22   ..   ..   £18

12   15

Romano-Celtiberian Coinage
CITERIOR PROVINCE

15 **Emporiai** (the Indigetes). 218-133 B.C. Æ 31. Helmeted hd. of Minerva r., Iberian letters before. R. Pegasos galloping r., his hd. in the form of a seated genius; above, wreath; beneath, Iberian legend. *Heiss* 38   ..   ..   £20

16   17

16 — Æ 19.   *Obv.*   Similar.   R. Lion prancing r., Iberian legend beneath.   *Heiss* 52
              £18

17 **Tarraco** (the Cosetani). 204-154 B.C. Æ *drachm.* Young male hd., beardless, r. R. Two horses galloping r., the nearer with rider holding palm; beneath, Iberian legend. *Heiss* 1   ..   ..   £85

18 — Æ 27.   *Obv.*   Similar.   R. Horseman galloping r., holding palm; beneath, Iberian legend.   *Heiss* 4   ..   ..   £12

19 — Æ 16.   *Obv.*   Similar to 17, but with three pellets behind.   R. Forepart of Pegasos r., three pellets above, Iberian legend beneath.   *Heiss* 14 ..   ..   £10

20 **Ilerda.** 204-154 B.C. Æ 32. Beardless male hd. r., three dolphins around. R.
Horseman galloping r., holding palm; beneath, Iberian legend. *Heiss* 4   £14

21   22

21 — Æ 24. *Obv.* Similar, but without dolphins. R. Wolf stg. r., Iberian legend above.
Heiss 15-17   ..   ..   £14
22 **Celsa.** 204-154 B.C. Æ 29. Beardless male hd. r., three dolphins around. R.
Horseman galloping r., holding palm; beneath, Iberian legend. *Heiss* 1-3 ..   £15
23 80-72 B.C. (Sertorian War). Æ 32. Beardless male hd. r., two dolphins before, CEL.
behind. R. Same as last. *Heiss* 9-10 ..   ..   £20

24   25   28

24 **Saguntum** (the Arsenses). 214-204 B.C. Æ *hemidrachm.* Beardless male hd. r., laur.,
club over shoulder, dolphin before. R. Bull butting r., shell above, Iberian legend in ex.
Heiss p. 288, 4   ..   ..   £125
25 204-154 B.C. Æ *drachm.* Hd. r. with short beard, dolphin before, plough behind.
R. Horseman galloping r., holding arrow; beneath, Iberian legend. *Heiss* p. 248, 1-2
   £75
26 — Æ 25. Same as last. *Heiss* p. 249, 3-6   ..   ..   £15
27 — Æ 16. Scallop-shell. R. Dolphin r., Iberian legend beneath. *Heiss* 5 ..   £8
See also no. 56.
28 **Osca** (the Celsitani). 204-154 B.C. Æ *drachm.* Hd. r. with short beard, Iberian
letters behind. R. Horseman galloping r., holding spear couched; beneath, Iberian
legend. *Heiss* 1-2 ..   ..   £50
29 — Æ 25. *Obv.* Similar, but with dolphin instead of letters behind. R. Same as last;
also with star in field behind rider. *Heiss* 4   ..   ..   £12
See also no. 59.

30   33

30 **Turiaso.** 204-154 B.C. *Æ drachm.* Hd. r. with short beard, A behind, crescent beneath, Δ before. R. Horseman galloping r., holding spear couched; beneath, Iberian legend. *Heiss* 3   ..   ..   £60

31 — Æ 25. Hd. r. with short beard, A behind, dolphin before. R. Same as last. *Heiss* 4
                                                                             £12

32 **Cascantum.** 204-154 B.C. Æ 25. Hd. r. with short beard, A before, plough behind. R. Horseman galloping r., holding spear couched; beneath, Iberian legend. *Heiss* 1
                                                                    £18

33 **Calagurris.** 204-154 B.C. Æ 26. Beardless male hd. r., star and crescent before, dolphin behind. R. Horseman galloping r., holding spear couched; beneath, Iberian legend. *Heiss* 1-3   ..   ..   £25

34 **Numantia** (the Aregoradenses). After 133 B.C. (?). *Æ drachm.* Beardless male hd. r., Θ behind. R. Horseman galloping r., holding spear couched; beneath, Iberian legend. *Heiss* p. 241, 1-2   ..   ..   £85

34   36

35 — Æ 24. Beardless male hd. r., dolphins before and behind. R. Similar to last, but the Iberian legend is in two lines. *Heiss* p. 241, 7-8 ..   ..   £15

36 **Bilbilis.** 204-154 B.C. Æ 28. Beardless male hd. r., dolphin before, Π behind. R. Horseman galloping r., holding spear couched; beneath, Iberian legend. *Heiss* 4
                                                                       £12

37 **Ercavica.** 204-154 B.C. Æ 24. Beardless male hd. r., Iberian letters before, plough behind. R. Horseman galloping r., holding spear couched; beneath, Iberian legend. *Heiss* 2   ..   ..   £15

38 **Segobriga.** 204-154 B.C. *Æ drachm.* Beardless male hd. r., crescent behind, M beneath. R. Horseman galloping r., holding spear couched; beneath, Iberian legend. *Heiss* 1-3   ..   ..   £75

39   42

Segobriga *continued*

39 — Æ 28. Beardless male hd. r., dolphin before, palm behind, M beneath. ℞. Same as
   last. *Heiss* 4 .. .. £15

40 **Carthago Nova** (the Sethitani). 204-154 B.C. Æ 27. Beardless male hd. r., three
   dolphins around. ℞. Horseman galloping r., holding palm; beneath, Iberian legend.
   Heiss p. 150, 1 .. .. £20

41 — Æ 21. *Obv.* Same. ℞. Horse, with bridle, galloping r., Iberian legend beneath.
   Heiss p. 150, 3 .. .. £24

42 **Saetabis.** 204-154 B.C. Æ 25. Beardless male hd. r., laur., palm behind. ℞.
   Horseman galloping r., holding spear couched; beneath, Iberian legend. *Heiss* 3
   £14

ULTERIOR PROVINCE

43 **Iliberis.** 204-154 B.C. Æ *drachm.* Beardless male hd. r. ℞. Two horses galloping l.,
   the nearer with rider holding shield; in ex., Iberian legend. *Heiss* 1-3 .. £85

44 — Æ 26. Beardless male hd. r., dolphin behind. ℞. Horseman galloping l., holding
   spear and shield; beneath, Iberian legend. *Heiss* 10-13 .. .. .. £14

45 **Ebura Cerealis.** 204-154 B.C. Æ 29. Helmeted male hd. r., laurel-branch before.
   ℞. Triskeles of human legs with facing hd. at centre; beneath, Iberian legend. *Heiss* 3-5
   £20

Later Coinage—the Phoenician Cities
ULTERIOR PROVINCE

46   49

46 **Gades.** 2nd-1st Cent. B.C. Æ 27. Hd. of Herakles (Melkart) l., wearing lion's skin, club behind. R. Two tunny fish l., varying symbols between, Phoenician legends above and beneath. *Heiss* 5-8 ..   ..   £14

47 — Æ 20. *Obv.* Same. R. Tunny fish l., Phoenician legends above and beneath. *Heiss* 20-22   ..   ..   £12

48 — Æ 16. *Obv.* Same. R. Dolphin l., Phoenician legends above and beneath. *Heiss* 28-9, 31   ..   ..   £10

49 **Abdera.** 2nd-1st Cent. B.C. Æ 25. Two tunny fish l., Phoenician legend between. R. Tetrastyle temple. *Heiss* 5-7 ..   ..   £15

50   51

50 **Malaca.** 2nd-1st Cent. B.C. Æ 24. Hd. of Hephaistos r., wearing pointed cap, pincers behind, Phoenician legend before or behind. R. Rad. hd. of Helios facing. *Heiss* 1-3
                   £12

51 — Æ 21. *Obv.* Similar, but Hephaistos wears flat cap. R. Star within wreath. *Heiss* 6-7 ..   ..   £12

52 **Sexsi.** 2nd-1st Cent. B.C. Æ 27. Hd. of Herakles (Melkart) l., wearing lion's skin, club behind. R. Two tunny fish r., star and crescent between, Phoenician legends above and beneath. *Heiss* 2   ..   ..   £14

53 — — *Obv.* Same. R. Phoenician legend on tablet, tunny fish and star above, dolphin and crescent beneath. *Heiss* 3, 5 ..   ..   £15

8

54 **Emporiai.** 2nd-1st Cent. B.C. (after 133). Æ 27. Helmeted hd. of Minerva r.
R. Pegasos flying r., wreath above, EMPOR. beneath. *Heiss* 55 .. .. .. £15

55 — — Similar to last, but with legend C.CAT. C.O. CAP. Q. on *obv.* *Heiss* 57 .. £18

55   56

56 **Saguntum.** 2nd-1st Cent. B.C. Æ 30 (*as*). SAGVNTINV. Helmeted hd. of Roma(?) r.
R. Prow r., Victory flying r. above, caduceus before, Iberian legend beneath. *Heiss* 15
£30

57 **Valentia** (Roman colony founded in 138 B.C.). After 138 B.C. Æ 30 (*as*). T . AHI .
T . F . L . TRINI L . F . Q. Type similar to last. R. Cornucopiae and thunderbolt in saltire,
VALENTIA beneath. *Heiss* 3 .. .. £30

58 — Æ 21 (*semis*). Helmeted hd. of Roma r., s behind. R. Similar to last, but legend
abbreviated to VAL. *Heiss* 4 .. .. £25

59 **Osca.** *Circa* 39-37 B.C. Æ *denarius.* Hd. r. with short beard, OSCA behind. R.
DOM . COS . ITER . IMP. Sacrificial implements. *Heiss* 7 .. .. .. £150
   *Cn. Domitius Calvinus was proconsul in Spain, with headquarters at Osca. He campaigned
   against the Cerretani and was saluted* Imperator.

60 **Castulo.** 2nd-1st Cent. B.C. Æ 28. L . QV . L . F . Q . ISCE. Beardless male hd. l.
R. Artemis Tauropolos seated facing on bull galloping r.; beneath, M . C . F. *Heiss* 22
£25

ULTERIOR PROVINCE

61 **Corduba.** 1st Cent. B.C. Æ 22 (*quadrans*). Diad. hd. of Venus r., CN . IVLI L . F . Q. before, three pellets behind. R. Cupid stg. facing, hd. l., holding torch and cornucopiae; to r., CORDVBA; to l., three pellets. *Heiss* 1 .. .. £15

62 **Obulco.** 1st Cent. B.C. Æ 21. Laur. hd. of Apollo r., OBVL. before, NIC. behind. R. Bull stg. r., crescent above. *Heiss* 27-8 .. .. £10

63 — — Eagle stg. r., wings spread, on tablet inscribed OBVLCO. R. Bull galloping r. *Heiss* 32 .. .. £15

64 **Carteia** (Roman colony founded in 171 B.C.). 2nd-1st Cent. B.C. Æ 24 (*semis*). Laur. hd. of Neptune (?) r., s behind. R. Prow r., Q . / C . MINI above, CA͞RTEI. beneath. *Heiss* 16 .. .. £12

65 — —*Obv.* Same. R. Dolphin r., Q . OPS above, CARTEIA beneath. *Heiss* 7 .. £11

66 — Æ 18 (*sextans*). Hd. of Hercules r., wearing lion's skin, two pellets before. R. CARTEIA. Dolphin l., two pellets above. *Heiss* 2 .. .. £10

67   69

67 — Æ 22. Turreted female hd. r., CARTEIA before. R. Fisherman seated l. on rock, basket at his side, with fish on the end of his line; D. — D. in field. *Heiss* 19 .. .. £15

68 — Æ 19. *Obv.* Similar, but with trident behind. R. Winged genius riding on dolphin r., IIII . VIR above, EX D . D. beneath. *Heiss* 23 .. .. £9

69 — — Dolphin l., with trident behind; beneath, CARTEIA. R. Rudder placed horizontally, IIII . VIR above, D . D. beneath. *Heiss* 24 .. .. £7

ÞÞ = A	✗ = I	ꓷꓤ = R
< = C	ꓤ = K	♀♀ = Ř
ꝿ = G (I)	✳ = H O	ꟽ = S
✗ = D (A)	ꓥꓥ = L	╫ = T (I)
ꞓ = E	Ꝟ = M	Ш = TO, TU
↑ = U, V	ꓦ = N	Ƴ = N
ꓕ = Z ?	☐ = O ?	ꓥꓥꓨꓨ = CA, GA
Η = O	ꓩ = B (I)	ꓛꓛ = GE
◇⊙○ = CO	ϟ = S	ǀ = BA, VA
Ꝋ = TH	ꓷ = QO, QU	ΔΔ = DU, TU

TABLE OF IBERIAN LETTERS (after HILL)

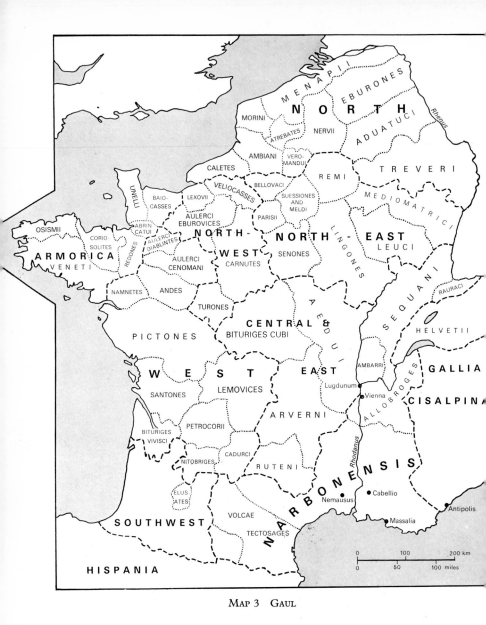

MAP 3   GAUL

GAUL

Greek contact with Gaul dated from *circa* 600 B.C. when the Phokaians founded the city of Massalia (Marseilles) on the Mediterranean coast.   Two hundred years later the Massiliots formed an alliance with the Roman Republic, an arrangement which was destined to be of inestimable value to the Romans as it protected the vital communications with Spain.   In the latter part of the Second Century B.C. Massalia found itself seriously threatened by the Celtic tribes.   The Romans utilized this situation to intervene in the affairs of southern Gaul, and the Ligurian tribes were conquered by 123 B.C., the Allobroges and the Arverni two years later.

These successes led to the formation of the Roman province of Gallia Transalpina—the *provincia* whose memory is perpetuated by present-day Provence. In 118 B.C. Narbo Martius (Narbonne) was founded as a Romany colony and trade with the interior of the country rapidly began to florish as Roman businessmen established themselves in the *provincia*. The final conquest of the whole of Gaul was carried out by Julius Caesar between 58 and 50 B.C. These remarkable campaigns are immortalized in Caesar's famous "Commentaries."

The coins of the Gaulish Celts, and indeed the Celtic peoples of other regions, do not really belong under the classification of Greek coins; but as many of the types are derived from Greek prototypes, and as the Celtic coinage as a whole plays an important part in the numismatic history of the Mediterranean World in the later Hellenistic period, it has been thought that it would be useful to include a selection of these issues within the scope of this catalogue.

Greek Coinage

70 **Massalia** (founded by the Phokaians *circa* 600 B.C.). *Circa* 450-400 B.C. Æ *obol.* Archaic hd. of Apollo r., wearing helmet ornamented with wheel. R. Wheel with four spokes. *Forrer (Keltische Numismatik der Rhein- und Donaulande)* 154. *De la Tour (Atlas de Monnaies Gauloises)* 520 ..   ..   £125

71 — — Archaic hd. of Artemis l. R. Crab, м beneath. *De la Tour* 511   ..   £150

N.B. Of an earlier date than these two types are the small silver pieces of archaic style such as those found in the famous Auriol Hoard of 1867 (see De la Tour, plate I). Some of these coins obviously originated from mints in Asia Minor, Greece and Italy, but others may have been produced in southern Gaul, mostly likely at Massalia.

72   73

72 After *c.* 400 B.C. Æ *obol.* Youthful male hd. (of Apollo ?) l. R. Wheel with four spokes, M⸗ A in two of the quarters. *Forrer* 156. *De la Tour* 580   ..   ..   ..   £35

73 *Circa* 375-200 B.C. Æ *drachm.* Hd. of Artemis r., of fine early style, hair adorned with olive-sprigs. R. Lion stg. r., ΜΑΣΣΑ above. *Forrer* 159. *De la Tour* 785 ..   £140

74 — — Similar, but of later and poorer style. *De la Tour* 820   ..   ..   £60

These drachms were extensively imitated by the Celtic tribes (see Forrer 160-67). The barbarous copies are, in fact, much commoner today than their Greek prototypes.

75 After *c.* 200 B.C. Æ *drachm.* Laur. hd. of Artemis r., bow and quiver at shoulder. R. Lion stg. r., ΜΑΣΣΑ above, trident-head beneath. *De la Tour* 844 ..   ..   £40

76 — — *Obv.* Similar, but hair adorned with olive-sprigs. R. Lion stg. r., ΜΑΣΣΑ / ΛΙΗΤΩΝ above and in ex.; in field to r., A. *De la Tour* 944   ..   ..   ..   £40

77   78

77 — — Diad. and dr. bust of Artemis r., bow and quiver at shoulder. R. Similar to last, but with ΤΑ monogram instead of A in field to r. *De la Tour* 992   ..   £35

78 *Circa* 200-49 B.C. Æ 24. Laur. hd. of Apollo l., quiver behind. R. Bull charging r., bow above, ΜΑΣΣΑΛΙΗΤΩΝ in ex. *De la Tour* 1515, *variety* £15

79 — Æ 21. Hd. of Athena r., wearing crested helmet. R. Μ - A either side of tripod above which, small wheel; in field to l., cornucopiae. *De la Tour* 1914   ..   £12

Coinage of the Gaulish Tribes

Most of these issues fall probably within the period late Second Century to mid-First Century B.C. Denominations other than gold are uncertain, and referred to merely by their diameters in millimetres—Æ 16, Æ 18, *etc.*

80 **SOUTHERN REGION. The Longostaletae.** Æ 26. Hd. of Hermes r., caduceus behind. ℞. Tripod-lebes, ΛΟΓΓΟΣΤΑ - ΛΗΤΩΝ to r. and to l. *Forrer, p.* 90. *De la Tour* 2355 .. .. £45

81 **Kings of the Narbonensian District.** Kaiantolos. Æ 27. Beardless male hd. r., club behind. ℞. Lion leaping r., ΚΑΙΑΝΤΟΛΟΥ / ΒΑΣΙΛΕΩ beneath. *Forrer* 168. *De la Tour* 2416 .. .. £90

82　　　　　　86

82 **The Elusates.** Æ 19. Vestiges of hd. r. ℞. Degraded Pegasos l. *Forrer* 533. *De la Tour* 3587 .. .. £120
This type is probably inspired by the drachms of Emporiai in Spain (see nos. 4-6).

83 **The Volcae Tectosages.** Æ 15. Degraded hd. l. ℞. Cross dividing the field into four segments; in upper segments, pellet and pellet with crescent; in lower, axe and pellet. *Forrer* 133. *De la Tour* 3263 .. .. £100
This type is probably inspired by the drachms of Rhoda in Spain (see no. 7).

84 **The Arverni.** N *stater* (12 carats fine). Bare male hd. l., beardless. ℞. Horse prancing l., lyres in field above and beneath. *De la Tour* 3740 .. .. £750

85 — of Vercingetorix. *Obv.* Similar, but with legend VERCINGETORIXS. ℞. Horse prancing l., crescent above, amphora beneath. *De la Tour* 3778 .. £10,000
Vercingetorix, chief of the Arverni, led the great Gallic revolt against Roman rule in 52 B.C. He was defeated by Caesar and kept in captivity for six years before adorning the dictator's triumph: later he was put to death.

86 **The Allobroges.** Æ 15. Helmeted hd. (of Roma?) l. ℞. Hippocamp l. *Forrer* 536 *var.* *De la Tour* 2917 *var.* £75

87 *Potin* 19 (cast). Hd. l., of crude style. ℞. Triquetra of fishes' tails. *Forrer* 480. *De la Tour* 2935 .. .. £15

88 **CENTRAL AND EASTERN REGIONS. The Bituriges Cubi.** N *stater* (10 carats fine). Hd. of Apollo l., hair in pronounced curls. ℞. Horse prancing l., bird with wings spread above; beneath, three circles, each with pellet at centre, and ABVCATO - S. *Forrer* 452 *var.* *De la Tour* 4173 .. .. £650

89 Æ 16. Hd. l. ℞. Horse pacing l., dagger above, pentagram beneath. *Forrer* 89. *De la Tour* 4097 .. .. £75

90　　　　　　91

90 **The Aedui.** Æ 15. Helmeted hd. (of Roma?) l. ℞. Horse pacing l., ΚΑΛ above, ΕΔ beneath. *Forrer* 188 .. .. £75

91 — Hd. l., ATPILI II. before. ℞. Horse prancing l., ORCITIRIX above, dolphin beneath. *Forrer* 200. *De la Tour* 4805 .. .. £150

92 *Potin* 19 (cast). Hd. l., of crude style. ℞. Eagle stg. facing, wings spread, hd. r., holding serpent in its beak. *De la Tour* 5275 .. .. £15

93 **The Ambarri.** N stater (15 carats fine). Laur. hd. of Apollo r. R. Biga galloping r., charioteer holding goad; beneath, blundered version of the legend ΦIΛIΠΠΟΥ. *Forrer* 57 (*pp. 32 and* 323) £500
This type is an unusually close copy of the coin which served as a model for a large proportion of the Celtic gold coinage—the stater of Philip II of Macedon.

94   97   100

94 **The Sequani.** R 15. Hd. l., hair in ringlets. R. SEQVANO IOTVOS (usually incomplete). Boar stg. l. *Forrer* 203. *De la Tour* 5351 .. .. £150
95 — Helmeted hd. (of Roma?) l., Q . DOCI before. R. Horse galloping l., Q . DOCI above, SAM . F. beneath. *Forrer* 204-5. *De la Tour* 5405 .. .. £80
96 — Hd. l., of crude style, TOGIRIX before. R. Horse galloping l., TOGIR. above, serpent beneath. *Forrer* 206. *De la Tour* 5550 .. .. £120
97 *Potin* 17. Helmeted hd. r., TOG. before. R. Lion springing r., TOG. beneath. *Forrer* 208. *De la Tour* 5629 .. .. £14
98 **The Rauraci.** N stater (14 carats fine). Laur. hd. of Apollo r. R. Biga galloping r., charioteer holding goad; beneath, triquetra. *Forrer* 61 (*pp. 33 and* 324) .. £525
99 **League against Ariovistus and the Helvetii.** R 16. Helmeted hd. of Roma r., DVRNAC. before. R. Horseman galloping r., holding spear, EBVRO beneath. *Forrer* 211. *De la Tour* 5743 .. .. £150
100 — Similar, but with different legends—BRIC on *obv.*, COMAN on *rev.* *Forrer* 212 *var.* *De la Tour* 5807 .. .. £80
101 — Similar, but with different legends—DVRNACVS on *obv.*, DONNVS on *rev.* *Forrer* 213. *De la Tour* 5795 .. .. £70
102 **WESTERN REGION. The Santones.** Electrum *stater.* Hd. of Apollo r. R. Human-headed horse galloping r., vestiges of charioteer behind; above, circle of pellets with pellet at centre; beneath, outstretched hand. *Forrer* 453. *De la Tour* 4512
£550

103   104   105

103 R 15. Helmeted hd. (of Roma?) l., ARIVOS before. R. Horse prancing r., SANTONO above; beneath, circle of pellets with pellet at centre. *Forrer* 215. *De la Tour* 4525
£175
104 **The Lemovices.** R 16. Hd. l. R. Horse pacing l.; above, human hd. l.; beneath, pellet within circle. *Forrer* 146. *De la Tour* 4572 *var.* £70
105 **The Pictones.** R 18. Female hd. r. R. Horseman galloping r., holding shield; beneath, lily-ornament. *Forrer* 145. *De la Tour* 4446.. .. .. .. £120

106   107

106 **The Namnetes** or **the Andecavi.** *N stater* (15 carats fine). Hd. r., surrounded by human-headed serpents (usually four); above and beneath, vestiges of supporting framework. R. Human-headed horse galloping r., charioteer behind; beneath, pellet in annulet. *De la Tour* 6723   ..   ..   £850

107 **The Osismii.** *Billon stater.* Stylised hd. r., human-headed serpents around, boar r. above. R. Human-headed horse galloping l.; above, curved ornament with two human heads attached; beneath, boar r. *Forrer* 463. *De la Tour* 6541   ..   £40

108 **The Redones.** *N stater* (16 carats fine). Laur. hd. of Apollo r., wreath accentuated. R. Naked rider on horse galloping r., holding shield and sword (?); beneath, lyre; before, star ornament with eight rays. *Forrer* 184. *De la Tour* 6759 ..   ..   £750

109   110

109 **The Baïocasses.** *Billon stater.* Stylised hd. r., similar to 107, but the serpents are not human-headed. R. Human-headed horse galloping r., stylised charioteer above, holding whip; in field to r., x within square; beneath horse, boar r. *Forrer* 540. *De la Tour* 6967 ..   ..   £40

110 **Channel Isles.** *Billon stater.* Hd. r., with curly hair. R. Stylised horse galloping r., boar r. beneath. *De la Tour, pl.* XXVII, J.62 ..   ..   £20

111   113   114

111 *Billon quarter stater.* Similar, but on *rev.* the horse has reins; beneath, lyre instead of boar. *De la Tour, pl.* XXVI, J.34   ..   ..   £40

112 **NORTHERN REGION. The Carnutes.** *R 14.* Helmeted hd. of Minerva l. R. Horse galloping l., ↑ above and beneath. *Forrer* 195. *De la Tour* 5980   ..   £70

113 Æ 16. Male bust r., CATAL before. R. Lion springing r., boar l. below, ornaments in field. *De la Tour* 6331   ..   ..   £14

114 Æ 17. Hd. r., resembling Herakles in lion's skin. R. Eagle (on l.) and eaglet (on r.), wings spread; pentagram, pelleted wheel and serpent in upper field. *De la Tour* 6088
                                                             £12

115 **The Aulerci Eburovices.** *N quarter stater.* Hd. l., with ꝫ-shaped ornaments in hair. R. Horse galloping r., charioteer holding goad above; beneath, wolf (?) r. *De la Tour* 7018 ..   ..   £450

115 116

116 **The Veliocasses.** N *quarter stater.* Vestiges of human hd. r., with pronounced eye, and star in place of ear. R. Horse galloping r., sun disk above. *De la Tour* 7245
£300

117 120

117 Æ 19. Naked male figure in kneeling-running attitude r.; various symbols in field. R. Human-headed horse galloping r., disks above and beneath. *Forrer* 385. *De la Tour* 7283 .. .. £25
The figure on the obv. may be derived from the Herakles on the tetradrachms of Thasos (see no. 1751).

118 **The Caletes.** N *stater* (18 carats fine). Disintegrated hd., represented merely by rough striations across the field. R. Stylised horse galloping l., charioteer holding goad above, lyre beneath. *Forrer* 447. *De la Tour, pl.* XXXV, 8694. *Mack (The Coinage of Ancient Britain)* 7 .. .. £1,200
Gallo-Belgic invaders brought coins of this type and the next to Britain c. 115 B.C.

119 N *quarter stater* (20 carats fine). Similar. *Forrer* 448. *De la Tour, pl.* XXXV, 8697. *Mack* 8. *Seaby (Standard Catalogue of British Coins)* 4.. .. .. .. £600

120 **The Ambiani.** N *half stater.* Stylised hd. of Herakles r. in lion's skin. R. Galloping biga driven r. by charioteer, blundered legend in exergue. *Forrer* 181. *De la Tour, pl.* LV, D.22 .. .. £450
This type is derived from the gold staters of Taras in Calabria (see no. 381).

121 **The Morini.** N *stater* (16 carats fine). *Obv.* Plain. R. Crude disjointed horse galloping r., various symbols in the field, and often with an ornamental exergual line. *Forrer* 472. *De la Tour* 8710. *Mack* 27. *Seaby* 7 .. .. £450
Coins of this type were brought to Britain in large quantities by Gallo-Belgic invaders at the time of Caesar's conquest of Gaul (c. 57 B.C.). Some specimens are of cruder style than usual and it is probable that these were actually struck in Britain (see Mack 27A).

122 **The Atrebates.** N *stater.* Laur. hd. of Apollo r., of very crude style and scarcely recognizable. R. Very crude disjointed horse galloping r., various symbols in the field. *De la Tour* 8597. *Mack* 26. *Seaby* 5 .. .. £700
These were also brought to Britain by Belgic invaders, though about 40 years earlier than the Morini staters and in smaller quantities. They were used as the prototype for the first British gold coinage, the "Westerham" and "Chute" types (see nos. 154 and 155).

123 *Potin* 22 (cast). Branch design derived probably from the diadem and hair of a human hd.; border of pellets and annulets. R. Horse (?) stg. l. within circle of annulets. *De la Tour* 8636 .. .. £15

124 **The Veromandui.** Æ 15. Hd. l., SOLOS before. ℞. Lion, of crude style, springing l., tongue extended; above, SOLOS. *De la Tour* 8570-72 .. .. £15

125 **The Nervii.** *N stater* (12 carats fine). Disintegrated hd. of Apollo, of completely unrecognizable form. ℞. Crude disjointed horse galloping r., various symbols in field including large wheel above. *Forrer* 458. *De la Tour* 8760 .. .. .. £450

126 **The Aduatuci.** Æ 18. Swastica with curved limbs and pellet within circle at centre; around, four more circles containing pellets. ℞. Horse prancing l. *De la Tour* 8868 £15

127 128

127 **The Treveri.** *N stater*. Disintegrated hd. of Apollo, of V-shaped form suggestive of a human eye. ℞. Horse galloping l.; in field, various symbols, each surrounded by pelleted frame. *De la Tour* 8799 .. .. £400

128 — *Obv.* Similar. ℞. Horse prancing l. above tablet inscribed POTTINA; in field above, v surrounded by pelleted frame; beneath, x; to r., rad. disk. *Forrer* 462. *De la Tour* 8825 .. .. £600

129 Æ 18. Young male hd. r., diad. ℞. Bull stg. l., l. foreleg raised; above, GERMANVS; in ex., INDVTILLI F. *Forrer* 175. *De la Tour, pl.* XXXVII, 9248.. .. .. £14

130 131

130 **The Parisii.** *N stater* (14 carats fine). Stylised hd. r., curved ornament in field before. ℞. Crude disjointed horse galloping l.; above, ornament resembling a billowing sail divided into small squares, each containing pellet; beneath, circle of large pellets, with pellet at centre. *Forrer* 542. *De la Tour* 7777 .. .. £750

131 **The Bellovaci.** *N stater* (20 carats fine). Laur. hd. of Apollo l., with wreath and hair much accentuated and occupying most of the field. ℞. Crude disjointed horse galloping l., vestiges of charioteer above, rosette ornament beneath. *Forrer* 441. *De la Tour* 7886. *Mack* 3. *Seaby* 1 .. .. £1,600

    Coins of this type and the next were brought to Britain in the first wave of Gallo-Belgic invasions, probably about 125 B.C. *Specimens found in this country are usually very worn and have been clipped.*

132 *N quarter stater*. Similar. *De la Tour* 7892. *Mack* 4. *Seaby* 2 .. .. £625

133   135

133 **The Suessiones.** Æ 17. Helmeted hd. l. R. Pegasos flying l., CRICIRV beneath. *De la Tour, pl.* XXXII, 7951   ..   ..   £15

134 **The Meldi.** Æ 18. Hd. l., EPENOS before. R. Horse galloping r.; above, eagle with wings spread; beneath, ЄΠΗΝΟС. *De la Tour* 7617   ..   ..   £25

135 **The Remi.** N *stater.* Disintegrated hd. of Apollo, of unrecognizable form apart from large eye. R. Crude disjointed horse, with triple tail, galloping r., vestiges of charioteer above; various symbols in field including large wheel beneath. *De la Tour* 8020. *Mack* 34a. *Seaby* 8   ..   ..   £600

136 *Potin* 21 (cast). Warrior, with flying pig-tail, advancing r., holding torque and spear. R. Bear(?) stg. r., devouring prey, uncertain object above. *Forrer* 70. *De la Tour, pl.* XXXII, 8124   ..   ..   £14

137 Æ 16. Three young male busts jugate l., REMO before. R. Biga galloping l., REMO beneath horses. *Forrer* 467. *De la Tour* 8040 ..   ..   £15

138   141

138 **The Mediomatrici.** N *quarter stater* (14 carats fine). Hd. of Janus. R. Horse prancing l., vestiges of charioteer above, large star beneath. *Forrer* 543. *De la Tour* 8937
£400

139 Æ 16. Young male bust r., diad. (?). R. Horseman galloping r., holding spear (?), MEDIO beneath. *De la Tour* 8946..   ..   ..   £40

140 **The Leuci.** N *stater* (9 carats fine). Very crude laur. hd. of Apollo r., s-ornament above, the wreath accentuated. R. Very crude horse stg. r., looking back; various symbols in field including large palm above horse's body. *Forrer* 456. *De la Tour, pl.* XXXVII, 9000 ..   ..   £600

141 *Potin* 19 (cast). Hd. l., of crude style. R. Crude boar stg. l., lily growing beneath. *Forrer* 48. *De la Tour* 9078   ..   ..   £10

142 **The Lingones.** *Potin* 20 (cast). Bucranium between ƨ and s. R. Bear (?) stg. r., devouring serpent. *De la Tour, pl.* XXXIII, 8351   ..   ..   £15

143 **The Senones.** *Potin* 18 (cast). Grotesque hd. l. R. Crude horse prancing l. *De la Tour* 7434   ..   ..   £12

144 Æ 16. Hd. r., GIAMILOS before. R. Bird stg. l. with hd. lowered, tree (?) in background; above, SIINV; in field, pentagram, two annulets containing pellets, and pellet. *De la Tour* 7565   ..   ..   £15

Coinage of the Roman Colonies, etc.

145 **Antipolis.** *Lepidus.* Æ 16. Laur. hd. of Venus (?) r., ΙΣ ΔΗΜ. before. ℞. Victory
 stg. r., crowning trophy; to r., ΛΕΠ.; in ex., ΑΝΤΙΠ. *De la Tour* 2179 ..   ..   £30
    *This type was struck in 44/3 B.C., whilst Lepidus was governor of Transalpine Gaul and
    prior to the formation of the Second Triumvirate.*

146 **Cabellio.** *Time of Augustus.* Æ 15. Female hd. r., CABE before; all within wreath.
 ℞. Helmeted hd. of Mars (?) r., COL. before. *De la Tour* 2563..   ..   ..   £20

147 — Æ 13. COL . CABE. Turreted bust of Tyche r. ℞. IMP . CAESAR . AVGVST . COS . XI.
 Cornucopiae. *De la Tour* 2556 (*mis-numbered 2256 on plate*) £20

148 **Nemausus.** *Time of Augustus.* Æ 10. Helmeted bust r., with short beard. ℞.
 NEM. / COL. in two lines. *De la Tour* 2718   ..   ..   £90

149 — Æ 16 (*semis*). *Obv.* Similar, but with S (=*semis*) behind. ℞. Figure stg. l., feeding
 serpent from patera and resting l. arm on stick; to r., NEM . COL. *De la Tour* 2735
                                                                                      £20

150 *Augustus and Agrippa.* Æ 26 (*as*). Hds., back to back, of Augustus r., wearing oak-
 wreath, and Agrippa l., wearing rostral crown; above, IMP.; beneath, DIVI F. ℞. Crocodile
 r., chained to palm-tree, the tip of which bends to r.; in field above, wreath, streamers and
 COL. — NEM.; beneath, palm branches. *De la Tour* 2806 ..   ..   ..   £25

151 — — Similar, but with P. — P. in *obv.* field and Augustus wears laurel-wreath, whilst on
 rev. the tip of the palm-tree bends to l. *De la Tour* 2837   ..   ..   ..   £25

152 **Vienna (Colonia Julia Viennensis).** *Octavian and Divus J. Caesar.* Æ 30 (*as*).
 IMP . CAESAR DIVI F . DIVI IVLI. Bare hds. of Octavian r. and Caesar l. back to back.
 ℞. Prow r., with mast and elaborate superstructure; above, C . I . V. *De la Tour* 2943
                                                                                      £90

153 **Lugdunum.** *Octavian and Divus J. Caesar.* Æ 31 (*as*). IMP . CAESAR DIVI F . DIVI
IVLIVS.   Palm between hds., back to back, of Octavian r., bare, and Caesar l., laur.   ℞.
Prow r., surmounted by obelisk on base; in field above, rad. disk; beneath, COPIA. *De la
Tour* 4669 . .   . .   £110

N.B. Prices given in this catalogue are for **fine** examples of coins in base metal
and for **very fine** examples of coins struck in precious metals.

There is no relationship between the values stated and the condition of the coins
used as illustrations.

MAP 4   BRITAIN

BRITAIN

Coinage was first brought to this country by Belgic invaders from northern Gaul in the last quarter of the Second Century B.C. Subsequent waves of invasions introduced coins of several different types to Britain and these are listed in this catalogue under the Gaulish tribes by whom they were issued (see nos. 118, 119, 121, 122, 131 and 132).

The first coinage to be produced in this country, *circa* 90 B.C., was based on the gold staters of the Atrebates, and other British issues followed, all closely modelled on Continental prototypes. However, the British tribes retained their independence for almost a century after Caesar's conquest of Gaul, and in consequence of this the Celtic coinage here ultimately developed its own distinct characteristics. These later issues, many of which bear rulers' names, will be listed in the forthcoming "Greek Imperial" catalogue, most of them belonging to the early Roman Imperial Period.

N.B. The late Commander R. P. Mack, in the 1975 edition of "The Coinage of Ancient Britain", attributes all the main Gallo-Belgic types found in this country to the Ambiani tribe, instead of giving them to the Bellovaci, Atrebates, Morini, etc., as in earlier editions. This brought his work into line with the late Derek Allen's "Origins". For the purposes of the present catalogue, however, it has been decided to retain, for the time being, the more traditional attributions of these types. (*See above under* GAUL)

Early Uninscribed Issues
(First half of the First Century B.C.)

154   155

154 **SOUTHERN DISTRICT. Westerham type.** *N stater.* Laur. hd. of Apollo r., of very crude style and scarcely recognizable. R. Very crude disjointed horse galloping l., large pellet beneath; exergual line ornamented with zig-zag pattern. *Mack (The Coinage of Ancient Britain)* 28. *Seaby (Standard Catalogue of British Coins)* 19 .. £600
    This is the earliest British gold stater and, like the other early types, is modelled on the coinage of the Gaulish Atrebates (see no. 122).

155 **Chute type.** *N stater.* Obv. Similar. R. Very crude disjointed horse galloping l., crab-like symbol beneath; exergual line curved. *Mack* 32. *Seaby* 20.. .. £600

156   157

156 **Yarmouth (Isle of Wight) type.** *N stater.* Obv. Similar, but of still cruder style. R. Very crude horse r., with triple-ended tail, its fore-legs crossed, its hind-legs connected to a single foot. *Mack* 31. *Seaby* 21 .. .. £900

157 **Geometric type: Sussex group.** *N quarter stater.* Unintelligible design. R. Cross formed by thin vertical line and thicker crooked object, various symbols in the angles. *Mack* 40. *Seaby* 49 .. .. £300

158 **— Kentish group.** *N quarter stater.* Obv. Plain. R. Uncertain object resembling a trophy surmounted by a crested helmet; in upper field to r., three-quarters of a square. *Mack* 43. *Seaby* 49 .. .. £300

159   161

159 **EASTERN DISTRICT. Clacton type 2.** *N stater.* Laur. hd. of Apollo r., of very
crude style and scarcely recognizable. R. Horse galloping r.; beneath, pellet, sometimes
with two curved lines attached; exergual line curved and ornamented with zig-zag pattern.
Mack 46, 46A. *Seaby* 25 .. .. £600

160 **Clacton type 1.** *N stater. Obv.* Similar. R. Very crude disjointed horse l., rosette
ornament beneath; exergual line same as last. *Mack* 47. *Seaby* 24 .. .. £1,000

161 **Norfolk Wolf type.** *N stater. Obv.* Similar. R. Wolf-like animal, with bristly
mane, stg. r., hd. lowered; beneath, pellet and crescent; exergual line curved and ornamented. *Mack* 49. *Seaby* 28 .. .. £1,800

162 **NORTH MIDLANDS DISTRICT. North East Coast type.** *N stater. Obv.*
Similar. R. Crude disjointed horse galloping r., pellet and crescent beneath; numerous
pellets, etc., in the field; exergual line ornamented with zig-zag pattern. *Mack* 50.
Seaby 26 .. .. £800

163 — — *Obv.* Similar. R. Similar, but the horse gallops to l. *Mack* 52. *Seaby* 27
£1,000

Later Uninscribed Issues
(Second half of the First Century B.C.)

164 **The Atrebates and Regni.** *N stater* of the British "Remic" type. Laur. hd. of
Apollo r., of very crude style and scarcely recognizable. R. Crude disjointed horse, with
triple tail, galloping r., vestiges of charioteer above; beneath, large wheel. *Mack* 58.
Seaby 41 .. .. £600

165   167

165 — — Similar, but *obv.* plain. *Mack* 59. *Seaby* 42 .. .. £550

166 *N quarter stater* of the British "Remic" type. *Obv.* Similar to 164. R. Triple-tailed
horse prancing r., floral ornament above, rosette beneath; in field to r., annulet, with
pellet at centre, connected to horse's chest. *Mack* 71. *Seaby* 51 .. .. £400

167 *R* 12 (weight *c.* 1·16 gm.). Helmeted hd. r. R. Horse prancing r., ram's horns (?) above,
large wheel beneath. *Mack* 89. *Seaby* 58 .. .. £550

168 *R* 8 (weight *c.* 0·25 gm.). Similar. *Mack* 90. *Seaby* 59 .. .. .. £350

169   171

169 **The Catuvellauni.** *N stater* of the Whaddon Chase type. Vestiges of laur. hd. of
Apollo r., in the form of a cruciform ornament. R. Horse, of improved style, galloping r.,
curved ornament and pellets above, pellet within circle of dots beneath; straight exergual
line. *Mack* 134. *Seaby* 31 .. .. £600

170 — of the Later Whaddon Chase type. *Obv.* Plain. ℞. Horse, with two tails, galloping r., pellet within annulet above and beneath. *Mack* 143. *Seaby* 32 .. .. £700

171 — of the Wonersh type. Cruciform wreath ornament with two crescents, back to back, at centre. ℞. Horse prancing r., "Catherine-wheel" ornament above, large wheel of eight spokes beneath. *Mack* 148. *Seaby* 37 .. .. £800

172   174

172 **The Durotriges.** Æ *stater* based on the Westerham type gold stater. Similar to 154. *Mack* 317. *Seaby* 60 .. .. £175

173 Æ *quarter stater* based on the Geometric type gold quarter stater. Similar to 157. *Mack* 319. *Seaby* 61 .. .. £190

174 **The Dobunni.** N *stater* based on the British "Remic" type stater. Branched emblem, perhaps representing ear of corn. ℞. Similar to 164. *Mack* 374. *Seaby* 43 £1,000

175   176

175 Æ 13 (weight *c.* 1·16 gm.). Hd. r., of crude style but quite recognizable. ℞. Triple-tailed horse galloping l., horned object above, crude cock's hd. l. beneath. *Mack* 378. *Seaby* 63 .. .. £400

176 **The Iceni.** N *stater* of the Freckenham type. Two crescents back to back, each enclosing pellet; five-pointed star above and beneath. ℞. Horse galloping r., vestiges of charioteer (?) above, large floral ornament beneath. *Mack* 397. *Seaby* 38 .. £1,000

177 — — Cross composed of pellets. ℞. Horse galloping r., wheels above and beneath. *Mack* 400. *Seaby* 40 .. .. £1,200

178   179

178 — — Voided cross composed of curved lines, each limb decorated with row of dots; at centre, trefoil design within circle. ℞. Horse galloping r., wheel beneath; above, zig-zag ornament within semi-circle; ornamental exergual line. *Mack* 401. *Seaby* 39 £1,000

179 Æ 14 (weight *c.* 1·13 gm.). Boar stg. r., three pellets beneath. ℞. Four-tailed horse galloping r., three pellets and rosette above. *Mack* 408 *var.* *Seaby* 72 .. £250

180 Æ 9 (weight *c.* 0·53 gm.). Boar stg. r. ℞. Bridled horse galloping r., pellets and ring ornament above. *Mack* 411. *Seaby* 73 .. .. £325

181 Æ 14 (weight *c.* 1·23 gm.). Hd. r., of crude style, branch behind, pellets before. ℞. Horse galloping r., triangle within beaded compartment above, diamond-shaped ornament beneath. *Mack* 413. *Seaby* 74 .. .. £110

The Iceni *continued*

182 Æ 13 (weight *c.* 1·25 gm.).   Cruciform wreath ornament, with two crescents, back to
back, and two annulets at centre.   R. Horse galloping l., wheel above, annulet beneath.
Mack 415.   *Seaby* 75   ..   ..   £80

183   185

183 **The Coritani.** *N stater* of the South Ferriby type.   Vestiges of the Apollo hd. type,
degraded to the point of abstraction.   R. Extremely crude disjointed horse galloping l.;
above, rectangular compartment enclosing four pellets.   *Mack* 448.   *Seaby* 29   £1,000

184 Æ 15 (weight *c.* 1·16-1·39 gm.).   Boar stg. r., large rosette ornament above, annulets
above and beneath.   R. Horse galloping l., pellet within large circle of dots above,
annulets above and beneath.   *Mack* 405A.   *Seaby* 66 ..   ..   £400

185 Æ 13 (weight *c.* 1·30 gm.).   Boar stg. r., two crescents above.   R. Horse galloping l.;
above, crescent and annulet containing two pellets.   *Mack* 451.   *Seaby* 66   ..   £400

186   188   189

186 Æ 14 (weight *c.* 1·13 gm.).   *Obv.* Plain.   R. Crude horse prancing r., seven pellets
above.   *Mack* 454.   *Seaby* 69   ..   ..   £200

187 Æ 12 (weight *c.* 0·45-0·55 gm.).   *Obv.* Plain.   R. Horse prancing r., three pellets
beneath.   *Mack* 455.   *Seaby* 70 ..   ..   £200

188 **Potin coins of Kent** — crude casts in an alloy of tin and bronze, based on the cast
potin issues of the so-called Sequani type, and originating probably in Kent.   Diameter
c. 18 mm.   *Obv.* Crude hd. of Apollo to l. or to r., the eye represented by large annulet
with pellet at centre.   R. Crude bull charging r. or to l., two crescents above, exergual
line beneath.   *Mack* 12 and 17.   *Seaby* 83   ..   ..   £25

189 — Diameter *c.* 13 mm.   Types similar to last, but degraded to such an extent that the head
appears as little more than two concentric circles with large pellet at centre, the bull as a
square enclosing a large pellet.   *Mack* 24-5.   *Seaby* 84..   ..   ..   ..   £125

The small Potin coins remained in use right down to the time of the Roman conquest in
A.D. 43: *they have been found in excavations associated with Claudian remains.*

N.B. Prices given in this catalogue are for **fine** examples of coins in base metal
and for **very fine** examples of coins struck in precious metals.

There is no relationship between the values stated and the condition of the coins
used as illustrations.

CELTIC COINS OF CENTRAL EUROPE
AND ASIA MINOR

The Celtic peoples occupying the lands of Central Europe, especially those of the Upper Rhine and Danube districts, produced a considerable imitative coinage using, for the most part, Macedonian regal issues for prototypes. The bulk of this coinage belongs to the Third and Second Centuries B.C. but the issue of some types extended into the First Century. In addition to coins of Philip II, Alexander III, etc., other series imitated by the Celts include silver issues of Thasos, Larissa, the Paeonian Kingdom, Tarsos and the Roman Republic. The copies of the Tarsos staters were struck by the Celts who crossed to Asia Minor and settled in the area known as Galatia in the first half of the Third Century B.C.

190 **RAETIA. Imitation of Alexander III of Macedon.** *N stater.* Helmeted hd. of Athena r. R. Nike stg. r., holding wreath; fragments of blundered inscription in field to l. and to r. *Forrer* 354 ..   ..   £900

191 *N half stater.* Hd. l., wearing head-dress surmounted by four coil-shaped ornaments; curved ornament before. R. Crude figure of Nike stg. l. *Forrer* 356..   ..   £600

192 **Imitation of Antigonos Gonatas of Macedon** (?). *R drachm.* Hd. r., BIAT beneath chin. R. Crude figure of Athena Alkidemos advancing l., brandishing spear and holding shield; to r., CIECIN; in lower field, Π — E. *Forrer* 360 ..   ..   £400

193   195   196

193 **THE BOII.** "Rainbow-cup" *N stater* (17 carats fine), of concave fabric. Bird's head l., large pellet above and beneath; all within wreath-like border. R. Six large pellets within circle formed by torques. *Forrer* 5   ..   ..   £1,000

194 — *N quarter stater* (14 carats fine), of concave fabric. Torque composed of crescents with pellet at each end. R. Five pellets within torque. *Forrer* 397..   ..   ..   £500

195 **RHINE VALLEY.** "Rainbow-cup" electrum *stater*, of concave fabric. Triskeles-design within torque composed of V-shaped ornaments with circle and pellet at each end. R. Eight circles, five containing pellets, the other three annulets; zig-zag border. *Forrer* 399 ..   ..   £700

196 **THE BOII AND THE MARCOMANNI.** *N stater,* of concave fabric, in the form of a mussel-shell, with *obv.* in relief and *rev.* incuse. *Forrer* 388 ..   ..   ..   £750

197 — BIATEC across field, hand above. R. Scallop-shell design, incuse. *Forrer* 390
   £1,500

198 **NORICUM. Imitation of Patraos of Paeonia.** *R stater.* Barbarous laur. hd. of Apollo r. R. Crude horse and rider galloping l. *Forrer* 304 ..   ..   £125

199 — Crude laur. hd. of Apollo l., the wreath accentuated. R. Horseman galloping r., holding spear; beneath, rosette of pellets and NEMET. *Forrer* 310 ..   ..   £350

200 **Imitation of Philip II of Macedon.** *R drachm.* Laur. hd. of Apollo r. R. Horse, with large ears, trotting r.; above, large star; beneath, torque. *Forrer* 312 ..   £110

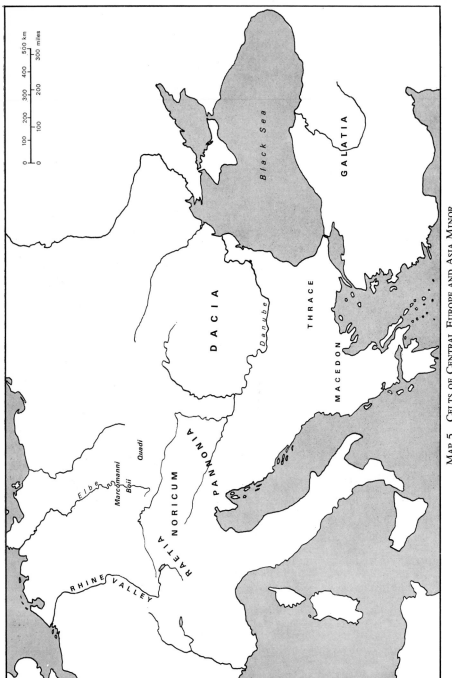

MAP 5   CELTS OF CENTRAL EUROPE AND ASIA MINOR

201 **NORICUM AND PANNONIA.** Æ *tetradrachm.* Jugate male heads r., the one in foreground laur., the other helmeted. R. Horseman galloping r., BIATEC between two lines beneath. *Forrer* 239 .. .. £350

    The obverse of this type is inspired by the Roman Republican denarius of Q. Fufius Kalenus and Mucius Cordus, issued in 70 B.C.

202 — Bare male hd. r., beardless. R. Wolf stg. r., DEVIL beneath. *Forrer* 550 .. £1,000

                203   204

203 **PANNONIA. Imitation of Philip II of Macedon.** Æ *tetradrachm.* Laur. hd. of Zeus r., of somewhat crude style. R. Youth on horse pacing r., holding palm-branch; beneath, race-torch; above and before, blundered version of ΦIΛIΠΠOY. *Forrer* 263 *var.*
    £200

204 — *Obv.* Similar, but of cruder style. R. Crude horse and rider pacing l., cross in upper field to r., star and crescent beneath. (*British Museum*) £175

205 — *Obv.* Similar, but of very crude style; the wreath and the eye are prominent. R. Very crude horse and rider pacing l., ⋈ beneath. *Forrer* 292 .. .. .. £150

                206   209

206 — Janiform hd. of Zeus. R. Horse and helmeted rider pacing r., of somewhat barbarous style. *Forrer* 328 .. .. £500

207 **THE QUADI.** Æ *denarius.* Laur. hd. of Apollo r. R. Hound running r., spear and ISTVWI beneath. *Forrer* 229 .. .. £65

    This type is copied from two Roman Republican denarii, the obv. from that of L. Calpurnius Piso Frugi, 90 B.C., the rev. from C. Postumius, 74 B.C.

208 — Diad. hd. of Juno r., s . c. behind. R. Victory in triga r., VA . BA͡EB. in ex. *Forrer* 233
    £75

    This is a copy of the Roman Republican denarius of C. Naevius Balbus, 79 B.C.

209 **THE ARAVISCI.** Æ *denarius.* Bearded hd. of the Genius of the Roman People r. R. Globe between rudder and thunderbolt, RAVIꟻ beneath. *Forrer* 223, *var.* .. £90

    This type is based on the Roman Republican denarius of Cn. Cornelius Lentulus Marcellinus, c. 76–75 B.C.

210 **DANUBIAN CELTS. Imitation of Alexander III of Macedon.** Æ *tetradrachm.*
   Hd. of Herakles r. in lion's skin, of somewhat crude style. ℞. Crude figure of Zeus
   seated l., holding eagle and sceptre. *Forrer* 330..   ..   ..   £100
211 Æ *drachm.* Similar. *Forrer* 332   ..   ..   £75

212 **Imitation of Philip III of Macedon.** Æ *tetradrachm,* of concave fabric. *Obv.* Almost
   plain, though with very faint traces of the hd. of Herakles. ℞. Similar to last; monogram
   in field to l., letter beneath seat, blundered version of ΦΙΛΙΠΠΟΥ to r. *Forrer* 336
              £125

                213   214

213 **Imitation of Lysimachos of Thrace.** N *stater.* Crude hd. of deified Alexander the
   Great r. ℞. Crude figure of Athena seated l., holding Nike and spear, trident beneath;
   the vertical inscriptions of the original are represented as dashes. *Forrer* 376
              £800
   This type is inspired not by the original coinage of Lysimachos but by the later issues of the
   Black Sea mints.

214 **Imitation of Larissa in Thessaly.** Æ *stater.* Female hd. facing. ℞. Horse prancing
   l., slight indications of rider. *Forrer* 319..   ..   ..   £350

215 **Imitation of Thasos.** Æ *tetradrachm.* Crude hd. of young Dionysos r. ℞. Crude
   figure of Herakles stg. l., holding club and lion's skin; blundered version of the legend
   ΗΡΑΚΛΕΟΥΣ ΣΩΤΗΡΟΣ ΘΑΣΙΩΝ; monogram in field to l. *Forrer* 405   ..   ..   £100

216 — Similar, but of still cruder style, and the inscription on *rev.* is quite unintelligible.
   Forrer 412   ..   ..   £150

217 **Imitation of Macedon as a Roman Protectorate.** Æ *tetradrachm.* Crude hd. of
   Artemis r. at centre of Macedonian shield. ℞. Club dividing blundered version of the
   legend ΜΑΚΕΛΟΝΩΝ / ΠΡΩΤΗΣ; all within wreath. *Forrer* 380 ..   ..   ..   £200

218 **DACIA. Imitation of Philip II and Alexander III of Macedon.** Æ *tetradrachm,* of thin, spread, concave fabric. Very crude hd. of Herakles r. in lion's skin. ℞. Very crude horse and rider r. *Forrer* 345, *var.* £175

219 **GALATIA. Imitation of Tarsos in Cilicia.** Æ *stater.* Female hd. facing, wearing necklace. ℞. Helmeted and bearded hd. of Ares r., blundered Aramaic inscription before. *Forrer* 423   ..   ..   £650

N.B. Prices given in this catalogue are for **fine** examples of coins in base metal and for **very fine** examples of coins struck in precious metals.

There is no relationship between the values stated and the condition of the coins used as illustrations.

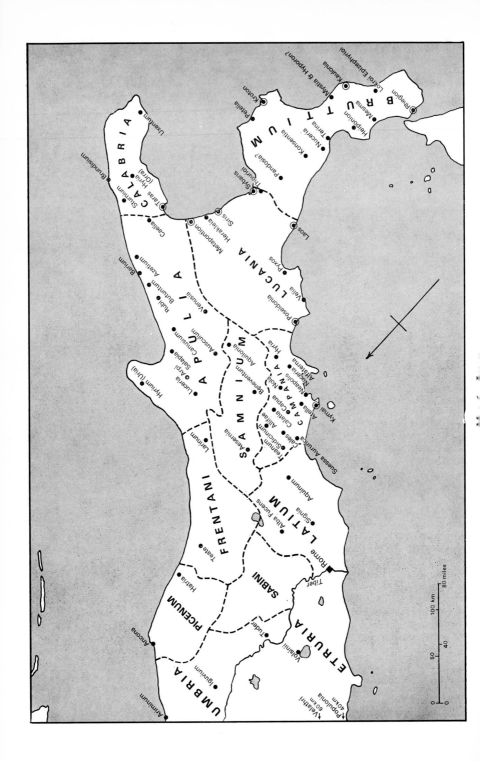

ITALY

Numerous Greek colonies were established in southern Italy in the centuries preceding the introduction of coinage, the earliest foundations dating from the Eighth Century B.C. The first coins appeared *circa* 530 B.C. and were of the curious brockage-type fabric, the obverse design being repeated, more or less exactly, on the reverse though in concave form instead of in relief. It has been suggested that the invention of this unique method of coin production could have been the brain-child of no less a celebrity than the famous Samian mathematician Pythagoras, who migrated to Italy at about this time.

The political history of Italy in the last centuries of the First Millennium B.C. was dominated by the gradual expansion of Roman power. The city on the Tiber which, in the early days of the Greek colonies, had merely been a southern outpost of the Etruscan Empire began, in the Fourth Century, to reveal its imperialistic ambitions. No one at that stage could have foreseen, or would have believed possible, the final outcome of this movement: within three centuries Rome was destined to become mistress of the whole Mediterranean world, and in Italy she was supreme from the end of the Third Century when Hannibal's offensive was finally frustrated. The coinages of the Greek cities gradually ceased as they came under Roman sway, but they undoubtedly had a considerable influence on the first Roman silver issues. These so-called "Romano-Campanian" didrachms were deliberately intended to replace the Greek didrachms in southern Italy and some were actually produced by Greek mints acting under instructions from the Roman government.

Archaic Period

220 **CAMPANIA. Kymai** (=Cumae: a Chalkidian colony, founded *c.* 750 B.C. and thus one of the earliest Greek settlements in the west). *Circa* 490 B.C. Æ *drachm.* Lion's scalp between two boars' heads. R. VK / ME. Mussel-shell. *Sambon (Les monnaies antiques de l'Italie), p.* 150 .. .. £1,250

221 — N *hemiobol* (*c.* 0·35 gm.). Corinthian helmet l. R. ΛЯ / ME. Mussel-shell. *B.M.C. 1. 1* £400

222 **CALABRIA. Taras** (known to the Romans as Tarentum; a Spartan colony founded *c.* 708 B.C.). 510-500 B.C. Æ *stater.* TARAϢ (retrograde). Hyakinthos, naked, kneeling l., holding flower and lyre. R. Similar to *obv.*, but incuse and kneeling r.; no legend. *B.M.C. 1. 33. Evans (The "Horsemen" of Tarentum), pl.* I, 2 .. .. .. £5,000

223   224

223 500-473 B.C. Æ *stater.* TARAϢ (retrograde). Taras seated r. on dolphin; beneath, scallop-shell. R. Wheel of four spokes. *B.M.C. 1. 35. Evans pl.* I, 3 .. £350

224 — — *Obv.* Similar, but without shell. R. Hippocamp r., scallop-shell beneath. *Evans pl.* I, 4, *var.* £375

225   227

225 — — TARAϢ. Taras seated l. on dolphin, arms extended; beneath, scallop-shell. R. Female hd. l., of Spartan style, within circle. *B.M.C. 1. 53. Evans, pl.* I, 6 .. £1,250

226 — Æ *diobol* (*c.* 1·3 gm.). TAPAϢ (retrograde). Dolphin r., scallop-shell beneath. R. TAPA (retrograde). Hippocamp r. *B.M.C. 1. 55* £100

227 — Æ *litra* (*c.* 0·8 gm.). Scallop-shell. R. TARAϢ (retrograde). Dolphin r., scallop-shell beneath. *B.M.C. 1. 60* £50

Taras *continued*

228 — Æ *obol* (*c.* 0·7 gm.).   Scallop-shell.   R. Wheel of four spokes.   *B.M.C. 1.* 56
£50

229 — Æ *hemilitron* (*c.* 0·35 gm.).   Scallop-shell.   R. Dolphin r., Λ beneath.   *B.M.C. 1.* 64
£40

230 — Æ *quarter litra* (*c.* 0·2 gm.).   Large T; three pellets in field.   R. Same as *obv.*   *B.M.C. 1.* 66 .. .. £35

231 — Æ *quarter obol* (*c.* 0·13 gm.).   Wheel of four spokes.   R. Same as *obv.*   *B.M.C. 1.* 68 .. .. £35

232   235

232 **LUCANIA.   Laos** (a colony of Sybaris).   500-480 B.C.   Æ *stater*.   ΛΑΣ (retrograde). Man-headed bull stg. r.   R. ΝΟΜ (retrograde).   Man-headed bull stg. l., looking back. *B.M.C. 1.* 2.. .. .. £1,250

233 — Æ *third* (*c.* 2·7 gm.).   Man-headed bull stg. l., barleycorn (?) in ex.   R. Man-headed bull walking r.   *B.M.C. 1.* 6 .. .. £450

234 — Æ *sixth* (*c.* 1·35 gm.).   Man-headed bull stg. l., looking back.   R. ΛΑΣ.   Acorn. *B.M.C. 1.* 7.. .. .. £250

235 **Metapontion** (called Metapontum by the Romans, this city was an Achaean colony of very early foundation; refounded from Sybaris, early Sixth Century B.C.).   530-510 B.C. Æ *stater*, of thin, spread fabric.   Ear of corn, in high relief, ΜΕΤΑ to r.   R. Same as *obv.*, but incuse and without legend.   *B.M.C. 1.* 9 .. .. £350

236   238

236 — Æ *third* (*c.* 2·7 gm.).   Ear of corn, grasshopper to l., ΜΕΤΑ to r.   R. Ear of corn, incuse. *Noe* (*The Coinage of Metapontum*) 106 .. .. £125

237 — Æ *twenty-fourth* (*c.* 0·35 gm.).   Ear of corn.   R. Ear of corn, incuse.   *B.M.C. 1.* 37. *Noe* 60 .. .. £45

238 510-480 B.C.   Æ *stater*, of smaller, more compact fabric.   Ear of corn, ram's hd. to l., ΜΕΤΑ (retrograde) to r.   R. Ear of corn, incuse.   *B.M.C. 1.* 27.   *Noe* 222 .. £200

239 — Æ *sixth* (*c.* 1·35 gm.).   Ear of corn, ΜΕΤ. (retrograde) to l.   R. Bucranium, incuse. *B.M.C. 1.* 39.   *Noe* 294-5 .. .. £125

240 — Æ *twelfth* (*c.* 0·68 gm.).   Ear of corn.   R. Barley-grain, incuse.   *Noe* 303   £65

241 **Poseidonia** (a colony of Sybaris, founded in the Seventh Century B.C.). 530-510 B.C.
Æ *stater.* ΠΟΜ (retrograde). Poseidon, naked but for chlamys over shoulders, advancing r., brandishing ornamented trident. ℞. ΠΟΜ (retrograde). Same figure as on *obv.*, but incuse, and viewed from the other side—thus, advancing l.; trident not ornamented. *B.M.C. 1.* 1 .. .. £5,000

242 — Æ *half stater* or *drachm.* Similar, but with pistrix in field to r. on *obv.* *B.M.C. 1.* 16
£2,500

243 — Æ *twelfth (c.* 0·6 gm.). Poseidon kneeling r., naked but for chlamys over shoulders, brandishing trident. ℞. Large ΟΠ. *B.M.C. 1.* 20 .. .. £250

244 **Siris and Pyxos** (the former an Ionian colony dating from the early Seventh Century B.C.; the latter a city of quite uncertain origin). 530-520 B.C. Æ *stater.* ΜΣΡΣΝΟΜ (retrograde). Bull stg. l., looking back. ℞. ΠΥΧΟΕΜ. Similar to *obv.*, but incuse and stg. r. *B.M.C. 1.* 1 .. .. £6,000
Siris was attacked and destroyed by Metapontion, Kroton and Sybaris some time before the destruction of Sybaris itself in 510 B.C.

245 **Sybaris** (founded by the Achaeans *c.* 720 B.C., it was the richest and most important of the Greek colonies in Italy until its destruction by Kroton in 510 B.C.). 530-510 B.C. Æ *stater.* Bull stg. l., looking back, VM in ex. ℞. Similar to *obv.*, but incuse and stg. r.; no legend. *B.M.C. 1.* 1 .. .. £700

246 — Æ *third (c.* 2·7 gm.). Similar. *B.M.C. 1.* 9 .. .. £250

247 — Æ *sixth (c.* 1·35 gm.). *Obv.* Similar. ℞. Amphora, incuse. *B.M.C. 1.* 15
£200

248 — Æ *twelfth (c.* 0·65 gm.). *Obv.* Similar. ℞. Large M/V. *B.M.C. 1.* 13 .. £125
N.B. See also no. 261.

248   249

249 **Velia** (founded *c.* 540 B.C. by Phokaians who had fled from Asia Minor following the Persian conquest). 520-500 B.C. Æ *drachm.* Forepart of lion r., devouring prey. ℞. Incuse square. *Historia Numorum, p.* 88 .. .. £300

Velia *continued*

250 500-450 B.C. *Æ didrachm.* Lion crouching r., large B above. ℞. VEΛH. Female hd. r., hair bound with string of beads. *B.M.C. 1.* 2 .. .. £250

251 — *Æ drachm.* *Obv.* Female hd. r., hair rolled behind. ℞. YEΛH. Owl stg. r., hd. facing, on olive-branch. *B.M.C. 1.* 16 .. .. £200

252 **BRUTTIUM. Kaulonia** (a very early Achaean colony). 530-480 B.C. *Æ stater.* KAVΛ. Apollo, naked, walking r., holding laurel-branch in r. hand and bearing on his l. arm a small running naked figure, also carrying branch; in field to r., stag stg. r., looking back. ℞. Similar to *obv.*, but incuse and reversed, and without legend. *B.M.C. 1.* 9. £2,500

253 — *Æ third* (*c.* 2·7 gm.). Similar, but with legends KAVΛO (retrograde) on *obv.* and KAVΛ (incuse and retrograde) on *rev.* *B.M.C. 1.* 15. *Noe (The Coinage of Caulonia)* 205 £750

254 — *Æ twelfth* (*c.* 0·68 gm.). Triskeles. ℞. VAϞ / OΛ in two lines, pellets in field. *B.M.C. 1.* 16. *Noe* 206 .. .. £125

255   257

255 **Kroton** (an Achaean colony, founded in 710 B.C.). 530-510 B.C. *Æ stater*, of thin, spread fabric. ϘPO. Delphic tripod, with three handles, and legs terminating in lions' feet; between legs, two serpents. ℞. Similar to *obv.*, but incuse apart from the handles which are in relief; no legend or serpents between legs. *B.M.C. 1.* 3 .. .. £450

256 510-480 B.C. *Æ stater*, of smaller, more compact fabric. Delphic tripod between stork stg. r. and ϘPO (retrograde). ℞. Delphic tripod, incuse. *B.M.C. 1.* 18 .. £175

257 — — *Obv.* Similar, but without stork. ℞. Eagle flying r., incuse. *B.M.C. 1.* 35 £300

258 — *Æ third* (*c.* 2·7 gm.). Similar to 256. *B.M.C. 1.* 28.. .. .. .. £90

259 — *Æ twenty-fourth* (*c.* 0·35 gm.). ϘPO. Delphic tripod. ℞. Delphic tripod, incuse. *B.M.C. 1.* 30 .. .. £40

260 — — Similar to 257. *B.M.C. 1.* 41 .. .. £45

261 **Kroton and Sybaris** in alliance. 530-510 B.C. Æ *stater*. ϙPO. Delphic tripod. ℞. Bull stg. r., looking back, incuse; in ex., VM. *B.M.C. 1. p.* 357, 2 ..   ..   £1,000

Sybaris was destroyed by Kroton in 510 B.C.

262 **Rhegion** (a Chalkidian colony, founded *c.* 720 B.C.). 494-480 B.C. (time of Anaxilas). *Æ drachm*. Lion's hd. facing. ℞. RECION (retrograde). Calf's hd. l. *B.M.C. 1.* 1-2
£500

263 — *Æ tetradrachm* (of Attic weight). Similar, but with legend RECINON (retrograde) on *rev. Historia Numorum, p.* 108 ..   ..   £1,500

Anaxilas was also ruler of Zankle-Messana in Sicily, where coins of similar types were struck.

262   264   268

Classical and Hellenistic Periods: Precious Metal Issues

264 **ETRURIA. Uncertain mints.** 5th-4th Cent. B.C. Æ 25 units (*c.* 1·35 gm.). Lion's hd. r., tongue protruding; beneath and behind, XXV. ℞. Plain. *S.N.G. Lloyd* 10
£325

265 — *Æ* 5 units (*c.* 11 gm.). Monster, represented as forepart of lion l., terminating in serpent's body and hd. ℞. Plain. *Not in B.M.C., but acquired by B.M. in* 1956
£1,250

266 — *Æ* 20 units (*c.* 22·7 gm.). XX. Sepia emerging from amphora, two helmets in background. ℞. Plain. *Numismatic Chronicle,* 1900, *p.* 2 ..   ..   £2,250

267 — *Æ* 20 units (*c.* 16·5 gm.). Chimaera crouching l., with lion's hd., goat's body and the tail of a dragon. ℞. Plain. *B.M.C. 1. p.* 7, 1 ..   ..   £1,750

268 — *Æ* 5 units (*c.* 4 gm.). Hare springing r. ℞. Plain. *B.M.C. 1. p.* 7, 3   ..   £400

269 4th-3rd Cent. B.C. Æ 10 units (*c.* 4·25 gm.). Laur. hd. of Apollo (?) l., x behind. ℞. Plain. *B.M.C. 1. p.* 3, 14 ..   ..   £250

270 — *Æ* 5 units (*c.* 2 gm.). Hippocamp r., dolphin and star above, ([=V] beneath. ℞. Plain. *S.N.G. ANS* 18 ..   ..   £175

271 — *Æ* 2½ units (*c.* 1 gm.). Lion's hd. l., tongue protruding. ℞. Plain. *B.M.C. 1. p.* 8, 6   ..   ..   £85

272 **Populonia.** 5th-4th Cent. B.C. *Æ didrachm* of 10 units. Gorgon-head facing, x beneath. ℞. Plain. *B.M.C. 1. p.* 6, 30 ..   ..   £350

273 — *Æ drachm* of 5 units. Similar, but with V instead of X on *obv. Sambon (Les Monnaies Antiques de l'Italie), p.* 49, 38   ..   ..   £250

274 4th Cent. B.C. *Æ didrachm* of 20 units. Similar, but with X : X between two annulets beneath the Gorgon-head. *B.M.C. 1 .p.* 3, 9-12   ..   ..   ..   £225

275   276

275 4th-3rd Cent. B.C. *Æ didrachm* of 20 units. Gorgon-head facing, xx beneath. ℞. Irregular x-marks in field. *B.M.C. 1. p.* 2, 6 ..   ..   £250

276 — — Hd. of young Herakles facing, wearing lion's skin knotted round neck; in lower field, x — x. ℞. Club. *B.M.C. 1.* 1-2 ..   ..   £300

Populonia *continued*

277　Æ *didrachm.* Gorgon-head facing, xx beneath. ℞. Star and crescent, x : x above, Etruscan legend *Puplana* (=Populonia) in semi-circle belwo. *Not in B.M.C., but acquired by B.M. in* 1958　..　..　..　..　..　..　..　..　..　£450

278　　　　　　　　　　282　　　　　　　285

278　— — Hd. of Athena three-quarter face to l., wearing triple-crested helmet; in lower field, x — x. ℞. Similar to last. *B.M.C. 1. p.* 396, 1 ..　..　..　..　..　£600

279　**Volsinii.** 300-265 B.C. Æ 20 units (*c.* 4·6 gm.). Young male hd. l., wreathed with myrtle; in lower field, x — x. ℞. Bull walking l., crowned by dove flying above; in field to l., star; in ex., Etruscan legend *Velznani*. *B.M.C. 1. p.* 11, 1　..　..　£1,000

280　**Thezi** or **Thezle** (location uncertain). 5th-4th Cent. B.C. Æ 5 units (*c.* 11 gm.). Winged Gorgon running l., hd. facing, holding serpent in each hand. ℞. Archaic wheel, with axle-beam crossed by two bands; between bands, ϴE — ιι. *B.M.C. 1. p.* 12, 1
　　　　　　　　　　　　　　　　　　　　　　　£2,500

281　— Æ 4 units (*c.* 9·4 gm.). ϴEILE. Hd. and shoulders of bull r. ℞. Hippocamp r. *B.M.C. 1. p.* 397, 1 ..　..　..　..　..　..　..　£1,500

282　**LATIUM. Alba Fucens** (occupied by a Roman colony in 303 B.C.). 303-263 B.C. Æ unit (*c.* 1·2 gm.). Hd. of Hermes r., wearing winged petasos. ℞. ALBA. Griffin running r. *B.M.C. 1.* 2-3..　..　..　..　..　..　..　£150

283　— Æ half unit (*c.* 0·6 gm.). Hd. of Athena r., wearing crested Corinthian helmet. ℞. ALBA. Eagle stg. r. on thunderbolt, looking back. *B.M.C. 1.* 1　..　..　£85

284　**Signia.** 300-280 B.C. Æ half unit (*c.* 0·6 gm.). Hd. of Hermes r. wearing winged petasos, dolphin beneath, caduceus before. ℞. SEIC. Mask of Seilenos l. and boar's hd. r. joined back to back. *B.M.C. 1.* 1-2　..　..　..　..　..　£125

286　　　　　　　　　　　　　287

285　**CAMPANIA. Allifae.** 400-350 B.C. Æ *litra.* Laur. hd. of Apollo (?) r., three dolphins around. ℞. ΑΛΛΙΒΑΝΟΝ. Skylla r., mussel beneath. *B.M.C. 1. p.* 73, 1-5
　　　　　　　　　　　　　　　　　　　　　　　£110

286　**Cales** (occupied by a Roman colony in 334 B.C.). After 268 B.C. Æ *didrachm.* Hd. of Athena r., wearing crested Corinthian helmet, wing behind. ℞. Nike in biga galloping l., CALENO in ex. *B.M.C. 1.* 5　..　..　..　..　..　..　£350

287　**Capua** (probably an Etruscan foundation, *c.* 600 B.C.). 216-211 B.C. Electrum *three-quarter drachm* (*c.* 2·6 gm.). Janiform female hd. ℞. Zeus in quadriga galloping r., driven by Nike. *Jenkins and Lewis* (*Carthaginian Gold and Electrum Coins*) 490　£600

　　This was struck during the Second Punic War, when Capua was in revolt against Rome and giving assistance to Hannibal.

288 **Kymai** (=Cumae: the city was captured by the Samnites in 423 B.C.).   480-423 B.C.
Æ didrachm.   Diad. female hd. r., of archaic style.   Ɍ. ƎM / KV.   Mussel-shell; marine-
plant above.   *B.M.C. 1. 2* £450

289   290

289 — — Lion's scalp between two boars' heads.   Ɍ. κVMAIOИ.   Mussel-shell; barleycorn
above.   *B.M.C. 1. 7* £850
290 — — Diad. female hd. l., of early fine style.   Ɍ. κYMAIOИ.   Mussel-shell; fish l.
above.   *B.M.C. 1. 9* £325
291 — *Æ obol* (c. 0·52 gm.).   Hd. of Athena r., wearing Corinthian helmet.   Ɍ. Mussel-
shell, κVM above, barleycorn beneath.   *B.M.C. 1. 18* £110
292 — *Æ ¼ obol* (c. 0·13 gm.).   Wheel-device with three spokes, pellet in each of the three
segments.   Ɍ. Dolphin r., κΛ beneath.   *B.M.C. 1. 24* £45
293 — *Æ ⅛ obol* (c. 0·07 gm.).   Corinthian helmet r.   Ɍ. Mussel-shell, VИ above.   *B.M.C.*
1. 25-6   ..   ..   £45
293A **Fenseris** (possibly identical with Veseris, on the slopes of Vesuvius).   *Circa* 330 B.C.
Æ didrachm.   Hd. of Hera three-quarter face to r., wearing broad stephanos.   Ɍ. ZENΣEP.
Bellerophon on Pegasos r., spearing Chimaera.   *Historia Numorum, p. 37*   ..   £850
294 **Hyria.**   400-335 B.C.   *Æ didrachm.*   Hd. of Athena r., wearing crested Athenian
helmet bound with olive-wreath.   Ɍ. Man-headed bull walking l., YPINAI above.
B.M.C. 1. 9 ..   ..   £200

295   297

295 — — Hd. of Hera three-quarter face to r., wearing broad stephanos, richly ornamented,
and necklace.   Ɍ. Man-headed bull walking r., YPINA (retrograde) above.   *B.M.C. 1. 13*
£350
296 **Neapolis** (originally a Rhodian colony of very early foundation under the name of
Parthenope, the city was recolonized by Kymaians *c.* 600 B.C. and its name finally changed
to Neapolis *c.* 450 B.C.   Allied with Rome from 326 B.C.).   450-340 B.C.   *Æ didrachm.*
Obv. Hd. of Athena, as 294.   Ɍ. NEΠOLITEΣ.   Man-headed bull stg. r., r. fore-leg raised.
B.M.C. 1. 1-2   ..   ..   £450
297 — — *Obv.* Similar.   Ɍ. Man-headed bull walking l., NEOΠOL above, ITEΣ (retrograde) in
ex.   *B.M.C. 1. 7* £450
298 — — Hd. or nymph r., wearing wreath.   Ɍ. Man-headed bull walking r., NEOΠOΛ
above.   *B.M.C. 1. 5* £500

299   304

Neapolis *continued*

299 Æ *didrachm.* Hd. of nymph r., wearing broad diadem, earring and necklace; E behind. Ꝑ. Man-headed bull stg. r., hd. facing, crowned by Nike flying r. above; in ex., ΝΕΟΠΟΛΙΤΗΞ. *B.M.C. 1.* 27 .. .. £225

300 — — *Obv.* Similar, but with dolphins around; hair very wavy. Ꝑ. Similar to last, but with legend ΝΕΟΠΟΛΙΤΩΝ; beneath bull, ΘΕ. *B.M.C. 1.* 89 .. .. .. £200

301 — Æ *obol* (c. 0·6 gm.). ИΕΟ. Hd. of Athena r., wearing Corinthian helmet. Ꝑ. ИΕΟ. Forepart of man-headed bull (river-god) swimming r. *B.M.C. 1.* 17 .. .. £90

302 — — *Obv.* Hd. of Athena, as 294. Ꝑ. Similar to last, but with legend ΝΕΟΠΟ (retrograde). *B.M.C. 1.* 22 .. .. £90

303 — — Laur. hd. of Apollo r. Ꝑ. ΝΕ. Hd. of man-headed bull facing. *B.M.C. 1.* 44
                            £100

304 — — Hd. of Athena r., wearing crested and winged helmet. Ꝑ. ΝΕΟΠΟ. Forepart of man-headed bull (river-god) swimming l. *B.M.C. 1.* 95 .. .. .. £85

305 — — Laur. hd. of Apollo l., symbol behind. Ꝑ. ΝΕΟΠΟΛ. Herakles kneeling r., strangling lion. *B.M.C. 1.* 138 .. .. £90

306 — Æ ⅛ *obol* (c. 0·075 gm.). Female hd. r., wearing sphendone. Ꝑ. ΝΕ. Mussel-shell. *B.M.C. 1.* 24 .. .. £45

307 340-241 B.C. Æ *didrachm.* Diad. hd. of nymph r., wearing earring and necklace; behind, bunch of grapes; beneath, o. Ꝑ. Man-headed bull walking r., hd. facing, crowned by Nike flying r. above; beneath, o; in ex., ΝΕΟΠΟΛΙΤΗΣ. *B.M.C. 1.* 54 .. £130

308 — — *Obv.* Similar, but with small figure of Artemis r. behind hd., and ΧΑΡΙ beneath. Ꝑ. Similar to last, but with ΜΥ monogram beneath bull, and ΝΕΟΠΟΛΙΤΩΝ in ex. *B.M.C. 1.* 80 .. .. £140

309 — — Diad. hd. of nymph l., wearing earring and necklace; behind, eagle l., looking back. Ꝑ. Similar to last, but with ΙΣ beneath bull. *B.M.C. 1.* 116 .. .. .. £110

310   311

310 — — *Obv.* Similar, but with oinochoë l. behind. Ꝑ. Similar to last, but with ΒΙ beneath bull. *B.M.C. 1.* 105 .. .. £120

311 **Nola** (conquered by the Romans in 313 B.C.). 360-325 B.C. Æ *didrachm.* Hd. of nymph r., wearing broad diadem, earring and necklace. Ꝑ. Man-headed bull walking r., hd. facing, crowned by Nike flying r. above; in ex., ΝΩΛΑΙΟΣ. *B.M.C. 1.* 3 .. £250

312 — — Hd. of Athena r., wearing crested Athenian helmet bound with olive-wreath, monogram behind. Ꝑ. Man-headed bull walking r., ΝΩΛΑΙΩΝ above, monogram beneath. *B.M.C. 1.* 8 .. .. £275

313   314

313 *Circa* 270 B.C. Æ *obol* (*c.* 0·65 gm.). ΝΩΛΑΙ. Laur. hd. of Apollo l. R. Man-headed bull walking r., hd. facing, crowned by N ke flying r. above; ΜΙ beneath. *B.M.C. 1.* 10, *var.* £100

314 **Nuceria Alfaterna** (an Oscan town, captured by the Romans in 308 B.C.). 280-268 B.C. Æ *didrachm.* Young male hd. l., with ram's horn, kantharos behind; Oscan legend around. R. Naked male figure stg. l., holding horse l. by bridle, sceptre in l. hand. *B.M.C. 1.* 4-5 .. .. £300

315   316

315 **Phistelia** (site and history unknown). 380-350 B.C. Æ *didrachm.* Female hd. three-quarter face to r., wearing necklace, hair loose. R. Man-headed bull stg. l., Oscan legend above, dolphin l. in ex. *B.M.C. 1.* 2-3 .. .. £900

316 — Æ *obol* (*c.* 0·6 gm.). Young male hd., without neck, three-quarter face to r. R. Oscan legend. Barleycorn between mussel-shell and dolphin. *B.M.C. 1.* 4-6 £70

317 — — Similar, but with legend ΦΙΣΤΕΛΙΑ on *obv.*, and the neck of the young male hd. is represented. *B.M.C. 1.* 7-9 .. .. £80

318   320

318 **Suessa Aurunca** (occupied by a Roman colony in 313 B.C.). 280-268 B.C. Æ *didrachm.* Laur. hd. of Apollo r., star behind. R. Naked rider trotting l., holding palm and leading a second horse on his r.; in ex., ΣΥΕΣΑΝΟ. *B.M.C. 1.* 7 .. .. £375

319 **Teanum Sidicinum.** 280-268 B.C. Æ *didrachm.* Oscan legend *Tianud.* Hd. of young Herakles r., wearing lion's skin, club beneath. R. Nike in triga cantering l., Oscan legend *Sidikinud* in ex. *B.M.C. 1.* 1 .. .. £500

320 — — *Obv.* Similar, but without legend, and with strung bow instead of club. R. Similar to last, but with Oscan legend *Tianud* in ex. *B.M.C. 1.* 7 .. .. .. £400

321 **APULIA. Arpi** (allied with Rome in 326 B.C., but supported Hannibal 217-213 B.C. during the second Punic War). 3rd Cent. B.C. Æ *didrachm.* ΑΡΠΑΝΩΝ. Hd. of Persephone l., wearing barley-wreath, ear of barley behind. R. Horse prancing l., large star above, ΔΑΣΟΥ beneath. *B.M.C. 1.* 1 .. .. £450

Arpi *continued*

322 Æ *obol* (*c.* 0·65 gm.).   Hook; in field to r., A.   Ŗ. Bridled horse prancing r., A above.
B.M.C. 1. 3 ..   ..   £120

        323   325   326

323 **Caelia.** 3rd Cent. B.C.   Æ *trihemiobol* (*c.* 1 gm.).   Helmeted hd. of Athena r.   Ŗ.
KAI.   Herakles kneeling r., strangling lion, club behind.   *B.M.C. 1.* 1   ..   £140

324 — Æ *hemiobol* (*c.* 0·33 gm.).   KAI.   Bull's hd. facing.   Ŗ. Lyre.   *Historia Numorum,*
p. 46 ..   ..   £65

325 **Canusium.** *Circa* 300 B.C.   Æ *three-quarter obol* (*c.* 0·5 gm.).   Amphora between
flower and oinochoë.   Ŗ. Lyre between K — A.   *B.M.C. 1.* 2 ..   ..   ..   £90

326 **Rubi.** 3rd Cent. B.C.   Æ *trihemiobol* (*c.* 1 gm.).   Hd. of Athena r., wearing Corinthian
helmet.   Ŗ. PY.   Ear of barley, cornucopiae to r.   *B.M.C. 1.* 1   ..   ..   £85

327 — Æ *hemiobol* (*c.* 0·33 gm.).   Bull's hd. facing.   Ŗ. Thunderbolt between P — Y.
B.M.C. 1. 2-3   ..   ..   £40

328 — — Rad. hd. of Helios facing.   Ŗ. Two crescents, back to back, between P — Y; above,
ΛΛ; beneath, pellet.   *B.M.C. 1.* 4 ..   ..   £45

                329   331

329 **CALABRIA.**   **Taras** (=Tarentum: the most important Greek city in southern Italy
during the fifth and fourth centuries B.C., Taras finally surrendered to the Romans in
272 B.C. despite the dynamic intervention of King Pyrrhos of Epeiros). 460-420 B.C.
Æ *didrachm.*   Taras seated r. on dolphin, l. arm extended; scallop-shell beneath, ΤΑΡΑΝΤΙΝΩΝ
around.   Ŗ. Male figure, naked to waist, seated l., holding distaff and sceptre.   *Evans*
(*The "Horsemen" of Tarentum*) *pl.* I, 9.   *B.M.C. 1.* 76 ..   ..   £300

330 — — ΤΑΡΑ (retrograde).   Taras seated l. on dolphin, r. arm extended; beneath, crayfish l.   Ŗ. Dionysiac male figure, naked to waist, seated l. on chair, offering bird, held in r.
hand, to panther's cub which jumps before him.   *Evans pl.* I, 12.   *B.M.C. 1.* 81
                                                                                          £350

331 — — ΤΑΡΑ.   Taras seated r. on dolphin, l. arm extended, a profusion of waves in lower
field; T in field to r.   Ŗ. Naked horseman galloping r., holding whip: the horse is somewhat elongated and has short legs.   *Evans* I, A.1   ..   ..   £400

332 — Æ *litra* (*c.* 0·85 gm.).   Scallop-shell.   Ŗ. Hd. of Taras r., hair tied in knot behind.
B.M.C. 1. 89   ..   ..   £75

333 — Æ *hemilitron* (*c.* 0·35 gm.).   Similar.   *B.M.C. 1.* 96..   ..   ..   ..   £45

334 420-380 B.C.   Æ *didrachm.*   Naked horseman l., dismounting from horse cantering l.;
he holds shield and spear with l. hand; in field to l., Σ.   Ŗ. Taras seated l. on dolphin,
holding crested helmet, shield and spear; beneath, ΤΑΡΑΣ.   *Evans* II, C.1.   *B.M.C.*
1. 263   ..   ..   £225

335 — — Naked horseman cantering l., holding small shield in l. hand.   Ŗ. ΤΑΡΑΣ (retrograde).   Taras seated l. on dolphin, pointing downwards with r. hand and holding oar with
l.; beneath, waves.   *Evans* II, D.1   ..   ..   £250

336 — — Naked youth on horse stg. l., r. foreleg raised; he crowns the horse with r. hand and
holds small shield in l.   Ŗ. ΤΑΡΑΣ (retrograde).   Taras seated r. on dolphin, brandishing
trident held in r. hand and pointing downwards with l.   *Evans* II, K.1.   *B.M.C. 1.* 200
                                                                                          £275

337   340

337 380-345 B.C. Æ *didrachm*. Naked youth galloping r. ℞. Taras seated l. on dolphin, holding akrostolion, TAPAΣ beneath. *Evans* III, B.2 .. .. £250

338 — — Naked boy on horse pacing l., crowned by Nike flying l. behind him; in background, a second horse also paces l., its bridle held by the boy; in field to l., κ; beneath horse, ΦI. ℞. TAPAΣ. Taras seated sideways on dolphin l., turning to the r. and aiming trident at tunny-fish beneath; waves below, A in field to r. *Evans* III, G.1 .. .. £450

339 — — Naked youth galloping r., holding whip behind him; beneath, ΔOP. ℞. Taras, as a child, seated l. on dolphin, holding wreath; beneath, TAPAΣ. *Evans* III, Q.1 .. £200

340 344-334 B.C. N *stater*. Hd. of Amphitrite r., wearing stephane and light veil, TAPA and dolphin before, A behind. ℞. Naked boy seated on horse pacing r. which he crowns with his r. hand; in upper field to l., rudder; beneath, purple-shell, Σ and KYΛIK. *Evans pl.* V, 2. *B.M.C.* 1. 7 .. .. £7,500
This type was struck at the time when the Spartan king Archidamos was assisting the Tarentines against their aggressive neighbours, the Messapians.

341   342

341 — Æ *didrachm*. Naked boy seated on horse stg. r. which he crowns with his r. hand; beneath, a second boy kneeling r., picking pebble from the horse's l. fore-hoof; in field to r., Φ. ℞. TAPAΣ. Taras seated sideways on dolphin l., holding kantharos, shield and trident; beneath, Π and waves. *B.M.C.* 1. 184 .. .. £300

342 — — Naked warrior, helmeted, stg. facing, hd. r., behind his horse which stands r.; he holds spear and large shield; in field to r., ⊢. ℞. TAPAΣ. Taras seated sideways on dolphin l., holding trident and small shield; beneath, A and waves. *Evans* IV, D.1
£250

343 — — Naked boy on horse prancing r., crowned by Nike flying r.; the horse is embraced by a second boy stg. behind it; beneath, I. ℞. Taras seated l. on dolphin, holding vase; behind, κ; beneath, TAPAΣ. *Evans* IV, F.3. *B.M.C.* 1. 172 .. .. .. £250

344 — — Naked horseman, helmeted, prancing l., holding two spears and shield; Nike stands before, attempting to restrain the rearing steed by rein and forelock; above, TAPANTINΩN; in field to r., ⊢A; beneath, M and KAΛ. ℞. TAPAΣ. Taras seated r. on dolphin, wearing chlamys, hurling dart and holding two spears; beneath, KAΛ and waves. *Evans* IV, G.1. *B.M.C.* 1. 272 .. .. £300

345 — — Naked horseman prancing r., brandishing spear with r. hand and holding shield and two more spears in l.; behind, ⊢ ; before, A; beneath, KAΛ / A. ℞. TAPAΣ. Taras seated r. on dolphin, holding crested helmet with both hands; large star in field on either side; beneath, KAΛ. *Evans* IV, H.2. *B.M.C.* 1. 211 .. .. £225

Taras *continued*

346 334-302 B.C. N *hemilitron* (*c.* 0·43 gm.). Rad. hd. of Helios three-quarter face to r.
R. Thunderbolt between TAP and AΠOΛ. *Evans pl.* V, 5. *B.M.C. 1.* 30-32 ..   £250

347 — R *didrachm.* *Obv.* Similar to 345, but with R behind and ΦI beneath. R. Taras, as a
child, seated l. on dolphin, holding distaff; to l., ΦIΛIΣ; to r., eagle stg. l.; beneath, waves.
Evans V, A.5. *B.M.C. 1.* 235 ..   ..   £225

*The last two types were issued at the time of the Italian campaign of the Epeirote King
Alexander the Molossian, 334-330 B.C. Ostensibly the champion of the Tarentines, Alexander
soon revealed wider ambitions, but his career was abruptly terminated by his death in battle
against the Lucanians and Bruttians.*

348 — N *stater.* TAPA. Hd. of Amphitrite r. wearing stephane and light veil, dolphin before
and behind; ΩY (?) beneath. R. The Dioskouroi on horses pacing l., side by side; above,
two stars; in ex., ΣA. *B.M.C. 1.* 5   ..   ..   £4,500

349 — R *didrachm.* *Obv.* Similar to 345, but with ΣA beneath horse. R. Taras seated l. on
dolphin, holding kantharos and trident; in field to l., Ω / Σ; to r., TAPAΣ; beneath, small
dolphin l. *Evans* V, B.15. *B.M.C. 1.* 229-31 ..   ..   £225

350 — — Naked boy seated on horse stg. r., its r. foreleg raised; he crowns the horse with his
r. hand; beneath, AΠH. R. Similar to last, but with Φ in field to r. and TAPAΣ beneath.
Evans V, F.1. *B.M.C. 1.* 140   ..   ..   £200

351   354   358

351 FRACTIONAL SILVER DENOMINATIONS, mostly of the fourth century B.C.
Diobol (*c.* 1·2 gm.). Hd. of Athena r., wearing crested helmet. R. TAPANTINΩN. Herakles
stg. r., strangling lion; behind, bow and club; between legs, K. *B.M.C. 1.* 352   £45

352 — Hd. of Herakles r., wearing lion's skin. R. Herakles kneeling r., grappling with lion and
wielding club with r. hand. *B.M.C. 1.* 371   ..   ..   £75

353 — Two horses' heads back to back; above and beneath, two small crescents back to back.
R. Same as *obv.*, but without crescents; beneath, N. *B.M.C. 1.* 383 ..   ..   £65

354 *Litra* (*c.* 0·7 gm.). Scallop-shell. R. Diad. female hd. r. *B.M.C. 1.* 391 ..   £60

355 — Scallop-shell. R. Dolphin l., tripod beneath. *B.M.C. 1.* 398   ..   ..   £35

356 *Obol* (*c.* 0·6 gm.). Kantharos, with four pellets around and K in field to l. R. Kantharos,
with five pellets around. *B.M.C. 1.* 443 ..   ..   £30

357 — Kantharos, four pellets around; in field to r., K. R. Kantharos, four pellets around; in
field to l., cornucopiae. *B.M.C. 1.* 444 ..   ..   £30

358 — Horse's hd. r., ⊢ before. R. Same as *obv.* *B.M.C. 1.* 418..   ..   ..   £30

359 *Hemilitron* (*c.* 0·35 gm.). Scallop-shell. R. Dolphin r., bee beneath. *B.M.C. 1.* 452
£30

360 *Hemiobol* (*c.* 0·3 gm.). One-handled vase l. R. K within olive-wreath. *B.M.C. 1.* 466
£25

361 ⅓ *litra* (*c.* 0·23 gm.). Two crescents back to back, four pellets around. R. Two crescents
back to back, dividing K — A; pellet above and beneath. *B.M.C. 1.* 457   ..   £25

362   363

362 302-281 B.C. *A´ stater*. Hd. of young Herakles r., wearing lion's skin, club beneath.
R. Biga galloping r., driven by Taras (?) wearing chlamys and holding trident; above,
NIKAP; in ex., TAPANTINΩN. *Evans pl.* V, 12. *B.M.C.1.* 11 .. .. .. £1,750
363 — *R didrachm*. Naked boy, often of effeminate appearance, seated on horse stg. r.
which he crowns with his r. hand; in upper field to l., ΣA; beneath horse, ΦIΛI / APXOΣ.
R. TAPAΣ. Taras seated l. on dolphin, holding bunch of grapes; beneath, AΓA. *Evans* VI,
A.3. *B.M.C.1.* 131-2 .. .. £125
364 — — Naked horseman cantering l., holding small shield in l. hand; in field to r., ΣI;
beneath horse, ΦIΛOKΛHΣ. R. TAPAΣ. Taras seated l. on dolphin, holding wreath;
beneath, ΛY. *Evans* VI, C.3. *B.M.C.1.* 206 .. .. £125

365   368

365 — — Naked horseman galloping r.; in upper field to l., EY; beneath horse, APIΣTIAΣ.
R. TAPAΣ. Taras, as a child, seated l. on dolphin, holding bunch of grapes and distaff;
beneath, KΛH. *Evans* VI, F.2. *B.M.C.1.* 120 .. .. £125
366 — *R didrachm*, of the Campano-Tarentine type. Diad. hd. of nymph l., wearing earring
and necklace. R. Naked boy seated on horse pacing r. which he crowns with his r. hand;
beneath, TA and dolphin r. *Evans pl.* VI, 13. *B.M.C.1.* 282-3 .. .. £120
*This unusual type was, perhaps, the result of a monetary alliance between Taras and
Neapolis. The issue probably continued well into the third century B.C.*

367   368

367 — *R drachm*. Hd. of Athena r., wearing crested helmet ornamented with Skylla. R.
Owl, with closed wings, stg. r. on olive-spray; to l., TAP; to r., IOP and club. *B.M.C.1.*
308 .. .. £90
368 281-272 B.C. *A´ stater*. Laur. hd. of Zeus r., N̄K behind. R. TAPANTINΩN. Eagle, with
wings open, stg. r. on thunderbolt; in field to r., AΠOΛ and helmet r. *B.M.C.1.* 4
£2,000

369   370

Taras *continued*

369 — *N quarter stater* (*c.* 2·15 gm.). Laur. hd. of Apollo r., N̂K before. ℞. Similar to last, but with ÂP and spear-head in field to r., and IA beneath thunderbolt. *Evans pl.* V, 15. *B.M.C. 1.* 22 .. .. £500

370 — ℞ *didrachm* (wt. now reduced from *c.* 7·9 gm. to 6·5 gm.). Naked boy on horse pacing l.; before them, naked male figure stg. r., crowning the horse; in upper field to r., ΓΥ; beneath horse, ΑΡΙ / ΣΤΙ / Π. ℞. ΤΑΡΑΣ. Taras seated r. on dolphin, holding arrow and bow; beneath, elephant r. *Evans* VII, B.1. *B.M.C. 1.* 174-5 .. .. £150

371   375

371 — — The Dioskouroi on horses prancing l., monogram above, ΣΑΛΩΝΟΣ beneath. ℞. ΤΑΡΑΣ. Taras seated l. on dolphin, holding wreath-bearing Nike in r. hand, and shield and two spears in l.; in field to l., ΓΥ; beneath dolphin, waves. *Evans* VII, D.1. *B.M.C. 1.* 98-9 .. .. £150

372 — — Naked youth galloping r., holding behind him lighted torch; beneath, ⱶΗΡΑΚΛΗΙ. ℞. ΤΑΡΑΣ. Taras seated r. on dolphin, wearing chlamys, brandishing dart in raised r. hand, and holding two others in l.; in field to l., monogram; beneath dolphin, kantharos and Α. *Evans* VII, M.1. *B.M.C. 1.* 126 .. .. £100

373 — ℞ *drachm.* Hd. of Athena l., wearing crested helmet ornamented with Skylla. ℞. ΤΑΡΑΝΤΙΝΩΝ. Owl, with open wings, stg. r. on thunderbolt; in field to r., ΣΩΣ; beneath thunderbolt, ΔΙ. *Evans p.* 162, 6. *B.M.C. 1.* 317 .. .. .. £85

374 272-235 B.C. ℞ *didrachm.* Naked boy seated on horse pacing l. which he crowns with his r. hand; behind, N̂K; beneath, ΦΙΛΟΚΡΑ. ℞. Taras seated l. on dolphin, holding kantharos and trident, ΑΠΟΛ behind, ΤΑΡΑΣ beneath. *Evans* VIII, A.6. *B.M.C. 1.* 159-60 .. .. £90

375 — — Naked horseman prancing r., brandishing spear with r. hand and holding shield and two more spears in l.; behind, ΔΙ; beneath, ΑΡΙ — ΣΤΟ / ΚΑ — ΗΣ. ℞. Similar to last, but with hd. of nymph l. in field to r., instead of ΑΠΟΛ. *Evans* VIII, D.1. *B.M.C. 1.* 214 £90

376 — — Naked warrior, wearing helmet and holding large shield, seated on horse stg. l., its r. foreleg raised; in field to l., ΕΥΦ; beneath, ΑΡ — ΙΣΤΩΝ. ℞. Taras seated l. on dolphin, holding hippocamp and trident; behind, ΙΩΠ; beneath, ΤΑΡΑΣ. *Evans* VIII, M.1. *B.M.C. 1.* 195 .. .. £100

377 — ℞ *drachm.* Hd. of Athena r., wearing crested helmet ornamented with Skylla. ℞. Owl, with closed wings, stg. r. on Ionic capital; to l., ΝΙΚΟΚΡΑΤΗΣ; to r., ΤΑΡ and ΑΝ. *Evans p.* 182, 6 .. .. £100

378 235-228 B.C. ℞ *didrachm.* Warrior, wearing cuirass, galloping r., brandishing short spear; behind, wreath; beneath, ΟΛΥΜΠΙΣ. ℞. Taras seated l. on dolphin, holding kantharos and cornucopiae; behind, tripod; beneath, Τ — ΑΡΑΣ. *Evans* IX, C.1. *B.M.C. 1.* 274-5 .. .. £125

379 — — Warrior, in full military costume, hd. facing, on horse prancing r., holding wreath-bearing Nike in r. hand; behind, elaborate monogram; beneath, ΚΑΛΛΙΚΡΑ / ΤΗΣ. ℞. Taras seated l. on dolphin, holding wreath-bearing Nike and trident; behind, N̂E; beneath, ΤΑΡΑΣ. *Evans* IX, H.1. *B.M.C. 1.* 276-7 .. .. £125

379   383

380 — Æ *drachm*. *Obv*. Similar to 377, but with κ on flap of helmet. ꝶ. Owl, with closed wings, stg. r. on olive-spray; to l., ΟΛΥΜΠΙΣ; to r., monogram. *Evans p*. 196, 1. *B.M.C. 1*. 315 .. .. £100

381 212-209 B.C. *N stater*. Hd. of young Herakles r., wearing lion's skin. ꝶ. ΤΑΡΑΝΤΙΝΩΝ. Biga galloping r., driven by Taras (?) wearing chlamys and holding trident; beneath horses, ΑΡΙ; below, thunderbolt. *Evans pl*. X, 15. *B.M.C. 1*. 10 .. .. £1,500

382 — *N third stater* (*c*. 2·85 gm.). Hd. of Athena r., wearing crested Corinthian helmet. ꝶ. Similar to last, but without legend; beneath horses, dolphin r.; above, star. *Evans pl*. X, 16. *B.M.C. 1*. 21 .. .., ... £600

383 — Æ *drachm* (*c*. 3·5 gm.). Naked boy seated on horse pacing r. which he crowns with his r. hand; in l. hand, long palm-branch; beneath horse, ΚΡΙΤΟ — Σ. ꝶ. Taras seated l. on dolphin, holding wreath-bearing Nike and trident; monograms in field on either side; beneath, ΤΑΡΑΣ. *Evans* X, C.1. *B.M.C. 1*. 302 .. .. £150

384 — Æ *hemidrachm* (*c*. 1·75 gm.). Naked boy seated on horse stg. r. which he crowns with his r. hand; above, Nike flying r., crowning him; beneath horse, ΣΩΚΑΝ / ΝΑΣ. *Evans* X, F.1. *B.M.C. 1. p*. 400, 3 .. .. £175

The last four types were struck during the Hannibalic occupation of Taras in the second Punic War.

384   386   390

385 **LUCANIA. The Lucani.** 212-207 B.C. Æ *drachm* (*c*. 3·1 gm.). Hd. of Athena r., wearing crested Corinthian helmet. ꝶ. Ear of corn, with leaf; to l., ΛΟΥΚΑ; to r., owl. *Historia Numorum, p*. 70 .. .. £350

This type also belongs to the period of Hannibal's presence in southern Italy.

386 **Herakleia** (founded jointly by Taras and Thourioi in 433 B.C., it later became the seat of the general assembly of the Italiot Greeks: finally surrendered to the Romans in 272 B.C.). 433-380 B.C. Æ *diobol* (*c*. 1·3 gm.). Hd. of young Herakles r., wearing lion's skin. ꝶ. ΗΕ (retrograde). Lion running r. *B.M.C. 1*. 3 .. .. .. £90

387 — — Hd. of Athena r., wearing crested Athenian helmet ornamented with hippocamp. ꝶ. ΗΕ. Herakles kneeling r., strangling lion. *B.M.C. 1*. 9 .. .. .. £75

388 400-370 B.C. Æ *didrachm*. Female hd. r., hair bound with olive; surrounded by aegis with border of serpents intertwined. ꝶ. ΗΡΑΚΛΕΙΩΝ. Herakles, naked, reclining l. on rocks, holding wine-cup; club at his side. *B.M.C. 1*. 15 .. .. .. £2,500

389 370-281 B.C. Æ *didrachm*. Hd. of Athena r., wearing crested Athenian helmet ornamented with Skylla hurling stone; before, Δ / Κ / Φ. ꝶ. ⊢ΗΡΑΚΛΗΙΩΝ. Herakles, naked, stg. facing, hd. and body turned to r., strangling lion with both hands; between legs, owl r.; in field to l., club and ΚΑΛ. *B.M.C. 1*. 28 .. .. £750

390 — — Hd. of Athena three-quarter face to r., wearing triple-crested helmet and necklace. ꝶ. Similar to last, but Herakles is about to strike the lion with club wielded in r. hand; no symbols or letters in field. *B.M.C. 1*. 27 .. .. £750

391   392   396

Herakleia *continued*

391 — Æ *drachm.* HPAKΛHIΩN. Hd. of Athena r., wearing crested Corinthian helmet ornamented with Skylla; behind, K. ℞. ⊢ HPAKΛHIΩN. Herakles, naked, stg. facing, holding club and bow, lion's skin over l. arm; in field to l., vase above AΘA. *B.M.C. 1.* 33-4 .. £225

392 — Æ *diobol* (*c.* 1·2 gm.). *Obv.* Similar to 387, but hd. to l., and helmet ornamented with Skylla. ℞. ⊢ HPAKΛHIΩN. Herakles stg. r., strangling lion. *B.M.C. 1.* 41 .. £60

393 — Æ *obol* (*c.* 0·6 gm.). *Obv.* Similar to 388. ℞. Club and strung bow crossed, five pellets around. *B.M.C. 1.* 25 .. .. £150

394 — Æ *hemiobol* (*c.* 0·35 gm.). Four crescents back to back; four pellets around, another at centre. ℞. EH. Club and strung bow crossed. *B.M.C. 1.* 11 .. .. £35

395 — — Corn-grain surmounted by owl stg. l. ℞. Plough r., ⊢ HPA above. *B.M.C. 1.* 44 .. .. £40

396 281-268 B.C. Æ *didrachm* (wt. now reduced from *c.* 7·9 gm. to 6·5 gm.). AΓAΣIΔAM. Hd. of Athena r., wearing crested Corinthian helmet ornamented with griffin; behind, monogram. ℞. ⊢ HPAKΛEIΩN. Herakles, naked, stg. l., resting on club and holding cornucopiae; to l., Nike flying to crown him; below, ⊢ A. *B.M.C. 1.* 46 .. £275

397 — Æ *drachm.* *Obv.* Similar to 389, but without letters in field. ℞. ⊢ HPAKΛHIΩN. Owl stg. l. on olive-branch, rose between its legs. *B.M.C. 1.* 40 .. .. .. £225

398   403

398 **Metapontion** (=Metapontum: captured by the Lucanians *c.* 300 B.C. and later passed under Roman control; supported Hannibal, 212-207 B.C., during the second Punic War). 480-400 B.C. Æ *stater.* Ear of corn, META to l., locust to r. ℞. Apollo, naked, stg. facing, hd. l., holding laurel tree resting on altar, and bow with two arrows; behind, flower growing. *B.M.C. 1.* 49. *Noe* (*The Coinage of Metapontum*) 319 .. £750

399 — Æ *half stater* or *drachm* (*c.* 3·9 gm.). Ear of corn, META to r. ℞. Apollo, naked, stg. facing, hd. r., r. hand on hip, holding strung bow in l.; all within laurel-wreath. *B.M.C. 1.* 52. *Noe* 320 .. .. £900

400 — Æ *twelfth* or *obol* (heavy series, *c.* 0·75 gm.). Ear of corn. ℞. Hd. of man-headed bull r., annulet before and behind. *B.M.C. 1.* 57. *Noe* 347 .. .. .. £75

401 — — (light series, *c.* 0·6 gm.). Ear of corn, ME to l. ℞. Three crescents back to back; three pellets around, another at centre. *Noe* 352 .. .. £85

402 — Æ *twenty-fourth* or *hemiobol* (*c.* 0·38 gm.). Ear of corn. ℞. Ear of corn, ME to r., ivy-leaf to l. *Noe* 362 .. .. £45

403 400-350 B.C. Æ *stater.* Hd. of Apollo Karneios r., with ram's horn and ear, wreathed with olive. ℞. Ear of corn, META to r., leaf to l. *Noe* 341 .. .. .. £900

404 — — Youthful female hd. r., of great charm, wearing double fillet which crosses above the ear. ℞. Same as last. *Noe* 366 .. .. £750

405 — — Mature female hd. l. (Demeter), wearing corn-wreath and necklace. ℞. Ear of corn, META to l., praying mantis to r. *Noe* 398 .. .. £600

406 — — Youthful female hd. r., wearing fillet and ear-ring; ⊢ YΓIEIA on truncation of neck. ℞. Ear of corn, ME to r., T and leaf to l. *Noe* 413 .. .. £400

407   411

407 — — *by Aristoxenos.* Hd. of Demeter l., wearing olive-wreath, ear-ring and necklace; ΑΡΙΣΤΟΞΕ on truncation of neck. ℞. Ear of corn, META to r., leaf to l.   *Noe* 422   £650
This artist also produced dies for the mint of Herakleia.

408 — — Hd. of young Herakles r., wearing lion's skin. ℞. Ear of corn, META to l., locust to r. *Noe* 430 .. .. £500

409 — — *by Aristoxenos.* Hd. of Demeter r., hair bound with single ear of barley, and wearing necklace; behind, corn-grain; on truncation of neck, ΑΡΙ. ℞. Ear of corn, ΜΕΤΑΠΟΝ to r., locust to l. *B.M.C. 1.* 83. *Noe* 439 .. .. £650

410 — — Laur. hd. of Apollo r., ΑΠΟΛ on truncation of neck, Σ beneath. ℞. Ear of corn, META to l., leaf to r. *Noe* 461 .. .. £550

411 — — Hd. of young Dionysos r., wreathed with ivy; ΠΟΛΥ on truncation of neck, Σ behind. ℞. Ear of corn, META to r., owl alighting on leaf to l. *B.M.C. 1.* 93. *Noe* 464   £650

412 — Æ *sixth* or *diobol* (*c.* 1·3 gm.). Similar to 403, but with META to l. and leaf to r. on *rev. B.M.C. 1.* 68. *Noe* 363 .. .. £150

413 350-330 B.C. *N third stater* (*c.* 2·85 gm.). ΛΕΥΚΙΠΠΟΣ. Bearded hd. of Leukippos r., wearing crested Corinthian helmet ornamented with Skylla. ℞. Two ears of corn, each with leaf on outer side; between them, ΣΙ. *B.M.C. 1.* 1 .. .. .. £1,500
Leukippos was the legendary founder of Metapontion.

414   416

414 — Æ *distater* or *tetradrachm* (*c.* 15·6 gm.). Bearded hd. of Leukippos r., wearing Corinthian helmet ornamented with Nike in galloping quadriga; behind, forepart of lion r. and ΑΠΗ. ℞. Ear of corn; ΜΕΤΑΠΟΝΤΙΝΩΝ to r., leaf with club and ΑΜΙ to l. *B.M.C. 1.* 75
£1,000

415 — Æ *stater.* ΛΕΥΚΙΠΠΟΣ. Similar hd. of Leukippos, but helmet plain; behind, dog l.; beneath, Ɔ. ℞. Ear of corn; META to l., leaf with dove and ΑΜΙ to r. *B.M.C. 1.* 79
£250

416 330-300 B.C. Æ *stater.* Hd. of Demeter r., wearing corn-wreath, ear-ring and necklace. ℞. Ear of corn; META to l., leaf with plough and ΜΑΝ to r. *B.M.C. 1.* 98 .. £175

417 — — Hd. of Demeter three-quarter face to r., wreathed with corn and wearing stephane, ear-rings and necklace. ℞. Similar to last, but with bucranium and ΑΘΑ in place of plough and ΜΑΝ. *B.M.C. 1.* 117 .. .. £300

Metapontion *continued*

418 — *Æ stater*. Hd. of Demeter r., wreathed with corn and wearing light veil, ear-ring and necklace; A — π either side of neck. ℞. Ear of corn; ΜΕΤΑ with προ beneath to r., leaf and tripod to l. *B.M.C. 1.* 121　　..　..　..　..　..　..　..　£225

419　　　　　　　　421　　　　　　　　423

419 — *Æ sixth* or *diobol* (*c.* 1·2 gm.). Young male hd. l., with ram's horn, A before. ℞. Ear of corn; ΜΕΤΑ to l., leaf, owl and π to r. *B.M.C. 1.* 157..　..　..　..　£85

420 — — Hd. of Demeter r., wreathed with corn and wearing ear-ring and necklace. ℞. Ear of corn, ΜΕΤΑ to l., leaf and plough to r. *B.M.C. 1.* 159　..　..　..　£85

421 — — Hd. of Athena r., wearing a Corinthian helmet. ℞. ΜΕΤΑ. Ear of corn, with leaf to r. above which cornucopiae. *B.M.C. 1.* 163 ..　..　..　..　..　£85

422 After 300 B.C. *Æ half stater* or *drachm* (*c.* 3 gm.). Hd. of Athena (?) r., wearing winged helmet and ear-ring. ℞. Ear of corn, ΛΥΚ monogram to l., leaf and club to r. *B.M.C. 1.* 150 ..　..　..　..　..　..　..　..　..　..　£200

423 212-207 B.C. *Æ half stater* or *drachm* (*c.* 3·6 gm.). Hd. of Athena r., wearing crested Corinthian helmet: very late style. ℞. Ear of corn, ΜΕΤΑ to l., leaf and owl to r. *Hunterian Catalogue* I, *pl.* VI, 25. *Evans* (*The "Horsemen" of Tarentum*), *pp.* 206-7 ..　£275

This type belongs to the period of Hannibal's presence in southern Italy during the second Punic War.

424

424 **Poseidonia** (captured by the Lucanians, very early in the 4th Cent. B.C., who corrupted the name of the city to Paestum: finally received a Roman colony in 273 B.C.). 480-400 B.C. *Æ stater*. ΠΟΜΕΣ. Poseidon, naked but for chlamys over shoulders, advancing r., brandishing trident. ℞. ΠΟΜΕΣΔΑΝ (retrograde). Bull stg. l.; all within shallow circular incuse. *B.M.C. 1.* 32 ..　..　..　..　..　..　£225

425 — *Æ third* (*c.* 2·7 gm.). Similar, but with legend ΠΟΜ on *obv.*, and without inscription on *rev. B.M.C. 1.* 43 ..　..　..　..　..　..　..　£150

426 — *Æ sixth* (*c.* 1·3 gm.). ΠΟΜΕΙ. Poseidon advancing r., as 424, but with olive-branch in field to l. ℞. ΠΟΜΕΣ. Bull stg. l., olive-sprig before, dolphin r. in ex. *B.M.C. 1.* 53
£65

427 — *Æ twelfth* (*c.* 0·6 gm.). ΠΟΜ (retrograde). Poseidon advancing r., as 424. ℞. ΠΟΜ. Same figure as on *obv.*, but viewed from the other side—thus, advancing l. *B.M.C. 1.* 56
£45

428 — *Æ twenty-fourth* (*c.* 0·35 gm.). ΠΟΣΕ. Poseidon, naked, advancing r., brandishing trident. ℞. Bull stg. l., dolphin l. above. *B.M.C. 1.* 58 ..　..　..　£35

426　　　　　　　　428　　　　　　　　429

429 **Sybaris** (the city had been destroyed in 510 B.C., but in 453 it was rebuilt with the aid of the Poseidonians: five years later, however, it was destroyed for the second time by Kroton. In 443, with the help of the Athenians, they city arose yet again, but later its name was changed to **Thourioi**—see below). 453-448 B.C. Æ *sixth* (*c.* 1·3 gm.). MV (retrograde). Poseidon, naked, advancing r., brandishing trident. Ŗ. Dove r. within wreath. *B.M.C. 1.* 21 .. .. £175

430 — — Poseidon, naked but for chlamys over shoulders, advancing r., brandishing trident. Ŗ. YM. Bull walking l. *B.M.C. 1.* 22 .. .. £150

431 — — VM. Poseidon, naked, advancing r., brandishing trident and carrying chlamys on extended l. arm. Ŗ. MOΠ. Bull stg. r. *B.M.C. 1. p.* 287, 1 .. .. .. £200
This type commemorates the alliance with Poseidonia.

432   435   438

432 **Thourioi** (an Athenian colony founded in 443 B.C. close to the site of the ruined Sybaris, it initially bore the name of **New Sybaris**, but this was later changed to Thourioi). 443-425 B.C. Æ *third* (*c.* 2·7 gm.). Hd. of Athena r., wearing crested Athenian helmet bound with olive-wreath. Ŗ. Bull stg. r., looking back; in ex., ΣΥΒΑΡΙ. *B.M.C. 1.* (*Sybaris*) 31 .. .. £200

433 — Æ *sixth* (*c.* 1·3 gm.). Similar, but with legend ΣΥΒΑ on *rev.* *B.M.C. 1.* (*Sybaris*) 33-4 £150

434 — Æ *twenty-fourth* (*c.* 0·35 gm.). *Obv.* Similar. Ŗ. ΣΥΒΑ. Hd. of bull r. *B.M.C. 1.* (*Sybaris*) 35 .. .. £85

435 425-400 B.C. Æ *stater*. *Obv.* Similar. Ŗ. Bull butting r., ΘΟΥΡΙΩΝ above, tunny-fish r. in ex. *B.M.C. 1.* 2 .. .. £250

436 — — *Obv.* Similar, but with small Φ in upper field to r. Ŗ. Bull walking l., hd. lowered, ΘΟΥΡΙΩΝ above, tunny-fish l. in ex.; beneath bull, bird r.; on its flank, small Φ. *B.M.C. 1.* 14-15 .. .. £450
Specimens of this type exhibit great delicacy of style.

437 — Æ *third* (*c.* 2·7 gm.). *Obv.* Similar, but with A instead of Φ in field to r. Ŗ. Bull walking l., hd. lowered, ΘΟΥΡΙΩΝ above, tunny-fish l. in ex. *B.M.C. 1.* 19 .. £100

438 — Æ *sixth* (*c.* 1·3 gm.). *Obv.* Similar, but without letter in field. Ŗ. Similar to last, but with bull and tunny-fish to r. *B.M.C. 1.* 21 .. .. £75

439 — Æ *twelfth* (*c.* 0·65 gm.). *Obv.* Same as last. Ŗ. Bull stg. r., looking back; above, ΘΟΥ. *B.M.C. 1.* 25 .. .. £45

440 400-350 B.C. Æ *distater* or *tetradrachm* (*c.* 15·8 gm.). Hd. of Athena r., wearing crested Athenian helmet ornamented with Skylla; in upper field, before crest, Φ. Ŗ. Bull butting r., ΘΟΥΡΙΩΝ above, tunny-fish r. in ex.; on flank of bull, small ΥΕ. *B.M.C. 1.* 26. *Noe* (*The Thurian distaters*) B2 .. .. £700

441 — — *Obv.* Similar, but facing l., and without Φ in field. Ŗ. Bull butting l., ΘΟΥΡΙΩΝ above, tunny-fish l. in ex. *Noe* E4 .. .. £750

442 — Æ *stater*. *Obv.* Similar to 440. Ŗ. Bull walking l., hd. lowered, ΘΟΥΡΙΩΝ above, tunny-fish l. in ex.; beneath bull, bird l. *B.M.C. 1.* 50 .. .. £250

443 — — *Obv.* Similar to 440, but without Φ in field, and with M on flap of helmet. Ŗ. Bull butting r., ΘΟΥΡΙΩΝ above, tunny-fish r. in ex.; along exergual bar, in minute letters, ΜΟΛΟΣΣΟΣ. *B.M.C. 1.* 59 .. .. £425
The signature "Molossos" may be that of an engraver.

444 — Æ *sixth* (*c.* 1·2 gm.). *Obv.* Similar to 440, but without Φ in field. Ŗ. Bull butting r., ΘΟΥΡΙΩΝ above, fish r. in ex. *B.M.C. 1.* 100 .. .. £60

445   447

Thourioi *continued*

445 350-281 B.C. *Æ distater.* Hd. of Athena r., wearing crested Athenian helmet ornamented with Skylla holding rudder; behind neck, ΙΠ; in field to l., *wreath-bearing Nike.* R. Bull butting r., ΘΟΥΡΙΩΝ and flaming race-torch above, two tunny-fishes r. in ex. *B.M.C. 1.* 35 .. .. £650

    This type may be connected with the Italian campaign of the Epeirote King Alexander the Molossian, 334-330 B.C., in the course of which he achieved a great victory over the Lucanians.

446 — — *Obv.* Similar, but Skylla hurls rock, and without the ΙΠ or Nike. R. Bull butting r., ΘΟΥΡΙΩΝ and ΣΙ above; in ex., tripod between two dolphins. *B.M.C. 1.* 45. *Noe* K6 £600

447 — *Æ stater. Obv.* Similar, but Skylla holds trident; on flap of helmet, bird r. R. Bull butting r., ΘΟΥΡΙΩΝ and ΣΟΣ above, hippocamp r. in ex. *B.M.C. 1.* 86 .. £200

448 — — Hd. of Athena r., wearing crested Athenian helmet ornamented with griffin; behind, ΣΙ. R. Bull butting r., ΘΟΥΡΙΩΝ and ΕΥΦΑ above, ΔΑ beneath; in ex., thyrsos r. *B.M.C. 1.* 97 .. .. £225

449   450

449 — *Æ sixth. Obv.* Similar to 447 but without bird on helmet-flap. R. Bull butting r., ΘΟΥΡΙΩΝ and Η above, tunny-fish r. in ex. *B.M.C. 1.* 109 .. .. .. £60

450 281-268 B.C. *Æ stater* (wt. now reduced from *c.* 7·9 gm. to 6·5 gm.). Laur. hd. of Apollo r., hair long. R. Bull butting r., ΘΟΥΡΙΩΝ and tripod in ex., ΑΡΙ above. *B.M.C. 1.* 99 .. .. £350

451   453

451 **Velia** (unlike many of the Greek cities of southern Italy, Velia was never captured by the Lucanians, and in 275 B.C. became a Roman ally). 450-400 B.C. *Æ didrachm.* ΥΕΛΗ. Female hd. r., hair bound with narrow stephane. R. Lion crouching r., ΥΕΛΗ in ex. *B.M.C. 1.* 20 .. .. £300

452 — *Æ drachm.* Diad. female hd. r., Δ behind. R. ΥΕΛΗ. Owl stg. r., hd. facing, on olive-branch. *B.M.C. 1.* 27 .. .. £175

453 400-350 B.C. *Æ didrachm.* Hd. of Athena r., wearing crested Athenian helmet bound with olive-wreath and inscribed ΗΡΑ; in upper field, before crest, Ε. R. ΥΕΛΗΤΕΩΝ. Stag kneeling l., being attacked by lion l. which stands on his back and bites the base of his neck; in field to r., Δ. *B.M.C. 1.* 38 .. .. £400

    The letters on the helmet are probably the signature of an engraver.

454 — — Hd. of Athena l., wearing crested Athenian helmet ornamented with griffin; before neck, crab; behind, Θ. ℞. ΥΕΛΗΤΩΝ. Lion walking r., Θ beneath. *B.M.C. 1.* 50

£275

455   457

455 — — *by Kleudoros.* Hd. of Athena three-quarter face to l., wearing winged and crested Phrygian helmet inscribed ΚΛΕΥΔΩΡΟΥ. ℞. Lion stg. l., devouring piece of meat held between fore-paws; above, Α; beneath, ᛌΓ; in ex., ΥΕΛΗΤΩΝ. *B.M.C. 1.* 71   .. £350

456 — — Hd. of Athena l., wearing Phrygian helmet ornamented with female Centaur; behind, ᛌΕ. ℞. Lion stg. l., as last; above, Α; beneath, ᛌΕ; in ex., ΥΕΛΗΤΩΝ. *B.M.C. 1.* 74 .. .. £250

457 — ℞ *drachm.* Hd. of Athena r., wearing crested Athenian helmet bound with olive-wreath; above, Δ. ℞. ΥΕΛΗ. Owl stg. r., hd. facing, on olive-branch. *B.M.C. 1.* 35

£225

458 — ℞ *diobol* (c. 1 gm.). Female hd. r., wearing sphendone, ear-ring and necklace, Θ behind. ℞. ΥΕΛΗ. Owl stg. r., hd. facing, wings spread; in field to r., Σ. *B.M.C. 1.* 114 .. .. £100

459 350-281 B.C. ℞ *didrachm by Philistionos.* Hd. of Athena r., wearing crested Corinthian helmet ornamented with galloping quadriga; on band beneath crest, ΦΙΛΙΣΤΙΩΝΟΣ. ℞. Lion stg. l. on bones of carcass, gnawing prey; above, Nike flying l., ΦΙ behind her; in ex., ΥΕΛΗΤΩΝ. *B.M.C. 1.* 88 .. .. £375

460 — ℞ *didrachm.* Hd. of Athena r., wearing crested Athenian helmet ornamented with griffin; above, Δ. ℞. Lion walking r., pentagram between Φ — Ι above, ΥΕΛΗΤΩΝ in ex. *B.M.C. 1.* 102 .. .. £175

461 — — Hd. of Athena l., wearing crested Athenian helmet ornamented with Pegasos; above, Α; behind, ΙΕ within square frame. ℞. ΥΕΛΗΤΩΝ. Lion attacking stag, as 453, but no letter in field. *B.M.C. 1.* 111-12 .. .. £200

462   463

462 **BRUTTIUM. Kaulonia** (destroyed by Dionysios I of Syracuse in 388 B.C.). 480-388 B.C. ℞ *stater.* ΚΑVΛ (retrograde). Apollo, naked, walking r., holding laurel-branch in r. hand and bearing on his l. arm a small figure running r.; before, stag stg. r., looking back. ℞. ΚΑVΛ (retrograde). Stag stg. r.; before, sapling growing. *B.M.C. 1.* 18 .. .. £200

463 — — *Obv.* Similar, but without the small figure or the stag, and with a fillet hanging over Apollo's extended l. arm; monogram in field to l.; no legend. ℞. ΚΑVΛΩΝΙΑΤΑΣ. Stag stg. r. *B.M.C. 1.* 27 .. .. £225

464   465

Kaulonia *continued*

464 — Æ *third* (c. 2·6 gm.). *Obv.* Similar to 462, but with legend KAV. ℞. Stag stg. r.;
above, KAV (retrograde); before, sapling growing. *B.M.C. 1.* 38   ..   ..   £85

465 — Æ *sixth* (c. 1·3 gm.). Apollo, naked, walking r., holding laurel-branch in r. hand,
l. arm extended; before, stag stg. r., looking back. ℞. KAV (retrograde). Stag stg. r.,
barleycorn before. *B.M.C. 1.* 42..   ..   ..   £60

466 **Kroton** (suffered greatly from attacks by Dionysios I of Syracuse in the early part of the
4th Cent., and later was involved in continual warfare with the Bruttians: captured by
Agathokles of Syracuse in 299 B.C., and finally fell to the Romans twenty-two years later).
480-420 B.C. Æ *stater.* Tripod; stork stg. r. in field to l.; ϘPO to r. ℞. Same as *obv.*
B.M.C. 1. 45   ..   ..   £200

467   470

467 — — Tripod; kantharos in field to l., ϘPO to r. ℞. Tripod; DA in field to l., thymiaterion
to r. *B.M.C. 1.* 47 ..   ..   £250

This type may record an alliance between Kroton and the Sicilian city of Zankle-Messana.

468 — Æ *sixth* or *diobol* (c. 1·3 gm.). Tripod; ϘPO (retrograde) in field to r. ℞. Pegasos
flying l., Ϙ beneath. *B.M.C. 1.* 52   ..   ..   £90

469 — Æ *twelfth* or *obol* (c. 0·65 gm.). Tripod; stork stg. r. in field to l.; ϘPO (retrograde) to
r. ℞. Hare running r., annulet above and beneath. *B.M.C. 1.* 61   ..   ..   £75

470 420-400 B.C. Æ *stater.* Eagle stg. l, looking back, perched on the nose of stag's hd. r.
℞. Tripod; ivy-leaf to l., ϘPO to r. *B.M.C. 1.* 68   ..   ..   ..   £375

471 — — Eagle stg. l., wings spread, holding serpent in talons. ℞. Tripod; ϘPO to l., ear of
barley to r. *B.M.C. 1.* 73 ..   ..   £350

472 400-379 B.C. Æ *stater.* Eagle stg. l. on olive-branch, its hd. raised and flapping its
wings. ℞. Tripod; KPO to l., Δ to r. *B.M.C. 1.* 80   ..   ..   ..   £300

It may be noted that at this point the letter Ϙ is replaced by K in the mint-name.

473   474

473 — — Herakles, as the city-founder, naked, seated l. on rock, holding lustral branch and
club; before him, altar; behind, bow and quiver, and OΣΚΣΜΤΑΜ (=ΟΙΚΙΣΤΑΣ); in ex., two
fishes meeting. ℞. Tripod, filleted; to l., Apollo r., aiming arrow at the Python, coiled
and erect, in field to r.; in ex., KPOTON. *B.M.C. 1.* 85 ..   ..   ..   £1,000

*The archaic form of lettering on the obv. is used intentionally to complement the type of
Herakles as "Oikistas" or founder of the city.*

474 360-330 B.C. Æ *stater.* Hd. of Hera Lakinia three-quarter face to r., wearing stephanos
richly adorned with honeysuckle ornament and griffins' heads; to l., KPOTO. ℞. Herakles,
naked, reclining l. on rock, holding wine-cup; in field above, bow and club crossed.
B.M.C. 1. 89   ..   ..   £750

475 — — ΚΡΟΤΩΝΙΑΤΑΣ. Laur. hd. of Apollo r. ℞. Naked infant Herakles seated facing on bed, strangling two serpents which are coiled around his body. *B.M.C. 1.* 96-7
    £650

476 — ℞ *third* (*c.* 2·8 gm.). Hd. of young river-god Aesaros r., bound with taenia. ℞. Owl stg. l. on stalk of corn-ear, ΚΡΟ behind. *B.M.C. 1.* 103 ..   ..   £150

    477   479   480

477 — ℞ *sixth* or *diobol* (*c.* 1·5 gm.). Laur. hd. of Apollo r., with short hair. ℞. Tripod; ΚΡΟ to l., corn-ear to r. *B.M.C. 1.* 104 ..   ..   £100

478 330-299 B.C. ℞ *stater.* Laur. hd. of Apollo r., with flowing hair. ℞. Tripod; laurel-branch to l., ΚΡΟ to r. *B.M.C. 1.* 98-9 ..   ..   £300

479 299-281 B.C. ℞ *stater.* ΚΡΟΤΩΝΙΑΤΑΝ. Eagle stg. l. on olive-branch, wings spread. ℞. Tripod, filleted, with round cover; to l., ear of corn with leaf; to r., Python coiled and erect. *B.M.C. 1.* 83 ..   ..   £275

480 — ℞ *sixth* or *diobol* (*c.* 1·2 gm.). ΚΡΟΤΩ. Hd. of Athena r., wearing crested Corinthian helmet. ℞. ΟΙΚΙΣΤΑΣ. Herakles, as the city-founder, stg. r., wearing lion's skin and leaning on club with both hands; ♀ behind. *B.M.C. 1.* 108 ..   ..   ..   £110

481 281-277 B.C. ℞ *stater* (wt. now reduced from *c.* 7·9 gm. to 6·5 gm.). Eagle stg. l. on thunderbolt, looking back; in upper field, Φ — Ι. ℞. Tripod; ΚΡΟ to l., kerykeion to r. *S.N.G. Copenhagen* 1820 ..   ..   £225

       483   485

482 **Lokroi Epizephyrioi** (founded *c.* 680 B.C., but issued no coins until the middle of the 4th Cent.: was allied with Dionysios I of Syracuse, thus avoiding the ruin suffered by the other Greek cities at the time of the tyrant's intervention in Italian affairs, *c.* 388 B.C.: went over to the Romans in 277 B.C. during the Pyrrhic War, but in the Second Punic War was one of Hannibal's principal seaports until its capture by Scipio in 205 B.C.). CORINTHIAN TYPE COINAGE: 350-332 B.C. ℞ *stater.* ΛΟΚ. Pegasos flying r. ℞. Hd. of Athena r., wearing Corinthian helmet. *B.M.C. 12. (Colonies of Corinth) p.* 94, 1-2
    £175

    These Corinthian-type staters, etc., were used by the Lokroians for foreign commerce: the example in this had been set by Syracuse, their close ally.

483 — 332-300 B.C. ℞ *stater.* Pegasos flying l., thunderbolt beneath. ℞. ΛΟΚΡΩΝ. Hd. of Athena l., wearing Corinthian helmet. *B.M.C. 12. (C. of C.) p.* 95, 9-12 ..   £150

484 — 300-268 B.C. ℞ *stater.* *Obv.* Same as *rev.* of last, but of later style. ℞. Same as *obv.* of last. *B.M.C. 12. (C. of C.) p.* 95, 14 ..   ..   £150

485 COINAGE OF LOKROIAN TYPES: 350-332 B.C. ℞ *stater.* Laur. hd. of Zeus r., with short hair, ΙΕΥΣ beneath. ℞. Eirene seated l. on square cippus, holding caduceus; in ex., ΕΙΡΗΝΗ; behind, ΛΟΚΡΩΝ. *B.M.C. 1.* 1 ..   ..   £2,500

486 — 332-326 B.C. ℞ *stater.* Laur. hd. of Zeus l., with flowing hair, ΛΟΚΡΩΝ before. ℞. Eagle flying l., attacking hare held in its talons; thunderbolt before, A͡P behind. *B.M.C. 1.* 9 ..   ..   £375

Lokroi *continued*

487 — 326-300 B.C.   *Æ stater.*   Laur. hd. of Zeus r., with flowing hair, thunderbolt behind.
R. ΛΟΚΡΩΝ.   Eagle flying l., attacking hare held in its talons.   *B.M.C. 1.* 10-11   £300
These are frequently of very inferior work.

488 — 300-280 B.C.   *Æ stater.*   Eagle flying l., attacking hare held in its talons.   R. Large
thunderbolt; caduceus to l., ΛΟΚΡΩΝ to r.   *B.M.C. 1. 3* £350

        489   491   494

489 — — *Æ sixth* or *diobol* (c. 1·2 gm.).   Eagle stg. l., looking back, wings spread; before,
caduceus.   R. ΛΟΚ / ΡΩΝ in two lines, thunderbolt between.   *B.M.C. 1.* 18   ..   £90

490 — — *Æ twelfth* or *obol* (c. 0·7 gm.).   Eagle stg. l., wings closed; in field, Λ — ο.   R.
Thunderbolt between two annulets.   *B.M.C. 1.* 19   ..   ..   £75

491 — 277-268 B.C.   *Æ stater.* ΛΟΚΡΩΝ.   Laur. hd. of Zeus l., N̄E beneath.   R. Roma
seated r., holding parazonium and resting r. arm on shield, crowned by female figure
(Lokroi as Pistis) stg. l.; to l., ΡΩΜΑ; to r., ΠΙΣΤΙΣ.   *B.M.C. 1.* 16   ..   ..   £650
*This type records the Lokroian alliance with Rome following the expulsion of the Pyrrhic
garrison from the city.   These coins bear a marked resemblance to the issues of Pyrrhos from
the mint of Lokroi (280-277 B.C.)—see below under Epeiros.*

N.B.   Lokroi may have been the mint for the extensive issues of the Brettii at the time of
the Hannibalic occupation—see below under Brettian League.

492 **Mesma** (a colony of Lokroi).   350-300 B.C.   *Æ stater* of the Corinthian type.   Pegasos
flying l., M̄E beneath.   R. Hd. of Athena l., wearing Corinthian helmet, M beneath.
B.M.C. 12. (*Colonies of Corinth*) *p.* 97, 1   ..   ..   £250

493 **Pandosia** (it was in the vicinity of this city that Alexander the Molossian, King of Epeiros,
was killed in battle *c.* 330 B.C.: its coins, however, belong to an earlier period).   After
c. 400 B.C.   *Æ stater.*   Hd. of Hera Lakinia three-quarter face to r., wearing stephanos
richly adorned with honeysuckle ornament and foreparts of griffins.   R. ΠΑΝΔΟΣΙΝ.
Pan, naked, seated l. on rock, holding two spears, hound at his side; before, bearded term
r. with caduceus affixed; in upper field, Φ.   *B.M.C. 1.* 2   ..   ..   ..   £5,000

494 — *Æ third* (c. 2·5 gm.).   *Obv.* Similar, but the stephanos is adorned with rosettes.   R.
ΠΑΝΔΟΣΙ.   Pan, naked, seated l. on rock, between two hounds; in background, two
spears; before NIKO.   *B.M.C. 1.* 3   ..   ..   £1,500

            495   496

495 — *Æ sixth* (c. 1·2 gm.).   *Obv.* Same as last.   R. ΠΑΝΔΟΣΙΝ.   Pan, naked, seated r. on
rock, holding two spears; behind, NIKO.   *B.M.C. 1.* 4   ..   ..   £750

496 **Rhegion** (destroyed by Dionysios I of Syracuse in 387 B.C. and restored some years later
by Dionysios II, 356-350 B.C.).   480-466 B.C.   *Æ tetradrachm.*   Mule-car driven r. by
bearded charioteer, olive-leaf in ex.   R. RECINON (usually retrograde).   Hare running r.
B.M.C. 1. 4 ..   ..   £550

497 — *Æ obol* (c. 0·62 gm.).   Hare running r.   R. REC (retrograde) within circle of dots.
B.M.C. 1. 7 ..   ..   £90

498   501

498 466-415 B.C. Æ *tetradrachm*. Lion's scalp facing. R. RECINOS. Iokastos, the traditional founder of the City, naked to waist and seated l., holding staff and resting l. hand on
hip; all within laurel-wreath. *B.M.C. 1. 8* £1,250

499 — Æ *drachm*. Similar. *B.M.C. 1. 15* £275

500 — Æ *obol* (*c.* 0·75 gm.). Lion's scalp facing, ivy-leaf in field to r. R. RECI. within wreath.
B.M.C. 1. 21   ..   ..   £75

501 415-387 B.C. Æ *tetradrachm*. Lion's scalp facing. R. PHΓINON. Laur. hd. of Apollo
r., olive-sprig behind. *B.M.C. 1. 24* £1,500

502 — Æ *drachm*. Similar. *B.M.C. 1. 38* £450

503 — Æ *litra* (*c.* 0·87 gm.). Lion's scalp facing. R. PH between two olive-leaves with
berries. *B.M.C. 1. 32* £60

504 350-300 B.C. Æ *stater* of the Corinthian type. Pegasos flying l., P̄H beneath. R. Hd.
of Athena l., wearing Corinthian helmet, lyre behind. *B.M.C. 12.* (*Colonies of Corinth*)
p. 97, 1   ..   ..   £175

505 **Terina** (a colony of Kroton, Terina was founded in the Sixth Century but did not issue
coins before *c.* 480 B.C. It passed under the control of the Bruttians in 356 B.C., submitted to Rome in 272 B.C. and was burnt by Hannibal in 203 B.C.). 480-445 B.C. Æ
stater. TEPΣNA. Diad. hd. of the nymph Terina r., of archaic style. R. NΣKA (retrograde). Nike Apteros stg. l., holding branch and resting l. hand on hip; all within wreath.
B.M.C. 1. 1 ..   ..   £1,750

506 445-425 B.C. Æ *stater*. Hd. of the nymph Terina l., hair rolled and wearing ampyx; all
within wreath. R. TEPINAION. Winged Nike seated l. on overturned amphora, holding
wreath and caduceus. *B.M C. 1. 5* £1,250

507 425-400 B.C. Æ *stater*. ΓEPINAION. Hd. of the nymph Terina r., wearing sphendone,
hair in korymbos, Π behi d. R. Winged Nike stg. l., stooping forward and resting r.
foot on rock, holding caduceus, l. hand behind back, Π in field to l. *B.M.C. 1. 22*   £750

506   508

508 400-356 B.C. Æ *stater*. TEPINAIΩN. Hd. of the nymph Terina r., hair rolled and very
curly. R. Winged Nike seated l. on square cippus, bird perched on her extended r. hand,
l. resting on cippus. *B.M.C. 1. 41* £500

509 — Æ *sixth* (*c.* 1·15 gm.). Hd. of the nymph Terina r., wearing sphendone. R. Winged
Nike seated l. on square cippus, holding poppy. *B.M.C. 1. 34* £85

Terina *continued*

510 Late 4th Cent. B.C. (time of Agathokles of Syracuse?). Æ *third* (*c.* 2·3 gm.). *Obv.* Similar to 508, but hd. to l. and with triskeles behind neck. R. Similar to 508, but with Δ in field to l. *B.M.C. 1.* 46.. .. .. £110

510   512   513

511 **Brettian League** (the coinage of the Brettii, issued perhaps from Lokroi, belonging to the period of the Hannibalic occupation of Italy). 215-205 B.C. *N drachm* (*c.* 4·24 gm.). Diad. hd. of Poseidon l., trident behind, bucranium beneath. R. ΒΡΕΤΤΙΩΝ. Thetis (?) seated l. on seahorse swimming r.; she holds in her r. hand small figure of Eros drawing bow; in field to r., bee. *B.M.C. 1.* 1 .. .. £4,000

512 — *N hemidrachm* (*c.* 2·12 gm.). Hd. of Herakles l., bearded, wearing lion's skin, cornucopiae behind, Γ beneath. R. ΒΡΕΤΤΙΩΝ. Nike in galloping biga r., Γ and thunderbolt beneath. *B.M.C. 1.* 7 .. .. £2,750

513 — Æ *octobol* (*c.* 5·84 gm.). Jugate busts of the Dioskouroi r., each wearing chlamys and laur. pileus, cornucopiae and Γ behind. R. The Dioskouroi on horseback prancing r., their r. hands raised, holding palms in l., knotted staff beneath, Γ in field to l., ΒΡΕΤΤΙΩΝ in ex. *B.M.C. 1.* 8 .. .. £1,250

514 — Æ *drachm*? (*c.* 4·66 gm.). Hd. of winged Nike r., diad., plough behind. R. ΒΡΕΤΤΙΩΝ. Naked male figure (youthful Dionysos?), horned, stg. facing, crowning himself and holding long torch in l., thymiaterion in field to r. *B.M.C. 1.* 24 .. .. £110

515   516

515 — — Veiled hd. of Thetis (?) r., wearing stephanos, sceptre over l. shoulder, fly behind, Γ below. R. ΒΡΕΤΤΙΩΝ. Poseidon, naked, stg. l., r. foot on Ionic capital, holding sceptre in l. hand, eagle on wreath in field to l. *B.M.C. 1.* 14 .. .. £150

516 — Æ *hemidrachm*? (*c.* 2·18 gm.). Laur. hd. of Apollo r., anvil behind, Γ below. R. ΒΡΕΤΤΙΩΝ. Artemis stg. l., holding arrow and flaming torch, hound at her feet, star in field to l. *B.M.C. 1.* 33 .. .. £100

Classical and Hellenistic Periods: Base Metal Issues

517 **ETRURIA: Struck issues. Uncertain mints.** 350-2 0 B.C. Æ *uncia.* Wheel with six spokes, pellet between two of them. R. Hd. of bipennis between pellet and Etruscan letter. *B.M.C. 1., p.* 19, 5.. .. .. £40

518   521

518 — — 3rd Cent. B.C. Æ 19. Hd. of negro r. R. Elephant stg. r., bell suspended from neck, Etruscan letter beneath. *B.M.C. 1., p.* 15, 20 .. .. £20

519 — — — Æ 15. Young male hd. r., in dog's skin. R. Maltese dog running l., Etruscan letter beneath. *B.M.C. 1., p.* 15, 14 .. .. £18

520 — **Populonia.** 3rd Cent. B.C. Æ *sextans.* Diad. hd. of young Herakles r., club beneath. R. Two pellets in central field, bow and arrow above, club and Etruscan legend *Pupluna* (=Populonia) beneath. *B.M.C. 1.* 24 .. .. £75

521 — — — Æ *triens.* Hd. of Vulcan r., wearing laur. pilos, x behind. R. Four pellets between tongs and hammer, Etruscan legend *Pupluna* in semicircle below. *B.M.C. 1.* 26 £60

522 — **Peithesa.** 3rd Cent. B.C. Æ 14. Hd. of Hermes r., in winged petasos. R. Owl stg. r., hd. facing, Etruscan legend *Peithesa* around. *B.M.C. 1., p.* 13, 5 .. .. £25

523 **Cast issues (Aes Grave). Uncertain mints.** 3rd Cent. B.C. Æ *quadrans.* Wheel, with four spokes. R. Krater, Etruscan letter above, three pellets around foot. *B.M.C. 1., p.* 21, 3 .. .. £175

524 — — — Æ *uncia.* Wheel with four spokes, Etruscan letter between two of them. R. Same as *obv.*, but without letter. *B.M.C. 1., p.* 17, 9 .. .. £40

525 — **Velathri (Volaterrae).** 3rd Cent. B.C., Æ *semis.* Beardless Janiform hd., wearing flat petasos. R. Etruscan legend *Velathri* around ɔ (mark of value). *B.M.C. 1.* 1 £200

526 — — — Æ *sextans.* Similar. R. Club between two pellets, Etruscan legend *Velathri* around. *B.M.C. 1.* 12 .. .. £125

527 **UMBRIA. Ariminum.** After 268 B.C. Æ 19. Bearded hd. of Vulcan l., wearing wreathed pilos. R. Gaulish warrior advancing l., with sword and oval shield, ARIMN. in ex. *B.M.C. 1.* 8 .. .. £35

528 **Iguvium.** 3rd Cent. B.C. Æ *uncia* (cast). Bunch of grapes within circle. R. Pellet within circle. *B.M.C. 1.* 8 .. .. £45

529 **Tuder.** 3rd Cent. B.C. Æ *triens* (cast). Right hand bound with cestus, four pellets in
field. ℞. Umbrian legend *Tutere* between two clubs, upright; four pellets in field.
B.M.C. 1. 18   ..   ..   £100

530 — Æ *sextans* (cast, almond-shaped). Club or fish-spine. ℞. Two pellets. *B.M.C. 1.* 2
                                                                                   £75

                    531   532

531 — Æ 18. Hd. of Seilenos r., bound with ivy. ℞. Eagle l., with wings spread, Umbrian
legend *Tutere* to l. *B.M.C. 1.* 1 ..   ..   £15

532 **PICENUM. Ancona.** 290-268 B.C. Æ 20. Laur. hd. of Aphrodite r., м behind.
℞. ΑΓΚΩΝ. Bent r. arm, holding palm, two stars above. *B.M.C. 1.* 1 ..   ..   £25

533 **Hatria.** 3rd Cent. B.C. Æ *as* (cast). Hd. of bearded Seilenos facing, bound with ivy,
V in field to r. ℞. Sleeping dog r., HAT below, l in field to l. *B.M.C. 1.* 1   ..   £500

534 — Æ *uncia* (cast). Anchor. ℞. HAT around pellet. *B.M.C. 1.* 18   ..   ..   £65

535 **LATIUM. Aquinum.** 263-250 B.C. Æ 20. Hd. of Athena l., wearing crested
Corinthian helmet. ℞. AQVINO. Cock stg. r., star behind. *B.M.C. 1.* 1   ..   £15

*Coins of similar type were struck at certain other mints, such as Cales, Suessa Aurunca,
Teanum Sidicinum, etc., suggesting some kind of monetary alliance.*

536   539

536 **SAMNIUM. Aesernia.** After 263 B.C. Æ 20. VOLCANOM. Hd. of Vulcan l., wearing laur. pilos, tongs behind. R. Zeus in galloping biga r., hurling thunderbolt, AISERNINO in ex. *B.M.C. 1.* 4   ..   ..   £20

537 —— AIZERNINO. Laur. hd. of Apollo l., pentagram behind. R. Man-headed bull walking r., hd. facing, crowned by Nike flying r.; T beneath bull. *B.M.C. 1.* 5   £18

538 **Aquilonia.** *Circa* 268 B.C. Æ 21. Hd. of Athena r., in crested Corinthian helmet, shield behind, Oscan legend *Acudunniad* before. R. Warrior stg. l., holding patera, shield on l. arm. *B.M.C. 1.* 1   ..   ..   £25

539 **Beneventum.** After 268 B.C., Æ 20. BENVENTOD. Laur. hd. of Apollo l. R. ΠΡΟΠΟΜ. Horse prancing r., pentagram above. *B.M.C. 1.* 1 ..   ..   ..   £15

540   544

540 **FRENTANI. Frentrum.** *Circa* 268 B.C. Æ 21. Hd. of Hermes l., wearing winged petasos, Oscan legend *Frentrei* before. R. Pegasos flying l., tripod beneath, same Oscan legend in ex. *B.M.C. 1.* 1 ..   ..   £25

541 **Larinum.** *Circa* 268 B.C. Æ 19. Laur. hd. of Apollo l., ΛΑΡΙΝΩΝ before. R. Man-headed bull stg. r., hd. facing, crowned by Nike flying r. above. *B.M.C. 1.* 1 ..   £30

542 *Circa* 217 B.C. Æ *quincunx.* Hd. of Athena r., in crested Corinthian helmet. R. Warrior on horseback galloping l., with spear and shield, Oscan legend LADINOD beneath, five pellets in ex. *B.M.C. 1.* 2   ..   ..   £25

543 — Æ *triens.* Hd. of Zeus Dodonaios r., bound with oak-wreath. R. Eagle stg. r. on thunderbolt, LADINOD before, four pellets beneath. *B.M.C. 1.* 7   ..   £16

544 — Æ *sextans.* Laur. and veiled hd. of Thetis (?) r. R. Dolphin r., V above, LADINOD and two pellets beneath. *B.M.C. 1.* 9   ..   ..   £12

545   547

545 **CAMPANIA. Atella.** 250-217 B.C. Æ *sextans.* Laur. hd. of Zeus r., two pellets behind. R. Two warriors stg. face to face, each holding sword raised, taking oath over young pig held between them; two pellets in field to l., Oscan legend *Aderl* in ex. *B.M.C. 1.* 3 ..   ..   £40

546 **Calatia.** 250-210 B.C. Æ *sextans.* Laur. hd. of Zeus r., two stars behind. R. Selene in biga galloping r., two stars above, Oscan legend *Calati* in ex. *B.M.C. 1.* 1 ..   £40

547 **Cales.** After 268 B.C., Æ 20. CALENO. Laur. hd. of Apollo l., corn-ear behind. R. Man-headed bull walking r., hd. facing, lyre above, B beneath, CALENO in ex. *B.M.C. 1.* 17   ..   ..   £9

Cales *continued*

548 — Æ 20. Hd. of Athena l., wearing crested Corinthian helmet. ℞. CALENO. Cock stg. r., star behind. *B.M.C. 1.* 26   ..   ..   £8
See also nos. 535, 565 *and* 568.

549   551

549 **Capua.** Before 268 B.C. Æ 27. Laur. hd. of Zeus r. ℞. Eagle stg. r. on thunderbolt, wings open, Oscan legend *Kapu* in ex. *B.M.C. 1.* 8   ..   ..   £25

550 After 268 B.C. Æ *quadrans.* Hd. of Demeter r., bound with corn-wreath. ℞. Ox stg. r., hd. facing, three pellets above, Oscan legend *Kapu* in ex. *Sambon (Les Monnaies Antiques de l'Italie)* 1027   ..   ..   £20

551 — Æ *uncia.* Bust of Artemis r., wreathed with myrtle, bow and quiver at shoulder. ℞. Boar running r., pellet above, Oscan legend *Kapu* in ex. *B.M.C. 1.* 3   ..   £12

552 **Compulteria** or **Cubulteria.** 268-240 B.C. Æ 20. Laur. hd. of Apollo l., Oscan legend *Cupelternum* before. ℞. Man-headed bull standing r., hd. facing, crowned by Nike flying r. above, IΣ beneath. *B.M.C. 1.* 1   ..   ..   £20

553 **Neapolis.** 340-280 B.C. Æ 18. Laur. hd. of Apollo r. ℞. ΝΕΟΠΟΛΙΤΕΩΝ. Forepart of man-headed bull swimming r., star on shoulder. *B.M.C. 1.* 141   ..   ..   £10

554 320-280 B.C. Æ 17. ΝΕΟΠΟΛΙΤΩΝ. Laur. hd. of Apollo l., astragalos behind. ℞. Man-headed bull walking r., hd. facing, circular shield above, AΦ beneath bull, sword in sheath in ex. *Cf. Sambon* 639   ..   ..   £8

555   557

555 300-260 B.C. Æ 14. Beardless male hd. l., laur., cornucopiae behind. ℞. ΝΕΟΠΟ — ΛΙΤΩΝ either side of tripod. *B.M.C. 1.* 203   ..   ..   £4

556 270-250 B.C. Æ 13. ΝΕΟΠΟΛΙΤΩΝ. Laur. hd. of Apollo l., ME behind. ℞. Forepart of man-headed bull swimming r., dolphin r. above, NY / BI behind. *B.M.C. 1.* 182
£5

557 270-240 B.C. Æ 20. *Obv.* Similar, but with N behind. ℞. Man-headed bull walking r., hd. facing, crowned by Nike flying r. above; beneath bull, IΣ. *B.M.C. 1.* 212   £6

558 250-200 B.C. Æ 20. Laur. hd. of Apollo r., XAI behind. ℞. Omphalos surmounted by crested serpent, and lyre; in ex., ΝΕΟΠΟΛΙΤΩΝ and club. *B.M.C. 1.* 243   ..   £9

559 — Æ 15. Diad. bust of Artemis r., bow and quiver at shoulder, ΔH before. ℞. ΝΕΟΠΟΛΙ — ΤΩΝ on either side of cornucopiae. *B.M.C. 1.* 256   ..   ..   £5

560 — — Hd. of Dioskouros, beardless and with short hair, r., star behind. ℞. Horseman galloping l., AΣ beneath, ΝΕΟΠΟΛΙΤ. in ex. *B.M.C. 1.* 249   ..   ..   ..   £6

561   563

561 **Nola.** *Circa* 270 B.C. Æ 20. Laur. hd. of Apollo l., ΝΩΛΑΙ before, A behind. ℞. Man-headed bull walking r., hd. facing, crowned by Nike flying r. above, ΜΙ beneath. *B.M.C.*
1. 12 ..   ..   £12

562 **Nuceria Alfaterna.** 260-210 B.C. Æ 20. Oscan legend *Nuvkrinum Alafaternum;*
young male hd. l., diad. ℞. The Dioskouroi on horseback cantering l., Oscan legend of
uncertain meaning in ex. *B.M.C. 1*. 7 ..   ..   £25

563 — Æ 16. Oscan legend *Nuvkrinum;* laur. hd. of Apollo l. ℞. Hound r., on the scent;
Oscan legend *Alafaternum.* *B.M.C. 1*. 8   ..   ..   £15

564   568

564 **Suessa Aurunca.** 280-268 B.C. Æ 21. ΠΡΟΒΟΜ. Hd. of Hermes l., in winged
petasos. ℞. SVESANO. Herakles facing, body inclined to r., strangling lion; club between
his legs. *B.M.C. 1*. 18   ..   ..   £15

565 *Circa* 268 B.C. Æ 20. Hd. of Athena l., wearing crested Corinthian helmet. ℞.
SVESANO. Cock stg. r., star behind. *B.M.C. 1*. 16   ..   ..   £10
   See also nos. 535, 548 *and* 568.

566 260-240 B.C. Æ 19. SVESANO. Laur. hd. of Apollo l., N behind. ℞. Man-headed bull
walking r., hd. facing, crowned by Nike flying r. above, ΙΣ beneath. *B.M.C. 1*. 11
   ..   £12

567 **Teanum Sidicinum.** 280-268 B.C. Æ 20. Laur. hd. of Apollo l., wreath behind.
℞. Same type as last; beneath bull, pentagram; in ex., Oscan legend *Tianud.* *B.M.C.*
1. 11 ..   ..   £12

568 *Circa* 268 B.C. Æ 20. Hd. of Athena l., wearing crested Corinthian helmet. ℞. TIANO.
Cock stg. r., star behind. *B.M.C. 1*. 17 ..   ..   £12
   See also nos. 535, 548 *and* 565.

569   571

569 **APULIA. Arpi.** 3rd Cent. B.C. Æ 21. ΔΑΙΟΥ. Laur. hd. of Zeus l., thunderbolt
behind. ℞. Kalydonian boar running r., spear-head above, ΑΡΠΑΝΩΝ in ex. *B.M.C.*
1. 4 ..   ..   £9

570 — Æ 19. Bull butting r., ΠΟΥΛΛΙ beneath. ℞. ΑΡΠΑΝΟΥ. Horse prancing r. *B.M.C.*
1. 6 ..   ..   £8

571 **Ausculum.** Before 300 B.C. Æ 22. ΑΥ⊢ΥΣΚΛΙ. Horse's hd. l., bridled. ℞. Same
legend. Ear of barley. *B.M.C. 1*. 1   ..   ..   £12

572 3rd Cent. B.C. Æ 19. Hd. of young Herakles l. in lion's skin, club behind neck. ℞.
ΑΥΣΚΛΑ. Nike stg. r., holding wreath and palm. *B.M.C. 1*. 5 ..   ..   ..   £10

573 575

573 **Azetium.** 3rd Cent. B.C. Æ 20. Hd. of Athena r., wearing crested Corinthian helmet. R. ΑΙΕΤΙΝΩΝ. Owl stg. r., hd. facing, on top of Ionic column, olive-branch to r. *B.M.C. 1., p.* 154, *no.* 2 .. .. £24

574 — Æ 17. Eagle stg. r. on thunderbolt, wings spread. R. ΑΙΕΤ. Ear of barley. *B.M.C. 1., p.* 154, *no.* 1 .. .. £22

575 **Barium.** Late 3rd Cent. B.C. Æ *sextans.* Laur. hd. of Zeus r., two stars behind. R. ΒΑΡΙΝΩΝ. Prow r., upon which Eros r., leaning forward and drawing bow; beneath, dolphin r. *B.M.C. 1.* 1 .. .. £12

576 — Æ *uncia.* Similar, but only one star behind hd. on *obv.,* and no dolphin on *rev.* *B.M.C. 1.* 3 .. .. £10

577 **Butuntum.** 3rd Cent. B.C. Æ 21. Hd. of Athena r., wearing crested Corinthian helmet. R. ΒΥΤΟΝΤΙΝΩΝ. Ear of barley. *B.M.C. 1., p.* 157, *no.* 3 .. .. £12

578 — Æ 15. Owl stg. r., hd. facing, on laurel-branch. R. ΒΥΤΟΝΤΙΝΩΝ. Thunderbolt. *Grose* 417 .. .. £12

579 582

579 **Caelia.** 268-200 B.C. Æ *sextans.* Hd. of Athena r., wearing crested Corinthian helmet, two pellets above. R. ΚΑΙΛΙΝΩΝ. Trophy consisting of helmet, shield, spear, sword and cuirass; in field to l., club. *B.M.C. 1.* 3 .. .. £9

580 — Æ 14. *Obv.* Similar, but no mark of value. R. ΚΑΙ. Male figure advancing l., holding palm. *B.M.C. 1.* 8 .. .. £7

581 — — *Obv.* Same. R. The Dioskouroi on horseback galloping r., ΚΑΙΛΙ. in ex. *B.M.C. 1.* 9 .. .. £10

582 **Canusium.** 3rd Cent. B.C. Æ 21. Bare male hd. l. R. ΚΑΝΥΣΙΝΩΝ. Horseman, with spear couched, galloping r. *B.M.C. 1.* 4 .. .. £8

583 — Æ 13. Laur. hd. of Zeus r. R. Κ — Α on either side of club; all within olive-wreath. *Garrucci (Le monete dell'Italia antica), pl.* XCIV, 7 .. .. £7

584 **Hyrium** or **Uria.** 3rd Cent. B.C. Æ 13. Hd. of Athena r., wearing crested Corinthian helmet. R. ΥΡΙΑ — ΤΙΝΩΝ above and below rudder, lengthwise, l.; beneath rudder, dolphin r. *B.M.C. 1.* 1 .. .. £6

585 **Luceria** (finally fell into the hands of the Romans in 314 B.C.).   Early 3rd Cent. B.C.
Æ *as* (cast).   Hd. of young Herakles r., in lion's skin, club beneath.   R. Horse prancing
r., star above, V beneath.   *B.M.C. 1.* 23 ..   ..   £250

586 — Æ *uncia* (cast).   Frog, on raised field.   R. Ear of barley, pellet above, V beneath; all
on raised field.   *B.M.C. 1.* 47   ..   ..   £45

587 Late 3rd Cent. B.C.   Æ *quincunx* (struck).   Hd. of Athena r., wearing crested Corinthian
helmet, five pellets above.   R. LOVCERI between the spokes of a large wheel.   *B.M.C.*
1. 54 ..   ..   £18

588 **Neapolis** (a town known only from its coins).   Early 3rd Cent. B.C.   Æ 18.   Hd. of
young Dionysos r., wreathed with ivy, thyrsos over his shoulder.   R. ΝΕΑΠΟΛ.   Vine-
branch with bunch of grapes.   *B.M.C. 1., p.* 399, *no.* 1 ..   ..   £15

589 **Rubi.**   3rd Cent. B.C.   Æ 17.   Laur. hd. of Zeus r., ΓΡΟΣΕ • E behind.   R. Female
figure stg. l., holding phiale and cornucopiae, ΡΥ to r.   *B.M.C. 1.* 11 ..   ..   £8

590 — Æ 15.   Hd. of Athena r., wearing crested Corinthian helmet, Κ above.   R. ΡΥΒΑΣΤΕΙΝΩΝ.
Owl stg. r., hd. facing, on olive-branch, ΛΙ in field to r.   *B.M.C. 1.* 10 ..   ..   £8

591 **Salapia.**   3rd Cent. B.C.   Æ 22.   ΣΑΛΑΠΙΝΩΝ.   Laur. hd. of Apollo r., quiver at shoulder.   R. Horse prancing r., trident above, ΠΥΛΛΟΥ beneath.   *B.M.C. 1.* 3 ..   £12

592 — Æ 15.   ΣΑΛΑΠΙΝΩ.   Dolphin r.   R. Dolphin r.   *B.M.C. 1.* 7 ..   ..   £9

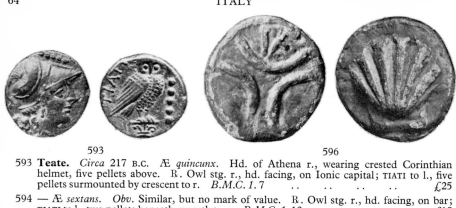

593   596

593 **Teate.** *Circa* 217 B.C. Æ *quincunx.* Hd. of Athena r., wearing crested Corinthian helmet, five pellets above. R. Owl stg. r., hd. facing, on Ionic capital; TIATI to l., five pellets surmounted by crescent to r. *B.M.C. 1.* 7 .. .. £25

594 — Æ *sextans.* *Obv.* Similar, but no mark of value. R. Owl stg. r., hd. facing, on bar; TIATI to l., two pellets beneath, wreath to r. *B.M.C. 1.* 13 .. .. .. £15

595 **Venusia** (captured and colonized by the Romans in 292 B.C.). Early 3rd Cent. B.C. Æ *sextans* (cast). Dolphin l., two pellets beneath. R. Same as *obv.* *B.M.C. 1.* 5
                                                                    £150

596 — Æ 34 (cast). Three crescents, back to back, V̄E above. R. Cockle-shell. *B.M.C. 1.* 8 .. .. £125

597   599

597 268-217 B.C. Æ *quincunx.* Laur. hd. of Zeus l., five pellets behind. R. Eagle, wings spread, stg. l. on thunderbolt, V̄E before. *B.M.C. 1.* 22.. .. .. .. £20

598 — Æ *quadrans.* Veiled hd. of Hera l., V̄E before, three pellets behind. R. Three crescents, back to back, star within each; pellet at centre. *B.M.C. 1.* 24 .. .. £15

599 **CALABRIA. Brundisium** (colonized by the Romans in 245 B.C., it became the chief port of embarkation for Greece and the East following the extension of the Appian Way). 245-217 B.C. Æ *sextans.* Laur. hd. of Poseidon r., crowned by small Nike, trident behind, two pellets beneath. R. BRVN. Taras seated on dolphin l., holding Nike and lyre, two pellets beneath. *B.M.C. 1.* 1 .. .. £20

600 217-200 B.C. Æ *quadrans.* *Obv.* Similar, but with three pellets beneath hd. R. Taras seated on dolphin l., holding Nike and lyre, BRVN. and three pellets beneath. *B.M.C. 1.* 22 .. .. £9

601   602

601 200-89 B.C. Æ *semis.* *Obv.* Similar, but with ∽ beneath hd. and with legend M . BIT. R. Taras seated on dolphin l., holding Nike and lyre, S in field to r., BRVN. beneath. *B.M.C. 1.* 14 .. .. £12

602 **Graxa** (site unknown). Before 200 B.C. Æ 15. Cockle-shell. R. Eagle stg. r. on thunderbolt, ΓΡΑ beneath, star in field to r. *B.M.C. 1., p. 222, no.* 8 .. .. £16

603 200-170 B.C.   Æ *quadrans*.   Laur. hd. of Zeus r., three pellets behind.   R. Two eagles stg. r. on thunderbolt, ΓΡΑ beneath, ΚΡΗ behind, three pellets before.   *B.M.C. 1., p.* 221, *no.* 3 ..   ..   £20

604 **Hyria** or **Orra** (on the Appian Way, between Taras and Brundisium).   217-200 B.C. Æ *quincunx*.   Hd. of Athena r., wearing triple-crested helmet.   R. Eagle stg. r. on thunderbolt, wings spread, five pellets beneath, ORRA before.   *B.M.C. 1.* 1 ..   £18

605 200-89 B.C.   Æ *quadrans*.   Laur. bust of Aphrodite r., sceptre over l. shoulder.   R. Eros flying r., holding fillet with both hands, ORRA and three pellets beneath.   *B.M.C. 1.* 8
£14

606 **Sturnium.**   2nd Cent. B.C.   Æ 15.   Cockle-shell.   R. Eagle stg. r. on thunderbolt, ΣΤΥ beneath.   *B.M.C. 1.* 1 ..   ..   £25

607 **Taras** (=Tarentum).   300-228 B.C.   Æ 22.   Laur. hd. of Zeus r.   R. ΤΑΡΑΝΤΙΝΩΝ. Nike stg. r., holding thunderbolt.   *B.M.C. 1.* 473   ..   ..   £15

608   611

608 — Æ 15.   Cockle-shell.   R. ΤΑΡΑΝ.   Taras seated on dolphin l., holding kantharos and cornucopiae.   *B.M.C. 1.* 479 ..   ..   £10

609 — — Kantharos between two stars.   R. Kantharos; ΤΑ in lower field to l.   *B.M.C. 1.* 482 ..   ..   £9

610 **Uxentum** (a town not mentioned by any ancient writer).   *Circa* 89 B.C.   Æ *as.* Janiform female hd., helmeted.   R. ΟΖΑΝ.   Herakles stg. l., holding club, cornucopiae and lion's skin, crowned by Nike on l.   *B.M.C. 1.* 5 ..   ..   £20

611 — Æ *semis*.   Hd. of Athena r., wearing crested Corinthian helmet, ω beneath.   R. ΟΙΑΝ. Herakles stg. l., holding club, cornucopiae and lion's skin, ear of corn and s in field to l. *B.M.C. 1.* 6 ..   ..   £12

612 **LUCANIA.   The Lucani.**   212-207 B.C.   Æ 27.   Hd. of Ares l., wearing crested Corinthian helmet, thunderbolt beneath.   R. ΛΟΥΚΑΝΟΜ.   Hera Hoplosmia advancing r., hd. facing, holding large shield, spear over l. shoulder.   *B.M.C. 1., p.* 224, *no.* 1
£35

613   616

613 — — Hd. of young Herakles r., wearing lion's skin, spear-head beneath.   R. Similar to last, but with legend ΛΥΚΙΑΝΩΝ and Hera's shield is smaller; in field to r., wolf's hd. r. *B.M.C. 1., p.* 224, *no.* 5 ..   ..   £35

614 — Æ 18.   ΝΙΚΑ.   Diad. hd. of Nike l.   R. ΛΟΥΚΑΝΟΜ.   Zeus advancing r., hurling thunderbolt and holding spear.   *B.M.C. 1., p.* 224, *no.* 2 ..   ..   ..   £20

615 **Herakleia.**   330-228 B.C.   Æ 20.   Hd. of Persephone l., wreathed with corn.   R. ΗΡΑΚΛΕΙΩΝ.   Ear of corn.   *B.M.C. 1.* 54 ..   ..   £18

616 — Æ 19.   Two figures of Herakles stg. l., each holding patera and club; ΗΡΑΚΛΕΙΩΝ in ex. R. Athena stg. l., holding patera and spear, altar at feet; shield and torch behind.   *B.M.C. 1.* 57 ..   ..   £14

Herakleia *continued*

617 — Æ 14. Hd. of Athena r., wearing crested Corinthian helmet. ℞. Marine divinity
(Glaukos ?) r., armed with helmet, shield and spear, star behind, ⊢ΗΡΑΚΛΕΙΩΝ beneath.
B.M.C. 1. 69 ..   ..   £10

618 — Æ 11. Hd. of young Herakles r., bound with wreath. ℞. ⊢Η. Club between strung
bow and quiver. *B.M.C. 1.* 71 ..   ..   £8

619   621

619 **Laos.** 4th Cent. B.C. Æ 23. ΛΑ. Female hd. r., wreathed with olive. ℞. Crow stg.
r., ΛΑΙΝΩΝ/Η behind, bull's hd. before. *B.M.C. 1.* 11 ..   ..   ..   £25

620 — Æ 15. ΛΑ. Veiled and dr. bust of goddess facing. ℞. Two crows passing one another
in opposite directions, Μ beneath. *B.M.C. 1.* 15 ..   ..   ..   £20

621 **Metapontion.** 350-300 B.C. Æ *obol.* ΜΕ. Hd. of Persephone r., wreathed with
corn. ℞. ΟΒΟΛΟΣ. Ear of corn; poppy-head in field to r. *B.M.C. 1.* 165 ..   £20

622   628

622 — Æ 17. Eagle stg. l., wings open, wreath in field to l. ℞. ΜΕΤΑ. Ear of corn, winged
thunderbolt to r. *B.M.C. 1.* 190 ..   ..   £9

623 — — Hd. of Persephone r., wreathed with corn. ℞. ΜΕΤΑ. Two ears of corn; dove
perched on leaf to r. *B.M.C. 1.* 199   ..   ..   £9

624 — Æ 15. Athena Promachos advancing l., with spear and shield. ℞. ΜΕΤΑ. Owl stg. l.,
hd. facing, on ear of barley. *B.M.C. 1.* 191 ..   ..   £8

625 — Æ 14. Hd. of young Herakles r., wearing lion's skin. ℞. ΜΕΤΑ. Ear of corn; in
field to r., torch with cross pieces at top. *B.M.C. 1.* 173 ..   ..   ..   £7

626 — Æ 13. Hd. of Athena r., wearing crested Corinthian helmet. ℞. ΜΕ. Three corn-
grains, arranged star-wise; fly in field. *B.M.C. 1.* 182 ..   ..   ..   £6

627 — Æ 11. Hd. of Artemis r., hair tied in knot, bow and quiver at shoulder. ℞. ΜΕΤΑ.
Kantharos; in field to r., ear of corn. *B.M.C. 1.* 194 ..   ..   ..   £6

628 **Poseidonia.** *Circa* 400 B.C. Æ 14. Poseidon advancing r., brandishing trident.
℞. Bull butting r., ΠΟΣΕΙΔΑ on raised band in ex. *B.M.C. 1.* 65 ..   ..   £12

629 — under the name of **Paestum** (Poseidonia was captured by the Lucanians at the
beginning of the 4th Cent. B.C. and they corrupted the name of the city to Paestum.
This mint had the unique privilege in Italy of being allowed to issue its own bronze coins
right down to the time of Augustus and Tiberius). 300-268 B.C. Æ 22. Laur. hd. of
Poseidon r., dolphin behind. ℞. ΠΑΙΣΤΑΝΟ. Winged Eros riding on dolphin l., holding
wreath and trident. *B.M.C. 1.* 2 ..   ..   £12

630   636   637

630 268-89 B.C. Æ *triens*. Hd. of young Dionysos r., crowned with vine-leaves and grapes four pellets behind. ℞. Cornucopiae; ΠΑΙΣ to r., four pellets and palm-branch to l. *B.M.C. 1*. 9 ..   ..   £9

631 — Æ *quadrans*. Diad. hd. of Poseidon r., three pellets behind. ℞. Dolphin r.; ΠΑΙΣ below, three pellets and caduceus above. *B.M.C. 1*. 13   ..   ..   £8

632 — — Similar, but on *rev.* ΠΑΕΣ and bow in case below the dolphin, three pellets above. *Grose* 1130 ..   ..   £9

633 — Æ *sextans*. Hd. of Demeter r., wreathed with corn. ℞. Forepart of wild boar running r., ΠΑΙΣ above, two pellets beneath. *B.M.C. 1*. 21   ..   ..   £8

634 — Æ *uncia*. Hd. of Artemis r., wearing stephane, bow and quiver at shoulder. ℞. ΠΑΙΣ. Ear of corn with three leaves, pellet in field to l. *B.M.C. 1*. 29 ..   ..   £6

635 After 89 B.C. Æ *semis*. Winged hd. of Nike r., PAE before, s behind. ℞. QT . RE . II . VIR. Palm-branch laid across wreath. *B.M.C. 1*. 54 ..   ..   £7

636 — — Wild boar r., pierced by javelin, s beneath, PAE in ex. ℞. L . ARTV / C . COMI / II . VIR in three lines, lituus and urceus above. *B.M.C. 1*. 58 ..   ..   ..   £8

637 — Æ *sextans*. Q . L . A̅V̅. Conjoined busts of the Dioskouroi r., each wearing laur. pilos, surmounted by star; all within wreath. ℞. LEX XXXX either side of ear of corn, two pellets beneath. *B.M.C. 1*. 72   ..   ..   £8

638   641

638 **Thourioi.** 400-350 B.C. Æ 14. Hd. of Athena r., wearing crested Athenian helmet wreathed with olive. ℞. ΘΟΥΡΙΩΝ. Bull butting r., tunny-fish l. in ex. *B.M.C. 1*. 127
£12

639 350-300 B.C. Æ 23. Hd. of Athena, as last, but the helmet is adorned with figure of Skylla, hurling stone. ℞. ΘΟΥΡΙΩΝ. Bull butting r.; tunny-fish r. in ex. *B.M.C. 1*. 134
£40

640 300-268 B.C. Æ 18. Laur. hd. of Apollo l. ℞. ΘΟΥΡΙΩΝ. Tripod-lebes. *B.M.C. 1*. 144   ..   ..   £9

641 — Æ 16. *Obv.* Similar. ℞. ΘΟΥΡΙΩΝ. Five-stringed lyre, monogram beneath. *B.M.C. 1*. 145   ..   ..   £8

642 — — Diad. hd. of Artemis r., quiver at shoulder. ℞. ΘΟΥΡΙΩΝ ΚΛΕΩΝ. Apollo, naked, stg. l., holding plektron and lyre. *B.M.C. 1*. 148   ..   ..   £8

643 — Æ 11. Hd. of Athena r., wearing crested Athenian helmet. ℞. ΘΟΥ. Bucranium, with pendent fillets. *B.M.C. 1*. 139   ..   ..   £7

644   645

644 — under the name of **Copia** (in 194 B.C. Thourioi received a Roman colony, and the name of the city was changed to Copia). 194-89 B.C. Æ *semis*. Veiled hd. of City-goddess r., s behind. ℞. L . C . Q . COΠIA. Cornucopiae. *B.M.C. 1*. 1   ..   £14

645 — Æ *quadrans*. Hd. of young Herakles r., in lion's skin, three pellets behind. ℞. Q . L . C . COΠIA. Cornucopiae, three pellets to l. *B.M.C. 1*. 4, *var.* £8

646 **Velia.** 350-300 B.C. Æ 20. Hd. of Athena l., wearing Phrygian helmet wreathed with olive. ℞. Forepart of lion l., devouring prey, ΥΕΛΗ in ex., ΦΑ above. *B.M.C. 1.* 117
£30

647 — Æ 16. Hd. of young Herakles r., in lion's skin. ℞. ΥΕΛΗ. Owl stg. r. on olive-branch, hd. facing. *B.M.C. 1.* 118 .. .. £10

648 — Æ 14. Laur. hd. of Zeus r. ℞. ΥΕΛΗ. Owl stg. facing, body inclined to r., wings spread. *B.M.C. 1.* 124 .. .. £8

649 — Æ 13. Hd. of Athena (?) r., of crude style, wearing crested helmet. ℞. ΥΕΛΗ. Tripod. *B.M.C. 1.* 133 .. .. £6

647 652

650 **BRUTTIUM. Konsentia** (captured by the Bruttians in 356 B.C. who made this city their metropolis). 400-356 B.C. Æ 19. Hd. of Ares r., wearing crested Corinthian helmet, ο above. ℞. ΚΩΣ. Thunderbolt; beneath, three crescents. *B.M.C. 1.* 1
£30

651 **Kroton.** Before 400 B.C. Æ 22. ϙΡΟ. Tripod. ℞. Octopus. *Garrucci (Le monete dell'Italia antica), pl.* 110, 16 .. .. £65

652 4th Cent. B.C. Æ 18. Hd. of Persephone r., wearing wreath of corn. ℞. ΚΡΟ around three crescents, horns outwards. *B.M.C. 1.* 117 .. .. £14

653 — — ΛΥΚΩΝ. Hd. of young Herakles r., in lion's skin, Η before. ℞. ΚΡΟ. Eagle flying r., attacking serpent which it holds in its talons; ivy-leaf in field to l. *B.M.C. 1.* 113 .. .. £14

654 — Æ 15. ΑΙΣΑΡΟΣ. Hd. of young river-god Aesaros r., hair long. ℞. ΚΡΟΤΩΝΙΑΤΑΝ. Thunderbolt, star above. *B.M.C. 1.* 112 .. .. £12

655 — — Hd. of young Herakles r., in lion's skin. ℞. Crab, ΚΡΟ beneath. *B.M.C. 1.* 115
£10

656 **Heiponion** (commonly called Hipponium this city, originally a colony of Lokroi, had a most troubled history: pillaged by Dionysios of Syracuse in 389 B.C., it was restored by the Carthaginians ten years later, only to be captured by the Bruttians in 350 B.C. Alexander of Epeiros liberated it twenty years later, Agathokles of Syracuse conquered it in 296 B.C., soon after which it fell to the Bruttians once more. Finally, in 272 B.C., it was garrisoned by the Romans). 379-350 B.C. Æ 17. ΙΕΙ. Hd. of Hermes r., wearing petasos tied under chin. ℞. Caduceus. *B.M.C. 1.* 4 .. .. £15

657 658

657 330-325 B.C. (time of Alexander of Epeiros). Æ 19. ΔΙΟΣ. Laur. hd. of Zeus r. ℞. ΕΙΠΩΝΙΕΩΝ. Amphora; in field to r., torch. *B.M.C. 1.* 12 .. .. .. £15

658 — Æ 16. Laur. hd. of Apollo r., monogram behind. ℞. ΕΙΠΟΝΙΕΩΝ ΠΑΝΔΙΝΑ. Goddess Pandina stg. l., holding wreath and sceptre. *B.M.C. 1.* 17 .. .. .. £15
The Goddess Pandina appears also on coins of Terina (see no. 698) though nothing is known of her.

659 *Circa* 296 B.C. (time of Agathokles of Syracuse). Æ 22. ΣΩΤΕΙΡΑ. Hd. of Athena r., wearing crested Corinthian helmet ornamented with Skylla. ℟. ΕΙΠΩΝΙΕΩΝ. Nike stg. l., holding wreath and sceptre. *B.M.C. 1.* 9 .. .. £15

660 — under the name of **Vibo Valentia** (in 192 B.C. Heiponion received a Roman colony, and its name was changed to Vibo Valentia). 192-89 B.C. Æ *as*. Laur. hd. of Zeus r., I behind. ℟. VALENTIA. Winged thunderbolt, star and I above. *B.M.C. 1.* 7   £15

661   663

661 — Æ *semis*. Hd. of Hera r., wearing stephane, s behind. ℟. VALENTIA. Double cornucopiae, s and dolphin in field to r. *B.M.C. 1.* 18 .. .. £10

662 — Æ *triens*. Hd. of Athena r., wearing crested Corinthian helmet, four pellets behind. ℟. VALENTIA. Owl stg. r., hd. facing; in field to r., four pellets and star. *B.M.C. 1.* 23
£8

663 — Æ *quadrans*. Hd. of bearded Herakles r., in lion's skin, three pellets behind. ℟. VALENTIA. Two clubs, their handles joined; in field to l., three pellets and star. *B.M.C. 1.* 27 .. .. £6

664 — Æ *sextans*. Laur. hd. of Apollo r., two pellets behind. ℟. VALENTIA. Lyre, two pellets in field to r. *B.M.C. 1.* 31 .. .. £6

665 **Lokroi Epizephyrioi.** 350-332 B.C. Æ 25. Laur. hd. of Zeus r., hair short. ℟. Eagle stg. l. on rock, wings closed. *B.M.C. 1.* 21 .. .. £35
The blanks for these coins were cast in strips, and individual specimens often retain traces of the connecting band.

666   669

666 300-268 B.C. Æ 28. Hd. of Athena r., in crested Corinthian helmet, ΛΕΥ behind. ℟. ΛΟΚΡΩΝ. Persephone enthroned l., holding phiale and sceptre surmounted by poppy-head; two stars in upper field, before and behind. *B.M.C. 1.* 35 .. .. £25

667 — Diad. hd. of Persephone r., long flaming torch behind. ℟. ΛΟΚΡΩΝ. Eagle stg. l. on thunderbolt, monogram before, palm filleted behind. *B.M.C. 1.* 33 .. £20

668 — Æ 24. ΔΙΟΣ. Laur. hd. of Zeus r., hair long; behind, thunderbolt. ℟. ΛΟΚ / ΡΩΝ above and beneath winged thunderbolt. *B.M.C. 1.* 24 .. .. £14

669 — — Hd. of Athena l., in Corinthian helmet. ℟. ΛΟΚΡΩΝ. Pegasos flying l., star above, monogram beneath. *B.M.C.* 12. (*Corinth*), *p.* 96, *no.* 20 .. .. £12

670 — Æ 19. Hd. of Athena l., wearing crested Corinthian helmet wreathed with olive. ℟. ΛΟΚΡΩΝ. Eagle stg. l. on thunderbolt, wings spread; in field to l., cornucopiae. *B.M.C. 1.* 37 .. .. £12

671 — — Conjoined busts of the Dioskouroi r., each wearing laur. pilos surmounted by star. ℟. ΛΟΚΡΩΝ. Zeus enthroned l., holding patera and sceptre, cornucopiae behind. *B.M.C. 1.* 40 .. .. £14

672   675

672 Mesma. 350-300 B.C. Æ 22. Hd. of Persephone three-quarter face to r., crowned with barley; oinochoë in field to l. R. ΜΕΣΜΑΙΩΝ. Laur. hd. of Apollo r., hair long. *B.M.C.1.*1 .. .. £75

673 — Æ 20. ΜΕΣ. Hd. of the Fountain-nymph Mesma r., hair rolled. R. Naked male figure (the River Metauros ?) seated l. on rock, a dog at his feet. *B.M.C.1.*3 .. £110

674 Mystia and Hyporon. *Circa* 300 B.C. Æ 19. Laur. hd. of Apollo r. R. ΜΥ ΥΠΩΡ. Tripod lebes. *Grose* 1841 .. .. £25

675 Nuceria. 350-270 B.C. Æ 22. Laur. hd. of Apollo r., ear of corn beneath. R. ΝΟΥΚΡΙΝΩΝ. Horse standing l., pentagram beneath. *B.M.C.1.*1 .. .. £20

676 — Æ 17. Young male hd. r., diad. R. ΝΟΥΚΡΙ . ΣΤΑΤΙΟΥ. Eagle stg. r., wings closed. *Cf. Historia Numorum, p.* 105 .. .. £15

677 Pandosia. After *c.* 400 B.C. Æ 11. Hd. of Hera Lakinia three-quarter face to l., wearing stephanos. R. ΠΑΝ. Incense altar. *B.M.C.1.*5 .. .. .. £25

678 Petelia (this city remained loyal to Rome during the war with Hannibal, and in consequence was allowed to continue issuing its own bronze currency throughout the 2nd Cent. B.C.). 280-216 B.C. Æ 20. Veiled hd. of Demeter r., wreathed with barley. R. ΠΕΤΗΛΙΝΩΝ. Naked Zeus facing, striding to l., hurling thunderbolt and holding sceptre; in field to l., star; to r., Η. *B.M.C.1.*5 .. .. £14

679 — Æ 11. Diad. hd. of bearded Herakles r. R. ΠΕΤΗΛΙΝΟΝ. Club. *B.M.C.1.*4
£6

680 204-89 B.C. Æ *quadrans.* Laur. hd. of Zeus r., three pellets behind. R. ΠΕΤΗΛΙΝΩΝ. Zeus striding r., brandishing thunderbolt and holding sceptre; monogram behind. *B.M.C.1.*1 .. .. £12

681 — Æ *sextans.* Laur. hd. of Apollo r., two pellets behind. R. ΠΕΤΗΛΙΝΩΝ. Artemis advancing l., holding flaming torch; palm-branch in field to l. *Grose* 1849 .. £10

682   683   684

682 — Æ *uncia.* Bearded hd. of Ares r., wearing crested Corinthian helmet, pellet behind. R. ΠΕΤΗΛΙΝΩΝ. Nike stg. l., holding wreath; monograms in field to l. *B.M.C.1.*2
£8

683 Rhegion. Before 387 B.C. Æ 11. Lion's scalp facing. R. ΡΗ within olive-spray with berries. *B.M.C.1.* 42 .. .. £10

684 350-270 B.C. Æ 20. Similar. R. ΡΗΓΙΝΩΝ. Laur. hd. of Apollo r., hair long; behind, omphalos. *B.M.C.1.*50 .. .. £15

685 — Æ 11. Similar. R. ΡΗΓΙΝΩΝ. Lyre. *B.M.C.1.*44 .. .. .. £8

686   689

686 270-203 B.C. Æ 23. Laur. hd. of Apollo l., hair long; behind, hook. ℞. ΡΗΓΙ — ΝΩΝ either side of tripod lebes. *B.M.C. 1.* 75   ..   ..   £15

687 — — Hd. of Artemis r., wearing stephane, bow and quiver at shoulder. ℞. ΡΗΓΙ / ΝΩΝ above and beneath lion walking r. *B.M.C. 1.* 81   ..   ..   ..   £25

688 — — *Obv.* Similar. ℞. ΡΗΓΙΝΩΝ. Young Asklepios, naked, stg. facing, holding branch of laurel and sceptre, bird perched on r. hand; in field to l., tripod lebes. *B.M.C. 1.* 88
                                                       £25

689 203-89 B.C. Æ *pentonkion.* Janiform female hd., laur., wearing polos. ℞. ΡΗΓΙΝΩΝ. Asklepios enthroned l., holding serpent-staff; Π and tripod in field to l. *B.M.C. 1.* 94
                                                       £25

690 — — Hd. of Athena l., wearing crested Athenian helmet ornamented with griffin. ℞. ΡΗΓΙΝΩΝ. Athena stg. l., holding Nike and shield, spear resting against l. shoulder; in field to l., thunderbolt and Π. *B.M.C. 1.* 95 ..   ..   £20

691 — Æ *tetras.* Jugate hds. r. of Apollo, laur., and Artemis, wearing stephane. ℞. ΡΗΓΙ — ΝΩΝ either side of tripod lebes, four pellets in field to r. *B.M.C. 1.* 98   ..   £35

692 — — Jugate laur. hds. r. of Asklepios and Hygieia. ℞. ΡΗΓΙΝΩΝ. Artemis stg. facing, holding spear and bow, hound at her feet; in field to r., ΙΙΙΙ and ear of corn. *B.M.C. 1.* 102   ..   ..   £10

693   696

693 — — Jugate busts of the Dioskouroi r., wearing laur. pilei, each surmounted by star. ℞. ΡΗΓΙΝΩΝ. Hermes stg. l., holding branch and caduceus, ΙΙΙΙ and cornucopiae in field to l. *B.M.C. 1.* 108 ..   ..   £9

694 — — *Obv.* Similar; spear-head behind. ℞. ΡΗΓΙΝΩΝ. Young Asklepios, naked, stg. l., holding branch and staff, bird perched on r. wrist; ΙΙΙΙ in field to l. *B.M.C. 1.* 110
                                                       £8

695 — Æ *trias.* Laur. hd. of Apollo r., palm-branch behind. ℞. ΡΗΓΙ / ΝΩΝ above and beneath wolf stg. r., about to spring; ΙΙΙ in field to r. *Grose* 1946 ..   ..   ..   £8

696 — — Laur. hd. of Asklepios r. ℞. ΡΗΓΙΝΩΝ. Hygieia stg. l., holding patera, from which serpent feeds, and raising her garment; in field to l., ΙΙΙ. *B.M.C. 1.* 113   £7

697 **Terina.** 4th Cent. B.C. Æ 18. Female hd. l., wearing earring and necklace, hair rolled. ℞. ΤΕΡΙ. Crab, crescent above. *B.M.C. 1.* 54   ..   ..   £20

Terina *continued*

698 — Æ 14. ΠΑΝΔΙΝΑ. Hd. of Pandina r., wearing sphendone, earring and necklace. ℞. ΤΕΡΙ. Winged Nike seated r. on square cippus, holding palm (?) and bird. *B.M.C. 1*. 60 ..   ..   £18
  The Goddess Pandina appears also on coins of Heiponion (see no. 658) though nothing is known of her.

699 — — Similar, but without inscription on *obv.*, and on *rev.* Nike is seated l. and rests l. hand on cippus, bird on r. *B.M.C. 1*. 61   ..   ..   £14

700 *Circa* 272 B.C. Æ 22. Lion's scalp facing. ℞. ΤΕΡΙΝΑΙΩΝ. Laur. hd. of Apollo l., short sword behind. *B.M.C. 1*. 58   ..   ..   £22

700   701

701 **Brettian League.** 215-205 B.C. Æ *sextans.* Hd. of Ares l., wearing crested Corinthian helmet, ear of corn beneath, two pellets behind. ℞. ΒΡΕΤΤΙΩΝ. Nike stg. l., holding palm and crowning trophy on l., cornucopiae between; in field to r., hammer. *B.M.C. 1*. 58 ..   ..   £20

702   703

702 — Æ 27. *Obv.* Similar, but with thunderbolt beneath, and no pellets. ℞. ΒΡΕΤΤΙΩΝ. Hera Hoplosmia advancing r., hd. facing, holding large shield, spear over l. shoulder; owl in field to r. *B.M.C. 1*. 43   ..   ..   £20

703 — Æ 22. Laur. hd. of Zeus r. ℞. ΒΡΕΤΤΙΩΝ. Naked warrior advancing r., holding spear and large oval shield; pine-torch in field to r. *B.M.C. 1*. 69   ..   ..   £18

704 — — *Obv.* Similar, but with ear of corn behind. ℞. ΒΡΕΤΤΙΩΝ. Eagle stg. l. on thunderbolt, wings spread; cornucopiae in field to l., crescent above. *B.M.C. 1*. 86 ..   £15

705   707

705 — Æ 20. ΝΙΚΑ. Diad. hd. of Nike l., ear of corn behind. ℞. ΒΡΕΤΤΙΩΝ. Zeus advancing r., hurling thunderbolt and holding sceptre; cornucopiae in field to r. *B.M.C. 1*. 96   £16

706 — Æ 18. Diad. hd. of Nike l., winged. ℞. ΒΡΕΤΤΙΩΝ (in ex.). Zeus in galloping biga l., hurling thunderbolt and holding staff; beneath, owl flying l. *B.M.C. 1*. 100 ..   £14

707 — Æ 15. Hd. of marine goddess l., wearing crab's shell head-dress, serpent behind. ℞. ΒΡΕΤ / ΤΙΩΝ above and beneath crab. *B.M.C. 1*. 108   ..   ..   ..   £14

SICILY

The first Greek colony to be planted on Sicilian soil was Naxos, founded by Chalkidians from Euboia *circa* 734 B.C. Shortly after this Syracuse, the greatest of the ancient cities of Sicily, was established by Corinthian colonists. Prior to the coming of the Greeks the island had been inhabited by Sicels, Sicani and Elymians, the last named having their centres at Segesta and Eryx.

Phoenician involvement in Sicilian affairs may go back earlier than the period of Greek colonization, but the first hostilities between the two rival powers only took place *c*. 580 B.C., when the Knidians attempted, unsuccessfully, to settle in the extreme west of the island. Throughout the 6th Century the Greek colonies quietly prospered. In 485 B.C. Gelon, tyrant of Gela, captured Syracuse and transferred his seat of government there. From this time dates the position of pre-eminence enjoyed by the Syracusans throughout the 5th Century in Greek Sicily. An Athenian attempt at Sicilian conquest, in the latter part of the century, ended in utter defeat before the walls of Syracuse in 413 B.C.; but this only left the field open for the Carthaginians who, in 409, landed ostensibly to support Segesta against Selinus. There followed a long and inconclusive struggle between the Carthaginians and Dionysios, tyrant of Syracuse, resulting in the division of the island under the terms of a peace made in 378 B.C. Agathokles, who made himself tyrant of Syracuse in 317 and was the first of the Sicilian tyrants to take the title of 'king', renewed the struggle with Carthage and actually carried the war into North Africa. He was unsuccessful in this venture, though he was still able to maintain his position at Syracuse. Hieron II (270-216 B.C.), king of Syracuse, made an alliance with the Romans in 263, giving the Italian imperialists a valuable base for military operations against the Carthaginians during the First Punic War (264-241). Rome's prize at the conclusion of the war was the island of Sicily, which thus became the first Roman province. Hieron was allowed to retain possession of his territory for the remainder of his life, but Syracuse was sacked by the Romans in 212 B.C., and following the destruction of Akragas two years later, the whole of Sicily came under Roman rule.

The coinage of Greek Sicily commences in the latter part of the 6th Century, emanating from mints such as Naxos, Zankle, Himera, Selinus and Akragas. During the Syracusan supremacy in the 5th Century, the Sicilian coinage reaches heights of artistic brilliance unsurpassed by any other series in Greek numismatics, culminating, towards the close of the period, in the exquisite work produced by great artists, such as Euainetos, Eukleidas and Kimon. During the 4th Century, the Carthaginians issued large numbers of tetradrachms in Sicily, for the payment of mercenaries in the wars against the Greeks. This series is usually referred to as the 'Siculo-Punic' coinage. Agathokles of Syracuse produced an extensive coinage in all metals, some types being finely engraved and of great beauty, but with the advent of Roman rule in the mid-3rd Century the artistic level of die-engraving quickly deteriorates. The Romans allowed many Sicilian mints the right of issuing bronze currency, even after the fall of Syracuse in 212 B.C., and the series extends well into the 2nd Cent. B.C.

Archaic Period

708   709

708 **Akragas** (known to the Romans as Agrigentum: second only in importance to Syracuse, Akragas was founded early in the 6th Century by colonists from Gela). 510-472 B.C. Æ *didrachm*. ΑΚRΑCΑΝΤΟΣ (retrograde). Eagle, with closed wings, stg. l. Ŗ. Crab. *B.M.C. 2.* 4 ..   ..   £325

709 — — *Obv.* Similar, but with legend ΑΚRΑ behind eagle. Ŗ. Crab; beneath, Corinthian helmet l. *B.M.C. 2.* 31 ..   ..   £200

709A — — Eagle, with closed wings, stg. r.; ΑΚ behind, RΑ before. Ŗ. Crab; beneath, diad. male hd. r., dividing CΑ — Σ. *B.M.C. 2.* 36 ..   ..   £275

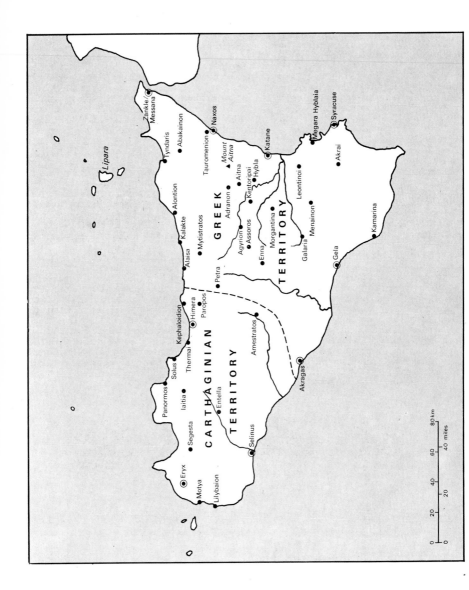

710   711

710 **Katane** (a Chalkidian colony from Naxos, Katane was captured by Hieron of Syracuse in 476 B.C. and re-colonized with Syracusans, who changed the name of the city to Aitna). Before 476 B.C. Æ *litra*. Hd. of bald Seilenos l., with pointed ears. ℞. KATANE. Thunderbolt with two curled wings, and disk on either side. *B.M.C. 2.* 8 .. £750

711 **Eryx** (originally a town of the native Elymians, Eryx appears to have been dependent upon Akragas during the earliest period of its coinage). Before 480 B.C. Æ *drachm*. ERVKINON (retrograde). Eagle, with closed wings, stg. r. on capital of column. ℞. Crab. *B.M.C. 2.* 1 .. .. £750

712 — Æ *litra*. Similar, but eagle stg. l. *B.M.C. 2.* 2 .. .. £125

713   714

713 **Gela** (the third city of ancient Sicily, after Syracuse and Akragas, Gela was founded *c.* 688 B.C. by colonists from Crete and Rhodes. The place was named from the river Gelas which flowed to the east of the settlement). 490-480 B.C. Æ *didrachm*. Naked horseman, wearing crested helmet, galloping r., brandishing spear held high in r. hand. ℞. ϹΕΛΑϹ (retrograde). Forepart of man-headed bull swimming r. (the river-god Gelas). *B.M.C. 2.* 16 .. .. £325

714 *Circa* 480 B.C. Æ *tetradrachm*. *Obv.* Similar; horseman wears conical helmet. ℞. ϹΕΛΑϹ. Man-headed bull (Gelas), shown at full length, prancing r. *Jenkins* (*The Coinage of Gela*) 101-103 .. .. £5,000

715   718

715 **Himera** (founded *c.* 650 B.C. by Chalkidian colonists from Zankle, Himera was captured in 482 B.C. by Theron, tyrant of Akragas). 530-482 B.C. Æ *drachm*. Cock strutting l. ℞. Incuse square, divided into eight triangular compartments alternately raised and depressed. *B.M.C. 2.* 2 .. .. £650

716 — — Cock stg. l., LV above. ℞. Hen stg. r., LV (retrograde) above; all within incuse square. *B.M.C. 2.* 19 .. .. £850

717 — Æ *obol* (*c.* 0·90 gm.). Same types as 715. *B.M.C. 2.* 9 .. .. .. £110

718 482-472 B.C. (tyranny of Theron and his son Thrasydaios). Æ *didrachm*. HIMERA. Cock stg. l. ℞. Crab. *B.M.C. 2.* 24 .. .. £300

719 — Æ *drachm*. Cock stg. l. ℞. HIMERA. Crab. *B.M.C. 2.* 27 .. .. £450

720 — — Similar. ℞. HIMERAION. Astragalos. *B.M.C. 2.* 29 .. .. .. £500

721 **Zankle/Messana** (a settlement of great antiquity, Zankle was a Sicel town even before the coming of Chalkidian colonists about 730 B.C. The name derives from the word for 'sickle'—the shape of the natural harbour. The city was captured by Samians, fleeing from the Persians, in 493 B.C. and they held the place for 4 years until their expulsion by Anaxilas, tyrant of Rhegion. Anaxilas renamed the city Messana). 520-493 B.C. *R drachm.* DANKLE beneath dolphin leaping l., within sickle-shaped band representing the harbour of Zankle. R. Same type incuse. *Hill (Coins of Ancient Sicily) pl.* I, *no.* 1
£1,500

722   724

722 — — *Obv.* Similar, but legend DANK, and the sickle-shaped band has four equidistant projections. R. Scallop-shell at centre of incuse key-pattern. *B.M.C. 2.* 1 ..   £900
723 — *R obol (c.* 0·90 gm.). *Obv.* As 721, but with legend DANK. R. As last. *B.M.C. 2.* 7
£150
724 493-489 B.C. (period of Samian occupation). *R tetradrachm.* Round shield, on which lion's scalp, facing. R. Prow of Samian galley l. *Lloyd Sylloge* 1081..   ..   £2,500
725 489-480 B.C. (tyranny of Anaxilas). *R tetradrachm.* Lion's head facing. R. MESSENION. Calf's head l. *B.M.C. 2.* 10   ..   ..   £1,500
Anaxilas was also ruler of Rhegion, on the Italian mainland, where coins of similar types were struck.
726 — *R litra.* Similar. R. MES within incuse circle. *B.M.C. 2.* 9   ..   ..   £125

727   729

727 **Naxos** (the earliest Greek settlement in Sicily, Naxos was founded by Chalkidians from Euboia *circa* 734 B.C.). 530-490 B.C. *R drachm.* Hd. of Dionysos l., with long pointed beard, wearing ivy-wreath. R. NAXION. Bunch of grapes hanging from stalk between two leaves. *B.M.C. 2.* 2 ..   ..   £6,000
728 — *R litra.* Similar, but without the leaves on *rev.* *B.M.C. 2.* 6   ..   ..   £1,000
729 **Selinus** (the most westerly of the Greek cities in Sicily, Selinus was founded *circa* 651 B.C. by colonists from Megara, and took its name from the wild celery plant—*selinon*—which grows abundantly in the area). 530-520 B.C. *R didrachm.* Selinon leaf, of crude, archaic form. R. Incuse square irregularly divided into five compartments. *Lloyd Sylloge* 1203..   ..   ..   £500

730   731

730 520-490 B.C. *R didrachm.* Selinon leaf, of more regular form, the veins clearly marked. R. Incuse square triangularly divided into eight compartments, alternately raised and depressed. *B.M.C. 2.* 5 ..   ..   £400

731 490-466 B.C. Æ *didrachm.* Similar. ℞. Incuse square containing selinon leaf, with inscription ΣE in the four corners. *B.M.C. 2.* 15 .. .. £650

732 — Æ *obol* (*c.* 0·70 gm.). Similar. ℞. Selinon leaf within border of dots. *B.M.C. 2.* 20

£110

733 — Æ *hemiobol* (*c.* 0·35 gm.). Similar. ℞. Rose (?) within circular incuse. *B.M.C. 2.* 22

£55

735   736

734 **Syracuse** (founded by Corinthian colonists *circa* 733 B.C., Syracuse was destined to become the dominant Greek state in Sicily. In 485 B.C. Gelon, tyrant of Gela, took possession of Syracuse and made it the seat of his power, ruling until his death seven years later). *Circa* 510 B.C. Æ *tetradrachm.* Slow quadriga driven r. by male charioteer, ΣVRAϘO / ΣION above. ℞. Plain quadripartite incuse square. *Boehringer (Die münzen von Syrakus)* 1 .. .. £3,000

735 510-490 B.C. Æ *tetradrachm.* Similar. ℞. Quadripartite incuse square, with archaic female hd. l. in circular incuse at centre. *B.M.C. 2.* 2 .. .. £2,250

736 — Æ *didrachm.* Naked rider on horse pacing r., leading a second horse on his far side; ΣVRA above. ℞. As last. *B.M.C. 2.* 3 .. .. £1,750

The numbers of horses on these coins indicate the denomination—four for the tetradrachm, two for the didrachm.

737 490-485 B.C. Æ *tetradrachm.* Slow quadriga driven r. by male charioteer holding goad; above, Nike flying r., crowning horses. ℞. ΣYRAϘOΣION. Diad. hd. of Artemis-Arethusa r., of archaic style, with hair indicated by dotted lines and falling in formal tresses over neck; four dolphins around. *B.M.C. 2.* 4 .. .. £2,000

738 — Æ *didrachm.* Naked rider on horse pacing r., leading a second horse on his far side. ℞. As last. *B.M.C. 2.* 5 .. .. £900

Classical and Hellenistic Periods: Precious Metal Issues

739 **Abakainon** (a Sicel town). 450-400 B.C. Æ *litra*. Laur. hd. of Zeus r. ℞. Boar stg. r., acorn before; ABA in ex., KAIN (retrograde) above. *B.M.C. 2.* 2 .. £175

740 — — Hd. of water-nymph three-quarter face to l., with flying hair. ℞. ABA. Sow stg. l., piglet at her feet. *B.M.C. 2.* 6 .. .. £200

741 **Akragas** (=Agrigentum: was a city of great wealth and importance in the 5th Century B.C., but in 406 it was sacked by the Carthaginians, a disaster from which it never fully recovered: finally fell to the Romans in 210 B.C.). 472-420 B.C. Æ *tetradrachm*. Eagle, with closed wings, stg. l.; AKRAC behind, ANTOΣ (retrograde) before. ℞. Crab. *B.M.C. 2.* 39 .. .. £600

742 — — Similar, but on *obv.* the eagle is standing on capital of Ionic column. *B.M.C. 2.* 44 £650

743 — — Similar to 741, but with dolphin beneath the crab on *rev.* *B.M.C. 2.* 41 £700

746 — Æ *litra*. Eagle, with closed wings, stg. l. on Corinthian capital; AK behind, RA (retrograde) before. ℞. Crab; beneath, ΛI. *B.M.C. 2.* 50 .. .. £100

741   747

747 420-413 B.C. Æ *tetradrachm*. AKRAΓANTINON. Eagle, wings spread, stg. l. on dead hare lying on rock, on which, corn-grain and scallop shell. ℞. Crab, between scallop shell and conch; beneath, large fish (gurnard) l. *B.M.C. 2.* 59 .. .. .. £7,500

748 413-406 B.C. ℕ *diobol*? (*c.* 1·35 gm.). Eagle, with closed wings, stg. l. on rocks, attacking serpent held in its talons; above, AKP; beneath, two pellets. ℞. Crab; beneath, ΣIΛA / NOΣ (the second line retrograde). *B.M.C. 2.* 1 .. .. £1,250

749 — Æ *dekadrachm*. Helios in chariot drawn l. by four prancing horses; AKPAΓAΣ and eagle flying l. above, crab beneath. ℞. Two eagles stg. l. on dead hare lying on rock: the one in foreground, its wings closed, lifts its head as if screaming; the other, with wings spread, is about to tear its prey with its beak; locust in field to r. (*British Museum*) £50,000

The occasion for the issue of this remarkable coin was, probably, the victory of Exainetos of Akragas in the Olympic games of 412 B.C.

750 — Æ *tetradrachm, by Myron* (?).   Fast quadriga r., driven by young male charioteer who is crowned by Nike flying l. above; beneath horses, MYP (artist's signature); in ex., Skylla r. Ṙ. ΑΚΡΑΓΑΝΤΙΝΟΝ.   Two eagles on dead hare, similar to rev. of last, but they stand to r., and the locust is in field to l. *B.M.C. 2.* 54   ..   ..   £6,500

751 — Æ *hemidrachm.*   Eagle, with spread wings, stg. r. on dead hare which it is about to tear with its beak. Ṙ. ΑΚΡΑ.   Crab; beneath, tunny-fish r. *B.M.C. 2.* 71   ..   £350

752   753

752 338-287 B.C.   Æ *hemidrachm.*   Crab, M above. Ṙ. Free horse cantering r., star above. *B.M.C. 2.* 76   ..   ..   £250

753 — Æ 1½ *litra.*   Laur. hd. of Zeus l., Δ behind. Ṙ. ΑΚΡΑΓΑΝΤΙΝΩΝ.   Eagle stg. erect r., wings spread. *B.M.C. 2.* 77   ..   ..   £140

754 — Æ *obol.*   Bearded hd. of river-god r., horned and wreathed with reeds. Ṙ. ΑΚΡΑΓΑΝ-ΤΙΝΩΝ.   Eagle, with spread wings, stg. r., looking back. *B.M.C. 2.* 79   ..   £85

755 279-241 B.C.   Æ *drachm.*   Laur. hd. of Zeus r. Ṙ. ΑΚΡΑΓΑΝΤΙΝΩΝ.   Eagle stg. r., wings spread, E in field to r. *B.M.C. 2.* 82   ..   ..   £250

756   757

756 — Æ *hemidrachm.*   Similar, but with A in field to r. on *rev.* *B.M.C. 2.* 85   ..   £150

757 **Kamarina** (a colony of Syracuse, founded *c.* 600 B.C.   Following its destruction by Gelon of Syracuse in 484 B.C.   Kamarina was re-colonized from Gela, *c.* 461.   The city was taken by the Carthaginians in 405 and its population evacuated to Syracuse.   It was finally destroyed by the Romans in 258 B.C. during the First Punic War).   460-450 B.C.   Æ *litra.*   ΚΑΜΑ (retrograde).   Athena stg. l., holding spear, shield behind. Ṙ. Nike flying r., swan at her feet before; all within olive-wreath. *B.M.C. 2.* 2   ..   £120

758   759

758 450-420 B.C.   Æ *tetradrachm.*   Galloping quadriga driven l. by Athena who is crowned by Nike flying r. above; in ex., crane flying l. Ṙ. ΚΑΜΑΡΙΝΑΙΟΝ (retrograde).   Hd. of bearded Herakles l., wearing lion's skin. *B.M.C. 2.* 10..   ..   ..   ..   £1,800

758A — Æ *litra.*   ΚΑΜΑΡΙΝΑ (retrograde).   Hd. of nymph Kamarina l., wearing sphendone ornamented with star. Ṙ. Swan flying l. over waves, its hd. bent down; amid waves, fish l. *B.M.C. 2.* 24   ..   ..   £175

759 420-413 B.C.   Æ *tetradrachm.*   Galloping quadriga driven r. by Athena who is crowned by Nike flying l. above; in ex., ΚΑΜΑΡΙΝΑ divided by two amphorae. Ṙ. Beardless hd. of young Herakles l., wearing lion's skin; before, upper part of strung bow. *B.M.C. 2.* 13   £1,800

Kamarina *continued*

760   413-405 B.C.   N 1⅓ *litra* (*c.* 1·17 gm.).   Hd. of Athena r., wearing crested helmet ornamented with hippocamp.   R. KA between two olive-leaves with berries.   *Weber Catalogue* 1248 .. .. £1,500

761   — Æ *tetradrachm, by Exakestidas*.   Galloping quadriga driven r. by Athena who is crowned by Nike flying l. above; on exergual band, EΞAKEΣTIΔAΣ; in ex., two amphorae. R. KAMAPINAION before beardless hd. of young Herakles l., wearing lion's skin.   *B.M.C. 2.* 14 .. .. £2,200

762   766

762   — Æ *didrachm*.   IΠΠAPIΣ (retrograde).   Hd. of river-god Hipparis l., horned; a fish, upwards, on either side.   R. KAMAPINA (retrograde).   The nymph Kamarina seated, looking l., on swan swimming l.; three fishes around, in lower field.   *B.M.C. 2.* 17
£2,000

763   — Æ *didrachm, by Euainetos*.   Hd. of river-god Hipparis, horned, three-quarter face to l.; a fish, downwards, on either side; artist's signature, EYAI, on neck; all within circle of waves.   R. KAMAPINA.   Nymph Kamarina on swan, as last, but with waves beneath, and two fishes instead of three.   *B.M.C. 2.* 16 .. .. £6,000

764   **Katane** (following its capture by Hieron of Syracuse, in 476 B.C., the name of this city was ehanged to Aitna; but on the expulsion of the new colonists, fifteen years later, the place reverted to its original name of Katane.   It was captured in 404 B.C. by Dionysios of Syracuse who sold the population into slavery.   Katane submitted to Rome during the First Punic War).   476-461 B.C. (under the name of **Aitna**).   Æ *tetradrachm*.   AITNAION. Hd. of Seilenos r., bald and with long, bushy beard, wreathed with ivy; beneath, scarabaeus beetle.   R. Zeus Aitnaios seated r. on throne covered with leopard skin, holding knotted vine-staff and winged thunderbolt; before, fir tree on top of which eagle perches r. (*Brussels*) .. .. (*Unique*)

765   — Æ *litra*.   Bald hd. of Seilenos l., without wreath.   R. AITN.   Winged thunderbolt. *B.M.C. 2.* 16 .. .. £750

766   461-450 B.C. (name of Katane now restored).   Æ *tetradrachm*.   Man-headed bull (river-god Amenanos) stg. r., about to be crowned by Nike flying r. above.   R. KATANAION. Nike advancing l., her wings spread, holding fillet and olive wreath, H in field to l.   *B.M.C. 2.* 6 .. .. £7,500

767   450-420 B.C.   Æ *tetradrachm*.   Slow quadriga driven r. by male charioteer holding goad. R. KATANAION.   Laur. hd. of Apollo r., hair turned up behind.   *B.M.C. 2.* 17   £1,500

768   420-413 B.C.   Æ *tetradrachm*.   *Obv.* Similar, but the horses are crowned by Nike flying r. above.   R. Laur. hd. of Apollo l., with short, wavy hair; KATANAION before, laurel-sprig behind.   *B.M.C. 2.* 24 .. .. £1,250

769   413-404 B.C.   Æ *tetradrachm*.   Quadriga l., horses in high action, driven by charioteer who is crowned by Nike flying r. above; H (=Herakleidas?) below triple exergual line. R. Young male hd. l., diad.; KATANAIΩN before.   *B.M.C. 2.* 27.. .. .. £3,000

770 — Æ *tetradrachm, by Euainetos.* Quadriga l., horses in high action, having just rounded the turning-column (meta) which is shown on the extreme right; the charioteer is crowned by Nike flying r. above who also holds tablet with artist's signature, EYAIN; crab below double exergual line. ℞. Laur. hd. of Apollo l., hair turned up behind; KATANAIΩN above, knotted fillet with bell attached before, crayfish behind. *B.M.C. 2.* 35   £6,500

771   772

771 — Æ *tetradrachm, by Herakleidas.* Laur. hd. of Apollo, three-quarter face to l., hair in rich profusion of loose curls; on r., artist's signature, HPAKΛEIΔAΣ. ℞. Quadriga l., horses in high action, driven by charioteer who is crowned by Nike floating r. above, erect; in ex., KATANAIΩN and fish l. *B.M.C. 2.* 32   ..   ..   £10,000

772 — Æ *drachm.* Quadriga galloping r., driven by charioteer who is crowned by Nike flying l. above; in ex., KATANAION. ℞. Hd. of young river-god Amenanos, horned, three-quarter face to r.; fish in lower field on either side. *B.M.C. 2.* 36   ..   ..   £2,500

773 — Æ *hemidrachm.* Hd. of Seilenos facing, bald and with pointed ears. ℞. KATANAIΩN. Laur. hd. of Apollo r., hair rolled behind. *B.M.C. 2.* 44   ..   ..   ..   £250

774 — Æ *litra.* Hd. of Seilenos l., crowned with ivy. ℞. KATANAIΩN. Winged thunderbolt. *B.M.C. 2.* 46   ..   ..   £150

774   777   778

775 **Kephaloidion** (captured in 409 B.C. by the Carthaginians who issued coins of Greek style bearing the mint name *Rash Melkarth*—'Promontory of Herakles'. The town was recovered by Dionysios of Syracuse after thirteen years of Carthaginian occupation). 409-396 B.C. Æ *tetradrachm.* Quadriga galloping r., driven by charioteer who is crowned by Nike flying l. above; in ex., Punic inscription. ℞. Hd. of Tanit r., wreathed with corn, four dolphins around (inspired by the Syracusan Arethusa of Euainetos). *B.M.C. 2., p.* 251, *no.* 6 ..   ..   £750

776 — Æ 2 *litrai.* EK KEΦAΛOIΔIOY. Hd. of young Herakles r., wearing lion's skin. ℞. HPAKΛEIΩTAN. Bull butting r. *Weber Catalogue* 1298 ..   ..   £300
     This type was issued by the exiled Greek inhabitants of Kephaloidion, but from which mint it is impossible to say.

777 **Enna** (a most sacred place, at the centre of the island, Enna was reputed to be the scene of the rape of Persephone). *Circa* 450 B.C. Æ *litra.* Slow quadriga driven r. by Demeter holding torch. ℞. HENNAION. Demeter stg. facing, hd. l., holding lighted torch over altar at her feet to l. *B.M.C. 2.* 1   ..   ..   £1,000

778 **Entella** (in 404 B.C. this town was captured by Campanian mercenaries who had been in the service of the Carthaginian invaders of Sicily). *Circa* 450 B.C. Æ *litra.* Female figure stg. l., sacrificing over lighted altar at her feet. ℞. ENTEΛ (sometimes retrograde). Man-headed bull (river-god Hypsas) stg. r. *B.M.C. 2.* 1-2 ..   ..   ..   £600

779 404-340 B.C. (period of Campanian occupation). Æ *drachm.* Free horse cantering r., large grain of corn below. ℞. KAMΠANΩN. Helmet l., with cheek pieces. *Grose* 2230-31
     £400
     These are sometimes overstruck on drachms of Katane.

780 **Eryx** (throughout most of the 5th Century Eryx seems to have been closely allied with the neighbouring city of Segesta: about 400 B.C. it was captured by the Carthaginians and remained in their hands for many years). 480-413 B.C. Æ *didrachm.* IRVKA IIB. Hound walking r., three corn-stalks in background. R. Hd. of Aphrodite r., hair in sphendone. *Grose* 2235 .. .. £750

781 782 784

781 — Æ *litra.* EPVKINON (retrograde). Female figure stg. l., both arms extended, lighted altar at feet. R. Hound prowling r., on the scent; ivy-branch above, volutes in ex. *B.M.C.* 2. 7 .. .. £250

782 413-400 B.C. Æ *litra.* Aphrodite enthroned l., holding dove with spread wings; behind, tree. R. EPVKINO. Hound stg. r., swastika above. *B.M.C.* 2. 10 .. .. £300

783 After 400 B.C. (period of Carthaginian occupation). Æ *obol.* Young male hd. l., beardless. R. Man-headed bull stg. l., Punic inscription above. *Jenkins* (*Coins of Punic Sicily*), *pl.* 24, *no.* 24 .. .. £150

784 **Galaria** (an ancient Sicel town). *Circa* 460 B.C. Æ *obol.* ΣOTER (retrograde). Zeus enthroned l., holding sceptre surmounted by eagle l., its wings closed. R. CAΛA. Young Dionysos stg. l., holding kantharos and vine-branch. *B.M.C.* 2. 1 .. .. £1,250

785 789

785 **Gela** (throughout most of the latter part of the 5th Century Gela enjoyed great prosperity; but in 405 B.C. the city was destroyed by the Carthaginians, a disaster from which it never fully recovered). 480-470 B.C. Æ *tetradrachm.* Slow quadriga driven r. by charioteer; above, Nike flying r., crowning the horses; double exergual line. R. CEΛAΣ. Forepart of man-headed bull (river-god Gelas) r., with long wavy beard. *Jenkins* (*The Coinage of Gela*) 104 .. .. £750

786 — Æ *drachm.* Naked horseman, holding whip, about to jump from horse prancing r. R. Similar to previous, but with legend CEΛOION. *Jenkins* 187 .. .. .. £1,250

787 — Æ *obol.* Forepart of man-headed bull r., CEΛ above. R. Wheel with four spokes. *Jenkins* 190. *B.M.C.* 2. 34 .. .. £100

788 — Æ *hexas* (c. 0·08 gm.). Horse's hd., unbridled, r. R. CE and two pellets. *Jenkins* 200 .. .. £35

789 465-450 B.C. Æ *tetradrachm.* Slow quadriga driven r. by charioteer who leans forward; in background, Ionic column on plinth (representing the 'terma' or turning-point of the race-course); in ex., ear of corn r. R CEΛAΣ. Forepart of man-headed bull r., with long beard. *Jenkins* 207 .. .. £1,000

790 — — *Obv.* Similar. R. Similar to previous, but the bull is crowned by Nike flying r. above; CEΛAΣ behind. *Jenkins* 218 .. .. £1,200

791 — Æ *litra.* Horse stg. r., rein trailing from mouth; above, wreath. R. CEΛAΣ. Forepart of man-headed bull r., corn-grain beneath. *Jenkins* 245. *B.M.C.* 2. 33 .. £125

792 450-440 B.C. *Æ tetradrachm.* Slow quadriga driven r. by tall charioteer who leans far forward; above, Nike flying r., crowning the horses; in ex., palmette with flanking tendrils. R. CEΛΑΣ. Forepart of man-headed bull r., of fine early classical style, with thick wavy beard. *Jenkins* 341. *B.M.C. 2.* 36 .. .. £600

793 — — Similar, but of much poorer style: the bull has small compact hd. and face, with short beard. *Jenkins* 366. *B.M.C. 2.* 39 .. .. £300

794 796

794 440-430 B.C. *Æ tetradrachm.* Slow quadriga driven r. by charioteer who leans forward; above, Nike flying r., crowning the horses; in ex., CEΛΟΙΟΝ (retrograde). R. Forepart of man-headed bull r., about to be crowned by the nymph Sosipolis on r., who stands facing, looking l., wearing peplos; above, ΣΟΣΙΠΟΛΙΣ (retrograde). *Jenkins* 371 £4,500

795 — — *Obv.* Similar, but the charioteer leans farther forward, and with barley-grain instead of legend in ex. R. CEΛΑΣ (retrograde). Forepart of man-headed bull r., of poor style, with short beard. *Jenkins* 382. *B.M.C. 2.* 14 .. .. £400

797 801

796 430-425 B.C. *Æ tetradrachm.* Slow quadriga driven r. by tall bearded charioteer who bows forward; three of the horses' hds. are distinctly shown; above, olive-wreath. R. CEΛΑΣ. Forepart of man-headed bull r., of fine compact style; beneath, goose (?) l. *Jenkins* 398. *B.M.C. 2.* 44 .. .. £500

797 — *Æ litra.* Bearded horseman, armed with spear and shield, on horse prancing l. R. CEΛΑΣ. Forepart of man-headed bull r. *Jenkins* 405. *B.M.C. 2.* 52 .. £150

798 425-420 B.C. *Æ tetradrachm.* Slow quadriga driven r. by winged Nike; above, large olive-wreath; in ex., ΓΕΛΩΙΟΝ. R. Hd. or river-god Gelas l., represented as a beardless youth, diad. and with small bull's horn above forehead; around, three large fish (mullets ?), one on either side, the other beneath. *Jenkins* 455. *B.M.C. 2.* 54 .. .. £7,500

799 — — *Obv.* Similar. R. Forepart of man-headed bull r., of fine style; before, long-legged bird (heron ?) stg. r. *Jenkins* 457 .. .. £1,750

800 — *Æ didrachm.* Mounted warrior, wearing Phrygian helmet, galloping r. past fallen hoplite whom he spears with javelin held in r. hand; the hoplite is naked but for crested helmet and holds large circular shield. R. Hd. of river-god Gelas l., similar to 798; behind, ΓΕΛΑΣ; all within olive-wreath. *Jenkins* 464. *B.M.C. 2.* 55 .. .. £2,500

801 420-415 B.C. *Æ tetradrachm.* Slow quadriga driven l. by bearded charioteer who leans forward; above, Nike flying l., crowning the horses; in ex., lizard l., about to catch a fly. R. ΓΕΛΑΣ. Forepart of man-headed bull l., of fine neat style. *Jenkins* 470. *B.M.C. 2.* 49 .. .. £1,250

Gela *continued*

802 — Æ *didrachm.* Mounted warrior, wearing helmet, chiton and chlamys, on prancing
horse r.; he looks round and thrusts down behind him with spear held in r. hand. ℞.
Similar to previous. *Jenkins* 479 ..   ..   £1,500

803 415-405 B.C. *N dilitron* (*c.* 1·75 gm.). Mounted warrior, wearing Phrygian helmet and
chiton, on horse pacing r.; he holds spear in l. hand. ℞. ΓΕΛΑΣ. Forepart of man-
headed bull r., grain of barley above. *Jenkins* 490. *B.M.C.* 2. 1   ..   ..   £1,750

804 — *N* 1⅓ *litra* (*c.* 1·15 gm.). ΓΕΛΑΣ. Forepart of man-headed bull l. ℞. ΣΩΣΙΠΟΛΙΣ.
Hd. of nymph Sosipolis r., hair in sphendone. *Jenkins* 492. *B.M.C.* 2. 2   ..   £1,250

805 — *N litra* (*c.* 0·88 gm.). Forepart of horse r., bridled. ℞. Similar to previous. *Jenkins*
491 ..   ..   £900

806   807

806 — Æ *tetradrachm.* ΓΕΛΩΙΩΝ. Galloping quadriga driven r. by winged Nike; above,
eagle flying r.; in ex., large pellet. ℞. ΓΕΛΑΣ (retrograde). Forepart of man-headed bull
r., large grain of barley above. *Jenkins* 483. *B.M.C.* 2. 57   ..   ..   £2,250

807 — — ΓΕΛΩΙΩΝ. Galloping quadriga driven l. by charioteer who crouches forward;
above, eagle flying l.; in ex., ear of wheat l. ℞. ΓΕΛΑΣ. Man-headed bull, depicted full
length, stg. l.; before, long corn-stalk with ears; in ex., large grain of barley. *Jenkins* 485
£3,500

808 339-310 B.C. (the city was refounded by Timoleon of Corinth in 339 B.C.). Æ *trihemiobol*
(*c.* 1·05 gm.). Forepart of man-headed bull r. ℞. ΓΕΛΩΙΩΝ. Ear of corn. *Jenkins* 539
£350

809   811

809 — — Bearded hd. of river-god Gelas r., with long horn above forehead; ΓΕΛΑΣ before.
℞. Horse prancing r. *Jenkins* 551. *B.M.C.* 2. 62   ..   ..   ..   £350

810 — Æ *litra.* ΕΥΝΟΜΙΑ. Hd. of Eunomia ('Law and Order') r., wearing sphendone.
℞. ΓΕΛΩΙΩΝ. Man-headed bull stg. r. on large ear of corn. *Jenkins* 536   ..   £350

811 — — Hd. of young Herakles r., wearing lion's skin; behind, astragalos. ℞. ΓΕΛΩΙΩΝ.
Bearded hd. of river-god Gelas l., wreathed with corn, and with bull's horn at temple.
Jenkins 541. *B.M.C.* 2. 60   ..   ..   £250

812 **Himera** (following the expulsion of the Akragantine tyrants, in 472 B.C., Himera enjoyed considerable prosperity until its destruction by the Carthaginians in 408 B.C.). *Circa* 472 B.C. Æ *tetradrachm*. Pelops, with pointed beard, driving slow quadriga r.; ΠΕΛΟΨ above; palm-branch with bunch of dates in ex. Ŗ. Nymph Himera stg. facing, looking r., holding out fold of peplos with her r. hand, l. hand raised in front of face; in field to r., IMERA (sometimes retrograde). *Lloyd Sylloge* 1016. *Weber Catalogue* 1349 ..   £7,500

813

814

813 465-415 B.C. Æ *tetradrachm*. Slow quadriga driven r. by charioteer who is crowned by Nike flying l. above; in ex., IMEPAION (retrograde). Ŗ. Nymph Himera stg. facing, looking l., her l. hand raised, r. hand holding patera over altar; on r., satyr stg. in basin, washing below fountain which pours from lion-head spout; corn-grain in field above; fish r. in ex. *B.M.C. 2.* 34   ..   ..   £2,250

814 — Æ *didrachm*. IMEPAION (retrograde). Naked youth seated sideways on horse galloping l., from which he is about to dismount; in ex., crane flying l. Ŗ. Nymph Himera stg. facing, looking l., her l. hand raised, r. hand holding patera over altar; corn-grain in field above; caduceus bound with fillet to r.; ΣΟΤΕΡ (retrograde) in ex. *B.M.C. 2.* 36
£2,500

815 — Æ *hemidrachm*. HIMEPAION (retrograde). Naked youth, blowing on shell and holding caduceus, seated on goat prancing l. Ŗ. Nike flying l., holding aplustre bound with fillet; legend — $\frac{NI}{AK}$ — around. *B.M.C. 2.* 38 ..   ..   £650

816   817   818

816 — Æ *litra*. Forepart of monster l., with bearded human hd., goat's horn, lion's paw and curled wing. Ŗ. HIMEPAION. Naked youth seated on goat prancing l. *B.M.C. 2.* 41
£250

817 — Æ *obol*. Male hd. l., bearded and wearing crested Athenian helmet. Ŗ. IMEPAION. Two greaves. *B.M.C. 2.* 45   ..   ..   £150

818 415-408 B.C. Æ *tetradrachm, by Mai* . . . Galloping quadriga driven r. by charioteer who is crowned by Nike flying l. above; Nike also holds tablet with artist's signature MAI . . .; in ex., hippocamp l. Ŗ. Nymph Himera sacrificing at altar and satyr washing below fountain, similar to 813, but of fine classical style and without the corn-grain and fish. *B.M.C. 2.* 48   ..   ..   £2,750

819 — Æ *litra*. IMEPAIΩN. Hd. of young Herakles r., wearing lion's skin. Ŗ. Athena stg. facing, wearing triple-crested helmet, holding spear and shield. *B.M.C. 2.* 49   £250

820 **Thermai** (the refugees from Himera were permitted by the Carthaginians to found a new settlement at the hot springs not far from the old city). 405-350 B.C. *Æ didrachm.* ΘΕΡΜΙΤΑΝ. Hd. of Hera r., wearing richly ornamented stephanos; behind, dolphin. R. Young Herakles, naked, holding club, seated l. on rock covered with lion's skin; behind, bow and quiver. *B.M.C. 2.* 1 .. .. £2,500

821 — *Æ obol.* Similar, but without dolphin on *obv. Weber Catalogue* 1365 .. £200

821   822

822 **Hipana** (a town of no great importance, near Panormos). *Circa* 450 B.C. *Æ litra.* ΙΠΑΝΑΤΑΝ (partly retrograde). Eagle, wings closed, stg. l. on Ionic capital. R. Dolphin l., scallop-shell beneath. *B.M.C. 2., p. 239, no.* 1 .. .. £1,250

823 **Leontinoi** (founded by Chalkidians from Naxos in 729 B.C., Leontinoi produced no coinage in the Archaic period. In the early part of the 5th Cent. the city was under the rule of the Gelan and the Syracusan tyrants, but in 466 B.C. it regained its independence. Enjoyed considerable prosperity until 422 B.C. when it was reduced to a state of dependency on Syracuse). *Circa* 480 B.C. *Æ tetradrachm.* Slow quadriga driven r. by charioteer who is crowned by Nike flying l. above; in ex., lion running r. R. LEONTINON. Laur. hd. of Apollo r., of superb late archaic style; three bay leaves around, one on either side, the other above; beneath, lion running r. *B.M.C. 2.* 10 .. .. .. £15,000

This masterpiece of late archaic art is probably by the same hand as the famous 'Demareteion' coinage of Syracuse.

824   825

824 480-475 B.C. *Æ tetradrachm.* Slow quadriga driven r. by charioteer; above, Nike flying r., crowning horses; in ex., lion running r. R. ΛΕΟΝΤΙΝΟΝ (retrograde). Female hd. r., wearing wreath, earring and necklace; around, four corn-grains. *B.M.C. 2.* 9 £2,000

825 475-466 B.C. *Æ tetradrachm. Obv.* Similar, but without lion in ex. R. ΛΕΟΝΤΙΝΟΝ. Lion's hd. r., with open jaws; around, four corn-grains. *B.M.C. 2.* 8.. .. £450

826 — *Æ didrachm.* Naked horseman cantering r., holding whip and bridle. R. Similar to previous. *B.M.C. 2.* 13 .. .. £500

827 828

827 — Æ *drachm*. Similar, but on *obv*. the horse is trotting, and the rider rests his r. hand on hip. *B.M.C. 2.* 16.. .. .. £300

828 — Æ *obol*. Lion's hd. facing. R. ΛΕΟΝ. Corn-grain. *B.M.C. 2.* 19 .. £120

829 — Æ *hemilitron*. Lion's hd. r., with open jaws. R. Corn-grain, dividing six pellets and Λ E. *B.M.C. 2.* 23 .. .. £100

830 — Æ *pentonkion*. *Obv*. Similar. R. Five pellets. *B.M.C. 2.* 24 .. .. £65

831 — Æ *hexas*. *Obv*. Similar. R. Two pellets. *B.M.C. 2.* 26 .. .. .. £35

832 833

832 466-425 B.C. Æ *tetradrachm*. Laur. hd. of Apollo r., hair turned up behind and bound with wreath. R. LEONTINON. Lion's hd. r., with open jaws; around, four corn-grains. *B.M.C. 2.* 28 .. .. £500

833 — — Similar, but of more advanced style with the hair of Apollo rolled behind, and the types to *left* instead of to right on both *obv*. and *rev*. *B.M.C. 2.* 36 .. .. £850

834 — — *Obv*. Similar, but type to r. R. LEONTINON. Lion's hd. r., with open jaws; three corn-grains around—above, before and beneath; behind, tripod-lebes. *B.M.C. 2.* 41 £1,400

835 — Æ *drachm*. Laur. hd. of Apollo l., hair turned up behind and bound with wreath. R. LEON. Lion's hd. r., with open jaws; three corn-grains around—above, before and beneath. *B.M.C. 2.* 44 .. .. £400

836 838

836 — Æ *litra*. Laur. hd. of Apollo r., hair in formal locks over temple, plaited behind. R. LEON. Corn-grain. *B.M.C. 2.* 50 .. .. £150

837 — — LEON. Lion's hd. r., with open jaws. R. Naked river-god (Lissos?) stg. l. before altar, holding patera and laurel-branch; behind, corn-grain. *B.M.C. 2.* 46 .. £150

838 425-422 B.C. Æ *tetradrachm*. Laur. hd. of Apollo r., of fine early classical style, hair short. R. ΛΕΟΝΤΙΝΟΝ. Lion's hd. r., with open jaws; three corn-grains around—one on each side, the other above; beneath, river-fish r. *B.M.C. 2.* 55 .. .. £1,750

Leontinoi *continued*

839 *Circa* 355 B.C. (time of Dion). Æ *stater* of the Corinthian type. Pegasos flying l.
R. ΛΕΟΝΤΙΝΟΝ. Hd. of Athena r., wearing Corinthian helmet, corn-grain behind.
B.M.C. 12. (Colonies of Corinth), p. 98, no. 1   ..   ..   £400

839   840

840 **Longane** (a town of uncertain location, possibly on the river Longanus near Mylai).
Circa 450 B.C. Æ *litra*. ΛΟΓΓΑΝΑΙΟΝ (retrograde). Hd. of young Herakles r., wearing
lion's skin. R. Hd. of young river-god (Longanus?) l., short horn above forehead.
B.M.C. 2. 1 ..   ..   £1,250

841 **Megara Hyblaia** (founded by colonists from Megara in Greece, the town was destroyed
by Gelon of Syracuse in 483 B.C. but was, apparently, resettled in the following century).
Circa 350 B.C. Æ *litra*. Female hd. r.; before, small naked female figure stg. l.   R. ΜΕΓΑ.
Man-headed bull stg. r., hd. facing. *Numismatic Chronicle, 1896, pl. IX, 2* ..   £1,000

842   844

842 **Messana** (the city was ruled by the tyrants of Rhegion—Anaxilas and then his son—
until 461 B.C. when the Messanians regained their independence. In 396 B.C. Messana
was destroyed by the Carthaginians under Himilco, a blow from which it only slowly
recovered during the 4th Cent.). 480-461 B.C. (tyranny of Anaxilas and his son). Æ
tetradrachm. Biga of mules driven r. by bearded charioteer; olive-leaf in ex. R.
ΜΕSSΕΝΙΟΝ. Hare bounding r. *B.M.C. 2. 14* £400

*This type was adopted at both Messana and Rhegion following Anaxilas' victory with the
mule-team at the Olympic Games of 480 B.C.*

843 — — Similar, but with Nike flying r. to crown mules on *obv.*, and with A above hare on
rev. B.M.C. 2. 16 ..   ..   £650

844 — Æ *didrachm*. Similar to 842, but without olive-leaf in ex. on *obv.   Weber Catalogue
1415* £500

845 — Æ *litra*. Hare bounding r. R. MES (retrograde) within olive-wreath. *B.M.C. 2. 24*
£110

846 *Circa* 461 B.C. (following the expulsion of the tyrants the city briefly reverted to its original
name of Zankle). Æ *tetradrachm*. Poseidon (?), naked but for chlamys over shoulders,
striding r., brandishing thunderbolt; to r., altar. R. ΔΑΝΚΛΑΙΟΝ. Dolphin leaping l.,
shell beneath. *Numismatic Chronicle, 1896, pl. VIII, 7*   ..   ..   ..   (*Unique*)

847   848

847 461-450 B.C.   Æ *tetradrachm*.   Biga of mules driven r. by seated male charioteer; above, Nike flying r., crowning mules; in ex., olive-leaf.   ℞. ΜΕΣΣΑΝΙΟΝ.   Hare bounding r.; beneath, spray of olive.   *B.M.C. 2*. 25   ..   ..   £350

848 — Æ *drachm*.   *Obv*. Similar.   ℞. ΜΕΣΣΑΝΙΟΝ (partly retrograde).   Hare bounding r.: all within olive-wreath.   *B.M.C. 2*. 31   ..   ..   £275

849 — Æ *litra*.   Hare bounding r., scallop-shell beneath.   ℞. ΜΕΣ within olive-wreath.   *B.M.C. 2*. 63   ..   ..   £90

850 450-425 B.C.   Æ *tetradrachm*.   Biga of mules driven r. by *standing* male charioteer; above, Nike flying r., crowning mules; in ex., olive-leaf with fruit.   ℞. ΜΕΣΣΑΝΙΟΝ.   Hare bounding r.; beneath, fly r.   *B.M.C. 2*. 44   ..   ..   £400

851 — — Biga of mules driven r. by standing *female* charioteer (city-goddess Messana); above, Nike stg. r. on reins, her wings spread; in ex., olive-leaf with fruit.   ℞. ΜΕΣΣΑΝΙΟΝ. Hare bounding r.; beneath, dolphin r.   *B.M.C. 2*. 37   ..   ..   £500

852   855

852 425-396 B.C.   Æ *tetradrachm*.   Biga of mules, seen in perspective, driven *left* by city-goddess Messana who is about to be crowned by Nike flying r. above, holding wreath; in ex., two dolphins meeting.   ℞. ΜΕΣΣΑΝΙΟΝ (retrograde).   Hare bounding l.; beneath, hd. of Pan l., with short horns.   *B.M.C. 2*. 49   ..   ..   £850

853 — — Biga of trotting mules driven l. by city-goddess Messana who is crowned by Nike flying r. above; nothing in ex.   ℞. ΜΕΣΣΑΝΙΟΝ.   Hare bounding r.; beneath, sea-horse l. *B.M.C. 2*. 53   ..   ..   £900

854 — — Biga of mules driven l. by city-goddess Messana; in ex., two dolphins meeting. ℞. ΜΕΣΣΑΝΙΟΝ (sometimes ΜΕΣΣΑΝΙΩΝ) in ex.   Hare bounding l.; above, eagle flying l.; beneath, stalk of corn.   *B.M.C. 2*. 46   ..   ..   £950

855 — Æ *drachm*.   Hd. of nymph Pelorias l., wreathed with corn; ΠΕΛΩΡΙΑΣ before, Α behind, dolphin l. beneath.   ℞. ΦΕΡΑΙΜΩΝ.   Pheraimon, son of Aeolos, naked but for helmet, advancing r., holding spear and large shield.   *B.M.C. 2*. 58   ..   ..   ..   £600

856 — Æ *obol*.   Hare bounding r., ΜΕΣ beneath.   ℞. Dolphin r., within olive-wreath.   *B.M.C. 2*. 33 ..   ..   £100

857 **Morgantina** (although a town of some importance, little is known of the history of Morgantina: it was of Sicel foundation). *Circa* 460 B.C. Æ *drachm.* Elderly male hd. r., bearded and bound with taenia. R. MORCANTIN (retrograde). Ear of corn. *Weber Catalogue* 1445 .. .. £1,500

858 — Æ *litra.* Similar, but with legend MORCANTINA (retrograde) on *rev. B.M.C. 2.* 1 £500

859 420-400 B.C. Æ *litra.* MOPΓANTINΩN. Hd. of Athena three-quarter face to r., wearing triple-crested helmet. R. MOPΓA. Nike seated l. on rock, holding wreath; beneath, corn-grain. *B.M.C. 2.* 4 .. .. £650

860 — — MOPΓANTINΩN. Hd. of Artemis r., quiver at shoulder. R. Horseman prancing l., thrusting with spear held high in r. hand. *B.M.C. 2.* 2.. .. .. .. £600

858 861

861 **Motya** (the chief naval base of the Carthaginians in Sicily, Motya was situated on a small islet, off the west coast, connected to the mainland by a causeway. It was destroyed by Dionysios of Syracuse in 397 B.C.). Before 415 B.C. Æ *didrachm.* MOTVAION. Naked youth seated sideways on horse galloping l., from which he is about to dismount. R. Female hd. r., hair bound with cord wound four times round the hd.; swastika before neck; around, three dolphins. *Jenkins (Coins of Punic Sicily), pl.* 1, *no.* 12. *Lloyd Sylloge* 1135.. .. .. £1,250
The obv. of this type is copied from the coinage of Himera, the rev. from that of Segesta or Syracuse.

862 — — Hound stg. r.; above, small female hd. r. R. Diad. female hd. r., hair rolled; before, corn-grain. *Jenkins, pl.* 2, *no.* 16 .. .. £750
This type is copied from the coinage of Segesta.

863 — Æ *obol.* Female hd. r., within wreath. R. Nymph stg. r. before altar. *Jenkins, pl.* 23, *no.* 2 .. .. £175

864 865

864 — — Eagle, wings closed, stg. l. on Ionic capital, holding serpent in beak; above, ivy-leaf. R. MOTVAION (retrograde). Dolphin l., scallop-shell beneath. *Jenkins, pl.* 23, *no.* 1. *B.M.C. 2.* 1 .. .. £150
This type is very similar to, and probably copied from, the litrai of Hipana (see no. 822*).*

865 415-405 B.C. Æ *didrachm.* Hound stg. r.; beneath, plant growing. R. MOTVAION. Female hd. r., hair rolled. *Jenkins, pl.* 3, *no.* 22. *B.M.C. 2.* 4.. .. .. £1,000
Copied from the coinage of Segesta.

866 — — *Obv.* Similar. R. Diad. female hd. r., with tall slender neck, hair rolled; before, Punic legend '*m t v*'; behind, ivy-leaf. *Jenkins, pl.* 3, *no.* 26. *B.M.C. 2., p.* 243, 5 £850

867 — Æ *obol.* Gorgon-head, with protruding tongue. R. Palm-tree; in lower field, Punic legend '*m t v*'. *Jenkins, pl.* 23, *no.* 4a. *B.M.C. 2., p.* 244, 12 .. .. £90

868   870

868 405-397 B.C. *Æ tetradrachm.* Eagle stg. r., wings closed; above, Punic legend '*m t v*'.
R. Crab; beneath, fish r. *Jenkins, pl. 5, no. 43.* *B.M.C. 2., p. 243, 2* £1,500
Copied from the coinage of Akragas.

869 — — Female hd. l., wearing sphendone, earring and necklace, hair in net behind; around,
four dolphins. R. Crab. *Jenkins, pl. 5, no. 46.* *Weber Catalogue 1452* ..   £1,250
*The obv. of this type is copied from the Arethusa head by Kimon on Syracusan deka-
drachms; the reverse from the coinage of Akragas.*

870 — *Æ didrachm.* Female hd. three-quarter face to r., wearing necklace and ampyx;
around, six dolphins. R. Crab; above, fish r.; beneath, Punic legend '*m t v*'. *Jenkins,
pl. 5, no. 49.* *B.M.C. 2., p. 244, 8*. £1,500
*This obv. type is copied from Kimon's famous facing head of Arethusa on a Syracusan
tetradrachm.*

871 — *Æ obol.* Similar to previous, but without dolphins on *obv.*, and without fish on *rev.*
Jenkins, pl. 23, no. 6. .   ..   .   £175

872 **Naxos** (after being subject to the tyrants Hippokrates, Gelon and Hieron for much of the
earlier part of the 5th Cent., Naxos regained its independence in 461 B.C. The city was
destroyed by Dionysios of Syracuse in 404 B.C.). 461-430 B.C. *Æ tetradrachm.* Hd. of
Dionysios r., wreathed with ivy and with long beard, hair in bunch behind. R. NAXION.
Naked Silenos squatting facing, body inclined to r., looking l., holding kantharos in raised
r. hand. *B.M.C. 2. 7* £9,000
This is one of the masterpieces of late archaic Greek numismatic art.

873 — *Æ drachm.* Obv. Same as last. R. Similar, but Silenos' body is inclined to l., and he
rests l. hand on knee. *B.M.C. 2. 10* £1,750

874 — *Æ litra.* Obv. Same as last. R. NAXI (retrograde). Bunch of grapes within ivy-
wreath. *B.M.C. 2. 13* £350

875 430-413 B.C. *Æ tetradrachm.* Bearded hd. of Dionysos r., of fine early classical style,
hair bound with broad band adorned with ivy-wreath. R. NAΞION. Naked Silenos
squatting, similar to 872, but of more advanced style, and he also holds thyrsos (in l. hand);
to l., vine growing, with leaves and fruit. *B.M.C. 2. 19* £6,000

Naxos *continued*

876 413-404 B.C. Æ *tetradrachm*. ΝΑΞΙΩΝ. Hd. of Maenad r., wearing ivy-wreath. R.
Naked Silenos squatting facing, looking l., holding kantharos, branch of ivy and wineskin; to l., vine growing. *Hill (Coins of Ancient Sicily) pl.* VIII, *no.* 17   ..   £7,500

877   881

877 — Æ *didrachm*. ΝΑΞΙΩΝ. Laur. hd. of Apollo l.; laurel-leaf with berry behind. R.
Naked Silenos squatting facing, body inclined to r., looking l., holding kantharos and
thyrsos; to l., vine growing; to r., term. *B.M.C.* 2. 20 ..   ..   ..   £1,500

878 — Æ *hemidrachm*. ΑΣΣΙΝΟΣ. Hd. of young river-god Assinos l., wreathed with vine-
leaves, and with short horn. R. ΝΑΞΙΩΝ. Naked Silenos squatting facing, body inclined
to r., looking l., holding kantharos and pipes. *B.M.C.* 2. 23 ..   ..   ..   £400

879 — Æ *litra*. ΝΑΞΙΩΝ. Hd. of river-god Assinos, as last. R. Bunch of grapes on stalk
with leaves and tendrils. *B.M.C.* 2. 26 ..   ..   £175

880 **Panormos** (the principal Phoenician city in Sicily, Panormos produced a limited coinage
in the latter part of the 5th Cent.; but following the great success of Carthaginian arms,
409-405 B.C., the issues of the mint became much larger.   The types are mostly copied
from the coinages of other Sicilian cities, such as Gela, Segesta and Syracuse).   Before
415 B.C. Æ *didrachm*. Hound stg. r.; above, small female hd. r. R. Diad. female hd.
r., hair rolled; around, three dolphins, and Punic legend '*sys*'. *Jenkins (Coins of Punic
Sicily), pl.* 2, *no.* Z1..   ..   ..   £1,000
    This type is copied from the coinage of Segesta.

881 — Æ *litra*. Poseidon seated r. on rock, holding trident and extending l. hand towards
dolphin in field to r.   R. Naked youth seated sideways, holding caduceus, on man-headed
bull galloping r.; beneath, Punic legend '*sys*'. *Jenkins, pl.* 24, *no.* 5. *B.M.C.* 2., *p.* 246, 1
£200

882 415-405 B.C. Æ *tetradrachm*. Slow quadriga driven r. by charioteer; above, Nike
flying r., crowning horses. R. ΠΑΝΟΡΜΙΤΙΚΟΝ (retrograde). Laur. hd. of Apollo r.
Jenkins, pl. 7, *no.* 6. *B.M.C.* 2. 1 ..   ..   £1,400
    This type is copied from the coinage of Katane.

883   885

883 — Æ *didrachm*. Hound stg. r., looking back; above, shell. R. ΠΑΝΟΡΜΙΤΙΚΟΝ (retrograde). Female hd. r., wearing sphendone; behind, swastika. *Jenkins, pl.* 6, *no.* 8.
B.M.C. 2. 2 ..   ..   £800
    Copied from the coinage of Segesta.

884 — Æ *litra*. ΠΑΝΟΡΜΟ (retrograde). Young male hd. r., wearing tainia, hair short.
R. Forepart of man-headed bull swimming r., shell beneath. *Jenkins, pl.* 24, *no.* 2.
B.M.C. 2. 5 ..   ..   £175
    Copied from the coinage of Gela.

885 405-380 B.C. Æ *tetradrachm*. Quadriga galloping l., driven by charioteer who is crowned
by Nike flying r. above; in ex., Punic legend '*sys*' and shell. R. Female hd. r., wearing
broad diadem round which the hair is rolled; dolphins before and behind; above, long
fish r. *Jenkins, pl.* 8, *no.* 21. *B.M.C.* 2., *p.* 247, 6   ..   ..   ..   £900
    Copied from the coinage of Syracuse.

886 — — Quadriga galloping r., driven by charioteer who is crowned by Nike flying l. above; in ex., hippocamp r. and Punic legend 'sys'. ℞. Female hd. l., hair in net, bound by sphendone, wearing earring and necklace; around, four dolphins. *Jenkins, pl. 10, no. 33. Weber Catalogue 1475* £700

The reverse of this type is closely copied from the Arethusa head by Kimon on Syracusan dekadrachms.

887   891

887 — ℞ *didrachm.* Hound stg. r., looking back; above, shell; beneath, Punic legend 'sys'. ℞. Female hd. r., wearing sphendone ornamented behind with stars. *Jenkins, pl. 6, no. 9. B.M.C. 2., p. 248, 18* £700

Copied from the coinage of Segesta.

888 — — Free horse prancing r.; above, Punic legend 'sys'. ℞. Young male hd. r., bare, with short curly hair; around, three dolphins. *Jenkins, pl. 6, no. 12. B.M.C. 2., p. 248, 20* £1,100

889 — ℞ *obol.* Young male hd. l. ℞. Man-headed bull stg. l., hd. facing; above, Punic legend 'sys'. *Jenkins, pl. 24, no. 14. B.M.C. 2., p. 249, 27* £150

890 — — Female hd. r., wearing sphendone; behind, swastika. ℞. Forepart of man-headed bull swimming r., shell beneath; before, Punic legend 'sys'. *Jenkins, pl. 24, no. 8. B.M.C. 2., p. 249, 23* £150

891 370-360 B.C. ℞ *tetradrachm.* Quadriga galloping l., driven by bearded charioteer crowned by Nike flying r. above; in front of charioteer, sign of Tanit; in ex., swan l., with spread wings. ℞. Female hd. r., of fine style, wearing ampyx; before, two dolphins. *Jenkins, pl. 10, no. 39. Weber Catalogue 1476* £750

Copied from the coinage of Syracuse.

892 360-340 B.C. ℞ *tetradrachm.* Slow quadriga driven l. by female charioteer, horses crowned by Nike flying l. above; in ex., Punic legend 'sys'. ℞. Female hd. l., wearing ampyx, short fluttering hair above; around, three dolphins. *Jenkins, pl. 11, no. 44. Weber Catalogue 1478* £550

893 340-320 B.C. ℞ *tetradrachm.* Quadriga galloping l., driven by charioteer who is crowned by Nike flying r. above; in ex., Punic legend 'sys'. ℞. Female hd. l., of fine style, wearing corn-wreath and large earring; around, three dolphins. *Jenkins, pl. 13, no. 63* £650

The reverse of this type is closely copied from the Syracusan dekadrachms by Euainetos.

894 320-300 B.C. ℞ *tetradrachm.* Obv. Similar to last, but with star in field above hd. of farthest horse. ℞. Female hd. l., similar to last, but of harsher style, and with four dolphins around; behind neck, small swastika. *Jenkins, pl. 13, no. 71. B.M.C. 2., p. 248, 13* £500

Panormos *continued*

895 — — *Obv.* Similar to 893, but with two dolphins in ex., on either side of the Punic legend. ℞. Female hd. l., similar to 893; of smooth and elaborate style, and with four dolphins around. *Jenkins, pl.* 14, *no.* 80. *B.M.C.* 2., *p.* 248, 11 .. .. £600

895   893   899

896 **Segesta** (a town of Elymian origin, Segesta was frequently in dispute with its southern neighbour, Selinus. These troubles were used as the excuse for the Athenian expedition to Sicily, defeated in 413 B.C., and for the disastrous Carthaginian invasion of 409 B.C. After this date Segesta was dependent on the Carthaginians). 480-461 B.C. Æ *didrachm* Hound stg. r., wearing collar, his nose to the ground. ℞. ΣΕCΕΣΤΑ ΙΙΒΕΜΙ (retrograde) Hd. of nymph Segesta r., of archaic style, with hair turned up under diadem. *B.M.C.* 2. 5 .. .. £600

897 — — Hound stg. l.; above, murex-shell. ℞. ΣΕCΕΣΤΑ ΙΙΒ (retrograde). Similar hd. of nymph Segesta, but facing l. *B.M.C.* 2. 7 .. .. £750

898 — Æ *trihemiobol.* Hound stg. l.; above, wheel. ℞. ΣΕΓΕΣΤΑ ΙΙΒ. Female hd. facing, hair loose. *B.M.C.* 2. 14 .. .. £175

899 — Æ *litra.* Hound bounding r., its hd. uplifted. ℞. ΣΕCΕΣΤΑ ΙΙΒ. Hd. of nymph Segesta r., similar to 896. *B.M.C.* 2. 11 .. .. £150

900 461-415 B.C. Æ *didrachm.* Hound walking r., on the scent; above, hd. of nymph Segesta r. ℞. ΣΕΓΕΣΤΑ ΙΙΒ. Diad. hd. of nymph Segesta r., hair rolled. *B.M.C.* 2. 28 £600

901   903

901 415-409 B.C. Æ *tetradrachm.* ΕΓΕΣΤΑΙΩΝ. Youthful huntsman (Pan or Krimissos), naked, stg. r., l. foot on rock, r. hand on hip, holding two javelins in l.; two hounds r. at his feet; before, term l. ℞. ΣΕΛΕΣΤΑ ΙΙΑ. Hd. of nymph Segesta r., with hair in sphendone ornamented with stars behind; beneath, stalk of barley. *B.M.C.* 2. 32 .. £5,000

902 — — Galloping quadriga driven r. by female charioteer, holding corn-ears, who is crowned by Nike flying l. above; in ex., ΣΕΛΕΣΤΑ ΙΙΑ and grasshopper r. ℞. Youthful huntsman, similar to *obv.* of previous coin, but with only one hound at his feet. *B.M.C.* 2. 34 £4,000

903 — Æ *litra.* Hd. of nymph Segesta three-quarter face to l., between two branches of olive. ℞. ΕΓΕΣΤΑΙΟΝ (retrograde). Hound stg. l.; above, Gorgoneion; before, murex-shell. *B.M.C.* 2. 43 .. .. £175

904 — Æ *hemilitron.* Forepart of crouching hound r. ℞. ΣΕΓΕ around large H. *B.M.C.* 2. 47 .. .. £90

905 — Æ *hexas.* Hd. of hound r. ℞. ΕΓΕ / ΣΤΑ and two pellets. *B.M.C.* 2. 48 .. £40

906 **Selinus** (this city enjoyed considerable prosperity in the mid-5th Cent. B.C. The coin types dwell upon the purification of the neighbouring marshlands, which were the cause of frequent epidemics in the city until the philosopher Empedokles advised the diversion of two local streams. The Carthaginians destroyed Selinus in 409 B.C.). 466-415 B.C. Æ *tetradrachm.* ΣΕΛΙΝΟΝΤΙΟΝ. Slow quadriga driven l. by Apollo and Artemis, standing side by side, the former discharging arrow from his bow. Ṛ. ΣΕΛΙΝΟΣ. Archaic figure of river-god Selinos, naked, walking l., holding phiale over altar in front of which stands sacrificial cock l.; in l. hand he holds lustral branch; behind, bull stg. l. on pedestal, selinon leaf above. *B.M.C. 2.* 25 ..   ..   £1,750

907 — — *Obv.* No legend. Quadriga driven by Apollo and Artemis, similar to last, but travelling to r., and with corn-grain in ex. Ṛ. ΣΕΛΙΝΟΝΤΙΟΝ. River-god Selinos, all as last, but the figure is of finer, early classical, style, and stands facing, hd. to l. *B.M.C. 2.* 31 ..   ..   £1,250

908 — Æ *didrachm.* ΣΕΛΙΝΟΤΙΟΝ (*sic*, and partly retrograde). Naked Herakles jumping r., seizing by its horn the Cretan bull which gallops r.; he wields club held in raised r. hand. Ṛ. ΗΥΨΑΣ. River-god Hypsas, naked, stg. facing, hd. l., holding phiale over altar round which snake twines; in l. hand he holds lustral branch; to r., crane running r., selinon leaf above. *B.M.C. 2.* 34 ..   ..   £900

909 — Æ *litra.* Nymph seated l. on rock, holding at arm's length a serpent which darts towards her; with her l. hand she raises her veil; in field above, selinon leaf. Ṛ. ΣΕΛΙΝΟΕΣ. Man-headed bull stg. r.; in ex., fish r. *B.M.C. 2.* 40 ..   ..   £175

910   911

Selinus *continued*

910   415-409 B.C.   Æ *tetradrachm.* Galloping quadriga driven r. by Nike; above, olive-wreath; in ex., ΣΕΛΙΝΟΝΤΙΟΝ and ear of corn.   R. ΣΕΛΙΝΟΝΤΙΟΝ. River-god Selinos, all as 907, but of the finest classical style. *B.M.C. 2.* 44   ..   ..   £2,000

911   — Æ *hemidrachm.* Hd. of bearded Herakles r., wearing lion's skin. R. Galloping quadriga driven l. by male charioteer; above, selinon leaf; in ex., ΣΕΛΙΝΟΝΤΙΟΝ. *B.M.C. 2.* 47 ..   ..   £350

912   — — *Obv.* Hd. of young Herakles, in lion's skin, three-quarter face to l. R. Same as last. *B.M.C. 2.* 48   ..   ..   £400

913   915

913 **Syracuse** (under the rule of the tyrant Gelon, 485-478 B.C., Syracuse rose to a position of pre-eminence amongst the Sicilian Greeks, especially after the great victory over the Carthaginian invaders at Himera in 480 B.C. She maintained her ascendancy throughout the 5th Century, though her influence was much curtailed at the close of the century when the Carthaginians gained a firm footing in the island. The 4th Century was a troubled period in Sicily, though the tyrant Agathokles, 317-289 B.C., tried valiantly to reassert Greek authority over the whole of the island. The Carthaginians were defeated by the Romans in the First Punic War, 264-241 B.C., and the victors took possession of Sicily. Syracuse, Rome's ally, was allowed to remain independent until 212 B.C. when the city was sacked by the Romans). 485-478 B.C. (tyranny of Gelon). Æ *tetradrachm.* Slow quadriga driven r. by male charioteer holding goad; above, Nike flying r., crowning horses. R. ΣΥΡΑΚΟΣΙΟΝ. Large hd. of Artemis-Arethusa r., hair slightly waved and turned up behind under diadem of beads; four dolphins around. *Boehringer* (*Die münzen von Syrakus*) 69. *B.M.C. 2.* 35   ..   ..   £400

914   — — Similar, but the hd. of Artemis-Arethusa is much smaller. *Boeh.* 123. *B.M.C. 2.* 29 ..   ..   £300

915   — Æ *didrachm.* Naked rider, bearded, on horse pacing r., leading a second horse on his far side. R. ΣΥΡΑΚΟΣΙΟΝ. Hd. of Artemis-Arethusa r., similar to 913, but only three dolphins around. *Boeh.* 98. *B.M.C. 2.* 20   ..   ..   £450

916   — Æ *drachm.* Naked rider, bearded, on horse pacing r. R. Similar to previous, but without dolphins. *Boeh.* 283. *B.M.C. 2.* 47 ..   ..   £300

917   — Æ *obol.* Hd. of Artemis-Arethusa r., hair turned up behind under diadem of beads. R. Wheel of four spokes. *Boeh.* 366. *B.M.C. 2.* 56 ..   ..   £65

918   — Æ *pentonkion. Obv.* Similar. R. Five pellets. *Boeh.* 371-2   ..   ..   £55

919   — Æ *hexas. Obv.* Similar. R. Two pellets. *Boeh.* 373   ..   ..   ..   £35

920 *Circa* 479 B.C. (special issue on the occasion of the Carthaginian defeat).   Æ *dekadrachm.*
Slow quadriga driven r. by male charioteer holding goad; above, Nike flying r., crowning
horses; in ex., lion springing r.   ℞. ΣVRAKOΣION around linear circle, within which hd.
of Artemis-Arethusa r., wearing olive-wreath; around, four dolphins.   *Boeh.* 376.
B.M.C. 2. 63   ..   ..   £75,000
   This famous piece, one of the classic rarities of the Greek coinage, is popularly known as the
'Demaretion'.   It is so-called because Demarete, wife of Gelon, intervened with her husband
on behalf of the defeated Carthaginians who, in gratitude, presented her with one hundred
talents of gold.   It was from the proceeds of this gift that the special coinage is supposed to have
been produced.   However, some scholars have assigned this issue to a slightly later period,
c. 465 B.C.

921   924

921 — Æ *tetradrachm.* Same as last. *Boeh.* 380. *B.M.C. 2.* 64 ..   ..   ..   £6,000
922 — Æ *obol.* Hd. of Artemis-Arethusa r., wreathed with olive. ℞. Wheel, with ΣV / RA
between the four spokes. *Boeh.* 402. *B.M.C. 2.* 66   ..   ..   £250
923 474-450 B.C. Æ *tetradrachm.* Slow quadriga driven r. by male charioteer who is crowned
by Nike flying l. above; in ex., pistrix (sea-serpent) r. ℞. ΣVRAKOΣION. Hd. of Artemis-
Arethusa r., hair waved in front and turned up behind under diadem of beads; four
dolphins around. *Boeh.* 439. *B.M.C. 2.* 69   ..   ..   £750
924 — — *Obv.* Similar, but Nike flies r. to crown horses instead of charioteer. ℞. ΣVRAKOΣION.
Hd. of Artemis-Arethusa r., hair bound with diadem of beads and rolled behind; four
dolphins around. *Boeh.* 517. *B.M.C. 2.* 84   ..   ..   £850
925 — — *Obv.* Same as last. ℞. ΣVRAKOΣION. Hd. of Artemis-Arethusa r., hair bound with
cord which passes thrice round the hd., and twice round back hair; four dolphins around.
Boeh. 570. *B.M.C. 2.* 94 ..   ..   £950
926 — — Galloping quadriga driven l. by male charioteer who is crowned by Nike flying r.
above; in ex., pistrix l. ℞. ΣVΡΑΚΟΣ (retrograde). Hd. of Artemis-Arethusa r., hair in
korymbos; four dolphins around. *Boeh.* 603. *B.M.C. 2.* 103..   ..   ..   £1,100

927   929

Syracuse *continued*

927 — Æ *didrachm.* Naked rider, bearded, on horse pacing r., leading a second horse on his far side; Nike flies r. behind to crown horseman; in ex., pistrix r. ℞. ΣΥΡΑΚΟΣΙΟΝ. Hd. of Artemis-Arethusa r., wearing diadem of beads, hair tied behind with double cord, loose tresses on cheek; four dolphins around. *Boeh.* 497. *B.M.C. 2.* 75   £750

928 — Æ *drachm.* Rider, wearing chlamys, on horse prancing l. ℞. ΣΥΡΑΚΟΣΙΟΝ. Hd. of Artemis-Arethusa r., hair in korymbos. *Boeh.* 607. *B.M.C. 2.* 106 ..   £500

929 — Æ *litra.* ΣΥRA before hd. of Artemis-Arethusa r., hair turned up behind under diadem of beads. ℞. Cuttle-fish. *Boeh.* 421. *B.M.C. 2.* 50 ..   ..   ..   £75

930 — Æ *pentonkion.* *Obv.* Similar, but without legend. ℞. Wheel of four spokes and five pellets—one at centre, the others in the angles of the spokes. *Boeh.* 431. *B.M.C. 2.* 79 ..   ..   £65

931 450-439 B.C. Æ *tetradrachm.* Slow quadriga driven r. by male charioteer holding goad; above, Nike flying r., crowning horses. ℞. ΣΥΡΑΚΟΣΙΟΝ. Hd. of Artemis-Arethusa r., hair enclosed in sakkos ornamented with maeander and zig-zag patterns; four dolphins around. *Boeh.* 644. *B.M.C. 2.* 113   ..   ..   £850

932 — — *Obv.* Similar. ℞. ΣΥΡΑΚΟΣΙΟΝ. Hd. of Artemis-Arethusa r., hair bound with cord wound around four times, forming an elongated coiffure; four dolphins around. *Boeh.* 671. *B.M.C. 2.* 121   ..   ..   £800

933   934

933 439-435 B.C. Æ *tetradrachm.* *Obv.* Similar, but Nike flies l. to crown charioteer. ℞. ΣΥΡΑΚΟΣΙΟΝ. Hd. of Artemis-Arethusa r., hair bound with sphendone, the long ends of which are wound three times round the hd.; four dolphins around. *Boeh.* 723. *B.M.C. 2.* 110   ..   ..   £1,000

934 425-413 B.C. Æ *tetradrachm, by Sosion* (unsigned). Galloping quadriga driven l. by charioteer who is crowned by Nike flying r. above; each horse is clearly visible, unlike earlier dies. ℞. ΣΥΡΑΚΟΣΙΟΝ. Hd. of Artemis-Arethusa l., hair elaborately bound and rolled, and wearing ampyx; four dolphins around. *Tudeer (Die tetradrachmenprägung von Syrakus in der Periode der Signierenden Künstler)* 1. *Grose* 2703 ..   ..   £2,500

935 — Æ *tetradrachm, by Eumenes.* Similar, but on *rev.* the ampyx is inscribed with the artist's signature, ΕΥΜΗ / ΝΟΥ. *Tudeer* 7. *B.M.C. 2.* 140 ..   ..   £3,000

936   938

936 — Æ *tetradrachm, by Euainetos and Eukleidas.* Galloping quadriga driven r. by female charioteer who is crowned by Nike flying l. above; the horses are shown in perspective, and the farthest one has broken his rein which trails on the ground; in ex., chariot-wheel; artist's signature EYAINETO in minute letters along exergual line. ℞. ΣΥΡΑΚΟΣΙΟΣ. Hd. of Artemis-Arethusa l., hair bound with sphendone, ornamented with swan in front, and stars and artist's signature EVKΛEI at the back; four dolphins around. *Tudeer* 37. *B.M.C.* 2. 190   ..   ..   £1,750

937 — Æ *tetradrachm, by Euainetos.* Galloping quadriga driven r. by bearded male charioteer, the horses seen in perspective, as last; above, Nike flying l., bearing a tablet inscribed EYAIN / ETO; in ex., two dolphins meeting. ℞. ΣΥΡΑΚΟΣΙΩΝ. Hd. of Artemis-Arethusa l., hair bound with sphendone, ornamented with dolphin in front and stars at the back; four dolphins around, the one before face inscribed EYAI. *Tudeer* 42. *B.M.C.* 2. 188
£2,500

938 — Æ *drachm, by Eumenes.* ΛΕΥΚΑΣΠΙΣ. Leukaspis, naked, rushing r., holding sword and oval shield. ℞. ΣΥΡΑΚΟΣΙΟΝ. Hd. of Artemis-Arethusa r., hair bound with diadem crossed; beneath, EVMENOV; four dolphins around. *B.M.C.* 2. 162 ..   ..   £1,000

939 413-405 B.C. Æ *tetradrachm, by Euth . . . . and Phrygillos.* Galloping quadriga driven r. by winged naked youth (Eros or Agon ?) who is crowned by Nike flying l. above; in ex., monster Skylla r., holding trident, and artist's signature EYΘ. ℞. ΣΥΡΑΚΟΣΙΟΝ. Hd. of Persephone (?) l., wearing wreath of corn with oak leaf and poppy head; beneath, ΦΡΥΓΙΛΛ / ΟΣ; four dolphins around. *Tudeer* 47. *B.M.C.* 2. 156-7   ..   ..   £3,000

940 — Æ *tetradrachm, by Phrygillos.* ΣΥΡΑΚΟΣΙΟΝ. Hd. of Artemis-Arethusa l., wearing sphendone, ornamented with stars behind and inscribed ΦΡΥ above the forehead; four dolphins around. ℞. Galloping quadriga driven l. by Persephone carrying flaming torch; she is about to be crowned by Nike flying r.; in ex., ear of corn. *Tudeer* 56. *B.M.C.* 2. 158   ..   ..   £5,000
     The head of Artemis-Arethusa here appears for the first time as the obverse type.

941 — Æ *tetradrachm, by Eukleidas.* *Obv.* Similar to *rev.* of last. ℞. ΣΥΡΑΚΟΣΙΩΝ. Hd. of Athena three-quarter face to l., hair hanging loose in curls, wearing richly ornamented triple-crested helmet inscribed with artist's signature EV — K — ΛEIΔ / A; four dolphins around. *Tudeer* 58. *B.M.C.* 2. 198-9 ..   ..   £10,000

942 — Æ *tetradrachm,* unsigned. *Obv.* Same as last. ℞. ΣΥΡΑΚΟΣΙΩΝ. Hd. of Artemis-Arethusa r., hair tied up into a tight topknot; four dolphins around. *Tudeer* 62. *B.M.C.* 2. 224 ..   ..   £2,000

Syracuse *continued*

943 — Æ *tetradrachm, by Parmenides* (unsigned). Galloping quadriga driven l. by charioteer, holding goad, about to be crowned by Nike flying r. above; broken chariot-wheel beneath horses' hooves; in ex., ear of corn. ℞. ΣΥΡΑΚΟΣΙΩΝ. Hd. of Artemis-Arethusa l., wearing sphendone ornamented with stars behind; beneath, small hd. of Silenos r.; four dolphins around. *Tudeer* 70. *B.M.C. 2.* 219 .. .. £1,500

944   945

944 — Æ *tetradrachm, by Kimon.* Hd. of Arethusa three-quarter face to l., hair flowing in loose tresses; artist's signature ΚΙΜΩΝ on hair-band across forehead; two dolphins on either side, only partially visible; above, outside border, ΑΡΕΘΟΣΑ. ℞. Galloping quadriga driven l. by male charioteer, looking back; above, Nike stepping r., on the heads of the two nearer horses, bearing wreath; behind, ΣΥΡΑΚΟΣΙΩΝ; beneath horses, fallen column; in ex., ear of corn. *Tudeer* 81. *B.M.C. 2.* 208 .. .. £12,500

> *The facing head of Arethusa on this type is generally considered to be Kimon's masterpiece and was much imitated in later periods.*

945 — Æ *drachm.* ΣΥΡΑΚΟΣΙΩΝ. Helmeted hd. of Athena three-quarter face to l., similar to *rev.* of 941, but without artist's signature. ℞. ΣΥΡΑΚΟΣΙΩΝ. Leukaspis, naked, advancing r., holding spear and large oval shield; in background, square altar beside which lies sacrificial ram; in ex., ΛΕΥΚΑΣΠΙΣ. *B.M.C. 2.* 226-7 .. .. £1,000

946 — Æ *hemidrachm.* *Obv.* Similar to last, but with legend abbreviated to ΣΥ. ℞. Galloping quadriga driven l. by charioteer, holding goad, crowned by Nike flying r. above; in ex., two dolphins meeting. *B.M.C. 2.* 231-2.. .. .. £450

947   948

947 405-380 B.C. (time of Dionysios the Elder). N 1⅓ *litra* (*c.* 1·17 gm.). ΣΥΡ. Hd. of young Herakles l., wearing lion's skin. ℞. Incuse square, quartered, with Σ — Υ / Ρ — Α in the corners; at centre, incuse circle containing female hd. l. *B.M.C. 2.* 135 £500

948 — N *obol* (*c.* 0·7 gm.). ΣΥΡΑ. Hd. of Athena l., wearing crested Athenian helmet. ℞. Aegis, with Gorgon's hd. facing. *B.M.C. 2.* 138 .. .. £750

949 — N *tritemorion* (*c.* 0·55 gm.). *Obv.* Similar to last, with legend ΣΥΡ. ℞. Similar to 947, but the incuse circle contains a wheel of four spokes. *B.M.C. 2.* 139 .. .. £550

950   951

950 — N *octobol* (=100 silver litrai =2 dekadrachms; *c.* 5·8 gm.), *by Kimon.* ΣΥΡΑΚΟΣΙΟΝ. Hd. of Artemis-Arethusa l., wearing sphendone ornamented with stars; behind, corn-grain and ΚΙ. ℞. ΣΥΡΑ. Herakles, naked, kneeling r., strangling the Nemean lion with both arms; behind, club; above, ivy-leaf. *B.M.C. 2.* 168 .. .. .. £3,000

951 — N *tetrobol* (=50 silver litrai=1 dekadrachm; *c.* 2·9 gm.), *by Euainetos.* ΣΥΡΑ. Hd. of young river-god Anapos l., Ε behind. ℞. ΣΥΡΑΚΟΣΙΩΝ on exergual line beneath free horse prancing r.; above, star. *B.M.C. 2.* 172 .. .. £1,500

952 — Æ *dekadrachm, by Kimon.* Galloping quadriga driven l. by charioteer, holding goad, crowned by Nike flying r. above; in ex., panoply of armour consisting of cuirass flanked by greaves, with shield on l. and crested helmet on r.; beneath, AΘΛΑ. ℞. ΣΥΡΑΚΟΣΙΩΝ. Hd. of Artemis-Arethusa l., wearing hair-band, inscribed ΚΙ, and net; around, four dolphins. *B.M.C. 2.* 204 .. .. £10,000

953 — Æ *dekadrachm, by Euainetos.* *Obv.* Similar to Kimon's work, though differing in style and treatment of the subject. ℞. ΣΥΡΑΚΟΣΙΩΝ. Hd. of Artemis-Arethusa, or Persephone, l., hair bound with wreath of corn-leaves; four dolphins around; beneath truncation, ΕΥΑΙΝΕ. *B.M.C. 2.* 175 .. .. £6,000

> *One of the most celebrated and admired coins of Antiquity, Euainetos' dekadrachm was extensively imitated by the engravers of many other mints in the Greek world.*

954 — Æ *dekadrachm, by Euainetos* (but unsigned). Similar, but without artist's signature on *rev.;* beneath chin, pellet; behind neck, star of eight rays. *B.M.C. 2.* 184 .. £4,500

955 956

955 — Æ *tetradrachm, by Eukleidas.* Galloping quadriga driven l. by charioteer holding goad, about to be crowned by Nike flying r. above; in ex., dolphin l. ℞. ΣΥΡΑΚΟΣΙΩΝ. Hd. of Artemis-Arethusa l., wearing sphendone, hair floating loosely above; four dolphins around; beneath truncation, scroll inscribed with artist's signature ΕΥΚΛΕΙ. *Tudeer* 88. *B.M.C. 2.* 194 .. .. £2,000

956 357-353 B.C. (time of Dion). Electrum 100 *litrai* (*c.* 7·2 gm.). ΣΥΡΑΚΟΣΙΩΝ. Laur. hd. of Apollo l., strung bow behind. ℞. Diad. hd. of Artemis r., quiver at shoulder; before, ΣΩΤΕΙΡΑ; behind, strung bow. *B.M.C. 2.* 252 .. .. £2,250

957   958   959

Syracuse *continued*

957 — Electrum 50 *litrai* (*c.* 3·6 gm.). Laur. hd. of Apollo l. ℞. ΣΥΡΑΚΟΣΙΩΝ. Tripod-lebes. *B.M.C. 2.* 254 .. .. £400

958 — Electrum 25 *litrai* (*c.* 1·8 gm.). Laur. hd. of Apollo l. ℞. ΣΥΡΑΚΟΣΙΩΝ. Lyre with five strings. *B.M.C. 2.* 266 .. .. £350

959 — Electrum 10 *litrai* (*c.* 0·72 gm.). Hd. of Artemis-Arethusa r., hair in sphendone. ℞. Cuttle-fish. *B.M.C. 2.* 270 .. .. £250

N.B. *On the basis of recent hoard evidence it seems likely that these electrum issues belong to a later period, during the reign of Agathokles (late 4th-early 3rd Cent. B.C.).*

         960   961

960 344-317 B.C. (time of Timoleon). *N hemidrachm* (=3 silver Corinthian staters = 30 litrai; *c.* 2·15 gm.). ΙΕΥΣ ΕΛΕΥΘΕΡΙΟΣ. Laur. hd. of Zeus Eleutherios l. ℞. ΣΥΡΑΚΟΣΙΩΝ. Pegasos flying l., ΑΡ monogram before, three pellets beneath. *B.M.C. 2.* 265.. £1,500

961 — *R stater* of the Corinthian type (=10 litrai). Pegasos flying l. ℞. ΣΥΡΑΚΟΣΙΩΝ. Hd. of Athena r., wearing Corinthian helmet; pellet in field to l. *B.M.C. 12.* (*Colonies of Corinth*), *p.* 98, *no.* 5 .. .. £250

962 — *R* 3 *litrai.* Pegasos flying l. ℞. ΣΥΡΑΚΟΣΙΩΝ. Laur. hd. of Artemis-Arethusa l., three dolphins around. *B.M.C. 2.* 272 .. .. £300

       963   964   967

963 — *R* 2½ *litrai.* ΣΥΡΑΚΟΣΙΩΝ. Hd. of Athena three-quarter face to l., wearing triple-crested helmet, three dolphins around. ℞. Naked rider on horse pacing r., star behind. *B.M.C. 2.* 280 .. .. £250

964 — *R* 2 *litrai.* ΣΥΡΑΚΟΣΙΩΝ. Janiform female hd., laur.; two dolphins in field to r. ℞. Free horse prancing r., ear of corn above, Ν beneath. *B.M.C. 2.* 283 .. £200

965 — *R* 1½ *litra.* ΣΥΡΑΚΟΣΙΩΝ. Hd. of Artemis-Arethusa l., hair rolled, three dolphins around. ℞. Forepart of Pegasos l., star above. *B.M.C. 2.* 276 .. .. £100

966 — *R litra.* Female hd. (Kyane?) l., hair rolled; behind, ΕΥ and lion's hd. l. ℞. ΣΥΡΑΚΟΣΙΩΝ. Cuttle-fish. *B.M.C. 2.* 279 .. .. £120

967 Reign of Agathokles, 317-289 B.C. (with title of ΒΑΣΙΛΕΟΣ = 'King' from 304 B.C.). *N drachm* (*c.* 4·3 gm.). Laur. hd. of young Apollo or Ares l., corn-ear behind. ℞. ΣΥΡΑΚΟΣΙΩΝ. Galloping biga driven r. by charioteer holding goad; beneath horses, triskeles. *B.M.C. 2.* 338 .. .. £1,000

968 — *N tetrobol* (*c.* 2·9 gm.). Similar, but also with Τ in ex. on *rev.* *B.M.C. 2.* 342

                                                             £600

969   970

969 — *N diobol* (*c.* 1·45 gm.). Hd. of Persephone l., wreathed with corn. ℞. ΣΥΡΑΚΟΣΙΩΝ. Bull walking l., hd. lowered. *B.M.C. 2.* 344   ..   ..   £500

970 — *N stater* (*c.* 5·7 gm.). Hd. of Athena r., wearing crested Corinthian helmet, ornamented with griffin. ℞. ΑΓΑΘΟΚΛΕΟΣ / ΒΑΣΙΛΕΟΣ above and beneath winged thunderbolt; ΤΡ monogram below. *B.M.C. 2.* 416   ..   ..   £1,500

971   972

971 — *Æ tetradrachm.* Hd. of Persephone l., wearing wreath of corn; three dolphins around; beneath truncation, ΝΙΚ monogram. ℞. Galloping quadriga driven l. by charioteer holding goad; above, triskeles; in ex., ΣΥΡΑΚΟΣΙΩΝ / *N. B.M.C. 2.* 346   ..   £850

972 — — Hd. of Persephone r., wearing wreath of corn, ΣΥΡΑΚΟΣΙΩΝ before. ℞. Nike, naked to the waist, stg. r., erecting trophy, a hammer held in her r. hand; behind, ΑΓΑΘΟΚΛΕΙΟΣ; in field to r., triskeles. *B.M.C. 2.* 378   ..   ..   £900

973 — — Similar, but on *obv.* the legend is ΚΟΡΑΣ and reads upwards behind the hd. of Persephone: on *rev.* the king's name (spelt ΑΓΑΘΟΚΛΕΟΣ) is in ex., and the monogram *N* appears in field to l. *B.M.C. 2.* 388   ..   ..   £950

974   975

974 — — Similar, but of rougher style: on *obv.* ΚΟΡΑΣ reads downwards; on *rev.* the triskeles is in field to l. in place of the monogram. *B.M.C. 2.* 387   ..   ..   ..   £450

These pieces of inferior style may have been struck in North Africa at the time of Agathokles' attack on Carthage.

975 — *Æ stater of the Corinthian type.* Hd. of Athena r., wearing crested Corinthian helmet, ornamented with griffin; behind, trophy. ℞. ΣΥΡΑΚΟΣΙΩΝ. Pegasos flying l., triskeles above, ear of corn beneath. *B.M.C. 12.* (*Colonies of Corinth*), *p.* 99, *no.* 11   ..   £200

This issue breaks with the traditions of the Corinthian type coinage as the Pegasos is here relegated to the reverse side of the coin.

976 — — (but weight now reduced to *c.* 6·9 gm. = 8 litrai). Hd. of Athena l., wearing Corinthian helmet. ℞. Pegasos flying l., triskeles beneath. *B.M.C. 12.* (*Colonies of Corinth*), *p.* 99, *no.* 14   ..   ..   £175

977 — *Æ drachm.* ΣΥΡΑΚΟΣΙΩΝ. Young male hd., laur., l.; behind, trophy. ℞. Triskeles; at centre, circle containing Gorgoneion. *B.M.C. 2.* 353   ..   ..   ..   £2,500

978 979

Syracuse *continued*

978 Reign of Hiketas, 288-279 B.C. *N drachm* (*c.* 4·3 gm.). ΣΥΡΑΚΟΣΙΩΝ. Hd. of Persephone l., hair rolled and wreathed with corn; behind, cornucopiae. Ŗ. Galloping biga driven r. by Nike; star above, ear of corn beneath; in ex., ΕΠΙ ΙΚΕΤΑ. *B.M.C. 2.* 434 £900

979 — Æ 15 *litrai*. Hd. of Persephone l., wreathed with corn; behind, amphora. Ŗ. ΣΥΡΑΚΟΣΙΩΝ (in ex.). Galloping quadriga driven l. by Nike; above, star. *B.M.C. 2.* 438. *Lloyd Sylloge* 1524 .. .. £2,000

980 Rule of Pyrrhos, 278-276 B.C. *N stater.* Hd. of Athena r., in crested Athenian helmet ornamented with griffin; behind, owl; beneath truncation, Α. Ŗ. ΠΥΡΡΟΥ ΒΑΣΙΛΕΩΣ. Nike stepping l., holding wreath and trophy; bucranium in field to l. *B.M.C. 7.* (*Epirus*), *p.* 111, *no.* 1 .. .. £7,000

981 982

981 — *N half-stater.* Hd. of Artemis r., quiver behind neck; to l., bee. Ŗ. ΠΥΡΡΟΥ ΒΑΣΙΛΕΩΣ· Nike, as last, but with crescent and head of torch above, and thunderbolt to l. *B.M.C. 7.* (*Epirus*), *p.* 111, *no.* 5 .. .. £3,500

982 — Æ *octobol.* Hd. of Persephone r., wreathed with corn; to l., star. Ŗ. ΠΥΡΡΟΥ ΒΑΣΙΛΕΩΣ. Athena Alkidemos advancing l., brandishing spear and holding shield; thunderbolt in field to l. *B.M.C. 7.* (*Epirus*), *p.* 112, *no.* 9 .. .. .. £400

983 985

983 Reign of Hieron II, 275-215 B.C. *N drachm* (=60 silver litrai; *c.* 4·3 gm.). Hd. of Persephone l., wreathed with corn; behind, poppy-head. Ŗ. Galloping biga driven r. by female charioteer holding goad; ΙΕΡΩΝΟΣ below. *B.M.C. 2.* 510 .. .. £900

984 — Æ *octobol* (*c.* 5·7 gm.). Hd. of Athena l., wearing crested Corinthian helmet ornamented with serpent; behind, wing. Ŗ. Pegasos flying l., Π and ΙΕΡΩΝΟΣ beneath. *B.M.C. 2.* 523 .. .. £300

985 — Æ 32 *litrai* (*c.* 28 gm.). Diad. hd. of Hieron l., beardless; behind, ear of corn. Ŗ. Galloping quadriga driven r. by Nike; above, ΒΑΣΙΛΕΟΣ; beneath, Ε; in ex., ΙΕΡΩΝΟΣ. *B.M.C. 2.* 525, *var.*.. .. .. £3,500

986 988

986 — Æ 8 *litrai* (*c.* 7 gm.). Diad. hd. of Gelon, son of Hieron, l., beardless. Ɍ. Galloping biga driven r. by Nike; above, ΣΥΡΑΚΟΣΙΟΙ; before, ΒΑ / Κ; beneath, ΓΕΛΩΝΟΣ. *B.M.C.* 2. 527 .. .. £250

987 — Æ 4 *litrai* (*c.* 3·5 gm.). *Obv.* Similar. Ɍ. ΣΥΡΑΚΟΣΙΟΙ ΓΕΛΩΝΟΣ. Eagle, wings closed, stg. r. on thunderbolt, behind, Ε; before, ΒΑ. *B.M.C.* 2. 534 .. .. £200

988 — Æ 16 *litrai* (*c.* 14 gm.). Diad. and veiled hd. l. of Philistis, wife of Hieron; behind, palm. Ɍ. Galloping quadriga driven r. by Nike; above, ΒΑΣΙΛΙΣΣΑΣ; beneath horses, Ε; in ex., ΦΙΛΙΣΤΙΔΟΣ. *B.M.C.* 2. 545 .. .. £375

989 — — *Obv.* Similar, but with thyrsos behind. Ɍ. Same as last, but the horses are walking, and without the Ε; in field to r., Α. *B.M.C.* 2. 553 .. .. £400

990 — Æ 5 *litrai* (*c.* 4·4 gm.). *Obv.* Same as 988. Ɍ. Galloping biga driven r. by Nike; above, ΒΑΣΙΛΙΣΣΑΣ; before, Ε; in ex., ΦΙΛΙΣΤΙΔΟΣ. *B.M.C.* 2. 559 .. .. £225

991 Reign of Hieronymos, 215-214 B.C. Ɲ *drachm* (=60 silver litrai; *c.* 4·3 gm.). Hd. of Persephone l., wreathed with corn. Ɍ. Winged thunderbolt; above, ΒΑΣΙΛΕΟΣ and ΚΙ; beneath, ΙΕΡΩΝΥΜΟΥ. *Historia Numorum, p.* 186 .. .. £2,500

992 — Ɲ *hemidrachm* (=30 silver litrai; *c.* 2·18 gm.). Same as last. *B.M.C.* 2. 636 £1,500

993 — Æ 24 *litrai* (*c.* 21 gm.). Diad. hd. of Hieronymos l., beardless; behind, cornucopiae. Ɍ. Same as last, but with ΜΙ instead of ΚΙ above thunderbolt. *B.M.C.* 2. 638.. £600

994 997

994 — Æ 10 *litrai* (*c.* 8·75 gm.). Similar, but without cornucopiae on *obv.*, and with ΑΦ instead of ΜΙ on *rev.* *B.M.C.* 2. 639 .. .. £250

995 — Æ 5 *litrai* (*c.* 4·4 gm.). *Obv.* Same as last. Ɍ. Same as 991. *B.M.C.* 2. 644 £225

996 Republic, 214-212 B.C. Æ 16 *litrai* (*c.* 14 gm.). Laur. hd. of Zeus l. Ɍ. Galloping quadriga driven r. by Nike; above, ΣΥΡΑΚΟΣΙΩΝ; beneath horses, ΣΛ; in ex., ΥΑ. *B.M.C.* 2. 650 .. .. £1,250

997 — Æ 12 *litrai* (*c.* 10·5 gm.). Hd. of Athena l., wearing crested Corinthian helmet ornamented with serpent. Ɍ. Artemis stg. l., discharging arrow from bow, hound running l. at her feet; behind, ΣΥΡΑΚΟΣΙΩΝ; in field to l., ΧΑΡ. *B.M.C.* 2. 653 .. .. £325

Syracuse *continued*

998 — ℛ 10 *litrai* (*c*. 8·75 gm.). Hd. of Persephone l., hair long and wreathed with corn; behind, flaming torch. ℞. Zeus stg. facing, looking r., r. hand resting on spear; to r., ΣΥΡΑΚΟΣΙΩΝ; to l., ΧΑΡ above eagle. *B.M.C.* 2. 661 .. .. £750

999 — ℛ 8 *litrai* (*c*. 7 gm.). *Obv.* Similar, but hair rolled and curly, and with owl behind. ℞. Galloping quadriga driven r. by Nike; above, ΑΡΚ monogram; beneath horses, ΑΙ; the quadriga resting on base inscribed ΛΥ; in ex., ΣΥΡΑΚΟΣΙΩΝ. *B.M.C.* 2. 658 £550

1000 — — *Obv.* Hd. of Athena, similar to 997, but helmet is ornamented with griffin and Α. ℞. Winged thunderbolt; above, ΣΥΡΑΚΟΣΙΩΝ; beneath, ΥΑΣ. *B.M.C.* 2. 656 .. £225

1001　　　　　　　　　　　1002

1001 — ℛ 6 *litrai* (*c*. 5·2 gm.). Hd. of bearded Herakles l., wearing lion's skin. ℞. Galloping biga driven r. by Nike; beneath, ΞΑ; in ex., ΣΥΡΑΚΟΣΙΩΝ. *B.M.C.* 2. 659 .. £500

1002 — ℛ 4 *litrai* (*c*. 3·5 gm.). Laur. hd. of Apollo l. ℞. ΣΥΡΑΚΟΣΙΩΝ. Nike advancing l., holding palm and trophy; in field to r., ΧΑΡ. *B.M.C.* 2. 660 .. .. .. £475

1003 — ℛ 2½ *litrai* (*c*. 2·2 gm.). *Obv.* Similar. ℞. ΣΥΡΑΚΟΣΙΟΙ. Female figure (Tyche ?) stg. l., looking upwards, her veil billowing out behind, holding scroll and branch; in field to l., Φ. *B.M.C.* 2. 664 .. .. £175

1004 — ℛ 1¼ *litra* (*c*. 1·1 gm.). Hd. of Artemis r., quiver at shoulder. ℞. ΣΥΡΑΚΟΣΙΟΙ. Owl stg. r., hd. facing; in field to l., Φ. *B.M.C.* 2. 667 .. .. £125

1005 — ℛ *litra* (*c*. 0·87 gm.). Hd. of Athena l., wearing crested Corinthian helmet. ℞. ΣΥΡΑΚΟΣΙΟΙ. Roman numeral XIII preceded by three pellets; beneath, Κ. *B.M.C.* 2. 669 .. .. £110

1006　　　　　　1008　　　　　　1010

1006 **Tauromenion** (a Sicel stronghold founded in 396 B.C., Tauromenion was occupied by the exiled inhabitants of Naxos in 358 B.C.). *Circa* 300 B.C. *N tritemorion* (*c*. 0·55 gm.). Hd. of Athena right, wearing crested Corinthian helmet. ℞. Owl stg. r., hd. facing; ΠΑ monogram in field. *B.M.C.* 2., *p*. 122, *no*. 6 .. .. £300

1007 — *N hemiobol* (*c*. 0·36 gm.). Laur. hd. of Apollo r. ℞. Lyre bound with fillet; ΠΑ monogram in field. *B.M.C.* 2., *p*. 122, *no*. 7 .. .. £200

1008 275-210 B.C. *N trihemiobol* (=15 silver litrai; *c*. 1·1 gm.). Laur. hd. of Apollo l.; behind, club. ℞. ΤΑΥΡΟΜΕ — ΝΙΤΑΝ either side of tripod-lebes; in field to r., ΕΥ. *B.M.C.* 2. 5 .. .. £400

1009 — ℛ *octobol* (*c*. 5·8 gm.). Hd. of Athena l., wearing crested Corinthian helmet ornamented with griffin; behind, Η. ℞. ΤΑΥΡΟΜΕΝΙΤΑΝ. Pegasos flying l., star beneath. *B.M.C.* 2. 9 .. .. £550

1010 — ℛ 4 *litrai* (*c*. 3·5 gm.). Laur. hd. of Apollo r., star behind. ℞. ΤΑΥΡΟΜΕ — ΝΙΤΑΝ either side of tripod-lebes. *B.M.C.* 2. 10 .. .. £225

1011 — ℛ *litra*. Bull's hd. facing. ℞. ΤΑΥΡΟΜ. Bunch of grapes. *B.M.C.* 2. 7 £125

Classical and Hellenistic Periods: Base Metal Issues

1012   1014

1012 **Abakainon.** 400-350 B.C. Æ 18. Female hd. r., hair in sphendone. ℞. ABAKAININΩN. Forepart of bull butting l. *B.M.C. 2.* 11..   ..   ..   £25

1013 After 241 B.C. Æ 22. Laur. hd. of Apollo r. ℞. — Bull walking r. *B.M.C. 2.* 13

                                                               £10

1014 **Akrai** (a dependency of Syracuse until 212 B.C.). After 210 B.C. Æ 20. Hd. of Persephone r., wreathed with corn. ℞. AKPAIΩN. Demeter stg. l., holding torch and sceptre. *B.M.C. 2.* 1, 2   ..   ..   £15

1015 **Adranon** (founded by Dionysios of Syracuse about 400 B.C.). 344-336 B.C. Æ *litra.* Laur. hd. of Apollo l., AΠOΛ beneath. ℞. No legend. Lyre, with seven strings. *B.M.C. 2., p. 3, no.* 1..   ..   ..   £120

          These are frequently overstruck on bronze litrai of Syracuse.

1016 — Æ 22 (*hemilitron*?). Hd. of young river-god Adranos l., with short horns, wearing tainia. ℞. AΔPANITAN (partly retrograde). Bull butting r. *B.M.C. 2.* 3   £40

1017 **Aitna** (the Syracusan colonists expelled from Katane in 461 B.C. founded a new settlement about ten miles to the north-west, and to this place they transferred the name of Aitna which they had previously bestowed upon Katane). Before 339 B.C. Æ 23. AITNAIΩN. Hd. of Athena r., wearing Corinthian helmet. ℞. Horse cantering r., M above. *Weber Catalogue* 1175   ..   ..   £60

1018 After 210 B.C. Æ *trias.* Rad. bust of Apollo r., wearing chlamys. ℞. AITNAIΩN. Warrior stg. facing, hd. l., holding spear and shield; three pellets in field to l. *B.M.C. 2.* 1 ..   ..   £20

1019 — Æ *hexas.* Hd. of Persephone r., wreathed with corn. ℞. — Cornucopiae; two pellets in field to l. *B.M.C. 2.* 7 ..   ..   £15

1020   1021   1022

1020 **Akragas** (=Agrigentum). Early 5th Cent. B.C. Æ *trias* (tooth-shaped, with flat base, and possibly a weight rather than an actual coin). On one side, two eagles' heads back to back, A beneath the one on l.; on the other, crab; on the base, three pellets. *B.M.C. 2., p.* 24, *nos.* 3, 4 ..   ..   £100

1021 — Æ *onkia* (almond-shaped, and possibly a weight, as last). On one side, eagle's hd. l.; on the other, crab's claw. *B.M.C. 2., p.* 24, *no.* 6   ..   ..   ..   £75

1022 425-406 B.C. Æ *hemilitron.* ΑΚΡΑΓΑΝΤΙΝΟΝ. Eagle r., its hd. thrown back, wings spread, holding tunny-fish in its talons. R. Crab, holding eel in l. claw; beneath, conch-shell and cuttlefish; six pellets around. *B.M.C. 2.* 86 ..   ..   ..   £45

1023 — Æ *trias.* ΑΚΡΑ. Eagle r., wings spread, holding in its talons hare, which it attacks with its beak. R. Crab; beneath, three pellets and crayfish l. *B.M.C. 2.* 102   £30

1024 — Æ *hexas. Obv.* Similar, but eagle holds bird instead of hare. R. Crab; beneath, two tunny-fishes l.; two pellets in field, to l. and to r. *B.M.C. 2.* 107 ..   ..   £20

1025   1026

1025 — Æ *onkia.* ΑΚΡΑ. Eagle stg. r. on tunny-fish, looking back, wings closed. R. Crab; beneath, perch r.; above, pellet. *B.M.C. 2.* 112..   ..   ..   ..   £14

1026 405-392 B.C. Æ *hemilitron* (restruck on coins of the previous issue). Hd. of young Herakles r., wearing lion's skin; all within incuse circle. R. Plain. *B.M.C. 2.* 117
                                                     £45

These countermarked issues were produced in the troubled period following the destruction of Akragas by the Carthaginians.

1027 338-287 B.C. Æ *hemilitron.* ΑΚΡΑΓΑΣ. Horned hd. of young river-god l., wearing diadem. R. Eagle, wings closed, stg. l. on Ionic capital, looking back; to l., crab; above, six pellets. *B.M.C. 2.* 125   ..   ..   £65

1028 — Æ 20. ΑΚΡΑΓΑΣ. Laur. hd. of Zeus l. ℞. Eagle l., wings spread, holding in its talons hare, which it attacks with its beak; behind, Δ. *B.M.C. 2.* 128 .. .. £30

1029 — Æ 15. Laur. hd. of Zeus r. ℞. ΑΚΡΑΓΑΝ / ΤΙΝΩΝ above and below winged thunderbolt. *B.M.C. 2.* 130 .. .. £12

1030 Reign of Phintias, 287-279 B.C. Æ 20. ΑΚΡΑΓΑΝΤΟΣ. Laur. hd. of Apollo l. ℞. ΦΙ. Two eagles stg. l. on hare, the farther one attacking the prey, the nearer throwing back its hd. *B.M.C. 2.* 131 .. .. £15

1031 — Æ 14. ΑΚΡΑΓΑΝΤΙ. Similar. ℞. ΦΙ. Eagle, wings closed, stg. r., looking back. *B.M.C. 2.* 133 .. .. £10

1032   1036

1032 — Æ 20. Hd. of Persephone l., wreathed with corn, N͞E behind. ℞. ΒΑΣΙΛΕΟΣ ΦΙΝΤΙΑ. Boar l., at bay. *B.M.C. 2.* 135 .. .. £16

1033 — — ΣΩΤΕΙΡΑ. Hd. of Artemis l., hair in knot behind, quiver at shoulder. ℞. Same as last. *B.M.C. 2.* 139 .. .. £20

1034 279-241 B.C. Æ 24. Laur. hd. of Apollo r. ℞. ΑΚΡΑΓΑΝΤΙΝΩΝ. Naked warrior advancing r., thrusting with spear held in r. hand. *B.M.C. 2.* 150 .. .. £20

1035 — Æ 22. *Obv.* Similar. ℞. — Tripod-lebes. *B.M.C. 2.* 148 .. .. £18

1036 — — ΑΚΡΑΓΑΝΤΙΝΩΝ. Diad. hd. of Zeus Soter r., bunch of grapes behind. ℞. ΔΙΟΣ ΣΩΤΗΡΟΣ. Eagle stg. r. on thunderbolt, looking back, wings closed. *B.M.C. 2.* 146 £22

1037 241-210 B.C. Æ 24. Laur. hd. of Zeus r. ℞. ΑΚΡΑΓΑΝΤΙΝΩΝ. Eagle stg. facing on thunderbolt, wings spread, looking r. *B.M.C. 2.* 155 .. .. £18

1038 — Æ 22. Hd. of Persephone r., wreathed with corn; ΑΣΚΛΑΠΙΟΣ before, ΑΚΡ monogram behind. ℞. — Asklepios stg. facing, r. hand extended. *B.M.C. 2.* 154 .. £16

1039 — Æ 19. Laur. hd. of Asklepios r. ℞. — Serpent twined round staff. *B.M.C.* *2.* 157 .. .. £14

1037   1041

1040 **Agyrion** (situated in the interior of the island, Agyrion had particular associations with Herakles, who is said to have visited the place during his wanderings in Sicily). 420-353 B.C. (time of the tyrant Agyris). Æ 23. Eagle stg. r., wings closed; behind, olive-spray. ℞. ΑΓ — ΥΡ — ΙΝ — ΑΙ between the four spokes of a wheel. *B.M.C. 2.* 2 £45

1041 — Æ 18. ΑΓΥΡΙΝΑΙΟΝ. Young male hd. r., with short hair. ℞. ΠΑΛΑΓΚΑΙΟΣ. Forepart of man-headed bull swimming r. *B.M.C. 2.* 3 .. .. £35

Agyrion *continued*

1042 345-399 B.C. (tyranny of Apolloniades). Æ 30. ΑΓΥΡΙΝΑΙΟΝ. Hd. of young Herakles r., in lion's skin. ℞. Forepart of man-headed bull stg. r. *B.M.C. 2.* 4 .. £100

1043 — Æ 28. Hd. of young Herakles r., wearing tainia, lion's skin tied round his throat. ℞. Leopard stg. r., devouring hare, ΑΓΥΡΙΝΑΙΩΝ in ex. *B.M.C. 2.* 6 .. .. £75

1044 339-300 B.C. Æ 26. ΖΕΥΣ ΕΛΕΥΘΕΡΙΟΣ. Laur. hd. of Zeus Eleutherios r. ℞. ΑΓΥΡΙΝΑΙΩΝ. Thunderbolt; eagle r. in field to r. *B.M.C. 2.* 9 .. .. £65

1045 After 241 B.C. Æ 23. ΕΠΙ ΣΩΠΑΤΡΟΥ. Laur. hd. of Zeus r., monogram before. ℞. ΑΓΥΡΙΝΑΙΩΝ. Iolaös stg. l., holding horn and pedum, crowned by Nike flying l. behind him; hound at his feet. *B.M.C. 2.* 11 .. .. £24

1046 **Alaisa** (founded in 403 B.C. by the Sicel chief Archonides). *Circa* 340 B.C. Æ *litra.* ΑΡΧΑΓΕΤΑΣ. Laur. hd. of Apollo l. ℞. ΣΥΜΜΑΧΙΚΟΝ. Lighted pine-torch between two stalks of barley. *B.M.C. 2., p.* 28, *nos.* 1, 2 .. .. £150

1047 — Æ *hemilitron.* ΣΙΚΕΛΙΑ. Hd. of nymph Sikelia l., wearing sphendone ornamented with star. ℞. Same as last. *B.M.C. 2., p.* 29, *no.* 3 .. .. £90

1048   1049

1048 — Æ 22. Griffin springing l. ℞. Horse prancing l., ΚΑΙΝΟΝ in ex. *B.M.C. 2., p.* 29, *no.* 6 .. .. £14

1049 After 241 B.C. Æ 21. Laur. hd. of Zeus l. ℞. ΑΛΑΙΣΑΣ ΑΡΧ. Eagle standing l., wings spread; bucranium in field to l. *B.M.C. 2.* 2 .. .. £15

1050 — — Laur. hd. of Apollo l., bow behind. ℞. ΑΛΑΙΣΑΣ. Apollo stg. l., holding wreath and lyre; ΑΡΧ monogram in field to l. *B.M.C. 2.* 5 .. .. £15

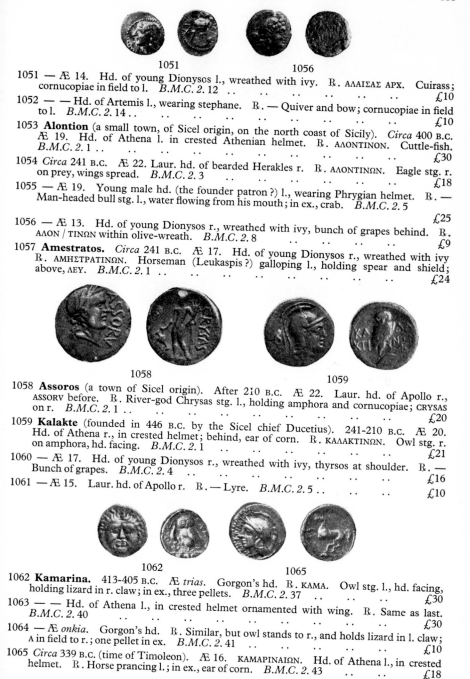

1051   1056

1051 — Æ 14. Hd. of young Dionysos l., wreathed with ivy. ℞. ΑΛΑΙΣΑΣ ΑΡΧ. Cuirass; cornucopiae in field to l. *B.M.C. 2. 12* £10

1052 — — Hd. of Artemis l., wearing stephane. ℞. — Quiver and bow; cornucopiae in field to l. *B.M.C. 2. 14* £10

1053 **Alontion** (a small town, of Sicel origin, on the north coast of Sicily). *Circa* 400 B.C. Æ 19. Hd. of Athena l. in crested Athenian helmet. ℞. ΑΛΟΝΤΙΝΟΝ. Cuttle-fish. *B.M.C. 2. 1* £30

1054 *Circa* 241 B.C. Æ 22. Laur. hd. of bearded Herakles r. ℞. ΑΛΟΝΤΙΝΩΝ. Eagle stg. r. on prey, wings spread. *B.M.C. 2. 3* £18

1055 — Æ 19. Young male hd. (the founder patron ?) l., wearing Phrygian helmet. ℞. — Man-headed bull stg. l., water flowing from his mouth; in ex., crab. *B.M.C. 2. 5*
  £25

1056 — Æ 13. Hd. of young Dionysos r., wreathed with ivy, bunch of grapes behind. ℞. ΑΛΟΝ / ΤΙΝΩΝ within olive-wreath. *B.M.C. 2. 8* £9

1057 **Amestratos.** *Circa* 241 B.C. Æ 17. Hd. of young Dionysos r., wreathed with ivy ℞. ΑΜΗΣΤΡΑΤΙΝΩΝ. Horseman (Leukaspis ?) galloping l., holding spear and shield; above, ΛΕΥ. *B.M.C. 2. 1* £24

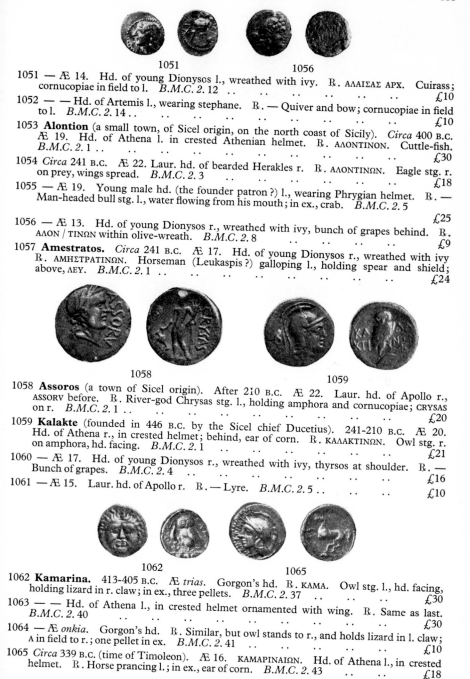

1058   1059

1058 **Assoros** (a town of Sicel origin). After 210 B.C. Æ 22. Laur. hd. of Apollo r., ASSORV before. ℞. River-god Chrysas stg. l., holding amphora and cornucopiae; CRYSAS on r. *B.M.C. 2. 1* £20

1059 **Kalakte** (founded in 446 B.C. by the Sicel chief Ducetius). 241-210 B.C. Æ 20. Hd. of Athena r., in crested helmet; behind, ear of corn. ℞. ΚΑΛΑΚΤΙΝΩΝ. Owl stg. r. on amphora, hd. facing. *B.M.C. 2. 1* £21

1060 — Æ 17. Hd. of young Dionysos r., wreathed with ivy, thyrsos at shoulder. ℞. — Bunch of grapes. *B.M.C. 2. 4* £16

1061 — Æ 15. Laur. hd. of Apollo r. ℞. — Lyre. *B.M.C. 2. 5* £10

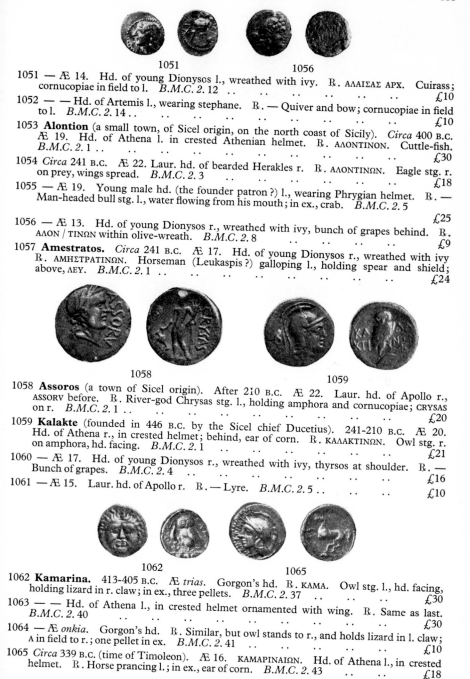

1062   1065

1062 **Kamarina.** 413-405 B.C. Æ *trias.* Gorgon's hd. ℞. ΚΑΜΑ. Owl stg. l., hd. facing, holding lizard in r. claw; in ex., three pellets. *B.M.C. 2. 37* £30

1063 — — Hd. of Athena l., in crested helmet ornamented with wing. ℞. Same as last. *B.M.C. 2. 40* £30

1064 — Æ *onkia.* Gorgon's hd. ℞. Similar, but owl stands to r., and holds lizard in l. claw; Α in field to r.; one pellet in ex. *B.M.C. 2. 41* £10

1065 *Circa* 339 B.C. (time of Timoleon). Æ 16. ΚΑΜΑΡΙΝΑΙΩΝ. Hd. of Athena l., in crested helmet. ℞. Horse prancing l.; in ex., ear of corn. *B.M.C. 2. 43* £18

1066   1067

1066 **The Campani** (Campanian mercenaries). 344-339 B.C. Æ *litra*. Bull butting l.;
above, monogram (of KAM ?). ℞. Star of sixteen rays. *B.M.C. 2.*, *p. 237, no. 2*   £50
   *These are overstruck on bronze litrai of Syracuse, obv. hd. of Athena, rev. star-fish and
dolphins.*

1067 **Katane.** 413-404 B.C. Æ *trias.* AMENANOΣ. Horned hd. of young river-god
Amenanos l. ℞. Winged thunderbolt dividing small K — A. *Gabrici (La monetazione
del bronzo nella Sicilia antica), pl. 2, 7* £35

1068   1070

1068 *Circa* 360 B.C. Æ 24. Hd. of Persephone l., wreathed with corn; three dolphins around.
   ℞. Man-headed bull stg. r. *Holm (Geschichte des sicilischen Münzwesens) 198*   £40
   The obv. is inspired by the Euainetos dekadrachms of Syracuse.

1069 After 212 B.C. Æ 21. River-god reclining l., holding cornucopiae and resting l. elbow
on amphora; branch over shoulder. ℞. KATANAIΩN. Caps of the Dioskouroi; between,
ΣΩ monogram and owl r. *B.M.C. 2.* 56 ..   ..   £15

1070 — Æ 13. Jugate hds. of Zeus Sarapis and Isis r. ℞. — Two ears of corn, with leaves.
   B.M.C. 2. 60   ..   ..   £9

1071   1072

1071 — Æ *litra.* Diad. hd. of Poseidon r., trident at shoulder. ℞. — Dolphin r., XII above.
   B.M.C. 2. 61   ..   ..   £12

1072 — Æ *dekonkion.* Jugate busts of Zeus Sarapis and Isis r.; ear of corn behind, X before.
   ℞. — Apollo stg. facing, holding laurel-branch and bow, and resting l. elbow on column;
quiver and omphalos at feet. *B.M.C. 2.* 62   ..   ..   £14

1073 — Æ *pentonkion.* Laur. hd. of Apollo r. ℞. — Isis stg. l., holding bird, dog at her feet;
Π in field to l. *B.M.C. 2.* 64   ..   ..   £14

1074 — Æ *hexas.* Laur. hd. of Apollo l., omphalos behind. ℞. — Isis stg. r., holding
patera (?) and bird; Π in field to r. *B.M.C. 2.* 65   ..   ..   £12

1075 — Æ 27. Laur. and rad. hd. of Zeus Sarapis r., with head-dress of globe, horns and
plumes. ℞. — Isis stg. facing, holding sceptre; monograms and figure of Harpokrates in
field to l., sistrum to r. *B.M.C. 2.* 88   ..   ..   £22

1076   1077

1076 — Æ 24. Janiform hd. of Sarapis, monograms in field. ℞. — Demeter stg. l., holding
corn-ears and torch. *B.M.C. 2.* 91 .. .. £21

1077 — Æ 20. ΚΑΤΑΝΑΙΩΝ. Hd. of Hermes r., wearing winged petasos. ℞. Nike advancing
l., holding wreath and palm; monograms in field. *B.M.C. 2.* 82 .. .. £14

1078 — — ΛΑΣΙΟ. Hd. of young Dionysos r., wreathed with ivy; monogram behind. ℞.
ΚΑΤΑΝΑΙΩΝ. The Katanean brothers, Amphinomos and Anapias, advancing l. and r.,
bearing their parents on their shoulders. *B.M.C. 2.* 70.. .. .. £16

*Lasios was probably a local name for the god Dionysos. The Katanean brothers received
divine honours after a miraculous escape whilst rescuing their parents during a violent eruption
of Mt. Aitna.*

1079   1080

1079 —-Æ 13. One of the Katanean brothers advancing l., carrying his father. ℞. — The
other brother advancing l., holding his mother in both arms. *B.M.C. 2.* 76.. £10

1080 **Kentoripai** (a Sicel city at the centre of a prosperous agricultural district). *Circa*
340 B.C. Æ *litra.* Hd. of Persephone l., wreathed with corn; four dolphins around.
℞. Panther stg. l., its back arched; in ex., ΚΕΝΤΟΡΙΠΙΝΩΝ. *B.M.C. 2.* 1 .. £125

These are normally restruck on the contemporary bronze litrai of Syracuse.

1081   1083

1081 After 241 B.C. Æ *dekonkion.* Laur. hd. of Zeus r., eagle behind. ℞. ΚΕΝΤΟΡΙΠΙΝΩΝ.
Winged thunderbolt; Λ beneath. *B.M.C. 2.* 3 .. .. £30

1082 — Æ *hemilitron.* Laur. hd. of Apollo r. ℞. — Lyre; six pellets in field, on either side.
B.M.C. 2. 7 .. .. £18

1083 — Æ *trias.* Diad. bust of Artemis r., bow and quiver at shoulder. ℞. — Tripod-
lebes; three pellets in field to l. *B.M.C. 2.* 9 .. .. £15

Kentoripai *continued*

1084 — Æ *hexas*. Bust of Demeter r., wreathed with corn; behind, tripod. ℞. — Plough r.,
bird r. on the share; two pellets in field to l. *B.M.C. 2.* 15   ..   ..   ..   £12

1085 — Æ 13. Laur. hd. of Apollo r. ℞. ΚΕΝΤΟ. Laurel-bough. *B.M.C. 2.* 19   £8

1086

1088

1086 **Kephaloidion** (the city was captured by the Romans in 254 B.C., during the First Punic
War). 254-212 B.C. Æ 20. Laur. hd. of bearded Herakles r. ℞. ΚΕΦΑ. Club between lion's skin (on l.) and bow and arrows in case (on r.). *B.M.C. 2.* 4   ..   £18

1087 — Æ 13. Bust of Hermes r., in winged petasos, caduceus at shoulder. ℞. ΚΕ — ΦΑ
divided by winged caduceus. *B.M.C. 2.* 5   ..   ..   £9

1088 **Enna.** *Circa* 340 B.C. Æ 26. ΔΑΜΑΤ. Hd. of Demeter r., wreathed with corn.
℞. ΕΝΝ. Hd. of sacrificial ox three-quarter face to r.; corn-grain above. *B.M.C. 2.* 2
£75

1089 After 258 B.C. Æ 17. ΕΝΝΑ. Similar to 1087. ℞. Male figure seated r., looking l.,
uncertain object in r. hand, l. grasping tree. *B.M.C. 2.* 8   ..   ..   ..   £18

1090 — Æ 28. L . MVNATIVS M . CESTIVS. Diad. and veiled hd. of Demeter l., wreathed with
corn. ℞. MVN . HENNAE. Hades and Persephone in galloping quadriga r. *B.M.C.*
2. 9 ..   ..   £35

1091 **Entella.** *Circa* 340 B.C. (under the occupation of Campanian mercenaries). Æ 20
ΕΝΤΕΛ. Hd. of Demeter r., wreathed with corn. ℞. ΚΑΜΠΑΝΩΝ. Pegasos flying l.;
helmet beneath. *B.M.C. 2.* 4   ..   ..   £30

1092

1095

1092 **Eryx.** 400-340 B.C. Æ *hexas*. ΙΡVΚΑ (retrograde). Male hd. r., bearded . ℞. Hound
stg. r.; two pellets in field, one above, the other below. *B.M.C. 2.* 17 ..   ..   £40

1093 After 241 B.C. Æ 22. Hd. of Aphrodite r., hair rolled. ℞. ΕΡΥΚΙΝΩΝ. Herakles
stg. l., holding club, lion's skin on l. arm. *B.M.C. 2.* 18   ..   ..   ..   £18

1094 **Gela.** 420-405 B.C. Æ *trias*. ΓΕΛΑΣ. Bull stg. l., hd. lowered; three pellets in ex.
℞. Wheel, with four corn-grains between the spokes. *Jenkins* (*The Coinage of Gela*) 495
£22

1095 — — *Obv.* Similar, but with Π instead of legend above bull. ℞. ΓΕΛΑΣ. Diad. hd. of
young river-god Gelas r., with horns. *Jenkins* 505. *B.M.C. 2.* 71-2 ..   ..   £25

1096 — Æ *onkia*. Bull stg. l., hd. lowered; above, ΓΕΛΑΣ and leaf; in ex., pellet. ℞. Hd. of young river-god Gelas r., hair floating; behind, corn-grain. *Jenkins* 517. *Weber* 1336
£12

1097

1099

1097 339-310 B.C. Æ 17 (*tetras* ?). Hd. of bearded Herakles r., wearing lion's skin; astragalos behind. ℞. ΓΕΛΩΙΩΝ. Bearded hd. of river-god Gelas l., horned, and wreathed with corn. *Jenkins* 544. *B.M.C. 2.* 75   ..   ..   £20

1098 — Æ 13 (*hexas* ?). Similar, but on *obv.* Herakles is beardless, and without astragalos. *Jenkins* 546. *B.M.C. 2.* 76   ..   ..   £10

1099 — Æ 14 (*trias* ?). ΓΕΛΩΙΩΝ. Hd. of Demeter three-quarter face to r., wreathed with corn. ℞. Type similar to 1097. *Jenkins* 549. *B.M.C. 2.* 77-8   ..   ..   £25

1100

1103

1100 — Æ 27 (*litra* ?). Naked warrior stg. r. astride ram which he is about to sacrifice with sword held in r. hand. ℞. Horse prancing r.; star above. *Jenkins* 552. *B.M.C. 2.* 79-80   ..   ..   £90

1101 2nd-1st Cent. B.C. (the city was destroyed by the Mamertini in *c.* 282 B.C., the survivors moving to the newly-founded **Phintias,** where the following were struck in a later age). Æ 22 (=unit). Beardless hd. of river-god r., crowned with reeds. ℞. ΓΕΛΩΙΩΝ. Warrior sacrificing ram, similar to *obv.* of previous; H in field to l. *Jenkins* 554. *B.M.C. 2.* 81-2
£20

1102 — Æ 19 (=half). Hd. of Demeter r., wreathed with corn. ℞. — Wheat ear. *Jenkins* 556. *B.M.C. 2.* 84   ..   ..   £14

1103 — Æ 20 (=unit, reduced). Similar to 1101, but of later style. *Jenkins* 558. *B.M.C. 2.* 83 ..   ..   £18
These are frequently countermarked with a bucranium on obv.

1104 — Æ 17 (=half). Similar to 1102, but with monogram before hd. of Demeter on *obv.* *Jenkins* 559. *B.M.C. 2.* 85   ..   ..   £12

1105

1107

1105 **Himera.** 450-420 B.C. Æ *hemilitron*. Gorgon's hd. facing. ℞. Six pellets. *B.M.C. 2.,* p. 39, 27-30   ..   ..   £35

1106 — Æ *pentonkion*. Similar, but with five pellets on *rev. B.M.C. 2.,* p. 39, 31 ..   £50

1107 — Æ *trias*. Similar, but with three pellets on *rev. B.M.C. 2.,* p. 39, 33   ..   £40

Himera *continued*

1108 420-408 B.C. Æ *hemilitron.* Naked youth, blowing shell and holding caduceus, seated on goat prancing r.; beneath, grasshopper. R. ΚΙΜΑΡΑ. Nike advancing l., wings spread, holding aplustre; six pellets in field to l. *B.M.C. 2.* 50..   ..   ..   £50

1109 — Æ *trias.* Similar, but with *obv.* type to left, and the mark of value (three pellets) is shown beneath the goat instead of grasshopper; legend on *rev.* reads ΙΜΕΡΑ. *B.M.C. 2* 52 ..   ..   £35

1110   1111

1110 — Æ *hemilitron.* ΙΜΕ. Hd. of nymph Himera l., wearing sphendone; six pellets before. R. Six pellets within laurel-wreath. *B.M.C. 2.* 54   ..   ..   £25

1111 **Thermai.** 407-340 B.C. Æ 15. Hd. of Hera r., wearing stephanos ornamented with honeysuckle. R. ΘΕΡΜΙΤΑΝ. Hd. of young Herakles r., in lion's skin. *B.M.C. 2.* 2   £18

1112 After 241 B.C. Æ 25. Turreted and veiled hd. of City r., cornucopiae behind. R. ΘΕΡΜΙΤΑΝ ΙΜΕΡΑΙΩΝ. Statue of the poet Stesichoros r., leaning on staff and reading book. *B.M.C. 2.* 9 ..   ..   £45

1113   1115

1113 — Æ 22. Hd. of bearded Herakles r. in lion's skin, club at shoulder. R. Three nymphs stg. facing, each holding the end of her peplos; in ex., ΘΕΡΜΙΤΑΝ. *B.M.C. 2.* 6   £40

1114 — Æ 20. *Obv.* Similar. R. ΘΕΡΜΙΤΑΝ. City-goddess stg. l., holding phiale and cornucopiae. *B.M.C. 2.* 7   ..   ..   £15

1115 **Hybla** (situated on the southern slopes of Mt. Aitna and one of three Sicilian cities bearing the same name). After 210 B.C. Æ 20. Veiled hd. of Hyblaia r., wearing modius; behind, bee. R. ΥΒΛΑΣ ΜΕΓΑΛΑΣ. Dionysos (?) stg. l., holding kantharos and sceptre, panther leaping up at feet. *B.M.C. 2.* 1 ..   ..   £25

1116   1118

1116 **Iaitia** (a Sicel fortress fifteen miles south-west of Panormos). After 241 B.C. Æ 24. ΙΑΙΤΙΝΩΝ. Hd. of bearded Herakles r., in lion's skin. R. Gorgoneion at centre of triskeles. *B.M.C. 2.* 1   ..   ..   £40

1117 — Æ 19. Hd. of young warrior r., wearing helmet surmounted by mural crown. R. ΙΑΙΤΙΝΩΝ. Warrior stg. l., with similar helmet, holding spear and shield. *B.M.C. 2.* 4 ..   ..   £25

1118 **Leontinoi.** 430-422 B.C. Æ *trias.* ΛΕΟΝ. Laur. hd. of Apollo r.; behind, laurel-leaf with berry. R. Tripod-lebes between two corn-grains; in ex., three pellets. *B.M.C. 2.* 56 ..   ..   £30

1119 After 210 B.C. Æ 23. Laur. hd. of Apollo r., quiver at shoulder. ℞. ΛΕΟΝΤΙΝΩΝ.
Demeter stg. l., holding corn-ears and torch, plough at feet. *B.M.C. 2.* 59 ..   £14

1120   1124

1120 — — Bust of Demeter facing, wreathed with corn-stalks, radiating; plough in field to
l. ℞. — Naked river-god seated r. on rock, holding cornucopiae and branch; crab in
field to l. *B.M.C. 2.* 64 ..   ..   £15

1121 — Æ 17. Jugate hds. of Apollo and Artemis r., plough behind. ℞. — Two ears of
corn bound together. *B.M.C. 2.* 68   ..   ..   £12

1122 — Æ 14. Laur. hd. of Apollo l., plough behind. ℞. — Lion walking l. *B.M.C. 2.* 72
£10

1123 — Æ 11. *Obv.* Similar. ℞. Two fishes l.; beneath, monogram of ΛΕΟΝΤΙΝΩΝ. *B.M.C.
2.* 76 ..   ..   £8

1124 **Lilybaion** (founded by the Carthaginians in 397 B.C. and populated by refugees from
Motya. Besieged by the Romans in the First Punic War and finally captured by them
in 241 B.C.). After 241 B.C. Æ 22. Laur. hd. of Apollo r., bow and quiver at shoulder.
℞. ΛΙΛΥΒΑΙΙΤΑΝ. Lyre. *B.M.C. 2.* 2 ..   ..   £14

1125 — Æ 15. Laur. hd. of Apollo r. ℞. — Tripod-lebes. *B.M.C. 2.* 1   ..   £8

1126 — Æ 28. ΛΙΛΥΒΑΙΙΤΑΙC. Veiled female hd. r., with mural crown, within triangular
enclosure. ℞. ΑΤΡΑΤΙΝΟ ΠΥΘΙΩΝ. Serpent coiled around tripod. *B.M.C. 2.* 4
£25

1127   1130

1127 **Menainon** (founded in 459 B.C., Menainon was subject to Syracuse for much of its
history down to the time of the Roman conquest at the end of the 3rd Century). After
210 B.C. Æ *pentonkion.* Laur. bust of Zeus-Sarapis r. ℞. ΜΕΝΑΙΝΩΝ. Nike in
galloping biga r., π beneath. *B.M.C. 2.* 9   ..   ..   £14

1128 — — Laur. bust of Apollo r., π behind. ℞. — Asklepios stg. facing, holding phiale and
serpent-staff. *B.M.C. 2.* 11   ..   ..   £15

1129 — Æ *tetras.* Veiled bust of Demeter r., wreathed with corn. ℞. — Two torches
crossed, Δ beneath. *B.M.C. 2.* 7 ..   ..   £12

1130 — Æ *trias.* Hd. of Herakles r., bearded. ℞. — Club; three pellets in field. *B.M.C.
2.* 2 ..   ..   £11

1131 — Æ *hexas*. Dr. bust of Hermes r., wearing winged petasos. ℞. — Caduceus; two pellets in field. *B.M.C. 2.* 4   ..   ..   £10

1132   1133

1132 **Messana.** 430-396 B.C. Æ 20. ΜΕΣΣΑΝΙΩΝ. Hare bounding l.; in ex., locust. ℞. Cuttle-fish. *B.M.C. 2.* 68   ..   ..   £40

1133 — Æ 17. Hd. of nymph Pelorias l., wearing sphendone; before, ΠΕΛΩΡΙΑΣ; two dolphins in field. ℞. ΜΕΣΣΑΝΙΟΝ. Trident between scallop-shell and hare. *B.M.C. 2.* 71, *var.*
£20

1134 343-338 B.C. Æ 26. ΜΕΣΣΑΝΙΩΝ. Hd. of nymph Messana l., hair bound with crossing fillets. ℞. Biga of mules driven r. by City-goddess holding palm; Δ in ex. *B.M.C. 2.* 67
£35

1135 — — ΠΟΣΕΙΔΑΝ. Laur. hd. of Poseidon l. ℞. ΜΕΣΣΑΝΙΩΝ. Ornamented trident-head between two dolphins downwards. *B.M.C. 2.* 73   ..   ..   £65

1136   1139

1136 300-288 B.C. Æ 23. ΠΕΛΩΡΙΑΣ. Hd. of nymph Pelorias l., wreathed with corn; before, two dolphins meeting. ℞. — Naked warrior advancing l., holding spear, shield on l. arm. *B.M.C. 2.* 81 ..   ..   £30

1137 — Æ 20. ΜΕΣΣΑΝΙΩΝ. Hd. of young Herakles l., in lion's skin. ℞. Lion prowling r.; club above, pine-torch in ex. *B.M.C. 2.* 79   ..   ..   £20

1138 — **under the Mamertini** (a force of Oscan mercenaries, named Mamertini, attacked and captured Messana about 288 B.C. The inhabitants were massacred and the new regime ruled the city until Roman times). 288-278 B.C. Æ 28. Laur. hd. of Ares r.; ΑΡΕΟΣ before, Macedonian helmet behind. ℞. ΜΑΜΕΡΤΙΝΩΝ. Bull butting l. *B.M.C. 2.* 17   £35

1139 — — *Obv.* Similar, but with spear-head behind. ℞. — Eagle, wings spread, stg. l. on thunderbolt. *B.M.C. 2.* 8   ..   ..   £30

1140 278-270 B.C. Æ 24. Hd. of young Herakles l. in lion's skin, bow behind. ℞. — Same as last. *B.M.C. 2.* 13   ..   ..   £15

1141 — Æ 19. ΑΔΡΑΝΟΥ. Bearded hd. of Adranos l., wearing Corinthian helmet. ℞. — Hound stg. r. *B.M.C. 2.* 2   ..   ..   £22

Adranos, whose temple was on Mt. Aitna, originated with the Phoenicians and his sacred animal was the dog.

1142   1143

1142 270-220 B.C. Æ *hexas.* Laur. hd. of Ares r.; ΑΡΕΟΣ before, two pellets behind. R. — Athena, in defensive pose, stg. r., holding spear and resting l. hand on shield. *B.M.C.* 2. 24 ..   ..   £22

1143 220-200 B.C. Æ *pentonkion.* Laur. hd. of Ares l. R. — Horseman (Dioskouros ?) stg. l., holding spear and touching the hd. of his horse stg. l. behind him; π in field to l. *B.M.C.* 2. 32   ..   ..   £20

1144   1146

1144 — — Laur. hd. of Zeus r. R. — Naked warrior charging r., holding spear and large circular shield; π in field to r. *B.M.C.* 2. 25   ..   ..   ..   £20

1145 — Æ 20. *Obv.* Similar, but with ΔΙΟΣ and ΤΡ monogram behind. R. — Hermes stg. l., holding phiale and caduceus, ram l. at feet. *B.M.C.* 2. 47   ..   ..   £15

1146 — Æ 11. Diad. hd. of Artemis r., bow and quiver at shoulder. R. — Omphalos; monograms in field. *B.M.C.* 2. 51   ..   ..   £10

1147 200-38 B.C. Æ *hemilitron.* Laur. hd. of Apollo r.; behind, lyre and six pellets. R. — Nike stg. l., holding wreath and palm. *B.M.C.* 2. 41   ..   ..   £18

1148   1151

1148 **Morgantina** (a city of Sicel foundation, of the history of which we possess little information). *Circa* 340 B.C. Æ 27. ΜΟΡΓΑΝΤΙΝΩΝ. Hd. of Athena r., in richly ornamented triple-crested helmet; behind, owl. R. Lion stg. r., tearing at stag's hd. on ground; serpent between his legs; Γ above. *B.M.C.* 2. 7 ..   ..   £100

1149 — Æ 20. Hd. of Sikelia r., wreathed with myrtle. R. ΜΟΡΓΑΝΤΙΝΩΝ (retrograde). Eagle, wings spread, stg. l. on serpent. *B.M.C.* 2. 11 ..   ..   ..   £26

1150 — Æ 15. ΑΛΚΟΣ. Laur. hd. of Alkos (=Apollo ?) r. R. ΜΟΡΓΑΝΤΙΝΩΝ. Tripod-lebes. *B.M.C.* 2. 12   ..   ..   £22

1151 **Motya.** 413-397 B.C. Æ *trias.* Gorgoneion; three pellets beneath. R. Palm-tree, and Punic legend 'm t v'. *B.M.C.* 2., *p.* 245, 16 ..   ..   ..   £30

1152 **Mytistratos.** *Circa* 340 B.C. Æ *hemilitron.* Bearded hd. of Hephaistos r., wearing pilos. R. VM and six pellets within olive-wreath. *B.M.C.* 2. 1   ..   £150

These are normally overstruck on contemporary coins of Syracuse, obv. Athena, rev. star-fish and dolphins.

1153 **Nakona** (site unknown: this city was captured and held by Campanian mercenaries in the 4th Cent. B.C.). Before *circa* 400 B.C. Æ *trias.* Seilenos seated on ass walking l., holding kantharos and thyrsos; three pellets in lower field. R. ΝΑΚΟΝΑΙΟΝ. Hd. of nymph r., hair bound by cord and wound four times round. *B.M.C.* 2. 1 ..   £35

Nakona *continued*

1154 — Æ *onkia*. *Obv*. Similar to *rev*. of last. R. Goat stg. r.; pellet above, ivy-leaf before.
Weber 1464 . .   . .   £25

1155   1157

1155 **Panormos** (the city was captured by the Romans in 254 B.C. during the First Punic
War). *Circa* 430 B.C. Æ *hemilitron*. Cock stg. r.; before, Punic legend '*sys*'. R. Six
pellets. *B.M.C. 2., p.* 249, 33   . .   . .   £45
1156 — Æ *trias*. Similar, but with three pellets on *rev*. *B.M.C. 2., p.* 249, 34   . .   £40
1157 *Circa* 330 B.C. Æ 22. Hd. of Hera l., wearing stephanos. R. Man-headed bull stg. l.,
hd. facing; radiate disk above, Punic legend '*sys*' in ex. *B.M.C. 2., p.* 250, 38   £35
1158 Before 254 B.C. Æ 18. Laur. hd. of Apollo l. R. Pegasos flying l.; Punic legend
'*sys*' below. *B.M.C. 2., p.* 250, 39   . .   . .   £18
1159 After 254 B.C. Æ 29. ΠΑΝΟΡΜΙΤΑΝ. Bust of Athena r., in Corinthian helmet. R.
Hd. of Persephone l., wreathed with corn. *B.M.C. 2.* 9   . .   . .   . .   £25
1160 — Æ 26. *Obv*. Similar, without legend. R. ΠΑΝΟΡΜΙΤΑΝ. Demeter (?) stg. l.,
holding phiale and cornucopiae. *B.M.C. 2.* 10 . .   . .   £10
1161 — Æ 24. *Obv*. Same as 1159. R. Triskeles, with Gorgoneion at centre; ears of corn
between the legs. *B.M.C. 2.* 11 . .   . .   £30

1162   1165

1162 — — Laur. hd. of Zeus l. R. ΠΑΝΟΡΜΙΤΑΝ. Eagle, wings spread, stg. l. on thunderbolt, looking back. *B.M.C. 2.* 13 . .   . .   £12
1163 — Æ 18. ΠΑΝΟΡΜΙΤΑΝ. Female hd. r., wearing stephane. R. Square altar with
horns. *B.M.C. 2.* 17   . .   . .   £10
1164 — Æ 17. Laur. hd. of Zeus r. R. ΠΑΝΟΡΜΙΤΑΝ. Warrior, in helmet and cuir.,
stg. l., holding phiale and spear, shield at feet. *B.M.C. 2.* 26 . .   . .   £9
1165 — Æ 13. Veiled hd. of Demeter l.; behind, two corn-ears. R. Prow r.; ΠΑΡ monogram above. *B.M.C. 2.* 23   . .   . .   £7
1166 — Æ 11. Hd. of Aphrodite r., wearing stephane. R. Dove stg. r.; ΠΑΡ monogram
above. *B.M.C. 2.* 25   . .   . .   £6

1167   1168

1167 — Æ *as*. Laur. hd. of Janus, I above. R. ПOR monogram within laurel-wreath. *B.M.C. 2.* 29   ..   ..   £18

1168 **Paropos.** After 241 B.C. Æ 20. Laur. hd. of Apollo l. R. ΠΑΡΩΠΙΝΩΝ. Hunter stg. l., holding phiale (?) and spear; hound running l. beyond; wing in field to l. *B.M.C. 2.* 1 ..   ..   £25

1169   1171

1169 **Petra.** *Circa* 340 B.C. Æ *litra*. ΠΕΤΡΙΝΩΝ. Hd. of Zeus Eleutherios r. R. Aphrodite seated r., r. hand resting on seat, holding dove on outstretched l. *B.M.C. 2., p.* 63, 15 (misattributed to Eryx) £200

1170 After 241 B.C. Æ 19. Hd. of bearded Herakles r., in lion's skin. R. ΠΕΤΡΕΙΝΩΝ. Female figure stg. l., r. hand raised, l. elbow resting on column. *B.M.C. 2.* 1   £25

1171 **Piakos.** *Circa* 420 B.C. Æ *hemilitron*. ΠΙΑΚΙΝ before hd. of young river-god l., horned and wreathed with olive; six pellets between the letters of the inscription. R. Dog r., seizing fallen fawn by the throat; leaf in field to r. *B.M.C. 2.* 1   ..   £50

1172 **Segesta.** 430-409 B.C. Æ *tetras*. Hd. of nymph Segesta r., hair tied behind by fillet; ivy-leaf behind. R. Hound stg. r., plant before; four pellets in field, above and below. *B.M.C. 2.* 49   ..   ..   £30

1173   1174

1173 — Æ *hexas*. ΗΕΞΑΣ (retrograde). Hd. of nymph Segesta r., wearing sphendone. R. Hound stg. r., looking back; two pellets in field, above and below. *B.M.C. 2.* 57

£22

One of the few instances of the name of the denomination appearing in full on a coin—see also no. 621, *obol of Metapontion.*

1174 After 241 B.C. (under Roman rule). Æ 22. Turreted and veiled bust of Segesta r. R. ΣΕΓΕΣΤΑΙΩΝ. Aeneas stg. r., holding sword and carrying Anchises on his shoulder. *B.M.C. 2.* 59   ..   ..   £17

The Segestans, like the Romans, claimed a Trojan descent.

1175 — Æ 19. *Obv.* Similar. R. — Horseman stg. l., spear over shoulder, holding his horse by the bridle. *B.M.C. 2.* 63   ..   ..   £13

1176 **Selinus.** 415-409 B.C. Æ *trias*. Horned hd. of young river-god l. R. Selinon leaf: three pellets around. *B.M.C. 2.* 50   ..   ..   £35

1177   1181   1183

1177 **Solus** (a Phoenician town not far from Panormos, and a dependency of Carthage until the First Punic War). Late 5th Cent. B.C. Æ *hemilitron*. ΣΟΛΟΝΤΙΝΟΝ. Hd. of bearded Herakles r., in lion's skin. ℞. Punic legend *'kfra'*. Cray-fish between six pellets. *B.M.C. 2., p.* 242, 2   ..   ..   £40

1178 — Æ *trias*. Similar, but with only three pellets on *rev*. *B.M.C. 2., p.* 242, 4   £25

1179 Late 4th Cent. B.C. Æ 20. Hd. of Persephone l., wreathed with corn. ℞. Bull pacing l.; in ex., Punic legend *'kfra'*. *B.M.C. 2., p.* 242, 7   ..   ..   £35

1180 — Æ 18. Hippocamp r., with curled wing. ℞. Hd. of young Herakles r., in lion's skin. *B.M.C. 2.* 1 ..   ..   £20

1181 — Æ 14. Hd. of Athena three-quarter face to r., wearing triple-crested helmet. ℞. Punic legend *'kfra'*. Naked archer kneeling r., about to discharge arrow from bow. *B.M.C. 2., p.* 242, 5 ..   ..   £25

1182 After 241 B.C. Æ 23. Hd. of Athena r., in Corinthian helmet. ℞. ϹΟΛΟΝ / ΤΙΝΥΝ in laurel-wreath. *B.M.C. 2.* 4   ..   ..   £21

1183 — Æ 18. Laur. hd. of Poseidon r., trident at shoulder. ℞. ϹΟΛΟΝΤΙΝΩΝ (retrograde). Naked warrior advancing l., holding spear and shield. *B.M.C. 2.* 5 ..   ..   £17

1184   1185

1184 **Syracuse.** 440–425 B.C. Æ *trias*. ΣΥΡΑ. Hd. of Arethusa r., hair in korymbos; dolphins before and behind. ℞. Cuttle-fish; three pellets around. *B.M.C. 2.* 126   £20

1185 Before 357 B.C. Æ 17. ΣΥΡΑ. Hd. of Arethusa l., hair bound with ampyx and sphendone ornamented with star. ℞. Quadripartite incuse square; at centre, incuse circle containing star. *B.M.C. 2.* 242 ..   ..   £25

1186   1187

1186 — — *Obv.* Similar, but no legend and without star on sphendone; behind, dolphin. ℞. ΣΥ — ΡΑ in the upper quarters of wheel with four spokes; dolphin in each of the lower quarters. *B.M.C. 2.* 243 ..   ..   £18

1187 357–344 B.C. Æ 18. Female hd. l., hair in sphendone; behind, spray of olive. ℞. Dolphin leaping r. above scallop-shell; ΣΥΡΑ between. *B.M.C. 2.* 301   ..   £24

1188 — Æ 15. Hd. of Arethusa l., hair bound with ampyx and sphendone. R. Cuttle-fish.
B.M.C. 2. 248   ..   ..   £12

1189 344-336 B.C. (time of Timoleon). Æ litra. ΣΥΡΑ. Hd. of Athena l., wearing Corinthian helmet bound with olive-wreath. R. Starfish between two dolphins. B.M.C. 2.
287 ..   ..   £40

1190
1192

1190 — — ΣΥΡΑΚΟΣΙΩΝ. Bearded hd. l. (Archias ?), wearing Corinthian helmet. R. Pegasos
flying l., dolphin l. beneath; between them, Σ. B.M.C. 2. 308 ..   ..   ..   £75
1191 — — ΙΕΥΣ ΕΛΕΥΘΕΡΙΟΣ. Laur. hd. of Zeus Eleutherios l., hair long. R. ΣΥΡΑΚΟΣΙΩΝ.
Free horse prancing l. B.M.C. 2. 311   ..   ..   £75
1192 — Æ hemilitron. ΙΕΥΣ ΕΛΕΥΘΕΡΙΟΣ. Laur. hd. of Zeus Eleutherios r., hair short.
R. ΣΥΡΑΚΟΣΙΩΝ. Thunderbolt; eagle stg. r. in field to r. B.M.C. 2. 313   ..   £30

1193
1195

1193 — Æ trias. ΣΥΡΑ. Hd. of Athena, as 1189, but also with dolphins, before and behind.
R. Hippocamp l., with curled wing. B.M.C. 2. 289   ..   ..   £18
1194 — — ΙΕΥΣ ΕΛΕΥΘΕΡΙΟΣ. Laur. hd. of Zeus Eleutherios l., hair short. R. ΣΥΡΑΚΟΣΙΩΝ.
Cuttle-fish. B.M.C. 2. 320   ..   ..   £24
1195 Reign of Agathokles, 317-289 B.C. Æ 23. Hd. of Kore l., wreathed with corn; behind,
corn-grain; before, ΣΥΡΑΚΟΣΙΩΝ. R. Bull butting l.; above, dolphin l. and ΝΙ; beneath,
another dolphin l. B.M.C. 2. 357   ..   ..   £22
1196 — Æ 15. Female hd. l., hair rolled; behind, scallop. R. Bull butting l.; in ex.,
ΣΥΡΑΚΟΣΙΩΝ; above, ΕΧ monogram. B.M.C. 2. 369   ..   ..   £10

1197   1199

Syracuse *continued*

1197 — Æ 19. ΣΥΡΑΚΟΣΙΩΝ. Laur. hd. of Apollo l.; behind, trophy; beneath, ΑΙ. ℞. Triskeles, with Gorgoneion in circle at centre. *B.M.C. 2.* 354.. .. .. £35

1198 — Æ 14. *Obv.* Similar, but without symbol and letters. ℞. Dog lying l., looking back; x in field to l. *B.M.C. 2.* 377 .. .. £18

1199 — Æ 18. *Obv.* Similar, but with pilos behind. ℞. Pegasos flying l.; A beneath. *B.M.C. 2.* 321 .. .. £18

1200   1202

1200 — Æ 22. ΣΩΤΕΙΡΑ. Bust of Artemis r., quiver at shoulder. ℞. ΑΓΑΘΟΚΛΕΟΣ / ΒΑΣΙΛΕΟΣ above and below winged thunderbolt. *B.M.C. 2.* 422 .. .. £14

1201 — — ΣΥΡΑΚΟΣΙΩΝ. Young male hd. (Herakles ?) r., wearing tainia. ℞. Lion prowling r.; above, club. *B.M.C. 2.* 389 .. .. £20

1202 — Æ 20. ΣΥΡΑΚΟΣΙΩΝ. Hd. of Athena r., in crested Corinthian helmet. ℞. Horseman, wearing Phrygian helmet, cantering r., holding spear couched. *B.M.C. 2.* 409 £25

1203 — Æ 22. *Obv.* Similar, but with trophy behind. ℞. Pegasos flying l., both wings visible; beneath, trident. *B.M.C. 2.* 412.. .. .. £22

1204 — Æ 14. Hd. of Athena l., in crested Corinthian helmet. ℞. ΣΥΡΑΚΟΣΙΩΝ. Winged thunderbolt. *B.M.C. 2.* 414 .. .. £10

1205 Democracy, 289-288 B.C. Æ 22. ΔΙΟΣ ΕΛΕΥΘΕΡΙΟΥ. Laur. hd. of Zeus Eleutherios l. ℞. ΣΥΡΑΚ / ΟΣΙΩΝ above and below winged thunderbolt. *B.M.C. 2.* 428 .. £28

1206 — — ΣΩΤΕΙΡΑ. Bust of Artemis l., quiver at shoulder. ℞. ΔΙΟΣ ΕΛΕΥ / ΘΕΡΙΟΥ above and below winged thunderbolt. *B.M.C. 2.* 426.. .. .. £25

1207   1209

1207 — — *Obv.* Similar, but bust to r. ℞. Same as 1205. *B.M.C. 2.* 405 .. £20

1208 — Æ 15. Similar, but bust of Artemis to l. on *obv.* *B.M.C. 2.* 408 .. .. £15

1209 Reign of Hiketas, 288-279 B.C. Æ 24. ΣΥΡΑΚΟΣΙΩΝ. Hd. of Persephone l., wreathed with corn. ℞. Galloping biga driven r. by charioteer; above, star. *B.M.C. 2.* 441 £24

1210 — — ΣΥΡΑΚΟΣΙΩΝ. Hd. of Demeter r., wreathed with corn; behind, flaming torch. ℞. Similar to last, but also with ΠΥ monogram and x in ex. *B.M.C. 2.* 457 .. £24

1211 — — ΔΙΟΣ ΕΛΛΑΝΙΟΥ. Laur. and beardless hd. of Zeus Hellanios l.; behind, thunderbolt. ℞. ΣΥΡΑΚΟΣΙΩΝ. Eagle stg. l. on thunderbolt, wings open. *B.M.C. 2.* 468 £24

1211   1213

1212 — — Similar, but with hd. of Zeus Hellanios to r., and with trophy behind; on *rev.*,
star in field to l. *B.M.C. 2.* 482 .. ..   £24

1213 Rule of Pyrrhos, 278-276 B.C. Æ 23. ΣΥΡΑΚΟΣΙΩΝ. Hd. of young Herakles l., in
lion's skin. ℞. Athena Promachos advancing r., brandishing spear and holding shield;
wreath in field to l. *B.M.C. 2.* 493 .. ..   £12

1214 — — Similar, but the legend is on *rev.* instead of *obv.*, and Athena Promachos brandishes
thunderbolt instead of spear; no symbol in *rev.* field. *B.M.C. 2.* 503 .. ..   £13

1215   1216

1215 — Æ 26. ΦΘΙΑΣ. Veiled hd. of Phthia l., crowned with oak; behind, thyrsos. ℞.
ΒΑΣΙΛΕΩΣ / ΠΥΡΡΟΥ above and below winged thunderbolt. *B.M.C. 7. (Epirus),p.* 112, 20
£35
*Phthia was the name of Pyrrhos' mother, and also of a district of Thessaly where the King's
family had originated.*

1216 — Æ 23. Hd. of Persephone r., wreathed with corn; behind, Θ. ℞. ΒΑΣΙΛΕΩΣ ΠΥΡΡΟΥ.
Demeter enthroned r., holding corn-stalk and sceptre; N in field to r. *B.M.C. 7. (Epirus),*
p. 113, 27 .. ..   £24

1217 — Æ 19. Hd. of Athena l., in crested Corinthian helmet; behind, owl . ℞. ΒΑΣΙΛΕΩΣ /
ΠΥΡΡΟΥ above and below ear of corn; all within oak-wreath. *B.M.C. 7. (Epirus), p.* 113,
27 .. ..   £18

1218 Reign of Hieron II, 275-215 B.C. Æ 19. ΣΥΡΑΚΟΣΙΩΝ. Hd. of Persephone l., hair
rolled and wreathed with corn. ℞. Bull butting l.; above, club and Δ; in ex., ΙΕ. *B.M.C.*
2. 618 .. ..   £14

1219 — Æ 15. Female hd. l., wearing ampyx and sphendone; behind, poppy-head. ℞.
Pegasos flying l., ΙΕΡΩΝΟΣ beneath. *B.M.C. 2.* 615 .. ..   £12

1220 — Æ 34. Diad. hd. of Hieron l., beardless. ℞. Galloping biga driven r. by Nike;
ΣΩ monogram beneath; ΙΕΡΩΝΟΣ in ex. *B.M.C. 2.* 578 .. ..   £125

1221   1223

Syracuse *continued*

1221 — Æ 27. *Obv.* Similar; beneath, Y. ℞. Horseman prancing r., holding spear couched; beneath, E; in ex., ΙΕΡΩΝΟΣ. *B.M.C. 2.* 583   ..   ..   £20

1222 — — Similar, but on *obv.* Hieron is laur., with bee behind, nothing beneath; on *rev.* AP monogram instead of E beneath. *B.M.C. 2.* 570   ..   ..   ..   £25

1223 — Æ 22. Hd. of Poseidon l., wearing tainia. ℞. Ornamented trident-head, between two dolphins, dividing ΙΕΡ — ΩΝΟΣ in lower field; o in field to l. *B.M.C. 2.* 603   £8

1224   1225

1224 Reign of Hieronymos, 215-214 B.C. Æ 22. Diad. hd. of Hieronymos l., beardless. ℞. ΒΑΣΙΛΕΟΣ / ΙΕΡΩΝΥΜΟΥ above and below winged thunderbolt, above which, ΑΠ. *B.M.C. 2.* 645   ..   ..   £16

1225 Republic, 214-212 B.C. Æ 22. Laur. hd. of Apollo l. ℞. The Dioskouroi on horseback cantering r., star above hd. of each; beneath, ΑΓ; in ex., ΣΥΡΑΚΟΣΙΩΝ. *B.M.C. 2.* 678   £18

1226 — Æ 19. Hd. of Poseidon l., wearing tainia. ℞. Ornamented trident-head, between two dolphins, dividing ΣΥΡΑ — ΚΟΣΙΩΝ; beneath, o — Φ. *B.M.C. 2.* 671   ..   £10

1227 — Æ 11. Laur. hd. of Apollo l.; behind, cornucopiae. ℞. ΣΥΡΑΚΟΣΙΩΝ. Tripodlebes. *B.M.C. 2.* 681   ..   ..   £6

1228 Under Roman Rule, after 212 B.C. Æ 27. Laur. hd. of Zeus r. ℞. ΣΥΡΑΚΟΣΙΩΝ. Simulacrum of Isis in triumphal quadriga r. *B.M.C. 2.* 685   ..   ..   £20

1229 — Æ 24. Laur. hd. of Zeus l. ℞. Galloping biga driven r. by Nike; above, crescent; in ex., ΣΥΡΑΚΟΣΙΩΝ. *B.M.C. 2.* 691   ..   ..   £12

1230   1231

1230 — Æ 20. Hd. of Athena r., wearing crested Corinthian helmet. ℞. ΣΥΡΑΚΟΣΙΩΝ. Nike facing, kneeling on back of prostrate bull, which she is about to sacrifice with sword held aloft in r. hand. *B.M.C. 2.* 698   ..   ..   £14

1231 — — Hd. of Sarapis r., wearing tainia. ℞. ΣΥΡΑΚΟCΙΩΝ. Isis stg. l., holding sistrum and sceptre. *B.M.C. 2.* 701   ..   ..   £14

1232 — Æ 17. Veiled hd. of Demeter r., wreathed with corn. ℞. ΣΥΡΑΚΟΣΙΩΝ. Two flaming torches, crossed. *B.M.C. 2.* 711   ..   ..   £10

1233 — Æ 19.   Rad. bust of Artemis r., bow and quiver at shoulder.   R. — Apollo, naked, stg. r., holding wreath and branch.   *B.M.C. 2.* 719   ..   ..   £14

1234 — Æ 17.   Laur. hd. of Apollo r.   R. — Sacrificial cap; Q in field to r.   *B.M.C. 2.* 716
£9

1235 — Æ 14.   Hd. of Persephone r., wreathed with corn.   R. ΣΥΡΑ / ΚΟΣΙ / ΩΝ in three lines within corn-wreath.   *B.M.C. 2.* 710   ..   ..   £7

1236   1239

1236 **Tauromenion.**   344-317 B.C.   Æ 26.   ΑΡΧΑΓΕΤΑΣ.   Laur. hd. of Apollo Archegetes l.   R. ΤΑΥΡΟΜΕΝΙΤΑΝ.   Man-headed bull walking l.   *B.M.C. 2.* 17   ..   ..   £45

1237 — Æ 20.   *Obv.* Similar; beneath, A.   R. — Bull butting l.; in ex., bunch of grapes.   *B.M.C. 2.* 20   ..   ..   £18

1238 — Æ 17.   *Obv.* Similar; without A.   R. — Forepart of bull butting l.   *B.M.C. 2.* 25
£15

1239 Time of Pyrrhos, 279-276 B.C.   Æ 22.   ΑΡΧΑΕΕΤΑ (*sic*).   Laur. hd. of Apollo Archegetes l.   R. ΤΑΥΡΟΜΕΝΙΤΑΝ.   Lyre; above, bunch of grapes.   *B.M.C. 2.* 27   ..   £14

1240 — — *Obv.* Similar; legend ΑΡΧΑΓΤΑΣ (*sic*).   R. — Tripod-lebes.   *B.M.C. 2.* 29   £12

1241   1243

1241 275-212 B.C.   Æ 26.   Bearded hd. of Herakles r., wearing tainia; behind, ΕΥ monogram.   R. ΤΑΥΡΟΜΕΝΙΤΑΝ.   Bull butting r.   *B.M.C. 2.* 33   ..   ..   £30

1242 — Æ 23.   Hd. of Athena l., wearing crested Corinthian helmet; behind, owl.   R. — Pegasos prancing l.   *B.M.C. 2.* 40   ..   ..   £14

1243 — — Laur. hd. of Apollo l.; behind, bee.   R. — Tripod-lebes.   *B.M.C. 2.* 46
£12

1244 — Æ 19.   Hd. of Athena r., wearing crested Corinthian helmet.   R. — Owl stg. r. on amphora.   *B.M.C. 2.* 53   ..   ..   £15

1245 **Tyndaris** (founded by Dionysios of Syracuse in 396 B.C. for the settlement of exiles from Greece expelled by the Spartans following the Peloponnesian War.   The city was named after Tyndareos, father of the Dioskouroi).   396-345 B.C.   Æ 22.   ΤΥΝΔΑΡΙΣ.   Hd. of Helen l., wearing stephane; behind, star.   R. One of the Dioskouroi on horse cantering r., palm over shoulder.   *B.M.C. 2.* 1   ..   ..   £40

Tyndaris *continued*

1246 *Circa* 344 B.C. Æ 17. TYNΔAPITAN. Laur. hd. of Apollo r. ℞. Cock stg. r.; before, grasshopper; behind, star. *B.M.C. 2.* 4 ..   ..   £30

1247 — Æ 22. TYNΔAPITAN. Hd. of Persephone l., wreathed with corn. ℞. The Dioskouroi on horseback galloping l.; above, ΣΩTHPEΣ. *B.M.C. 2.* 7   ..   £35

1248 254-210 B.C. Æ 22. Laur. hd. of Zeus r. ℞. The Dioskouroi stg. facing, each holding horse by the bridle; in ex., TYNΔAPITAN. *B.M.C. 2.* 9 ..   ..   ..   £24

1249 — Æ 18. *Obv.* Similar; behind, star. ℞. TYNΔAPITAN. Eagle stg. r. on thunderbolt, wings spread. *B.M.C. 2.* 11   ..   ..   £20

1250 — — Hd. of Athena r., wearing crested Corinthian helmet. ℞. — Hermes stg. l., holding patera and caduceus. *B.M.C. 2.* 15   ..   ..   £22

1251 — Æ 17. Hd. of Poseidon r., wearing tainia. ℞. — Ornamented trident. *B.M.C. 2.* 12 ..   ..   £18

1252 — — Female hd. r., veiled. ℞. — Pilei of the Dioskouroi, each surmounted by star. *B.M.C. 2.* 16   ..   ..   £20

1252   1254

1253 **ISLANDS OFF SICILY. Lipara** (occupied by Greek settlers in the 6th Cent. B.C., the island was captured by the Carthaginians about 288 B.C. and by the Romans in 252). *Circa* 350 B.C. Æ *litra.* Hd. of bearded Hephaistos r., wearing pilos. ℞. ΛIΠAPAION. Stern of galley going r. *Gabrici* (*La monetazione del bronzo nella Sicilia antica*) 1   £750

1254 — Æ *hemilitron. Obv.* Similar. ℞. ΛIΠAPAION (retrograde). Stern of galley going l.; in field above, six pellets. *B.M.C. 2.* 1 ..   ..   £500

1255 — Æ *trias. Obv.* Similar. ℞. ΛIΠAPAION around three pellets. *B.M.C. 2.* 7   £350

1256 — Æ *hexas. Obv.* Similar. ℞. ΛIΠ; two pellets in field, above and below. *B.M.C. 2.* 10 ..   ..   £175

1257   1258

1257 — Æ *onkia. Obv.* Similar. ℞. ΛI, with pellet between. *B.M.C. 2.* 14   ..   £85

1258 *Circa* 300 B.C. Æ *litra.* Young Hephaistos, naked, seated r. on stool, holding hammer and kantharos. ℞. ΛIΠAPAION. Dolphin leaping r. *B.M.C. 2.* 20 ..   ..   £60

1259 — Æ *hemilitron. Obv.* Similar, but the kantharos held by Hephaistos rests on stand; bunch of grapes in field to r. ℞. ΛIΠAPAIΩN. Dolphin leaping l. above waves. *B.M.C. 2.* 25 ..   ..   £50

1260   1265

1260 — Æ *hexas. Obv.* Similar to 1258. ℞. ΛΙΠ, with two pellets, above and below, connected by the ι of the legend. *B.M.C. 2.* 49   ..   ..   £25

1261 *Circa* 260 B.C.   Æ 20. Laur. hd. of young Ares l. ℞. ΛΙΠΑΡΑΙΩΝ. Ornamented trident-head. *B.M.C. 2.* 61   ..   ..   £20

1262 Time of Second Punic War, after 218 B.C.   Æ *hemilitron. Obv.* Similar to 1259, but without bunch of grapes. ℞. ΛΙΠΑΡΑΙΩΝ around six pellets. *B.M.C. 2.* 41   ..   £30

1263 — Æ *onkia. Obv.* Similar to 1258. ℞. ΛΙ, with pellet between. *B.M.C. 2.* 60
                                                                                            £17

1264 2nd-1st Cent. B.C.   Æ 20.   Laur. hd. of Poseidon l. ℞. ΛΙΠΑΡΑΙΩΝ. Young Hephaistos naked, stg. l., holding tongs and sceptre. *B.M.C. 2.* 74..   ..   ..   ..   £16

1265 — Æ 18.   Hd. of young Hephaistos r., in laur. pilos; behind, tongs. ℞. — Young Hephaistos running r., brandishing hammer and holding tongs. *B.M.C. 2.* 79   £14

1266 After *c.* 89 B.C.   Æ 18.   ΛΙΠΑΡΑΙΩΝ.   Hd. of young Hephaistos l., in laur. pilos. ℞.
Γ . ΜΑΡΚΙΟ . Γ . ΑϹΩΝΕΥ . ΔΥΟ . ΑΝΔΡ.   Tongs. *B.M.C. 2.* 81 ..   ..   ..   £15

1267 **Sardinia** (the island was largely under Carthaginian control from early times, but soon after the end of the First Punic War, in 238 B.C., it was taken by the Romans).   After 238 B.C. Æ 24.   Hd. of Persephone l., wreathed with corn. ℞. Three ears of corn; above, crescent and pellet. *Weber* 1789 ..   ..   £20

1268 — Æ 19. Similar. *Weber* 1791   ..   ..   £16

1269 — — *Obv.* Similar. ℞. Cow stg. r.; above, star. *Grose* 3065   ..   ..   £14

N.B. Prices given in this catalogue are for **fine** examples of coins in base metal and for **very fine** examples of coins struck in precious metals.

There is no relationship between the values stated and the condition of the coins used as illustrations.

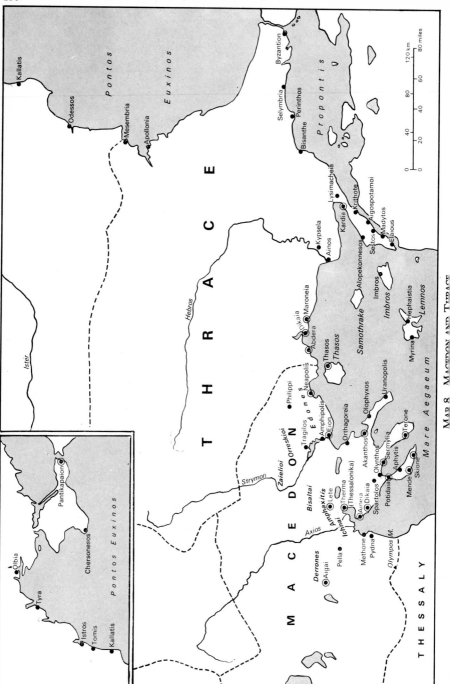

MAP 8. MACEDON AND THRACE

NORTHERN GREECE

The coastal regions of Macedon and Thrace were settled by Greek colonists during the Eighth and Seventh Centuries B.C. The interior was occupied by a number of indigenous tribes who, through prolonged contact with the Greek cities, gradually became partially Hellenized. The Macedonian kingdom, centred on the city of Aigai, was of no great importance in its early days, but under Alexander I (495-454 B.C.) its wealth and territorial extent were greatly enhanced. Philip II (359-336 B.C.) initiated the dynamic expansion of the Macedonian kingdom when, in 357, he captured Amphipolis, a city founded by the Athenians in 436 and situated close to the rich mining district of Mt. Pangaion. The power of the Greek cities of the Chalkidike peninsula was finally broken by Philip in 348 with the destruction of Olynthos, capital city of the Chalkidian League.

Archaic Period
GREEK CITIES OF THE CHALKIDIKE PENINSULA

1270 **Akanthos** (a colony from the Aegean Island of Andros, Akanthos was a prolific mint in the early period and probably had its own silver mines). 510-480 B.C. Æ *tetradrachm.* Bull kneeling r., hd. raised, attacked by lioness r. on his back. ℞. Quadripartite incuse square. *Price & Waggoner (Archaic Greek silver coinage: the "Asyut" hoard)* 153-8

£1,250

1271   1276

1271 — — Similar, but the bull's hd. is lowered and the lioness is to l., attacking his rump. *Price & Waggoner* 159. *B.M.C.* 5. 1. *Desneux (Les tetradrachmes d'Akanthos)* 16

£1,250

1272 — — Bull kneeling l., hd. uplifted, attacked by lion r. on his back; in ex., floral ornament. ℞. Quadripartite incuse square. *Price & Waggoner* 178-84. *Desneux* 38

£1,000

1273 — Æ *tetrobol.* Forepart of lioness r. ℞. Quadripartite incuse square. *B.M.C.* 5. 8

£200

1274 — Æ *obol.* Hd. and neck of lioness facing. ℞. Quadripartite incuse square. *B.M.C.* 5. 21 .. .. £75

1275 **Aineia** (traditionally founded by Aeneas during his flight from Troy). 490-480 B.C. Æ *tetradrachm.* Aeneas, carrying Anchises, advancing r., preceded by his wife, Kreusa, who carries Askanios and looks back; to l., AIN (retrograde) and ram's hd. r. ℞. Quadripartite incuse square. *Price & Waggoner* 194 .. .. £20,000

1276 — Æ *tetrobol.* Archaic hd. of bearded Aeneas r., wearing crested Corinthian helmet. ℞. Quadripartite incuse square. *B.M.C.* 5. 1 .. .. £300

1277 **Dikaia** (an Eretrian colony). 500-480 B.C. Æ *tetrobol.* Cow stg. r., scratching herself; floral ornament above. ℞. Incuse square of "mill-sail" pattern. *B.M.C.* 5. 1

£350

1278   1280

1278 **Mende** (a very early foundation, Mende was settled by colonists from Eretria in Euboia and was celebrated for its wine). 500-480 B.C. Æ *tetradrachm..* MIN. Ithyphallic ass stg. l.; crow perched r. on his back pecking at his rump. R. Five incuse triangles arranged in "mill-sail" pattern. *Price & Waggoner* 200-203. *B.M.C. 5.* 1   ..   ..   £1,500

1279 — Æ *tetrobol.* MIN. Ithyphallic ass stg. r.; vine with bunches of grapes in background. R. Similar to last, but only four incuse triangles. *Weber* 1923 ..   ..   ..   £225

1280 — Æ *tritemorion* (*c.* 0·5 gm.). Hd. of braying ass l. R. Incuse square divided diagonally by two broad bands. *Weber* 1929   ..   ..   £65

1281 — Æ *trihemitartemorion* (*c.* 0·3 gm.). Similar; incuse square divided by broad bands into four squares. *B.M.C. 5.* 3   ..   ..   £50

1282   1286

1282 **Potidaia** (a colony of Corinth, Potidaia derived its name from Poseidon, a statue of whom stood before the city). 500-480 B.C. Æ *tetradrachm.* Poseidon Hippios on horse stg. r.; he holds trident and reins; star beneath; ᴨ in field to r. R. Incuse square diagonally divided into four triangles. *B.M.C. 5.* 1   ..   ..   ..   £1,800

1283 — Æ *tetrobol.* *Obv.* Similar, but without star, and with legend ᴨO in field. R. Incuse square containing archaic hd. of Amazon r., wearing pointed fox-skin cap. *B.M.C. 5.* 2 ..   ..   £250

1284 — Æ *diobol.* Naked horseman r. on forepart of prancing horse; ᴨ in field. R. Incuse square containing archaic female hd. r., with long hair. *B.M.C. 5.* 9 ..   ..   £140

1285 **Skione** (traditionally founded by Protesilaos on his way to the Trojan War, Skione was probably established by colonists from Euboia). *Circa* 500 B.C. Æ *tetradrachm.* Stag kneeling r., hd. raised, attacked by lion l. on its back. R. Quadripartite incuse square. *Price & Waggoner* 192-3 ..   ..   £2,500

1286 500-480 B.C. Æ *tetrobol.* SKION (retrograde). Forepart of lion r., looking back. R. Quadripartite incuse square, with pellets at centre. *B.M.C. 5.* 2 ..   ..   £400

1287 **Sermylia.** 500-480 B.C. Æ *tetradrachm.* Naked horseman galloping r., brandishing spear; large globule behind. R. Quadripartite incuse square. *Price & Waggoner* 220   £4,500

1288 **Terone** (a prosperous city, Terone gave assistance to Xerxes at the time of the Persian invasion of Greece, 480 B.C.). 500-490 B.C. Æ *tetradrachm* (Thraco-Macedonian weight standard, *c.* 14·5 gm.). Amphora, with ribbing on shoulder. R. Quadripartite incuse square. *Price & Waggoner* 221 ..   ..   £2,500

1289 490-480 B.C. Æ *tetradrachm* (Attic standard, *c.* 17 gm.). Amphora, with bunch of grapes hanging from each handle. R. Same as last. *B.M.C. 5.* 1   ..   ..   £2,250

| 1290 | 1291 |

1290 — — Similar, but with a third bunch of grapes, hanging from neck of amphora, and with legend H — E in obv. field.   *B.M.C. 5.* 3 ..   ..   £2,500

A city named Herakleia is known to have existed in the vicinity of Terone and it is possible that these coins were struck there.

1291 — Æ *tetrobol.*   Oinochoë l.   R. Quadripartite incuse square.   *B.M.C. 5.* 4-6   £150

OTHER MACEDONIAN CITIES

| 1292 | 1293 | 1294 |

1292 **Aigai** (this city was the original capital of the Macedonian kingdom and following the defeat of the Persians in 479 B.C. these 'civic' issues were superseded by the regal coinage of Alexander I).   500-480 B.C.   Æ *stater.*   Goat kneeling r., looking back; above, $\overline{AE}$.   R. Quadripartite incuse square.   *B.M.C. 5.* 1 ..   ..   £2,500

1293 — Æ *trihemiobol* (?).   Similar, but with annulet above goat instead of monogram   *B.M.C. 5.* 4 ..   ..   £75

1294 **Eion** (a port at the mouth of the River Strymon).   *Circa* 480 B.C.   Æ *drachm.*   Goose and its young stg. r. and l. respectively, the latter looking back; annulet between them.   R. Incuse square.   *B.M.C. 5.* 1 ..   ..   £650

1295 — Æ *trihemiobol* (?).   Goose stg. r., looking back.   R. Incuse square.   *B.M.C. 5.* 5   £100

1296 — Æ *obol* (?).   Two geese stg. breast to breast, their heads turned back; between them, Λ.   R. Incuse square.   *B.M.C. 5.* 4   ..   ..   £90

| 1297 | 1298 |

1297 **Lete** (the following types have traditionally been assigned to this mint, but Lete was a city of no great importance and the attribution is open to serious doubt).   530-480 B.C.   Æ *stater.*   Naked ithyphallic satyr advancing r., seizing by her r. wrist a nymph, who looks back at him and raises her l. arm; six pellets in field.   R. Incuse square roughly divided into four triangles.   *B.M.C. 5.* 2 ..   ..   £800

1298 — — Similar, but larger, more grotesque, figures and the satyr caresses the nymph's r. shoulder; three pellets in field; on *rev.* the square is clearly divided diagonally into four triangles.   *B.M.C. 5.* 6 ..   ..   £500

1299   1303

Lete *continued*

1299 — — *Obv.* Similar, but the figures are more carefully engraved and the satyr caresses the nymph's chin. ℞. Quadripartite incuse square. *B.M.C. 5.* 22   ..   ..   £600

1300 — — ΛΕΤΑΙΟΝ (retrograde). Centaur kneeling r., carrying in his arms a nymph who raises her r. hand in protest. ℞. Crested helmet r. within incuse square. *Weber* 1821
£2,500
The attribution to Lete of this type is, of course, beyond doubt because of the obv. legend.

1301 — Æ *trihemiobol* (?). Naked satyr squatting r.; two pellets in field. ℞. Incuse square, diagonally divided into four triangles. *B.M.C. 5.* 26   ..   ..   £125

1302 — — Naked satyr in kneeling-running attitude r. ℞. Quadripartite incuse square. *B.M.C. 5.* 29   ..   ..   £100

1303 **Neapolis** (founded by the Thasians to guard their mining interests on the mainland, Neapolis subsequently passed under Athenian control). 510-480 B.C. Æ *stater*. Gorgon's hd. facing, with tongue protruding. ℞. Incuse square, divided diagonally into four triangles. *B.M.C. 5.* 1   ..   ..   £1,250

1304 — — Similar, but with quadripartite incuse square of "mill-sail" pattern on *rev.* *B.M.C. 5.* 6 ..   ..   £900

1305   1308

1305 — Æ *drachm.* Similar; Λ in upper field to l. on *obv.* *B.M.C. 5.* 8   ..   ..   £250

1306 — Æ *trihemiobol* (?). Similar, but without letter in *obv.* field. *B.M.C. 5.* 12-13   £125

1307 **Therma** (better known by its later name of Thessalonika, this city is supposed to have been a colony of Corinth, hence the attribution to it of the following types depicting Pegasos). 510-480 B.C. Æ *tetradrachm.* Pegasos walking l. ℞. Quadripartite incuse square. *B.M.C. 5.,p.* 137, 4   ..   ..   £2,250

1308 — Æ *tetrobol.* Forepart of Pegasos flying r.; floral ornament above. ℞. Quadripartite incuse square. *B.M.C. 5.,p.* 138, 8-9   ..   ..   £240

1309 — Æ *hemiobol.* Similar, but without the floral ornament on *obv.* *B.M.C. 5.,p.* 138, 10-12   ..   ..   £45

1310   1311

1310 **Uncertain mints.** Æ *tetradrachm, circa* 490 B.C. Two archaic female figures stg. face to face, supporting between them an amphora; rose (?) in lower field to r. ℞. Quadripartite incuse square. *B.M.C. 5.,p.* 135, 1   ..   ..   £5,000

1311 Æ *didrachm, circa* 525 B.C. Archaic winged male figure (daimon), naked, in kneeling-running attitude r.; rose before. ℞. Quadripartite incuse square. *B.M.C. 5.,p.* 136, 2
£2,000

THRACO-MACEDONIAN TRIBES

1312 The Derrones. 500-480 B.C. Æ *dodekadrachm* (c. 40·5 gm.). ΔΕΡΡΟΝΙΚΟΝ. Two bulls walking l., drawing cart; in background, Ares, helmeted, stg. l., holding shield and spear. ℞. Quadripartite incuse square. *Price & Waggoner* 25, 26 .. .. £8,500

1313 — Æ *tetradrachm.* ΔΕΡΡΟΝΙΚΟΝ. Bull walking l. ℞. Quadripartite incuse square. *Price & Waggoner* 38 .. .. £3,500

1314 — Æ *tetrobol.* Forepart of bull kneeling l. ℞. Quadripartite incuse square. *Price & Waggoner* 39 .. .. £250

1315   1317

1315 *Circa* 475 B.C. Æ *dodekadrachm.* King seated in car drawn r. by two oxen; above, crested Corinthian helmet; below, rose. ℞. Triskeles; three palmettes in the angles. *B.M.C. 5., p.* 150, 1.. .. .. £6,500

1316 The Ichnai. 490-480 B.C. Æ *octadrachm* (c. 29·5 gm.). ΙΧΝΑΙΟΝ. Two bulls stg. l. side by side, the nearer with hd. lowered, the farther with hd. raised; between them, naked archaic male figure (Ares ?) l., his hands resting on the bulls. ℞. Wheel of four spokes within incuse square. *Price & Waggoner* 40-44.. .. .. £5,000

1317 After 480 B.C. Æ *stater.* ΙΧΝΑΙΟΝ (retrograde). Warrior l., wearing crested helmet and armour, restraining horse prancing l. ℞. Wheel of four spokes. *B.M.C. 5., p.* 76, 1
£1,500

3118   1321

1318 The Bisaltai. 475-465 B.C. Æ *octadrachm.* ΓΙΣΑΛΤΙΚΩΝ (partly retrograde). Naked warrior (Ares ?), holding two spears, stg. r. on far side of bridled horse r. ℞. Quadripartite incuse square. *B.M.C. 5., p.* 140, 2 .. .. £5,000

1319 — Æ *tetradrachm.* Horseman, wearing kausia and holding two spears, seated on horse pacing r. ℞. Quadripartite incuse square. *B.M.C. 5., p.* 142, 6 .. .. £2,000

1320 — Æ *octobol.* Similar to 1318, but without legend. *B.M.C. 5., p.* 141, 5 .. £275

1321 — Æ *tetrobol.* Similar to 1319. *B.M.C. 5., p.* 142, 7.. .. .. .. £225

The Bisaltai *continued*

1322 Mosses, king of the Bisaltai? Æ *octobol.* *Obv.* Similar to 1318, but without legend, and the warrior wears short chlamys. R. ΜΟΣΣΕΩ around raised quadripartite square; all within incuse square. *B.M.C. 5., p.* 143, 3 .. .. £500

The identification of Mosses is quite uncertain, and his connection with the Bisaltai has been questioned by Doris Raymond in 'Macedonian Regal Coinage to 413 B.C.', p. 115, note 14.

1322   1323

1323 **The Edones.** 475-465 B.C. Æ *octadrachm,* in the name of King Getas. Two bulls walking r. side by side, the farther with hd. raised; between them, naked male figure (Hermes ?) stg. r., holding two goads; traces of legend ΒΑΣΙΛΕV ΗΔΩΝΕΩΝ above and in ex., in fine letters. R. ΓΕΤΑ ΒΑΣΙΛΕV ΗΔΩΝΕΩΝ around raised quadripartite square; all within incuse square. *Weber* 1853 .. .. £7,500

Getas may have ruled over the Ichnai as well, as another type is known with reverse similar to 1316 above.

1324 **The Orreskioi.** 510-480 B.C. Electrum *stater.* Centaur stg. r., looking back, holding nymph in his arms. R. Deep incuse square, quartered. *B.M.C. 14. (Ionia), p.* 9, 42 £5,000

The attribution to this tribe is conjectural, though the type is clearly Thracian.

1325 — Æ *stater.* Centaur kneeling r., carrying in his arms a nymph l. who raises her r. hand in protest. R. Quadripartite incuse square, of 'swastika' form. *Price & Waggoner* 62-80 .. .. £750

1326   1329

1326 — — *Obv.* Similar, but with legend ΩΡΗΣΚΙΩΝ (retrograde). R. Quadripartite incuse square. *B.M.C. 5.* 5 .. .. £1,000

1327 — — *Obv.* As last. R. Crested helmet r. within incuse square. *Weber* 1797 £1,250

1328 — Æ *obol.* Bull kneeling l.; above, ΡΟ; to l., Η. R. Quadripartite incuse square. *Weber* 1799 .. .. £100

1329 475-465 B.C. Æ *octadrachm.* ΟΡΡΗΣΚΙΟΝ. Two bulls stg. r., side by side, the farther with hd. raised; between them, naked male figure (Hermes ?) stg. r., holding two spears. R. Quadripartite incuse square. *B.M.C. 5.* 2 .. .. £5,000

1330 — Æ *stater.* Male figure, bearded and wearing short chiton and kausia, stg. r., restraining horse prancing r.; ΩΡΗΣΚΙΟΝ before. R. Quadripartite incuse square. *B.M.C. 5.* 4 .. .. £2,500

1331 **The Zaielioi.** *Circa* 490 B.C. Æ *stater.* ΤΑΙΕΛΕΩΝ. Centaur with nymph, as 1325; pellet in field above. ℞. Quadripartite incuse square, of 'swastika' form. *B.M.C. 5., p.* 149, 1 ..   ..   £2,000

1332 **The Pernaioi.** *Circa* 490 B.C. Æ *stater.* Similar, but with *obv.* legend ΠΕΡΝΑΙΩΝ (retrograde), and with flower growing beneath Centaur; no pellet in field. *B.M.C. 5., p.* 148, 1 ..   ..   £2,000

1333 **The Dionysioi.** *Circa* 490 B.C. Æ *stater.* Similar to 1325, but with legend ΔΙΟΝΥ... (retrograde) on *obv.* *Babelon (Traité), pl. XLVI* £2,000

1334 **The Laiai.** *Circa* 490 B.C. Æ *stater.* Similar, but with legend ΛΑΕΙΤΙΚΟΝ (retrograde). *Price & Waggoner* 94 ..   ..   *(Unique)*

THRACE

1335 **Abdera** (originally a colony of Klazomenai, of 7th Century foundation, Abdera only rose to be a place of importance with an influx of refugees from Teos about 544 B.C.). 530-500 B.C. Æ *octadrachm.* Griffin seated l., r. foreleg raised; kantharos before. ℞. Rough quadripartite incuse square. *May (The Coinage of Abdera)* 11. *Weber* 2365
£5,500

1336 — Æ *tetradrachm.* Griffin seated l. on dotted exergual line. ℞. Same as last. *May* 15
£1,500

1337 — Æ *didrachm.* Griffin seated l. on plain exergual line, r. foreleg raised. ℞. Same as last. *May* 18 ..   ..   £450

1339   1342

1338 — Æ *obol.* Similar. *May* 27 ..   ..   £75

1339 500-480 B.C. Æ *octadrachm.* Griffin seated l. on abacus of column (?), r. foreleg raised; ΑΡΧ before. ℞. Quadripartite incuse square. *May* 50. *B.M.C. 3., p.* 228, 1a   £4,500

1340 — Æ *tetradrachm.* Similar, but with ΕΡ instead of ΑΡΧ on *obv.* *Price & Waggoner* 143. *(Not in May)* £1,750

1341 — Æ *drachm.* Griffin seated l. on short thick base, r. foreleg raised. ℞. Quadripartite incuse square. *May* 55 ..   ..   £200

1342 — Æ *obol.* Griffin seated l., r. foreleg raised very high. ℞. Same as last. *May* 57. *B.M.C. 3.* 18 ..   ..   £75

1343 **Maroneia** (named after Maron, a priest of Apollo, who features in the *Odyssey*, Maroneia was noted for the fine quality of its wine). 500-480 B.C. Æ *diobol*. Forepart of prancing horse l. R. Quadripartite incuse square. *Grose* 3942 ..   ..   £150

1344 — Æ *obol*. Horse trotting r.; pellet in field above. R. Same as last. *Grose* 3944   £100

1345   **1347**

1345 **Dikaia** (a coastal town and port situated east of Abdera). 515-490 B.C. Æ *stater*. Hd. of bearded Herakles r., of archaic style, clad in lion's skin. R. Incuse square divided diagonally into four triangles. *B.M.C. 3.* 1   ..   ..   £2,000

1346 — Æ *diobol*. Similar. *B.M.C. 3.* 2   ..   ..   £150

1347 490-480 B.C. Æ *distater*. *Obv.* Similar, but hd. to left. R. Quadripartite incuse square. *Weber* 2353   .. ..   £4,000

1348 **THRACIAN CHERSONESE: Cherronesos.** 500-480 B.C. Æ *tetradrachm*. Lion stg. r., looking back, one forepaw raised. R. Incuse square containing archaic hd. of Athena l., wearing helmet with large crest. *Weber* 2400   ..   ..   £4,500

1349   **1351**   **1356**

1349 — Æ *tetrobol*. Forepart of lion r., looking back, paws raised R. Quadripartite incuse square, the alternate depressions deeper. *B.M.C. 3.* 1 ..   ..   ..   £75

1350 — Æ *diobol*. Similar. *B.M.C. 3.* 2   ..   ..   £50

1351 **TAURIC CHERSONESE: Pantikapaion** (founded in the 6th Century, Pantikapaion was a colony of Miletos). 500-480 B.C. Æ *drachm* (*c.* 3·5 gm.). Lion's scalp facing. R. Quadripartite incuse square of 'swastika' pattern. *Weber* 2682   ..   £175

1352 — Æ *hemidrachm*. Similar. *Weber* 2683   ..   ..   ..   £125

1353 — Æ *obol*. Lion's scalp facing. R. Quadripartite incuse square. *Weber* 2684   £50

1354 — Æ *hemiobol*. Similar, but with pellet in each of the alternate quarters of the square. *B.M.C. 3., p.* 87, 5 (attributed to Apollonia) £35

ISLANDS OF THE THRACIAN SEA

1355 **SAMOTHRAKE** (i.e. the Thracian Samos; this island was the home of the famous mysteries of the Kabeiroi). 500-480 B.C. Æ *hemidrachm*. Sphinx seated l., r. forepaw raised. R. Quadripartite incuse square, the alternate depressions deeper. *Price & Waggoner* 61   ..   ..   £300

1355A — Æ *didrachm*. *Obv.* Similar, but with legend AΣ in field to l. R. Quadripartite incuse square, each quarter containing a raised granulated surface. *Schwabacher* (*Ein fund archaischen Münzen von Samothrake*), *pl.* 11, 1   ..   ..   £2,500

1356 **THASOS** (a rich and fertile island off the southern coast of Thrace, Thasos possessed prolific gold mines and had a controlling interest in many of the silver mines on the mainland). 520-510 B.C. Æ *stater* (lumpy fabric). Naked ithyphallic satyr in kneeling-running attitude r., carrying in his arms a struggling nymph who raises her r. hand in protest. R. Rough quadripartite incuse square. *B.M.C. 3.* 1 ..   ..   ..   £700

1357   1361

1357 510-490 B.C. Æ *stater* (flat fabric). Similar; the incuse square more clearly cut, but the divisions not plainly discernible, sometimes resulting in a 'swastika' pattern. *B.M.C. 3. 5. Weber* 2500. *Price & Waggoner* 100-126.. .. .. £400

1358 — Æ *drachm*. Similar. *B.M.C. 3.* 12. *Grose* 4200 .. .. £200

1359 — Æ *obol* (c. 0·65 gm.). Two dolphins swimming in opposite directions, one above the other, the one above to r.; three pellets in field . Ꝝ. Quadripartite incuse square, as 1357. *B.M.C. 3.* 18 .. .. £65

1360 — Æ *hemiobol* (c. 0·32 gm.). Dolphin r. Ꝝ. As last. *B.M.C. 3.* 23 .. £40

1361 490-480 B.C. Æ *stater*. Similar to 1357, but the incuse square is more regular, with the quadripartite divisions clearly visible. *B.M.C. 3.* 2. *Price & Waggoner* 127-8 £425

N.B. *None of these issues (1356-61) bears an inscription, and the attribution to Thasos is by no means certain. However, the known wealth of the Thasians and the extent of this coinage render it likely that the mint was situated on this island.*

Classical and Hellenistic Periods
MACEDONIAN CITIES

1362   1364

1362 **Akanthos.** 480-465 B.C. Æ *tetradrachm*. Bull kneeling l., looking back, attacked by lion r. on his back; above, ϴ; in ex., floral ornament. Ꝝ. Quadripartite incuse square. *B.M.C. 5.* 3. *Desneux (Les tetradrachmes d'Akanthos)* 79 .. .. .. £1,000

1363 — — Bull kneeling l., hd. raised, attacked by lion r. on his back; above, scallop shell. Ꝝ. Quadripartite incuse square. *B.M.C. 5.* 5. *Desneux* 88 .. .. .. £ 1,100

1363A — Æ *tetrobol*. Forepart of lion r., devouring prey; floral ornament above. Ꝝ. Quadripartite incuse square. *B.M.C. 5.* 10 .. .. £150

1364 465-424 B.C. Æ *tetradrachm*. *Obv.* Similar to 1363, but with ivy-leaf above. Ꝝ. AKANΘION around quadripartite linear square; all within incuse square. *B.M.C. 5.* 6. *Desneux* 93 .. .. £1,400

1365 — — *Obv.* Similar, but with ΔI on bull's rump and fish l. in ex.; nothing above. Ꝝ. Same as last. *Desneux* 103 (*Berlin*) £1,600

1366 — Æ *diobol*. Hd. of Athena r., wearing crested Athenian helmet. Ꝝ. AKAN in the four quarters of a quadripartite incuse square. *B.M.C. 5.* 20 .. .. .. £125

Akanthos *continued*

1367 424-380 B.C. *AR tetradrachm* (reduced weight, *c.* 14·5 gm.).   Bull kneeling l., hd. raised, attacked by lion r. on his back; beneath bull, EVK; wavy line in ex. R. ΑΚΑΝΘΙΟΝ around quadripartite linear square; all within incuse square. *B.M.C.* 5. 22. *Desneux* 118
                                                                                                    £1,250

1368 — — Bull kneeling l., hd. turned to face the spectator, attacked by lion r. on his back. R. ΑΚΑΝΘΙΟΝ on raised band around quadripartite linear square, each quarter of which contains a raised granulated surface; all within incuse square. *B.M.C.* 5. 28. *Desneux* 158..   ..   ..   £1,750

1367   1369   1372

1369 — *AR tetrobol.* Forepart of bull kneeling l., looking back; above, swastika. R. Shallow quadripartite incuse square. *B.M.C.* 5. 35   ..   ..   £75

1370 — *AR obol.* Laureate hd. of Apollo r. R. ΑΚΑΝΘΙΟΝ. Seven-stringed lyre. *B.M.C.* 5. 40, 41   ..   ..   £100

1371 *Bronze Coinage.* After *c.* 400 B.C. Æ 15. Hd. of Athena r., wearing crested helmet R. A K / A N in the four quarters of a wheel. *B.M.C.* 5. 42, 43..   ..   ..   £12

1372 — Æ 12. *Obv.* Similar, but hd. l. R. A K / A N in the four quarters of a linear square. *B.M.C.* 5. 47, 49   ..   ..   £10

1373 **Aineia.** After 424 B.C. *AR tetrobol.* Hd. of Aeneas l., of fine style and with short beard, wearing crested Corinthian helmet. R. ΑΙΝΕΑΣ around quadripartite linear square; all within incuse square. *B.M.C.* 5. 3, 4..   ..   ..   £250

1374 *Bronze Coinage.* Before 348 B.C. Æ 15. Bearded hd. of Ascanius, son of Aeneas, r., wearing Phrygian cap. R. ΑΙΝΕΙΑΤΩΝ. Bull butting r. *B.M.C.* 5. 5..   ..   £20

1373   1375

1375 **Amphaxitis** ('autonomous' issues in the time of the Macedonian kings Philip V and Perseus). *Circa* 196-168 B.C. *AR tetradrachm.* Macedonian shield with wheel-like ornaments, composed of six crescents joined by central pellet, at centre and in circle around. R. ΜΑΚΕΔΟΝΩΝ / ΑΜΦΑΞΙΩΝ above and below club r.; above, two monograms; all within oak-wreath. *Price (Coins of the Macedonians) pl. XIV*, 79   ..   ..   £1,500

1376 — Æ 22. Hd. of young Herakles r. in lion's skin. R. ΑΜΦΑ / ΞΙΩΝ above and below club r., within oak-wreath; monogram beneath. *B.M.C.* 5. 1, 2   ..   ..   £15

1377 **Amphipolis** (founded by the Athenians in 436 B.C. to protect their mining interests in the north, Amphipolis surrendered to the Spartan general Brasidas in 424. The city preserved its independence until 357 when it was captured by Philip II, King of Macedon). *Circa* 410-357 B.C. *N half stater.* Young male hd. l., bound with tainia. R. ΑΜΦΙΠ-ΟΛΙΤΕΩΝ on raised frame containing race-torch, to r. of which is small bunch of grapes. *Grose* 3203   ..   ..   £5,000

1378 — Æ *tetradrachm.* Hd. of Apollo three-quarter face to r., of vigorous classical style, laur. and with hair dishevelled. ℞. ΑΜΦΙΠΟΛΙΤΕΩΝ on raised frame containing race-torch; all within incuse square. *Jenkins (Ancient Greek Coins) no. 213/4* £7,500

1379 — — *Obv.* Similar, but of later, more delicate style; in field to r., forepart of dog l. ℞. Same as last, but with small Α in field to r. of race-torch. *B.M.C. 5. 1* .. £8,000

1380 — Æ *drachm.* Similar to 1378. *B.M.C. 5. 7* £600

1381 — Æ *tetrobol.* *Obv.* Similar, but hd. three-quarter face to *left.* ℞. Α Μ / Φ Ι above and below race-torch; all in laurel-wreath contained within incuse square. *B.M.C. 5. 8*
£400

1382 — Æ *obol.* Young male hd. r., bound with tainia. ℞. Α Μ / Ι Φ above and below dolphin r.; all in linear square contained within incuse square. *B.M.C. 5. 10* .. £125

| 1381 | 1383 | 1384 |

1383 196-168 B.C. ('autonomous' issues in the time of the Macedonian Kings Philip V and Perseus). Æ *tetrobol.* Macedonian shield with wheel-like ornament at centre composed of four crescents joined by central pellet. ℞. ΜΑΚΕ / ΔΟΝΩΝ above and below stern of galley; star in field above. *B.M.C. 5., p. 10, 19* £50

1384 — — Hd. of Mainad r., wreathed with vine-leaves and grapes. ℞. Similar to last, but without star, and with Μ in field to r. *B.M.C. 5., p. 10, 26* £45

1385 *Circa* 168 B.C. (struck on the occasion of the dissolution of the Macedonian monarchy and the establishment, by the Romans, of four separate Macedonian republics). Æ *tetradrachm.* Hd. of Zeus r., of the finest Hellenistic style, wearing oak-wreath. ℞. ΜΑΚΕΔΟΝΩΝ ΠΡΩΤΗΣ. Artemis Tauropolos, holding torches, reclining r. on bull prancing l., fillet over its hd.; monograms in lower field. *Historia Numorum, p. 238. Price (Coins of the Macedonians) pl. XIV, 81* .. .. - £7,000

1386 158-149 B.C. (from the reopening of the silver mines to the revolt of Andriscus). Æ *tetradrachm.* Macedonian shield, at centre of which bust of Artemis Tauropolos r., bow and quiver at her shoulder. ℞. ΜΑΚΕΔΟΝΩΝ / ΠΡΩΤΗΣ above and below club r.; in field above, ΗΡ monogram; beneath, Ν; all within oak-wreath, to l. of which, thunderbolt. *B.M.C. 5., p. 7, 5* £120

1387   1388

Ampipholis *continued*

1387 — Æ *tetrobol.* Macedonian shield, at centre of which MA / KE above and below club r.
R. Macedonian helmet l., with cheek-pieces; two monograms in field to l.; monogram and
trident to r. *B.M.C. 5., p.* 9, 11 ..   ..   £50

1388 149 B.C. (on the occasion of the Roman embassy to Andriscus). Æ *tetradrachm. Obv.*
Similar to 1386. R. LEG / MAKEΔONΩN above and below club r.; hand holding olive-
branch in field above; all within oak-wreath. *B.M.C. 5., p.* 17, 69 ..   ..   £500

1389   1390

1389 148 B.C. (on the defeat of Andriscus by the Roman general Metellus). Æ *tetradrachm.*
Obv. Similar, but Artemis wears a wreath of victory. R. MAKE / ΔONΩN above and below
club r.; monogram in field above; all within oak-wreath. *B.M.C. 5., p.* 16, 66 £500

1390 *Bronze Coinage.* Before 357 B.C. Æ 18. Laur. hd. of Apollo r. R. AM / ΦI above and
below race-torch; all within linear square. *B.M.C. 5.,* 11 ..   ..   ..   £12

1391 — Æ 11. Young male hd. r., bound with tainia. R. Similar to last, but AM / IΘ.
B.M.C. 5. 14 ..   ..   £8

1392   1394

1392 196-168 B.C. Æ 26. Hd. of young Dionysos r., wreathed with ivy. R. MAKE / ΔONΩN
above and below goat stg. r.; two monograms in field above, another to l.; AMΦI monogram to r. *B.M.C. 5., p.* 11, 32 ..   ..   £12

1393 — Æ 20. Laur. hd. of Apollo r. R. MAKE / ΔONΩN on either side of tripod surmounted
by laurel-sprays; AMΦI monogram in field to l. *B.M.C. 5., p.* 11, 37 ..   ..   £8

1394 168-149 B.C., and later. Æ 22. Diad. hd. of Artemis Tauropolos r., bow and quiver
at shoulder. R. AMΦIΠOΛITΩN. Two goats on their hind legs, contending, face to face.
B.M.C. 5. 36 ..   ..   £10

1395 — Æ 19. Hd. of young Herakles r. in lion's skin. R. — Centaur prancing r., hurling
stone and holding branch; monogram beneath. *B.M.C. 5.* 19 ..   ..   ..   £9

1396 — — Hd. of Poseidon r., wearing tainia. R. AMΦIΠO / ΛITΩN above and below club r.;
P in field above; all within oak-wreath. *B.M.C. 5.* 23 ..   ..   £8

1397 — — Hd. of young Dionysos r., wreathed with ivy.   Ɍ. ΑΜΦΙΠΟ / ΛΕΙΤΩΝ above and
below goat stg. r.   *B.M.C. 5.* 41 ..   ..   £8

1398 — Æ 15.   Hd. of young river-god Strymon r., horned and crowned with reeds.   Ɍ.
ΑΜΦΙΠΟ / ΛΙΤΩΝ above and below dolphin r.; monogram in field above; plough and
monogram beneath; all within oak-wreath.   *B.M.C. 5.* 31   ..   ..   ..   £7

1399   1401

1399 **Aphytis** (a city famous for its temple dedicated to Zeus Ammon).   Before 348 B.C.
Æ 17.   Hd. of Zeus Ammon, bearded and with ram's horns, three-quarter face to l.
Ɍ. ΑΦΥΤΑΙΩΝ.   Kantharos.   *B.M.C. 5.* 1   ..   ..   £20

1400 — — Hd. of Zeus Ammon r.   Ɍ. ΑΦΥ above two eagles stg. face to face; astragalos
between them.   *B.M.C. 5.* 3   ..   ..   £14

1401 After 168 B.C.   Æ 22.   Hd. of Zeus Ammon r.   Ɍ. ΑΦΥΤΑΙ.   Eagle stg. r., wings closed.
B.M.C. 5. 4 ..   ..   £12

    The Bottiaians—see below, under Pella and Spartolos.

1403   1405

1403 **Dikaia.**   *Circa* 475-450 B.C.   Æ *tetradrachm.*   Cow stg. r., its hd. turned back to lick
its r. hind leg, which is raised; above, dove and mouse r.; in ex., turtle r.   Ɍ. ΔΙΚΑΙΑ
above octopus; all within incuse square.   *Price (Coins of the Macedonians) pl. V,* 27
£4,000

1404 — Æ *tetrobol.*   Cock stg. r.   Ɍ. Octopus in shallow incuse square.   *Grose* 3199
£350

1405 Before 348 B.C.   Æ 17.   Hd. of nymph r., wreathed with corn.   Ɍ. ΔΙΚΑΙ ΟΠΟΛ.
Bull stg. r.   *Historia Numorum, p.* 214.   *Robinson and Clement (Olynthus excavation
report) p.* 281   ..   ..   £25

1405A **Herakleia Sintika.**   Late 5th Cent. B.C.   Æ *trihemidrachm?* (*c.* 4·9 gm.).   Herakles
kneeling l., wrestling with Nemean lion.   Ɍ. ΗΡΑΚΛΕΙΑ around quadripartite linear square
containing ΔΑΜ in three of its quarters; all within incuse square.   *Price (Coins of the
Macedonians) pl. VI,* 36   ..   ..   £750

1406 **Mende.**   480-465 B.C.   Æ *tetradrachm.*   ΜΙΝ.   Ithyphallic ass stg. r.; crow perched l.
on his back, pecking at his rump; in background, vine with bunch of grapes.   Ɍ. Four
incuse triangles arranged in "mill-sail" pattern.   *Weber* 1922 ..   ..   ..   £1,750

Mende *continued*

1407　465-424 B.C.　Æ *tetradrachm.* Dionysos reclining l. on back of ass stg. r., holding kantharos in r. hand; beneath, dog r.; before, crow perched r. on vine.　Ɍ. MENΔAION around vine with five bunches of grapes; all within shallow incuse square.　*B.M.C. 5.* 4
£2,000

1408　　　　　　　　　　　　　　　　1409

1408　— —　*Obv.* Similar, but without dog beneath ass; before, Seilenos advancing r., carrying wineskin and thyrsos.　Ɍ. MENΔAION around linear square within which vine with five bunches of grapes, cicada above; all within incuse square.　*Price (Coins of the Macedonians) pl. VI,* 33　..　..　..　..　..　..　..　..　..　£2,500

1409　— —　Dionysos reclining l., looking r., an back of ass stg. r.; he holds kantharos in r, hand; in ex., caduceus and NI.　Ɍ. Similar to last, but only four bunches of grapes on vine. and without cicada.　*Noe (The Mende/Kaliandra hoard)* 93　..　..　£2,250

1410　—　Æ *tetrobol.* Dionysos, naked, stg. r. behind ass r., which he holds by the ears. Ɍ. MENΔAION around crow stg. r.; all within incuse square.　*B.M.C. 5.* 6　..　£275

1411　— Æ *obol.*　Forepart of ass r.　Ɍ. Kantharos within incuse square.　*B.M.C. 5.* 7　£80

1412　　　　　　1413　　　　　　1416

1412　424-358 B.C.　Æ *tetrobol.* Dionysos reclining l. on back of ass walking r., holding kantharos in r. hand; beneath, astragalos; before, corn-grain.　Ɍ. MENΔAIH around amphora; all within incuse square.　*B.M.C. 5.* 10　..　..　..　£250

1413　*Bronze Coinage.*　Before 358 B.C.　Æ 15.　Hd. of young Dionysos r., wreathed with ivy. Ɍ. MENΔ.　Two amphorae; ivy-branch on either side.　*B.M.C. 5.* 12 ..　..　£15

1414　— Æ 10.　*Obv.* Similar.　Ɍ. MEN.　Amphora.　*B.M.C. 5.* 13　..　..　£10

1415　**Methone.**　Before 354 B.C.　Æ 10.　Female hd. l., hair rolled.　Ɍ. MEΘΩ.　Lion stalking r.　*Robinson and Clement (Olynthus excavation report)* p. 220　..　..　£15

1416　**Neapolis.**　411-348 B.C.　Æ *drachm.*　Gorgon's hd. facing, with tongue protruding. Ɍ. NEOΠ.　Young female hd. (Artemis Parthenos ?) r., laur., of exquisite style.　*B.M.C. 5.* 14 ..　..　..　..　..　..　..　..　£300

1417　— Æ *hemidrachm.*　Similar, but the female hd. on *rev.* is bound with cord.　*B.M.C. 5.* 17 ..　..　..　..　..　..　..　..　£125

1418　*Bronze Coinage.*　Before 348 B.C.　Æ 11.　Similar to last, but with bird behind the female hd. on *rev.*　*B.M.C. 5.* 33 ..　..　..　..　..　£10

1419　**Olophyxos** (situated near the summit of Mt. Athos).　*Circa* 375-348 B.C.　Æ 14. Hd. of nymph r., hair rolled and bound with band.　Ɍ. OΛOΦYΞIΩN.　Eagle stg. r., wings closed; all within linear square.　*Robinson and Clement (Olynthus excavation report)* p. 221　..　..　..　..　..　..　..　£20

1420 **Olynthos** (a colony of Chalkis, Olynthos became the centre of opposition to Athenian imperialism in the North, and was the headquarters of the Chalkidian League formed *c.* 432 B.C. The city was captured and destroyed by Philip II, king of Macedon, in 348 B.C.). Before 432 B.C. Æ *tetrobol.* Free horse, with loose rein, prancing r. ℞. OΛVN. Eagle flying upwards, hd. turned to r., holding serpent in beak and talons; all in incuse square. *B.M.C. 5.* 2   ..   ..   £250

1421 — Æ *diobol.* Forepart of prancing horse l. ℞. Eagle flying upwards, hd. turned to l., holding serpent in beak and talons; all in incuse square. *B.M.C. 5.* 4 ..   ..   £110

1422 — **coinage of the Chalkidian League** (432-348 B.C.). 432-420 B.C. Æ *tetrobol.* Laur. hd. of Apollo r., A behind. ℞. XAΛKIΔEΩN around lyre; all within incuse square. *Robinson-Clement* 14. *B.M.C. 5.* 14   ..   ..   £150

1423 — Æ *hemiobol.* Laur. hd. of Apollo l. ℞. XAΛ — KI either side of tripod; all within incuse square. *Robinson-Clement, pl. II, b.* *B.M.C. 5.* 28   ..   ..   ..   £40

1424   1425

1424 420-392 B.C. Æ *tetradrachm.* Laur. hd. of Apollo l., of the finest classical style. ℞. XAΛKIΔEΩN around lyre. *Robinson-Clement* 22. *B.M.C. 5.* 3   ..   ..   £1,500

1425 — Æ *tetrobol.* Laur. hd. of Apollo r. ℞. Similar to last. *Robinson-Clement* 66. *B.M.C. 5.* 18   ..   ..   £175

1426 — Æ *diobol.* Similar. ℞. XAΛKI — ΔEΩN either side of tripod. *Robinson-Clement, pl. IX, a-b* £90

1427 392-379 B.C. N *stater.* Laur. hd. of Apollo l. ℞. XAΛKIΔEΩN around lyre. *Robinson-Clement* I. *B.M.C. 5.* 1   ..   ..   £7,500

1428 — Æ *tetradrachm.* Similar. *Robinson-Clement* 70. *Weber* 1905 ..   ..   £1,250

1429   1430

1429 379-348 B.C. N *stater.* Laur. hd. of Apollo r. ℞. XAΛKIΔEΩN around lyre; EΠI EYΔΩPIΔA beneath. *Robinson-Clement* IV. *B.M.C. 5.* 2   ..   ..   £8,000

1430 — Æ *tetradrachm.* Similar, but with EΠI APIΣTΩNOΣ beneath lyre on *rev.* *Robinson-Clement* 134. *B.M.C. 5.* 10   ..   ..   £1,400

1431 — Æ *tetrobol.* Similar, but with EΠI OΛYMΠIO beneath lyre on *rev.* *Robinson-Clement* 110. *B.M.C. 5.* 25..   ..   ..   £200

1432 — Æ *diobol.* Laur. hd. of Apollo r. ℞. XAΛKI — ΔEΩN either side of tripod; in ex., EΠI ΣTPATΩNOΣ. *Robinson-Clement, pl. XIII, a-e.* *Weber* 1912   ..   ..   £110

Olynthos *continued*

1433 *Bronze Coinage.* Before 348 B.C.   Æ 16.   Laur. hd. of Apollo l.   R. ΧΑΛΚΙΔΕΩΝ.
Lyre.   *B.M.C. 5.* 31   ..   ..   £12

1434 — Æ 11.   Laur. hd. of Apollo r.   R. — Tripod.   *B.M.C. 5.* 32, 33 ..   ..   £8

1435 **Orthagoreia** (perhaps the same place as the earlier Stageira).   *Circa* 350 B.C.   Æ *stater.*
Hd. of Artemis r., quiver at shoulder.   R. ΟΡΘΑΓΟ — ΡΕΩΝ either side of facing helmet,
with cheek-pieces, surmounted by star; beneath, ΗΓ monogram.   *B.M.C. 5.* 1-4
£350

1436   1438

1436 — Æ *triobol.*   Hd. of Artemis three-quarter face to l., quiver at r. shoulder.   R. Similar
to last, but without monogram.   *B.M.C. 5.* 5   ..   ..   £175

1437 — Æ 14.   Laur. hd. of Apollo r.   R. Similar to last.   *B.M.C. 5.* 6 ..   ..   £9

1437A **Pelagonia** (capital of the fourth republic after the fall of the monarchy in 168 B.C.).
168-149 B.C.   Æ 22.   Laur. hd. of Zeus r.   R. ΜΑΚΕΔΟΝΩΝ / ΤΕΤΑΡΤΗΣ above and below
club r.; monograms in field above and beneath; all within oak-wreath.   *B.M.C. 5.,*
p. 8, 10   ..   ..   £30

1438 **Pella** (became the capital of the Macedonian kingdom under Archelaus, in succession to
Aigai.   Following the Roman conquest, in 168 B.C., Pella was the capital of the third
republic.   Its issues are often in the name of the Bottiaians, the original inhabitants of
the district in which Pella was situated).   196-168 B.C. ('autonomous' issues in the time of
the Macedonian Kings Philip V and Perseus).   Æ *triobol.*   Macedonian shield with wheel-
like ornament at centre composed of five crescents.   R. Stern of galley inscribed
ΒΟΤΤΕΑΤΩΝ.   *B.M.C. 5., p.* 64, 1 ..   ..   £75

1439   1441

1439 *Circa* 90-75 B.C.   Æ *tetradrachm.*   Hd. of Alexander the Great r., with horn of Ammon
and flowing hair; ΜΑΚΕΔΟΝΩΝ beneath, Β (reversed) behind.   R. AESILLAS / Q. above club
between money-chest and quaestor's chair; all within olive-wreath.   *Price* (*Coins of the
Macedonians*) *pl. XVI,* 84 ..   ..   £150

1440 *Bronze Coinage.*   196-168 B.C.   Æ 22.   Hd. of Athena r. in crested helmet.   R. ΒΟΤΤΕ /
ΑΤΩΝ above and beneath bull feeding r.   *B.M.C. 5., p.* 64, 5   ..   ..   ..   £12

1441 — — Hd. of Zeus r., wearing oak-wreath.   R. ΜΑΚΕ / ΔΟΝΩΝ above and below winged
thunderbolt; ΒΟΤ monogram beneath.   *B.M.C. 5., p.* 13, 48   ..   ..   ..   £12

1442 — Æ 20. Hd. of Pan r., pedum at his shoulder. ℞. вот monogram above two goats kneeling r.; all within oak-wreath. *B.M.C. 5., p.* 13, 46   ..   ..   ..   £14

1443 168-158 B.C. Æ 20. Hd. of Athena r., wearing richly ornamented crested helmet. ℞. ΓΑΙΟΥ ΤΑΜΙΟΥ. Bull feeding r.; monogram above, вот monogram beneath. *B.M.C. 5., p.* 18, 76 ..   ..   £12

1444 158-149 B.C., and later. Æ 22. *Obv.* Similar. ℞. Nike in galloping biga r.; star above, corn-ear beneath; in ex., ΠΕΛΛΗΣ. *B.M.C. 5.* 1, 2   ..   ..   ..   £10

1445   1447

1445 — — Bust of Pan r., pedum at his shoulder. ℞. ΠΕΛ — ΛΗΣ either side of Athena Alkidemos advancing r.; two monograms in field, to l. and to r. *B.M.C. 5.* 5..   £10

1446 — — Similar to 1443, but with *rev.* legend ΠΕΛΛΗΣ and two monograms in field, beneath bull and to r. *B.M.C. 5.* 17   ..   ..   £8

1447 — Æ 15. Laur. hd. of Apollo r. ℞. ΠΕΛ — ΛΗΣ either side of tripod. *B.M.C. 5.* 14   £8

1448   1449

1448 **Philippi** (following Philip II's capture of Amphipolis in 357 B.C. and his acquisition of the mining area of Mt. Pangaion, the mining centre of Krenides was given the name of Philippi in the king's honour). 357-330 B.C. *N stater.* Hd. of young Herakles r. in lion's skin. ℞. Tripod with fillet; ΦΙΛΙΠΠΩΝ to l., laurel-branch above, Phrygian cap to r. *B.M.C. 5.* 1   ..   ..   £6,000

1449 — Æ *tetradrachm.* *Obv.* Similar. ℞. Tripod with fillet; ΦΙΛΙΠΠΩΝ to r., laurel-branch above, club to l.; in ex., ΗΡΑ. *Weber* 1990   ..   ..   £1,400

1450 — Æ *drachm.* *Obv.* Similar. ℞. Tripod with fillet; ΦΙΛΙΠΠΩΝ to l., laurel-branch above, strung bow to r. *B.M.C. 5.* 4   ..   ..   £250

1451 — Æ *hemidrachm.* Similar. *B.M.C. 5.* 5   ..   ..   £100

1452 — Æ 18. *Obv.* Similar. ℞. Tripod; ΦΙΛΙΠΠΩΝ to r., club and barleycorn to l. *B.M.C. 5.* 8 ..   ..   £9

1453 **Potidaia** (captured by Philip II in 356 B.C.). Before 356 B.C. Æ 12. Hd. of Athena l. in Corinthian helmet. ℞. ΠΟΤΙΔ. Trident-head. *Robinson-Clement, p.* 307 *and pl. XXX*, 31   ..   ..   £14

1453A Pydna (originally a Greek foundation, Pydna early fell into the hands of the Macedonian kings, though it enjoyed two brief spells of autonomy in the first half of the 4th Cent.). 389-379 B.C. Æ 17. Hd. of young Herakles r. in lion's skin. ℞. ΠΥΔΝΑΙΩΝ. Eagle stg. r., attacking serpent held in talons. *B.M.C. 5.* 1-3 .. .. .. £12

1453B 364-357 B.C. Æ 17. Female hd. r., hair in sphendone. ℞. — Owl stg. r., hd. facing, on olive-branch. *B.M.C. 5.* 4 .. .. £14

1454 Spartolos (the original inhabitants of Bottiaia were expelled from their territory by the Macedonian kings in the 5th Cent. B.C. They settled near Olynthos, their chief city being Spartolos, though they retained the name of Bottiaians which appears on the coins. Evidence has recently come to light suggesting that some, if not all, of the bronze issues were produced by the Olynthos mint). Late 5th Cent. B.C. Æ tetrobol. Hd. of Demeter r., diad. and wreathed with corn. ℞. ΒΟΤΤΙΑΙΩΝ. Forepart of bull kneeling r.; all within incuse square. *B.M.C. 5., p.* 63, 1 .. .. £275

1455 Before 348 B.C. Æ 15. Laur. hd. of Apollo r. ℞. ΒΟΤΤΙΑΙΩΝ. Lyre. *B.M.C. 5., p.* 63, 2, 3 .. .. £14

1456 — Æ 12. Diad. hd. of Artemis r. ℞. Similar to last. *B.M.C. 5., p.* 63, 4 .. £10

1457   1458   1459

1457 Terone (captured by Philip II in 348 B.C.). *Circa* 480-455 B.C. Æ *tetrobol.* Oinochoë l. dividing Τ — Ε. ℞. Shallow quadripartite incuse square, the surface granulated. *B.M.C. 5.* 7, 8 .. .. £150

1458 *Circa* 404-380 B.C. Æ *tetrobol.* Seilenos kneeling l., drinking from oinochoë. ℞. Goat stg. r., ΤΕ in field; all within incuse square. *B.M.C. 5.* 9 .. .. .. £225

1459 — Æ *obol.* ΤΕ. Oinochoë l. ℞. Goat's hd. r., within incuse square. *B.M.C. 5.* 10 £65

1460 Before 348 B.C. Æ 15. Laur. hd. of Apollo r. ℞. Two oinochoës. *Robinson-Clement, p.* 315 *and pl. XXX*, 36 .. .. £15

1461 — Æ 12. *Obv.* Similar. ℞. Oinochoë r. *Robinson-Clement, pl. XXX*, 37.. £10

1462 Thessalonika (called Therma in an earlier period, the city received its more famous name in 315 B.C. in honour of Kassander's wife Thessalonika, daughter of Philip II. After the fall of the monarchy it became the capital of the second republic, established by the Romans). 158-149 B.C. Æ *tetradrachm.* Macedonian shield, at centre of which bust of Artemis Tauropolos r. ℞. ΜΑΚΕΔΟΝΩΝ / ΔΕΥΤΕΡΑΣ above and below club r.; two monograms in field, above and beneath; all within oak-wreath. *B.M.C. 5., p.* 8, 9 £750

1463 *Circa* 90-75 B.C. Æ *tetradrachm.* Hd. of Alexander the Great r., with horn of Ammon and flowing hair; MAKEΔONΩN beneath, Θ behind. R. AESILLAS / Q. above club between money-chest and quaestor's chair; all within olive-wreath. *B.M.C. 5., p.* 19, 81-83
£125

1464 — — *Obv.* Similar. R. Similar to last, but with SVVRA LEG. / PRO Q. instead of AESILLAS / Q. *B.M.C. 5., p.* 20, 87 .. .. £600

1465 *Bronze Coinage.* 158-149 B.C., and later. Æ 22. Hd. of young Dionysos r., wreathed with ivy. R. ΘΕΣΣΑΛΟ / NIKHΣ. Bunch of grapes; two monograms in field; all within ivy-wreath. *B.M.C. 5.* 3 .. .. £10

1466

1469

1466 — — *Obv.* Similar. R. ΘΕΣΣΑΛΟ / NIKHΣ. Goat stg. r.; monogram above. *B.M.C. 5.* 12 .. .. £8

1467 — — Hd. of Athena r., wearing richly ornamented crested helmet. R. ΘΕΣΣΑΛΟ / NIKHΣ. Bull feeding r. *B.M.C. 5.* 19 .. .. £9

1468 — Æ 17. Diad. hd. of Artemis r. R. ΘΕΣΣΑΛΟ / NIKEΩN. Strung bow behind quiver; monogram above. *B.M.C. 5.* 24 .. .. £8

1469 After 88 B.C. Æ *as.* Laur. hd. of Janus; I above. R. ΘΕΣΣΑΛΟ / NIKHΣ. Two Centaurs prancing, back to back, each holding branch. *B.M.C. 5.* 34 .. .. .. £15

1470

1472

1470 **Tragilos.** *Circa* 450-410 B.C. Æ *hemiobol* (*c.* 0·36 gm.). Ear of corn. R. TR / IA in the quarters of an incuse square. *B.M.C. 5., p.* 130, 1 .. .. £75

1471 — Æ *tetartemorion* (*c.* 0·18 gm.). Bunch of grapes. R. Similar to last. *B.M.C. 5., p.* 130, 4 .. .. £50

1472 *Bronze Coinage. Circa* 400-357 B.C. Æ 17. Hd. of Hermes r., wearing petasos. R. TRAIΛION. Rose; crescent in field to r. *B.M.C. 5., p.* 131, 11 .. .. £12

1473 — Æ 10. Hd. of Hermes l., wearing petasos. R. TP / AI in the four quarters of the field. *B.M.C. 5., p.* 131, 8 .. .. £8

1474 **Uranopolis** (founded on Mt. Athos by Alexarchos, brother of the Macedonian king
Kassander). *Circa* 300 B.C. Æ *didrachm*. Radiate globe, representing the sun. ℞.
OYPANIΔΩN. Aphrodite Urania seated facing on globe, holding long filleted sceptre sur-
mounted by ring; in field to l., conical object surmounted by star. *B.M.C. 5.* 1   £750

1475 — Æ 17. Eight-rayed star, representing the sun. ℞. OYPANIΔΩN ΠΟΛΕΩΣ. Aphrodite
Urania seated facing on globe, holding long sceptre. *B.M.C. 5.* 2   ..   ..   £15

1476 — Æ 13. Star and crescent, representing the sun and moon. ℞. Similar to last.
B.M.C. 5. 5 ..   ..   £12

THE MACEDONIAN KINGDOM (ALEXANDER I-PERDIKKAS III)
(For the later kings, including the empire of Philip II, Alexander the Great,
and their successors, see Vol. 2 of this catalogue, under 'Hellenistic Monarchies')

1477   1480

1477 **Alexander I,** 495-454 B.C. (king of Aigai, Alexander enlarged his kingdom after the
retreat of the Persians in 479 B.C., and was the first of the Macedonian rulers to place his
name on the coinage). Æ *octadrachm.* Warrior (Ares ?), holding two spears, stg. r. on
far side of bridled horse r. ℞. ΑΛΕΞΑΝΔΡΟ around raised quadripartite square; all within
incuse square. *Raymond* (*Macedonian regal coinage to* 413 B.C.) 50. *B.M.C. 5.* 1
                                                                              £4,500

1478 — Mounted warrior on horse pacing r., holding two spears. ℞. Similar to last. *Raymond* 1   ..   ..   £5,000

1479 Æ *tetradrachm.* *Obv.* Similar to last, but with A beneath horse on exergual line. ℞.
Forepart of goat kneeling r. in linear square; all within incuse square. *Raymond* 64.
Price, pl. X, 47   ..   ..   £2,000

1480 — *Obv.* Similar, but without A. ℞. Granulated incuse square containing crested helmet
r. *Raymond* 11. *Weber* 2010   ..   ..   £2,000

1481 — *Obv.* Similar, but horse pacing *left.* ℞. Goat's hd. r., caduceus behind, within linear
square; all in incuse square. *Raymond* 17. *B.M.C. 5., p.* 158, 1   ..   ..   £2,000

1482   1483   1484

1482 Æ *octobol.* Warrior stg. r. beside horse, as 1477. ℞. Inscription around quadripartite
square, as 1477. *Raymond* 75. B.M.C. 5. 4   ..   ..   £450

1483 Æ *heavy tetrobol* (*c*. 2·45 gm.).   Mounted warrior on horse pacing r., holding two spears. R. Forepart of lion r. within shallow incuse square.   *Raymond* 118.   *B.M.C. 5.*, *p*. 161, 19
£200

1484 Æ *light tetrobol* (*c*. 2·18 gm.).   Horse pacing r.; A on exergual line beneath.   R. Crested helmet r. in linear square within shallow incuse.   *Raymond* 83.   *B.M.C. 5.*, *p*. 160, 10
£200

1485 Æ *trihemiobol* (*c*. 1·05 gm.).   Hd. and forelegs of prancing horse l.   R. Similar to last. *Raymond, pl. IX, e*.   *B.M.C. 5.*, *p*. 160, 16   ..   ..   £140

1486 Æ *obol*.   Hd. of young warrior r., wearing petasos.   R. Quadripartite incuse square. *Raymond, pl. IX, d*.   *B.M.C. 5*. 15   ..   ..   £110

1487 **Perdikkas II**, 454-413 B.C. (son and successor of Alexander, Perdikkas was instrumental in the formation of the Chalkidian League, in 432, following the Athenian foundation of Amphipolis four years earlier).   Æ *light tetrobol*.   Horse pacing r.   R. Crested helmet r. in linear square within shallow incuse.   *Raymond* 143.   *B.M.C. 5.*, *p*. 159, 6 ..   £150

1488   1490

1488 — Similar, but with *double* linear square on *rev*.   *Raymond* 162.   *B.M.C. 5.*, *p*. 159, 8
£175

1489 — Similar to last, but horse *prancing* on *obv*., and with inscription ΠΕΡΔΙΚ around helmet on *rev*.   *Raymond* 173.   *B.M.C. 5*. 1   ..   ..   £225

1490 Æ *heavy tetrobol*.   Mounted warrior on horse pacing r., holding two spears; plant growing beneath.   R. Forepart of lion l. within shallow incuse square.   *Raymond* 198.   *B.M.C. 5.*, *p*. 161, 20   ..   ..   £150

1491 — Similar, but without plant on *obv*., and with caduceus r. above forepart of lion (which faces r.) on *rev*.   *Raymond* 203.   (*British Museum*) £150

1492 — Mounted warrior on horse prancing r., holding two spears; Π beneath.   R. Forepart of lion r. within shallow incuse square.   *Raymond* 217.   *B.M.C. 5.*, *p*. 161, 27   £200

1493 Æ *obol*.   Horse stg. r., tethered to a ring above.   R. ΠΕΡ around forepart of lion r.; all within shallow incuse square.   *Raymond, pl. XI, e*.   *B.M.C. 5*. 2   ..   ..   £110

1494   1496   1497

1494 **Archelaus,** 413-399 B.C. (son of Perdikkas, Archelaus transferred the capital of his Kingdom from Aigai to Pella.   He strengthened Macedonia by building roads and fortresses, but his philhellenic policies were cut short by his assassination after only 14 years of rule).   Æ *tetradrachm* (reduced weight, *c*. 10·6 gm.).   Mounted warrior on horse prancing l., holding two spears.   R. ΑΡΧΕΛΑΟ around forepart of goat kneeling r., looking back; all in linear square within incuse square.   *B.M.C. 5*. 1, 2   ..   ..   £750

1495 — Young male hd. (Ares?) r., wearing tainia.   R. ΑΡΧΕΛΑΟ above and before bridled horse stg. r., l. foreleg raised; all in linear square within incuse.   *B.M.C. 5*. 3-5   £300

1496 Æ *tetrobol*.   Free horse prancing l.   R. ΑΡΧΕΛΑΟ before and above crested helmet l.; all in double linear square within incuse.   *B.M.C. 5*. 7, 8   ..   ..   ..   £250

1497 Æ *diobol*.   Hd. of bearded Herakles r., in lion's skin.   R. Forepart of wolf r., devouring prey; club above, ΑΡΧ before.   *B.M.C. 5*. 10   ..   ..   £200

Archelaus *continued*

1498 Ɍ *obol* (?). *Obv.* Similar, but young Herakles, beardless. Ɍ. ΑΡΧΕ. Wolf's hd. r., club beneath. *B.M.C. 5.* 11 .. .. £125

1499 Æ 15 (Archelaus was the first Macedonian King to issue bronze coins). Lion's hd. facing. Ɍ. ΑΡΧΕ. Forepart of butting bull r. *Robinson-Clement, pl. XXXI,* 2 £25

1500 **Aeropos,** 396-392 B.C. (a period of confusion followed the assassination of Archelaus in 399 B.C. Eventually Aeropos, guardian of the dead King's infant son Orestes, seized the throne and reigned for about four years). Types similar to 1495, but with inscription ΑΕΡΟΠΟ on *rev.* *Berlin Cat.* II, *pl.* VIII, 75 .. .. £1,000

1501 Æ 15. Young male hd. r., wearing kausia. Ɍ. ΑΕΡ above horse stg. r. *Price, pl.* X, 53 £25

1502   1504   1507

1502 Æ13. *Obv.* Similar. Ɍ. ΑΕΡΟ above forepart of lion r. *B.M.C. 5.* 2 .. £20

1503 **Amyntas II,** 392-390 B.C. (an illegitimate son of Archelaus). Ɍ *tetradrachm.* Types similar to 1495, but with inscription ΑΜΥΝΤΑ on *rev.* *B.M.C. 5.* 1 .. .. £600

1504 Æ 13. Young male hd. r., bare. Ɍ. ΑΜΥΝΤΑ above Corinthian helmet r. *B.M.C. 5.* 3, 4 £20

1505 **Pausanias,** 390-389 B.C. (son of Aeropos). Ɍ *tetradrachm.* Young male hd. (Ares ?) r., wearing tainia. Ɍ. ΠΑΥΣΑΝΙΑ above and before free horse stg. r., caduceus on its hind-quarter; all in linear square within incuse. *B.M.C. 5.* 1 .. .. .. £500

1506 Æ 15. *Obv.* Similar. Ɍ. ΠΑΥΣΑΝΙΑ. Forepart of boar r. *Weber* 2031 .. £20

1507 Æ 17. — Ɍ. — Forepart of lion r. *B.M.C. 5.* 4 .. .. .. £20

1508   1509

1508 **Amyntas III,** 389-383 and 381-369 B.C. (a great-grandson of Alexander I, Amyntas dethroned the usurper Pausanias in 389 B.C. He was temporarily expelled from his Kingdom by the Illyrians in 383, but returned two years later with Spartan assistance). Ɍ *tetradrachm* (often plated). Hd. of bearded Herakles r., in lion's skin. Ɍ. ΑΜΥΝΤΑ above and before free horse stg. r.; all in linear square within incuse. *B.M.C. 5.* 1-4 £300

Martin Price, in 'Coins of the Macedonians' (p. 21), makes the interesting suggestion that this type belongs to the reign of the infant Amyntas IV (359-357 B.C.), for whom Philip II was regent. This can scarcely be considered proven, however, and the style of the coins seems to be more akin to the issues of the early part of the 4th Cent. B.C.

1509 Ɍ *tetradrachm.* Mounted warrior on horse prancing r., brandishing spear; sometimes with caduceus on horse's hind-quarter. Ɍ. ΑΜΥΝΤΑ above lion stg. l., holding in his jaws a broken spear, the point of which pierces his r. foot. *B.M.C. 5.* 14-16 .. £450

1510   1511

1510 Ɍ *triobol.* Hd. of young Herakles r., in lion's skin. Ɍ. ΑΜΥΝΤΑ. Eagle stg. l., looking back, wings closed; all within linear square. *B.M.C. 5.* 5-8 .. .. .. £175

1511 Æ 13. Hd. of bearded Herakles r., in lion's skin. Ɍ. ΑΜΥΝΤΑ. Forepart of boar r.; above, club r. *B.M.C. 5.* 11 .. .. £12

1512 Æ 15. Hd. of young Herakles r., in lion's skin. R. AMYNTA above eagle stg. r., wings closed, devouring serpent held in talons. *B.M.C. 5.* 17-22 .. .. .. £12

1513 Æ 10. *Obv.* Similar. R. AMYNTA. Bow and club, crossed. *B.M.C. 5.* 23 .. £10

1514 1515

1514 **Perdikkas III,** 365-359 B.C. (Amyntas III's son, Alexander II, was assassinated by Ptolemy within a year of coming to the throne. Ptolemy then ruled as guardian for Alexander's brothers Perdikkas III and Philip II, until the former murdered him, in 365 B.C. Perdikkas was killed fighting the Illyrians six years later, to be succeeded by his brother Philip, an event of momentous importance for the future of the Greek World). Æ *tetradrachm.* Hd. of young Herakles r., in lion's skin. R. ΠΕΡΔΙΚΚΑ. Free horse trotting r.; beneath, club r. *B.M.C. 5.* 1.. .. .. £400

1515 Æ 20. *Obv.* Similar. R. ΠΕΡΔΙΚ / ΚΑ above and below lion stg. r., holding broken spear in his jaws. *B.M.C. 5.* 2, 3 .. .. £17

1516 Æ 15. —R. ΠΕΡΔΙΚΚΑ. Eagle stg. l., looking back, wings closed. *B.M.C. 5.* 8 £15

[For the later Macedonian Kings, Philip II to Perseus, see Vol. 2 of this catalogue, under 'Hellenistic Monarchies'].

KINGDOM OF PAEONIA

(In the troubled period following the death of Perdikkas III, in 359 B.C., the Paeonians asserted their independence of the Macedonian Kingdom and managed to retain their freedom until 286 B.C.).

1517 1519

1517 **Lykkeios,** *c.* 359-340 B.C. Æ *tetradrachm.* Laur. hd. of Apollo r. R. ΛΥΚΚΕΙΟΥ. Herakles, naked, stg. l., fighting with lion, upright, r., which he is about to club; in field to r., bow and quiver. *B.M.C. 5.* 1, 2 .. .. £750

1518 — Laur. hd. of Zeus r. R. Similar to last. *Historia Numorum, p.* 236. *Glendining-Seaby auction,* 11 Dec. 1974, *lot* 33.. .. .. £800

1519 Æ *drachm.* Laur. hd. of Apollo r. R. ΛΥΚΚΕ / ΙΟΥ above and below lion running r. on bent exergual line; crescent beneath lion. *B.M.C. 5.* 3 .. .. .. £300

1520 **Patraos,** *c.* 340-315 B.C. Æ *tetradrachm.* Laur. hd. of Apollo r., with short hair. R. ΠΑΤΡΑΟΥ (sometimes retrograde). Armed warrior on horse prancing r., spearing fallen enemy, who holds spear and shield; bell in field to l. *B.M.C. 5.* 4 .. £125

1521

1522

Patraos *continued*

1521 Æ *drachm.* Young male hd. r., wearing tainia. ℞. ΠΑΤΡΑΟΥ. Forepart of running boar r.; beneath, monogram. *B.M.C. 5.* 13 .. .. £175

1522 Æ *tetrobol. Obv.* Similar to 1520. ℞. Eagle, wings closed, stg. r.; ΠΑΤΡΑΟΥ before, monogram behind. *B.M.C. 5.* 16 .. .. £150

1523 **Audoleon**, *c.* 315-286 B.C. Æ *tetradrachm.* Hd. of Athena three-quarter face to r., wearing triple-crested helmet. ℞. ΑΥΔΩΛΕΟΝΤΟΣ. Free horse trotting r.; monogram beneath. *B.M.C. 5.* 4-6 .. .. £650

1524   1525

1524 — (Attic standard, *c.* 17 gm., issued after 305 B.C.). Hd of young Herakles r., in lion's skin. ℞. ΑΥΔΩΛΕΟΝΤΟΣ ΒΑΣΙΛΕΩΣ. Zeus seated l., holding eagle and sceptre; monogram in field to l. *B.M.C. 5.* 19 .. .. £1,250

1525 Æ *didrachm.* Hd of Athena r., in crested Corinthian helmet. ℞. Similar to 1523, but horse bridled. *B.M.C. 5.* 9 .. .. £350

1526 Æ *drachm.* Similar to 1523, but hd. of Athena is three-quarter face to *left. B.M.C. 5.* 13, 14 .. .. £175

1527 Æ *tetrobol.* Similar to 1523, but with *rev.* type forepart of galloping free horse r. *B.M.C. 5.* 17 .. .. £140

1528 Æ 16. Laur. hd. of Apollo r. ℞. ΒΑΣΙΛΕΩΣ / ΑΥΔΩΛΕΟΝΤΟΣ above and below forepart of lion running r., looking back at star. *Weber* 2247 .. .. £20

N.B. The coinage of the Paeonian Kings was extensively imitated by the Celtic tribes of the interior—see, for example, nos. 198 and 199 above.

THRACE

1529   1530

1529 SOUTHERN THRACE: Abdera. *Circa* 480-465 B.C. Æ *tetradrachm.* ΣΜΟΡ. Griffin seated l., r. foreleg raised; dancing satyr before. ℞. Shallow quadripartite incuse square. *May (The coinage of Abdera)* 110. *B.M.C. 3.* 4 .. .. .. £1,600

1530 — Æ *drachm.* ΔΕΟ. Griffin seated l., r. foreleg raised. ℞. Shallow quadripartite incuse square. *May* 93. *B.M.C. 3.* 11 .. .. £200

1531 — Æ *triobol.* *Obv.* Similar, but without legend; curved wing. ℞. Bull's hd. and shoulders l. within incuse square. *May* 114. *Grose* 3998 .. .. .. £150

1532 — — *Obv.* As last. ℞. Lion's scalp facing within incuse square. *May* 115. *Grose* 3996 £125

1533 — Æ *obol.* *Obv.* As last. ℞. Rough quadripartite incuse square. *May* 120. *B.M.C. 3.* 14 .. .. £75

1534 — — Griffin striding l. ℞. Eagle's hd. l. within incuse square. *May* 125 (*British Museum*) £90

1535   1539

1535 *Circa* 465-450 B.C. Æ *tetradrachm.* Griffin seated l., r. foreleg raised; before, scarab downwards, dragging ball after it. ℞. ΕΠΙ ΦΙΤΤΑΛΟ around quadripartite linear square; all within shallow incuse square. *May* 126. *B.M.C. 3.* 23 .. .. .. £2,250

1536 — — ΚΑΛΛΙΔΑΜΑΣ. Griffin seated l. on tunny-fish, r. foreleg raised. ℞. ΑΒΔΗΡΙΤΕΩΝ around quadripartite linear square; all within shallow incuse square. *May* 148. *B.M.C. 3.* 19 .. .. £2,000

1537 — Æ *triobol.* Similar to 1531, but bull's hd. to *right* on *rev.* *May* 188. *Grose* 3997 £150

1538 — Æ *hemiobol.* Forepart of griffin l., both forelegs raised. ℞. Scallop shell within incuse square. *May* 198. *Grose* 4000 .. .. £50

1539 *Circa* 440-410 B.C. Æ *tetradrachm* (wt. reduced to *c.* 14 gm.). Griffin springing l. ℞. ΜΕΛΑΝΙΠΠΟΣ around linear square containing hd. of Athena r., in crested helmet wreathed with olive; all within incuse square. *May* 217. *B.M.C.* 27 .. £3,000

1540   1543

Abdera continued

1540 — — *Obv.* Similar. ℞. ΝΙΚΟΣΤΡΑΤΟΣ around linear square containing naked warrior advancing r., with spear and shield; all within incuse square. *May* 219. *B.M.C. 3.* 28
£3,000

1541 — *R tetrobol.* Griffin rearing l. ℞. ΑΝΑΞΙΔΙΚΟΣ around linear square containing goat's hd. l.; all within incuse square. *May* 210. *B.M.C. 3.* 40 .. .. .. £200

1542 — *R triobol.* Similar to 1531, but Griffin's wing is pointed. *May* 244. *B.M.C. 3.* 50
£150

1543 *Circa* 410-385 B.C. *R stater* (*c.* 12·5 gm.). Griffin springing l. ℞. ΔΙΟΝΥΣΑΣ around hd. of bearded Dionysos r., wreathed with ivy; all in linear frame within incuse square. *May* 287 (*British Museum*) £2,000

1544 — — *Obv.* Similar, but with ΑΒΔΗΡΙ above. ℞. ΠΥ / ΘΩΝ either side of tripod; all within shallow incuse square. *May* 345. *B.M.C. 3.* 32 .. .. .. £2,250

1545   1548

1545 — *R half stater.* ΑΒΔΗΡΙΤΕΩΝ. Griffin seated l., r. foreleg raised. ℞. ΕΠΟΡΧΑΜΟ around linear square containing lion stg. r.; all within shallow incuse square. *May* 256. *B.M.C. 3.* 36 .. .. £750

1546 — *R tetrobol.* Griffin rearing l., ΑΒΔ behind. ℞. ΕΠΙ ΠΡΩΤΕΩ around three sides of linear square containing three stalks of barley; all within shallow incuse square. *May* 356. *B.M.C. 3.* 45 .. .. £225

1547 — *R diobol.* Griffin rearing l. ℞. Ram's hd. l.; ΚΛΕ above, ΑΝ (retrograde) below; all within shallow incuse square. *May* 303. *B.M.C. 3., p.* 231, 52a £110

1548 *Circa* 385-375 B.C. *R stater* (wt. reduced to *c.* 11·2 gm.). ΑΒΔΗΡΙ above Griffin seated l. ℞. ΠΟΛΥΚΡΑΤΗΣ (partly retrograde) behind Artemis stg. r., holding laurel-branch and bow and arrow, stag r. at her side; all within incuse square. *May* 458. *B.M.C. 3., p.* 231, 52b £1,750

1549 — *R hemidrachm.* Griffin springing l. ℞. ΜΟΛΠΑΓΟΡΗΣ around linear square containing hd. of young Dionysos r., wreathed with ivy. *May* 410 (*British Museum*) .. £200

1550 *Circa* 373-360 B.C. *N half stater.* ABΔHPITEΩN behind laur. hd. of Apollo r. ℞.
   EΠI / IKEΣIOY above and below Griffin seated l.   *May* 463 (*Oxford*) ..   .. (*Unique*)

1551   1553

1551 — *R stater.* EΠI / ΠAYΣANIΩ above and below Griffin seated l. ℞. ABΔHPI / TEΩN
   either side of laur. hd. of Apollo r.; all within shallow incuse square. *May* 481. *B.M.C.*
   3. 53   ..   .. £750
1552 — *R hemidrachm.* EΠI ΦA / NEΩ above and below Griffin rearing l. ℞. ABΔHPITEΩN
   around linear square containing laur. hd. of Apollo r. *May* 495. *B.M.C. 3. 55*   £175
1553 *Circa* 360-347 B.C. *R stater* (wt. further reduced to *c.* 10·2 gm.). ABΔH / PITEΩN above
   and below Griffin seated l. ℞. EΠI IΠΠΩ / NAKTOΣ either side of laur. hd. of Apollo r.,
   scallop-shell beneath. *May* 543. *B.M.C. 3. 64* £500
1554 — *R hemidrachm. Obv.* Similar. ℞. EΠI ΔIONYΣAΔOΣ around linear square containing
   laur. hd. of Apollo r. *May* 536. *B.M.C. 3. 72* £150

1555   1557

1555 *Bronze Coinage.* 410-385 B.C. Æ 16. Griffin springing l. ℞. EΠI MANΔPΩNOΣ. Hd.
   of young river-god (?) r. *May* 281 (*British Museum*) £17
1556 — Æ 13. *Obv.* Similar. ℞. ΠPΩ / THΣ either side of stalk of barley. *May* 375   £12
1557 385-375 B.C. Æ 10. *Obv.* Similar. ℞. ΠEIΘEΣIΛEΩΣ. Eagle stg. r., attacking serpent
   held in talons. *May* 421. *B.M.C. 3. 87* £10
1558 373-360 B.C. Æ 15. *Obv.* Similar. ℞. ABΔHPITEΩN around laur. hd. of Apollo r.; all
   within circular incuse. *May* 462. *B.M.C. 3. 79* £10
1559 360-347 B.C. Æ 10. Griffin seated l., r. foreleg raised. ℞. EΠI ΔIONYΣAΔOΣ around
   quadripartite linear square, with pellet in each quarter. *B.M.C. 3. 85*   .. £8
1560 **Agathopolis.** 4th Cent. B.C. Æ 17. Young male hd. r., bound with tainia. ℞.
   AΓAΘO. Owl stg. r.; spear-head r. beneath. *B.M.C. 3. 1, 2* £20

1561 **Aigospotamoi** (i.e. *the goat's river*; the scene of the great Athenian naval defeat by
   Lysander at the end of the Peloponnesian War). 4th Cent. B.C. Æ 20. Hd. of Demeter
   l., wearing wreathed and ornamented kalathos. ℞. AIΓOΣΠO. Goat stg. l. *B.M.C. 3. 2*
   £22

              1562   1565

1562 **Ainos** (a prosperous city and trading centre, situated on a peninsula at the mouth of the
river Hebros). *Circa* 474-449 B.C. Æ *tetradrachm.* Hd. of youthful Hermes r.,
wearing petasos ornamented with row of beads above brim. Ɍ AINI above goat walking r.;
crescent and ivy-leaf before; all within incuse square. *May (Ainos, its history and
coinage)* 54. *B.M.C. 3.* 2 ..   ..   £3,000

1563 — Æ *drachm.* Similar, but with amphora before goat on *rev. May* 33. *B.M.C. 3.* 6
                                                                              £600

1564 — Æ *diobol.* *Obv.* Similar. Ɍ. A-I divided by caduceus placed diagonally across incuse
square. *May* 76 (*British Museum*) £200

1565 *Circa* 435-405 B.C. Æ *tetradrachm.* Similar to 1562, but of later style, and with
caduceus before goat on *rev. May* 254 (*British Museum*) £2,000

1566 — Æ *tetrobol.* *Obv.* Similar. Ɍ. AIN above goat stg. r.; bipennis (double-axe) before.
May 120. *B.M.C. 3.* 7   ..   ..   £400

              1567   1568

1567 — Æ *diobol.* Similar to last, but with club before goat on *rev. May* 137 (*British
Museum*) £175

1568 *Circa* 405-357 B.C. Æ *tetradrachm.* Hd. of youthful Hermes facing, inclined slightly
to l., wearing petasos ornamented with row of beads above brim. Ɍ. AINION above goat
stg. r.; trophy before; all within shallow incuse square with rounded corners. *May* 381.
B.M.C. 3. 17   ..   ..   £4,000

              1569   1571

1569 —— Æ *tetrobol.* Similar, but with hydria instead of trophy on *rev.*, and the goat leans
forward. *May* 354. *Weber* 2317. (*British Museum*) £500

1570 — Æ *diobol.* Similar, but with corn-grain instead of hydria on *rev.*, and with legend
AINI. *May* 335 (*British Museum*)..   ..   ..   £225

1571 *Circa* 357-342 B.C. Æ *drachm.* Hd of youthful Hermes three-quarter face to r.,
wearing broad petasos upturned behind. Ɍ. High-backed throne l., surmounted by
cult-image of Hermes Perpheraios l.; AINION to r.; kantharos to l. *May* 438. *B.M.C. 3.*
23   ..   ..   £750

1572 *Bronze Coinage.* 400-342 B.C. Æ 14. Hd of Hermes l., in close-fitting petasos.
Ɍ. Caduceus; A-I / NI in field, hydria to r. *May* 5   ..   ..   £14

1573 — Æ 12. Similar, but hd. to r. Ɍ. Caduceus; A-I / N-I in field. *May* 1   ..   £12

1574   1576

1574 280-200 B.C.   Æ 23.   Hd of Hermes r., wearing wide petasos.   R. Caduceus; A-I / N-I /
   O-N in field, ear of corn to r.   *B.M.C. 3*. 32   ..   ..   £18

1575 2nd-1st Cent. B.C.   Æ 23.   Hd. of Poseidon r., bound with tainia; monogram beneath.
   R. AINIΩN.   Hermes, naked, stg. l., holding purse and caduceus; before, flaming altar.
   B.M.C. 3. 45   ..   ..   £12

1576 **Alopekonnesos** (on the western shores of the Chersonese).   Before *c.* 341 B.C.   Æ 14.
   Hd. of young Dionysos r., wreathed with ivy.   R. Kantharos; AΛΩ in field, club to l.
   B.M.C. 3. 1 ..   ..   £18

1577 **Bisanthe** (a colony of Samos, situated on the European coast of the Propontis, west of
   Perinthos).   After *c.* 280 B.C.   Æ 20.   Veiled hd. of Demeter r.   R. BIΣAN / ΘHNΩN
   within corn-wreath.   *Weber* 2541 ..   ..   £14

1578 — Æ 15.   Hd. of Athena r., in Corinthian helmet.   R. BI.   Owl stg. r.   *B.M.C. 3*. 1   £12

1579   1580

1579 **Byzantion** (a prosperous city, through its control of the vital grain trade from the Black
   Sea, Byzantion was founded by Megarian colonists about 657 B.C. and was besieged by
   Philip of Macedon, 340/339 B.C.).   416-357 B.C.   Æ *drachm* or *siglos* (*c.* 5·4 gm.).   Cow
   stg. l., on dolphin l., r. foreleg raised; above, ΠY.   R. Incuse square of "mill-sail" pattern.
   B.M.C. 3. 1-8   ..   ..   £100

1580 357-340 B.C.   Æ *tetradrachm* (*c.* 15·3 gm.).   *Obv.* Similar, but also with monogram to l.,
   between cow's forelegs.   R. Quadripartite incuse square, with granulated surface.
   B.M.C. 3. 12   ..   ..   £450

1581 — Æ *drachm* (*c.* 3·8 gm.).   Similar to 1579, but also with trident between cow's forelegs
   on *obv.*   *B.M.C. 3*. 13, 14 ..   ..   £75

1582 — Æ *tetrobol* (*c.* 2·5 gm.).   Similar to 1579.   *B.M.C. 3*. 15, 16   ..   ..   £50

1583 — Æ *hemidrachm* (*c.* 1·9 gm.).   Forepart of advancing cow l. on dolphin; above, ΠY.
   R. Ornamented trident-head.   *B.M.C. 3*. 23, 24   ..   ..   £40

1584 — Æ *diobol* (*c.* 1·2 gm.).   Similar to 1579.   *B.M.C. 3*. 17-21   ..   ..   £30

1585 After *c.* 280 B.C. (at this time the Byzantines were subject to continual threats by Gaulish
   invaders, who were bought off by the payment of huge annual tributes.   The impoverished
   city had to resort to countermarking foreign coins in place of a proper currency).   Æ
   drachm of Alexander the Great of Macedon, *obv.* hd. of young Herakles, *rev.* Zeus enthroned, countermarked on the *obv.* with ΠY above prow of galley r., within circular
   incuse   ..   ..   ..   · £65

1586   1587

Byzantion *continued*

1586 — Æ *tetradrachm* of Ptolemy I of Egypt, *obv*. diad. hd. of Ptolemy, *rev*. eagle on thunderbolt, countermarked on the *obv*. with monogram incorporating mint mark and magistrate's
name, within circular incuse. *B.M.C. 3., p.* 110, 1-3 .. .. £200

1587 *Circa* 250-200 B.C. Æ *tetradrachm*. Veiled hd. of Demeter r., wreathed with corn.
R. Poseidon seated r. on rocks, holding aplustre and trident; π behind, monogram before,
ΕΠΙ ΟΛΥΜΠΙΟΔΩΡΟΥ beneath. *B.M.C. 3.* 26 .. .. £900

1588 — Æ *octobol* (*c.* 5·3 gm.). Similar; different monogram on *rev*. *B.M.C. 3.* 27 £350

1589 2nd Cent. B.C. Æ *tetradrachm*, restoring the type of King Lysimachos of Thrace.
Hd. of deified Alexander the Great r., with horn of Ammon. R. ΒΑΣΙΛΕΩΣ / ΛΥΣΙΜΑΧΟΥ
either side of Athena seated l., holding Nike; monogram in field to l., ΒΥ on throne, trident
l. beneath. *Müller (Die Münzen des thrakischen Königs Lysimachos)* 160. *Jenkins
(Ancient Greek Coins)* 677/8 .. .. £150

1590 — *N stater*. Similar; different monogram on *rev*. *Müller* 162 .. .. £800

1591 *Bronze Coinage*. Before 340 B.C. Æ 17. Cow stg. l. on dolphin l.; ΠΥ above. R.
Trident between two dolphins. *B.M.C. 3.* 28 .. .. £14

1592 — Æ 14. Cow's hd. l. R. Three dolphins around ΠΥ. *B.M.C. 3.* 29 .. £12

1593 — Æ 10. Similar, but cow's hd. r. *B.M.C. 3.* 30 .. .. .. £10

1594 *Circa* 250-200 B.C., and later. Æ 24. Laur. hd. of Apollo r. R. Tripod; ΕΠΙ ΜΕΝΙΣΚΟΥ
to l., ΠΥ and monogram to r. *B.M.C. 3.* 31 .. .. £14

1595 — — Veiled hd. of Demeter r., wreathed with corn. R. ΒΥΙΑΝΤΙΩΝ. Cornucopiae;
to l., ΕΠΙ ΕΚΑΤΟΔΩΡ. *B.M.C. 3.* 34, 35 .. .. £16

1596 — Hd. of Poseidon r., wearing tainia. R. ΕΠΙ / ΔΙΟΣΚΟΥΡΙ above and below
trident l.; π in field. *B.M.C. 3.* 32, 33 .. .. £15

1597 — Æ 19. Laur. hd. of Apollo l. R. Obelisk of Apollo Karinos; ΕΠΙ / ΦΩΚΡΙ to l.,
ΒΥΙΑΝ to r. *Weber* 2564 .. .. £12

1596   1598

1598 **Kardia** (an important city of the Chersonese, Kardia was originally a colony of Miletos.
It was destroyed by Lysimachos in 309 B.C.). *Circa* 350 B.C. Æ 20. Hd. of Demeter l.,
wreathed with corn. R. ΚΑΡΔΙΑ above lion l., gnawing at its prey; in ex., corn-grain and
star. *B.M.C. 3.* 3 .. .. £12

1599 — — Hd. of Demeter three-quarter face to l., wreathed with corn. ℞ ΚΑΡΔΙΑ above
lion stg. l., looking back; corn-grain beneath. *B.M.C. 3.* 11 ..   ..   ..   £15

1600 — Æ 13. Lion r. ℞. ΚΑΡ / ΔΙΑ and corn-grain; all within linear square. *B.M.C. 3.* 14
£10

1601 —— Similar, but lion's *head* only on *obv.* *B.M.C. 3.* 17 ..   ..   ..   £10

1602   1605   1607

1602 **Cherronesos** (possibly the same place as the later Kardia). 400-350 B.C. Æ *hemidrachm* (*c.* 2·4 gm.). Forepart of lion r., looking back, paws raised. ℞. Quadripartite
incuse square, the alternate depressions deeper and each containing pellet. *B.M.C.
3., p.* 183, 8, 9 ..   ..   £45

1603 — — Similar; A above pellet and bunch of grapes in the alternate depression. *B.M.C. 3.*
18 ..   ..   £45

1604 — — Similar; ΑΓ monogram above pellet and helmet in the depressions. *B.M.C. 3.* 25
£45

1605 — — Similar; VE monogram beside pellet and bee in the depressions. *B.M.C. 3.* 41
£45

1606 — — Similar; X beside pellet and amphora in the depressions. *B.M.C. 3.* 48   £45

1607 *Bronze Coinage.* Mid-4th Cent. B.C. Æ 11. Lion's hd. l. ℞. ΧΕΡ / ΡΟ and corn-grain;
pellet beneath. *B.M.C. 3.* 53 ..   ..   £9

1608 — — Hd. of Athena r., wearing crested helmet. ℞. Similar to last, but with small
corn-grain instead of pellet beneath. *B.M.C. 3.* 57 ..   ..   £10

1609 **Krithote** (situated near Gallipoli). *Circa* 350 B.C. Æ 22. Hd. of Demeter three-
quarter face to r. ℞. ΚΡΙΘΟΥ / ΣΙΩΝ above and below corn-grain; all within corn-wreath.
B.M.C. 3. 1 ..   ..   £18

1610 — Æ 20. Hd of Athena l., in Corinthian helmet. ℞. ΚΡΙ and corn-grain. *B.M.C. 3.* 2
£14

1611   1612   1616

1611 **Kypsela** (the modern Ipsala, situated on the Hebros about 20 miles upstream of Ainos).
Circa 400 B.C. Æ 13. Hd. of Hermes r., in close-fitting petasos. ℞. ΚΥΨΕ. Two-
handled vase; pentagram above. *B.M.C. 3.* 1 ..   ..   £18

1612 **Dikaia.** 480-450 B.C. Æ *stater.* Hd of bearded Herakles r., clad in lion's skin.
℞. ΔΙΚ (retrograde). Hd. and neck of bull l.; all within shallow incuse square. *B.M.C.
3.* 3 ..   ..   £2,500

1613 — Æ *drachm.* *Obv.* Similar. ℞. Cock stg. r. in dotted square within incuse square.
Weber 2359 ..   ..   £750

1614 — Æ *hemidrachm.* Similar, but cock holds worm in beak. *Weber* 2360 ..   £300

1615 **Late 5th Cent. B.C.** Æ *tetrobol.* Female hd. l., hair rolled. ℞. ΔΙΚΑΙΑ around hd. and
neck of bull r.; all within incuse square. *B.M.C. 3.* 4 ..   ..   £350

1616 **Elaious** (the southernmost town of the Thracian Chersonese, Elaious was situated
close to the entrace to the Hellespont). *Circa* 350 B.C. Æ 18. Prow r., with eye.
℞. ΕΛΑΙ within olive-wreath. *Grose* 4156 ..   ..   £12

1617 — Æ 15. Hd. of Athena r., in Corinthian helmet. ℞. ΕΛΑΙΟΥΣΙΩΝ. Owl stg. r., hd.
facing; monogram below. *Grose* 4157 ..   ..   £10

1618   1620

1618 **Lysimacheia** (founded by Lysimachos in 309 B.C., close to the site of Kardia which he had destroyed, this city became the principal residence and European mint of the King of Thrace). 309-281 B.C., and probably later. Æ *octobol*. Hd. of young Herakles r., in lion's skin. ℞. ΛΥΣΙΜΑΧΕΩΝ. Nike stg. facing, hd. l., holding wreath and palm; monograms in lower field, to l. and r. *Weber* 2452 .. .. £750

1619 — Æ 25. Diad. hd. of Lysimachos r. ℞. ΛΥΣΙ / ΜΑΧΕΩΝ above and below lion springing r.; monogram beneath. *B.M.C. 3.* 1 .. .. £20

1620 — — Hd. of young Herakles r., in lion's skin. ℞. ΛΥΣΙΜΑ / ΧΕΩΝ either side of Artemis stg. r., holding two long torches. *B.M.C. 3.* 2 .. .. £17

1621 — Æ 22. Veiled hd. of Demeter r., wreathed with corn. ℞. ΛΥΣΙΜΑΧΕΩΝ. Nike stg. l., holding wreath and palm. *B.M.C. 3.* 6 .. .. £14

1622 — Æ 19. Hd. of Athena r., in Corinthian helmet. ℞. ΛΥΣΙ / ΜΑΧΕΩΝ above and below lion advancing r. *B.M.C. 3.* 11 .. .. £12

1623 — Æ 15. Lion's hd. r. ℞. ΛΥ / ΣΙ. Ear of corn; monogram to l. *B.M.C. 3.* 16 £10

1624 **Madytos** (on the European coast of the Hellespont, opposite Abydos). *Circa* 350 BC.. Æ 19. Bull butting l.; fish l. above. ℞. ΜΑΔΥ. Dog seated r.; ear of corn behind; magistrate's name in ex. *B.M.C. 3.* 1 .. .. £18

1625 **Maroneia.** *Circa* 480-450 B.C. Æ *didrachm*. Forepart of prancing horse r. ℞. ΜΑΡΩΝΙΤΩΝ around quadripartite linear square; all within incuse square. *B.M.C. 3.* 15 £850

1626 — Æ *drachm*. Forepart of prancing horse l.; ΜΑΡΩ before. ℞. Shallow quadripartite incuse square, the surface granulated. *Weber* 2325 .. .. £500

1627 — — *Obv.* Similar, but legend ΜΑΡ, and two large pellets in field above and below horse. ℞. Ram's hd. l., in dotted square; all within incuse square. *B.M.C. 3.* 6 .. £450

1625   1628

1628 *Circa* 440-410 B.C. Æ *tetradrachm* (*c.* 14 gm.). Horse prancing l.; above, ΜΑΡΩΝ and kantharos. ℞. ΕΠΙ ΜΗΤΡΟΔΟΤΟ around linear square containing vine; all within incuse square. *B.M.C. 3.* 11 .. .. £1,750

1629 — Æ *didrachm.* Forepart of prancing horse l. ℞. Similar to last, but with magistrate's name ΠΟΣΕΙΔΙΠΠΟΣ. *B.M.C. 3.* 17 .. .. £900

1630 — Æ *drachm. Obv.* Similar, but also with legend ΜΑΡΩ (retrograde). ℞ Vine-branch with grapes, in dotted square; all within incuse square. *B.M.C. 3.* 19.. .. £400

1631 *Circa* 385-360 B.C. Æ *stater* (*c.* 11 gm.). Horse prancing l., with loose rein; ΜΑΡΩ above. ℞. ΕΠΙ ΙΚΕΣΙΟ around three sides of linear square, caduceus along the fourth; vine with bunches of grapes within square; all within incuse square. *B.M.C. 3.* 24
£650

1632 — Æ *quarter stater.* Forepart of prancing horse l.; H-P in field. ℞. M-A either side of bunch of grapes attached to vine-branch; all in dotted square within incuse. *B.M.C. 3.* 33
£150

1633 — — ΜΑΡΩ. Forepart of prancing horse r. ℞. ΕΠΙ ΑΡΙΣΤΟΛΕΩ around dotted square containing vine-branch with grapes. *B.M.C. 3.* 41, 42 .. .. .. £175

1634 — Æ *eighth stater.* Forepart of prancing horse l. ℞. ΜΑΡ-ΩΝ. Tripod-lebes; all within incuse square. *B.M.C. 3.* 46, 47 .. .. £125

1635 After 148 B.C. (following the defeat of Andriscus and the organization of Macedonia into a Roman province, the output of the great silver mines was sent to the Thracian mints of Maroneia and Thasos for conversion to coin). Æ *tetradrachm.* Hd. of young Dionysos r., wreathed with ivy and with band across forehead. ℞. ΔΙΟΝΥΣΟΥ ΣΩΤΗΡΟΣ ΜΑΡΩΝΙΤΩΝ. Dionysos, naked, stg. l., holding grapes and two narthex wands; two monograms in field, to l. and r. *B.M.C. 3.* 48-63 .. .. £175
These issues were imitated by the Danubian Celts of the interior.

1636 *Bronze Coinage. Circa* 400-350 B.C. Æ 15. Horse prancing r.; monogram beneath. ℞. ΜΑΡΩΝΙΤΩΝ around three sides of linear square containing vine; monogram beneath. *B.M.C. 3.* 65 .. .. £8

1637 — Æ 18. Hd. of young Dionysos r., wreathed with ivy. ℞. ΕΠΙ ΠΥΘΟΝΙΚΟ ΜΑΡΩΝΙΤΩΝ around dotted square containing bunch of grapes. *B.M.C. 3.* 71 .. .. £14

Maroneia *continued*

1638 After 148 B.C.   Æ 24.   Similar to 1635, but only one monogram, to l., on *rev.   B.M.C. 3.
72 ..   ..   £12

1639 — — Laur. hd. of Apollo r.   ℞. ΜΑΡΩΝΙΤΩΝ.   Asklepios stg. facing, hd. l., holding
serpent-staff; two monograms to l.   *B.M.C. 3.* 83   ..   ..   £15

1640 — Æ 20.   Laur. hd. of bearded Herakles r., club at shoulder.   ℞. ΜΑΡΩ / ΝΙΤΩΝ above
and below bridled horse galloping r.; two monograms in field.   *B.M.C. 3.* 87..   £10

1641 **Mesembria** (a walled stronghold of the Samothrakians, of little importance, not to be
confused with the Megarian colony, of the same name, on the west coast of the Black Sea).
2nd-1st Cent. B.C.   Æ 20.   Hd. of young Dionysos r., wreathed with ivy.   ℞. ΜΕΣΑΜ /
ΒΡΙΑΝΩΝ.   Bunch of grapes.   *Historia Numorum, p.* 248   ..   ..   ..   £25

1642 **Perinthos** (a Samian colony, midway along the northern coastline of the Propontis).
Circa 350 B.C.   Æ *stater* (*c.* 10·5 gm.).   Laur. hd. of Zeus r.   ℞. ΠΕΡΙΝ.   Foreparts of
two horses joined back to back; ΚΙΣ and monogram beneath.   *Historia Numorum, p.* 270
£2,500

1643 — Æ 20.   Hd. of Athena r., in Corinthian helmet.   ℞. ΠΕΡΙΝ / ΘΙΩΝ.   Foreparts of two
horses, as last.   *B.M.C. 3.* 1   ..   ..   £15

1644 2nd-1st Cent. B.C.   Æ 23.   Bearded bust of Herakles (?) r., wearing tainia.   ℞.
ΠΕΡΙΝΘΙΩΝ.   Apollo stg. l., holding laurel-branch and lyre resting on column.   *B.M.C. 3.*
2   ..   ..   £18

1645 — Æ 20.   Jugate busts of Sarapis and Isis r.   ℞. — Harpokrates, naked, stg. l., r. hand
raised to mouth, and holding cornucopiae.   *B.M.C. 3.* 3   ..   ..   ..   £22

1646 — Æ 15.   Hd. of Hermes r., in winged petasos.   ℞ — Winged caduceus.   *B.M.C. 3.* 6
£8

1647   1648

1647 **Selymbria** (on the north coast of the Propontis, about 20 miles east of Perinthos).
Circa 480-450 B.C.   Æ *drachm.*   Cock walking l.; ΣΑ above.   ℞. Quadripartite incuse
square.   *B.M.C. 3.* 1   ..   ..   £450

1648 — — Cock stg. l.   ℞. ΣΑ-ΛΥ either side of ear of corn.   *Weber* 2601 ..   ..   £500

1649   1651

1649 **Sestos** (in the Thracian Chersonese, on the shores of the Hellespont at the point where
Xerxes and the Persian army crossed to Europe in 480 B.C.).   *Circa* 300 B.C.   Æ 20.   Hd.
of Demeter l., wreathed with corn.   ℞ Hermes stg. l., holding caduceus; ΣΗ to r., corn-ear
to l.   *B.M.C. 3.* 2   ..   ..   £14

1650 — Æ 11.   Term of Hermes between corn-grain and caduceus.   ℞. Σ-Η either side of
amphora.   *B.M.C. 3.* 6 ..   ..   £8

1651 After *c.* 150 B.C.   Æ 18.   Laur. hd. of Apollo l.   ℞. ΣΗΣ-ΤΙΑ either side of tripod-lebes.
B.M.C. 3. 11   ..   ..   £10

1652 — Æ 16.   Hd. of Hermes l., in winged petasos.   ℞. Lyre; ΣΗ to r.   *Weber* 2465   £9

1653 — Æ 9.   *Obv.* Similar.   ℞. Caduceus; ΣΗ to r.   *Weber* 2469..   ..   ..   £7

1654   1655

1654 **BLACK SEA AREA: Apollonia Pontika** (a colony of Miletos, the city boasted a fine
temple of Apollo with a statue by the sculptor Kalamis).   450-400 B.C.   Æ *drachm.*
Anchor; crayfish to r.   ℞ 'Swastika' pattern, partly incuse.   *B.M.C. 15.* (*Mysia*) *p.* 8, 1
£140

1655 — — *Obv.* Similar, but crayfish to l., A to r.   ℞. Gorgoneion.   *B.M.C. 15.* (*Mysia*)
p. 8, 5-7   ..   ..   £90

1656 400-350 B.C.   Æ *tetradrachm.*   Laur. hd. of Apollo l., hair rolled.   ℞. Anchor; A and
magistrate's name to l., crayfish to r.   *B.M.C. 15.* (*Mysia*) *p.* 9, 13   ..   ..   £1,250

1657 — Æ *diobol.*   Laur. hd. of Apollo facing.   ℞. Anchor; A to l., crayfish to r.   *B.M.C. 15.*
(*Mysia*) *p.* 9, 15   ..   ..   £75

1658 — Æ 18.   Apollo seated l. on omphalos, r. hand resting on bow.   ℞. Anchor; to l.,
A and magistrate's name; to r., crayfish.   *B.M.C. 15.* (*Mysia*) *p.* 10, 17   ..   £18

1659   1664

1659 **Kallatis** (a colony of Herakleia Pontika).   3rd Cent. B.C. (after 281).   Æ *octobol.*   Hd.
of young Herakles r., in lion's skin.   ℞. ΚΑΛΛΑΤΙ between monogram, ear of corn and club
(above), and bow in case (below).   *B.M.C. 3.* 1   ..   ..   £225

1660 — Æ *tetrobol.*   *Obv.* Similar.   ℞. ΚΑΛΛΑ between bow in case (above), and club and ear
of corn (below).   *B.M.C. 3.* 2   ..   ..   £140

1661 2nd Cent. B.C.   N *stater*, restoring the type of King Lysimachos of Thrace.   Hd. of
deified Alexander the Great r., with horn of Ammon.   ℞. ΒΑΣΙΛΕΩΣ / ΛΥΣΙΜΑΧΟΥ either
side of Athena seated l., holding Nike; monogram to l., ΚΑΛ on throne, trident l. beneath.
Müller (*Die Münzen des thrakischen Königs Lysimachos*) 266   ..   ..   ..   £1,000

1662 — Æ *tetradrachm.*   Similar, but with ΚΑΛ and corn-ear in ex. (nothing on throne).
Müller 257 ..   ..   £200

1663 — Æ 14.   Hd. of Athena r., in crested Corinthian helmet.   ℞. ΚΑΛΛΑ between club and
corn-ear; above, A.   *B.M.C. 3.* 5   ..   ..   £10

1664 **Cherronesos** (another colony of Herakleia Pontika, situated close to Sebastopol).
3rd Cent. B.C.   Æ *didrachm.*   Hd. of young Herakles r., in lion's skin.   ℞. ΧΕΡ . Artemis
enthroned l., holding arrow, bow and quiver over shoulder; before, ΑΠΟΛΛΩΝΙΟ.   *B.M.C.*
3. 1   ..   ..   £375
These are sometimes countermarked on the obv.

1665   1666

Cherronesos *continued*

1665 — Æ *drachm.* Hd. of Artemis r., wearing turreted crown, quiver at shoulder. ℞. Stag
stg. r.; XEP before, MOIPIOΣ in ex. *B.M.C. 3.* 3 ..   ..   £225

1666 — Æ 22. Artemis in galloping quadriga r. ℞. Warrior kneeling l., in defensive attitude,
holding spear and large shield; beneath, XEP; behind, I. *B.M.C. 3.* 5, *variety*   £20

1667 — — Artemis kneeling r., holding arrows and bow. ℞. Griffin prancing l.; XOPEIO
above, XEP below. *B.M.C. 3.* 6 ..   ..   £17

1668 — — Artemis kneeling l. on prostrate stag which she spears; XEP below. ℞. Bull
butting l.; beneath, club and quiver, ΔIAΓOPA between. *B.M.C. 3.* 7   ..   £18

1669   1673

1669 **Istros** (a Milesian colony, its large output of silver coinage in the first half of the 4th
Cent. suggests that it was a place of commercial importance). 400-350 B.C. Æ *stater*
(*c.* 5·75 gm.).   Two young male heads facing, side by side, one upright, the other inverted.
℞. IΣTPIH. Sea-eagle stg. l. on dolphin l., which it attacks with its beak; beneath, A.
B.M.C. 3. 2 ..   ..   £225
*The curious obv. type has been variously interpreted as representing the Dioskouroi, the
rising and setting sun, and the supposed two branches of the river Danube (or Ister).*

1670 — Æ *quarter stater.* Similar, but without A on *rev. B.M.C. 3.* 13 ..   ..   £75

1671 2nd-1st Cent. B.C. Æ *stater*, restoring the type of King Lysimachos of Thrace. Hd. of
deified Alexander the Great r., with horn of Ammon. ℞. BAΣIΛEΩΣ / ΛYΣIMAXOY either
side of Athena seated l., holding Nike; ΔI to l., IΣ on throne, trident l. beneath. *Müller*
(*Die Münzen des thrakischen Königs Lysimachos*) 285   ..   ..   £1,250

1672 *Bronze Coinage.* 3rd-2nd Cent. B.C. Æ 14. Bearded hd. of river-god Ister three-
quarter face to r. ℞. IΣTPI. Sea-eagle attacking dolphin, as 1669. *B.M.C. 3.* 15   £14

1673 **Mesembria** (an important colony of Megara, Mesembria was situated on the Black Sea
coast, north of Apollonia Pontika). 450-350 B.C. Æ *diobol.* Crested helmet facing.
℞. META in the four quarters of a radiate wheel. *B.M.C. 3.* 2   ..   ..   £85

1674 — Æ *hemiobol.* Similar. *B.M.C. 3.* 4 ..   ..   £35

1675 400-350 B.C. Æ 17. Similar. *B.M.C. 3.* 5 ..   ..   £14

1676 3rd-2nd Cent. B.C. Æ 18. Diad. female hd. r. ℞. METAM / BPIANΩN either side of
Athena Alkidemos advancing l., brandishing spear and holding shield. *B.M.C. 3.* 8-10
£10

1677 — Æ 20. Similar, but with legend MEΣAM / BPIANΩN. *B.M.C. 3.* 12   ..   £10

N.B. Prices given in this catalogue are for **fine** examples of coins in base metal
and for **very fine** examples of coins struck in precious metals.

There is no relationship between the values stated and the condition of the coins
used as illustrations.

1678   1681

1678 Odessos (a colony of Miletos). After *circa* 200 B.C. Æ *tetradrachm*. Bearded hd. of the 'Great God' of Odessos r., wearing tainia. ℞. ΘΕΟΥ / ΜΕΓΑΛΟΥ either side of the Great God stg. l., holding phiale and cornucopiae; ΟΔΗ in field to l., ΚΥΡΣΑ in ex. *Historia Numorum, p.* 276, *fig.* 167 ..   ..   £6,000

1679 — Æ 22. Laur. hd. of the Great God r. ℞. Rider on horse pacing r.; monogram below, ΟΔΗΣΙΤΩΝ in ex. *Grose* 4416   ..   ..   £22

1680 — Æ 18. Laur. hd. of Apollo r. ℞. ΟΔΗΣΙΤΩΝ. The Great God reclining l., holding phiale and cornucopiae, thyrsos before; above, monogram. *B.M.C. 3*. 3 ..   £15

1681 Olbia (another Milesian colony, Olbia was situated close to the mouths of the Hypanis and Borysthenes rivers, in an ideal trading position—hence its prosperity in Hellenistic times). 3rd-1st Cent. B.C. Æ *stater*. Hd. of Demeter l., bound with corn-ears. ℞. ΟΛΒΙΟ beneath sea-eagle flying l., looking back, holding dolphin l. in its talons. *B.M.C. 3*. 1   ..   ..   £600

1682 — Æ 70 (cast). Gorgon's hd. facing, with protruding tongue. ℞. ΑΡΙΧ around sea-eagle flying r., holding dolphin in its talons. *Weber* 2603   ..   ..   £1,250

1683 — Æ 33 (cast). *Obv.* Similar, but tongue not protruding. ℞. ΑΡΙΧ in the angles formed by the four spokes of a wheel. *Weber* 2605   ..   ..   ..   £300

1684   1685

Olbia *continued*

1684 — Æ, in the shape of a dolphin: length 35mm. (*British Museum*) £200

1685 — Æ 24. Bearded hd. of river-god Borysthenes l. ℞. Battle-axe and bow in case; ολβιο to r., monogram to l. *B.M.C. 3.* 10   ..   ..   £14

1686 — Æ 19. Laur. hd. of Apollo r. ℞. ολβιο. Lyre; ᴀ in field to r., ɛɪ-ⱶ ᴘ beneath. *Weber* 2619. *Berlin Cat.* 131   ..   ..   £14

1687 — Æ 17. Hd. of Demeter r., wreathed with corn. ℞. ολβιο (retrograde). Sea-eagle stg. r. on dolphin, which it attacks with its beak. *B.M.C. 3.* 13   ..   ..   £12

1688 — Æ 13. Turreted hd. of Tyche l. ℞. ολβιο. Naked archer kneeling l., discharging arrow. *B.M.C. 3.* 17   ..   ..   £12

1689 **Pantikapaion** (it would seem, on the evidence of the coins, that this Milesian colony originally bore the name Apollonia). 5th Cent. B.C. *Æ hemidrachm* (*c.* 1·5 gm.). Lion's scalp facing. ℞. ᴀποᴧ in the quarters of a quadripartite incuse square. *B.M.C. 3., p.* 87, 2 (attributed to Apollonia) £75

1690 — *Æ drachm.* Similar, but with the legend πᴀɴᴛ on *rev. Berlin Cat., p.* 9   £150

1691 — *Æ diobol* (?). Lion's scalp facing. ℞. πᴀɴᴛ above ram's hd. r.; all in incuse square. *Grose* 4444   ..   ..   £90

1692   1695

1692 4th Cent. B.C. *N stater* (*c.* 9 gm.). Bearded hd. of Pan three-quarter face to l. ℞. πᴀɴ. Griffin stg. l. on stalk of corn, hd. facing, holding spear in his mouth. *B.M.C. 3.* 1 £5,000

1693 — — Similar, but on *obv.* hd. of Pan to l., wreathed with ivy. *B.M.C. 3.* 3   £4,500

1694 — *N sixth stater.* Hd. of young Pan l. ℞. πᴀɴ. Forepart of griffin l.; ear of corn beneath. *B.M.C. 3.* 4   ..   ..   £750

1695 — *Æ drachm?* (*c.* 3·4 gm.). *Obv.* Similar to 1692. ℞. πᴀɴ. Hd. and neck of bull to l. *B.M.C. 3.* 6   ..   ..   £450

1696 — *Æ tetrobol?* (*c.* 2·35 gm.). Bearded hd. of Pan r. ℞. πᴀɴᴛɪ. Lion's hd. r. *B.M.C. 3.* 8   ..   ..   £275

1697 3rd-2nd Cent. B.C. *Æ didrachm* (of base metal). Hd. of young Dionysos r., wreathed with ivy. ℞. πᴀɴᴛɪ / κᴀπᴀɪ / ᴛⱳɴ in three lines, bunch of grapes above; all within ivy-wreath above which, monogram. *B.M.C. 3.* 11..   ..   ..   £150

1698 — *Æ hemidrachm.* Laur. hd. of Apollo r. ℞. πᴀɴᴛɪκᴀπᴀɪᴛⱳɴ. Forepart of galloping horse r. *B.M.C. 3.* 14   ..   ..   £125

1699 *Bronze Coinage.* 4th Cent. B.C. Æ 28. Hd. of young Pan l., wreathed with ivy. R. ΠΑΝ. Hd. and neck of bull to l. *B.M.C. 3.* 16 .. .. £20

1700   1702

1700 — Æ 20. Bearded hd. of Pan r. R. ΠΑΝ. Forepart of griffin l.; beneath, sturgeon l. *B.M.C. 3.* 20 .. .. £16

1701 — — Hd. of young Pan l., wreathed with ivy. R. ΠΑΝ. Lion's hd. l.; beneath, sturgeon l. *B.M.C. 3.* 21, 22 .. .. £15

1702 — Æ 15. Hd. of young Pan r. R. ΠΑΝ. Forepart of Pegasos r. *B.M.C. 3.* 25 £12

1703 3rd-2nd Cent. B.C. Æ 30. Hd. of Mithras (?) r., in Phrygian cap bound with diadem. R. ΠΑΝ ΤΙΚΑΠΑΙΤΩΝ. Dionysos stg. l., holding bunch of grapes and thyrsos, panther at feet; monogram to l. *B.M.C. 3.* 34 .. .. £18

1704 — Æ 22. Laur. hd. of Apollo r. R. — Tripod-lebes, against which rests thyrsos; monogram to r. *B.M.C. 3.* 35 .. .. £12

1705 — Æ 18. Bearded hd. of Pan l., wreathed with ivy. R. ΠΑΝΤΙ. Cornucopiae between caps of the Dioskouroi. *B.M.C. 3.* 39, 40 .. .. £10

1706 — Æ 15. ΠΑΝΤΙΚΑΠ between the eight rays of a star. R. Tripod-lebes. *B.M.C. 3.* 48, 49 .. .. £10

1707 — Æ 13. Diad. male hd. r., beardless. R. ΠΑΝ. Bow in case. *B.M.C. 3.* 44-6 £9

1705   1709

1708 **Tomis** (another colony of Miletos). 2nd-1st Cent. B.C. *N stater*, restoring the type of King Lysimachos of Thrace. Hd. of deified Alexander the Great r., with horn of Ammon. R. ΒΑΣΙΛΕΩΣ / ΛΥΣΙΜΑΧΟΥ either side of Athena seated l., holding Nike; ΔΙΟ to l., ΤΟ on throne, trident l. beneath. *Müller (Die Münzen des thrakischen Königs Lysimachos)* 277 .. .. £1,100

1709 — Æ 27. Bearded hd. of the 'Great God' of Odessos r., wearing tainia. R. Eagle stg. r., ΤΟΜΙ above, ΤΙΜΟ below; all within oak-wreath. *B.M.C. 3.* 1 .. .. £25

1710 **Tyra** (situated about twenty miles inland, on the river Dniester, Tyra was another Milesian colony). 3rd Cent. B.C. Æ *octobol?* (*c.* 5·5 gm.). Veiled hd. of Demeter, three-quarter face to l., ears of corn in hair. R. ΤΥΡΑΝΟΝ above bull butting l. *Grose* 4313 *Pick (Die antiken Münzen Nord-Griechenlands) pl. XII,* 10 .. .. .. £750

1711 2nd-1st Cent. B.C. Æ 20. Hd. of Demeter facing, wreathed with corn. R. ΤΥΡΑ. Cista mystica. *Historia Numorum, p.* 273 .. .. £24

THRACIAN KINGS

1712   1715

1712 **Sparadokos**, *circa* 425 B.C. (King of the Odrysai, brother of Sitalkes). Æ *tetradrachm.*
Bearded horseman (the King?) seated on horse pacing l., holding two spears; in field to r.,
Corinthian helmet l. R. Eagle stg. l., attacking serpent, within square surrounded by
raised band inscribed ΣΠΑΡΑΔΟΚΟ; all within incuse square. (*British Museum*)   £4,000

1713 Æ *drachm.* ΣΠΑΡΑΔΟΚΟ. Free horse pacing l., astragalos beneath. R. Eagle flying l.,
holding serpent in beak; all within incuse square. *Weber* 2710   ..   ..   £750

1714 Æ *diobol.* ΣΠΑ. Forepart of galloping horse l. R. Similar to last. *B.M.C. 3.* 3   £200

1715 **Seuthes I**, after 424 B.C. (son of Sparadokos). Æ *didrachm.* Bearded horseman
(the King?) galloping r., brandishing spear(?). R. ΣΕΥΘΑ / ΚΟΜΜΑ in two lines. *B.M.C.*
3. 1 ..   ..   £1,500

1716 **Metokos**, *circa* 400 B.C. (mentioned by Xenophon under the name of Medokos). Æ *dio-*
bol. ΜΗΤΟΚΟ. Bearded hd. of Dionysos r. R. Bipennis; bunch of grapes in field.
Historia Numorum, p. 282 ..   ..   £300

1717 **Amadokos II**, 359-351 B.C. (issued his coinage from the Greek city of Maroneia).
Æ 23. Bipennis, the handle forming the "T" of the legend ΑΜΑΤΟΚΟ; above, caduceus.
R. ΕΠΙ ΔΗΜΟΚΡΙΤΟ around dotted square containing vine with grapes; all within incuse
square. *B.M.C. 3.* 1 (*Amadokos I*) £40

1718   1720

1718 **Teres III**, *circa* 350 B.C. (also struck his coinage at Maroneia). Æ 20. Bipennis, the
handle forming the "T" of the legend ΘΗΡΕΩ. R. ΕΠ ... Ρ ΙΟ around dotted square containing vine with grapes; all within incuse square. *Weber* 2714   ..   ..   £45

1719 **Saratokos**, *circa* 400 B.C. (dynast in Thasos?). Æ *diobol.* Naked Satyr kneeling l.,
holding kantharos. R. ΣΑΡΑΤΟ. Amphora; all within incuse square. *B.M.C. 3.* 1
(*Saratos*) £250

1720 **Bergaios**, early 4th Cent. B.C. (a dynast in the Pangaean district). Æ *drachm* (*c.* 3·25
gm.). Satyr kneeling to front, looking r., carrying in his arms a nymph l. R. ΒΕΡΓΑΙΟΥ
around quadripartite incuse square; all within incuse square. *B.M.C. 3.* 1 ..   £750

1721 Æ 10. Bearded hd. of Seilenos r. R. ΒΕΡΓ below fish r. *B.M.C. 3.* 2, 3 ..   £18

1722   1723

1722 **Ketriporis**, *circa* 356 B.C. (mentioned in an inscription found at Athens as an ally of the
Athenians against Philip II of Macedon). Æ 15. Bearded hd. of Dionysos r., wreathed
with ivy. R. ΚΕΤΡΙΠΟΡΙΟΣ. Kantharos; crescent above, thyrsos to l. *B.M.C. 3.* 2   £22

1723 **Kotys I**, 382-359 B.C. (King of the Odrysai, Kotys appears to have issued his coins from the mint of Kypsela). Æ *trihemiobol*? (*c.* 0·85 gm.). Male hd. l., bearded. ℞. ΚΟΤΥ Two-handled vase. *B.M.C. 3.* 1, *variety* £200

1724 Æ 20. Horseman cantering r., r. hand raised. ℞. ΚΟΤΥΟΣ around two-handled vase; all within incuse square. *B.M.C. 3.* 2 .. .. £25

1725 **Seuthes III**, *circa* 324 B.C. (King of the Odrysai). Æ 21. Laur. hd. of Zeus (?) r. ℞. ΣΕΥΘΟΥ. Horseman cantering r., wreath beneath. *B.M.C. 3.* 1, 2 .. £20

[**Lysimachos**, 323-281 B.C.: see Part 2 of this Catalogue, under 'Hellenistic Monarchies']

1726   1727

1726 **Kersibaulos**, early 3rd Cent. B.C. Æ *tetradrachm*, in imitation of the type of Alexander the Great. Hd. of young Herakles r., in lion's skin. ℞. ΒΑΣΙΛΕΩΣ ΚΕΡΣΙΒΑΥΛΟΥ. Zeus seated l., holding eagle and sceptre; large shield before, ΓΙ beneath throne. *B.M.C. 3.*, p. 239, 1 .. .. £1,500

1727 **Kavaros**, *c.* 219-200 B.C. (the last Gaulish King in Thrace). Æ 20. Laur. hd. of Apollo r. ℞. ΒΑΣΙΛΕΩΣ ΚΑΥΑΡΟΥ. Nike stg. l., crowning king's name and holding palm; monogram to l. *B.M.C. 3.* 1, 2 .. .. £20

1728 **Mostis**, 2nd Cent. B.C. Æ *tetradrachm*, based on the type of Lysimachos. Diad. and dr. bust of Mostis r. ℞. ΒΑΣΙΛΕΩΣ / ΜΟΣΤΙΔΟΣ either side of Athena enthroned l., holding Nike; in ex., ΕΠΙ ΣΑΔΑΛΟΥ / ΕΤΟΥΣ ΛΗ; in field to l., ΙΜ. *B.M.C. 3.* 1 .. .. £4,000

1729 Æ 22. Jugate heads of Zeus and Hera r. ℞. ΒΑΣΙΛΕΩΣ ΜΟΣΤΙΔΟΣ. Eagle stg. l. on thunderbolt; monogram to r. *Weber* 2740 .. .. £24

1730 Æ 19. Laur. hd. of Apollo r. ℞. — Horse trotting l.; monogram above. *B.M.C. 3.* 2 £18

1731 **Kotys III**, 57-48 B.C. Æ 13. Diad. hd. of King r. ℞. ΚΟΤΥΟC. Eagle stg. l. on thunderbolt. *Historia Numorum, p.* 286 .. .. £12

1732 **Akrosandros**, *circa* 100 B.C. (possibly a King of the Getae). Æ 22. Jugate heads of Demeter and Persephone r. ℞. ΒΑΣΙΛΕ ΑΚΡΟΣΑΝΔΡ. Two ears of corn. *Historia Numorum, p.* 289 .. .. £25

1733　　　　　　　　　　　　1734

1733 **Koson,** mid-1st Cent. B.C. (an unknown dynast, possibly Scythian, whose coinage seems to be inspired by silver denarii issued in 54 B.C. by M. Junius Brutus—see Crawford 433/1). *N stater.* Three togate figures advancing l., the first and third each carrying an axe over l. shoulder; ΚΟΣΩΝ in ex. ℞. Eagle stg. l. on sceptre, holding wreath in one claw. *B.M.C. 3.* 2 .. .. £650

ISLANDS OF THE THRACIAN SEA

1734 **IMBROS** (colonized by Athenians in the 6th Cent. B.C.). Late 4th Cent. B.C. Æ 14. Hd. of Demeter r., wreathed with corn. ℞. ΙΜΒΡΟΥ. Naked ithyphallic figure of Hermes Imbramos stg. r. before altar, holding branch andj phiale; kantharos in field to r. *B.M.C. 3.* 1 .. .. £13

1735 — Æ 9. Hd. of Athena r., in Corinthian helmet. ℞. ΙΜΒΡΟΥ. Owl stg. r. *B.M.C. 3.* 5 .. .. £7

1736 **LEMNOS** (a large island in the Aegean sea, sacred to Hephaistos). *Circa* 375 B.C. Æ 14. Male hd. r., bearded. ℞. ΛΗΜΝΙ. Ram walking r.; all within incuse square. *Berlin Cat., p.* 279 .. .. £14

1737　　　　　　　　　　　　1743

1737 **Hephaistia** (the chief town of the island). *Circa* 300 B.C. Æ 17. Hd. of Athena r., in Corinthian helmet. ℞. ΗΦΑΙ / ΣΤΙ. Ram stg. r. *B.M.C. 3.* 1, 2 .. .. £11

1738 — Æ 13. *Obv.* Similar. ℞. ΗΦΑ. Owl stg. facing. *B.M.C. 3.* 5 .. .. £9

1739 *Circa* 280-190 B.C. Æ 18. Diad. male hd. r., beardless (Antiochos III of Syria ?). ℞. ΗΦ. Race-torch between caps of the Dioskouroi; caduceus in field to r. *B.M.C. 3.* 7 £12

1740 — Æ 14. Rad. hd. of Helios r. ℞. ΗΦΑΙ above thyrsos, placed horizontally, from which is suspended bunch of grapes. *Weber* 2487 .. .. £10

1741 **Myrina** (another town of Lemnos). *Circa* 300 B.C. Æ 14. Hd. of Athena r., in Corinthian helmet. ℞. ΜΥΡΙ. Owl stg. facing; olive-branch in field to r. *B.M.C. 3.* 2 £11

1742 **SAMOTHRAKE** (i.e. the Thracian Samos; this island was the home of the famous mysteries of the Kabeiroi). After *c.* 280 B.C. *R didrachm.* Hd. of Athena r., in crested Corinthian helmet. ℞. Kybele enthroned l., holding patera and sceptre, lion beneath throne; behind, ΣΑΜΟ; before, ΜΗΤΡΩΝΑ. *B.M.C. 3.* 1 .. .. .. £900

1743 — Æ 19. Similar, but without lion on *rev.*, and ΣΑΜΟ before, ΠΥΘΟΚ behind. *B.M.C. 3.* 2, 3 .. .. £14

1744 — Æ 13. *Obv.* Similar. ℞. Forepart of ram r.; ΣΑΜΟ above, ΑΚΗΡΙ behind. *B.M.C. 3.* 6, 7 .. .. £11

1745 2nd-1st Cent B.C. Æ 19. Bust of Athena r., wearing Corinthian helmet and aegis; behind, star on globe. ℞. ΣΑΜΟΘΡΑΚΩΝ. Kybele enthroned, similar to 1742. *B.M.C. 3.* 11 .. .. £13

1746   1748

1746 **THASOS.** 463-411 B.C. Æ *stater.* Naked ithyphallic Satyr in kneeling-running attitude r., carrying in his arms a struggling nymph who raises her r. hand in protest; the Satyr has long beard and both figures have flowing hair indicated by streaming lines. R. Quadripartite incuse square. *B.M.C. 3.* 24 .. .. £425

1747 — — Similar, but the *obv.* is of later, finer, style: the nymph, her hair bound with fillet, no longer struggles and her r. arm is extended behind the Satyr's back; he is bearded but bald-headed; A in field to r. *B.M.C. 3.* 29, 30 .. .. £650

1748 — Æ *drachm.* Similar, but without letter in *obv.* field. *B.M.C. 3.* 32-4 .. £200

1749 — — Similar, but the Satyr kneels to front, his hd. turned r. towards the nymph· *B.M.C. 3.* 35 .. .. £250

1750   1752   1754

1750 411-350 B.C. N *drachm* (c. 3·9 gm.). Bearded hd. of Dionysos l., wreathed with ivy. R. ΘΑ / ΣΙΟΝ behind and before bearded Herakles, clad in lion's skin, kneeling r., shooting with bow; bunch of grapes in field to r.; all within incuse square. *Weber* 2509 £3,500

1751 — Æ *tetradrachm.* Similar, but on *rev.* the legend ΘΑΣΙΟΝ is behind Herakles, and with shield in field to r. *B.M.C. 3.* 36 .. .. £2,500

1752 — Æ *didrachm.* Similar to last, but hd. of Dionysos to r. on *obv.*, and club in field to r. on *rev.* *B.M.C. 3.* 39, *variety* £600

1753 — Æ *drachm.* Similar to 1751, but with owl in field to r. on *rev.* *B.M.C. 3.* 46 £225

1754 — Æ *hemidrachm.* Janiform hd. of bald and bearded Satyr. R. ΘΑΣΙ (sometimes retrograde). Two amphorae, one of them upside-down; all within incuse square. *B.M.C. 3.* 51, 52 .. .. £250

1755   1758

1755 — Æ *trihemiobol.* Satyr kneeling l., holding kantharos. R. ΘΑΣ / ΙΩΝ either side of amphora; all within incuse square. *B.M.C. 3.* 53-6 .. .. £75

1756 — Æ *tritemorion* (c. 0·45 gm.). Hd. of bald and bearded Satyr r. R. ΘΑΣΙ. Two dolphins swimming l. and r., one above the other; all within incuse square. *B.M.C. 3.* 60 £60

1757 — Æ *hemiobol* (c. 0·30 gm.). Hd. of nymph l. R. ΘΑ / Σ below dolphin l.; all within incuse square. *B.M.C. 3.* 64 .. .. £45

1758 After c. 280 B.C. Æ *hemidrachm.* Bearded hd. of Dionysos r., wreathed with ivy. R. ΘΑΣΙ/ΩΝ above and below club r.; all within laurel-wreath. *B.M.C. 3.* 66 .. £65

Thasos *continued*

1759 After 148 B.C. (following the defeat of Andriscus and the organization of Macedonia into a Roman province, the output of the great silver mines was sent to the Thracian mints of Maroneia and Thasos for conversion to coin). Æ *tetradrachm.* Hd. of young Dionysos r., wreathed with ivy and with band across forehead. ℞. ΗΡΑΚΛΕΟΥΣ ΣΩΤΗΡΟΣ ΘΑΣΙΩΝ. Herakles, naked, stg. l., holding club, lion's skin over l. arm; monogram in field to l. *B.M.C. 3.* 67-78 .. .. £130

These issues were extensively imitated by the Danubian Celts of the interior—see nos. 215 and 216.

1760 1764

1760 *Bronze Coinage.* Before 357 B.C. Æ 10. Hd. of young Herakles r., in lion's skin. ℞. ΘΑΣΙΟΝ / ΗΠΕΙΡΟ above and below strung bow and club. *B.M.C. 3., p.* 226, 112 £18

These were struck at the mining centre of Krenides for circulation in the Thasian territory on the mainland.

1761 Before 350 B.C. Æ 11. Bearded hd. of Herakles r., in lion's skin. ℞. ΘΑΣΙΟΝ. Club, and strung bow within which, amphora. *B.M.C. 3.* 92.. .. .. .. £10

1762 After 280 B.C. Æ 18. Similar, but on *rev.* the legend reads ΘΑΣΙΩΝ, and with monogram in field. *B.M.C. 3.* 95 .. .. £12

1763 — Æ 23. Veiled hd. of Demeter r., wreathed with corn. ℞. ΘΑΣΙΟΝ. Jugate heads of the Kabeiroi r.; all within vine-wreath. *B.M.C. 3.* 102.. .. .. .. £15

1764 After 148 B.C. Æ 19. Diad. bust of Artemis r., bow and quiver at shoulder. ℞. ΘΑΣΙΩΝ. Herakles, naked, advancing r., drawing bow; monogram in field to r. *B.M.C. 3.* 105-6 .. .. £13

1765 — Æ 14. Amphora. ℞. ΘΑΣΙΟΝ. Cornucopiae. *B.M.C. 3.* 107-8 .. £8

N.B. Prices given in this catalogue are for **fine** examples of coins in base metal and for **very fine** examples of coins struck in precious metals.

There is no relationship between the values stated and the condition of the coins used as illustrations.

MAP 9   ILLYRIA

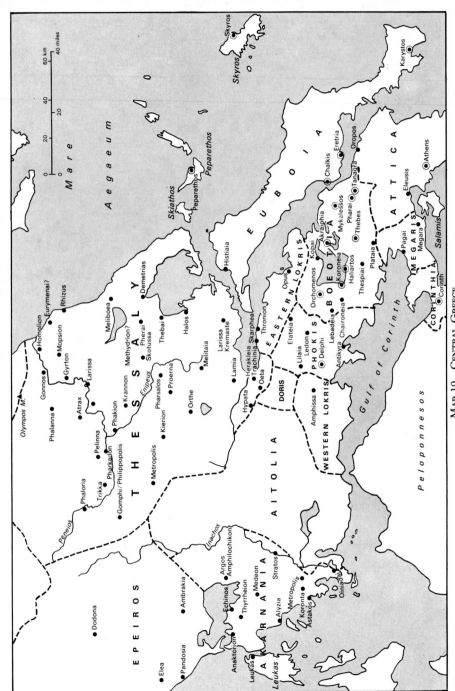

MAP 10   CENTRAL GREECE

ILLYRIA AND CENTRAL GREECE

Comprising fourteen districts, arranged in the following approximate geographical sequence: Illyria; Epeiros; Corcyra; Thessaly; Akarnania; Aitolia; Lokris; Phokis; Boeotia; Euboia; Attica; Megaris; Aigina; Corinthia.

Archaic Period

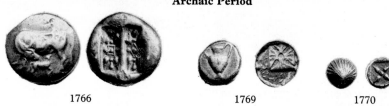

1766   1769   1770

1766 **CORCYRA** (the island-state of Corcyra, situated in the Ionian sea about twelve miles off the coast of Epeiros, was colonized by Corinthians, but became independent of its mother-city early in the 6th Cent. B.C.).   525-500 B.C.   Æ *stater.*   Cow stg. l., looking back at calf, which it suckles.   R. Two incuse rectangles, separated by central bar, each containing stellate pattern.   *B.M.C. 7.* 10   ..   ..   £750

1767 500-475 B.C.   Æ *stater.*   Similar, but cow stands to r. on *obv.*   *B.M.C. 7.* 1   £750

1768 — Æ *drachm.*   Forepart of cow running r.   R. Stellate pattern within incuse square.   *B.M.C. 7.* 18-20   ..   ..   £250

1769 — Æ *hemidrachm.*   Amphora.   R. Similar to previous.   *B.M.C. 7.* 24-26 ..   £125

1770 — Æ *trihemiobol.*   Scallop-shell.   R. Similar to previous.   *B.M.C. 7.* 27-30   £75

1771 — Æ *hemiobol* (c. 0·45 gm.).   Vase, without handles.   R. Similar to previous.   *B.M.C. 7.* 31, 32   ..   ..   £65

1772 — Æ *tetartemorion* (c. 0·23 gm.).   Similar.   *B.M.C. 7.* 33   ..   ..   £50

1773 **ISLANDS OFF THESSALY. Peparethos** (a small island, about twenty miles in circumference, Peparethos was famous for the quality of its wines).   500-480 B.C.   Æ *tetradrachm.*   Large bunch of grapes.   R. Bearded hd. of Herakles l., wearing lion's skin; all in dotted square within incuse square.   *Weber* 2956-7.   *Price & Waggoner (Archaic Greek silver coinage: the "Asyut" hoard)* 232   ..   ..   ..   £3,500

1774   1776

1774 — — Large bunch of grapes between two smaller ones.   R. Crested Corinthian helmet r., within incuse square.   *Weber* 2958   ..   ..   £3,500

The attribution of these coins to Peparethos must be considered doubtful. Martin Price ("Asyut hoard", p. 49) would prefer to assign them to a mint in the wine-producing area of Macedon.

1775 **Skyros** (a rocky and barren island, about thirty miles north-east of Euboia).   490-480 B.C.   — *tetradrachm.*   Fig leaf flanked by two rearing goats.   R. Star-shaped floral design within incuse square.   *Price & Waggoner* 233   ..   ..   *(Only two specimens known)*

1776 **PHOKIS. Delphi** (the chief town of Phokis, Delphi was named after Delphos, son of Apollo.   It was famed throughout the ancient world as the home of the oracle of Apollo).   500-480 B.C.   Æ *trihemiobol.* (c. 1·5 gm.).   Ram's hd. l.; dolphin l. beneath.   R. Goat's hd. r., within incuse square.   *B.M.C. 8.* 1   ..   ..   £200

1777 — Æ *obol* (c. 1 gm.).   Tripod.   R. Phiale, in incuse square.   *B.M.C. 8.* 5 ..   £140

Delphi *continued*

1778 *Circa* 480 B.C. Æ *tridrachm* (*c.* 18·5 gm.). ΔΑΛΦΙΚΟΝ. Two rams' heads in juxta-
position, downwards; above, two dolphins meeting. ℞. Four deep incuse squares, each
containing dolphin and flower. *Price & Waggoner* 239-45   (*Only ten specimens known*)
    *It has been suggested that this unusual reverse type represents the ceiling of the temple of
Apollo at Delphi.*

1779   1783

1779 **BOEOTIA** (being of a federal character, the coinage of this region exhibits a remarkable
uniformity—the obverse type being, almost without exception, the distinctive Boeotian
shield).
    Thebes (the principal city of Boeotia, Thebes was frequently in conflict with Athens and
actually assisted the Persian invaders in 480/479 B.C.). 520-500 B.C. Æ *drachm* (*c.* 6 gm.).
Boeotian shield. ℞. Incuse square, divided into eight triangular compartments. *B.M.C.
8., p.* 32, 1-6 ..   ..   £100

1780 — Æ *hemidrachm*. Similar. *B.M.C. 8., p.* 33, 7, 8 ..   ..   £85

1781 — Æ *obol* (*c.* 1 gm.). Similar. *B.M.C. 8., p.* 33, 9, 10   ..   ..   ..   £65

1782 — Æ *hemiobol*. Similar, but with half-shield on *obv.* *B.M.C. 8., p.* 33, 13 ..   £50

1783 500-480 B.C. Æ *stater* (*c.* 12 gm.). Boeotian shield. ℞. Incuse square, of 'mill-sail'
pattern; at centre, Θ. *B.M.C. 8.* 1, 2   ..   ..   £300

1784 — — Similar, but with ΘΕΒΑ in the four deeper divisions of the incuse square. *B.M.C.
8.* 3   ..   ..   £350

1785 — — Similar to 1783, but the rim of the shield is divided into twelve segments. *B.M.C.
8.* 4-7   ..   ..   £300

1786 — Æ *drachm*. Similar to 1783. *B.M.C. 8.* 8, 9   ..   ..   £140

1787 — Æ *hemidrachm*. Similar. *B.M.C. 8.* 10   ..   ..   £120

1788 — Æ *obol*. Boeotian shield. ℞. Θ within incuse square. *B.M.C. 8.* 11, 12   £85

1789   1791

1789 — Æ *hemiobol*. Similar, but with half-shield on *obv.* *B.M.C. 8.* 13-16   ..   £60

1790 — Æ *tetartemorion* (*c.* 0·25 gm.). Similar to 1788. *B.M.C. 8.* 17 ..   ..   £40

1791 **Akraiphia** (situated on the eastern shore of Lake Kopais). 500-480 B.C. Æ *obol*.
Boeotian shield. ℞. A within incuse square. *B.M.C. 8.* 1 ..   ..   ..   £120

1792 — Æ *hemiobol*. Half-Boeotian shield. ℞. AK monogram within incuse square. *B.M.C.
8.* 2, 3   ..   ..   £90

1793 **Koroneia** (situated on a hill at the entrance of a valley close to Mt. Helikon). 500-480 B.C. Æ *drachm*. Boeotian shield. ℞. Incuse square, of 'mill-sail' pattern; at centre, ♀. *Head (Coinage of Boeotia), p.* 14 .. .. £225

1794 1795

1794 — Æ *obol*. Boeotian shield. ℞. ♀ within incuse square. *B.M.C. 8.* 1, 2 .. £100

1795 **Haliartos** (one of the few Boeotian towns to remain loyal to the Hellenic cause, Haliartos was razed to the ground by the Persians in 480 B.C.). 520-500 B.C. Æ *drachm*. Boeotian shield, with aspirate (initial letter of the mint) on either side, within the openings. ℞. Incuse square, divided into eight triangular compartments. *B.M.C. 8.* 1, 2 .. £175

1796 1801

1796 500-480 B.C. Æ *stater*. Boeotian shield. ℞. Incuse square, of 'mill-sail' pattern; at centre, aspirate (initial letter of the mint). *B.M.C. 8.* 3-5 .. .. .. £325

1797 — — Similar, but the rim of the shield is divided into eight segments. *B.M.C. 8.* 6
£350

1798 — Æ *drachm*. Similar. *B.M.C. 8.* 7, 8 .. .. £175

1799 — Æ *hemidrachm*. Similar. *B.M.C. 8.* 9 .. .. £140

1800 — Æ *obol*. Similar, but with *rev.* type aspirate within incuse square. *B.M.C. 8.* 10
£100

1801 **Mykalessos** (mentioned by Homer in the *Iliad*—'and the spreading lawns of Mykalessos' —ii. 498). 500-480 B.C. Æ *stater*. Boeotian shield. ℞. Incuse square, of 'mill-sail' pattern; at centre, M. *Weber* 3206 .. .. £500

1802 1804

1802 **Pharai** (only four miles from the more important town of Tanagra, Pharai appears to have achieved considerable prosperity in the archaic period). 500-480 B.C. Æ *stater*. Boeotian shield. ℞. Incuse square, of 'mill-sail' pattern; at centre, Φ. *B.M.C. 8.* 1 £450

1803 — Æ *drachm*. Similar. *Head (Coinage of Boeotia), p.* 16 .. .. .. £225

1804 **Tanagra** (second only to Thebes amongst the towns of Boeotia, Tanagra was famous for its fighting-cocks). 520-500 B.C. Æ *drachm*. Boeotian shield, with T-A in the side-openings. ℞. Incuse square, divided into eight triangular compartments. *B.M.C. 8.* 1
£175

1805 — — Similar, but with T-T on *obv*. *B.M.C. 8.* 2, 3 .. .. £175

1806 — Æ *hemidrachm*. Similar. *B.M.C. 8.* 4 .. .. £150

1807 — Æ *obol*. Similar, but with T in only one side-opening of the shield. *B.M.C. 8.* 5
£110

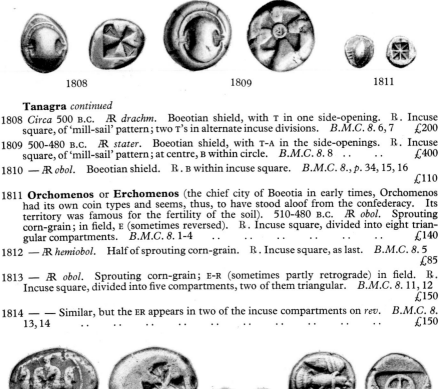

1808   1809   1811

Tanagra *continued*

1808 *Circa* 500 B.C. Æ *drachm.* Boeotian shield, with T in one side-opening. ℞. Incuse
      square, of 'mill-sail' pattern; two T's in alternate incuse divisions. *B.M.C. 8.* 6, 7   £200

1809 500-480 B.C. Æ *stater.* Boeotian shield, with T-A in the side-openings. ℞. Incuse
      square, of 'mill-sail' pattern; at centre, B within circle. *B.M.C. 8.* 8 ..   ..   £400

1810 — Æ *obol.* Boeotian shield. ℞. B within incuse square. *B.M.C. 8., p.* 34, 15, 16
                                                                                    £110

1811 **Orchomenos** or **Erchomenos** (the chief city of Boeotia in early times, Orchomenos
      had its own coin types and seems, thus, to have stood aloof from the confederacy. Its
      territory was famous for the fertility of the soil). 510-480 B.C. Æ *obol.* Sprouting
      corn-grain; in field, E (sometimes reversed). ℞. Incuse square, divided into eight trian-
      gular compartments. *B.M.C. 8.* 1-4 ..   ..   £140

1812 — Æ *hemiobol.* Half of sprouting corn-grain. ℞. Incuse square, as last. *B.M.C. 8.* 5
                                                                                    £85

1813 — Æ *obol.* Sprouting corn-grain; E-R (sometimes partly retrograde) in field. ℞.
      Incuse square, divided into five compartments, two of them triangular. *B.M.C. 8.* 11, 12
                                                                                    £150

1814 — — Similar, but the ER appears in two of the incuse compartments on *rev.* *B.M.C. 8.*
      13, 14 ..   ..   £150

1816   1815   1818

1815 — — Similar, but the ER appears within plain incuse square on *rev.* *B.M.C. 8.* 15   £160

1816 **EUBOIA. Chalkis** (the principal city of the island, and mother-city of numerous
      far-flung colonies). 540-510 B.C. Æ *tridrachm stater* (*c.* 16·8 gm.). Four-horse chariot
      to front, driven by Hera. ℞. Incuse square, of 'mill-sail' pattern. *Principal Coins,*
      I. B. 24 ..   ..   £7,500

1817 510-480 B.C. Æ *tridrachm stater.* Eagle flying l. ℞. Wheel of four spokes within
      incuse square. *Price & Waggoner* 253 ..   ..   £5,000

1818 — Æ *half stater.* Eagle flying r., carrying snake wound round its body. ℞. Wheel of
      four spokes within incuse triangle. *Weber* 3350 ..   ..   £1,800

1819 — Æ *hemidrachm* (*c.* 2·75 gm.). *Obv.* Similar. ℞. ΨAL in three quarters of a four-
      spoked wheel; all within incuse square. *B.M.C. 8.* 37 ..   ..   £350

1820 **Eretria** (the second city of the island and, like Chalkis, very active in colonizing, Eretria
      was destroyed by the Persians in 490 B.C.). 540-510 B.C. Æ *tetradrachm.* Cow stg. l.,
      hd. turned back, scratching itself with l. hind-hoof; swallow perched on its back. ℞. In-
      cuse square, of 'Union Jack' pattern. (*British Museum*) ..   ..   ..   (*Unique*)
         When published by G. K. Jenkins (Num. Chron. 1955, p. 136) this type was assigned to the
      Eretrian colony of Dikaia in Macedon: a Euboian attribution has since been shown to be more
      likely.

1821   1828

1821 510-490 B.C. Æ *tetradrachm.* *Obv.* Similar; beneath cow, E (reversed). R. Sepia, within incuse square. *B.M.C. 8.* 21   ..   ..   £3,500

1822 — Æ *didrachm.* Cow stg. r., hd. turned back, scratching itself with r. hind-hoof; E beneath. R. Similar to last. *B.M.C. 8.* 23-24   ..   ..   ..   £1,250

1823 — Æ *drachm.* Similar, but without E on *obv.*, and with E-R in lower field on *rev.* *B.M.C. 8.* 27   ..   ..   £650

1824 — Æ *diobol.* Similar to 1821, but without swallow on cow's back, and E not reversed. *B.M.C. 8.* 30, 31   ..   ..   £200

1825 — Æ *obol.* Cow's hd. facing. R. Sepia, within incuse square. *B.M.C. 8.* 33-8   £125

1826 **Karystos** (situated in the far south of the island, Karystos was famous for its marble). 540-510 B.C. Æ *tetradrachm.* Cow stg. l., hd. turned back, scratching itself with l. hind-hoof; swallow perched on its back; beneath cow, KAP. R. Incuse square, of 'Union Jack' pattern. *Price & Waggoner* 250   ..   ..   (*Unique*)

1827 510-480 B.C. Æ *tetradrachm.* Cow stg. l., hd. turned back. R. Cock stg. r., KA above; all within incuse square. *Price & Waggoner* 252   ..   ..   ..   £3,500

1828 — Æ *didrachm.* Cow stg. r., hd. turned back, suckling calf. R. Cock stg. r., K before; all within incuse square. *B.M.C. 8.* 1   ..   ..   £1,500

1829   1834

1829 **ATTICA.** **Athens** (this most famous of all Greek cities was, for much of the latter half of the 6th Cent. B.C., under the rule of the tyrants Peisistratos, Hippias and Hipparchos. The establishment of democratic government in 510 B.C. was the occasion for the introduction of the famous 'owls'—tetradrachms with head of Athena on obverse, owl on reverse. In the second decade of the 5th Century there was an especially large output of these coins, coinciding with the discovery of vast quantities of ore at the Laurion silver mines and the build-up of Athenian naval power in anticipation of the struggle with Persia). 545-515 B.C. ('Wappenmünzen' coinage). Æ *didrachm.* R. Wheel of four spokes. R. Incuse square, divided diagonally into four triangles. *B.M.C. 8.* (*Chalkis*) 6-9. *Seltman* (*Athens: its history and coinage before the Persian invasion*) 35   ..   ..   £1,250

1830 — Æ *drachm.* Similar. *B.M.C. 8.* (*Chalkis*) 10-16. *Seltman, p.* 158   ..   £450

1831 — Æ *obol.* Similar. *B.M.C. 8.* (*Chalkis*) 19-35. *Seltman, p.* 158   ..   £110

1832 — Æ *didrachm.* Amphora. R. Incuse square, as 1829. *B.M.C. 8., p.* 137, 1. *Seltman* 13   ..   ..   £1,750

1833 — Æ *drachm.* Hindquarters of horse r. R. As last. *B.M.C. 8., p.* 136, 1-3. *Seltman p.* 158   ..   ..   £650

1834 — Æ *didrachm.* Gorgon's hd. facing. R. As last, but with panther's hd. facing in one quarter of the incuse square. *B.M.C. 8.* (*Eretria*) 6. *Seltman* 89   ..   £2,500

1835 515-510 B.C. ('Wappenmünzen' coinage). Æ *tetradrachm.* Gorgon's hd. facing. R. Bull's hd. facing, within incuse square. *B.M.C. 8.* (*Eretria*) 14. *Seltman* 315 £7,500

1836   1838

Athens *continued*

1836 — — *Obv.* Similar. ℞. Panther's hd. and paws facing; all within incuse square.
B.M.C. 8. (Eretria) 15-18. *Seltman* 323 .. .. £7,000

1837 510-505 B.C. (first issue of 'owls'). *Æ tetradrachm.* Hd. of Athena r., in *unwreathed*
crested helmet: well modelled and in high relief. ℞. Owl stg. r., hd. facing; AΘE to r.,
olive-spray in upper field to l.; all within incuse square. *B.M.C. 11.* 23. *Seltman* 303
(group H) £3,500

1838 — — Similar, but on *rev.* the owl stands to *left*, with AΘE (retrograde) to l., and olive-
spray in upper field to r. *B.M.C. 11.* 22. *Seltman* 300 (group H) £3,500

1839   1842

1839 505-490 B.C. *Æ tetradrachm. Obv.* Similar, but crest-support on helmet is ornamented
with line of small chevrons and dots. ℞. Owl, well proportioned, stg. r., hd. facing; to r.,
AΘE (with slanting bars to the epsilon); in upper field to l., olive-spray; all within incuse
square. *Seltman* 330 (group L) £1,750

1840 — *Æ drachm.* Similar. *Price & Waggoner* 266. *Seltman, pp.* 199-200 .. £450

1841 — *Æ hemidrachm. Obv.* Similar. ℞. Unhelmeted hd. of Athena Ergane r.; AΘE
behind; two olive-leaves before; all within incuse square. *Price & Waggoner* 267.
Seltman, p. 200 .. .. £400

1842 490-482 B.C. *Æ tetradrachm. Obv.* Similar, but style somewhat coarser: the chevrons
and dots on the crest-support are a little more exaggerated. ℞. Owl stg. r., hd. facing;
to r., AΘE (with square epsilon); in upper field to l., olive-spray (often spiky), with two
leaves and berry; all within incuse square. *B.M.C. 11.* 16. *Seltman* 402 (group M) £1,000

1843 — *Æ drachm.* Similar. *B.M.C. 11.* 27. *Seltman, p.* 181 (group Gi) .. £400

1844 482-480 B.C. *Æ tetradrachm. Obv.* Similar, but of coarse style, with thick lips, and the
chevrons and dots even more exaggerated. ℞. Similar to 1842: the leaves of the olive-
spray are usually very broad. *B.M.C. 11.* 3. *Seltman* 61 (group C) £1,000

1845   1846

1845 — — As last, but helmet has row of studs along the side. *B.M.C. 11.* 8. *Seltman* 146
(group F) £1,000

1846 *Circa* 480 B.C. *Æ tetradrachm.* Similar to 1844, but of very crude, almost barbarous,
style: on *rev.* the alpha, when visible, is shown sideways, and the theta is often represented
as a rosette of pellets. *Seltman* 97 (group E) £750

1847   1848

1847 **AIGINA** (the island-state of Aigina, situated midway between Attica and the coastline of Argolis, was probably the first place in European Greece to issue coinage. From Aigina the practice quickly spread to Athens and Corinth, Euboia, and other important centres. The Aiginetic weight standard, based on a didrachm-stater of about 12·6 gm., was widely adopted in Crete and Asia Minor, as well as Greece). 550-530 B.C. Æ *stater*. Smooth-shelled turtle, with single row of dots down the middle. R. Incuse square, divided irregularly by thin criss-cross lines. *Num. Chron.*, 1950, *pl.* XI, 1. (*British Museum*) £500

1848 530-510 B.C. Æ *stater*. *Obv*. Similar. R. Rough incuse square, with undeveloped pattern. *B.M.C. 11. 7.*   *Price & Waggoner* 424 .. .. £400

1849   1851

1849 510-490 B.C. Æ *stater*. *Obv*. Similar. R. Incuse square, of 'Union Jack' pattern. *B.M.C. 11. 3.*   *Price & Waggoner* 429 .. .. £350

1850 — Æ *triobol*. Similar. *B.M.C. 11. 47* £140

1851 — Æ *stater*. *Obv*. Similar. R. Incuse square, divided into eight triangular compartments, of which five are sunken. *B.M.C. 11. 28.*   *Price & Waggoner* 441 .. £300

1852 — Æ *drachm*. Similar. *B.M.C. 11. 43* £250

1853 — Æ *obol*. Similar. *B.M.C. 11. 73* £90

1854   1858

1854 — Æ *stater*. *Obv*. Similar. R. Incuse square, of 'mill-sail' pattern, the eight triangular compartments alternately raised and sunken. *B.M.C. 11. 12.*   *Price & Waggoner* 478
£300

1855 — Æ *drachm*. Similar. *B.M.C. 11. 41* £250

1856 — Æ *triobol*. Similar. *B.M.C. 11. 46* £150

1857 490-485 B.C. Æ *stater*. *Obv*. Similar. R. Incuse square, of 'proto-skew' pattern (*i.e.* with one or more of the dividing lines wedge-shaped). *Price & Waggoner* 514 £325

1858 485-480 B.C. Æ *stater*. *Obv*. Similar. R. Small incuse square, of 'skew' pattern, divided by straight lines into five compartments. *Price & Waggoner* 541 .. £350

1859   1860

1859 **CORINTHIA: Corinth** (one of the richest and most important cities of ancient Greece,
Corinth gained its wealth from the control of the isthmus connecting Peloponnesos
and central Greece. It was the mother-city of many important colonies, including
Syracuse, Corcyra and Leukas). 545-525 B.C. Æ *stater* (=3 drachms, *c.* 8·5 gm.).
Pegasos, with curled wing, flying r.; koppa beneath. ℞. Incuse square, of 'mill-sail'
pattern, the eight triangular compartments alternately raised and sunken. *Ravel (Les
'poulains' de Corinthe)* 1. *B.M.C. 12.* 1 .. ..   £1,500

1860 525-500 B.C. Æ *stater*. Pegasos, with curled wing, flying l.; koppa (ϙ) beneath. ℞. Quadripartite incuse square, of 'swastika' pattern. *Ravel* 39. *B.M.C. 12.* 16   ..   £600

1861 — — Similar, but Pegasos walking l. *Ravel* 22. *B.M.C. 12.* 2   ..   ..   £750

1862 — Æ *drachm* (*c.* 2·85 gm.). Similar to 1860. *B.M.C. 12.* 29.. .. ..   £175

1863 — Æ *hemidrachm*. Forepart of flying Pegasos l., with curled wing; koppa (ϙ) beneath
℞. 'Swastika' incuse, as 1860. *B.M.C. 12.* 37 .. ..   £125

1864 — Æ *obol* (*c.* 0·5 gm.). Similar to 1860. *B.M.C. 12.* 40   ..   ..   ..   £90

1865 — Æ *hemiobol*. Hd. of Pegasos r. ℞. 'Swastika' incuse, as 1860. *B.M.C. 12.* 47   £45

1866   1867   1870

1866 500-480 B.C. Æ *stater*. Pegasos, with curled wing, flying r.; koppa beneath. ℞. Hd.
of Athena r., in Corinthian helmet; all in linear square within incuse square. *Ravel* 105
B.M.C. 12. 49 .. ..   £250

1867 — — Pegasos, with curled wing, flying l.; koppa beneath. ℞. *Small, compact* hd. of
Athena r., in Corinthian helmet; all within incuse square (no linear square). *Ravel* 138.
B.M.C. 12. 56 .. ..   £225

N.B.   *In the following period, after* 480 B.C., *the Corinthian staters are very similar, but for
the head of Athena, which has developed a markedly elongated appearance—see below under
'Classical and Hellenistic periods'.*

1868 — — Similar, but hd. of Athena l. *Ravel* 153. *B.M.C. 12.* 53   ..   ..   £225

1869 — — Similar to 1867, but Pegasos r. *Ravel* 158-9. *B.M.C. 12.* 66.. ..   £225

1870 — Æ *drachm*. Pegasos, with curled wing, flying l.; koppa beneath. ℞. Hd. of Athena
r., in Corinthian helmet; all in linear square within incuse square. *B.M.C. 12.* 87   £200

1871 — — Similar, but Pegasos to r., and no linear square on *rev*. *B.M.C. 12.* 89   £200

1872 — Æ *hemidrachm*. Forepart of flying Pegasos r., with curled wing; koppa beneath.
℞. Similar to 1870. *B.M.C. 12.* 95 .. ..   £125

1873 — — Similar, but hd. of Athena l. *B.M.C. 12.* 96 .. ..   £125

Classical and Hellenistic Periods

1874   1876

1874 **ILLYRIA. Amantia** (the Amantes were an Illyrian tribe descended from the Abantes of Phokis). 238-168 B.C. Æ 20. Hd. of Zeus of Dodona r., wreathed with oak; behind, ΘOI. ℞. AMAN / TΩN above and below thunderbolt; ΞE beneath; all within oak-wreath. *B.M.C.* 7. 1 ..   ..   £18

1875 — Æ 18. Jugate heads of Zeus and Dione r. ℞. AMAN / TΩN above and below coiled serpent; all within oak-wreath. *B.M.C.* 7. 3 ..   ..   £20

1876 **Apollonia** (a colony of Corcyra, on the Adriatic coast). *Circa* 400 B.C. Æ *stater*. Cow stg. r., looking back at calf, which it suckles. ℞. A Π on two sides of square containing double stellate pattern. *B.M.C.* 7. 1   ..   ..   £350

1877   1878

1877 *Circa* 350 B.C. Æ *stater* of the Corinthian type. Pegasos, with pointed wing, flying r. ℞. Hd. of Athena r., wearing Corinthian helmet over leather cap; AΠOΛ before, lyre behind. *B.M.C.* 12. (*Colonies of Corinth*), *p.* 100, 1 ..   ..   ..   £250

1878 3rd-2nd Cent. B.C., after 229 (period of Roman protectorate). Æ *drachm* (*c.* 3·25 gm.). Cow stg. l., looking back at calf, which it suckles; above, NIKΩN; below, caduceus. ℞. AΠOΛ APIΣTIΠΠOY around square containing double stellate pattern. *B.M.C.* 7. 7   £35

1879 — — Similar, but cow to r., with ΛONAΞ above; *rev.* legend AΠOΛ MOΣXOY. *B.M.C.* 7. 25, 26 ..   ..   £35
    This extensive series bears the names of many moneyers and eponymous magistrates, on obv. and rev. respectively.

1880 — Æ *hemidrachm*. Forepart of cow stg. r., EK above. ℞. AΠOΛ . . . AΓEOΣ around square containing double stellate pattern. *B.M.C.* 7. 43 ..   ..   ..   £65

1881 — — AI / NEA above and below fire of the Nymphaeum. ℞. AΠOΛΛΩ / NIATAN either side of pedum. *B.M.C.* 7. 44, 45   ..   ..   £75

1882 1st Cent. B.C. Æ *drachm* (*c.* 4 gm.). Laur. hd. of Apollo l., ΔΩPIΩNOΣ before. ℞. Three nymphs hand in hand, dancing round the fire of the Nymphaeum; AΠOΛ in field, ANΔPOMA / XOΣ in ex. *B.M.C.* 7. 66 ..   ..   £100

1883 — Æ *hemidrachm*. Hd. of Athena l., in Corinthian helmet, ANΔPΩNOΣ before. ℞. AΠOΛΛΩ / NIATAN either side of obelisk; TI / MHN on r. and l. *B.M.C.* 7. 73, 74   £75

1884 *Bronze Coinage.* 400-350 B.C. Æ 13. Lyre. ℞. AΠOΛ / ΛΩNOΣ either side of obelisk *B.M.C.* 7. 2 ..   ..   £15

1885   1889

Apollomia *continued*

1885 3rd-2nd Cent. B.C. Æ 27. Diad. hd. of Artemis l., bow and quiver at shoulder; ΞΕ below, monogram and ΧΑΙΡΗΝ behind. Ŗ. ΑΠΟΛΛΩ / ΝΙΑΤΑΝ either side of tripod-lebes; all within laurel-wreath. *B.M.C. 7. 56* £15

1886 — Æ 23. Hd. of young Dionysos l., wreathed with ivy; monogram before, ΞΕ and monogram behind. Ŗ. ΑΠΟΛΛΩ / ΝΙΑΤΑΝ either side of cornucopiae. *B.M.C. 7. 58, 59*   £12

1887 — Æ 17. Laur. hd. of Apollo r. Ŗ. Obelisk; ΑΠΟ-ΛΛΩ / ΝΙΑ-ΤΑΝ in field; all within laurel-wreath. *B.M.C. 7. 49* £9

1888 **Byllis.** 238-168 B.C. Æ 15. Hd. of Zeus of Dodona r., wreathed with oak. Ŗ. Serpent entwined round cornucopiae; ΒΥΛ-ΛΙΟ / Ν-ΩΝ in field; all within oak-wreath. *B.M.C. 7. 1* ..   .. ᾽ £15

1889 — Æ 13. Young male hd. r., helmeted. Ŗ. ΒΥΛ / ΛΙΣ behind and before eagle stg. r. on thunderbolt. *B.M.C. 7. 4* £12

1890   1893

1890 **Epidamnos-Dyrrhachium** (Epidamnos, a colony of Corcyra founded *c.* 623 B.C., was the chief town of the Dyrrhachii, in whose name its coins were issued. The Romans changed the name of the place to Dyrrhachium, and it became the main port of arrival in Greece for ships from Brundisium, in Italy). 400-350 B.C. Æ *stater.* Cow stg. r., looking back at calf, which it suckles. Ŗ. ΔΥΡ and club around square containing double stellate pattern. *B.M.C. 7. 1* £150

1891 — — Similar, but cow to l., with lizard l. above. *B.M.C. 7. 19* £175

1892 — — Similar, but cow to r., with ΜΕ above; on *rev.*, ΔΥΡ is retrograde. *B.M.C. 7. 22, 23*   £175

1893 350-300 B.C. Æ *stater* of the Corinthian type. Pegasos, with pointed wing, flying r. Ŗ. Hd. of Athena r., wearing Corinthian helmet over leather cap; ΔΥΡΡΑΧΙΝΩΝ before; club and Σ (reversed) behind. *B.M.C. 12. (Colonies of Corinth), p. 100, 3*   ..   £160

1894 — — Pegasos r., as last, but with Δ beneath. Ŗ. Hd. of Athena r., as last, but with dolphin before, club behind and Δ-ΥΡ in lower field. *B.M.C. 12. (Colonies of Corinth), p. 101, 6* £140

1895 — — *Obv.* Similar. Ŗ. Hd. of Athena r., as 1893, but with dolphin before, and club and Ε (reversed) behind. *B.M.C. 12. (Colonies of Corinth), p. 101, 12* £140

1896 250-229 B.C. Æ *drachm.* Hd. of young Herakles r., in lion's skin. Ŗ. ΔΥΡ (retrograde). Pegasos flying r. *B.M.C. 12. (Colonies of Corinth), p. 103, 27-31* £55

1897 — — Similar, but ΛΥΡ not retrograde, and with monogram beneath Pegasos. *B.M.C.*
12. (*Colonies of Corinth*), *p.* 102, 18   ..   ..   £55

1898 — — *Obv.* Similar. ℞. Pegasos flying r.; thunderbolt to l.; monogram and bow in case
beneath. *B.M.C. 12.* (*Colonies of Corinth*), *p.* 103, 37 ..   ..   £55

1899 3rd-2nd Cent. B.C., after 229 (period of Roman protectorate). *Æ drachm* (*c.* 3·25 gm.).
Cow stg. r., looking back at calf, which it suckles; above, ΕΥΝΟΥΣ; to r., cornucopiae; in ex.,
rudder. ℞. ΛΥΡ ΑΜΥΝΤΑ around square containing double stellate pattern. *B.M.C. 7.* 32,
33 ..   ..   £30

1900   1902

1900 — — Similar, but with ΑΡΙΣΤΩΝ above, corn-ear to r. and bunch of grapes in ex. on *obv.;*
and with ΛΥΡ ΔΑΜΗΝΟΣ on *rev.* *B.M.C. 7.* 51 ..   ..   £30

1901 — — Similar, but with ΦΙΛΩΝ and hd. of Isis above, corn-ear and grapes to r. on *obv.;*
and with ΛΥΡ ΦΑΝΙΣΚΟΥ on *rev.* *B.M.C. 7.* 122 ..   ..   £30

*This very large series, like the contemporary issues of Apollonia (nos. 1878-9), bears the
names of numerous moneyers and eponymous magistrates.*

1902 — *Æ hemidrachm.* Forepart of cow stg. r., ΛΛ above. ℞. ΛΥΡ ΛΥΣΙΠΠΟΥ around square
containing double stellate pattern. *B.M.C. 7.* 151 ..   ..   £50

1903 — Æ 18. Hd. of Zeus of Dodona r., wreathed with oak. ℞. ΑΓΑΘΟ / ΚΛΕΟC either side
of tripod-lebes, ΛΥΡ beneath; all within oak-wreath. *B.M.C. 7.* 158, 159 ..   £9

1904 — Æ 15. Rad. hd. of Helios r. ℞. ΛΥΡ. Prow r., ΦΙΛΙΠ / ΠΟΥ above and below. *B.M.C.*
7. 183   ..   ..   £8

1905 — Æ 13. Hd. of young Herakles l., in lion's skin. ℞. ΛΥΡ ΞΕΝΙCΚΟΥ. Bow, club and
quiver. *B.M.C. 7.* 172, 173   ..   ..   £7

1906 **Lissos** (at the mouth of the river Drilon, Lissos was founded by Dionysios of Syracuse in
385 B.C.). 211-197 B.C. Æ 13. Goat stg. ℞. ΛΙΣΣΙΤΑΝ. Thunderbolt. *Num. Chron.*,
1880, *pl. XIII*, 3   ..   ..   £20

1907 After 168 B.C. Æ 18. Hd. of Hermes (?), wearing petasos. ℞. — Galley. *Historia
Numorum*, *p.* 315 ..   ..   £25

1908 **Orikos** (traditionally founded by Euboians returning from Troy, Orikos was a port near
the mouth of the river Aous). 238-168 B.C. Æ 20. Hd. of Zeus of Dodona r., wreathed
with oak; Α beneath chin. ℞. ΩΡΙΚΙΩΝ. Eagle stg. l. on thunderbolt, Τ behind hd.; all
within oak-wreath. *Grose* 5073 ..   ..   £17

1909 — Æ 17. Laur. hd. of Apollo r. ℞. — Obelisk of Apollo Agyieos; all within wreath.
B.M.C. 7. 1-3   ..   ..   £15

1910 — Æ 13. Hd. of Athena r., in Corinthian helmet; behind, Κ. ℞. — Thunderbolt.
B.M.C. 7. 5 ..   ..   £12

1912 **Skodra** (situated on the river Barbana, about 17 miles from the coast, Skodra was the
residence of the Illyrian King Genthios). After 168 B.C. Æ 17. Hd. of Zeus of Dodona
r., wreathed with oak. ℞. ΣΚΟΔΡΕΙ / ΝΩΝ above war-galley. *B.M.C. 7.* 1 ..   £18

1913   1916

1913 ILLYRIAN KINGS. Monunios, *c.* 300-280 B.C. Æ *stater* of *Epidamnos-Dyrrhachium.* Cow stg. r., looking back at calf, which it suckles; above, jaw-bone of Calydonian boar. R. Square containing double stellate pattern; ΒΑΣΙΛΕΩΣ / ΜΟΝΟΥΝΙΟΥ above and below; spear-head to l., club to r. *B.M.C. 7., p.* 80, 1 ..   ..   £350

1914 Genthios, *c.* 197-168 B.C. (became king of Illyria following the Roman victory over Philip V of Macedon). Æ 15. Macedonian shield. R. ΒΑΣΙΛΕΩΣ ΓΕΝΘΙΟΥ. Helmet. *Historia Numorum, p.* 317 ..   ..   £25

1915 Æ 13. Hd. of Genthios, wearing kausia. R. — Thunderbolt. *Historia Numorum, p.* 317   ..   ..   £25

1916 Ballaios, *c.* 167-135 B.C. Æ *drachm*? (*c.* 3·5 gm.). Bare hd. of Ballaios l. R. ΒΑΣΙΛΕΩΣ ΒΑΛΛΑΙΟΥ. Artemis advancing l., holding torch and two spears. *B.M.C. 7., p.* 81, 5   £200

1917 Æ 18. Similar, but Artemis holds only one spear. *B.M.C. 7., p.* 81, 8   ..   £24

1918   1919

1918 Æ 14. Bare hd. of Ballaios r. R. ΒΑΛΛΑΙΟΥ (partly retrograde). Artemis stg. l., holding torch. *B.M.C. 7., p.* 81, 2   ..   ..   £22

1919 ILLYRIAN ISLANDS: ISSA (colonized by Parians, in 385 B.C., with the help of Dionysios of Syracuse). 4th Cent. B.C. Æ 24. Hd. of Athena r., in Corinthian helmet. R. Goat stg. r., ΙΣ above. *B.M.C. 7., p.* 82, 1-4 ..   ..   £20

1920 — Æ 22. Amphora, ΙΣ above. R. Vine-branch, with bunch of grapes and leaves. *B.M.C. 7., p.* 82, 8 ..   ..   £18

1921   1922

1921 2nd Cent. B.C. Æ 19. Young male hd. r., bare. R. Ι-Σ either side of kantharos. *B.M.C. 7., p.* 82, 10..   ..   ..   £16

1922 — **PHAROS** (colonized at the same time as the neighbouring island of Issa). 4th Cent. B.C. Æ *tetrobol*? (*c.* 2·65 gm.). Laur. hd. of Zeus l. R. Goat stg. l. *B.M.C. 7., p.* 83, 1   ..   ..   £175

1923 — Æ 23. Similar, but with serpent before goat. *B.M.C. 7., p.* 83, 2, 3   ..   £20

1924 — Æ 20. Hd. of Persephone l., wreathed with corn. R. Goat stg. l., ΦΑ in ex. *B.M.C. 7., p.* 83, 7 ..   ..   £18

1925   1926

1925 2nd Cent. B.C. Æ 19. Young male hd. l., laur. R. Φ-A either side of kantharos. *B.M.C. 7., p.* 84, 12-14 .. .. £15

1926 **Herakleia** (a town on the island of Pharos). 4th Cent. B.C. Æ 24. Hd. of young Herakles r., in lion's skin. R. Bow and club, HPAKΛ beneath; large pellet at centre. *B.M.C. 7., p.* 78, 1-4 .. .. £30

1927   1929

1927 **ILLYRO-PAEONIAN REGION** (a little-known area, comprising mountainous country on the borders of Illyria and Paeonia, it possessed rich silver deposits. The centre of the mining industry was the town of Damastion, the site of which has yet to be discovered). **Damastion.** 395-380 B.C. Æ *tetradrachm* (*c.* 13·5 gm.). Laur. hd. of Apollo l. R. ΔAMA / ΣTINΩ either side of tripod-lebes; all within incuse square. May (*The Coinage of Damastion*) 12. *B.M.C. 7.* 1 .. .. £550
  This coinage is inspired by the types of the Chalkidian League, issued from Olynthos.

1928 — Æ *drachm.* Female hd. l., wearing sphendone. R. ΔAMAΣTINΩN. Portable ingot. *May* 5. *B.M.C. 7.* 10 .. .. £450
  The female head on these coins is copied from the silver drachms of Larissa, in Thessaly.

1929 380-360 B.C. Æ *tetradrachm.* Laur. hd. of Apollo l., with long flowing hair. R. Similar to 1927, but the tripod is of more massive form, and there are only slight indications of the incuse square. *May* 32. *B.M.C. 7.* 2 .. .. £500

1930 — Æ *tetrobol.* Laur. hd. of Apollo r. R. ΔAMA / ΣTINΩ either side of tripod-lebes; all within incuse square. *May* 5. *B.M.C. 7.* 13 .. .. £200

1931   1934

1931 360-345 B.C. Æ *tetradrachm.* Laur. hd. of Apollo r. R. Tripod stg. on thick base inscribed HPAKΛ, EIΔO in field to r.; to l., knife and KH. *May* 53a (*British Museum*) £500

1932 — — *Obv.* Similar, but of much poorer style. R. Tripod stg. on thick base inscribed ΔAMAΣT, NΩN in field to r.; to l., KHΦI. *May* 60d. *B.M.C. 7.* 8 .. .. £450

1933 — Æ *drachm.* Female hd. r., with necklace and ear-ring, hair in net behind. R. ΔAMAΣTINΩ. Portable ingot, inscribed KHΦ. *May* 10i (*Ashmolean, Oxford*) .. £350

1934 — Æ *tetrobol.* Similar to 1932, but on *rev.* the base is inscribed ΔAMA, ΣTIN in field to r., and KHΦ to l. *May* 9c. *B.M.C. 7.* 15 .. .. £175

1935   1936

Damastion *continued*

1935 345-330 B.C.   Æ *tetradrachm*.   Laur. hd. of Apollo l.   R. ΔΑΜΑΣ / ΤΙΝΩΝ either side of
tripod stg. on base; between the legs, two swastika symbols.   *May* 73e.   *B.M.C.* 7. 3
£450

1936 — Æ *drachm*.   Female hd. r., wearing stephane, hair-net and ear-ring.   R. ΔΑΜΑΣΤΙΝΩΝ.
Portable ingot, inscribed with swastika symbol.   *May* 17b.   *B.M.C.* 7. 12 ..   £350

1937 — Æ *tetrobol*.   Hd. of Apollo (?) r., of crude style.   R. ΔΑΜ / ΤΙΝ either side of pick-axe.
May 15b.   *B.M.C.* 7. 17 ..   ..   £150

1938   1940

1938 330-323 B.C.   Æ *tetradrachm*.   Laur. hd. of Apollo r., of barbarous style.   R. ΔΑΜ / ΑΣΤΙ
(retrograde) either side of tripod, stg. on base which is inscribed ΚΑΚΙΟ.   *May* 107a.
B.M.C. 7. 6 ..   ..   £400

1939 **"Daparria"** (whether this name represents a town or a ruler we cannot be sure, but the
coins are strongly influenced by those of Damastion, and may even have been struck there).
365-360 B.C.   Æ *tetrobol*.   Laur. hd. of Apollo r., with short hair.   R. ΔΑΠ / ΑΡΡΙΑ either
side of tripod-lebes.   *May*, *p.* 164, 2.   *B.M.C.* 7., *p.* 87, 2 (*Uncertain places*) ..   £350

1940 335-330 B.C.   Æ *tetradrachm*.   Laur. hd. of Apollo l.   R. ΔΑΠΑ / ΡΡΙΑ (partly retrograde)
either side of tripod-lebes.   *May*, *p.* 164, 5.   *Weber* 2985   ..   ..   ..   £750

1941   1943

1941 **Pelagia** (the site of this town is not known, and its earlier issues, down to *c.* 323 B.C., were
struck probably at the mint of Damastion).   360-350 B.C.   Æ *tetradrachm*.   Laur. hd. of
Apollo r.   R. ΠΕΛΑΓΙΤΑΟΝ around highly ornamented circular shield (Macedonian).
May, *p.* 170, 1   ..   .. (*Unique*)

1942 — Æ *drachm*.   Female hd. r., hair in net (?) behind R.   ΠΕΛΑΓΙΤΕΩΝ.   Portable ingot.
May, *p.* 173, 2 (*Ashmolean*, *Oxford*) £500

1943 330-323 B.C.   Æ *tetradrachm*.   Laur. hd. of Apollo r., of crude style.   R. Crude tripod;
ΠΕΛΑ to r., ΓΙ between legs; knife to l.   *May*, *p.* 174, 6.   *B.M.C.* 7. 2 ..   ..   £650

1944 323-310 B.C.   Æ *tetradrachm*.   Stylized laur. hd. of Apollo l., with exaggerated jaw and
receding forehead.   R. ΕΛΛ (retrograde).   Disintegrated tripod; crescent above, knife to
r.   *May*, *p.* 181, 11   ..   ..   £500

1945 310-300 B.C.   Æ *tetradrachm*? (wt. now reduced to *c*. 7 gm., but individual specimens fluctuate considerably from this norm). Hd. of young Herakles r., in lion's skin. R. Similar to last. *May, p.* 184, 13 .. .. £450
    This obv. type was copied from the posthumous coinage of Alexander the Great.

1946   1952

1946 300-280 B.C.   Æ *tetradrachm*? Similar, but the hd. of Herakles is further adorned, with the horn of Ammon: more stylized treatment. *May, p.* 186, 21. *B.M.C.* 7. 3 (*Gaulish imitation*) £450
    The horn of Ammon, on obv., is inspired probably by the coinage of Lysimachos of Thrace. The issue terminates with the Gallic invasion, c. 280 *B.C.*

1947 **Simon** (an unknown dynast, whose coinage was issued from Damastion). *Circa* 355 B.C. Æ *tetradrachm*. Laur. hd. of Apollo r. R. ΣΙΜΩ / ΝΟΣ either side of tripod-lebes. *May, pl. IX, A* .. .. (*Unique*)

1948 **Nikarchos** (another dynast, issuing coinage from the Damastion mint). *Circa* 360 B.C. Æ *tetradrachm*. Laur. hd. of Apollo r. R. ΝΙΚΑ / ΡΧΟΥ either side of trident-head. *May, pl. IX, B* .. .. (*Unique*)

1949 **The Tenestini** (an unknown tribe of the Illyro-Paeonian region). *Circa* 335 B.C. Æ *tetradrachm*. Stylized laur. hd. of Apollo r. R. ΤΕΝΕΣ / ΤΙΝΩΝ (partly retrograde) either side of tripod-lebes on base. *May, pl. IX, C* .. .. (*Unique*)

1950 **The Sarnoates** (this tribe occupied an area close to Pelagia, whose coinage they used as a model for their own). *Circa* 315 B.C. Æ *tetradrachm*. Laur. hd. of Apollo l. R. ΣΑΡΝΟΑΤΩΝ. Disintegrated tripod, upside down; ΦΑΙ monogram between legs, knife in field to l., crescent beneath. *May, pl. IX, E* .. .. (*Unique*)

1951 "**Darado**" (although definitely belonging to this area, the name *Darado* is unknown in history and could represent either a town or some local ruler). *Circa* 350 B.C. Æ *drachm*. Female hd. l., wearing sphendone. R. ΔΑΡ / ΑΔΟ within square frame. *May, pl. XII, G* £550

1952 **EPEIROS. Ambrakia** (an important colony of Corinth, Ambrakia was founded *c.* 660 B.C., and became the capital of the kingdom of Epeiros under Pyrrhos). 480-456 B.C. Æ *stater* of the Corinthian type. Pegasos, with curled wing, flying r.; A beneath. R. Hd. of Athena r., wearing Corinthian helmet; all within incuse square. *Ravel* (*The 'Colts' of Ambracia*) 1. *Weber* 3828 .. .. £200

1953 — — Similar, but with ivy-branch behind hd. of Athena. *Ravel* 9. *B.M.C.* 12. (*Colonies of Corinth*), p. 104, 1 .. .. £200

1954 456-426 B.C.   Æ *stater*. Pegasos, with curled wing, flying l.; A to l.; beneath, serpent coiled round tortoise. R. Hd. of Athena l., wearing Corinthian helmet which is sur-mounted by bull butting l.; A in upper field to l.; all within incuse square. *Ravel* 17. *B.M.C.* 12. 17 .. .. £350

Ambrakia *continued*

1955 — — Pegasos, with pointed wing, flying l.; A beneath. ℞. Hd. of Athena l., wearing Corinthian helmet; behind, kantharos; all within incuse square. *Ravel* 28. *B.M.C. 12.* 37 .. .. £175

1956 426-404 B.C. ℛ *stater.* Pegasos, with pointed wing, flying r. ℞. Hd. of Athena r., wearing Corinthian helmet, bound with olive, over leather cap; caduceus behind, A before; traces of incuse square. *Ravel* 45. *B.M.C. 12.* 46 .. .. £175

1957 — — *Obv.* Similar, but with A beneath. ℞. Hd. of Athena r., wearing Corinthian helmet over leather cap; behind, owl stg. r. *Ravel* 74. *B.M.C. 12.* 15 .. £150

1958   1960

1958 404-360 B.C. ℛ *stater.* *Obv.* Similar. ℞. Hd. of Athena l., wearing Corinthian helmet over leather cap; ΑΜΒΡΑΚΙΩΤΑΝ before; behind, girl stg. l., holding kottabos pole. *Ravel* 106. *B.M.C. 12.* 5.. .. .. £250

1959 — — *Obv.* Similar. ℞. Hd. of Athena r., wearing Corinthian helmet over leather cap; behind, prow r.; before, A; traces of incuse square. *Ravel* 113. *B.M.C. 12.* 39, 40 £125

1960 360-338 B.C. (at which date the mint was closed, following the occupation of the town by the forces of Philip II of Macedon). ℛ *stater.* Pegasos, with curled wing, pacing r.; A beneath. ℞. Hd. of Athena l., wearing Corinthian helmet over leather cap; behind, hd. of Achelous facing. *Ravel* 137. *B.M.C. 12.* 19 .. .. £150

1961 — — Pegasos, with pointed wing, stg. r., its l. hoof examined by naked male figure (Bellerophon) squatting r. beneath. ℞. Hd. of Athena r., wearing Corinthian helmet over leather cap; A behind. *Ravel* 147. *B.M.C. 12.* 57 .. .. £300

1962 — — Pegasos, with pointed wing, flying l.; A beneath. ℞. Hd. of Athena l., wearing crested Corinthian helmet over leather cap; behind, spear-head. *Ravel* 167. *B.M.C. 12.* 42 .. .. £200

1963   1964

1963 238-168 B.C. ℛ *drachm.* Laur. and veiled hd. of Dione l. ℞. A — M either side of obelisk of Apollo, bound with tainia; all within laurel-wreath. *B.M.C. 7. (Epirus)* 1-3 £120

1964 — Æ 18. Similar, but hd. of Dione to r., and on *rev.* the obelisk, which is without tainia, divides the legend A — M / B — P. *B.M.C. 7.* 5-7 .. .. £9

1965 — Æ 14. Hd. of Athena r., wearing crested Corinthian helmet. ℞. A — M either side of obelisk; all within laurel-wreath. *B.M.C. 7.* 11, 12 .. .. £7

1966 — Æ 19. Hd. of young Herakles r., in lion's skin. ℞. Apollo Aktios seated l., holding bow; in field, A — M / B — P. *B.M.C. 7.* 15-17 .. .. £9

1967 — Æ 21. Laur. hd. of Apollo r. ℞. Zeus advancing r., brandishing thunderbolt and holding aegis; monogram to l.; in field, A — M / B — P. *B.M.C. 7.* 25, 26 .. £10

1968 — Æ 19. Laur. hd. of Zeus r. ℞. Griffin running r.; A — M / B — P in field; ΔΑΜΙΩΝ in ex. *B.M.C. 7.* 29, 30 .. .. £11

1969 **The Athamanes** (originally a Thessalian tribe, the Athamanes were driven out of their homeland, and settled in Epeiros). 220-190 B.C. Æ 17. Veiled and diad. hd. of Dione r. R. AΘAMANΩN. Athena standing left, holding owl and spear. *B.M.C. 7.* 1-4   £14

1970 — Æ 16. Laur. hd. of Apollo r. R. AΘAMA. Hd. and shoulders of bull l., hd. facing. *Weber* 2999   .. ..   £15

1971   1972

1971 **Kassope** (situated in the south of the country, in the district of Thesprotia, north-west of the Ambrakian gulf). 4th Cent., before 342 B.C. Æ 20. KAΣΣΩΠAIΩN. Hd of Aphrodite r., wearing stephanos ornamented with honeysuckle. R. Dove flying l.; ΠOΛ / Y in field to r.; all within laurel-wreath. *B.M.C. 7.* 3   .. .. ..   £14

1972 238-168 B.C. Æ *drachm* (*c.* 5 gm.). Hd. of Zeus r., wreathed with oak; monogram behind. R. KAΣΣΩ / ΠAIΩN either side of eagle stg. r. on thunderbolt; all within oak-wreath. *B.M.C. 7.* 8   .. ..   £125

1973 — Æ 18. Hd. of bearded Dionysos r., wreathed with ivy; IEPΩ before. R. KAΣΣΩ / ΠAIΩN either side of amphora; all within wreath. *B.M.C. 7* 14, 15   .. ..   £16

1974 **Dodona** (the home of the most ancient oracle in Greece, dedicated to Zeus). After 168 B.C. Æ 25. Hd. of Zeus of Dodona r., wreathed with oak; before, IEPEYΣ. R. MENEΔHMOΣ / APΓEAΔHΣ before and behind diad. bust of Artemis r. *B.M.C. 7., p.* 93, 68, 69   .. ..   £20
These were struck in the names of priests of the temple of Zeus Naios after the devastation of Epeiros by the Romans.

1975   1977

1975 **Elea** (situated on the coast, in the district of Thesprotia). 4th Cent., before 342 B.C. Æ 20. Hd. of Persephone three-quarter face to l., wreathed with corn. R. Kerberos stg. l.; ΘE below. *B.M.C. 7.* 4   .. ..   £22

1976 — Æ 14. Pegasos flying r. R. EΛEAT. Trident; ear of corn to r. *B.M.C. 7.* 1   £15

1977 **The Molossi** (the most powerful tribe in Epeiros, their kings eventually extended their rule over the whole country. The famous Molossian hounds were much prized for hunting). 4th Cent., before 342 B.C. Æ *tetrobol* (*c.* 2·25 gm.). Molossian hound stg. r. R. MOΛOΣΣΩN (retrograde). Thunderbolt. *Hist. Num., p.* 321   .. ..   £250

1978 — Æ 20. Hd. of Athena l., in crested Athenian helmet. R. Eagle stg. l. on thunderbolt, wings closed; MOΛOΣΣΩN behind. *B.M.C. 7.* 1   .. ..   £18

1979   1982

The Molossi *continued*

1979 — Æ 19. ΜΟΛΟΣΣΩΝ around rim of circular shield, on which, thunderbolt. ℞. Thunderbolt within laurel-wreath. *B.M.C. 7.* 3, 4 ..   ..   £20

1980 **Pandosia** (on the Acheron river in the district of Thesprotia). 238-168 B.C. Æ 19. ΑΓΙΑΣ. Hd. of Dodonaean Zeus l., wreathed with oak. ℞. ΠΑΝ beneath thunderbolt; all within oak-wreath. *B.M.C. 7.* 1 ..   ..   £18

1981 **Phoenike** (situated in the north of the country, in a marshy area, Phoenike became a place of considerable importance after the end of the monarchical period, and may have been the capital of the Epeirote Republic). 238-168 B.C. Æ 21. Hd. of Zeus r., hair bound with tainia. ℞. ΦΟΙΝΙ / ΚΑΙΕΩΝ above and below thunderbolt; all within oak-wreath. *B.M.C. 7.* 1, 2 ..   ..   £22

1982 — Æ 19. Diad. bust of Artemis r., bow and quiver at shoulder. ℞. ΦΟΙΝΙ / ΚΑΙΕΩΝ either side of spear-head; all within oak-wreath. *B.M.C. 7.* 3 ..   ..   ..   £18

1983 **EPEIROTE KINGS. Alexander,** son of Neoptolemos, 342-330 B.C. (King of the Molossians, Alexander was made ruler of the whole of Epeiros by Philip II of Macedon. In the last four years of his reign he intervened in the politics of southern Italy, but was killed in battle against the Lucanians and Bruttians near Pandosia in Bruttium). *N stater.* Hd. of Zeus Dodonaios r., of exquisite style, wreathed with oak. ℞. ΑΛΕΞΑΝΔΡΟΥ / ΤΟΥ ΝΕΟΠΤΟΛΕΜΟΥ either side of thunderbolt; spear-head in field to l. *B.M.C. 7.* 1   £7,500

> *Struck at Taras, in southern Italy, the probable mint for all of Alexander's coinage in gold and silver.*

1984   1987

1984 *N twelfth-stater* (c. 0·7 gm.). Rad. hd. of Helios three-quarter face to l. ℞. ΑΛ / ΕΞ above and below thunderbolt. *B.M.C. 7.* 2   ..   ..   £500

1985 *Æ stater* (c. 10·7 gm.). Similar to 1983, but the symbol on *rev.* is eagle stg. r., in field to r. *B.M.C. 7.* 3   ..   ..   £2,250

1986 *Æ trihemiobol.* Similar to 1984, but the legend on *rev.* is ΑΛΕΞΑΝ / ΔΡΟΥ above and below thunderbolt. *B.M.C. 7.* 5, 6 ..   ..   £150

1987 Æ 17. Eagle stg. r.; tripod behind, olive-spray before. ℞. ΑΛΕΞΑ / ΤΟΥ ΝΕ above and below thunderbolt; all within olive-wreath. *B.M.C. 7.* 7, 8 ..   ..   ..   £15

1988   1991

1988 **Pyrrhos,** 295-272 B.C. (one of the greatest generals of antiquity, Pyrrhos spent much of his reign campaigning outside his kingdom. He achieved notable victories against the Romans in Italy, and against the Carthaginians in Sicily, though he was eventually worsted by the former. For a brief period he also ruled the Macedonian kingdom). Æ *tetradrachm.* Hd. of Zeus Dodonaios l., wreathed with oak; below, Θ and monogram. ℞. ΒΑΣΙΛΕΩΣ / ΠΥΡΡΟΥ either side of Dione enthroned l., holding long sceptre; in ex., A *B.M.C. 7.* 6 ..   ..   £1,750
This and the next were struck at Lokroi, in southern Italy, between 280 and 277 B.C.

1989 Æ *didrachm.* Hd. of Achilles l., wearing crested helmet ornamented with griffin; A below. ℞. ΒΑΣΙΛΕΩΣ / ΠΥΡΡΟΥ above and below Thetis seated l. on hippocamp r., holding shield of Achilles. *B.M.C. 7.* 8 ..   ..   £1,250

1990 Æ 25. Hd. of Zeus Dodonaios r., wreathed with oak. ℞. ΒΑΣΙΛΕΩΣ / ΠΥΡΡΟΥ above and below thunderbolt; all within oak-wreath. *B.M.C. 7.* 40   ..   ..   ..   £14

1991 Æ 20. *Obv.* Similar, but hd. l. ℞. Thunderbolt; B above, ΠΥΡ monogram beneath; all within oak-wreath. *B.M.C. 7.* 44-7 ..   ..   £12

N.B. *For other coins of Pyrrhos, in gold, silver and bronze, see under Syracuse (nos.* 980-982 1213-17) *and under 'Hellenistic Monarchies' in Part 2 of this Catalogue.*

1992   1995

1992 **EPEIROTE REPUBLIC.** Before 238 B.C. Æ 17. Bull butting r., ΑΠΕΙΡΩΤΑΝ in ex. ℞. Thunderbolt, within wreath. *B.M.C. 7.* 1 ..   ..   £14

1993 — Æ 27. Hd. of Zeus Dodonaios r., wreathed with oak. ℞. Thunderbolt; ΑΠ monogram above, cornucopiae beneath; all within oak-wreath. *B.M.C. 7.* 3   ..   £20

1994 — Æ 20. Laur. hd. of Zeus l. ℞. A / Π above and below thunderbolt; all within oak-wreath. *B.M.C. 7.* 5 ..   ..   £15

1995 238-168 B.C. Æ *didrachm* (*c.* 10 gm.). Jugate hds. r. of Zeus Dodonaios, wreathed with oak, and Dione, veiled and diad.; behind, ΜΕ monogram. ℞. ΑΠΕΙ / ΡΩΤΑΝ above and below bull butting r.; all within oak-wreath. *B.M.C. 7.* 10, 11   ..   ..   £550

1996   2001

Epeirote Republic *continued*

1996 — *R drachm.* Hd. of Zeus Dodonaios r., wreathed with oak; EK monogram behind. R. ΑΠΕΙ / PΩTAN either side of eagle stg. r. on thunderbolt; all within oak-wreath. *B.M.C.* 7. 23, 24 .. .. £90

1997 — *R tetrobol.* Zeus and Dione, similar to 1995, but with EK monogram behind. R. ΑΠΕΙ / PΩTAN above and below thunderbolt; all within oak-wreath. *B.M.C.* 7. 42, 43   £150

1998 — *R diobol. Obv.* As 1996. R. As last. *B.M.C.* 7. 44, 45 .. .. £85

1999 — Æ 23. Hd. of Zeus Dodonaios l., wreathed with oak. R. As last. *B.M.C.* 7. 47   £9

2000 — Æ 19. Zeus and Dione, similar to 1995, but with ΘE monogram behind. R. As last. *B.M.C.* 7. 59 .. .. £12

2001 — Æ 17. Hd. of Dione r., veiled and wearing laur. stephanos; ANT monogram behind. R. ΑΠΕΙ / PΩTAN either side of tripod-lebes; all within laurel-wreath. *B.M.C.* 7. 53 £9

2002 — — Diad. bust of Artemis r., bow and quiver at shoulder; EK monogram behind, ΣΩ before. R. ΑΠΕΙ / PΩTAN above and below spear-head r.; all within laurel-wreath. *B.M.C.* 7. 65, 66 .. .. £8

2003 — Æ 13. Hd. of young Herakles r., in lion's skin. R. ΑΠΕΙ / PΩTAN above and below club r.; all within oak-wreath. *B.M.C.* 7. 60 .. .. £7

2004   2007

2004 **CORCYRA** (surrendered to the Romans in 229 B.C.). 475-450 B.C. *R stater.* Cow stg. l., looking back at calf, which it suckles. R. Incuse square, containing double stellate pattern. *B.M.C.* 7. 34-40.. .. .. £200

2005 — *R hemidrachm.* Amphora. R. Star within incuse circle. *B.M.C.* 7. 45, 46 £85

2006 — *R diobol.* Amphora. R. Kantharos, wreathed with ivy; above, K. *B.M.C.* 7. 55-7   £75

2007 450-400 B.C. *R stater. Obv.* As 2004. R. K on one side of square, containing double stellate pattern. *B.M.C.* 7. 60-65 .. .. £150

2008 — *R drachm.* Forepart of cow stg. r. R. Star-shaped floral pattern, within triple border. *B.M.C.* 7. 70 .. .. £120

2009 — *R hemidrachm.* Amphora, wreathed; ivy-leaf in field to l. R. Star; K between two of the rays. *B.M.C.* 7. 72-4 .. .. £65

2010   2014

2010 — — KOP. Diad. hd. of Hera r. R. As last. *B.M.C.* 7. 79 .. .. .. £85

2011 — *R diobol. Obv.* As 2009. R. As 2006. *B.M.C.* 7. 83, 84.. .. .. £60

2012 — — Diad. hd. of Hera r. R. Kantharos, wreathed with ivy; above, Δ (=diobol). *B.M.C. 7.* 88 .. .. £75

2013 — — Gorgoneion. R. Similar to last, but without ivy-wreath. *B.M.C. 7.* 89 £80

2014 — Æ *trihemiobol*. Ram's hd. r.; ivy-leaf below. R. Bunch of grapes; κ (reversed) in field to l. *B.M.C. 7.* 92 .. .. £55

2015 — Æ *obol*. Diad. hd. of Hera r. R. 'Swastika' pattern, incuse. *B.M.C. 7.* 97, 98 £45

2016 — — Scallop-shell. R. As last. *B.M.C. 7.* 99 .. .. £50

2017   2020

2017 400-350 B.C. Æ *stater*. Cow stg. r., looking back at calf, which it suckles; above, star. R. ΚΟΡ and spear-head around square, containing double stellate pattern. *B.M.C. 7.* 126-9 .. .. £150

2018 — Æ *hemidrachm*. Amphora, with bunch of grapes attached to each handle; above ivy-leaf. R. Star; ΚΟΡ between rays. *B.M.C. 7.* 143 .. .. £50

2019 — Æ *diobol*. Amphora, with bunch of grapes attached to handle. R. Kantharos; ΚΟΡ in field. *B.M.C. 7.* 144 .. .. £60

2020 350-300 B.C. Æ *stater* of the Corinthian type. Pegasos, with pointed wing, flying r. R. Hd. of Athena r., wearing Corinthian helmet over leather cap; ΚΟΡ before; amphora behind. *B.M.C. 12.* (*Colonies of Corinth*), *p.* 112, 1 .. .. £200

2021 — — *Obv.* Similar; κ beneath Pegasos. R. Hd. of Athena, as last; behind, Λ and vine-spray with leaf. *B.M.C. 12.* (*Colonies of Corinth*), *p.* 112, 3, 4 .. .. .. £175

2022   2023

2022 — Æ *stater* of Corinth, countermarked by Corcyra. Pegasos, with pointed wing, flying r.; beneath, rectangular countermark containing ΚΟΡ monogram. R. Hd. of Athena, as last; behind, amphora. *B.M.C. 12.* (*Colonies of Corinth*), *p.* 112, 6 £175

2023 300-229 B.C. Æ *didrachm* (wt. reduced to the Corinthian standard, *c.* 5·2 gm.). ΚΟΡΚΥΡΑΙ. Forepart of cow stg. r. R. Upright oblong figure containing double stellate pattern; in field to l., bunch of grapes and κ; to r., kantharos and ι. *B.M.C. 7.* 193-4 £100

2024 — Æ *drachm*. Cow stg. r., looking back at calf, which it suckles; above, ΦΙ. R. ΚΟΡ and pedum around square containing stellate pattern. *B.M.C. 7.* 197 .. £75

2025 — — Amphora; in field to l., κ and kantharos; to r., ι and oinochoë. R. Star; ΚΟΡΚΥΡΑΙ between the rays. *B.M.C. 7.* 198-9 .. .. £75

Corcyra *continued*

2026 — *R diobol.* Hd. of young Dionysos r., wreathed with ivy. R. ко. Thyrsos, bound with fillet to which ivy-leaf is attached. *B.M.C. 7.* 203-4 .. .. £65

2027   2033

2027 After 229 B.C. (period of Roman protectorate). *R didrachm. Obv.* Similar. R. Pegasos flying r.; beneath, two monograms (one of ко P). *B.M.C. 7.* 349-64 £100

2028 — *R octobol?* (*c.* 3·25 gm.). Veiled and laur. hd. of Dione r. R. Pegasos flying r., ΣΩ monogram beneath; all within laurel-wreath. *B.M.C. 7.* 373 .. .. £95

2029 — *R drachm.* Hd. of Aphrodite l.; ко P monogram behind. R. Pegasos flying l. *B.M.C. 7.* 378-80 .. .. £85

2030 — *R tetrobol?* (*c.* 1·7 gm.). Laur. hd. of Apollo r. R. Pegasos flying r.; beneath, ΘΕ monogram and ко P monogram. *B.M.C. 7.* 383-5 .. .. £80

2031 — — Hd. of Aphrodite l., hair bound with cord; behind, ΑΝΔ monogram. R. Pegasos flying l.; beneath, ко P monogram. *B.M.C. 7.* 387-8 .. .. £75

2032 — — Hd. of young Dionysos r., wreathed with ivy; behind, ΑΙ monogram. R. Pegasos flying r.; beneath, bunch of grapes. *B.M.C. 7.* 395 .. .. £85

2033 *Bronze Coinage.* 400-350 B.C. Æ 20. Forepart of cow stg. r.; ко P above. R. Oblong incuse, containing stellate pattern. *B.M.C. 7.* 100 .. .. £20

2034 — Æ 19. *Obv.* Similar. R. Bunch of grapes. *B.M.C. 7.* 117-20 .. .. £16

2035 — Æ 17. Hd. of young Herakles r., in lion's skin. R. ко. Bunch of grapes. *B.M.C.* 7. 101 .. .. £15

2036 — — ко. Amphora. R. Bunch of grapes. *B.M.C. 7.* 104-16 .. .. £10

2037 350-300 B.C. Æ 18. ко. Amphora. R. ΣΩ. Bunch of grapes. *B.M.C. 7.* 156-60
                                                                            £10

2038   2043

2038 — — *Obv.* As 2033. R. As last. *B.M.C. 7.* 169-71 .. .. £12

2039 — — Eagle stg. r., looking back, wings closed; bunch of grapes in field to l. R. ко P. Nike advancing l., holding akrostolion and wreath. *B.M.C. 7.* 179-81 .. £13

2040 — — Dionysos galloping r. on panther, brandishing thyrsos. R. ко P. Satyr stg. r., emptying amphora into krater. *B.M.C. 7.* 182-6 .. .. £14

2041 — — Similar, but with another amphora in place of krater on *rev. B.M.C. 7.* 187-92
                                                                            £14

2042 300-229 B.C. Æ 22. Hd. of young Dionysos l., wreathed with ivy. R. ко P. Krater bound with ivy-wreath. *B.M.C. 7.* 297 .. .. £15

2043 — Æ 18. Forepart of galley r.; ко PKYPA above. R. ко. Kantharos; bunch of grapes above, ΦΙ in field. *B.M.C. 7.* 256. . .. . £12

   The coins of this type are of unusual interest, as the names appearing on obv. are of actual galleys which competed in races off Corcyra during various religious festivals. Sixteen different names are recorded on coins listed in the British Museum Catalogue alone.

2044 — — Bull's hd. facing; star above. ℞. ΚΟΡ monogram within ivy-wreath. *B.M.C. 7.*
213-14 .. .. £14

2045 — — Hd. of Aphrodite r., hair tied in bun. ℞. Ornamental trident-head; Κ — ΟΡ in
lower field. *B.M.C. 7.* 287 .. .. £13

2046 — Æ 15. Star. ℞. Kantharos; ΚΟΡ monogram to l., pedum to r. *B.M.C. 7.* 225 £10

2047 — — Laur. and veiled hd. of Dione r. ℞. Prow of galley r., inscribed ΝΙΚΑ; before,
ΚΟΡ monogram. *B.M.C. 7.* 305 .. .. £10

2048 — Æ 13. Rudder; star above, ΚΟΡ monogram beneath. ℞. Ornamental trident-head.
B.M.C. 7. 229-31 .. .. £8

2049 229-48 B.C. Æ 19. Hd. of young Dionysos r., wreathed with ivy. ℞. Kantharos;
ΚΟΡ monogram to l., ΑΥ monogram to r. *B.M.C. 7.* 417 .. .. .. £9

2050   2054

2050 — — *Obv.* Similar. ℞. Amphora; bunch of grapes above, ΚΟΡ monogram to l. *B.M.C.*
7. 422-4 .. .. £10

2051 — — Laur. and veiled hd. of Dione r. ℞. ΚΟ. Bull's hd. facing; star above, Δ to l.;
all within laurel-wreath. *B.M.C. 7.* 441-3 .. .. £9

2052 — — *Obv.* Similar. ℞. Aplustre; ΚΟΡ monogram to l., ΦΙΝ monogram to r. *B.M.C.*
7. 472-6 .. .. £10

2053 — — Laur. hd. of Poseidon r., trident at shoulder. ℞. Bull's hd. facing; between ΚΡ
monogram and Ο; all within laurel-wreath. *B.M.C. 7.* 452 .. .. .. £8

2054 — Æ 22. Hd. of young Herakles r., in lion's skin. ℞. Prow of galley r.; ΚΟΡΚΥ / ΡΑΙΩΝ
above, ΑΡΙΣΤΕΑΣ below. *B.M.C. 7.* 488-92 .. .. £14

2055 — Æ 18. ΚΟΡΚΥΡΑΙΩΝ. Aplustre. ℞. ΝΙΚΑ / ΝΩΡ in two lines across field. *B.M.C. 7.*
521-3 .. .. £11

2056   2057

2056 **THESSALY** (a vast plain enclosed by mountain barriers and drained by the river
Peneios, Thessaly was famed for its horses and horsemen). **The Ainianes.** 400-344
B.C. Æ *hemidrachm.* Laur. hd. of Zeus r. ℞. ΑΙΝΙΑΝΩΝ. Warrior facing, body inclined
to l., looking r., hurling javelin and holding petasos. *B.M.C. 7.* 1 .. .. £200

2057 168-146 B.C. (struck after the dissolution of the Aitolian League, to which the Ainianes
had belonged). Æ *didrachm?* (*c.* 7·5 gm.). Hd. of Athena Parthenos r., wearing richly
ornamented triple-crested helmet (copied from the contemporary coinage of Athens).
℞. ΑΙΝΙΑΝΩΝ. Phemios (mythical king of the Ainianes) facing, body inclined to l.,
looking r., adjusting his sling, two javelins at his side; to r., ΘΕΡΣΙΠΠΟΣ and palm. *B.M.C.*
7. 9 .. .. £400

2058 — Æ *tetrobol?* (*c.* 2·5 gm.). Hd. of Athena r., in crested Corinthian helmet. ℞. Similar
to last, but without magistrate's name and symbol in field to r. *B.M.C. 7.* 14 £150

The Ainianes *continued*

2059 — — ΤΟΛΜΑΙΟΣ. Laur. hd. of Zeus l. ℞. ΑΙΝΙΑΝΩΝ. Warrior hurling javelin, as 2056; ΑΓ monogram to r. *B.M.C. 7.* 15, 16   ..   ..   £130

2060 — Æ 19. Laur. hd. of Zeus l. ℞. ΑΙΝΙΑΝΩΝ. Phemios adjusting sling, as 2058. *B.M.C. 7.* 18   ..   ..   £15

2061 **Halos** (said to have been founded by the hero Athamas, whose children, ordered by an oracle to be sacrificed, were rescued by the ram with the golden fleece). 400-344 B.C. Æ 17. Hd. of Zeus Laphystios l. ℞. ΑΛΕΩΝ. Helle (daughter of Athamas) seated sideways on ram flying r. *B.M.C. 7.* 1   ..   ..   £20

2062   2064

2062 3rd Cent. B.C. Æ 20. Diad. hd. of Zeus Laphystios r. ℞. ΑΛΕΩΝ. Phryxos (son of Athamas) clinging to ram flying r.; ΑΧ monogram in field to l. *B.M.C. 7.* 2   ..   £17

2063 **Atrax** (situated on the river Peneios, ten miles west of Larissa). 400-344 B.C. Æ *hemi-drachm.* Female hd. l., hair rolled. ℞. ΑΤΡΑΓΙΟΝ. Horse stg. r. *B.M.C. 7.* 1   £250

2064 — Æ 18. Hd. of Apollo r., with short hair. ℞. ΑΤΡΑΓΙΩ. Horse stg. r. *Weber* 2797 £20

2065 — Æ 11. Bearded hd. of Atrax(?) r. ℞. ΑΤΡΑΓΙΩΝ. Bull butting r. *Weber* 2796 £14

2066 **Kierion** (this town originally bore the name Arne). 400-344 B.C. Æ *trihemiobol.* Laur. hd. of Zeus r. ℞. ΚΙΕΡΙΕΙΩΝ. Nymph Arne kneeling r., looking back, playing with astragali; Φ in field to r. *B.M.C. 7.* 1   ..   ..   £150

2067 — — Similar, but with *obv.* type hd. of nymph Arne r., hair rolled, and without Φ on *rev.* *B.M.C. 7.* 2 ..   ..   £150

2068   2072

2068 — Æ *obol.* Horse grazing r. ℞. ΚΙΕ. Naked warrior (Ajax ?) advancing r., holding sword and shield. *Weber* 2798   ..   ..   £120

2069 — Æ 14. Hd. of Poseidon l., bound with tainia. ℞. ΚΙΕΡΙΕΙΩΝ. Nymph Arne kneeling, as 2067. *Weber* 2799   ..   ..   £17

2070 3rd Cent. B.C. Æ 20. Laur. hd. of Apollo r. ℞. — Zeus striding r., brandishing thunderbolt and holding eagle; to r., small figure of nymph Arne kneeling, playing with astragali. *B.M.C. 7.* 3, 4 ..   ..   £15

2071 **Krannon** (situated near the source of the river Onchestos, the citizens of Krannon held Poseidon in especially high regard). 480-400 B.C. Æ *drachm.* Hero Thessalos, naked, stg. r., subduing unruly bull r.; Ν above, ΑΧ below. ℞. ΚΡΑΝΟ. Horse of Poseidon stg. l., trident in background; all within incuse square. *Weber* 2800 ..   ..   ..   £450

2072 — Æ *hemidrachm.* ΚΡΑΝ. Hero Thessalos stg. r., subduing forepart of unruly bull r. ℞. ΚΡΑΝΟ. Forepart of horse of Poseidon galloping l., trident at his side; all within incuse square. *B.M.C. 7.* 1   ..   ..   £225

2073 400-344 B.C. Æ 18. Horseman galloping r. ℞. Hydria, mounted on wheels; Κ — ΡΑ / ΝΝΟ in field. *B.M.C. 7.* 5..   ..   ..   £18

2074 — Æ 15. Similar. ℞. Bull butting r.; trident above, ΚΡΑΝ in ex. *B.M.C. 7.* 2   £14

2075 2077

2075 3rd Cent. B.C. Æ 19. Laur. hd. of Poseidon r. R. KPA. Horseman galloping r. *B.M.C. 7. 7* £14

2076 — Æ 22. Bust of hero Thessalos r., wearing petasos and chlamys. R. ΚΡΑΝΝΩΝΙΩΝ. Horseman galloping r.; ΠΕΛ monogram below. *B.M.C. 7. 8* £15

2077 **Demetrias** (founded by Demetrios Poliorketes in 290 B.C. on the shores of the Pagasaean bay, Demetrias rose to be a place of considerable importance and a royal residence of the Macedonian Kings). *Circa* 290 B.C. Æ *hemidrachm*. Hd. of Artemis r., quiver at shoulder. R. ΔΗΜΗ / ΤΡΙΕΩΝ above and below prow of galley r.; ΑΣ (?) monogram to l. *B.M.C. 7. 1* £175

2078 — Æ *obol*. Diad. and horned hd. l. (Demetrios Poliorketes?). R. ΔΗΜΗΤΡΙΕΩΝ. Naked warrior advancing l., holding spear and shield. *Weber* 2804 .. .. £250

For coins struck at Demetrias in the 2nd Cent. B.C., see below under 'The Magnetes.'

2079 2082

2079 **Ekkarra.** *Circa* 350 B.C. Æ 12. Laur. hd. of Zeus l. R. ΕΚΚΑΡΡΕΩΝ. Artemis stg. facing, leaning on spear. *Weber* 2805 .. .. £25

2080 **Eurea.** *Circa* 350 B.C. Æ 20. Female hd. facing, wreathed with vine. R. ΕΥΡΕΑΙΩΝ. Vine-branch with bunch of grapes; A in field. *Hist. Num.. p.* 294 .. .. £40

2081 **Eurymenai.** 3rd-2nd Cent. B.C. Æ 20. Hd. of young Dionysos r., wreathed with ivy. R. ΕΥΡΥΜΕΝΑΙΩΝ. Vine-tree; krater in field. *Hist. Num., p.* 294 .. £35

2082 **Gomphi / Philippopolis** (a strong fortress commanding the chief pass from Thessaly to Epeiros, Gomphi was renamed Philippopolis by Philip II of Macedon, but later reverted to its old name. Nearby stood a famous temple, dedicated to Zeus Akraios). *Circa* 350 B.C. Æ *drachm*. Hd. of Hera (?) three-quarter face to r., wearing stephanos. R. ΦΙΛΙΠΠΟΠΟΛΙΤΩΝ. Zeus Akraios seated l. on rock, holding sceptre; thunderbolt in field to l. *B.M.C. 7. 1* £750

2083 *Circa* 300 B.C. Æ 18. Similar, but with *rev.* legend ΛΟΜΦ. *B.M.C. 7. 2* £18

2084 — Æ 22. Hd. of nymph three-quarter face to l., hair floating. R. ΓΟΜΦΕΩΝ. Zeus enthroned l., holding thunderbolt and sceptre. *B.M.C. 7. 4* £18

2085 2086

2085 **Gonnos** (a strongly fortified town on the river Peneios, at the entrance to the pass of Tempe). *Circa* 300 B.C. Æ 18. Laur. hd. of Zeus r. R. ΓΟΝΝΕΩΝ. Ram stg. r. *Weber* 2806 .. .. £30

2086 **Gyrton** (on the river Peneios, about five miles north of Larissa). 400-344 B.C. Æ 18. Young male hd. r., bare, conjoined with horse's hd. in background. R. ΓΥΡΤΩΝΙΟΝ before hd. of nymph l., hair in sphendone. *B.M.C. 7. 1, var. Weber* 2807 .. £35

Gyrton *continued*

2087 — — Young male hd. r., in crested helmet; ΠE before. ℞. ΓΥΡΤΩΝΙΩΝ. Hd. of
Aphrodite r., wearing stephane; ιΠ behind. *B.M.C. 7., p.* 203, 1*a* £25

2088 — — Laur. hd. of Apollo l. ℞. ΓΥΡΤΩΝΙΩΝ before female hd. l., bound with tainia.
B.M.C. 7. 2 .. .. £20

2089 — Æ 20. Laur. hd. of Zeus l. ℞. ΓΥΡΤΩΝΙΩΝ. Horse trotting l.; ΠΜ monogram
below. *B.M.C.* 7. 5 .. .. £15

2090   2094

2090 **Herakleia Trachinia** (a Spartan stronghold commanding the route from the south,
the town was renowned as a residence of Herakles). 400-344 B.C. Æ *obol*. Lion's hd. l.
℞. ΗΡΑ (retrograde) above club l.; beneath, ivy-leaf. *B.M.C.* 7. 1 .. .. £110

2091 — Æ *hemiobol*. Similar, but ΗΡΑ not retrograde, and with crayfish r. instead of ivy-leaf
on *rev.* *B.M.C.* 7. 4 .. .. £75

2092 — Æ 19. Similar to 2090, but ΗΡΑ not retrograde, and with two ivy-leaves beneath
club on *rev.* *B.M.C.* 7. 6 .. .. £18

2093 — Æ 15. Lion's hd. l. ℞. ΗΡΑ above club r.; all within olive-wreath. *B.M.C.* 7. 7, 8
£12

2094 **Homolion** (situated at the foot of Mt. Homole). *Circa* 300 B.C. Æ 21. Hd. of the hero
Philoktetes r., in conical hat. ℞. ΟΜΟΛΙΕΩΝ. Coiled serpent, hd. r.; bunch of grapes in
upper field. *Weber* 2814 .. .. £22

2095 — Æ 17. Similar, but with *rev.* legend ΟΜΟΛΙΚΟΝ, and without grapes in *rev.* field.
Grose 4579 .. .. £20

2096   2099

2096 **Hypata** (the chief town of the Ainianes). *Circa* 350 B.C. Æ 14. Laur. hd. of Zeus r.;
thunderbolt behind. ℞. ΥΠΑΤΑΙΩΝ. Athena standing left, holding Nike, spear and
shield. *B.M.C.* 7., p. 203, 1 .. .. £18

2097 **Lamia** (situated on the river Achelous, close to the Maliac gulf, Lamia was the chief
town of the Malians). 400-344 B.C. Æ *hemidrachm*. Hd. of young Dionysos l.,
wreathed with ivy. ℞. ΛΑΜΙΕ / ΩΝ either side of amphora; ivy-leaf above, prochous in
field to r. *B.M.C.* 7. 2, 3 .. .. £140

2098 — Æ *obol*. Similar. *B.M.C.* 7. 4 .. .. £110

2099 302-286 B.C. Æ *drachm*. Young male hd. r., wearing ear-ring, hair bound with tainia.
℞. ΛΑΜΙΕΩΝ. Philoktetes, naked, seated l. on rock, holding bow in case. *B.M.C.* 7. 8, 9.
Weber 2824 .. .. £300

2100 *Bronze Coinage*. 400-344 B.C. Æ 15. Hd. of nymph Lamia r., hair rolled. ℞. ΛΑΜΙ.
Wounded Philoktetes seated l. on ground, his r. hand raised to his conical hat; bird below,
bow in case to l. *B.M.C.* 7. 6, 7 .. .. £20

2101 — — *Obv.* Similar. ℞. ΛΑΜΙΕΩΝ. Philoktetes, naked, kneeling r., shooting with bow
and arrow; club behind him, two birds before. *B.M.C.* 7. 10-12 .. .. £18

See below, under 'Malienses', for coins struck at Lamia in the name of the Malians.

2102   2106

2102 **Larissa** (the most important town in Thessaly, Larissa was named after a daughter of Pelasgos, and was built on the right bank of the Peneios. It began issuing coins at an earlier date than most other places in the area). 475-460 B.C. Æ *drachm.* Horse stg. l. biting its r. foreleg; above, cicada l. Ŗ. ΛΑΡΙΣΑΙΟΝ. Sandal of Jason l.; double-axe in field above; all within incuse square. *B.M.C. 7.* 1   ..   ..   £2,500

2103 — Æ *hemidrachm.* Beardless hd. of Jason l., in kausia. Ŗ. Similar to last, but without double-axe in field. *Weber* 2825 ..   ..   £1,500

2104 — Æ *obol.* Hd. of nymph Larissa l. Ŗ. Sandal of Jason l.; ΛΑΡΙ above, Ι below; all within incuse square. *B.M.C. 7.* 3   ..   ..   £400

2105 — — Hd. and shoulders of bull l. Ŗ. Horse's hd. r.; ΛΑ before; all within incuse square. *B.M.C. 7.* 4 ..   ..   £350

2106 460-400 B.C. Æ *drachm.* Naked youth stg. r., restraining unruly bull prancing r.; rose beneath bull. Ŗ. ΛΑΡΙ. Horse prancing l.; all within incuse square. *B.M.C. 7.* 6
£275

The obv. type depicts the Thessalian sport of bull-wrestling.

2107 — — *Obv.* Similar, but type l.; beneath bull, plant growing from ground; in ex., ΤΟ. Ŗ. ΛΑ / ΡΙΣΑΙ above and below horse prancing r.; all within incuse square. *B.M.C. 7.* 19
£250

2108 — Æ *hemidrachm.* Naked youth stg. r., restraining forepart of bull prancing r.; rose beneath. Ŗ. ΛΑΡΙ. Forepart of horse prancing r.; all within incuse square. *B.M.C. 7.* 8
£200

2109   2111

2109 — Æ *trihemiobol.* Horseman pacing r., holding two spears. Ŗ. ΛΑΡΙΣΑ. Nymph Larissa seated r., holding patera, l. hand raised; all within incuse square. *B.M.C. 7.* 11
£150

2110 — Æ *obol.* Horse pacing r.; above, lion's hd. r. Ŗ. ΛΑΡΙ. Nymph Larissa stg. r., supporting on her l. knee a hydria, which she has filled from lion-headed fountain behind her; all within incuse square. *B.M.C. 7.* 15   ..   ..   £110

2111 400-360 B.C. Æ *drachm.* Youth running l., naked but for chlamys billowing out behind him, restraining unruly bull prancing l. Ŗ. ΛΑΡΙ / ΣΑΙΑ above and below horse galloping r.; all within incuse square. *B.M.C. 7.* 31   ..   ..   £225

2112 — Æ *diobol.* Horseman prancing l., holding spear. Ŗ. ΛΑΡΙΣΑ. Nymph Larissa seated r., r. hand raised behind hd., holding mirror in l.; all within incuse square. *B.M.C.* 7. 39 ..   ..   £175

2113 — Æ *trihemiobol.* Similar. *B.M.C. 7.* 40   ..   ..   £150

2114 — Æ *obol.* Horse pacing r. Ŗ. ΛΑΡΙ (partly retrograde). Nymph Larissa r., stooping to fasten her sandal; hydria on ground before; all within incuse square. *B.M.C. 7.*44 £110

Larissa *continued*

2115 — — *Obv.* Similar, but with Σ (reversed) / o in field. ℞. ΛΑΡΙΣΑ (retrograde). Nymph Larissa seated l. on hydria, tossing ball into the air; all within incuse square. *B.M.C.* 7. 23
£110

2116 — — Bull's hoof on circular shield. ℞. Bearded hd. of Asklepios r.; erect serpent before. *Weber* 2844 .. .. £140

2117　　　　　　　　　　2118

2117 360-350 B.C. Æ *drachm.* Hd. of nymph Larissa l., hair rolled. ℞. ΛΑΡΙΣΑΙΑ. Horse galloping r. *B.M.C.* 7. 48.. .. .. £300

2118 — — Hd. of nymph Larissa r., hair in sphendone. ℞. ΛΑΡΙΣΑΙΑ. Horse galloping r., about to be mounted by Thessalian youth stg. r., in background, grasping the reins; all within incuse square. *B.M.C.* 7. 52 .. .. £350

2119　　　　　　　　　　2124

2119 350-325 B.C. (under Macedonian domination). Æ *didrachm.* Hd. of nymph Larissa three-quarter face to l., wearing necklace; hair confined by fillet and floating loosely, with ampyx in front. ℞. ΛΑΡΙΣΑΙΩΝ. Horse trotting r. *B.M.C.* 7. 55 .. .. £950

2120 — Æ *drachm.* *Obv.* Similar. ℞. ΛΑΡΙΣΑΙΩΝ. Horse grazing r., l. forefoot raised. *B.M.C.* 7. 57-60 .. .. £175

2121 — — Similar, but with plant growing from ground beneath horse. *B.M.C.* 7. 61 £200

2122 — — *Obv.* Similar. ℞. ΛΑΡΙΣΑΙΩΝ. Mare stg. r.; foal r. beside her, in background. *B.M.C.* 7. 63, 64 .. .. £225

2123 — — Similar to 2120, but hd. of nymph Larissa is three-quarter face to *right*, and horse's forefoot is not raised. *B.M.C.* 7. 71 .. .. £200

2124 — — *Obv.* As last. ℞. Horse grazing r.; ΛΑΡΙ above, ΣΙΜΟ beneath. *B.M.C.* 7. 77
£350

The name on rev. is of Simos, Tetrarch of Larissa, 352-344 B.C.

2125 — — Bull rushing r.; ΛΑΡΙΣΑΙΩΝ above. ℞. Thessalian horseman, wearing chlamys and kausia, on horse galloping r. *B.M.C.* 7. 54 .. .. £400

2126　　　　　　　　　　2128

2126 — — Hd. of Aleuas, legendary leader of Thessaly, three-quarter face to l., in richly ornamented conical helmet; to r., ΑΛΕΥ and double-axe. ℞. Eagle stg. l. on thunderbolt, looking back; ΛΑΡΙΣΑΙΑ to r., ΕΛΛΑ to l. *B.M.C.* 7. 53 .. .. £750
This may have been issued at about the time of Alexander the Great's accession in 336 B.C.

2127 — Æ *hemidrachm.* Hd. of nymph Larissa three-quarter face to l., as 2119. Ɽ.
ΛΑΡΙΣΑΙΩΝ. Mare stg. r. *B.M.C. 7.* 65 ..   ..   £200

2128 — Æ *trihemiobol.* *Obv.* Similar. Ɽ. ΛΑΡΙΣΑΙΩΝ. Thessalian horseman, wearing
chlamys and kausia, on horse prancing r. *B.M.C. 7.* 69, 70   ..   ..   ..   £150

2129 *Bronze Coinage.* 360-325 B.C. Æ 17. Hd. of nymph Larissa r., hair rolled. Ɽ.
ΛΑΡΙΣΑΙΩΝ. Horse grazing r., l. forefoot raised. *B.M.C. 7.* 89   ..   ..   £14

2130   2134

2130 — Æ 12. Hd. of nymph Larissa l., hair tied behind. Ɽ. Similar to last. *B.M.C. 7.* 95-
7 ..   ..   £12

2131 — Æ 22. Hd. of nymph Larissa three-quarter face to l., as 2119. Ɽ. ΛΑΡΙΣΑΙΩΝ
(partly retrograde). Horse trotting r.; ear of corn beneath. *B.M.C. 7.* 79, 80   £20

2132 — Æ 18. *Obv.* Similar. Ɽ. Legend as last. Thessalian horseman r., holding spear,
horse prancing; beneath, Ξ. *B.M.C. 7.* 86   ..   ..   £18

2133 After 146 B.C. Æ 15. ΘΕΣΣΑΛΩΝ. Herakles, naked, seated l. on rock, r. hand raised
to hd., holding bow in l. Ɽ. ΛΑΡΙΣΑ. Nymph Larissa stg. l., r. hand raised to forehead.
Hist. Num., p. 299. *Cf. Grose* 4634   ..   ..   £15

See below, under 'Thessalian League', for other coins of the 2nd Cent. B.C. struck, probably,
at Larissa.

2134 **Larissa Kremaste** (situated in the south of Thessaly, Larissa Kremaste was built on a
height, hence its name. It was taken by Demetrios Poliorketes in 302 B.C., during his
invasion of Thessaly). 302-286 B.C. Æ 19. Hd. of Achilles (?) l., hair loose. Ɽ.
ΛΑΡΙ. Thetis riding on hippocamp l., bearing shield of Achilles with ΑΧ monogram.
B.M.C. 7. 1, 2   ..   ..   £20

2135 — Æ 14. Hd. of nymph l., hair rolled. Ɽ. ΛΑΡΙ below harpa r.; all within olive-wreath.
B.M.C. 7. 4, 5   ..   ..   £14

2136   2138

2136 **The Magnetes** (following Flamininus' proclamation of the freedom of Greece in 196 B.C.,
the Magnetes commenced the issue of a federal currency from their chief town, Demetrias).
196-146 B.C. Æ *drachm* (*c.* 4·2 gm.). Laur. hd. of Zeus r.; HPA monogram behind.
Ɽ. Artemis seated l. on prow of galley, holding bow; ΜΑΓΝΗΤΩΝ below; dolphin to l.;
ΣΕ and ΕΥΤ monograms to r. *B.M.C. 7.* 1   ..   ..   £200

2137 — Æ *hemidrachm.* Bust of Artemis r., hair tied behind; bow and quiver at shoulder.
Ɽ. ΜΑΓΝΗ / ΤΩΝ above and below prow of galley r.; ΑΧ monogram to r. *Grose* 4638-9
£150

2138 — Æ 22. Laur. hd. of Zeus l. Ɽ. ΜΑΓΝΗΤΩΝ. Centaur stg. r., r. hand held before
him, holding branch in l.; plough to l., ΗΔ monogram below. *B.M.C. 7.* 11 ..   £14

2139 — Æ 17. Laur. hd. of Apollo l. Ɽ. Artemis advancing r., holding torch; behind,
ΜΑΓΝΗΤΩΝ and Α. *Weber* 2872 ..   ..   £12

2140 — Æ 14. Hd. of Artemis r., hair tied behind. Ɽ. ΜΑΓΝΗΤΩΝ. Poseidon stg. l.,
holding dolphin and resting on trident. *Grose* 4643 ..   ..   £10

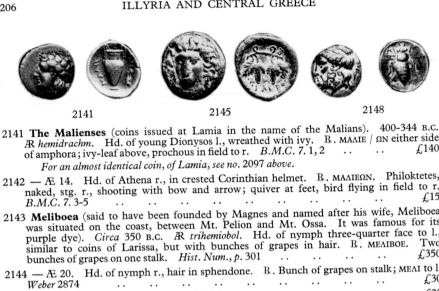

2141   2145   2148

2141 **The Malienses** (coins issued at Lamia in the name of the Malians). 400-344 B.C.
Æ *hemidrachm*. Hd. of young Dionysos l., wreathed with ivy. ℞. ΜΑΛΙΕ / ΩΝ either side
of amphora; ivy-leaf above, prochous in field to r. *B.M.C. 7*. 1, 2 ..   ..   £140
For an almost identical coin, of Lamia, see no. 2097 above.

2142 — Æ 14. Hd. of Athena r., in crested Corinthian helmet. ℞. ΜΑΛΙΕΩΝ. Philoktetes,
naked, stg. r., shooting with bow and arrow; quiver at feet, bird flying in field to r.
B.M.C. 7. 3-5 ..   ..   £15

2143 **Meliboea** (said to have been founded by Magnes and named after his wife, Meliboea
was situated on the coast, between Mt. Pelion and Mt. Ossa. It was famous for its
purple dye). *Circa* 350 B.C. Æ *trihemiobol*. Hd. of nymph three-quarter face to l.,
similar to coins of Larissa, but with bunches of grapes in hair. ℞. ΜΕΛΙΒΟΕ. Two
bunches of grapes on one stalk. *Hist. Num., p.* 301 ..   ..   ..   £350

2144 — Æ 20. Hd. of nymph r., hair in sphendone. ℞. Bunch of grapes on stalk; ΜΕΛΙ to l.
Weber 2874 ..   ..   £30

2145 — Æ 18. Similar to 2143. *B.M.C. 7*. 1 ..   ..   £25

2146 — Æ 11. Similar to 2144. *Grose* 4645 ..   ..   £15

2147 **Melitaia** (originally called Pyrrha, this town was situated on the northern slopes of
Mt. Othrys, close to the river Enipeos). *Circa* 350 B.C. Æ *drachm*. Laur. hd. of Zeus
r. ℞. ΜΕΛΙΤΕ . . . Bull grazing r.; all within shallow incuse square. *Hist. Num., p.* 301
£650

2148 — Æ 15. Laur. hd. of Zeus l. ℞. Bee; Μ — Ε / Λ — Ι in field. *Weber* 2875-6   £17

2148A **Methydrion** (site uncertain, but probably in the vicinity of Pherai). 450-400 B.C.
Æ *drachm*. Forepart of prancing horse r. ℞. ΜΕΘΥ. Corn-grain in its husk; all within
incuse square. *Babelon (Traité) pl. XLIII*, 15 ..   ..   £500
*For similar coins of this federal currency, see under Pherai (nos. 2201-3) and Skotussa
(nos. 2217-18).*

2149   2150

2149 **Methylion** (a town known only from its coinage). *Circa* 350 B.C. Æ 20. Young male
hd. r., hair short. ℞. ΜΕΘΥΛΙΕΩΝ. Horseman cantering r., holding spear; small figure
of Athena Promachos in field. *Hist. Num., p.* 302 ..   ..   £45

2150 **Metropolis** (formed by the union of several small towns, Metropolis was a centre for
the worship of Aphrodite). 400-344 B.C. Æ *trihemiobol*. Hd. of Aphrodite three-
quarter face to l. ℞. ΜΗΤΡΟΠΟΛΙΤΩΝ. Apollo Kitharoedos advancing r., playing lyre.
B.M.C. 7. 2 ..   ..   £250

2151 — Æ *obol*. Hd. of bearded river-god (?) facing. ℞. ΜΗΤΡΟ. Aphrodite Kastnietis
seated l. on rock, beneath tree; she holds thyrsos. *B.M.C. 7*. 1 ..   ..   £175

2152 3rd Cent. B.C. Æ 19. Laur. hd. of Apollo r. ℞. ΜΗΤΡΟΠΟΛΙΤΩΝ. Forepart of bull l.,
looking back; ΟΙ monogram beneath. *B.M.C. 7*. 3 ..   ..   £18

2153 — — Obv. Similar. ℞. — Aphrodite Kastnietis stg. l., holding dove, Eros stg. at her
feet; ΟΙ monogram in upper field to l. *B.M.C. 7*. 4 ..   ..   £18

2154   2158

2154 **Mopsion** (situated on a hill between Larissa and Tempe, the town was named after Mopsos, one of the Kalydonian hunters and a companion of the Argonauts). *Circa* 350 B.C. Æ 20. Hd. of Zeus three-quarter face to r.; thunderbolt in field to r. ℞. ΜΟΨΕΙΩΝ. The Lapith Mopsos, naked, stg. facing, wielding club about to strike Centaur rearing l., holding boulder over hd. with both hands. *Grose* 4648 .. .. £50

2155 **The Oetaei** (Mt. Oeta, in the south of Thessaly, was the scene of the death of Herakles). 400-344 B.C. ℞ *hemidrachm.* Lion's hd. l., spear-head in mouth. ℞. ΟΙΤΑΩΝ (retrograde). Herakles, naked, stg. facing, holding club in both hands. *B.M.C.* 7. 1, 2 £225

2156 — ℞ *obol. Obv.* Similar. ℞. ΟΙΤΑ. Bow and quiver. *B.M.C.* 7. 3, 4 .. £125

2157 196-146 B.C. ℞ *didrachm* (*c.* 7·75 gm.). *Obv.* Similar. ℞. ΟΙΤΑΙ / ΩΝ either side of Herakles, naked, stg. facing, resting r. hand on club and holding apple. *Weber* 2883 £650

2158 — ℞ *tetrobol* (*c.* 2·5 gm.). *Obv.* Similar. ℞. ΟΙΤΑΙ / ΩΝ either side of Herakles, naked, stg. facing, holding club in both hands. *B.M.C.* 7. 8, 9 .. £200

2159 *Bronze Coinage. Circa* 350 B.C. Æ 15. *Obv.* Similar. ℞. ΟΙΤ / ΑΩΝ above and below knife and spear. *B.M.C.* 7. 5 .. .. £15

2160 196-146 B.C. Æ 13. Similar, but with legend ΟΙΤΑΙ / ΩΝ. *B.M.C.* 7. 10 .. £10

2161 — Æ 17. Young male hd. r., laur. ℞. ΟΙΤΑΙ / ΩΝ above and below spear-head and jaw-bone of Kalydonian boar; ΠΑΡ monogram in centre field. *B.M.C.* 7. 11 .. £13

        2162   2165   2166

2162 **Orthe** (a place mentioned only by Pliny). 3rd Cent. B.C. Æ 18. Hd. of Athena r., in crested Athenian helmet. ℞. Ο — Ρ (retrograde) either side of trident; all within olive-wreath. *Weber* 2884 .. .. £20

2163 — Æ 22. *Obv.* Similar, but Corinthian helmet. ℞. ΟΡΘΙΕΙΩΝ. Forepart of horse r., springing from rock, upon which trees are growing; all within olive-wreath. *Grose* 4655 £30

2164 **Pelinna.** 400-344 B.C. ℞ *drachm.* Thessalian horseman, holding spear, on horse prancing l. ℞. ΠΕΛΙΝΝΑ. Warrior retreating l., looking back, holding spear and shield; sword at waist; all within incuse square. *B.M.C.* 7. 2, 3 .. .. .. £450

2165 — ℞ *trihemiobol. Obv.* Similar, but the horseman holds two spears, and the horse is galloping. ℞. ΠΕΛΛΙ. Warrior advancing l., holding spear in r. hand, spear and shield in l.; all within incuse square. *B.M.C.* 7. 1 .. .. £200

2166 — Æ 15. Horseman galloping r., spearing prostrate enemy. ℞. ΠΕΛΙΝΝΑΕ. Warrior advancing l., holding shield, sword at waist. *B.M.C.* 7. 5 .. .. .. £18

2167 3rd Cent. B.C. Æ 20. Veiled female hd. r. ℞. ΠΕΛΙΝΝΑΙΩΝ. Thessalian horseman, with couched spear, charging r.; ΜΑ monogram below. *B.M.C.* 7. 6 .. .. £15

2168 **The Perrhaebi** (descended from a warlike Pelasgic tribe who had migrated from Euboia to the mainland, the Perrhaebi lived in the north of Thessaly, close to the Macedonian border). 480-400 B.C. ℞ *drachm.* Naked Thessalian youth l., trying to restrain unruly bull prancing l. ℞. Horse prancing r., ΠΕ above; all within incus squaree. *Grose* 4660 .. .. £350

2169　　　　　　　　　　　　　2171

The Perrhaebi *continued*

2169 — Æ *hemidrachm.* Thessalian youth, wearing chlamys, stg. r., trying to restrain forepart of unruly bull r. R. ΠΕ / ΡΑ (partly retrograde) above and below forepart of prancing horse r.; all within incuse square. *B.M.C. 7.* 1 .. .. £250

2170 — Æ *trihemiobol.* Thessalian horseman, holding two spears, on horse pacing l. R. ΠΕΡΑ (retrograde). Thetis (?) seated l., holding helmet; all within incuse square. *B.M.C. 7.* 3 .. .. £200

2171 — Æ *obol.* Horse galloping l. R. ΠΕ / ΡΑ (partly retrograde). Athena advancing r., holding spear and shield; all within incuse square. *B.M.C. 7.* 5 .. .. £150

2172 — — Forepart of bull running r.; all within wreath. R. ΠΕΡ (retrograde). Horse's hd. r.; all within incuse square. *B.M.C. 7.* 10 .. .. £150

2173 196-146 B.C. Æ *drachm* (*c.* 4 gm.). Laur. hd. of Zeus r. R. ΠΕΡΡΑΙΒΩΝ. Hera enthroned r., holding sceptre; ΣΩ monogram in field to r. *Grose* 4665.. .. £225

2174 — Æ 21. Similar, but without monogram in *rev.* field. *Weber* 2892 .. £18

2175 **The Petthali** (unknown apart from their coinage, and an inscription). *Circa* 350 B.C. Æ 14. Laur. hd. of Zeus r. R. ΠΕΤΘΑΛΩΝ. Forepart of horse springing r. from rock; beneath, trident. *Hist. Num., p.* 304 .. .. £30

2176 **Phakion** (a mountain fortress on the right bank of the Peneios, in central Thessaly) 3rd Cent. B.C. Æ 20. Hd. of nymph r., wreathed with corn. R. ΦΑΚΙΑΣΤΩΝ. Horseman trotting r., r. hand raised. *B.M.C. 7.* 1, 2 .. .. £30

2177　　　　　　　　　　　　　2180

2177 **Phalanna** (on the Peneios, a few miles upstream from Larissa). 400-344 B.C. Æ *drachm.* Young male hd. r., with short hair. R. ΦΑΛΑΝΝΑΙΩΝ. Horse trotting r. *B.M.C. 7.* 1 .. .. £350

2178 — Æ *hemidrachm.* Similar. *B.M.C. 7.* 2 .. .. £225

2179 — Æ *trihemiobol.* Similar. *B.M.C. 7.* 3 .. .. £150

2180 *Circa* 350 B.C. Æ 19. *Obv.* Similar, but with T behind hd. R. ΦΑΛΑΝΝΑΙΩΝ. Hd. of Nymph Phalanna r., hair in sakkos. *B.M.C. 7.* 10, *var.* £18

2181 **Phaloria** (situated on the left bank of the Peneios, north of Trikka). 302-286 B.C. Æ 22. Laur. hd. of Apollo r. R. ΦΑΛΩΡΙΑΣΤΩΝ. Apollo (?) seated l. on rock, holding arrow and branch. *Hist. Num., p.* 305 .. .. £30

2182 **Pharkadon** (on the left bank of the Peneios, not far from Pelinna). 480-450 B.C. Æ *hemidrachm.* Naked Thessalian youth stg. r. on far side of forepart of bull r., which he attempts to restrain. R. ΦΑΡΚΑ (retrograde). Forepart of horse prancing r.; all within incuse square. *Grose* 4672 .. .. £175

2183

2187

2183   450-400 B.C.   Æ *hemidrachm.*   Similar, but the youth stands on nearside of bull, and the rev. legend is ΦΑ / ΡΚ (partly retrograde).   *B.M.C. 7. 3* £125

2184   — Æ *obol.*   Horse pacing r.   Ŗ. ΦΑΡ / ΚΑΔΟ either side of Athena stg. r., spear over shoulder, shield resting against her; all within incuse square.   *B.M.C. 7. 8* ..   £120

2185   *Circa* 350 B.C.   Æ 17.   Hd. of nymph l., hair rolled.   Ŗ. ΦΑΡΚΑΔ (retrograde).   Horseman prancing r.   *B.M.C. 7., p. 204, 9a* £18

2186   — — Horse grazing r.   Ŗ. Crescent enclosing star; ΦΑΡΚΑ / ΔΟΝΙΩΝ beneath.   *B.M.C. 7. 9* £20

2187   **Pharsalos** (one of the more important towns of Thessaly, Pharsalos was built on the northern slopes of Mt. Narthakios.   It was the scene of Caesar's famous victory over Pompey in 48 B.C.).   480-450 B.C.   Æ *hemidrachm.*   Hd. of Athena r., of archaic style, in close-fitting crested helmet ornamented with serpents.   Ŗ. ΦΑR before horse's hd. r.; all within incuse square.   *B.M.C. 7. 1* £140

2188   — Æ *obol.*   Similar.   *B.M.C. 7. 5* £100

2189

2191

2189   450-400 B.C.   Æ *hemidrachm.*   *Obv.* Similar, but of more advanced style, though still archaic; helmet plain.   Ŗ. ΦΑΡΣΑ around horse's hd. r.   *Weber 2904* £160

2190   400-344 B.C.   Æ *drachm.*   Hd. of Athena r., of fine style, in close-fitting crested helmet ornamented with laurel-wreath.   Ŗ. ΦΑ / ΡΣ (partly retrograde).   Forepart of galloping horse r.   *Weber 2906* £300

2191   — — *Obv.* Similar, but the helmet is ornamented with wing; behind, ΤΗ / ΙΠ.   Ŗ. ΦΑΡΣ. Horseman prancing r., holding whip; in ex., ΤΕΛΕΦΑΝΤΟ (retrograde).   *B.M.C. 7. 6*   £275

2192   — Æ *hemidrachm.*   *Obv.* As last, but with Τ / ΙΠ behind.   Ŗ. ΦΑΡΣ. Horse's hd. r. *B.M.C. 7. 11* £175

2193   — Æ *trihemiobol.*   Hd. of Athena three-quarter face to l., wearing triple-crested helmet. Ŗ. ΦΑΡΑΣ (*sic*).   Horseman prancing r., striking with whip.   *B.M.C. 7. 17* ..   £175

2194   — Æ *obol.*   Hd. of Athena l., in close-fitting crested helmet ornamented with figure of Skylla.   Ŗ. ΦΑΡΣΑ.   Horse's hd. r.   *B.M.C. 7. 18* £110

2195   — Æ 22.   Similar to 2193, but hd. of Athena is between spear and shield.   *B.M.C. 7. 24* £20

2196   — Æ 18.   *Obv.* Similar to 2194.   Ŗ. ΦΑ / ΡΣ (partly retrograde).   Horseman prancing r., striking with whip.   *B.M.C. 7. 19* £15

2197   — Æ 12.   Hd. of Athena r., in close-fitting crested helmet.   Ŗ. — Horse's hd. r. *Weber 2912* £11

2198   2202

2198 **Pherai** (situated west of Mt. Pelion, Pherai was the second city of Thessaly, after Larissa. In the 4th Cent. B.C. its tyrants extended their power over most of the region).   480-450 B.C.   Æ *drachm*.   Naked Thessalian youth stg. r., restraining unruly bull prancing r. R. ΦERI (*sic*).   Horse prancing l., water pouring on to his back from lion's head fountain behind; all within incuse square.   *B.M.C. 7*. 2 ..   ..   £350

2199 — — *Obv.* Similar, but type left, and the youth raises his r. leg.   R. ΦERAION.   Horse prancing l.; all within incuse square.   *Grose* 4691   ..   ..   ..   £350

2200 — Æ *hemidrachm*.   Naked youth stg. l. on far side of forepart of bull l., which he attempts to restrain.   R. ΦERA.   Forepart of horse springing r. from rock; all within incuse square.   *B.M.C. 7*. 3   ..   ..   £225

2201 450-400 B.C.   Æ *drachm*.   Forepart of prancing horse l.   R. Corn-grain in its husk; Φ above, E below; all within incuse square.   *B.M.C. 7*. 4   ..   ..   £450

2202 — Æ *hemidrachm*.   Forepart of horse springing r. from rock.   R. Corn-grain in its husk; ΦE (retrograde) above, ΘA beneath; all within incuse square.   *B.M.C. 7*. 9   £225

2203 — Æ *obol*.   Horse's hd. l.   R. Corn-grain in its husk; Φ above, E (reversed) below; all within incuse square.   *B.M.C. 7*. 10   ..   ..   £120

For similar coins of this federal currency (i.e. nos. 2201-3), see under Methydrion (no. 2148A) and Skotussa (nos. 2217-18).

2204   2207

2204 Early 4th Cent. B.C.   Æ *hemidrachm*.   Hd. of Hekate l., wreathed with myrtle; behind, torch.   R. ΦERAIOYN.   Nymph Hypereia stg. l., resting her r. hand on lion's head fountain; AΣ / TO within wreath to l.   *B.M.C. 7*. 20, 21   ..   ..   £300

2205 Late 4th Cent. B.C.   Æ *hemidrachm*.   Hd. of Hekate three-quarter face to l., holding torch in r. hand.   R. Hekate seated facing, holding torch, on horse galloping r.; lion's head fountain behind; ΦERAIΩN below.   *Weber* 2926   ..   ..   £400

2206 *Bronze Coinage.*   Early 4th Cent. B.C.   Æ 20.   Lion's hd. r.   R. ΦERAI.   Hekate seated facing, on horse pacing l., holding torch in each hand.   *Weber* 2920   ..   ..   £24

2207 — Æ 17.   Hd. of Hekate r., wreathed with myrtle; torch before.   R. ΦERAION.   Lion's head fountain r., water gushing from mouth.   *B.M.C. 7*. 12   ..   ..   ..   £17

2208 Late 4th Cent. B.C.   Æ 23.   Similar to 2205.   *B.M.C. 7*.23 ..   ..   ..   £22

2209 — **Alexander,** tyrant of Pherai, 369-357 B.C. (a prince notorious for his cruelty, Alexander was murdered by his wife, Thebe).   Æ *didrachm*.   Hd. of Hekate three-quarter face to r., wreathed with myrtle, holding torch in r. hand.   R. AΛEΞANΔPOY.   Warrior on horseback prancing r., holding spear; bipennis on horse's flank, and beneath.   *B.M.C. 7*. 14 ..   ..   £2,500

2210 Æ *drachm*.   Hd. of Hekate r., hair rolled; hand holding torch before.   R. AΛEΞANΔPOY. Lion's hd. r.   *B.M.C. 7*. 15, 16   ..   ..   £650

2211 Æ *obol*.   Wheel of four spokes.   R. Bipennis, dividing A — AE in lower field.   *Weber* 2924   ..   ..   £150

2209   2214

2212 Æ 15. Forepart of bull r., hd. facing. ℞. ΑΛΕΞΑΝ / ΔΡΟΥ above and below forepart of horse prancing r. *B.M.C.* 7. 18 ..   ..   £15

2213 Æ 14. Young male hd. r., wearing kausia. ℞. ΑΛΕΞΑΝΔΡΟΥ. Leg and hoof of horse r. *Weber* 2925 ..   ..   £20

2214 — **Teisiphonos,** tyrant of Pherai, *c.* 357-352 B.C. (a brother of Thebe, he seized power after Alexander's assassination.). Æ 15. Similar to 2212, but with legend ΤΕΙΣΙΦΟΝΟΥ. *Hist. Num., p.* 309 ..   ..   £45

2215 **Proerna** (on the western slopes of Mt. Narthakios). 3rd Cent. B.C. Æ 20. Female hd. facing. ℞. ΠΡΩΕΡΝΙΩΝ. Demeter stg. l., holding corn-ears and torch. *Hist. Num., p.* 309   ..   ..   £35

2216   2217

2216 **Rhizus** (in common with several other towns in the area, the inhabitants of Rhizus were removed from their homes by Demetrios Poliorketes, in 290 B.C., in order to populate his new foundation, Demetrias). *Circa* 350 B.C. Æ 14. Hd. of Artemis r. ℞. ΡΙΖΟΥΣΙΩΝ between the rays of a star. *Hist. Num., p.* 309   ..   ..   £25

2217 **Skotussa** (near the source of the river Onchestos, Skotussa was situated between Pherai and Pharsalos. The great Roman victory over Philip V of Macedon, in 197 B.C., took place close by, at Kynoskephalai). 450-400 B.C. Æ *drachm.* Forepart of horse prancing l. ℞. ΣΚΟ. Corn-grain in its husk; all within incuse square. *Weber* 2927 ..   £500

2218 — Æ *hemidrachm.* Similar, but horse to *right.* *B.M.C.* 7. 1   ..   ..   £250

     For similar coins of this federal currency, see under Methydrion (no. 2148A) and Pherai (nos. 2201-3).

2219 400-367 B.C. Æ *hemidrachm.* Bearded hd. of Herakles r., wearing lion's skin. ℞. Forepart of horse r., l. leg raised; Σ — ΚΟ in lower field. *B.M.C.* 7. 2   ..   £275

2220 3rd Cent. B.C. Æ *hemidrachm.* Female hd. facing. ℞. ΣΚΟΤΟΥΣΣΑΙΩΝ. Poseidon seated on rock, holding trident and dolphin. *Hist. Num., p.* 310   ..   £300

2221 *Bronze Coinage.* 400-367 B.C. Æ 21. Female hd. three-quarter face to l., with flowing hair. ℞. ΣΚΟΤΟΥΣΣΑΙΩΝ. Bunch of grapes on branch. *Grose* 4702 ..   £25

2222 3rd Cent. B.C. Æ 22. Bearded hd. of Herakles r., wearing lion's skin. ℞. ΣΚΟΤΟΥΣ / ΣΑΙΩΝ above and below club l. *B.M.C.* 7. 4   ..   ..   £20

2223 — Æ 19. Hd. of Ares r., in close-fitting helmet ornamented with plume. ℞. ΣΚΟΤΟΥΣ / ΣΑΙΩΝ above and below horse prancing r. *B.M.C.* 7. 5 ..   ..   ..   £18

2224 Thebai (close to the shores of the Pagasaean bay, Thebai was a town of some importance, possessing a good harbour. The famous sanctuary of Protesilaos was about ten miles distant, at Phylake). 302-286 B.C. Æ *hemidrachm.* Veiled hd. of Demeter r., wreathed with corn. ℞. ΘΗΒΑΙΩΝ. Protesilaos, holding sword and shield, leaping ashore r. from prow of galley. *B.M.C. 7.* 1 .. .. £300

2225 — Æ 14. Similar, but Demeter is not veiled; ΑΧ monogram between Protesilaos' legs on *rev. B.M.C. 7.* 2 .. .. £17

2224   2226

2226 Trikka (a centre for the worship of Asklepios, Trikka was named after a daughter of the river-god Peneios). 480-420 B.C. Æ *hemidrachm.* Naked Thessalian youth stg. r., restraining forepart of unruly bull prancing r. ℞. ΤΡΙΚΚΑΙΟΝ (partly retrograde). Forepart of horse prancing r.; all within incuse square. *B.M.C. 7.* 1 .. .. £140

2227 — Æ *obol.* Horse prancing l. ℞. ΤΡΙΚΑ. Athena stg. l., holding patera over altar, and spear; all within incuse square. *B.M.C. 7.* 10 .. .. £110

2228 — — *Obv.* Similar. ℞. ΤΡΙΚΚΑ. Fountain-nymph Trikka stg. r., opening cista before her. *B.M.C. 7.* 12.. .. .. £125

2229 420-400 B.C. Æ *hemidrachm.* Similar to 2226, but of more advanced style, and with legend ΤΡΙΚΚΑΙΩΝ. *B.M.C. 7.* 14.. .. .. £165

2230 400-344 B.C. Æ 20. Hd. of Nymph Trikka r., hair in sphendone. ℞. ΤΡΙΚΚΑΙΩΝ. Asklepios seated r., feeding serpent with bird held in outstretched r. hand. *B.M.C. 7.* 17 £20

2227   2232

2231 Thessalian League (following the great victory of the Roman general Flamininus over Philip V of Macedon, in 197 B.C., the freedom of the Greeks was proclaimed at Corinth and a number of new autonomous coinages were initiated. Those in the name of the Thessali were struck probably at **Larissa**). 196-146 B.C. Æ *double victoriatus* (=1½ *denarii*), usually *c.* 6-6·5 gm. Hd. of Zeus r., crowned with oak; monogram behind. ℞. ΘΕΣΣΑ / ΛΩΝ behind and before Athena Itonia advancing r., brandishing spear and holding shield; Π — Ο / Λ — Ι in lower field. *B.M.C. 7.* 4 .. .. .. £65

2232 — — *Obv.* Similar, but without monogram. ℞. ΘΕΣΣΑ / ΛΩΝ behind and before Athena Itonia r., as last; ΚΛΕΙΠ — ΠΟΣ across upper field; ΓΟΡΓΩΠΙΑΣ in ex. *B.M.C. 7.* 13, 14 £65

2233 — — *Obv.* Similar, but with ΠΤΟΛΕΜΑΙΟΥ behind hd. of Zeus. ℞. ΘΕΣΣΑ / ΛΩΝ and Athena Itonia, as last; ΑΡΙ — ΣΤΟ across upper field; ΚΛ — ΗΣ in lower field. *B.M.C. 7.* 22 .. .. £75

The names appearing on these issues, of which a large number have been recorded, are of the Strategoi of the League (on obv.) and magistrates (on rev.).

2234   2235

2234 — Æ *drachm.* (*c.* 4 gm.). Laur. hd. of Apollo r.; ΤΥ monogram behind. ℞. ΘΕΣΣΑ /
ΛΩΝ and Athena Itonia, as last; Μ — Α in lower field. *B.M.C.* 7. 40 .. .. £65

2235 — — Hd. of Athena r., in crested Corinthian helmet; ΑΓΑ above. ℞. ΘΕΣ / ΣΑΛΩΝ above
and below horse trotting r. *B.M.C.* 7. 47, 48 .. .. £75

2236 — Æ *hemidrachm.* Hd. of Zeus r., crowned with oak; behind, ΣΥ monogram. ℞.
ΘΕΣΣΑ / ΛΩΝ behind and before Athena Itonia r., as 2231; Π — Ο / Λ — Υ in lower field.
B.M.C. 7. 44 .. .. £65

2237 — Æ 22. Laur. hd. of Apollo r. ℞. ΘΕΣΣΑ / ΛΩΝ behind and before Athena Itonia r.,
as 2231; ΗΡ monogram in field to r. *B.M.C.* 7. 50, 51 .. .. £10

2238 — Æ 17. Hd. of Athena r., in crested Corinthian helmet; ΙΠΠΑΙ / ΤΑΣ above and
beneath. ℞. As 2235. *B.M.C.* 7. 62 .. .. £8

2239 — Æ 26. Laur. hd. of Zeus r. ℞. ΘΕΣΣΑ / ΛΛΩΝ either side of centaur prancing r.,
seizing by the bridle a horse rearing r.; ΕΥΒΙΟΤΟΥ above. *Weber* 2945.. .. £20

2240 **ISLANDS OFF THESSALY. Peparethos.** 350-300 B.C. Æ 15. Hd. of young
Dionysos r., wreathed with ivy. ℞. Amphora; ΠΕ / Π — Α / Ρ — Η in field. *B.M.C.* 7. 7
£14

2241   2245

2241 — Æ 14. Hd. of bearded Dionysos r., wreathed with ivy. ℞. Kantharos; Π — Ε in
field. *B.M.C.* 7. 1-3 .. .. £14

2242 — Æ 11. *Obv.* Similar to 2240. ℞. Thyrsos and cross-piece of torch, combined;
Π — Ε / Π — Α in field. *B.M.C.* 7. 8 .. .. £12

2243 **Skiathos** (situated between Peparethos and the mainland of Thessaly). *Circa* 350 B.C.
Æ 17. Hd. of Hermes r., wearing tainia. ℞. ΣΚΙ / ΑΘΙ either side of caduceus; tripod in
field to r. *B.M.C.* 7. 1 .. .. £18

2244 — Æ 14. Gorgoneion. ℞. Σ — Κ either side of caduceus. *B.M.C.* 7. 5 .. £16

2245 **AKARNANIA** (a district of western Greece, between the river Achelous and the Ionian
Sea; it's cities formed a confederacy, initially led by Stratos, towards the end of the 5th
Cent. B.C.). **Alyzia** (situated on the coast, opposite Leukas, Alyzia possessed a temple of
Herakles containing a statue of the god by Lysippos). Mid-4th to mid-3rd Cent B.C.
Æ *stater* of the Corinthian type. Pegasos, with pointed wing, flying r. ℞. Hd. of Athena r., wearing Corinthian helmet over leather cap; ΑΛΥΙΑΙΩΝ before;
pudenda virilia behind. *B.M.C.* 12. (*Colonies of Corinth*), *p.* 114, 6 .. .. £250

Alyzia *continued*

2246 — Æ 18. Hd. of Athena r., in crested Athenian helmet. R. ΑΛΥ. Hd. of bearded Herakles r., in lion's skin; club behind. *B.M.C. 7*. 1 .. .. £20

2247   2250

2247 **Anaktorion** (situated on a promontory at the entrance to the Ambrakian gulf). *Circa* 450 B.C. Æ *drachm* of the Corinthian type. Pegasos, with curled wing, flying r.; F (digamma) beneath. R. Archaic hd. of Aphrodite r., hair turned up behind under diadem; all within incuse square. *Weber* 3836 .. .. £200

2248 350-300 B.C. Æ *stater* of the Corinthian type. Pegasos, with pointed wing, flying l.; ANA monogram beneath. R. Hd. of Athena l., wearing Corinthian helmet, bound with olive-wreath, over leather cap; behind, lyre. *B.M.C. 12.* (*Colonies of Corinth*), *p.* 116, 17 £125

2249 — — *Obv.* Similar, but Pegasos r., and with ivy-leaf beneath. R. ΑΝΑΚΤΟΡΙΩΝ before hd. of Athena l., wearing crested Corinthian helmet over leather cap; behind, tripod. *B.M.C. 12.* 13 .. .. £140

2250 — — *Obv.* As last, but with AN monogram beneath. R. Hd of Athena r., wearing Corinthian helmet over leather cap; behind, AN monogram and tripod enclosed by wreath. *B.M.C. 12.* 35-7 .. .. £110

2251 — Æ *drachm.* *Obv.* As last. R. ΑΚΤΙΑΣ. Female hd. three-quarter face to r. *B.M.C. 12.* 7 .. .. £175

2252 — Pegasos, with pointed wing, flying l.; AN monogram beneath. R. Hd. of Aphrodite l., hair bound with cord and tied at back. *B.M.C. 12.* 46 .. .. £125

2253 — Æ *hemidrachm.* Forepart of Pegasos l., with curled wing; ANA monogram beneath. R. Female hd. l., wearing tainia over which hair is rolled. *B.M.C. 12.* 48 .. £95

2254 300-250 B.C. Æ *stater.* *Obv.* As 2252. R. Hd. of Athena l., wearing Corinthian helmet over leather cap; ΛΥΣ before; ΑΓ monogram beneath; AN monogram and thymiaterion behind. *B.M.C. 12.* 54-8 .. .. £110

2255 — — Similar, but on *rev.*, ΑΡΙ before hd. of Athena, and ΔΩ and flaming altar behind. *B.M.C. 12.* 66-8 .. .. £110

2256 250-167 B.C. Æ *drachm?* (*c.* 2·3 gm.). Laur. hd. of Zeus r. R. ΑΝΑ monogram; Λ above, Υ beneath; all within laurel-wreath. *B.M.C. 7.* (*Acarnania*), *p.* 171, 1 £85

2257 — Æ 19. Laur. hd. of Apollo l.; ΛΥΣΙ before. R. ΑΝΑΚΤΟΡΙΕΩΝ. Lyre; thymiaterion in field to l. *B.M.C. 7.* 3 .. .. £18

2257   2258

2258 **Argos Amphilochikon** (founded by the Argive Amphilochos, Argos was situated near the eastern shores of the Ambrakian gulf). Mid-4th to mid-3rd Cent. B.C. Æ *stater* of the Corinthian type. Pegasos, with pointed wing, flying l.; A beneath. R. Hd. of Athena l., wearing Corinthian helmet over leather cap; ΑΡΓΕΙ above; crested Corinthian helmet behind. *B.M.C. 12.* (*Colonies of Corinth*), *p.* 122, 8 *and* 9 .. .. £130

2259 — — Similar, but with ΑΜΦΙ instead of ΑΡΓΕΙ on *rev.*, and with ΑΒΡ and spear behind hd. of Athena. *B.M.C. 12.* 15 .. ..   £150

2260 — Æ 19. Hd. of Hermes (?) r., with short hair. ℞. ΑΡΓΕΙΩΝ. Dog r., at bay; wreath below. *B.M.C. 7. (Acarnania), p.* 172, 1.. .. ..   £15

2261 — Æ 15. Hd. of Athena r., in crested Athenian helmet. ℞. ΑΡΓΕΙΩΝ. Owl stg. l.; spear-head in field to l. *B.M.C. 7. 9* £10

2262   2263

2262 **Astakos.** *Circa* 350 B.C. Æ *stater* of the Corinthian type. Pegasos, with pointed wing, flying r. ℞. Hd. of Athena r., wearing Corinthian helmet over leather cap; ΑΣ beneath; crayfish behind. *B.M.C. 12. (Colonies of Corinth), p.* 123, 1 .. .. ..   £250

2263 **Koronta** (?). 300-250 B.C. Æ *stater* of the Corinthian type. Pegasos, with pointed wing, flying l. ℞. Hd. of Athena, as last, but to left; behind, κ and Macedonian shield ornamented with thunderbolt. *B.M.C. 12. (Colonies of Corinth), p.* 124, 1 *and* 2   £250

2264 **Echinos** (?). 300-250 B.C. Æ *stater* of the Corinthian type. *Obv.* Similar. ℞. Hd. of Athena, as 2262; behind, fish-hook and ε. *B.M.C. 12. (Colonies of Corinth), p.* 124, 1
£225

2265 **Leukas** (founded by the Corinthians in the 7th Cent. B.C., Leukas was a town of considerable importance — the head of the Akarnanian Confederacy from the end of the 4th Century). 480-450 B.C. Æ *stater* of the Corinthian type. Pegasos, with curled wing, flying l.; ʌ beneath. ℞. Hd. of Athena r., of archaic style, wearing Corinthian helmet; all within incuse square. *B.M.C. 12. (Colonies of Corinth), p.* 125, 1 *and* 2 ..   £225

After Corinth itself, Leukas was the most prolific mint for Pegasos staters.

2266 — — Similar, but Pegasos to right, and with ivy-leaf behind hd. of Athena on *rev.* *B.M.C. 12.* 7 .. ..   £225

2267 — Æ *trihemiobol* (*c.* 0·7 gm.). *Obv.* As last. ℞. τ — ρ / н — ι around Gorgoneion; all within incuse square. *B.M.C. 12.* 136 .. ..   £110

2268 — Æ *obol* (*c.* 0·47 gm.). *Obv.* As 2265. ℞. Incuse square, quartered. *B.M.C. 12.* 141
£65

2266   2269

2269 450-420 B.C. Æ *stater.* *Obv.* As 2265. ℞. Hd. of Athena l., wearing Corinthian helmet over leather cap; before, ʌ; behind, phiale; all within incuse square. *B.M.C. 12.* 15 .. ..   £200

Leukas *continued*

2270 — — Pegasos, with pointed wing, flying l.; ʌ beneath. R. Hd. of Athena l., as last; behind, A; olive-sprays in lower field to l. and to r.; all within incuse square. *B.M.C. 12.* 21 ..   ..   £200

2271 — R *drachm.* Pegasos, with curled wing, flying r.; ʌ beneath. R. Hd. of Aphrodite l., wearing ampyx; ʌ behind. *B.M.C. 12.* 111   ..   ..   £150

          2272   2277

2272 — R *triobol.* Forepart of Pegasos l., with curled wing; ʌ beneath. R. Hd. of Aphrodite l., wearing sphendone. *B.M.C. 12.* 119   ..   ..   £110

2273 — R *diobol. Obv.* As 2271. R. ΔIO. Pegasos, with curled wings, to front; all within incuse square. *B.M.C. 12.* 123 ..   ..   £110

2274 420–350 B.C. R *stater.* Pegasos, with pointed wing, flying l.; ʌ beneath. R. Hd. of Athena l., wearing Corinthian helmet over leather cap; before, ΛΕΥΚΑΔΙΩΝ. *B.M.C. 12.* 27   £140

2275 — — *Obv.* Similar. R. Hd. of Athena l., as last, but with ΛΕΥ before, and wreath behind. *B.M.C. 12.* 38 ..   ..   £125

2276 — — Pegasos, with curled wing, flying r.; ʌ beneath. R. Hd. of Athena l., as last; above, Σ; behind, bunch of grapes. *B.M.C. 12.* 47   ..   ..   ..   £150

2277 — — Similar to 2274, but without legend before hd. of Athena on *rev.*, and with ʌ and caduceus behind. *B.M.C. 12.* 51-5   ..   ..   £110

2278 — R *drachm.* Pegasos, with pointed wing, flying r.; ʌ beneath. R. Hd. of Aphrodite r., hair in net; ʌ behind. *B.M.C. 12.* 114   ..   ..   £85

2279 — R *diobol. Obv.* Similar, but Pegasos to left. R. Pegasos, with curled wing, pacing l.; ʌ beneath. *B.M.C. 12.* 132   ..   ..   £75

2280 — R *trihemiobol. Obv.* As last. R. Gorgoneion. *B.M.C. 12.* 138-40   ..   £75

          2281   2283

2281 350–300 B.C. R *stater. Obv.* As last. R. Hd. of Athena r., wearing Corinthian helmet over leather cap; behind, A and amphora surmounted by bunch of grapes hanging from vine. *B.M.C. 12.* 89   ..   ..   £95

2282 — — — R. Hd. of Athena, as last, but to left; behind, ʌ and mast with yard (stylis), wreathed; beneath, ΑΓ monogram. *B.M.C. 12.* 97, 98 ..   ..   ..   £95

2283 After 167 B.C. R *didrachm* (*c.* 8·3 gm.). Statue of Aphrodite Aineias r., on base, holding aplustre; at her side, stag r.; behind, sceptre surmounted by dove; all within laurel-wreath. R. Prow of galley r.; above, ΛΕΥΚΑΔΙΩΝ, ΛΥΣΙΜΑΧΟΣ and female hd.; below, ΑΚΑΡ monogram. *B.M.C. 7. (Acarnania), p.* 180, 94   ..   ..   £200

More than forty different magistrates' names have been recorded for this series.

2284 — Æ *octobol*? (*c.* 4·85 gm.). Hd. of young Herakles r., in lion's skin. ℞. Club r.; ΛΕΥΚΑΔΙΩΝ above, ΔΑΜΥΛΟΣ and ΑΡ monogram beneath; all within oak-wreath. *B.M.C. 7.* 104 ..   ..   £300

2285 *Bronze Coinage.* 350-250 B.C. Æ 21. Hd. of man-headed bull r. (river-god Achelous); behind, ΑΚ monogram. ℞. Chimaera l.; ΛΕ monogram beneath. *B.M.C. 7.* 15-18

                          £14

These, and the next type, are usually overstruck on coins of Philip II of Macedon.

2286 — Æ 19. Hd. of Athena l., in crested Corinthian helmet; Λ behind. ℞. Chimaera at bay, l. *B.M.C. 7.* 1-10 ..   ..   £12

2287 — Æ 17. Bellerophon riding r. on Pegasos, thrusting with spear. ℞. Chimaera at bay, r.; in ex., ΛΕΥ. *B.M.C. 7.* 33 ..   ..   £10

2288 — Æ 14. Pegasos flying r.; Λ beneath. ℞. Ornamental trident-head. *B.M.C. 7.* 57

                          £7

2289 — — Horse's hd. l.; Λ in field. ℞. Dolphin l.; trident beneath. *B.M.C. 7.* 64-6   £8

      2290   2292

2290 — Æ 19. Laur. hd. of Apollo l.; Ξ behind. ℞. Prow of galley l.; ΛΕΥ above, Ξ beneath. *B.M.C. 7.* 69 ..   ..   £9

2291 *After 167 B.C.* Æ 19. Similar to 2283, statue of Aphrodite Aineias / prow, but without wreath on *obv.*, and with magistrate's name ΔΑΜΟΚΡΑΤΗΣ on *rev.;* no monogram before prow. *B.M.C. 7.* 108-9 ..   ..   £8

2292 — Æ 23. Bust of young Herakles r., in lion's skin, club at shoulder. ℞. Lyre; ΛΕΥΚΑΔΙΩΝ to l.; ΜΑΡ monogram and ΔΙΩΝ to r. *B.M.C. 7.* 127-8 ..   ..   £12

2293 — Æ 17. *Obv.* Similar, but without club. ℞. Club; ΛΕΥΚΑΔΙΩΝ and corn-ear above; ΔΗΜΑΡΕΤΟΣ beneath; all within oak-wreath. *B.M.C. 7.* 145-8 ..   ..   £7

2294 — Æ 14. Flaming altar, wreathed. ℞. ΛΕΥΚΑ / ΔΙΩΝ. Dove stg. r., ΛΑΚΡΑΤΗΣ beneath; all within myrtle-wreath. *B.M.C. 7.* 194-6 ..   ..   £10

For other coins struck at Leukas, see below under Akarnanian Confederacy (nos. 2309-14).

2295 **Medeon** (?) — situated in the interior of the country, north-west of Stratos. 350-300 B.C. Æ 19. Laur. hd. of Apollo l., ΜΕ beneath. ℞. Α within laurel-wreath. *B.M.C. 7.* 1 ..   ..   £20

2296 — Æ 15. Hd. of Athena r., in crested helmet. ℞. ΜΕ. Owl stg. l.; ΦΙ in field. *B.M.C.* 7. 6, 7 ..   ..   £14

2297   2298

2297 **Metropolis** (on the eastern shores of the Ambrakian gulf). 300-250 B.C. Æ *stater* of
the Corinthian type. Pegasos, with pointed wing, flying l.; MH monogram beneath.
R. Hd. of Athena l., wearing Corinthian helmet over leather cap; behind, AΣ monogram
and Macedonian shield ornamented with figure of fighting Athena. *B.M.C. 12. (Colonies
of Corinth)*, p. 138, 1   ..   ..   £250
These are sometimes countermarked on the rev., with a star or with an AM monogram.

2298 **Oiniadai** (in the extreme south of the country, near the mouth of the Achelous, Oiniadai
was close to the Aitolian border). 219-211 B.C. Æ 23. Laur. hd. of Zeus r.; AP monogram beneath, star behind. R. Bearded hd. of man-headed bull r. (river-god Achelous);
OINIAΔAN above, AKAP monogram behind. *B.M.C. 7.* 6, 7   ..   ..   £10

2299 **Stratos** (the chief town of the Akarnanian Confederacy, until its capture by the Aitolians
circa 300 B.C.). 450-400 B.C. Æ *drachm* (c. 2·3 gm.). Bearded hd. of river-god Achelous
three-quarter face to l. R. ΣTPA (retrograde). Hd. of nymph Kallirrhoe facing; all
within incuse square. *B.M.C. 7.* 1   ..   ..   £350
2300 350-300 B.C. Æ 19. Hd. of nymph Kallirrhoe (?) r. R. ΣTPATIΩN. Hd. of Achelous r.,
as 2298. *B.M.C. 7.* 2, 3 ..   ..   £22
For other coins struck at Stratos, see below under Akarnanian Confederacy (nos. 2306-8).

2301   2303

2301 **Thyrrheion** (situated east of Anaktorion, near the southern shores of the Ambrakian
gulf, Thyrrheion rose to be a place of some importance in the 3rd and 2nd Cents. B.C.).
350-250 B.C. Æ *stater* of the Corinthian type. Pegasos, with pointed wing, flying l.;
Θ beneath. R. Hd. of Athena l., wearing Corinthian helmet over leather cap; Θ — Y in
field; AY beneath; amphora behind. *B.M.C. 12. (Colonies of Corinth)*, p. 139, 4 £125
2302 250-167 B.C. Æ *stater* of the Corinthian type, but reduced weight (c. 6·8 gm.). Pegasos,
with pointed wing, flying r.; Π beneath. R. Hd. of Athena r., wearing Corinthian helmet
over leather cap; Δ before; small hd. of river-god Achelous r. behind. *B.M.C. 12.
(Colonies of Corinth)*, p. 113, 3   ..   ..   £140
2303 After 167 B.C. Æ *stater* (c. 9·5 gm.). Beardless hd. of river-god Achelous r.; MENANΔPOΣ
behind. R. ΘYPPEIΩN behind Apollo Aktios, naked, enthroned l., holding bow; monogram in field to l. *Weber* 3112 ..   ..   £500

2304 *Bronze Coinage.* 350-300 B.C. Æ 18. Hd. of Athena l., in crested helmet. ℞.
ΘΥΡΡΕΙΩΝ. Owl stg. l., hd. facing; torch in field to l. *B.M.C. 7.* 3 ..   ..   £14

2305   2308

2305 After 167 B.C. Æ 18. ΘΥΡΡΕΙΩΝ. Hd. of Athena r., in crested Corinthian helmet.
℞. ΧΕΡ / ΣΥΣ either side of owl stg. r., hd. facing. *B.M.C. 7.* 14   ..   ..   £12

2306 **Akarnanian Confederacy.** 400-350 B.C. Æ *tetrobol?* (*c.* 1·9 gm.). Bearded hd. of
river-god Achelous three-quarter face to l. ℞. A — K either side of hd. of nymph Kallirrhoe three-quarter face to l. *B.M.C. 7., p.* 168, 1 ..   ..   £250

2307 350-300 B.C. Æ *drachm?* (*c.* 2·2 gm.). Bearded hd. of river-god Achelous r. ℞.
ΚΑΛΛΙΡΟΑ around large F; all within incuse square. *B.M.C. 7., p.* 189, 2 *and* 3 (*wrongly
attributed to Oiniadai*) £200

2308 — Æ *triobol?* (*c.* 1·1 gm.). Hd. of bearded Herakles l., in lion's skin. ℞. Large T
between two bunches of grapes and I R (retrograde); all within incuse square. *B.M.C. 7.,
p.* 189, 5 ..   ..   £175

Nos. 2306-8 *were struck probably at Stratos.*

2309   2310

2309 300-250 B.C. Æ *stater* of the Corinthian type. Pegasos, with pointed wing, flying l.;
AK monogram beneath. ℞. Hd. of Athena l., wearing Corinthian helmet over leather cap;
behind, bunch of grapes on vine-branch. *B.M.C.* 12. (*Colonies of Corinth*), *p.* 113, 1-3
(*pl. XXX,* 5 *and* 6) £140

This type was issued from the Leukas mint.

2310 250-167 B.C. Æ *stater* (*c.* 10 gm.). Beardless hd. of river-god Achelous r.; ΛΥΚΟΥΡΓΟΣ
behind. ℞. ΑΚΑΡΝΑΝΩΝ behind Apollo Aktios enthroned l., holding bow; AP monogram
in field to l. *B.M.C. 7., p.* 168, 4 *and* 5 ..   ..   £375

2311 — Æ *half stater.* Similar. *B.M.C. 7., p.* 169, 10 ..   ..   £225

2312 — Æ *drachm?* (*c.* 4 gm.). *Obv.* Similar, but with ΑΚΑΡΝΑΝΩΝ behind. ℞. ΜΕΝΝΕΙΑΣ
behind Artemis advancing r., carrying long torch in both hands; race-torch in field to r.
B.M.C. 7., p. 169, 13 ..   ..   £300

2313 — Æ 22. Hd. of young Herakles r., in lion's skin. ℞. Bearded hd. of river-god
Achelous r.; trident r. above, A behind. *B.M.C. 7., p.* 169, 16-18, 20 ..   ..   £8

2314 — — Hd. of Athena l., in crested helmet. ℞. Bearded hd. of river-god Achelous l.;
trident l. above. *B.M.C. 7., p.* 170, 21-4..   ..   ..   £8

Nos. 2310-14 *were struck probably at Leukas.*

2315   2317

2315 **AITOLIA** (the warlike people of this district produced no coinage until the 3rd Cent. B.C., when the Gallic invasion of Greece occasioned the inauguration of a Federal currency). 279-168 B.C. *N stater.* Hd. of Athena r., wearing crested Corinthian helmet decorated with griffin; behind, owl. ℞. ΑΙΤΩΛΩΝ behind Aitolia, represented as an armed Amazon, seated r. on pile of shields; she holds spear and Nike; ΑΠΩ monogram in field to r.   *B.M.C. 7.* 1   ..   ..   £5,000

2316 — *N half stater.* Hd. of young Herakles r., in lion's skin. ℞. Similar to last, but in field to r., small figure of Artemis advancing r., holding torch; monogram in ex. *B.M.C. 7.* 3   £2,500

2317 — *R tetradrachm.* *Obv.* As last. ℞. ΑΙΤΩΛΩΝ behind Aitolia, as an Amazon, seated r. on pile of Macedonian and Gaulish shields; she holds spear and sword; Gaulish carnyx lies beneath her feet; Λ in field to l., ΑΥ monogram and ΣΕ to r. *B.M.C. 7.* 8 ..   £750

2318   2320

2318 — *R stater* (c. 10·25 gm.). Young male hd. r., wearing oak-wreath intertwined with diadem; ΦI beneath. ℞. ΑΙΤΩΛΩΝ behind naked warrior stg. l., r. foot on rock, holding spear. *B.M.C. 7.* 9   ..   ..   £325

      The head on obv. has been variously identified as that of Antiochos III of Syria, or Demetrios Aitolos, son of Antigonos Gonatas of Macedon.

2319 — *R half stater.* Laur. bust of Artemis r., bow and quiver at shoulder; ΦI behind. ℞. ΑΙΤΩΛΩΝ behind Aitolia, as an Amazon, seated r., hd. facing, on pile of Gaulish shields; she holds spear and sword; Δ and trophy of Gaulish arms in field to r. *B.M.C. 7.* 12 £300

2320 — *R quarter stater.* Hd. of Aitolia r., wearing kausia; Λ — Ω in field. ℞. ΑΙΤΩΛΩΝ above Kalydonian boar r., at bay; in ex., spear-head r. *B.M.C. 7.* 17, 18   ..   £65

2321 — Æ 18. *Obv.* As last, but without legend. ℞. ΑΙΤΩ / ΛΩΝ above and beneath spear-head l.; bunch of grapes in lower field to r. *B.M.C. 7.* 34, 35 ..   ..   £9

2322 — — Laur. hd. of Aitolos (?) r. ℞. ΑΙΤΩ / ΛΩΝ above and beneath spear-head and jaw-bone of boar r.; ΚΛΕΙ in central field, bunch of grapes to l. *B.M.C. 7.* 58-61 ..   £8

2323 — — Hd. of Athena r., in crested Corinthian helmet. ℞. ΑΙΤΩ / ΛΩΝ either side of Herakles stg. facing, holding club and lion's skin; Φ in upper field to l. *B.M.C. 7.* 70, 71   £7

2324 — Æ 17. *Obv.* Similar to 2322. ℞. ΑΙΤΩ / ΛΩΝ either side of trophy; monogram in field to l. *B.M.C. 7.* 39 ..   ..   £9

2325   2326

2325 LOKRIS OPUNTIA and EPIKNEMIDIA (there were two separate districts occupied by the Lokrians — eastern Lokris, opposite the coastlines of Thessaly and Euboia, inhabited by the Opuntians and the Epiknemidians; and western Lokris, on the Corinthian gulf, called Lokris Ozolis). **Opus** (the chief town of the Opuntians). 387-369 B.C. *Æ obol.* ΟΠ / ΟΝ either side of amphora between grapes and ivy-leaf. Ꭱ. Star. *B.M.C. 8.* 4-6   ..   ..   £50

2326 369-338 B.C. *Æ stater* (*c.* 12·25 gm.). Hd. of Persephone l., wreathed with corn (imitated from the Syracusan coinage of Euainetos). Ꭱ. ΟΠΟΝΤΙΩΝ. Ajax, son of Oileus, naked but for helmet, advancing r., holding sword and large shield decorated with serpent; broken spear on ground. *B.M.C. 8.* 14-16   ..   ..   ..   £550

2327 — — Similar, but hd. of Persephone to r., and with kantharos between legs of Ajax (no spear). *B.M.C. 8.* 8   ..   ..   £500

2328   2332

2328 — — *Obv.* As last. Ꭱ. Similar to 2326, but the shield of Ajax is decorated with griffin, and the spear is unbroken. *B.M.C. 8.* 28   ..   ..   £550

2329 — *Æ half stater. Obv.* As 2326. Ꭱ. ΟΠΟΝΤΙΩΝ. Ajax advancing l., holding spear and large shield ornamented with Gorgoneion. *Weber* 3145   ..   ..   £750

2330 — *Æ quarter stater.* Similar to 2327. *B.M.C. 8.* 9-12   ..   ..   £125

2331 338-300 B.C. *Æ stater.* Similar to 2326, but with legend ΛΟΚΡΩΝ instead of ΟΠΟΝΤΙΩΝ; the shield is undecorated and the spear unbroken; ΥΠΟ monogram between legs of Ajax. *B.M.C. 8.* 38   ..   ..   £750

2332 — *Æ quarter stater.* Hd. of Athena r., in crested Corinthian helmet. Ꭱ. ΛΟΚΡΩΝ. Ajax, bare-headed, advancing r., holding sword and large shield decorated with sea-horse; trident before. *B.M.C. 8.* 42-4   ..   ..   £175

2333 — *Æ obol.* Similar to 2325, but with legend ΛΟ / ΚΡ instead of ΟΠ / ΟΝ. *B.M.C. 8.* 45-9   ..   £70

Following the battle of Chaeroneia, 338 B.C., the coins were issued in the name of the Lokrians in general, rather than just the Opuntians, though doubtless Opus remained the mint.

2334 *Bronze Coinage.* 350-338 B.C. Æ 13. Hd. of Athena r., in crested Corinthian helmet. Ꭱ. ΟΠΟΝΤΙΩΝ. Bunch of grapes. *B.M.C. 8.* 37   ..   ..   ..   £12

2335 338-300 B.C. Æ 14. Hd. of Hermes l., in petasos. Ꭱ. ΥΠΟΚ ΛΟΚΡΩΝ. Bunch of grapes. *B.M.C. 8.* 41   ..   ..   £15

The Epiknemidians were earlier called Hypoknemidii.

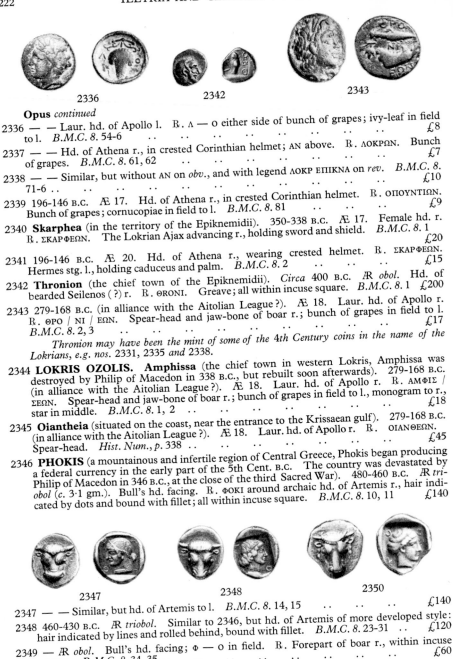

2336   2342   2343

Opus *continued*

2336 — — Laur. hd. of Apollo l. ℞. Λ — O either side of bunch of grapes; ivy-leaf in field to l. *B.M.C. 8.* 54-6 ..   ..   £8

2337 — — Hd. of Athena r., in crested Corinthian helmet; AN above. ℞. ΛΟΚΡΩΝ. Bunch of grapes. *B.M.C. 8.* 61, 62 ..   ..   £7

2338 — — Similar, but without AN on *obv.*, and with legend ΛΟΚΡ ΕΠΙΚΝΑ on *rev.* *B.M.C. 8.* 71-6 ..   ..   £10

2339 196-146 B.C. Æ 17. Hd. of Athena r., in crested Corinthian helmet. ℞. ΟΠΟΥΝΤΙΩΝ. Bunch of grapes; cornucopiae in field to l. *B.M.C. 8.* 81 ..   ..   £9

2340 **Skarphea** (in the territory of the Epiknemidii). 350-338 B.C. Æ 17. Female hd. r. ℞. ΣΚΑΡΦΕΩΝ. The Lokrian Ajax advancing r., holding sword and shield. *B.M.C. 8.* 1 £20

2341 196-146 B.C. Æ 20. Hd. of Athena r., wearing crested helmet. ℞. ΣΚΑΡΦΕΩΝ. Hermes stg. l., holding caduceus and palm. *B.M.C. 8.* 2 ..   ..   £15

2342 **Thronion** (the chief town of the Epiknemidii). *Circa* 400 B.C. Æ *obol.* Hd. of bearded Seilenos (?) r. ℞. ΘΡΟΝΙ. Greave; all within incuse square. *B.M.C. 8.* 1 £200

2343 279-168 B.C. (in alliance with the Aitolian League?). Æ 18. Laur. hd. of Apollo r. ℞. ΘΡΟ / ΝΙ / ΕΩΝ. Spear-head and jaw-bone of boar r.; bunch of grapes in field to l. *B.M.C. 8.* 2, 3 ..   ..   £17

Thronion may have been the mint of some of the 4th Century coins in the name of the Lokrians, e.g. nos. 2331, 2335 and 2338.

2344 **LOKRIS OZOLIS. Amphissa** (the chief town in western Lokris, Amphissa was destroyed by Philip of Macedon in 338 B.C., but rebuilt soon afterwards). 279-168 B.C. (in alliance with the Aitolian League?). Æ 18. Laur. hd. of Apollo r. ℞. ΑΜΦΙΣ / ΣΕΩΝ. Spear-head and jaw-bone of boar r.; bunch of grapes in field to l., monogram to r., star in middle. *B.M.C. 8.* 1, 2 ..   ..   £18

2345 **Oiantheia** (situated on the coast, near the entrance to the Krissaean gulf). 279-168 B.C. (in alliance with the Aitolian League?). Æ 18. Laur. hd. of Apollo r. ℞. ΟΙΑΝΘΕΩΝ. Spear-head. *Hist. Num., p.* 338 ..   ..   £45

2346 **PHOKIS** (a mountainous and infertile region of Central Greece, Phokis began producing a federal currency in the early part of the 5th Cent. B.C. The country was devastated by Philip of Macedon in 346 B.C., at the close of the third Sacred War). 480-460 B.C. Æ *triobol* (*c.* 3·1 gm.). Bull's hd. facing. ℞. ΦΟΚΙ around archaic hd. of Artemis r., hair indicated by dots and bound with fillet; all within incuse square. *B.M.C. 8.* 10, 11 £140

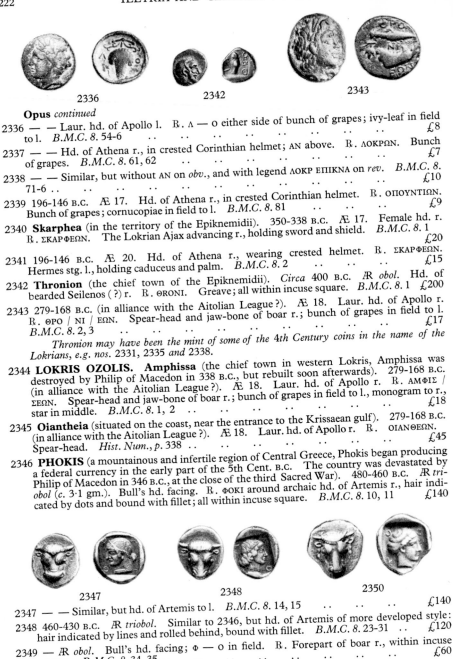

2347   2348   2350

2347 — — Similar, but hd. of Artemis to l. *B.M.C. 8.* 14, 15 ..   ..   £140

2348 460-430 B.C. Æ *triobol.* Similar to 2346, but hd. of Artemis of more developed style: hair indicated by lines and rolled behind, bound with fillet. *B.M.C. 8.* 23-31 .. £120

2349 — Æ *obol.* Bull's hd. facing; Φ — O in field. ℞. Forepart of boar r., within incuse square. *B.M.C. 8.* 34, 35 ..   ..   £60

2350 430-421 B.C. Æ *triobol.* Bull's hd. facing, bound with fillet. ℞. ΦΟΚΙ around hd. of Artemis r., of fine style, wearing ampyx; all within incuse square. *B.M.C. 8.* 52, 53 £175

2351 — Æ *obol*. Bull's hd. r.; ΦO above. R. As 2349. *B.M.C. 8.* 54 .. .. £65

2352 — Æ *hemiobol*. Bull's hd. r.; ΦO behind. R. Corinthian helmet r., within incuse square. *B.M.C. 8.* 61-3 .. .. £45

2353

2355

2353 357-346 B.C. (period of the third Sacred War). Æ *triobol*. Bull's hd. facing. R. Laur. hd. of the Delphian Apollo r.; Φ — Ω in lower field; lyre behind. *B.M.C. 8.* 78-83 £140

2354 — Æ *obol*. Similar. *B.M.C. 8.* 84-6 .. .. £70

2355 *Bronze Coinage.* 371-357 B.C. Æ 14. Hd. of Athena three-quarter face to l., wearing triple-crested helmet. R. Φ within olive-wreath. *B.M.C. 8.* 66-74 .. .. £9

2356 357-346 B.C. Æ 22 (*trichalkon*). ΦΩΚΕΩΝ. Three bull's heads, arranged in triangular pattern. R. T within laurel-wreath. *B.M.C. 8.* 91-3 .. .. £30

2357 — Æ 17. Bull's hd. facing, bound with fillet. R. ΦΩ within laurel-wreath. *B.M.C. 8.* 94-6 .. .. £14

2358 — Æ 13. Similar. *B.M.C. 8.* 97-100 .. .. £10

2359 — Æ 15. *Obv.* Similar. R. ONY / MAP / XOY in three lines within laurel-wreath. *B.M.C. 8.* 103 .. .. £18
  Onymarchos was strategos of the Phokians from 354-2 *B.C.*

2360 3rd-2nd Cent. B.C. Æ 19. *Obv.* Similar. R. Laur. hd. of Apollo r., ΦΩΚΕΩΝ behind. *B.M.C. 8.* 109 .. .. £12

2361 **Antikyra** (situated on the Corinthian gulf, this town originally bore the name Kyparissa). 2nd Cent B.C. Æ 15. Similar to previous, but with AN above bull's hd. on *obv*. *B.M.C. 8., p.* 23, 107 .. .. £17

2362 **Delphi.** 480-460 B.C. Æ *trihemiobol* (*c.* 1·5 gm.). Ram's hd. r.; dolphin r. beneath. R. Goat's hd. facing between two dolphins; all within incuse square. *B.M.C. 8.* 11 £225

2363 460-448 B.C. Æ *tritemorion*, i.e. ¾ *obol* (*c.* 0·75 gm.). Hd. of negro (Delphos) r. R. Three T's, arranged star-wise, within incuse square. *Weber* 3192 .. .. £175

2364 421-355 B.C. Æ *trihemiobol*. Ram's hd. l.; dolphin l. beneath. R. Goat's hd. facing between two dolphins; ΔΑΛ above, tripod in field to l. *B.M.C. 8.* 19 .. .. £250

2365 2366

Delphi *continued*

2365 336 B.C. Æ *stater*, in the name of the Amphiktyonic council. Veiled hd. of Demeter l.,
wreathed with corn. ℞. AMΦIKTIONΩN. Apollo seated left on the Delphian omphalos;
r. elbow resting on lyre in background, holding laurel-branch in l. hand; tripod in field to
l. *B.M.C. 8., p.* 27, 22 ..   ..   £3,500
*These were struck on the occasion of the re-minting of all the old coins in the Delphic
treasury in order to defray the cost of work on the new temple.*

2366 **Elateia** (the second town of Phokis, after Delphi, Elateia was situated in an important
pass from Boeotia). 2nd Cent. B.C. Æ 17. Bull's hd. facing, bound with fillet; EA
above. ℞. ΦΩKEΩN. Laur. hd. of Apollo r. *B.M.C. 8., p.* 23, 105-6..   ..   £17

2367 — Æ 19. Male hd. l., bearded. ℞. EΛATEΩN. Statue of Athena stg. r., brandishing
spear and holding shield; bull's hd. facing in field to r. *B.M.C. 8.* 1 ..   ..   £15

2368 **Ledon** (destroyed during the third Sacred War, but later rebuilt). 2nd Cent. B.C.
Æ 18. Similar to 2366, but with ΛE instead of EΛ above bull's hd. *Hist. Num., p.* 343
                                                  £20

2369 **Lilaia** (situated near the source of the river Kephissos). 2nd Cent. B.C. Æ 18.
Similar, but with ΛI above bull's hd. *Hist. Num., p.* 343   ..   ..   ..   £20

2370 **BOEOTIA. Thebes** (this great city was the arch-rival of Athens, and supported
Sparta during the Peloponnesian war. Later, the Thebans defeated their former allies
and became the most powerful state in Greece (371 B.C.). This position was soon usurped
by Philip II of Macedon who inflicted a crushing defeat on the combined forces of Thebes
and Athens in 338 B.C. Two years later Thebes was utterly destroyed by Alexander the
Great, and although partially restored by Kassander it never again recovered its political
influence in Greece). 480-456 B.C. Æ *stater*. Boeotian shield. ℞. Amphora, within
incuse square. *B.M.C. 8.* 18 ..   ..   £350

2371 — Æ *drachm*. Similar. *B.M.C. 8.* 19 ..   ..   £175

2372 — Æ *obol*. Similar. *B.M.C. 8.* 20-22 ..   ..   £100

2373 — Æ *hemiobol*. Half Boeotian shield. ℞. Ivy-leaf, within incuse square. *B.M.C. 8.* 23
                                                   £75

2374   2377

2374 456-446 B.C. Æ *stater*. Similar to 2370, but with Θ — E either side of amphora on *rev.*
B.M.C. 8. 26   ..   ..   £325

2375 — Æ *hemidrachm*. Similar, but with Θ only, to l. of amphora. *B.M.C. 8.* 27   £140

2376 — Æ *hemiobol*. As last, but with half Boeotian shield on *obv.* *B.M.C. 8.* 28   £75

2377 446-426 B.C. Æ *stater*. Boeotian shield. Ɽ. ΘEBAION. Young Herakles, naked, kneeling r., stringing his bow; all within incuse square. *B.M.C. 8.* 30   ..   £2,500

2378 — — Boeotian shield. Ɽ. ΘEBAION. Bearded Herakles, naked, striding r., wielding club and holding the Delphic tripod; all within incuse square. *B.M.C. 8.* 36   £3,000

2379   2382

2379 ·· — Boeotian shield. Ɽ. ΘEBA. Harmonia, wife of Kadmos, seated r., l. foot on stool, holding crested Corinthian helmet; all within incuse square. *B.M.C. 8.* 42 ..   £3,500

2380 —· Æ *hemidrachm*. Boeotian shield. Ɽ. Θ — E (retrograde) either side of kantharos, B above; all within incuse square. *B.M.C. 8.* 43   ..   ..   ..   £140

2381 — Æ *obol*. Boeotian shield. Ɽ. Large Θ, within incuse square. *B.M.C. 8.* 47   £90

2382 426-395 B.C. Æ *stater*. Boeotian shield. Ɽ. Bearded hd. of Herakles l., in lion's skin; Θ — E in lower field; all within incuse square. *B.M.C. 8.* 49   ..   ..   ..   £750

2383 — — Boeotian shield, ornamented with club. Ɽ. Bearded hd. of Dionysos r., wreathed with ivy; Θ — E in lower field; all within incuse square. *B.M.C. 8.* 63   ..   £500

2384   2387

2384 — — *Obv.* Similar. Ɽ. Amphora, the upper part fluted; Θ —E in field; all within incuse square. *B.M.C. 8.* 72   ..   ..   £250

2385 — Æ *hemidrachm*. Boeotian shield. Ɽ. Kantharos, club above; ΘE — BH in lower field; all within incuse square. *B.M.C. 8.* 78   ..   ..   £80

2386 — Æ *hemiobol*. Half Boeotian shield. Ɽ. Θ — E either side of bunch of grapes. *B.M.C. 8.* 81 ..   ..   £45

2387 395-387 B.C. Electrum *hemidrachm*. Bearded hd. of Dionysos r., wreathed with ivy. Ɽ. Infant Herakles, naked, seated facing, looking l., strangling two serpents; club beneath, Θ — E in field; all within incuse square. *B.M.C. 8.* 89 ..   ..   £5,000

2388 — Electrum *obol*. Similar, but on *rev*. infant Herakles kneels r., and without club beneath; all within incuse circle. *B.M.C. 8.* 90 ..   ..   £2,000

2389 — Æ *stater*. Boeotian shield. Ɽ. Amphora, the upper part fluted; Θ — E in lower field, bow to l. *B.M.C. 8.* 94   ..   ..   £250

2390 — — Boeotian shield. Ɽ. Amphora, as last; Θ above, E to r.; all within a wreath of ivy. *B.M.C. 8.* 99   ..   ..   £500

2391　　　　　　2392　　　　　2393

Thebes *continued*

2391 — — Boeotian shield. R. Infant Herakles, naked, seated facing, looking r., strangling two serpents; ΘE beneath, bow in field to r.　*B.M.C. 8.* 103　·· 　··　··　£1,000

2392 — Æ *tritemorion* (*c.* 0·7 gm.). Three Boeotian half-shields, Θ at centre. R. Similar to *obv.*, but each half-shield is ornamented with club.　*B.M.C. 8.* 105-6 ..　··　£85

2393 — Æ *hemiobol.* Half Boeotian shield, ornamented with club. R. Θ — E either side of amphora, B above; club in field to l.　*B.M.C. 8.* 107-8 ..　··　··　··　£55

2394 — Æ *tetartemorion* (*c.* 0·25 gm.). Boeotian shield, ornamented with club. R. Θ — E either side of kantharos; club above.　*B.M.C. 8.* 110 ..　··　··　··　£65

2395　　　　　　　　2396

2395 379-371 B.C.　Æ *stater.* Boeotian shield. R. BO — IΩ either side of amphora, the upper part fluted; above, bow and arrow.　*B.M.C. 8., p.* 36, 46　··　··　£200

    These federal issues were formerly attributed to the period following the great Theban defeat by Philip of Macedon in 338 B.C.

2396 — Æ *hemidrachm.* Boeotian shield. R. BO — I either side of kantharos; above, club r.; in field to r., crescent.　*B.M.C. 8., p.* 37, 50-54 ..　··　··　··　··　£75

2397 — Æ *obol.* Similar.　*B.M.C. 8., p.* 37, 55-6 ..　··　··　··　··　£50

2398 371-338 B.C.　Æ *stater.* Boeotian shield. R. Amphora, the upper part fluted; FA — ΣT across field; corn-grain above.　*B.M.C. 8.* 120-1　··　··　··　£175

2399 — — Similar, but with EΠ — AMI in *rev.* field, and with rose instead of corn-grain above amphora.　*B.M.C. 8.* 135 ..　··　··　··　··　··　··　£225

2400 — — Similar, but HI — KE in field, ivy-leaf hanging from each handle of amphora, and olive-spray in field to r. (nothing above).　*B.M.C. 8.* 147　··　··　··　£175

    Over forty different magistrates' names have been recorded for this series. That of Epaminondas (no. 2399) may represent the great Theban general who achieved the brilliant victory over the Spartans in 371 B.C.

2401 — Æ *obol.* Boeotian shield, ornamented with club. R. Hd. of young Herakles r., clad in lion's skin; before, ΘE (=magistrate's name, *not* mint name).　*B.M.C. 8.* 169-70
£110

2402   2405

2402 288-244 B.C. (Demetrios Poliorketes granted the Thebans their freedom from Macedonian domination in 288 B.C.). Æ *tetradrachm* (*c.* 17 gm.). Laur. hd. of Zeus r.
R. ΒΟΙΩΤΩΝ. Poseidon enthroned l., holding dolphin and trident; Boeotian shield on
side of throne. *B.M.C. 8.*, *p.* 38, 63   ..   ..   £6,000

2403 221-197 B.C. Æ *half stater* (*c.* 5 gm.). Hd. of Persephone three-quarter face to r.,
wreathed with corn. R. ΒΟΙΩΤΩΝ. Poseidon, naked, stg. facing, looking r., holding
trident and dolphin; to r., ΑΔ monogram and Boeotian shield. *B.M.C. 8.*, *p.* 40, 75   £140

2404 196-146 B.C. Æ *half stater*. Laur. hd. of Poseidon r. R. ΒΟΙΩΤΩΝ. Nike stg. l.,
holding wreath and trident; ΑΡΧΕ monogram to l. *B.M.C. 8.*, *p.* 42, 102   ..   £120

2405 *Bronze Coinage*. 379-371 B.C. Æ 14. Boeotian shield. R. ΒΟΙΩΤΩΝ. Ornamented
trident-head; dolphin and ivy-leaf in field to r. *B.M.C. 8.*, *p.* 38, 57   ..   ..   £12

2406 371-338 B.C. Æ 13. Hd. of young Herakles r., clad in lion's skin. R. ΘΕΟ / ΤΙ above
and beneath club and arrow, both l. *B.M.C. 8.* 174   ..   ..   £9

2407 — — *Obv.* Similar, but hd. l. R. ΟΛΥΜ above club and caduceus, both l. *B.M.C. 8.* 193
£9

2408 315-288 B.C. Æ 11. *Obv.* As 2406. R. ΘΗΒΑΙΩΝ between thyrsos l., above, and club l.,
beneath. *B.M.C. 8.* 201-6   ..   ..   £9

2409 — Æ 10. Boeotian shield. R. ΘΗΒΑΙΩΝ. Trident. *B.M.C. 8.* 207-9   ..   £8

2410   2412

2410 288-244 B.C. Æ 21. Hd. of Athena r., in crested Corinthian helmet. R. Trophy;
ΒΟΙΩΤΩΝ to r. *B.M.C. 8.*, *p.* 39, 64-5   ..   ..   £15

2411 — Æ 18. Hd. of Herakles, as 2406. R. ΒΟΙΩΤΩΝ. Winged Athena stg. r., brandishing
thunderbolt and holding aegis; ΑΦ monogram to l., Boeotian shield to r. *B.M.C. 8.*, *p.* 39,
67-9 ..   ..   £13

2412 — Æ 17. Hd. of young Dionysos r., wreathed with ivy. R. ΒΟΙΩΤΩΝ. Apollo seated
l. on basis surmounted by tripod; he holds bow; wreath in field to l. *B.M.C. 8.*, *p.* 40,
72-3 ..   ..   £12

2413 221-197 B.C. Æ 18. Hd. of Persephone, as 2403. R. ΒΟΙΩΤΩΝ. Poseidon, naked,
stg. l., r. foot set on rock, and holding trident. *B.M.C. 8.*, *p.* 41, 81-9. .   ..   £10
These are normally overstruck on Macedonian regal coins of Antigonos Doson.

2414 196-146 B.C. Æ 15. Boeotian shield, ornamented with club. R. Similar to 2404,
but without monogram in field. *B.M.C. 8.*, *p.* 43, 105-7   ..   ..   ..   £8

2415 — Æ 13. Boeotian shield. R. ΒΟΙΩΤΩΝ. Trident-head; dolphin in field to r. *B.M.C.*
8., *p.* 43, 108-11   ..   ..   £8

2416 146-27 B.C. Æ 15. ΘΗΒΑΙΩΝ. Lyre. R. Torch between two corn-ears and poppy-
heads. *B.M.C. 8.* 210-11. .   ..   .   £9

2417   2419

2417 **Akraiphia.** *Circa* 455 B.C.   Æ *stater*. Boeotian shield.   R. A — K either side of
kantharos, above which, laurel-leaf; all within incuse square. *B.M.C. 8.* 4 ..   £650

2418 **Chaironeia** (close to the Phokian border, Chaironeia was the scene of Philip of Macedon's great victory over the Thebans in 338 B.C.). *Circa* 375 B.C.   Æ *hemidrachm*.
Loeotian shield.   R. X / AI above and below club l. *Grose* 5525   ..   ..   £200

2419 **Kopai** (on the northern shores of lake Kopais). *Circa* 375 B.C.   Æ *obol*. Boeotian
shield.   R. ΚΩΠΑΙΩΝ. Forepart of charging bull r. *B.M.C. 8.* 1   ..   ..   £150

2420 **Koroneia.** *Circa* 455 B.C.   Æ *hemidrachm*. Boeotian shield.   R. K — O / R — O in the
corners of an incuse square containing Gorgoneion. *B.M.C. 8.* 6   ..   ..   £275

2421 *Circa* 375 B.C.   Æ *obol*. Boeotian shield.   R. K — O either side of Gorgoneion. *B.M.C.*
8. 7 ..   ..   £125

2422   2425

2422 — — Similar. R. K — O (retrograde) either side of hd. of Athena three-quarter face to
to r., wearing triple-crested helmet. *B.M.C. 8.* 12   ..   ..   £175

2423 — Æ 22. Boeotian shield. R. KOP in large letters across field. *Hist Num.*, p. 345
£40

2424 **Haliartos.** *Circa* 455 B.C.   Æ *stater*. Boeotian shield, the rim studded with nails.
R. ARI (retrograde). Amphora, wreathed with ivy; all within incuse square. *B.M.C. 8.*
11 ..   ..   £650

2425 *Circa* 375 B.C.   Æ *stater*. Boeotian shield, ornamented with trident. R. ARIARTION.
Poseidon Onchestios, naked, striding r., thrusting downwards with trident held in r. hand.
B.M.C. 8. 12   ..   ..   £850

2426 — Æ 24. Boeotian shield. R. API in large letters across field. *B.M.C. 8.* 13   £40

2427 **Lebadeia** (situated west of lake Kopais, close-by the famous oracle of Trophonios).
Circa 375 B.C.   Æ *diobol*. Boeotian shield.   R. Λ — E / B — A either side of thunderbolt.
Head (*Coins of Boeotia*), p. 46   ..   ..   £250

2428 — Æ 20. Boeotian shield. R. ΛEB in large letters across field. *Hist. Num.*, p. 346 £40

2429 146-27 B.C.   Æ 15. Hd. of Athena l., wearing crested Corinthian helmet. R. ΛE.
within olive-wreath. *B.M.C. 8.* 1   ..   ..   £15

2430 **Mykalessos.** *Circa* 375 B.C.   Æ *obol*. Boeotian shield.   R. M — Y either side of
thunderbolt. *B.M.C. 8.* 1, 2   ..   ..   £140

2431 — Æ *hemiobol*. Similar, but with half Boeotian shield on *obv*. *Head* (*Coins of Boeotia*),
p. 47 ..   ..   £100

2432 Orchomenos or **Erchomenos** (this ancient town was destroyed by Thebes *c.* 364 B.C.).
Circa 375 B.C. Æ *stater.* Boeotian shield. R. Horse galloping r.; EPX beneath, ear of
corn and EYΛOPO above. *B.M.C. 8.* 20 .. .. £1,000

2433 — — Boeotian shield, ornamented with ear of corn. R. EP — XO either side of amphora,
the upper part fluted; above, EY. *B.M.C. 8.* 24 .. .. £400

2434 — Æ *hemidrachm.* Boeotian shield. R. EPX within corn-wreath. *B.M.C. 8.* 21 £200

2435 — Æ *tritemorion.* Three sprouting corn-grains; EP beneath. R. Horse prancing r.
B.M.C. 8. 25-6 .. .. £100

2436 — Æ *hemiobol.* Half corn-grain; ivy-leaf to l. R. Ear of corn; E — R in lower field.
B.M.C. 8. 30-31 .. .. £70

2437   2440

2437 — Æ 22. Boeotian shield. R. OPX in large letters across field. *B.M.C. 8.* 38 £40

2438 — Æ 14. Boeotian shield, ornamented with ear of corn. R. EPXO between the alternate
rays of eight-rayed star. *B.M.C. 8.* 36-7 .. .. £17

*From the extent of this coinage (2432-8) it would seem likely that it was produced down to
the time of the destruction of the town.*

2439 146-27 B.C. Æ 13. Veiled bust of Hera r., sceptre at shoulder. R. EP / XO either side
of tripod; all within laurel-wreath. *B.M.C. 8.* 39 .. .. £12

2440 **Pharai.** *Circa* 375 B.C. Æ *obol.* Boeotian shield. R. Amphora; Φ — A in lower
field; corn-ear to l. *B.M.C. 8.* 4, 5 .. .. £100

2441   2443

2441 **Plataia** (close to the Attic border, Plataia was the scene of the memorable defeat of the
Persians in 479 B.C. The town was destroyed by Thebes *c.* 372 B.C.). *Circa* 375 B.C.
Æ *hemidrachm.* Boeotian shield. R. Hd. of Hera r., wearing stephanos; behind, ΠΛΑ.
B.M.C. 8. 1 .. .. £500

2442 — Æ 22. Boeotian shield. R. ΠΛΑ in large letters across field. *B.M.C. 8.* 3 £50

2443 **Tanagra.** 480-460 B.C. Æ *stater.* Boeotian shield, with T — A in the side-openings,
and T on rim. R. BOI in three quarters of a four-spoked wheel, within incuse circle.
B.M.C. 8. 9 .. .. £400

*This type would seem to suggest that during the troubled period of the Persian wars, and
their aftermath, Tanagra aspired to the leadership of the Boeotians (see also no. 1809).*

2444 — — Similar, but with T in one side-opening of shield on *obv.*, and TA in two opposite
quarters of wheel on *rev.* *B.M.C. 8.* 12 .. .. £375

Tanagra *continued*

2445 — Æ *hemidrachm.* As last. *B.M.C. 8.* 17 .. .. £150

2446 — Æ *obol.* Boeotian shield. ℞. Four-spoked wheel, within incuse square. *B.M.C. 8.* 18-21 .. .. £90

2447 2452

2447 *Circa* 455 B.C. Æ *stater.* Boeotian shield. ℞. Forepart of prancing horse r.; T — A in upper field; all within incuse square. *B.M.C. 8.* 23 .. .. £550

2448 — Æ *hemidrachm.* Similar, but type to l. on *rev.* *B.M.C. 8.* 26 .. .. £200

2449 — Æ *obol.* Boeotian shield. ℞. T — A either side of horse's hd. r.; all within incuse square. *B.M.C. 8.* 27 .. .. £100

2450 *Circa* 375 B.C. Æ *stater.* Boeotian shield. ℞. Forepart of prancing horse r., bound with wreath; T — A in upper field. *B.M.C. 8.* 29 .. .. £750

2451 — Æ *obol.* Boeotian shield. ℞. T — A either side of forepart of prancing horse l. *B.M.C. 8.* 40 .. .. £85

2452 — — Similar. ℞. Stern of galley l.; TA above. *B.M.C. 8.* 47 .. .. £110

2453 — Æ *hemiobol.* Half Boeotian shield. ℞. T — A either side of horse's hd. r. *B.M.C. 8.* 41 .. .. £60

2454 — Æ 22. Boeotian shield. ℞. TAN in large letters across field. *B.M.C. 8.* 49 £45

2455 2460

2455 **Thespiai** (situated on the south-eastern slopes of Mt. Helikon, Thespiai opposed the Persian invaders in 480 B.C. and was burnt by them. The town possessed the famous statue of Eros by Praxiteles). *Circa* 375 B.C. Æ *stater.* Boeotian shield. ℞. ΘΕΣΠΙΚΟΝ. Hd. of Aphrodite Melainis r.; large crescent before, smaller one beneath. *B.M.C. 8.* 9
£2,000

2456 — Æ *hemidrachm.* Similar, but with legend ΘΕΣ, and without small crescent beneath Aphrodite's hd. *B.M.C. 8.* 10, 11 .. .. £450

2457 — Æ *obol.* Boeotian shield. ℞. ΘΕΣΠΙ around two crescents, back to back. *B.M.C. 8.* 1, 2 .. .. £85

2458 — — Similar. ℞. Crescent, with ΘΕΣ between the horns. *B.M.C. 8.* 4-7 .. £75

2459 — — Boeotian shield, ornamented with crescent. ℞. Θ. Hd. of Aphrodite Melainis r. *B.M.C. 8.* 12 .. .. £150

2460 — Æ 22. Boeotian shield. ℞. ΘΕΣ in large letters across field. *B.M.C. 8.* 13 £45

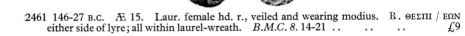

2461 146-27 B.C. Æ 15. Laur. female hd. r., veiled and wearing modius. ℞. ΘΕΣΠΙ / ΕΩΝ either side of lyre; all within laurel-wreath. *B.M.C. 8.* 14-21 .. .. .. £9

2462 **EUBOIA** (some of the later archaic issues of Euboian mints — see nos. 1816-28 — may have extended down to *c.* 465 B.C., when the expanding influence of Athens brought about a cessation of coinage in the island). **Eretria** (became the capital and mint of the Euboian League, formed in 411 B.C.). 411-404 B.C. Æ *stater* (*c.* 11·9 gm.). Hd. of nymph Euboia r., hair rolled. R. Cow seated r.; bunch of grapes above, EYB below; all within incuse square. *Weber* 3389. *Wallace* (*The Euboian League and its Coinage*) 10
£1,250

2463   2466

2463 400-395 B.C. Æ *tetradrachm* (*c.* 16·5 gm.). Hd. of nymph Euboia r., hair rolled. R. Cow stg. r.; EYB above. *Wallace* 15 (*British Museum*) £2,000

2464 — Æ *drachm.* *Obv.* Similar. R. Cow's hd. and neck three-quarter face to r.; EY above, B to r. *B.M.C.* 8., p. 94, 3. *Wallace* 28 .. .. £200

2465 — Æ *hemidrachm.* Similar. *B.M.C.* 8., p. 94, 6. *Wallace* 36 .. .. £140

2466 357-267 B.C. Æ *drachm* (*c.* 3·75 gm.). Hd. of nymph Euboia r., in high relief, hair rolled. R. Cow's hd. and neck three-quarter face to r., *fillet hanging from each horn;* EY above. *B.M.C.* 8., p. 95, 7. *Wallace* 44 .. .. £250

2467 — — Similar, but hd. of nymph to l., and in normal relief. *B.M.C.* 8., p. 95, 8. *Wallace* 63 .. .. £125

2468 — — As last, but with small hd. of Seilenos facing in field to r. on *rev.* *B.M.C.* 8., p. 95, 13. *Wallace* 119 .. .. £125

2469 — Æ *hemidrachm.* Hd. of nymph Euboia r., hair rolled; E behind. R. Cow's hd. and neck three-quarter face to r., fillet hanging from each horn; EY above. *B.M.C.* 8., p. 96, 15-16. *Wallace* 144 .. .. £100

2470 — Æ *diobol.* Hd. of nymph Euboia l., hair rolled; E behind. R. EYB. Two bunches of grapes on vine-branch. *B.M.C.* 8., p. 96, 18. *Wallace* 151 .. .. .. £90

               2471   2473

2471 196-146 B.C. Æ *octobol.* Hd. of Artemis r., bow and quiver at shoulder. R. Cow seated r.; EPETPI — EΩN above, ΦANIAΣ in ex. *B.M.C.* 8. 42 .. .. .. £500

2472 — Æ *tetrobol.* Hd. of nymph Euboia r., hair rolled. R. Two bunches of grapes on vine-branch; EPETPIEΩN above, ΦANIAΣ beneath. *B.M.C.* 8. 43 .. .. .. £175

2473 — Æ *triobol.* *Obv.* Similar. R. Cow's hd. and neck three-quarter face to r., fillet hanging from each horn; EPETPI above, ΦANIAΣ beneath. *B.M.C.* 8. 45 .. £120

2474 *Bronze Coinage.* 4th Cent. B.C. Æ 14. Hd. of nymph Euboia r., hair rolled. R. EY / BO either side of hd. and neck of cow three-quarter face to r.; above, two bunches of grapes. *B.M.C.* 8., p. 97, 32. *Wallace, pl. XIV,* 3 .. .. £14

2475 3rd Cent. B.C. Æ 17. Cow stg. l.; star above, ME monogram beneath. R. EYBOEΩN. Two bunches of grapes on vine-branch; star above. *B.M.C.* 8., p. 98, 34. *Wallace, p.* 128, 2 .. .. £12

2476 196-194 B.C. Æ 15. Cow seated l.; star above, ΔHMAPXOΣ beneath. R. As last. *B.M.C.* 8., p. 98, 38. *Wallace, pl. XIV,* 12 .. .. £12

2477   2480   2481

Eretria *continued*

2477 194-180 B.C. Æ 17. Veiled hd. (of Isis ?) r. ℞. EYBOI / EΩN. Bull butting r.; grain of wheat in ex., to r. of legend. *B.M.C. 8.,p.* 98, 40. *Wallace, pl. XV,* 9 ..   £9

2478 180-168 B.C. Æ 17. *Obv.* Similar, but hd. l. ℞. Cow seated l.; AΛEΞ / IΠΠOΣ above, EPETPIEΩN in ex. *B.M.C. 8.* 47 ..   ..   £10

2479 *Circa* 150 B.C. Æ 14. Veiled hd. (of Isis ?) three-quarter face to r. ℞. EYBOI / EΩN above and below prow r., ornamented with star and cornucopiae. *B.M.C. 8.,p.* 99, 47. *Wallace, pl. XV,* 17..   ..   ..   £12

2480 — Æ 11. Hd. of Hermes r., in petasos. ℞. EYBOI / EΩN either side of corn-ear. *B.M.C. 8.,p.* 99, 48. *Wallace, pl. XV,* 21   ..   ..   £8

2481 **Chalkis.** 340-294 B.C. Æ *drachm* (*c.* 3·7 gm.). Hd. of Hera (?) l., hair rolled. ℞. XAΛ. Eagle flying l., carrying snake in talons and beak; race-torch above. *B.M.C. 8.* 40 ..   ..   £65

2482 — — Hd. of Hera (?) r., hair rolled. ℞. XAΛ. Eagle flying r., carrying snake in talons and beak; trophy beneath. *B.M.C. 8.* 50-52 ..   ..   £50

2483   2486

2483 — — Similar, but of poorer style, and the legend retrograde; TH monogram above eagle, no symbol beneath. *B.M.C. 8.* 61-8 ..   ..   £35

  These may belong to a somewhat later period than the issues represented by nos. 2481-2.

2484 — Æ *hemidrachm.* *Obv.* As 2482. ℞. XA. Eagle flying r., attacking hare held in its talons; crescent above. *B.M.C. 8.* 57-8 ..   ..   £45

2485 — Æ *obol.* *Obv.* Similar. ℞. XA. Eagle stg. r.; corn-grain(?) before. *B.M.C. 8.* 60   ..   £50

2486 196-146 B.C. Æ *tetradrachm.* Veiled and diad. hd. of Hera r. ℞. Hera in slow quadriga r.; XAΛKIΔEΩN above, ΞENOKPATHΣ in ex.; all within oak-wreath. *B.M.C. 8.* 85 £1,500

2487 — Æ *octobol.* Hd. of Hera(?) r., hair rolled. ℞. Eagle stg. r., wings spread; snake, erect, before; XAΛKI to l., MENEΔH to r. *B.M.C. 8.* 86 ..   ..   ..   £300

2488 *Bronze Coinage.* 3rd Cent. B.C. Æ 14. Hd. of Hera(?) three-quarter face to r., wearing diad. surmounted by five disks (representing the planets ?). ℞. XAΛ (retrograde). Eagle flying r., carrying snake in talons and beak. *B.M.C. 8.* 70   ..   ..   £10

2489 2nd Cent. B.C.   Æ 17.   Hd. of Hera(?) r., hair rolled and confined by net of pearls.
R. ΧΑΛ.   Eagle and snake, as last; trident in field to r.   *B.M.C. 8.* 83 ..   ..   £10

2490 — — Similar, but with legend ΧΑΛΚΙ / ΔΕΩΝ, and no symbol in *rev.* field.   *B.M.C. 8.* 92-5
£10

2491   2494

2491 — Æ 23.   ΧΑΛΚΙ.   Charioteer driving slow quadriga r.   R. ΘΕΟ / ΚΛΗΣ / ΠΑΥΣΑ / ΝΙΟΥ
within laurel-wreath.   *B.M.C. 8.* 89-91 ..   ..   £18

2492 — Æ 17.   ΧΑΛ.   Hd. of Hera(?) three-quarter face to r., on capital of Ionic column.
R. Eagle flying r., carrying snake in talons and beak; ΦΙΛΙΣ above, ΑΑΘ beneath.   *B.M.C.
8.* 96-103   ..   ..   £11

2493 — Æ 13.   Circular shield, ornamented with eagle r., attacking erect serpent.   R.
Prow r.; ΧΑΛ monogram above.   *B.M.C. 8.* 105 ..   ..   £12

2494 **Histiaia** (situated in the far north of the island, Histiaia did not begin producing coinage
until the mid-4th Cent. B.C.   From its extensive silver issues in the Hellenistic age it
would appear to have been a place of considerable commercial importance).   350-340 B.C.
Æ drachm (c. 3·5 gm.).   Hd. of nymph Histiaia r., wreathed with vine.   R. Cow stg. r.;
vine with two bunches of grapes in background; race-torch in field to r., ΙΣΤΙ in ex.
B.M.C. 8. 2, 3   ..   ..   £140

2495   2496

2495 340-330 B.C.   *Æ tetrobol* (c. 2·75 gm.).   *Obv.* Similar, but hair in sphendone.   R.
ΙΣΤΙΑΙΕΩΝ.   Nymph Histiaia seated r. on stern of galley, ornamented with wing, holding
naval standard; bunch of grapes in field to l.   *B.M.C. 8.* 24-5 ..   ..   ..   £100
*This type, from which the huge Histiaian issues of the following century were copied,
commemorated the expulsion, with Athenian help, of the pro-Macedonian tyrant Philistides in
340 B.C.*

2496 3rd Cent. B.C.   *Æ tetrobol* (c. 2-2·4 gm.).   Hd. of nymph Histiaia r., wreathed with vine,
hair rolled.   R. ΙΣΤΙΑΙΕΩΝ.   Nymph Histiaia seated r. on galley, as last; beneath, trident-
head and M.   *B.M.C. 8.* 47-8   ..   ..   £30

2497 — — Similar, but with aplustre beneath galley on *rev.*   *B.M.C. 8.* 65-8   ..   £30

2498 — — Similar, but galley is ornamented with thunderbolt instead of wing, and with ΣΩ
monogram beneath.   *B.M.C. 8.* 113   ..   ..   £35
*The precise date of this extensive coinage is difficult to determine and is the subject of
controversy.   The bulk of it would appear to belong to the latter part of the century, and it
may have commenced with the cessation of silver issues for the Euboian League circa 267 B.C.
There are numerous imitations, of poor style and rough execution, which would seem to have
been produced in Macedon just prior to the Roman victory over Perseus in 168 B.C.*

2499 *Bronze Coinage.*   350-340 B.C.   Æ 14.   Hd. of nymph Histiaia r., wreathed with vine;
star behind.   R. ΙΣΤΙ.   Cow stg. r.; trophy above.   *B.M.C. 8.* 7   ..   ..   £14

2500   2504

Histiaia *continued*

2500 — — *Obv.* Similar, but without star. R. ΙΣΤΙ. Forepart of cow r.; above, small forepart of horse r. *B.M.C. 8.* 12 .. .. £12

2501 340-330 B.C. Æ 15. Hd. of nymph Histiaia r., wreathed with vine, hair in sphendone.
R. ΙΣΤΙ. Cow's hd. and neck three-quarter face to r., flllet hanging from each horn;
bunch of grapes in field to l. *B.M.C. 8.* 29-33 .. .. £13

2502 3rd Cent. B.C. Æ 14. Hd. of nymph Histiaia r., wreathed with vine, hair rolled. R.
Similar to last, but without symbol in field. *B.M.C. 8.* 132 .. .. .. £12

2503 2nd Cent. B.C. Æ 17. *Obv.* Similar. R. ΙΣΤΙΑΙΕΩΝ. Bunch of grapes. *B.M.C. 8.*
134-5 .. .. £10

2504 **Karystos.** *Circa* 350 B.C. R *didrachm.* Cow stg. r., hd. turned back, suckling calf.
R. ΚΑ / ΡΥΣ above and before cock stg. r. *B.M.C. 8.* 6, 7 .. .. .. £650

2505   2509

2505 — R *drachm.* Bearded hd. of Herakles r., clad in lion's skin. R. Cow seated l.; ΚΑΡΥ
above, club r. beneath. *B.M.C. 8.* 8, 9 .. .. £400

2506 — R *hemidrachm.* *Obv.* Similar. R. ΚΑ — ΡΥ either side of palm-tree; club in field to l.
B.M.C. 8. 10 .. .. £250

2507 — R *diobol.* Cow's hd. and neck three-quarter face to r. R. Two palm-trees; ΚΑΡΥ
across field. *B.M.C. 8.* 11 .. .. £140

2508 — R *tritemorion* (*c.* 0·45 gm.). Laur. hd. of Apollo r. R. Κ — Α either side of three
palm-trees, joined at base. *B.M.C. 8.* 12 .. .. £90

2509 *Circa* 300 B.C. R *didrachm.* Cow stg. r., hd. turned back, suckling calf. R. Cock stg.
r.; ΚΑΡΥΣΤΙΩΝ before, ΞΕΦ monogram behind. *B.M.C. 8.* 13 .. .. .. £750

2510   2514

2510 196-146 B.C. N *drachm* (*c.* 3·2 gm.). Bearded hd. of Herakles r., clad in lion's skin.
R. Cow seated l.; ΚΑΡΥ and trident l. above; club l. beneath. *B.M.C. 8.* 17 .. £4,000

2511 — R *didrachm.* Male hd. r., beardless, bound with royal diad. R. Nike in galloping
biga l.; ΚΑΡΥΣΤΙΩΝ in ex., trident within wreath above. *B.M.C. 8.* 18 .. £1,250

2512 — R *drachm.* Bearded hd. of Herakles r., clad in lion's skin. R. Bull rushing r.;
ΚΑΡΥ beneath, ΑΡΙΣΤΩΝ above; all within oak-wreath. *Grose* 5658 .. .. £450

2513 *Bronze Coinage.* Late 4th Cent. B.C. Æ 18. *Obv.* Similar. R. Hd. and neck of cow three-quarter face to r.; KA above. *B.M.C. 8.* 15 .. .. £15

2514 3rd Cent. B.C. Æ 18. Similar, but hd. of Herakles beardless, and with monogram in *rev.* field to r. *B.M.C. 8.* 19-21 .. .. £14

2515 2nd Cent. B.C. Æ 17. Veiled hd. (of Isis?) r. R. KA / PY above and beneath dolphin r. *B.M.C. 8.* 26 .. .. £11

2516 **ATTICA.   Athens** (throughout most of the 5th Cent. B.C., after the Persian defeat and withdrawal in 479, Athens was mistress of the Aegean world and became a great cultural, as well as political, centre. The long drawn-out Peloponnesian War, 431-404 B.C., drained Athens of her wealth and ended with the capture of the city by the Spartans. Although prosperous again in the 4th Cent., Athens never fully regained her importance in international affairs, and in Hellenistic times became dependent first on Macedon, then Rome). 478-449 B.C. Æ *dekadrachm,* issued *c.* 467-5. Hd. of Athena r., wearing crested helmet ornamented with three olive-leaves and floral scroll. R. AΘE. Owl stg. facing, wings spread; olive-twig in upper field to l.; all within incuse square. *Starr (Athenian Coinage 480-449 B.C.)* 62. *B.M.C. 11.* 40 .. .. £30,000

2517	2518

2517 — Æ *tetradrachm,* issued *c.* 478-72. *Obv.* Similar, but helmet is ornamented with four olive-leaves, and the crest-support has line of small chevrons and dots. R. Owl stg. r., hd. facing; to r., AΘE; to l., olive-twig and crescent; all within incuse square. *Starr 6 (British Museum)* £1,250

2518 — — issued *circa* 470. *Obv.* Similar to 2516. R. As last. *Starr 18 (British Museum)* £1,250

2519	2520

2519 — — issued *c.* 465-60. Similar, but the hd. of Athena and the owl are somewhat larger. *Starr 95 (British Museum)* £1,250

2520 — — issued *c.* 460-55. Similar, but the types less carefully engraved, and Athena's hair straighter on forehead: flans more spread than those of earlier issues. *Starr 111 (British Museum)* £750

2521   2522

Athens *continued*

2521 — — issued *c.* 455-49. Similar, but Athena's hd., which almost fills the field, has hair drawn across the forehead in parallel curves, with no trace of waving: on *rev.*, the owl's tail is still composed of three *separate* feathers, as on earlier varieties. *Starr* 204 (*British Museum*) £500

2522 — Æ *didrachm*, issued *c.* 467-5. *Obv.* Similar to 2516. R. Owl stg. r., hd. facing; to r., AΘE; to l., olive-twig, half of which is outside the incuse square enclosing the type; all within incuse circle. *Starr* 73. *B.M.C.* 11. 72 .. .. .. £2,500

2523 — Æ *drachm*, issued *c.* 470-67. Hd. of Athena, similar to 2516. R. Owl stg. r., hd. facing; to r., AΘE; to l., olive-twig; all within incuse square. *Starr* 45 (*Brit. Mus.*) £450

2524 — Æ *obol*, issued *c.* 460-55. Hd. of Athena, similar to 2516. R. Owl stg. r., hd. facing; to r., AΘE; to l., olive-leaf with berry; all within incuse square. *Starr, pl. XXIV, n* (*British Museum*) £150

2525 — Æ *hemiobol*, issued *c.* 455-49. Hd. of Athena, similar to 2516. R. Owl stg. r., hd. facing; to r., AΘE; to l., olive-leaf; all within incuse square. *Starr, pl. XXIV, z* (*British Museum*) £90

2526 449-413 B.C. Æ *tetradrachm.* Hd. of Athena r., wearing crested helmet ornamented with three olive-leaves and floral scroll; her hair is drawn across the forehead in parallel curves. R. Owl stg. r., hd. facing, in erect posture; the tail feathers represented as a single prong; to r., AΘE, in large, even lettering; to l., olive-twig and crescent; all within incuse square. *Cf. Starr, pl. XXII & XXIII.* *B.M.C.* 11. 62 .. .. .. £275

This enormous issue, the largest of any Greek state up to that time, seems to have begun when the Athenians appropriated 5,000 talents from the treasury of the Delian League in order to pay for rebuilding work on the city's temples. Over the following decades huge quantities of tetradrachms were minted to finance grandiose building projects, such as the Parthenon, and later to cover the costs of the disastrous Peloponnesian War, which ended in financial ruin for the Athenian state.

2527   2529   2533

2527 — Æ *drachm.* Similar, but without crescent behind owl. *B.M.C.* 11. 74 ..   £125

2528 — Æ *hemidrachm* (*triobol*). *Obv.* Hd. of Athena, similar to 2526. R. AΘE. Owl stg. facing, wings closed; olive-branch on either side, all within incuse circle. *B.M.C.* 11. 86 £100

2529 — Æ *trihemiobol.* *Obv.* Similar. R. AΘE. Owl stg. facing, wings spread; above, two olive-leaves; all within incuse circle. *B.M.C.* 11. 92 .. .. £75

2530 — Æ *obol*. *Obv*. Similar. R. Similar to 2526, but with olive-leaf and berry behind owl.
B.M.C. 11. 99   ..   ..   £65

2531 — Æ *hemiobol*. As last. B.M.C. 11. 120   ..   ..   £50

2532 406-404 B.C. (emergency issues during the final stages of the Peloponnesian War).
N *stater* (8·53 gm.).   Similar to 2526, but without crescent on *rev.*, and with olive-branch
to r. of owl. *Kraay* (*Coins of Ancient Athens*), *pl. III*, 10   ..   ..   ..   £7,500

2533 — N *quarter-stater* (*triobol*). As 2528. *Jenkins* (*Ancient Greek Coins*) 155/6 (*British
Museum*) £2,500

2534 — N *sixth-stater* (*diobol*). *Obv*. Hd. of Athena, similar to 2526. R. Two owls stg. r.
and l., their heads facing; olive-branch between them; AΘE beneath. *Kraay* (*Coins of
Ancient Athens*), *pl. III*, 11 (*Ashmolean Museum*)..   ..   ..   £2,000

2535   2537

2535 — *Tetradrachm* (struck in bronze, and silver-plated). Similar to 2526. *Starr, pl.
XXIII*, 12. B.M.C. 11. 61   ..   ..   £350

2536 — *Drachm* (struck in bronze, and silver-plated). Similar to 2527. *Starr, p.* 74   £150

2537 393-300 B.C. Æ *tetradrachm*. Hd. of Athena r., of more advanced style, the eye seen
in true profile; she wears crested helmet ornamented with three olive-leaves and floral
scroll. R. Owl stg. r., hd. facing; to r., AΘE; to l., olive-twig and crescent; all within
incuse square (which soon disappears as the series progresses). B.M.C. 11. 144   £140

*The volume of this coinage increased rapidly in the latter part of the century, and many
specimens are carelessly struck.*

2538   2542   2545

2538 — Æ *drachm*. Similar. B.M.C. 11. 152   ..   ..   £100

2539 — Æ *hemidrachm* (*triobol*). *Obv*. Similar. R. AΘE. Owl stg. facing, wings closed;
olive-branch on either side. B.M.C. 11. 168   ..   ..   £85

2540 — Æ *diobol*. *Obv*. Similar. R. AΘE. Double-bodied owl, hd. facing; in upper field
to l., olive-twig; traces of incuse square. B.M.C. 11. 177   ..   ..   ..   £75

2541 — Æ *obol*. *Obv*. Similar. R. AΘE. Four crescents, back to back; all within incuse
square. B.M.C. 11. 180 ..   ..   £75

2542 — Æ *tritartemorion* (¾ *obol*). *Obv*. Similar. R. AΘE. Three crescents arranged in
circle, enclosing the legend; all within incuse circle. B.M.C. 11. 187 ..   ..   £70

2543 — Æ *trihemitartemorion* (⅜ *obol*). *Obv*. Similar. R. AΘE. Kalathos; traces of incuse
square. B.M.C. 11. 193 ..   ..   £140

2544 — Æ *tetartemorion* (¼ *obol*). *Obv*. Similar. R. AΘE above crescent; all within incuse
square. B.M.C. 11. 199   ..   ..   £65

2545 — Æ *hemitartemorion* (⅛ *obol*). Similar to 2539. B.M.C. 11. 207   ..   ..   £90

*It is likely that these inconveniently small silver fractions of the obol (nos. 2542-5) ceased
to be issued by the middle of the 4th Century, when token bronze coinage was introduced.*

2546   2547

Athens *continued*

2546 300-262 B.C. *N stater*. Similar to 2537, but with kalathos in *rev.* field between owl and
AΘE. *B.M.C. 11.* 131 .. .. £6,000
    *These probably belong to the time of the tyrant Lachares, 295/4 B.C. Smaller de-
nominations in gold are also known.*

2547 — *R tetradrachm*. Similar to 2537, but generally very carelessly struck on mis-shapen
flans, which often assume an elongated form. *Kraay (Coins of Ancient Athens), pl. IV,* 6
£140

2548   2549

2548 229-200 B.C. *R tetradrachm*. Hd. of Athena, similar to 2537. R. Owl stg. r., hd.
facing; to r., AΘE; to l., olive-twig above bull's hd. facing. *B.M.C. 11.* 278 .. £250

2549 — *R pentobol*. Hd. of Athena r., in crested Corinthian helmet. R. AΘE. Owl stg. r.,
hd. facing, wings spread; amphora in field to r. *B.M.C. 11.* 158 .. .. £200

2550 — *R tetrobol*. Hd. of Athena r., in crested Athenian helmet ornamented with floral
scroll. R. AΘE. Two owls stg. r. and l., their heads facing. *B.M.C. 11.* 161 .. £150

2551 — *R triobol*. *Obv.* Similar. R. AΘE. Owl stg. facing, wings closed; olive-branch on
either side. *B.M.C. 11.* 173 .. .. £140

2551A *Circa* 190 B.C. *R tetradrachm*. Helmeted hd. of Athena Parthenos r. R. Owl stg. r.,
hd. facing; to l., olive-twig and winged thunderbolt; to r., AΘE and monogram. (*British
Museum — recent acquisitions* 1973-4, *p.* 69, *no.* 11) £1,000

2552 166-57 B.C. (the 'New Style' coinage). *N stater*, issued *c.* 87/6 B.C. Hd. of Athena Parthenos r., wearing triple-crested Athenian helmet, ornamented with Pegasos and foreparts of horses. ℞. Owl stg. r., hd. facing, on prostrate amphora; in field, A — ΘΕ / ΒΑΣΙ — ΛΕ / ΜΙ — ΘΡΑ / ΔΑ / ΤΗΣ / ΑΡΙΣ / ΤΙΩΝ; to r., star between two crescents; all within olive-wreath. *Thompson (The New Style Silver Coinage of Athens), pl.* 127. (*British Museum*) £7,500

The precise chronology of the Athenian 'New Style' coinage is still the subject of controversy, despite the comprehensive study of the series by Margaret Thompson. It would seem certain that no. 2552, on which 'King Mithradates' replaces the usual magistrate's name, belongs to the period of Athenian support for the Pontic King against the Romans (87-86 B.C.). On this basis, Miss Thompson's chronology requires to be down-dated by approximately three decades.

2553 — *R tetradrachm*, issued *c.* 157/6 B.C. Hd. of Athena Parthenos, as last. ℞. Owl stg. r., hd. facing, on prostrate amphora; A — ΘΕ in upper field; ΓΛΑΥΚ monogram and corn-ear to l., ΜΗΤ monogram to r.; all within olive-wreath. *Thompson* 50c. *B.M.C. 11.* 290
£175

2554 — — issued *c.* 144/3 B.C. *Obv.* Similar. ℞. Owl stg. r., hd. facing, on prostrate amphora, inscribed with Λ; in upper field, A — ΘΕ; to l., ΔΗ / ΜΗ above ΑΝ; to r., ΙΕ / ΡΩ and helmet surmounted by star; all within olive-wreath. *Thompson* 213. *B.M.C. 11.* 369
£175

The letter appearing on the amphora denotes the month of issue, those in the lower field possibly the origin of the bullion from which the issue was struck.

2555 — — issued *c.* 136/5 B.C. *Obv.* Similar. ℞. Owl stg. r., hd. facing, on prostrate amphora, inscribed Λ; in upper field, A — ΘΕ / ΤΙΜ — ΑΡΧΟΥ; to r., ΝΙΚΑΓΟ / ΦΑΝΟ / ΚΛΕ; to l., anchor and star; beneath amphora, ΜΕ; all within olive-wreath. *Thompson* 367c. *B.M.C. 11.* 503 .. .. £175

Athens *continued*

2556 — — issued *c.* 106/5 B.C. *Obv.* Similar. ℞. As last, but with A — ΘE / ANΔ — PEAΣ in upper field, XAPI / NAY / THΣ / ΔHM / HTP to l., K on amphora, and ΠE beneath; in field to r., Dionysos enthroned facing and Demeter (?) stg. facing, side by side. *Thompson* 805*d*. *B.M.C. 11.* 321　..　　..　　..　　..　　..　　..　　£190

2557 — — issued *c.* 96/5 B.C. *Obv.* Similar. ℞. As last, but with A — ΘE / API — ΣTI / ΩN in upper field, ΦI / ΛΩN / ΘE / O to l., E on amphora, and MH beneath; in field to r., Pegasos stg. l., hd. lowered. *Thompson* 961*e*. *B.M.C. 11.* 332 ..　　..　　..　　..　　£190

This magistrate (*Aristion*) *is probably the same man who is later associated with the issue in the name of King Mithradates (see no.* 2552). *The drinking Pegasos symbol is also a Pontic type.*

2558 — — issued *c.* 89/8 B.C. *Obv.* Similar. ℞. As last, but with A — ΘE / KO — IN / TOΣ in upper field, KΛE / AΣ / ΔIO / NYΣI to l., Γ on amphora, and ΔIO beneath; in field to r., Nike crowning seated Roma. *Thompson* 1128*b*. *B.M.C. 11.* 434 ..　　..　　..　　£250

The name KOINTOΣ *is the Greek rendering of the Latin '*Quintus*'.*

2559 — — issued *c.* 64/3 B.C. *Obv.* Similar. ℞. As last, but with A — ΘE / KAΛΛ — IMA / XOΣ in upper field, EΠI / KPA / THΣ to l., Λ on amphora, and HPA beneath; in field to r., Triptolemos in car drawn l. by winged serpents, star and crescent above. *Thompson* 1253. *B.M.C. 11.* 428　..　　..　　..　　..　　..　　..　　..　　£220

2560	2561	2563

2560 — Æ *drachm*, issued *c.* 138/7 B.C. *Obv.* Similar. ℞. Owl stg. r., hd. facing, on amphora inscribed H; in upper field, A — ΘE / HPA (to r.); in central field, API — ΣTO / EXE (to r.); club, lion's skin and bow in case in field to l; all within olive-wreath. *Thompson* 344*g*. *B.M.C. 11.* 336　..　　..　　..　　..　　..　　..　　..　　£175

2561 — Æ *hemidrachm*, issued *c.* 139/8 B.C. *Obv.* Similar. ℞. Owl stg. r., hd. facing, on club; in upper field, A — ΘE; to l., MI / KI; to r., ΘEO / ΦPA; all within olive-wreath. *Thompson* 328*a*. *B.M.C. 11.* 473..　　..　　..　　..　　..　　..　　£175

2562 *Bronze Coinage.* 350-262 B.C. Æ 14. Hd. of Athena r., wearing crested Athenian helmet ornamented with floral scroll. ℞. AΘ. Two owls stg. r. and l., their heads facing; all within olive-wreath. *B.M.C. 11.* 214..　　..　　..　　..　　..　　£12

2563 — Æ 13. *Obv.* Similar, but helmet is also ornamented with three olive-leaves. ℞. AΘE. Double-bodied owl, hd. facing; on either side, olive-twig; beneath, kalathos. *B.M.C. 11.* 224　..　　..　　..　　..　　..　　..　　..　　£12

2564   2567

2564 229-166 B.C. Æ 19. *Obv.* As last. R. AΘE. Owl stg. r., hd. facing, wings spread; amphora in field to r. *B.M.C. 11.* 247 .. .. £16

2565 — Æ 14. Hd. of Athena r., in crested Corinthian helmet. R. AΘ. Owl stg. r., hd. facing; all within corn-wreath. *B.M.C. 11.* 229.. .. .. .. £11

2566 166-57 B.C. Æ 22. Hd. of Athena Parthenos r., wearing triple-crested Athenian helmet, ornamented with Pegasos and foreparts of horses. R. AΘE. Owl stg. r., hd. facing, on prostrate amphora; all within olive-wreath. *B.M.C. 11.* 532 .. £14

2567 — Æ 19, issued c. 87/6 B.C. *Obv.* As 2565. R. AΘE. Zeus striding r., brandishing thunderbolt; star between two crescents in field to r. *B.M.C. 11.* 554.. .. £9

This type is associated with the precious-metal issues in the name of King Mithradates of Pontus (see no. 2552).

2568 — Æ 19. Hd. of Athena Parthenos r., as 2566. R. AΘE. Tripod between poppy-head and thunderbolt. *B.M.C. 11.* 566 .. .. £10

2569 — — — R. AΘE. Sphinx seated r.; all within olive-wreath. *B.M.C. 11.* 570 £14

2570 — Æ 15. *Obv.* Hd. of Athena Parthenos r., as 2566. R. AΘE beneath two owls stg. r. and l., their heads facing; all within olive-wreath. *B.M.C. 11.* 538 .. .. £10

2571 — Æ 13. Plemochoe, with corn-ear through each handle. R. AΘE. Kalathos; all within corn-wreath. *B.M.C. 11.* 637 .. .. £9

2572 — Æ 11. Hd. of Demeter r. R. AΘE. Pig stg. r. *B.M.C. 11.* 654-5 .. £8

2573 — Æ 10. Winged bust of Nike r. R. AΘE. Quiver and bow. *B.M.C. 11.* 611 £7

2574   2576   2578

2574 **Eleusis** (situated north-west of Athens, Eleusis possessed a magnificent temple of Demeter, and gave it's name to the famous Eleusinian mysteries, concerned with the cults of Demeter and Persephone). 3rd Cent. B.C. Æ 15. Triptolemos, favourite of Demeter, seated l. in winged car drawn by serpents, holding corn-ears. R. EΛEYΣI beneath boar stg. r. on bacchos; all within corn-wreath. *B.M.C. 11.* 1-7 .. £10

2575 — Æ 14. Similar, but Triptolemos *stands* in the winged car, and with legend EΛEY on *rev. B.M.C. 11.* 10 .. .. £12

2576 — Æ 18. *Obv.* As 2574. R. EΛEYΣI above boar stg. r. on bacchos; beneath, boar's hd. r. and ivy-leaf. *B.M.C. 11.* 12, 13 .. .. £9

2577 **Oropos** (on the northern coast of Attica, close to the Boeotian border and opposite Eretria in Euboia). 2nd-1st Cent. B.C. Æ 19. Laur. hd. of Apollo r. R. ΩPΩΠIΩN. Dolphin entwined round trident. *B.M.C. 11.* 1 .. .. £65

2578 **Salamis** (an island off the western coast of Attica, Salamis is chiefly famous for the great naval victory of the Greeks over the Persians in 480 B.C.). 350-318 B.C. Æ 18. Hd. of nymph Salamis r., wearing stephane. R. ΣA / ΛA either side of shield of Ajax, on which, sword in sheath. *B.M.C. 11.* 1, 2 .. .. £16

2579 — Æ 13. Hd. of Demeter r., wreathed with corn. R. As last. *B.M.C. 11.* 9 £14

2580   2581

2580 **MEGARIS.** **Megara** (situated midway between Athens and Corinth, Megara achieved considerable prosperity through commanding the trade routes between Central Greece and the Peloponnesos). 387-338 B.C. *Æ didrachm* (*c.* 7·9 gm.). Laur. hd. of Apollo l. ℞. ΜΕΓ / ΑΡΕ either side of lyre. *B.M.C. 11.* 1 ..   ..   £475

2581 — *Æ pentobol* (*c.* 3·25 gm.). *Obv.* Similar. ℞. Μ — Η — Ε — Γ — Α between five crescents arranged star-wise. *B.M.C. 11.* 2 ..   ..   £250

2582 — *Æ triobol* (*c.* 1·5 gm.). *Obv.* Similar. ℞. Μ — Ε — Γ between three crescents arranged star-wise. *B.M.C. 11.* 3 ..   ..   £150

2583 — *Æ diobol* (*c.* 1·15 gm.). *Obv.* Similar. ℞. Lyre. *B.M.C. 11.* 4, 5   ..   £125

2584 — *Æ obol* (*c.* 0·65 gm.). Similar. *B.M.C. 11.* 6 ..   ..   £100

2585 — *Æ hemiobol*. Similar, but with Μ — Ε in *rev.* field. *B.M.C. 11.* 7   ..   £85

2586   2590

2586 307-243 B.C. *Æ drachm* (*c.* 4·2 gm.). Laur. hd. of Apollo r. ℞. ΜΕΓΑ — ΡΕΩΝ either side of lyre. *B.M.C. 11.* 8, 9 ..   ..   £225

2587 — *Æ hemidrachm*. Similar. *B.M.C. 11.* 10 ..   ..   £140

2588 — Æ 19. Similar. *B.M.C. 11.* 12 ..   ..   £14

2589 — Æ 17. Laur. hd. of Apollo r. ℞. ΜΕΓΑ — ΡΕΩΝ either side of tripod. *B.M.C. 11.* 16, 17 ..   ..   £10

2590 — Æ 15. Prow l., surmounted by tripod; trident in field above. ℞. ΜΕΓ between two dolphins, swimming r. in circle. *B.M.C. 11.* 22..   ..   ..   ..   £9

2591 — — ΜΕΓΑ above prow l. ℞. Tripod between two dolphins. *B.M.C. 11.* 30   £8

2592 — Æ 14. *Obv.* Similar. ℞. Obelisk of Apollo Karinos between two dolphins. *B.M.C. 11.* 36 ..   ..   £10

2593 — Æ 10. Μ — Ε either side of tripod. ℞. Dolphin r. *B.M.C. 11.* 40-42   £7

For later coins of Megara, see below under Achaean League.

2594 **AIGINA** (although still a place of some importance in the 5th and 4th centuries, Aigina was eclipsed by Athens after the Persian Wars, and never regained her former position as one of the greatest trading states of the Greek World. The city was captured by the Athenians in 456 B.C., and a quarter of a century later the inhabitants were expelled from the island. In 404 B.C., after the fall of Athens, the exiles were restored to their homes). 480-456 B.C. *Æ stater*. Smooth-shelled turtle, with row of dots down the middle and across top of shell, in the form of a 'Τ'. ℞. Large incuse square, of 'skew' pattern, divided by straight lines into five compartments. *B.M.C. 11.* 85-104 ..   ..   ..   £325

These are sometimes countermarked on obv. with a symbol or monogram.

2595	— *Æ drachm*. Similar. *B.M.C. 11.* 105-6	..	..	..	..	..	£250
2596	— *Æ triobol*. Similar. *B.M.C. 11.* 107-12	..	..	..	..	..	£150
2597	— *Æ obol*. Similar. *B.M.C. 11.* 115-31	..	..	..	..	..	£110
2598	— *Æ hemiobol*. Similar. *B.M.C. 11.* 132-42 ..	..	..	..	..	£75

2599   2600

2599 *Circa* 457/6 B.C. *Æ stater*. *Obv*. Similar. ℞. Triskelis of human legs r., within incuse square. *B.M.C. 11.* 143 .. .. *(Unique)*
  This remarkable type may have been struck at the time of the Athenian siege of Aigina.

2600 445-431 B.C. *Æ stater*. Tortoise, with segmented shell. ℞. Incuse square of 'skew' pattern, as 2594. *B.M.C. 11.* 149 .. .. £450

2601 — *Æ obol*. Similar. *B.M.C. 11.* 177 .. .. £125

2602 — *Æ hemiobol*. Similar. *B.M.C. 11.* 182 .. .. £110

2603   2604

2603 404-340 B.C. *Æ stater*. Tortoise, with segmented shell. ℞. Incuse square, similar to 2594 and 2600, but the design more formalized, with the two principal lines of division crossing at right angles. *B.M.C. 11.* 165.. .. .. £400

2604 — — Similar, but with ΑΙΓ — I in the two upper divisions of the incuse square, and dolphin in the lower rectangular division. *B.M.C. 11.* 187 .. .. .. £450

2605 — *Æ drachm*. Similar to 2603, but with two pellets in the lower rectangular division of the incuse square. *B.M.C. 11.* 170 .. .. £225

2606   2610

2606 — — Tortoise, with segmented shell; Α — I in field. ℞. Incuse square, as 2603, but with Ν — I in the two upper divisions, and dolphin in the lower rectangular one. *B.M.C. 11.* 197 .. .. £250

2607 — *Æ triobol*. As 2605. *B.M.C. 11.* 171 .. .. £175

2608 — *Æ obol*. *Obv*. As 2606. ℞. As 2603, but with Δ — I in the two upper divisions of the incuse square. *B.M.C. 11.* 199 .. .. £125

2609 — Æ 14. Three dolphins encircling Α. ℞. Incuse square, as 2603. *B.M.C. 11.* 205
£15

2610 — — Two dolphins upwards, Α between. ℞. As last. *B.M.C. 11.* 206 .. £10

2611 — Æ 11. Similar, but with Ν — Ο in the two upper divisions of the incuse square. *B.M.C. 11.* 218-22 .. .. £10

2612   2616

Aigina *continued*

2612 3rd-2nd Cent. B.C. Æ 17. Bucranium. ℞. Dolphin r.; AI beneath. *B.M.C. 11.* 224
£12

2613 — — Prow r.; AIΓINA above. ℞. Ram's hd. l.; AIΓ monogram beneath. *B.M.C. 11.*
233 ..   ..   £14

2614 — — Laur. hd. of Zeus r. ℞. Archaic statue of Apollo r., naked, holding laurel-branch
and bow; A — I / Γ — I / N — H in field. *B.M.C. 11.* 236-7 ..   ..   ..   £10

2615 **CORINTHIA. Corinth** (the Corinthian mint was active throughout the 5th and 4th
Centuries, except for periods during the Peloponnesian War, when her hostile attitude
towards Athens may have restricted her supply of silver bullion.   The output of staters and
drachms increased dramatically in the second half of the 4th Cent., probably in connection
with Timoleon's successful intervention in Sicilian affairs, commencing 344 B.C.   Corinth
was occupied by the forces of Ptolemy I of Egypt from 308-306 B.C., and her silver coinage
ceased soon after.   She joined the Achaean League in the 3rd Cent., but later opposed
Rome and was utterly destroyed by the consul L. Mummius in 146 B.C.).   480-450 B.C.
Æ *stater* (= 3 drachms, *c.* 8·5 gm.). Pegasos, with curled wing, flying l.; koppa beneath.
℞. *Large, elongated* hd. of Athena r., in Corinthian helmet; all within incuse square.
Ravel (Les 'Poulains' de Corinthe) 177. *B.M.C. 12.* 57 ..   ..   £225

2616 — — Similar, but with X behind hd. of Athena. *Ravel* 184. *B.M.C. 12.* 61   £240

2617 — — Similar, but Pegasos flying r., and with koppa behind hd. of Athena. *Ravel* 292.
B.M.C. 12. 75   ..   ..   £240

2618 — — *Obv.* As last. ℞. Hd. of Athena l., of fine transitional style, hair short; wearing
Corinthian helmet; all within incuse square. *Ravel* 304 *(Paris and Berlin)* ..   £350

2619 450-430 B.C. Æ *stater*. *Obv.* As last. ℞. Hd. of Athena r., of fine early classical
style, wearing Corinthian helmet; behind, trident; all within incuse square. *Ravel* 306.
B.M.C. 12. 113   ..   ..   £300

2620 — — Pegasos, with *pointed* wing, flying l.; koppa beneath. ℞. Similar to last, but hd.
to l., and without symbol in field; Athena's hair hangs loosely behind. *Ravel* 322 *(Cambridge)* £325

2621   2622

2621 — — Pegasos, with curled wing, flying r.; koppa beneath. ℞. Hd. of Athena l., of
classical style, wearing Corinthian helmet *over leather cap.* *Ravel* 310. *B.M.C. 12.* 115
£275

2622 — Æ *half-stater* (*trihemidrachm*). Bellerophon riding on Pegasos, with pointed wing,
flying r.; koppa beneath. ℞. Chimaera r. *B.M.C. 12.* 116 ..   ..   ..   £450

2623 — Æ *drachm*. Pegasos, with pointed wing, flying r.; koppa beneath. R. Hd. of Aphrodite r., of classical style, hair rolled. *B.M.C. 12.* 118 .. .. £120

2624 — Æ *diobol*. Pegasos, with curled wing, flying l.; bunch of grapes above; koppa beneath. R. ΔIO. Pegasos, with curled wings, facing; all within incuse square. *B.M.C. 12.* 119
£100

2625 *Circa* 420 B.C. Æ *stater*. Pegasos, with pointed wing, flying l.; koppa beneath. R. Hd. of Athena l., wearing Corinthian helmet over leather cap; Δ in upper field to l. *Ravel* 333
£250

2626   2628

2626 400-350 B.C. Æ *stater*. Pegasos, with pointed wing, flying l.; koppa beneath. R. Hd. of Athena l., wearing Corinthian helmet over leather cap; behind, Phrygian cap. *Ravel* 373. *B.M.C. 12.* 134 .. .. £175

2627 — — Pegasos, with pointed wing, stg. r.; l. foreleg raised, hd. lowered as if to drink; koppa beneath. R. Hd. of Athena l., as last; behind, bucranium. *Ravel* 495. *B.M.C. 12.* 175 .. .. £225

2628 — — Pegasos, with curled wing, pacing l.; koppa on hind-quarter, another beneath. R. Hd. of Athena r., wearing Corinthian helmet over leather cap; behind, eagle's hd. r.; before, in upper field, dolphin r. *Ravel* 798. *B.M.C. 12.* 162.. .. .. £200

The large issues of this period are divided into series, distinguished by the symbol or symbols in the reverse field. More than sixty of these symbols have been recorded.

2629   2630

2629 350-306 B.C. Æ *stater*. Pegasos l., as 2626. R. Hd. of Athena l., wearing Corinthian helmet, bound with olive-wreath, over leather cap; in lower field, A — P; behind, boar l. *Ravel* 1017. *B.M.C. 12.* 247-8 .. .. £95

2630 — — *Obv.* Similar. R. Hd. of Athena l., wearing Corinthian helmet over leather cap; before, in lower field, I; behind, Nike flying l. *Ravel* 1030. *B.M.C. 12.* 350 £90

2631 — — *Obv.* Similar. R. Hd. of Athena l., as last; in field, Δ — I; behind, Artemis running r., carrying torch. *Ravel* 1081. *B.M.C. 12.* 317 .. .. £90

2632   2633

2632 — Æ *half-stater* (*trihemidrachm*). Bellerophon riding on Pegasos, with pointed wing, flying r.; koppa beneath. R. Chimaera l.; ΔI in lower field to r.; amphora beneath. *B.M.C. 12.* 319 .. .. £275

2633 — Æ *drachm*. Pegasos l., as 2626. R. Hd. of Aphrodite r., hair in sakkos; behind, A. *B.M.C. 12.* 231 .. .. £60

2634 2635

Corinth *continued*

2634 — — *Obv.* Similar. R. Hd. of Aphrodite l., wearing sphendone; A — P in lower field.
B.M.C. 12. 260 .. .. £60

2635 — R *hemidrachm.* Forepart of Pegasos l., with curled wing; koppa beneath. R. Veiled
hd. of Demeter l., wreathed with corn; A — P in lower field. B.M.C. 12. 265.. £45

2636 — — *Obv.* Similar. R. Hd. of Aphrodite l., hair bound with tainia; behind, Λ. B.M.C.
12. 368 .. .. £45

2637 — R *diobol.* Pegasos ,with pointed wing, flying l.; koppa beneath. R. Pegasos, with
curled wing, pacing l.; in lower field to l., I. B.M.C. 12. 358 .. .. .. £50

2638 — R *trihemiobol.* *Obv.* Similar. R. Gorgoneion; mouth closed; beneath, K (reversed).
B.M.C. 12. 364 .. .. £55

2639 — R *obol.* *Obv.* Similar. R. Trident; A — P in field. B.M.C. 12. 271 .. £45

In this period the issues are further distinguished by the addition of a letter, or letters, to the
symbol in the reverse field. These may represent the names of the responsible mint-officials.

2640 308-306 B.C. (period of Ptolemaic occupation). R *drachm.* Hd. of Alexander the
Great r., clad in elephant's skin. R. Athena Alkidemos advancing r., brandishing spear
and holding shield; ΑΛΕΞΑΝΔΡΟΥ behind; eagle stg. r. on thunderbolt and ΔO before.
Kraay (Archaic and Classical Greek Coins), pl. 14, 255 .. .. £500

Although not of Corinthian type, the only known specimens of this coin were found at
Chiliomodi, near Corinth, and the letters in the rev. field (ΔO) occur also on Corinthian staters
and drachms of this period (cf. Ravel 1091).

2641 2644

2641 306-300 B.C. R *stater.* Pegasos, with pointed wing, flying l.; koppa beneath. R.
Hd. of Athena l., wearing Corinthian helmet over leather cap; behind, AMY monogram and
Term l. *Ravel* 1107. *B.M.C. 12. 401* £110

2642 — — Similar, but with EY monogram and eagle stg. r. behind hd. of Athena. *Ravel*
1115. *B.M.C. 12. 396-7* £120

2643 — R *drachm.* *Obv.* Similar. R. Hd. of Aphrodite l., hair in sakkos; behind, AΠ monogram. *B.M.C. 12. 407-9* £70

2644 — — Pegasos, with pointed wing, flying r.; koppa beneath. R. Hd. of Aphrodite l.,
hair tied behind; AΦP monogram to r. *B.M.C. 12. 414* £75

2645   2648

2645 *Bronze Coinage.* Before 350 B.C. Æ 13. Pegasos, with pointed wing, flying r.; koppa beneath. R. Trident. *B.M.C. 12.* 423 .. .. £8

2646 — — Similar, but Pegasos l., and race-torch in field to r. on *rev. B.M.C. 12.* 441
£7

2647 350-300 B.C. Æ 13. *Obv.* As last. R. Trident; Δ — I in lower field; pine-cone to r. *B.M.C. 12.* 453 .. .. £6

2648 — Æ 18. Hd. of Athena l., wearing crested Corinthian helmet. R. KOPINΘIΩN. Trident. *B.M.C. 12.* 472 .. .. £9

2649 300-243 B.C. Æ 20. Hd. of Poseidon r., hair bound with marine plant. R. Bellerophon riding on Pegasos flying r.; beneath, HP monogram and koppa. *B.M.C. 12.* 479
£10

2650 — Æ 14. Hd. of Athena r., wearing crested Corinthian helmet. R. Pegasos flying r.; K beneath. *B.M.C. 12.* 476 .. .. £8

2651 — — Bearded hd. of Herakles r., wearing wreath. R. Forepart of Pegasos r.; beneath, HP monogram and koppa. *B.M.C. 12.* 481 .. .. £8

2652 — Æ 13. Pegasos, with pointed wing, flying l.; koppa beneath. R. Same as *obv. B.M.C. 12.* 477 .. .. £7

For later coins of Corinth, see below under the Achaean League.

N.B. Prices given in this catalogue are for **fine** examples of coins in base metal and for **very fine** examples of coins struck in precious metals.

There is no relationship between the values stated and the condition of the coins used as illustrations.

248

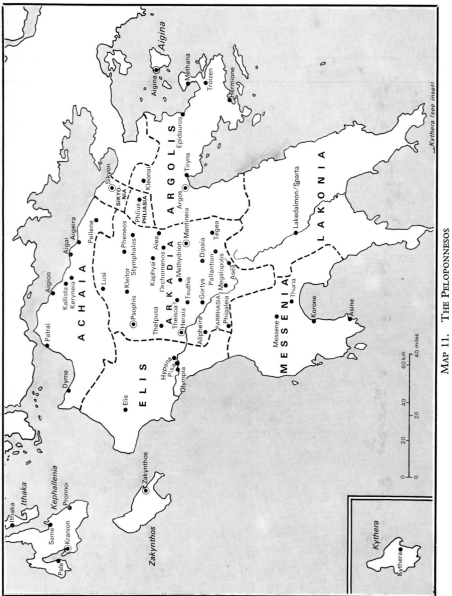

MAP 11. THE PELOPONNESOS

PELOPONNESOS

This southernmost area of Greece, the 'island of Pelops', was slow to develop its own coinages. In early times its needs were served by the vast quantities of silver staters put into circulation by the island mint of Aigina in the second half of the 6th Cent. B.C. It is hardly surprising, therefore, that when Peloponnesian coinage did begin to develop, in the following century, it was based on the Aiginetic weight standard (didrachm-stater of *c.* 12·6 gm.). However, large denominations were not normally struck, the triobol (hemidrachm) being the most frequently encountered Peloponnesian coin of the 5th Cent. The major exception to this was the mint of Elis which produced fine staters in connection with the Olympic festivals. In the 4th Cent. there was a flowering of coinage in the Peloponnese, especially after the fall of Sparta in 371 B.C., but by the end of the century the area had fallen under the control of the Macedonian kings. During the 3rd and 2nd Centuries many of the cities joined the Achaean League and produced coinages of a standardized federal type, but with the destruction of Corinth and formation of the Roman province of Achaia in 146 B.C., silver coinage ceased in Peloponnesos.

Archaic Period

2653   2655   2657

2653 **ARKADIA** (comprising much of the mountainous interior of the Peloponnese, and an area which witnessed some of the earliest developments in coinage in this part of Greece). **Heraia** (in the far west of the country, in the valley of the Alpheios, Heraia was named after Heraios, son of Lykaon). 500–480 B.C. Æ *triobol* (*hemidrachm*). Diad. and veiled hd. of Hera l. R. EPA (retrograde) across field; zigzag and pellets above and below; all within incuse square. *B.M.C. 10. 7* £225

2654 — Æ *obol*. Diad. and veiled hd. of Hera r. R. EP (retrograde) in dotted square; all within incuse square. *B.M.C. 10. 5* £110

2655 **Mantineia** (one of the most important towns of Arkadia, Mantineia possessed the oracular sanctuary of Poseidon Hippios). 490–480 B.C. Æ *triobol*. Bear prowling l. R. Triangular incuse, containing MA, three acorns and oak-leaf. *B.M.C. 10. 2* ..   £250

2656 — Æ *obol*. Bear's hd. l. R. MA and acorn, within incuse square. *B.M.C. 10. 5*   £120

2657 **Psophis** (originally called Phegia, this town was built in the narrow valley of the Erymanthos. In legend, it was the scene of Herakles' contest with the Erymanthian boar and the Keryneian stag). 500–480 B.C. Æ *tetrobol*. Stag prancing r. R. Fish r., mostly within dotted square; all in incuse square. *B.M.C. 10. 1* £275

2658 — Æ *obol*. Forepart of prancing stag r. R. Fish l.; O✳ above, hoof below; all within incuse square. *B.M.C. 10. 3* £140

2659   2662

2659 **SIKYONIA** (a small district in the north-east of Peloponnesos). **Sikyon** (the chief town of Sikyonia, Sikyon was a place of ancient foundation, described by Homer as forming part of the empire of Agamemnon). 490–480 B.C. Æ *drachm*. Dove alighting l. R. Large M (=letter *san*) within incuse square. *B.M.C. 10. 1* £200

2660 — Æ *hemiobol*. Dove stg. l. R. As last. *B.M.C. 10. 9* £60

2661 — Æ *tetartemorion* (¼ *obol*). Dove's hd. l. R. As last. *B.M.C. 10. 18* ..   £50

2662 **ARGOLIS** (the eastern part of the Peloponnese, between Arkadia and the Aegean sea). **Argos** (founded by Inachos, son of Oceanos, the ancient city of Argos was second only in importance to Sparta in Peloponnesos. Hera was especially revered by the Argives). 490–480 B.C. Æ *drachm*. Wolf l., at bay. R. Shallow incuse square, containing large A, and two deeper incuses in upper corners. *B.M.C. 10. 1, 2* £200

2663 — Æ *triobol*. Similar, but with forepart of wolf l. on *obv*. *B.M.C. 10. 3, 4* ..   £90

2664   2668   2672

2664 **ZAKYNTHOS** (an island of the Ionian sea, off the coast of Elis, Zakynthos receives frequent mention in Homer's writings. Its one city bore the same name as the island). 500-480 B.C. Æ *third-stater* (*c.* 3·8 gm.). I — A either side of amphora. ℞. Tripod, within incuse square. *B.M.C. 10.* 1 .. .. £300

2665 — Æ *sixth-stater*. Similar. *B.M.C. 10.* 2, 3 .. .. £175

2666 — —IA. Crescent; above, ivy-leaf. ℞. As last. *B.M.C. 10.* 8 .. .. £160

2667 — Æ *eighteenth-stater* (*c.* 0·66 gm.). As 2664. *B.M.C. 10.* 5 .. .. £85

2668 **KEPHALLENIA** (the largest island of the Ionian sea, Kephallenia is situated about ten miles north of Zakynthos. Of its four mint-towns, only one began its issues in the archaic period). **Kranion** (on the south coast of the island). 500-480 B.C. Æ *stater*. Ram's hd. r. ℞. Bow, within incuse square. *B.M.C. 10.* 1 .. .. £650

2669 — Æ *triobol*. KRANI above ram stg. l. ℞. As last. *B.M.C. 10.* 2 .. .. £125

2670 — Æ *trihemiobol*. Forepart of ram l. ℞. TR, within incuse square. *B.M.C. 10.* 11 £110

2671 — Æ *obol*. Similar to 2668, but ram's hd. l. *B.M.C. 10.* 12 .. .. .. £90

Classical and Hellenistic Periods

2672 **ARKADIA.** **The Arkadian League** (the first series of federal issues, down to *c.* 418 B.C., were formerly attributed to the mint of Heraia. It now seems clear, however, that three separate mints were active, possibly at Kleitor, Tegea and Mantineia). 480-465 B.C. Æ *triobol*. Zeus enthroned l., eagle on outstretched r. hand, holding sceptre in l. ℞. A — R (retrograde) before and behind hd. of Artemis l., hair in krobylos; all within incuse square. *Williams* (*The Confederate Coinage of the Arcadians in the Fifth Century B.C.*) 2. *B.M.C. 10.* 7 .. .. £250

2673 — Æ *obol*. Similar. *Williams* 24. *B.M.C. 10.* 8 .. .. £100

2674   2676   2677

2674 465-455 B.C. Æ *triobol*. *Obv.* Similar, but back-rest of throne is ornamented with swan's hd. ℞. ARKADIKON (retrograde). Hd. of Artemis l., hair bound with fillet from which project three olive-leaves; all within incuse square. *Williams* 51. *B.M.C. 10.* 19 £325

2675 — — *Obv.* As last. ℞. ARKA. Hd. of Artemis r., hair in bun behind; all within incuse square. *Williams* 75. *B.M.C. 10.* 38 .. .. £250

2676 — — *Obv.* Similar, but the eagle flies l., carrying snake, above Zeus' outstretched hand; throne has cross-stays. ℞. APKA. Hd. of Artemis l., hair in sakkos; all within incuse square. *Williams* 122. *B.M.C. 10.* 29 .. .. £275

2677 — Æ *obol*. *Obv.* As last, but without snake. ℞. ARKADIϘON (retrograde). Hd. of Artemis r., hair in bun behind; all within incuse square. *Williams* 100. *B.M.C. 10.* 32 £100

2678 455-445 B.C. Æ *triobol*. Zeus seated l. on throne without back-rest; eagle on out-stretched r. hand, holding sceptre in l. ℞. ARKADIKON (retrograde). Hd. of Artemis r., hair in plait down back of neck; all within incuse square. *Williams* 148. *B.M.C. 10*. 13
£250

2679 — — Similar, but Zeus enthroned *facing*, and legend not retrograde. *Williams* 152. *B.M.C. 10*. 14 .. .. £275

2680   2682

2680 — — Zeus stg. facing, hd. l., holding eagle and phiale; sceptre under l. arm. ℞. ARKADIKON. Hd. of Artemis three-quarter face to l.; hair in bun, visible to r.; all within incuse square. *Williams* 176. *B.M.C. 10*. 1 .. .. £350

2681 — Æ *obol*. Zeus enthroned r., holding eagle on outstretched r. hand, and sceptre in l. ℞. ARKA. Hd. of Artemis three-quarter face to r., hair in bun behind; all within incuse square. *Williams* 193 .. .. £140

2682 445-428 B.C. Æ *triobol*. Zeus enthroned l.; eagle flying l. above outstretched r. hand, holding sceptre in l. ℞. ARKA. Hd. of Artemis l., hair rolled; all within incuse square. *Williams* 285. *B.M.C. 10*. 24 .. .. £275

2683 — Æ *obol*. Zeus enthroned l., leaning forward, holding eagle on outstretched r. hand, and sceptre in l. ℞. Hd. of Artemis r., hair in plait down back of neck; A beneath chin; all within incuse square. *Williams* 273. *B.M.C. 10*. 6.. .. .. .. £100

2684 428-418 B.C. Æ *triobol*. Zeus seated l. on throne without back-rest, holding eagle on outstretched r. hand, and sceptre in l. ℞. A — P / K — A. Hd. of Artemis r., of fine classical style; hair rolled and wearing ampyx; all within incuse square. *Williams* 310. *B.M.C. 10*. 44 .. .. £300

2685 — Æ *hemiobol*. Bearded hd. of Zeus l. ℞. ARK. Hd. of Hermes r., in close-fitting cap; all within incuse square. *Williams* 315 .. .. £90

2686   2687

2686 370-280 B.C. Æ *stater*. Laur. hd. of Zeus l., of fine style. ℞. Naked Pan seated l., hd. facing, on rock inscribed OAY; he holds lagobolon in r. hand; ARK monogram in field to l.; syrinx on ground beside rock. *B.M.C. 10*. 48 .. .. £4,500

These may have been issued on the occasion of the 104th Olympiad (364 B.C.), when the Arkadians took over the Games on behalf of Pisa. These, and all subsequent issues in the name of the Arkadians, were struck at Megalopolis, a city founded c. 370 B.C. by Epaminondas.

2687 — Æ *triobol*. Laur. hd. of Zeus l.; I behind. ℞. Naked Pan seated l. on rock, r. hand raised, holding lagobolon in l.; ARK monogram in field to l., I to r. *B.M.C. 10*. 52   £90

2688 — Æ *obol*. Horned hd. of young Pan l. ℞. Large ARK monogram above syrinx. *B.M.C. 10*. 55-6 .. .. £50

The Arkadian League *continued*

2689 280-234 B.C. Æ *triobol.* Laur. hd. of Zeus l. Ɍ. Naked Pan seated l. on rock, r. hand raised, holding lagobolon in l.; to l., eagle flying l. *B.M.C. 10.* 76-7 .. .. £60

2690 — — Similar, but also with ARK monogram and Λ in *rev.* field. *B.M.C. 10.* 81 £60

2691 *Bronze Coinage.* 370-280 B.C. Æ 20. Horned hd. of young Pan r. Ɍ. Large ARK monogram above syrinx; A in field to l. *B.M.C. 10.* 62-3 .. .. .. £15

2692 — Æ 15. Similar, but hd. of Pan to l., and with ΘE in *rev.* field to l. *B.M.C. 10.* 70-71 £12

2693 — — Laur. hd. of Zeus l. Ɍ. Large ARK monogram above syrinx. *B.M.C. 10.* 74 £12

2694 280-234 B.C. Æ 18. *Obv.* Similar. Ɍ. Large ARK monogram above syrinx and thunderbolt; Π — M in field. *B.M.C. 10.* 87-8 .. .. £14

2869   2692   2695

2695 **Alea** (a small town, between Orchomenos and Stymphalos, but boasting several notable temples). *Circa* 370 B.C. Æ *obol.* Hd. of Artemis r., hair tied in top-knot. Ɍ. AΛ below strung bow. *B.M.C. 10.* 1 .. .. £150

2696 — Æ 14. Similar. *Weber* 4268 .. .. £17

For later coins of Alea, see below under Achaean League.

2697 **Kaphyai** (a few miles to the north-west of Orchomenos). 280-240 B.C. Æ 13. Hd. of Athena r.. in Corinthian helmet. Ɍ. ΚΑΦ within corn-wreath. *B.M.C. 10.* 1 £18

For later coins of Kaphyai, see below under Achaean League.

2698   2700

2698 **Kleitor** (in the north of the country, midway between Psophis and Pheneos). 418-400 B.C. Æ *triobol.* ΚΛΕΤΟ. Naked rider on horse prancing l. Ɍ. Formalized incuse, of 'mill-sail' pattern. *B.M.C. 10.* 2 .. .. £250

2699 — Æ *hemiobol.* Horse's hd. r. Ɍ. E within linear square; all in incuse square. *B.M.C. 10.* 1 .. .. £90

2700 362-300 B.C. Æ *triobol.* Radiate hd. of Helios facing. Ɍ. Bull butting r.; above, ΚΛΗ and centaur r. *B.M.C. 10.* 4-5 .. .. £175

2701 — Æ *obol.* Hd. of Athena l., in close-fitting crested helmet. Ɍ. ΚΛΗ (retrograde). Horse prancing r. *B.M.C. 10.* 8-9 .. .. £90

2702 — Æ 19. *Obv.* Similar. Ɍ. ΚΛΗ (retrograde). Horse prancing r. beside column; A above. *B.M.C. 10.* 10 .. .. £15

2703 — Æ 13. Radiate hd. of Helios facing. Ɍ. Large ΚΛΗ monogram. *B.M.C. 10.* 12-13 £12

For later coins of Kleitor, see below under Achaean League.

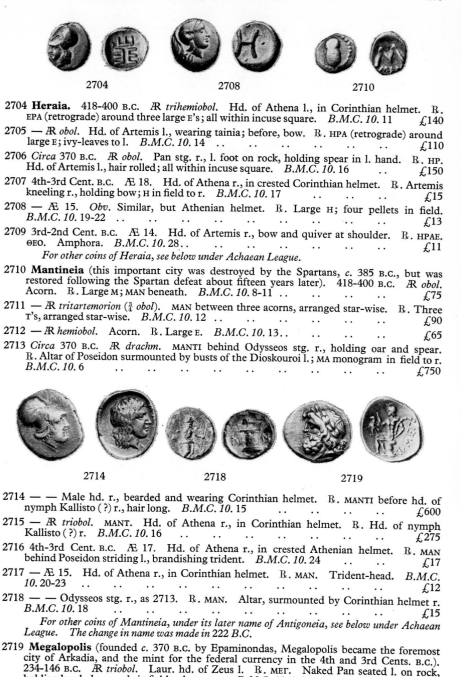

2704   2708   2710

2704 Heraia. 418-400 B.C. *Æ trihemiobol.* Hd. of Athena l., in Corinthian helmet. ℞. EPA (retrograde) around three large E's; all within incuse square. *B.M.C. 10.* 11   £140

2705 — *Æ obol.* Hd. of Artemis l., wearing tainia; before, bow. ℞. HPA (retrograde) around large E; ivy-leaves to l. *B.M.C. 10.* 14 ..   ..   £110

2706 *Circa* 370 B.C. *Æ obol.* Pan stg. r., l. foot on rock, holding spear in l. hand. ℞. HP. Hd. of Artemis l., hair rolled; all within incuse square. *B.M.C. 10.* 16   ..   £150

2707 4th-3rd Cent. B.C. *Æ 18.* Hd. of Athena r., in crested Corinthian helmet. ℞. Artemis kneeling r., holding bow; H in field to r. *B.M.C. 10.* 17   ..   ..   £15

2708 — *Æ 15.* Obv. Similar, but Athenian helmet. ℞. Large H; four pellets in field. *B.M.C. 10.* 19-22 ..   ..   £13

2709 3rd-2nd Cent. B.C. *Æ 14.* Hd. of Artemis r., bow and quiver at shoulder. ℞. HPAE. ΘΕΟ. Amphora. *B.M.C. 10.* 28..   ..   ..   £11

     For other coins of Heraia, see below under Achaean League.

2710 Mantineia (this important city was destroyed by the Spartans, *c.* 385 B.C., but was restored following the Spartan defeat about fifteen years later). 418-400 B.C. *Æ obol.* Acorn. ℞. Large M; MAN beneath. *B.M.C. 10.* 8-11 ..   ..   ..   £75

2711 — *Æ tritartemorion* (¾ obol). MAN between three acorns, arranged star-wise. ℞. Three T's, arranged star-wise. *B.M.C. 10.* 12 ..   ..   £90

2712 — *Æ hemiobol.* Acorn. ℞. Large E. *B.M.C. 10.* 13..   ..   ..   £65

2713 *Circa* 370 B.C. *Æ drachm.* MANTI behind Odysseos stg. r., holding oar and spear. ℞. Altar of Poseidon surmounted by busts of the Dioskouroi l.; MA monogram in field to r. *B.M.C. 10.* 6   ..   ..   £750

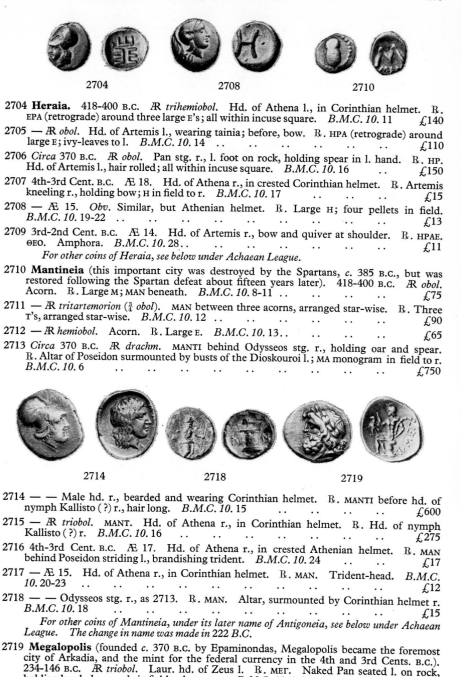

2714   2718   2719

2714 — — Male hd. r., bearded and wearing Corinthian helmet. ℞. MANTI before hd. of nymph Kallisto (?) r., hair long. *B.M.C. 10.* 15   ..   ..   ..   £600

2715 — *Æ triobol.* MANT. Hd. of Athena r., in Corinthian helmet. ℞. Hd. of nymph Kallisto (?) r. *B.M.C. 10.* 16 ..   ..   £275

2716 4th-3rd Cent. B.C. *Æ 17.* Hd. of Athena r., in crested Athenian helmet. ℞. MAN behind Poseidon striding l., brandishing trident. *B.M.C. 10.* 24 ..   ..   £17

2717 — *Æ 15.* Hd. of Athena r., in Corinthian helmet. ℞. MAN. Trident-head. *B.M.C. 10.* 20-23 ..   ..   £12

2718 — — Odysseos stg. r., as 2713. ℞. MAN. Altar, surmounted by Corinthian helmet r. *B.M.C. 10.* 18   ..   ..   £15

     For other coins of Mantineia, under its later name of Antigoneia, see below under Achaean League. The change in name was made in 222 B.C.

2719 Megalopolis (founded *c.* 370 B.C. by Epaminondas, Megalopolis became the foremost city of Arkadia, and the mint for the federal currency in the 4th and 3rd Cents. B.C.). 234-146 B.C. *Æ triobol.* Laur. hd. of Zeus l. ℞. MEΓ. Naked Pan seated l. on rock, holding lagobolon; eagle in field to l., ΔI to r. *B.M.C. 10.* 3-4 ..   ..   £50

Megalopolis *continued*

2720 — Æ 22. Similar. ℞. ΜΕΓ. Naked Pan seated l. on rock, holding lagobolon resting on ground; monograms in field to l. and to r.; all within oak-wreath. *B.M.C. 10.* 15 .... £15

2721 — Æ 18. Similar. ℞. ΜΕΓ beneath eagle stg. r. on thunderbolt; monograms in field to l. and to r.; all within oak-wreath. *B.M.C. 10.* 12 .. .. £12

For other coins of Megalopolis, see below under Achaean League.

2722   2725   2726

2722 **Orchomenos** (an ancient city north-west of Mantineia, Orchomenos refused to join the re-constituted Arkadian League in 370 B.C.). After 370 B.C. Æ 19. Artemis kneeling r., holding bow; hound seated r. behind her. ℞. ΕΡΧΟΜΕΝΙΩΝ. Kallisto seated l., falling back, pierced by arrow; young Arkas seated on ground beside her. *B.M.C. 10.* 1-2 £20

2723 — Æ 17. Male hd. r., bearded and wearing Corinthian helmet. ℞. Ε — Ρ either side of Artemis stg. r., shooting arrow. *B.M.C. 10.* 3-4 .. .. £17

2724 **Pallantion** (situated south-west of Tegea, Pallantion was said to have been founded by Pallas, son of Lykaon). 418-400 B.C. Æ *hemiobol.* Laur. hd. of Apollo r. ℞. Large Ε; ΠΑΛ (retrograde) to r. *B.M.C. 10.* 1 .. .. £140

For later coins of Pallantion, see below under Achaean League.

2725 **Parrhasia** (Parrhasia was a district in southern Arkadia — chief city Lykosura — though a town of this name is mentioned by Homer in the *Iliad*). 418-400 B.C. Æ *obol.* Male hd. r., with long hair and pointed beard. ℞. ΠΑΡ (retrograde) around large Π. *B.M.C. 10.* 1 .. .. £175

2726 **Pheneos** (an ancient town in the north-east of the country, at the foot of Mt. Kyllene, Pheneos was a centre for the worship of Hermes and of Demeter). 418-400 B.C. Æ *triobol.* Hd. of Hermes l., petasos at back of neck. ℞. ΦΕΝΙΚΟΝ. Bull feeding r. *B.M.C. 10.* 1 .. .. £375

2727 — Æ *obol.* Bust of Hermes r., petasos at back of neck. ℞. ΦΕ above ram stg. r.; beneath, ΑΡ. *B.M.C. 10.* 3 .. .. £120

2728 *Circa* 365 B.C. Æ *stater.* Hd. of Demeter r., wreathed with corn. ℞. ΦΕΝΕΩΝ. Hermes striding l., holding caduceus, looking back at the child Arkas held on his l. arm; ΑΡΚΑΣ in small letters in field to r. *B.M.C. 10.* 13 .. .. £5,000

The obv. type is inspired by the Syracusan dekadrachms by Euainetos.

2729 — Æ *drachm. Obv.* Similar, but hd. l. ℞. ΦΕΝΕΩΝ. Hermes seated l. on rock, holding caduceus. *B.M.C. 10.* 14 .. .. £750

2730 — Æ *triobol. Obv.* As last. ℞. ΦΕΝΙΚΟΝ above bull stg. r.; Π below. *B.M.C. 10.* 15 £325

2731 4th-3rd Cent. B.C. Æ 13. Forepart of ram r. ℞. Φ — Ε either side of caduceus. *B.M.C. 10.* 6 .. .. £14

2732 — Æ 15. Hd. of Hermes r., wearing petasos. ℞. ΦΕ above ram stg. r. *B.M.C. 10.* 7 £12

2733 — Æ 18. Hd. of Demeter l., wreathed with corn. ℞. Φ — E either side of caduceus. *B.M.C. 10.* 17-19 .. .. £13

2734 — — Bust of Artemis r., bow and quiver at shoulder. ℞. ΦΕΝΕΩΝ above horse feeding r.; ARK monogram below. *B.M.C. 10.* 22-3 .. .. £13
For later coins of Pheneos, see below under Achaean League.

2734   2735

2735 **Psophis.** 418-400 B.C. Æ *hemiobol.* Stag galloping r. ℞. Large E within dotted square; all in incuse square. *B.M.C. 10.* 5 .. .. £120

2736 2nd Cent. B.C. Æ 15. Hd. of Athena r., in crested Corinthian helmet. ℞. ΨΩΦΙ Stag stg. r. *Grose* 7005 .. .. £18

2737   2739

2737 **Stymphalos** (the ancient city of Stymphalos, south-east of Pheneos, was named after a grandson of Arkas. The celebrated Stymphalian birds dwelt on a nearby lake before their destruction by Herakles). *Circa* 400 B.C. Æ *triobol.* Hd. of young Herakles r., clad in lion's skin. ℞. ΣΤΥΜΦΑΛΙΟΝ. Hd. and neck of Stymphalian bird r., emerging from plants. *B.M.C. 10.* 1 .. .. £425

2738 — Æ *obol.* Similar. ℞. ΣΤΥΜΦΑΛΙΟΝ (retrograde). Hd. and neck of Stymphalian bird r.; T — Y in field. *B.M.C. 10.* 2-3 .. .. £150

2739 *Circa* 365 B.C. Æ *stater.* Laur. hd. of Artemis Stymphalia r., hair in korymbos. ℞. ΣΤΥΜΦΑΛΙΩΝ. Naked Herakles striding l., brandishing club and holding lion's skin and bow; ΣΟ between legs. *B.M.C. 10.* 6 .. .. £6,500

2740 — Æ 19. *Obv.* Similar, but not laur. ℞. ΣΤΥΜΦΑ between bow and quiver. *B.M.C. 10.* 7 .. .. £22
For later coins of Stymphalos, see below under Achaean League.

2741   2744

2741 **Tegea** (in the south-east of Arkadia, Tegea was an important city of very early foundation. It possessed a magnificent temple of Athena, by the architect Skopas). 418-400 B.C. Æ *trihemiobol.* Gorgoneion; T above. ℞. Three E's, back to back. *B.M.C. 10.* 1-2 £140

2743 — Æ *hemiobol.* Owl stg. r. ℞. Large E. *B.M.C. 10.* 5 .. .. .. £110

2744 *Circa* 370 B.C. Æ *triobol.* Hd. of Athena r., in crested Athenian helmet. ℞. ΤΕΓΕ. Owl stg. l. on olive-branch. *B.M.C. 10.* 6 .. .. £275

2745   2747

Tegea *continued*

2745 *Circa* 350 B.C. Æ *triobol*. Similar. R. TEΓEATAN. Kepheos (?), naked but for helmet, advancing r., holding sword and large shield decorated with figure of running hound; spear and κ (reversed) between his legs. *B.M.C. 10.* 11   ..   ..   ..   £250

2746 4th-3rd Cent. B.C. Æ 17. Hd. of Athena r., in crested Athenian helmet ornamented with Skylla. R. As 2744. *B.M.C. 10.* 8   ..   ..   ..   £13

2747 — — Hd. of Athena r., in crested Corinthian helmet. R. TEΓEA. Telephos, son of Herakles and Auge, seated l., suckled by doe stg. r.; M in field to l., owl to r. *B.M.C. 10.* 15 ..   ..   £15

2748 — — Diad. hd. of Eileithyia(?) l., lighted torch at shoulder. R. TEΓEA. Athena stg. r., placing hair of Medusa in hydria held by priestess Sterope stg. l. *B.M.C. 10.* 17   £17

2749   2751

2749 After 146 B.C. Æ 23. AΛEOΣ. Bearded hd. of Aleos r., wearing tainia. R. TEΓEATAN. Athena l. and Kepheos r., stg. face to face; between them, Sterope stg. r., holding hydria into which Athena places hair of Medusa; two monograms in field. *B.M.C. 10.* 20-21 £18

For other coins of Tegea, see below under Achaean League.

2750 **Thelpusa** (situated in western Arkadia, on the river Ladon, Thelpusa was named after a water-nymph, daughter of Ladon). *Circa* 370 B.C. Æ *obol*. Hd. of Demeter Erinys r.; θ before. R. EPIΩN above the horse Areion prancing r. *Weber* 4355 ..   £150

2751 After 146 B.C. Æ 18. Radiate hd. of Helios r. R. θEΛ within laurel-wreath. *B.M.C. 10.* 1 ..   ..   £12

For other coins of Thelpusa, see below under Achaean League.

2752 **PHLIASIA** (a small territory in the north-east of the Peloponnese — chief town, Phlius). **Phlius** (originally called Arantia, it was later re-named after Phlius, grandson of Temenos). 420-386 B.C. Æ *drachm*. ΦΛEIA. Bull pacing l., hd. lowered. R. ΣION. Wheel of four spokes; all within incuse square. *B.M.C. 10.* 1 ..   ..   ..   £450

2753   2756

2753 — — Similar, but bull butting l., hd. facing, and legends retrograde on both sides. *B.M.C. 10.* 6   ..   ..   £450

2754 — Æ *triobol*. Bull butting r. R. Large Φ, four pellets around; all in dotted square within incuse. *B.M.C. 10.* 4   ..   ..   £200

2755 — Æ *obol*. Bull butting l.; I above. R. Large Φ, four bunches of grapes around; all within incuse square. *B.M.C. 10.* 23   ..   ..   £100

2756 370-322 B.C. Æ *triobol*. Bull butting l. R. Φ within ivy-wreath. *B.M.C. 10.* 18-22   £175

2757 — Æ *trihemiobol.* Bull butting l.; I above. ℞. Wheel, with Φ and three bunches of grapes between the four spokes. *B.M.C. 10.* 24..   ..   ..   £140

2758 4th-3rd Cent. B.C. Æ 14. Bull butting l. ℞. Large Φ, pellet on either side. *B.M.C. 10.* 13-15   ..   ..   £11

2759 — Æ 18. Bearded hd. of Asopos r., crowned with reeds. ℞. Φ within ivy-wreath. *B.M.C. 10.* 26   ..   ..   £13

For later coins of Phlius, see below under Achaean League.

2760   2763

2760 **SIKYONIA. Sikyon** (in the 5th and 4th Cents. this important mint produced two large issues of silver staters and associated fractional denominations. The first was probably the principal war-coinage of the Peloponnesian allies during the long struggle with Athens). 450-430 B.C. Æ *hemidrachm.* Chimaera stg. l. ℞. Σ and T in two corners of incuse square containing dove flying r. *B.M.C. 10.* 3-4   ..   ..   £150

     The letter T on rev. is the mark of value (=triobol).

2761 — Æ *obol.* Forepart of Chimaera l. ℞. As last, but with Σ and O in *rev.* field. *B.M.C. 10.* 5..   ..   ..   £120

     The letter O is the mark of value (=obol).

2762 — Æ *hemiobol.* Dove stg. l. ℞. As last, but with Σ and H in *rev.* field. £75

     The letter H is the mark of value (=hemiobol).

2763 430-390 B.C. Æ *stater.* Chimaera stg. l.; ΣE beneath. ℞. Dove flying l., within olive-wreath. *B.M.C. 10.* 22   ..   ..   £375

2764 — — Similar, but with Chimaera r. on *obv.* and with A in *rev.* field. *B.M.C. 10.* 48-9   £350

2765   2769

2765 — Æ *drachm.* ΣE. Dove alighting l. ℞. Dove flying l., within olive-wreath. *B.M.C. 10.* 26-9   ..   ..   £120

2766 — —As 2763. *B.M.C. 10.* 66-7   ..   ..   £120

2767 — Æ *hemidrachm.* Chimaera stg. l.; ΣE beneath. ℞. Dove flying l.; Σ in field to r. *B.M.C. 10.* 76   ..   ..   £50

2768 — Æ *diobol.* As 2763. *B.M.C. 10.* 32-3   ..   ..   ..   £75

2769 — Æ *tritartemorion* (¾ *obol*). Archaic figure of Apollo kneeling r., holding bow and arrows. ℞. ΣE within olive-wreath. *B.M.C. 10.* 77-81   ..   ..   £60

2770 — Æ *hemiobol.* Lion walking l. ℞. Dove flying l., within olive-wreath. *B.M.C. 10.* 40   £45

                2771   2774

Sikyon *continued*

2771 360-330 B.C. Æ *stater*. Chimaera stg. l.; ΣI beneath, wreath above. R. Dove flying r.;
      AO in field; all within olive-wreath. *B.M.C. 10*. 106 ..   ..   £450

2772 — Æ *drachm*. Similar to 2765, but with legend ΣI on *obv*., and with E in *rev*. field.
      B.M.C. 10. 107-8 ..   ..   £120

2773 — — Similar to 2763, but with legend ΣI on *obv*., and with I in *rev*. field. *B.M.C. 10*.
      109-10   ..   ..   £120

2774 — Æ *hemidrachm*. Chimaera stg. l.; ΣI beneath. R. Dove flying l.; three pellets in
      field. *B.M.C. 10*. 120-22 ..   ..   £45

2775 — Æ *obol*. Dove alighting r., holding fillet in beak. R. Dove flying r.; ΣI behind.
      B.M.C. 10. 134   ..   ..   £35

2776 — — Laur. hd. of Apollo r. R. As last. *B.M.C. 10*. 166   ..   ..   ..   £50

                2777   2780

2777 Before 146 B.C. (issued contemporaneously with the coinage of the Achaean League).
      Æ *hemidrachm*. Dove flying l. R. Large Σ, with ΘPA / Σ — Y / KΛHΣ above, either side
      and beneath; all within shallow incuse square. *B.M.C. 10*. 194   ..   ..   £40
      Many different magistrates' names have been recorded for this series.

2778 *Bronze Coinage*. 4th-3rd Cent. B.C. Æ 18. Laur. hd. of Apollo r. R. Large Σ;
      E (reversed) to l.; all within olive-wreath. *B.M.C. 10*. 170-71 ..   ..   ..   £12

2779 — — Dove flying l. R. Tripod-lebes within olive-wreath. *B.M.C. 10*. 146   £13

2780 — Æ 17. Similar. R. ME beneath wreath; all within olive-wreath. *B.M.C. 10*. 151-2
                                                                                    £10

2781 — Æ 14. Dove flying r. R. ΣI within olive-wreath. *B.M.C. 10*. 140   ..   £8

2782 — — Dove flying l. R. Dove flying l., within olive-wreath. *B.M.C. 10*. 87-8   £9

2783 — Æ 13. Dove flying r. R. Large M; A above. *B.M.C. 10*. 102   ..   ..   £7

2784 Before 146 B.C. Æ 18. Laur. hd. of Apollo r. R. Dove flying l., holding fillet; ΣI
      behind; AINEAΣ above. *B.M.C. 10*. 234-5   ..   ..   £9

2785 — Æ 15. Dove flying l.; OΛYMΠI / AΔA above and behind. R. ΣI within olive-wreath.
      B.M.C. 10. 220   ..   ..   £7
      For other coins of Sikyon, see below under Achaean League.

2786   2788

2786 **ARGOLIS. Argos.** 465-430 B.C. Æ *triobol.* Forepart of wolf l., base beneath feet. R. Shallow incuse square, containing large A above which, two deeper incuses; three pellets in field. *B.M.C. 10.* 13 ..   ..   £75

2787 — — Similar, but without base beneath wolf's feet, and with ΣΟ in field to l.; no pellets on *rev.* *B.M.C. 10.* 16 ..   ..   £75

2788 — Æ *obol.* Wolf's hd. l. R. Similar to 2786, but with two pellets in field. *B.M.C. 10* 21 ..   ..   £60

2789 — Æ *hemiobol.* Large aspirate. R. Similar to 2786, but without pellets in field. *B.M.C. 10.* 27-8 ..   ..   £75

2790   2791

2790 370-330 B.C. Æ *stater.* Hd. of Hera r., wearing stephanos ornamented with floral motif. R. ΑΡΓΕΙΩΝ. Two dolphins l. and r., one above the other; between them, wolf l., at bay. *B.M.C. 10.* 33 ..   ..   £3,500

2791 — Æ *drachm. Obv.* Similar; Σ behind. R. ΑΡΓΕΙΩΝ. Diomedes moving stealthily to r., holding sword and carrying the Trojan Palladion on outstretched l. hand. *B.M.C. 10.* 44   £1,250

2792 — Æ *trihemiobol. Obv.* Similar; no letter behind. R. Palladion r.; A — P in field. *B.M.C. 10.* 48-9 ..   ..   £175

2793 — Æ *tritartemorion* (¾ *obol*). *Obv.* As last. R. Three Τ's (mark of value) around sacred key of the Heraion. *B.M.C. 10.* 42-3 ..   ..   £110

2794   2797

2794 3rd Cent. B.C. Æ *hemidrachm.* Forepart of wolf r. R. Large A; club beneath, Z — ΕΥ in field above; all within shallow incuse square. *B.M.C. 10.* 62-3 ..   ..   £45

2795 — — Forepart of wolf l.; Θ above. R. Similar to last, but with eagle on harpa beneath A, and with ΠΥΡ monogram in upper field to r. *B.M.C. 10.* 81..   ..   £45

2796 — Æ *obol.* Wolf's hd. r.; ΣΙ above. R. Large A, N — I in upper field; all within shallow incuse square. *B.M.C. 10.* 91 ..   ..   £50

2797 Before 146 B.C. (issued contemporaneously with the coinage of the Achaean League). Æ *hemidrachm.* Forepart of wolf r. R. Large A; harpa beneath; A — ΓΑ / Θ — Ο / ΚΛΕΟΣ in field; all within shallow incuse square. *B.M.C. 10.* 110 ..   ..   £40

Many different magistrates' names have been recorded for this series.

Argos *continued*

2798 *Bronze Coinage.* 4th-3rd Cent. B.C. Æ 18. Hd. of Hera r., wearing stephanos inscribed
APΓE. ℞. Athena Alkidemos advancing l., brandishing spear and holding shield. *B.M.C.*
10. 106-8 .. .. £12

2799 — Æ 13. Hd. of Hera l., wearing stephanos. ℞. Large A; club beneath. *B.M.C. 10.*
51-3 .. .. £10

2800 — — Wolf's hd. l. ℞. Large A; helmet beneath. *B.M.C. 10.* 101-2 .. £6

2801   2804   2805

2801 Before 146 B.C. Æ 16. Laur. hd. of Apollo r. ℞. Tripod-lebes; aspirate to l., club to r.;
EY — ΘY / M — E in field. *B.M.C. 10.* 131-2 .. .. £8

2802 — — Wolf's hd. r. ℞. Quiver; to l., helmet and wolf's hd. r.; to r., aspirate and XAP
monogram. *B.M.C. 10.* 138-9 .. .. £8

2803 — — Hd. of Hera r., wearing stephanos ornamented with floral motif. ℞. Quiver;
trident to l., prow to r.; Π — AM / ΦA — HΣ in field. *B.M.C. 10.* 140-41 .. £7

For other coins of Argos, see below under Achaean League.

2804 **Kleonai** (founded by Kleones, son of Pelops, Kleonai was situated at the foot of Mt.
Apesas, on the road from Corinth to Argos. Herakles was especially worshipped by the
inhabitants). *Circa* 450 B.C. *Æ obol.* Hd. of bearded Herakles l., clad in lion's skin.
℞. Large K, with conical-shaped object to l.; all within incuse square. *B.M.C. 10.* 1-5
£140

2805 — *Æ hemiobol.* Lion's hd. l. ℞. As last. *B.M.C. 10.* 7 .. .. .. £120

2806 — *Æ tetartemorion* (¼ *obol*). Bunch of grapes. ℞. As last, but the conical-shaped object
is to r. of K. *Grose* 6879 .. .. £90

2807 4th-3rd Cent. B.C. Æ 15. Hd. of young Herakles r., clad in lion's skin. ℞. KΛ / EΩ
within wreath of parsley. *B.M.C. 10.* 9-10 .. .. £13

For another type of Kleonai, see below under Achaean League.

2808 **Epidauros** (famous as the chief seat of the worship of Asklepios, god of medicine and
healing. A magnificent temple dedicated to the god was situated five miles outside the
city). 350-330 B.C. *Æ drachm* (of Aiginetic weight, *c.* 5·5 gm.). Laur. hd. of Asklepios
r. ℞. Asklepios enthroned l., holding sceptre and extending r. hand over serpent coiled
before him; dog lying r. beneath throne; E in field to r. *Grose* 6882 .. .. £750

*This representation of the god appears to be an exact copy of the famous chryselephantine
statue of Asklepios by the sculptor Thrasymedes.*

2809   2813

2809 — — (of Attic weight, *c.* 4·3 gm.). Laur. hd. of Apollo r. ℞. As last, but also with
ΘE beneath throne. *B.M.C. 10.* 7 .. .. £650

2810 — *Æ triobol.* Laur. hd. of Asklepios l. ℞. EΠ monogram within laurel-wreath. *B.M.C.*
10. 1-2 .. .. £200

2811 — *Æ obol.* Laur. hd. of Apollo r. ℞. E within laurel-wreath. *B.M.C. 10.* 3-5 £120

2812 — *Æ tetartemorion* (¼ *obol*). Large E. ℞. Large Π. *B.M.C. 10.* 6 .. .. £65

2813 4th-3rd Cent. B.C. Æ 18. Laur. hd. of Asklepios r. ℞. Epione, wife of Asklepios,
stg. l., pouring from phiale into patera; to l., EΠ monogram; to r., NAK monogram. *B.M.C.*
10. 14-15 .. .. £15

2814 — Æ 17.   Similar.   ℞. Dog seated r.; ΕΠ monogram above.   *B.M.C. 10.* 25   £14

2815 — Æ 11.   Similar.   ℞. ε within laurel-wreath; Π beneath.   *B.M.C. 10.* 19-20   £9
    For other coins of Epidauros, see below under Achaean League.

2816 **Hermione** (situated on the southern coastline of Argolis, Hermione possessed a cele-
    brated temple of Demeter Chthonia). 350-330 B.C.   Æ *triobol.*   Hd. of Demeter l.,
    wreathed with corn.   ℞. EP monogram, within corn-wreath.   *B.M.C. 10.* 1-2   £150

2817 — Æ *obol.*   Similar, but the corn-wreath on *rev.* contains torch between ε — P.   *B.M.C.
    10.* 3 ..   ..   £100

2818 — Æ 15.   Hd. of Demeter three-quarter face to r., wreathed with corn.   ℞. EP mono-
    gram, within corn-wreath.   *B.M.C. 10.* 4-6   ..   ..   £13

2819 — Æ 13.   As 2817.   *B.M.C. 10.* 8   ..   ..   £10
    For other coins of Hermione, see below under Achaean League.

2816   2820

2820 **Methana** (situated in a volcanic region on a peninsula north of Troizen).   4th-3rd.
    Cent. B.C.   Æ 15.   Hd. of Hephaistos r., in conical pilos.   ℞. ME monogram, within
    corn-wreath.   *B.M.C. 10.* 1   ..   ..   £14

2821 221-203 B.C. (under the name of **Arsinoe**).   Æ 19.   Hd. of Arsinoe, wife of Ptolemy IV,
    r.   ℞. ΑΡΣΙ.   Naked warrior stg. r., holding spear and leaning on shield.   *Weber* 4245
                                                                            £16

2822 **Tiryns** (one of the most ancient cities of Greece and the home of Herakles, Tiryns was
    destroyed by Argos *c.* 468 B.C.   The refugees fled south and established themselves at
    Halice where the later coinage was struck, though still in the name of the old city).
    350-330 B.C.   Æ *triobol.*   Archaistic hd. of Hera r.   ℞. Harpa and club, within wreath.
    Grose 6906 ..   ..   £275

2823   2827   2829

2823 — Æ *obol.*   Bearded hd. of Herakles l., clad in lion's skin.   ℞. Club.   *Weber* 4246   £150

2824 — Æ 17.   *Obv.* Similar, but hd. r.   ℞. τ — ι either side of palm-tree; all within incuse
    with straight sides and curved ends.   *B.M.C. 10.* 1   ..   ..   ..   £16

2825 — Æ 13.   Laur. hd. of Apollo r.   ℞. ΤΙΡΥΝΘΙΩΝ.   Palm-tree.   *B.M.C. 10.* 5   £11

2826 **Troizen** (situated in the south-east of the country, Troizen was another city of very early
    foundation, said to have been named after a son of Pelops).   *Circa* 450 B.C.   Æ *obol*
    (of Attic weight, *c.* 0·65 gm.).   Female hd. facing, with long hair.   ℞. ΤΡΟ and trident-
    head, within incuse square.   *B.M.C. 10.* 1   ..   ..   £120

2827 *Circa* 400 B.C.   Æ *drachm* (of Attic weight, *c.* 4 gm.).   Hd. of Athena(?) l., hair bound
    with tainia.   ℞. Ornate trident-head, ΤΡΟ to r.; all within incuse square.   *B.M.C. 10.* 3
                                                                            £275

2828 350-330 B.C.   Æ *hemidrachm* (of Attic weight, *c.* 2 gm.).   *Obv.* Similar, but also wearing
    earring.   ℞. Ornate trident-head; ΤΡΟ to r., three dolphins in field.   *B.M.C. 10.* 5-7
                                                                            £125

2829 — Æ *diobol.*   *Obv.* As last.   ℞. Double trident-head between ΤΡΟ and vine-twig.
    B.M.C. 10. 8   ..   ..   £90

Troizen *continued*

2830 — Æ *obol.* Hd. of Athena(?) l., hair bound with tainia. R. Ornate trident-head;
TPO to l. *B.M.C. 10.* 10-11   ..   ..   £65

2831 4th-3rd Cent. B.C. Æ 17. Hd. of Athena r., in crested Corinthian helmet. R. TPO.
Ornate trident-head; KA — Λ in field. *B.M.C. 10.* 15 ..   ..   £12

2832 — — Bearded hd. of Poseidon l.; EY monogram behind. R. Ornate trident-head between TPO and aplustre. *B.M.C. 10.* 17 ..   ..   £11

2833   2834

2833 **LAKONIA** (comprising the south-eastern portion of the Peloponnese, Lakonia is a
mountainous country.   The river Eurotas divides the mountain ranges, and in its valley
was situated Sparta, the chief city of Lakonia).   **Sparta** (also called **Lakedaimon** — the
principal city of Peloponnesos, Sparta was the arch-enemy of Athens and was the main
beneficiary from the Athenian defeat in 404 B.C. which ended the Peloponnesian War.
Spartan supremacy in Greece ended in 371 B.C. with their defeat by the Thebans at
Leuktra).   First half of 3rd Cent B.C. Æ *tetradrachm* (of Attic weight, *c.* 16·9 gm.).
Diad. hd. of beardless King (Areus ?) l. R. Λ — A either side of archaic image of Apollo of
Amyklai r.; he wears helmet and holds spear and bow; goat r. at his side; wreath in field
to l. *B.M.C. 10.* 1   ..   ..   £3,500

2834 Second half of 3rd Cent. B.C. Æ *tetradrachm* (of Rhodian weight, *c.* 15·5 gm.). Hd. of
the Apollo of Amyklai(?) r., wearing crested Corinthian helmet. R. Λ — A either side of
naked Herakles seated l. on rock, holding club resting on ground before him. *Weber*
4142 ..   ..   £3,000

2835 — Æ *trihemiobol*(?). Bearded hd. of Herakles r., clad in lion's skin. R. Club between
the two stars of the Dioskouroi. *B.M.C. 10.* 2-3   ..   ..   £140

2836   2838

2836 192-146 B.C. Æ *tetrobol.* Diad. hd. of bearded Herakles r. R. Λ — A either side of
amphora between caps of the Dioskouroi; monogram and O in lower field to l., KH to r.; all
within wreath. *B.M.C. 10.* 11-12   ..   ..   £75

2837 *Bronze Coinage.* 3rd Cent. B.C. Æ 23. Eagle stg. l. on thunderbolt, wings closed.
R. Λ — A either side of winged thunderbolt. *B.M.C. 10.* 4-5 ..   ..   ..   £16

2838 2nd-1st Cent. B.C. Æ 23. ΛΥΚΟΥΡΓΟC. Bearded hd. of Lykourgos r. R. Λ — A either
side of club and caduceus combined; AΓ monogram in field to l., H to r.; all within wreath.
B.M.C. 10. 14   ..   ..   £14

2839 — Æ 20. Diad. hd. of Apollo(?) r. R. Λ — A either side of eagle stg. r.; AP monogram
in field to l., ΦΙ to r. *B.M.C. 10.* 26-7   ..   ..   £10

2840 — Æ 18. Jugate hds. of the Dioskouroi r. Ŗ. Λ — A either side of two amphorae; ΔE in field to l., ι to r.; all within wreath. *B.M.C. 10.* 39 .. .. .. £11

2841 — Æ 15. Laur. hd. of bearded Herakles r. Ŗ. Λ — A either side of club; Σ — ι in lower field; all within wreath. *B.M.C. 10.* 42 .. .. £9

2842 — Æ 13. Hd. of Athena r., in crested Corinthian helmet. Ŗ. Λ — A either side of owl stg. r.; ΑΡΓ monogram in field to r.; all within wreath. *B.M.C. 10.* 44-5 .. £8

For other coins of Sparta, see below under Achaean League.

2840   2844

2843 **ISLAND OFF LAKONIA: KYTHERA** (about ten miles off the south-east extremity of the mainland, Kythera was, in early times, colonized by Phoenicians who introduced the worship of Aphrodite). 3rd-2nd Cent. B.C. Æ 20. Diad. hd. of Aphrodite r. Ŗ. ΚΥ. Dove flying r., holding wreath in claws. *B.M.C. 10.* 1 .. .. £14

2844 — Æ 15. Hd. of Aphrodite l. Ŗ. ΚΥ (retrograde). Dove flying r. *B.M.C. 10.* 5
£11

2845 2nd-1st Cent. B.C. Æ 22. Diad. bust of Aphrodite r.; ΗΡΙ behind. Ŗ. ΚΥΘΗΡΙΩΝ. Dove stg. r. *B.M.C. 10.* 13 .. .. £13

2846   2848

2846 **MESSENIA** (comprising the south-west portion of the Peloponnese, Messenia was, for centuries, under the domination of Sparta, its eastern neighbour. The Messenians were eventually freed from serfdom when the Spartans were defeated at Leuktra in 371 B.C.). **Messene** (founded by Epaminondas in 369 B.C., Messene was a strongly fortified city built on the slopes of Mt. Ithome. It is said that it was completed within the space of eighty-five days). 369-350 B.C. Æ *stater* (of Aiginetic weight, *c.* 12·2 gm.). Hd. of Demeter l., of fine classical style, wreathed with corn. Ŗ. ΜΕΣΣΑΝΙΩΝ. Zeus Ithomates, naked, striding r., brandishing thunderbolt and holding eagle. *B.M.C. 10.* 1 .. .. £4,500

The obv. type is inspired by the Syracusan dekadrachms by Euainetos.

2847 — Æ *obol.* *Obv.* Similar. Ŗ. M̄Ε — Σ either side of tripod. *B.M.C. 10.* 2 .. £150

2848 3rd Cent. B.C. Æ *tetradrachm* (of Attic weight, *c.* 16·9 gm.). Hd. of Demeter r., of late style, wreathed with corn. Ŗ. ΜΕΣΣΑΝΙΩΝ behind Zeus Ithomates r., as 2846; ΣΩΣΙΚΡΑ and tripod in field to r. *B.M.C. 10.* 11 .. .. £2,500

2849 2nd Cent. B.C. (before 146). Æ *tetrobol.* Diad. hd. of Zeus r. Ŗ. M̄Ε — Σ either side of tripod; all within wreath. *B.M.C. 10.* 13-14 .. .. £75

2850   2853

Messene *continued*

2850 — — Similar, but also with magistrate's name ΑΠ — ΟΛ / ΛΩ — ΝΙ / ΔΑ — Σ in *rev.* field.
B.M.C. 10. 17 .. ..   £75

2851 *Bronze Coinage.* 4th-3rd Cent. B.C. Æ 17. *Obv.* Similar to 2846. ℞. Large ME.
B.M.C. 10. 6 .. ..   £14

2852 — Æ 14. — ℞. M — E either side of tripod. B.M.C. 10. 4 .. .. ..   £11

2853 3rd-2nd Cent. B.C. Æ 23. Hd. of Demeter r., diad. and wreathed with corn. ℞.
Zeus Ithomates r., as 2846; before, M̄E and tripod; behind, ΔΑΜΙΩΝ and wreath. B.M.C.
10. 29-31 .. ..   £14

2854 — Æ 18. *Obv.* Similar. ℞. M̄E to r. of bunch of grapes on stalk; in field to r., ΔΙ
within wreath. B.M.C. 10. 39-40 .. ..   £10

For other coins of Messene, see below under Achaean League.

2855 **Korone** (situated on the western shores of the Messenian gulf, Korone was founded
c. 371 B.C., deriving its name from Koroneia in Boeotia). Before 184 B.C. Æ *tetrobol.*
Hd. of Athena r., in crested Corinthian helmet. ℞. K — OP either side of bunch of grapes;
all within ivy-wreath. B.M.C. 10. 1-2 .. ..   £110

2856 — Æ 20. *Obv.* Similar. ℞. ΚΟΡΩΝΑΙΩΝ. Bunch of grapes; OIT beneath. B.M.C. 10. 6
£15

For other coins of Korone, see below under Achaean League.

2857 **Thuria.** 2nd Cent. B.C. Æ 23. Diad. hd. of Zeus r. ℞. Athena stg. l., holding spear
and shield; to r., ΘΟΥ and wreath; to l., ΝΙΚΩΝΥΜΟΣ. B.M.C. 10. 2-3 .. ..   £16

2858 — Æ 11. Hd. of Athena r., in crested Corinthian helmet. ℞. ΘΟΥ within corn-wreath.
B.M.C. 10. 1 .. ..   £12

2859   2860

2859 **ELIS** (a fertile country in the north-west of the Peloponnese, Elis possessed the famous
festival centre of Olympia where the Greeks celebrated the Olympic Games every four
years.   The coinage in the name of the Eleans was issued not from the city of Elis itself,
but from the festival centre, in connection with each Olympic gathering. **Olympia.**
471-452 B.C. Æ *stater.* Eagle flying r., serpent entwined round body and held in beak.
℞. F — A either side of winged thunderbolt; all within circular incuse. *Seltman (The
Temple Coins of Olympia)* 2. B.M.C. 10. 3 .. ..   £1,250

2860 — — ϜΑΛΕΙΟΝ (retrograde). Eagle flying l., its wings inclined slightly forward; serpent
entwined, as last. ℞. F — A either side of archaic Nike running r., holding wreath; all
within circular incuse. *Seltman* 34. B.M.C. 10. 5 .. ..   £1,000

2861 — — *Obv.* Similar. ℞. ΟΛΥΝΠΙΚΟΝ (retrograde). Naked Zeus striding r., brandishing thunderbolt and holding eagle; all within incuse square. *Seltman* 37 ..   ..   £4,500

2862 — *Æ drachm.* Similar to 2859, but eagle flying l. on *obv.* *Seltman, pl. VIII,* 3   £350

2863 — *Æ hemidrachm.* As last. *B.M.C. 10.* 2   ..   ..   £150

2864 — *Æ obol.* Similar to 2859, but F — A retrograde on *rev.* *B.M.C. 10.* 4   ..   £100

2865   2866

2865 452-432 B.C. *Æ stater.* Eagle flying r., holding hare in talons. ℞. F — A / Λ — E (partly retrograde) in the corners of incuse square containing Nike seated l. on square base; her r. hand is extended and rests on lion's head fountain. *Seltman* 86. *B.M.C. 10.* 17   ..   ..   £1,500

2866 — — Zeus seated l. on rock, eagle alighting on extended r. hand, sceptre resting against r. shoulder. ℞. Eagle flying l., contending with serpent; FAΛ (partly retrograde) in field; all within incuse square. *Seltman* 101. *B.M.C. 10.* 13   ..   ..   ..   £2,000

2867   2871

2867 — *Æ hemidrachm.* FAΛEI before eagle flying l. ℞. F — A (retrograde) either side of Nike running r.; all within circular incuse. *B.M.C. 10.* 7   ..   ..   ..   £225

2868 — *Æ obol.* Eagle r., wings spread, attacking hare held in talons. ℞. F — A either side of winged thunderbolt; all within incuse square. *B.M.C. 10.* 21   ..   ..   £100

2869 432-421 B.C. *Æ stater.* *Obv.* Similar. ℞. F — A either side of Nike seated l. on steps, holding palm-branch; olive-spray in ex. *Seltman* 133. *B.M.C. 10.* 52   ..   £1,750

2870 — *Æ hemidrachm.* Eagle r., wings spread, looking back. ℞. F — A either side of winged thunderbolt; all within circular incuse. *B.M.C. 10.* 23-4   ..   ..   £150

2871 421-365 B.C. *Æ stater.* Laur. hd. of Zeus r., with short curly hair. ℞. F — A either side of winged thunderbolt; all within olive-wreath. *Seltman* 147. *B.M.C. 10.* 54 £5,000

     This head is thought to represent that of the celebrated chryselephantine statue in the temple of Zeus at Olympia — the work of the sculptor Pheidias.

2872 — — Large hd. of eagle l.; ivy-leaf beneath. ℞. As last. *Seltman* 154. *B.M.C. 10.* 40   £2,000

 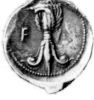  

2873   2874

Olympia *continued*

2873 — — Eagle stg. l., wings closed, attacking ram held in its talons; all on circular shield with raised rim. ℞. F — A (the latter incuse) either side of thunderbolt with furled wings. *Seltman* 171. *B.M.C. 10.* 36 .. .. £750

2874 — — Hd. of Hera r., wearing stephanos adorned with palmettes and lilies. ℞. F — A either side of thunderbolt; all within olive-wreath. *Seltman* 264. *B.M.C. 10.* 55 £300

Seltman suggests that the 'Hera' and Zeus' series were issued quite independently from mints situated within the temple precincts of the two deities. The 'Hera' coins with thunderbolt reverse were produced before circa 385 *B.C.*

2875 — — Hd. of Hera r., wearing stephanos adorned with palmettes and inscribed HPA; in field, F — A. ℞. Eagle stg. l., looking back, wings open; all within olive-wreath. *Seltman* 301. *B.M.C. 10.* 90 .. .. £650

The eagle reverse superseded the thunderbolt on the 'Hera' coinage circa 385 *B.C.*

2876   2878

2876 — Æ *drachm.* Large hd. of eagle r.; lizard r. beneath. ℞. F — A either side of thunderbolt; olive-leaves in field to l. and to r. *B.M.C. 10.* 43 .. .. £750

2877 — — Similar to 2875, but without olive-wreath on *rev.* *B.M.C. 10.* 91 .. £250

2878 — Æ *hemidrachm.* Eagle r., wings closed, attacking hare held in talons. ℞. F — A either side of winged thunderbolt. *B.M.C. 10.* 30 .. .. £150

2879 — — *Obv.* Similar to 2875, but without F — A in field. ℞. F — A either side of thunderbolt. *B.M.C. 10.* 69 .. .. £125

2880 — Æ *obol.* Large hd. of eagle r. ℞. As last. *B.M.C. 10.* 49 .. .. £140

2881 — — Hd. of Hera r., wearing stephane; F — A in field. ℞. Eagle's hd. and neck r., within olive-wreath. *B.M.C. 10.* 100 .. .. £175

2882 — Æ *hemiobol.* Hd. of Hera r., hair rolled; F — A in field. ℞. F — A either side of winged thunderbolt. *B.M.C. 10.* 80 .. .. £75

2883 — Æ *tetartemorion* (¼ *obol*). Large eagle's hd. l.; F / A above and below. ℞. F and olive-spray; all within incuse square. *B.M.C. 10.* 51 .. .. £90

2884   2887

2884 363-323 B.C.   Æ *stater*. ΦΑΛΕΙΩΝ before laur. hd. of Zeus l.   R. ΟΛΥΜΠΙΑ before hd. of
Olympia r., hair in sphendone. *Seltman* 175. *B.M.C. 10*. 71-2   ..   ..   £4,000

2885 — — *Obv*. Same.   R. Eagle r., wings closed, seated on Ionic capital. *Seltman* 176.
B.M.C. 10. 73-4   ..   ..   £3,500

2886 — — Laur. hd. of Zeus r.   R. Eagle r., wings closed, seated on ram's hd. r.; in field,
F — A / A — P.   *Seltman* 195.   *B.M.C. 10*. 122 ..   ..   £1,500

2887 — — Hd. of Olympia r., hair in sphendone; F — A in field.   R. Eagle stg. l., looking
back, wings closed; all within olive-wreath. *Seltman* 306. *B.M.C. 10*. 75   ..   £2,500

2888 — — Hd. of Hera l., wearing stephanos adorned with palmettes; F — A in field.   R.
Similar to last, but eagle not looking back. *Seltman* 339. *B.M.C. 10*. 113   ..   £1,250

2889   2892

2889 — — Hd. of Hera r., wearing stephanos inscribed ΦΑΛΕΙΩΝ.   R. Eagle l., looking back,
wings open; stg. on oval shield(?); all within olive-wreath. *Seltman* 350. *B.M.C. 10*. 101
                                              £850

2890 — Æ *hemidrachm*. Laur. hd. of Zeus l.   R. F — A either side of eagle stg. r. on shield(?),
wings closed; serpent in field to r. *Seltman, pl. VIII*, 29   ..   ..   ..   £200

2891 — Æ *obol*. Hd. of Hera r., wearing stephanos inscribed ΦΑ.   R. Eagle stg. r., wings
closed; F in field to r. *B.M.C. 10*. 111   ..   ..   £100

2892 — Æ *tritartemorion* (¾ *obol*). Hd. of Zeus r., bound with tainia.   R. Three τ's arranged
star-wise, F — A — Λ in the angles. *B.M.C. 10*. 81   ..   ..   ..   £90

2893 — Æ *tetartemorion* (¼ *obol*). Hd. of Olympia r., hair in sphendone.   R. F — A either
side of large τ. *Seltman, pl. VIII*, 24   ..   ..   £75

2894   2896

2894 323-271 B.C.   Æ *stater*. Laur. hd. of Zeus r.   R. Eagle stg. r., wings closed; F — A in
upper field; Α — ΠΙ in lower field; thunderbolt to l.; wreath to r. *Seltman* 216. *B.M.C.
10*. 120   ..   ..   £1,250

2895 — Æ *hemidrachm*. *Obv*. Similar.   R. F — A either side of eagle seated r. on Ionic capital;
Α in field to r. *Seltman, pl. VIII*, 30   ..   ..   £150

2896 271-191 B.C.   Æ *stater*. Laur. hd. of Zeus r.   R. Eagle stg. r., wings closed; F — A in
upper field; serpent and ΔΙ to r. *Seltman* 231. *B.M.C. 10*. 131   ..   ..   £900

Olympia *continued*

2897 — Æ *hemidrachm.* Laur. hd. of Zeus r. R. F — A / A — PI either side of thunderbolt; all within olive-wreath. *B.M.C. 10.* 125.. .. .. £75

2898 After 191 B.C. Æ *stater.* Laur. hd. of Zeus r., of coarse style. R. Eagle stg. r., wings closed; F — A / A — PI in upper field; thunderbolt to r. *Seltman* 240. *Weber* 4060 £750

2899 2905 2907

2899 — Æ *drachm.* Eagle r., wings spread, attacking hare held in talons; Σ in lower field to l. R. Winged thunderbolt; F — A / Σ — Ω in field; wreath to r. *B.M.C. 10.* 136 £140

2900 — Æ *hemidrachm.* *Obv.* As 2898. R. Eagle stg. r. on capital; F — A in upper field; ΣΩ to l. *B.M.C. 10.* 137 .. .. £85

2901 *Bronze Coinage.* 343-323 B.C. Æ 20. Laur. hd. of Zeus l. R. F — A either side of eagle stg. l., looking back, wings spread. *B.M.C. 10.* 115 .. .. .. £15

2902 3rd-2nd Cent. B.C. Æ 19. Laur. hd. of Zeus r. R. Horse pacing r.; FA beneath, AP above. *B.M.C. 10.* 129 .. .. £14

2903 — — Similar, but horse galloping. *B.M.C. 10.* 130 .. .. £14

2904 — — *Obv.* Similar. R. F — A either side of eagle stg. r., wings spread; serpent before; ΚΑΛ in field to l. *B.M.C. 10.* 141 .. .. £12

2905 2nd-1st Cent. B.C. Æ 18. Laur. hd. of Zeus r. R. FA / ΛΕΙ / ΩΝ within olive-wreath. *B.M.C. 10.* 150 .. .. £9

For other coins in the name of the Eleans, see below under Achaean League. These issues, however, were probably minted at the city of Elis rather than at Olympia.

2906 **Pisa** (the ancient city of Pisa, close to Olympia, had been destroyed by the Eleans early in the 6th Cent. When the Arkadians seized Olympia in 365 B.C. they revived the Pisatan state and gave it presidency over the Olympic Games of 364 B.C. The following year the Eleans regained control of Olympia, and Pisa lapsed back into obscurity). 365-363 B.C. N *trihemiobol* (*c.* 1·56 gm.). Laur. hd. of Zeus l. R. Three half-thunderbolts; Π — ΙΣ in the angles. *Seltman* 173 .. .. (*Unique*)

2907 — N *obol* (*c.* 1·04 gm.). *Obv.* Similar. R. ΠΙ — ΣΑ either side of thunderbolt. *Seltman* 174. *B.M.C. 10.* 1 .. .. (*Unique*)

2908 **ZAKYNTHOS.** 420-350 B.C. Æ *stater.* Laur. hd. of Apollo r. R. Tripod; ΙΑ to l., cock's hd. to r. *B.M.C. 10.* 11 .. .. £1,500

2909 — — *Obv.* Similar. R. ΙΑΚΥΝΘΟΣ. The hero Zakynthos, naked, seated r., playing lyre; Ξ to r. *B.M.C. 10.* 19 .. .. £3,500

2910 2911

2910 — — *Obv.* Similar, but Apollo's hair long, down back of neck. R. ΙΑΚΥΝΘΙΩΝ. Infant Iamos, son of Apollo, naked, kneeling r. between two serpents; he holds the one to r., and raises it to his lips. *B.M.C. 10.* 22 .. .. £6,500

2911 — — *Obv.* As last. R. ΔΙΩ / ΝΟΣ either side of tripod; beneath, between legs, Ι — A. *B.M.C. 10.* 33 .. .. £1,500

2912 — Æ *third-stater*. Laur. hd. of Apollo r. Ṛ. ɪ — ᴀ either side of tripod; all within laurel-wreath. *B.M.C. 10.* 26-7 ..   ..   £300

2913 — Æ *sixth-stater*. Laur. hd. of Apollo l. Ṛ. ɪ — ᴀ either side of tripod. *B.M.C. 10.* 13-14   ..   ..   £125

2914 — Æ *eighteenth-stater*. Laur. hd. of Apollo r. Ṛ. ɪᴀ. Two laurel-leaves. *B.M.C. 10.* 16 ..   ..   £90

2915 — Æ *thirty-sixth stater*. Laur. hd. of Apollo r. Ṛ. ɪᴀ / ʜ beneath and above laurel-leaf. *B.M.C. 10.* 18   ..   ..   £75

2915ᴀ 4th-3rd Cent. B.C. Æ *diobol*? (c. 1·2 gm.). Forepart of Pegasos l., with curled wing; ɪ beneath. Ṛ. Hd. of Aphrodite l. *B.M.C. 10.* 50   ..   ..   ..   £110

2916 3rd-2nd Cent. B.C. Æ *hemidrachm* (Attic weight, c. 2·1 gm.). Hd. of young Dionysos r., wreathed with vine. Ṛ. ɪᴀ above large crescent; trident in lower field to l. *B.M.C. 10.* 60
£120

2917 *Bronze Coinage*. 4th-3rd Cent. B.C. Æ 15. Lyre. Ṛ. ɪ — ᴀ either side of tripod. *B.M.C. 10.* 29   ..   ..   £12

2918 — — Laur. hd. of Apollo l. Ṛ. ɪ — ᴀ / ᴧ — ɪ within large ɪ. *B.M.C. 10.* 34-5   £10

2919 3rd-2nd Cent. B.C. Æ 15. Laur. hd. of Apollo r. Ṛ. ᴀ — ɪ either side of tripod; all within wreath. *B.M.C. 10.* 42 ..   ..   £8

2920 — — Similar. Ṛ. Forepart of Pegasos r., with curled wing; ɪᴀ beneath. *B.M.C. 10.* 52
£9

2921 — — Hd. of Artemis r., quiver at shoulder. Ṛ. ɪ — ᴀ either side of quiver; star to r.; all within wreath. *B.M.C. 10.* 72-3   ..   ..   £8

2922 2nd-1st Cent. B.C. Æ 19. Laur. hd. of Apollo r., hair in formal curls. Ṛ. ᴢ — ᴀ either side of tripod; all within wreath. *B.M.C. 10.* 77   ..   ..   £9

2923 **KEPHALLENIA. Kranion.** *Circa* 450 B.C. Æ *tetrobol*. Archaic female bust (Prokris ?) l., wearing stephane. Ṛ. Ram's hd. l., within incuse square. *B.M.C. 10.* 13
£225

2924 *Circa* 400 B.C. Æ *obol*. Ram's hd. r., ᴋ beneath. Ṛ. ᴋᴘᴀ. Ram's hoof r. *B.M.C. 10.* 15 ..   ..   £110

2925 — Æ *tritartemorion* (¾ *obol*). Gorgoneion. Ṛ. Three ᴛ's arranged star-wise; ᴋ — ᴘ — ᴀ in the angles. *B.M.C. 10.* 16   ..   ..   £100

2926 — Æ *hemiobol*. Ram's hd. r., ᴋ beneath. Ṛ. ᴋᴘᴀ. Large ʜ; ivy-leaf in field to l. *B.M.C. 10.* 17   ..   ..   £75

2927 *Circa* 350 B.C. Æ *obol*. Ram's hd. r. Ṛ. ᴋᴘᴀ. Ram's hoof r. *B.M.C. 10.* 32-6   £90

2928 *Bronze Coinage*. 4th-3rd Cent. B.C. Æ 17. Ram stg. l. Ṛ. Bow, within oblong-shaped incuse. *B.M.C. 10.* 18 ..   ..   £12

2929 — Æ 14. Crested helmet r. Ṛ. ᴋ in incuse square; all within linear circle. *B.M.C. 10.* 24-5 ..   ..   £13

270 PELOPONNESOS

Kranion *continued*

2930 — Æ 12. Ram's hd. l. R. KPA (retrograde). Ram's hoof r. *B.M.C. 10.* 37 £9

2931 — Æ 18. Kephalos, naked, stg. r., r. hand on hip, holding spear in l. R. Large KPA monogram. *B.M.C. 10.* 42-3 .. .. £11

2932

2934

2932 — Æ 19. Bull's hd. facing. R. Large X. *B.M.C. 10.* 48-9 .. .. .. £10

2933 — Æ 17. Ram stg. l. R. Large H; K above. *B.M.C. 10.* 57-8 .. .. £11

2934 **Pale** (situated in the south of Kephallenia, opposite Zakynthos). *Circa* 450 B.C. R *triobol.* Ram stg. l., Π before. R. Pine-cone between two leaves; all within incuse square. *B.M.C. 10.* 1 .. .. £175

2935 400-350 B.C. R *tetrobol.* Bare hd. of the hero Kephalos r.; Π — A in field. R. ΚΕΦΑΛΟΣ. Naked Kephalos seated r. on rock, holding spear. *B.M.C. 10.* 2-3 .. .. £200

2936 — — Hd. of Persephone (or Prokris ?) l., wreathed with corn; Π — A in field. R. Similar to last, but Kephalos is seated to l. *B.M.C. 10.* 8-10 .. .. £150

2937

2939

2937 — R *triobol.* Ear of corn; Π — A in field. R. Rudder between dolphin and spear-head. *B.M.C. 10.* 19-20 .. .. £140

2938 — R *diobol.* Similar to 2935, but without letters in *obv.* field. *B.M.C. 10.* 5-6 £110

2939 4th-3rd Cent. B.C. Æ 20. Hd. of Athena three-quarter face to r., wearing triple-crested helmet; Π — A in field. R. ΠΑ within laurel-wreath. *B.M.C. 10.* 24.. £16

2940 — Æ 17. Female hd. (Prokris ?) r., hair rolled; Π — A in field. R. Naked Kephalos seated l. on rock, holding spear. *B.M.C. 10.* 21-2 .. .. £13

2941 — — Hd. of Persephone l., wreathed with corn. R. ΠΑ monogram. *B.M.C. 10.* 27-31 £11

2942 — — Barleycorn within large letter Π. R. Dolphin r. above waves. *B.M.C. 10.* 37 £12

2943

2946

2943 **Pronnoi** (situated in the south-east of the island). *Circa* 370 B.C. R *triobol.* Bare hd. of the hero Kephalos l. R. ΠΡΩΝ / ΝΩΝ above and beneath club l. *B.M.C. 10.* 1-2 £175

2944 — R *trihemiobol.* Hd. of Prokris(?) l., hair rolled. R. Barleycorn within large ΠΡ monogram. *B.M.C. 10.* 3 .. .. £125

2945 — Æ 17. Laur. hd. of Zeus l. R. Π — P either side of pine-cone. *B.M.C. 10.* 7 £17

2946 Same (on the east coast of Kephallenia, opposite the island of Ithaka). *Circa* 400 B.C. Æ *tetrobol.* Laur. hd. of Kephalos l. ℞. ΣΑΜΑΙΩΝ. The hound, Lailaps, stg. r. *B.M.C. 10.* 1 ..   ..   £275

2947 — Æ *diobol.* Similar, but the hound's hd. is lowered. *B.M.C. 10.* 2   ..   £150

2948   2951

2948 370-350 B.C. Æ *triobol.* Hd. of Athena facing, in triple-crested helmet. ℞. ΣΑΜΑΙΩΝ. Ram stg. r. *B.M.C. 10.* 3-4   ..   ..   £175

2949 — Æ *obol.* Laur. hd. of Prokris(?) r. ℞. ΣΑ. The hound, Lailaps, stg. l. *B.M.C. 10.* 8 ..   ..   £110

2950 4th-3rd Cent. B.C. Æ 19. Similar to 2948, but hd. of Athena is three-quarter face to r. *B.M.C. 10.* 9   ..   ..   £13

2951 — Æ 17. Hd. of Kephalos r., bound with tainia. ℞. ΣΑΜΑΙΩΝ. The hound, Lailaps, seated r.; spear-head before. *B.M.C. 10.* 25-9 ..   ..   £13

2952 ITHAKA (a small island between Kephallenia and the Greek mainland, Ithaka was celebrated as the birthplace of Ulysses). 4th-3rd Cent. B.C. Æ 20. Hd. of Athena l., in Corinthian helmet. ℞. ΙΘΑ. Bearded hd. of Odysseos l., wearing conical pilos. *B.M.C. 10.* 1   ..   ..   £17

2953 — Æ 17. ΙΘΑ. Bearded hd. of Odysseos r., wearing conical pilos. ℞. Thunderbolt, within olive-wreath. *B.M.C. 10.* 7-9   ..   ..   £15

2954 — — Hd. of Athena r., in Corinthian helmet. ℞. ΙΘΑΚΩΝ. Odysseos stg. facing, holding spear. *B.M.C. 10.* 10-12..   ..   ..   £12

2955 — — Hd. of Odysseos, as 2953, but without legend. ℞. ΙΘΑ / ΚΩΝ either side of cock stg. r.; ΚΑ monogram before. *B.M.C. 10.* 18-21   ..   ..   ..   £14

2953   2956   2958

2956 ACHAIA (the northern coastal strip of the Peloponnese, Achaia was named after the Achaei, who took possession of the country about a century after the Trojan war. The Achaean League was formed in the early part of the 3rd Cent. B.C. to counter the influence of the Macedonian Kings). **Aigai** (situated on the river Krathis, Aigai was a town of very early foundation and possessed a celebrated temple of Poseidon). *Circa* 450 B.C. Æ *triobol.* ΑΙΓ (retrograde). Forepart of goat l. ℞. ΑΙΓΑΙΟΝ (retrograde). Bearded hd. of Dionysos r., wreathed with ivy; all within incuse square. *B.M.C. 10.* 1   £350

2957 *Circa* 370 B.C. Æ *triobol.* ΑΙΓ. Forepart of goat r. ℞. ΑΙΓΑΙΟΝ. Bearded hd. of Dionysos, of fine style, r., wreathed ith ivy. *B.M.C. 10.* 4   ..   ..   £225

2958 Aigeira (situated east of Aigai, Aigeira was built on a steep hillside. It received the former inhabitants of Aigai when their town was destroyed in the first half of the 4th Cent.). 4th-3rd Cent. B.C. Æ 14. Hd. of Athena r., in crested helmet. ℞. ΑΙΓΙ. Forepart of goat r.; all within wreath. *B.M.C. 10.* 1 ..   ..   £15

For later coins of Aigeira, see below under Achaean League.

2959   2961

Kranion *continued*

2959 **Aigion** (following the destruction of Helike in 373 B.C., Aigion became the capital of Achaia). After 146 B.C. Æ 23. ΑΙΓΙΕΩΝ. Laur. hd. of Zeus r. ℞. ΚΛΗΤΑΙΟΣ ΘΕΟΞΙΟΣ. The boy Zeus, naked, walking r., brandishing thunderbolt and holding eagle. *B.M.C. 10.* 4-5 .. .. £18
   For earlier coins of Aigion, see below under Achaean League.

2960 **Dyme** (in the far west of the country, near the entrance to the Corinthian Gulf). *Circa* 350 B.C. Æ *obol.* ΔΥ. Female hd. r., hair rolled. ℞. Amphora. *Hist. Num., p.* 414
                                                                                          £200

2961 — Æ 17. *Obv.* Similar, but no legend. ℞. ΔΥΜΑ. Flat-fish r. *B.M.C. 10.* 1   £17
   For later coins of Dyme, see below under Achaean League.

2962 **Patrai** (one of the principal ports on the Corinthian Gulf, Patrai originally bore the name Aroe). 146-32 B.C. Æ *triobol* (c. 2·33 gm.). Laur. hd. of Zeus r. ℞. ΑΓΥϹ / ΑΙ — ϹΧΡΙ / ωΝΟϹ in three lines, with ΠΑ monogram at centre; all within wreath. *B.M.C. 10.* 1 .. .. £65

2963   2966

2963 — — Diad. hd. of Aphrodite r. ℞. ΔΑ / ΜΑϹΙΑϹ in two lines above ΠΑΤΡΕ monogram; all within wreath. *B.M.C. 10.* 2-3 .. .. £50

2964 — Æ 22. Bearded hd. of Herakles r., wearing tainia. ℞. ΜΗΤΡΟΔωΡΟϹ ΜΕΝΕΚΛΕΟϹ ΠΑΤΡΕωΝ. Athena advancing r., with spear and shield; ΠΑΤΡΕ monogram to l., owl to r. *B.M.C. 10.* 8-11 .. .. £12

2965 — Æ 19. Bust of Athena r., in crested Corinthian helmet. ℞. ΛΥΚωΝ ΔΑΜΟΤΙΜΟΥ ΠΑΤΡΕωΝ. Poseidon advancing r., brandishing trident and holding dolphin; ΠΑΤΡΕ monogram to l. *B.M.C. 10.* 6 .. .. £12
   For earlier coins of Patrai, see below under Achaean League.

2966 **Pellene** (in the eastern part of Achaia, not far from Sikyon, Pellene was a strongly fortified town. It receives mention in Homer). 370-350 B.C. Æ *triobol.* Laur. hd. of Apollo r.; ΠΕ monogram behind. ℞. ΠΕΛ within laurel-wreath. *B.M.C. 10.* 3-4   £125

2967 — Æ 17. Laur. hd. of Apollo l. ℞. ΠΕ monogram above ram's hd. r.; all within laurel-wreath. *B.M.C. 10.* 8 .. .. £12
   For later coins of Pellene, see below under Achaean League.

2968 **ACHAEAN LEAGUE** (the original Confederacy would seem to date from the decade following the downfall of Sparta in 371 B.C. About 280 B.C. the League was reconstituted, though it appears not to have played a significant role in Greek politics for many years. Many Peloponnesian cities outside the borders of Achaia eventually became members of the League, and in the 2nd Century B.C., after the eclipse of Macedonian power, the Achaean League was the foremost state in Greece. In 146 B.C. war was declared on the Romans, resulting in the total destruction of the League and the sack of Corinth, its chief city). 370-360 B.C. Æ *stater.* Hd. of Artemis (?) l., hair elaborately rolled and tied in knot on top. ℞. ΑΧΑΙΩΝ. Zeus enthroned l., holding eagle on outstretched r. hand, and sceptre in l.; crested helmet in field to l. *Hist. Num., p.* 416 .. .. (*Unique*)

2968   2970

2969 — Æ *hemidrachm.* *Obv.* Similar. Ɍ. ΑΧΑΙΩΝ. Athena charging r., with spear and
shield. *B.M.C. 7. (Thessaly), p.* 48, 1 ..   ..   £750

2970 Late 3rd Cent. B.C. Æ *hemidrachm.* Laur. hd. of Zeus r. Ɍ. Large AX monogram
within laurel-wreath. *Clerk (Catalogue of the Coins of the Achaean League)* 1 / 1   £125

2971   2973

2971 196-146 B.C. (much of the vast later silver coinage of the Achaean League was thought to
have been produced in the 3rd Cent. B.C., in the years following the League's reconstitution
in 280.   However, hoard evidence strongly suggests a 2nd Century date for the entire
series, excepting no. 2970 above, commencing, perhaps, after Flamininus' proclamation of
the 'Freedom of Greece' in 196 B.C.). Æ *hemidrachm* of *Aigeira (Achaia).* Laur. hd. of
Zeus r. Ɍ. Large AX monogram; in field, A — Λ / K — I; above, forepart of goat r.; all
within laurel-wreath. *B.M.C. 10.* 13. *Clerk* 17 / 5 ..   ..   ..   £30

2972 — — of *Aigion (Achaia).* Similar, but with AI / O — TEI above and on either side of AX
monogram, and with thunderbolt below. *B.M.C. 10.* 22-3. *Clerk* 30/2   ..   £30

2973 — — — Similar, but with ΑΙΓΕΩΙΝ behind hd. of Zeus, and with ΑΡΙ / CTO — ΔΑ / ΜΟC
above, either side and below AX monogram. *B.M.C. 10.* 24-5. *Clerk* 44/16 ..   £35

2974 — — of *Dyme (Achaia).* Laur. hd. of Zeus r. Ɍ. Large AX monogram; above, ΔΥ;
to l., ANT monogram; below, fish r.; all within laurel-wreath. *B.M.C. 10.* 29. *Clerk* 55/4
£35

2975 — — of *Patrai (Achaia).* Similar, but with TAY monogram in *rev.* field to r. and trident
l. below the AX monogram. *B.M.C. 10.* 26. *Clerk* 49/4 *(attributed to Keryneia)*   £32

2976 — — — Similar, but with ΕΥ above AX monogram, A — ΠA on either side, and dolphin r.
below. *B.M.C. 10.* 41. *Clerk* 70/8 ..   ..   £30

2977 — — of *Pellene (Achaia).* Similar, but with ΠΕ monogram above AX monogram,
ΑΘ — ΦΙ on either side, and vase below. *Clerk* 90/4 ..   ..   £45

2978 — — of *Megara (Megaris).* Similar, but with lyre above AX monogram, and ΔΩ — PO
on either side. *B.M.C. 10.* 7-8. *Clerk* 120/3 ..   ..   £30

2979 — — of *Corinth.* Laur. hd. of Zeus l. Ɍ. Pegasos flying r.; below, ΑΠΩ monogram
and koppa above larger AX monogram; all within laurel-wreath. *B.M.C. 10.* 28. *Clerk*
112/2   ..   ..   £50

Achaean League *continued*

2980 — — — Laur. hd. of Zeus r. ℞. Large AX monogram; koppa to l., ΠΑΡΩ monogram below; all within laurel-wreath. *Clerk* 115/5 .. .. £40

2981 — — of *Sikyon*. Similar, but with ME monogram above AX monogram, N — I on either side, and dove flying r. below. *B.M.C. 10*. 44. *Clerk* 102/12 .. .. .. £38

2982   2985   2987

2982 — — of *Argos*. Similar, but with AKT monogram above AX monogram, and wolf's hd. r. below. *B.M.C. 10*. 87. *Clerk* 139/3 .. .. £35

2983 — — — Similar, but with I — Ω either side of AX monogram, and harpa below. *B.M.C. 10*. 89. *Clerk* 148/12 .. .. £35

2984 — — — Similar, but with club above AX monogram, and AKT monogram in field to r. *B.M.C. 10*. 90. *Clerk* 143/7 .. .. £35

2985 — — of *Epidauros (Argolis)*. Laur. hd. of Zeus r. ℞. Large AX monogram; above, coiled snake; in field, N — I; below, KO; all within laurel-wreath. *B.M.C. 10*. 92. *Clerk* 155/4 .. .. £38

2986 — — — Similar, but with cupping-vase above AX monogram, P — Ω in field, and IA below. *B.M.C. 10*. 95. *Clerk* 168/17 .. .. £38

2987 — — of *Sparta / Lakedaimon*. Laur. hd. of Zeus r. ℞. Large AX monogram between caps of the Dioskouroi; above, AΦ monogram; below, AYT monogram; all within laurel-wreath. *B.M.C. 10*. 84. *Clerk* 317/4 .. .. £40

2988 — — — Similar, with caps of the Dioskouroi, but with ΛΑ above AX monogram, and ME monogram and club below. *Clerk* 325/12 .. .. £40

2989 — — of *Messene*. Laur. hd. of Zeus l. ℞. Large AX monogram between N — Φ; below, M; all within laurel-wreath. *Clerk* 216/13 (*attributed to Megalopolis*) .. £35

2990   2993

2990 — — — Laur. hd. of Zeus r. ℞. Large AX monogram, M — E — Σ to l., above and to r.; all within laurel-wreath. *B.M.C. 10*. 77. *Clerk* 313/20 .. .. .. £35

2991 — — of *Korone (Messenia)*. Laur. hd. of Zeus l. ℞. Large AX monogram between Ξ — E; below, KO; all within laurel-wreath. *Clerk* 312/19 (*attributed to Messene*) £45

2992 — — of *Elis*. Laur. hd. of Zeus r. ℞. Large AX monogram; above, ΧΑΠ monogram; to l., FA; to r., TYP monogram; below, thunderbolt; all within laurel-wreath. *B.M.C. 10*. 62-3. *Clerk* 252/24 .. .. £30

2993 — — — Similar, but with F — A either side of AX monogram, and ΛY above (nothing below). *B.M.C. 10*. 53-4. *Clerk* 280/52 .. .. £30

2994 — — — Laur. hd. of Zeus r., ΘΡΑCΥΛΕωΝ behind. ℞. Large AX monogram; ANT monogram above; FA monogram to l.; XE monogram to r.; thunderbolt below; all within laurel-wreath. *B.M.C. 10*. 70. *Clerk* 272/44 .. .. £35

2995 — — of *Kaphyai (Arkadia)*. Laur. hd. of Zeus r. R. Large AX monogram between K — A; below, helmeted hd. of Athena r. and MAX monogram; all within laurel-wreath. *B.M.C. 10.* 109.   *Clerk* 176/3   ..   ..   £40

2996 — — of *Kleitor (Arkadia)*. Similar, but with facing hd. of Helios above AX monogram, KΛ — H on either side, and EΠΙ monogram below.   *Clerk* 179/1..   ..   ..   £50

2997   2998

2997 — — of *Lusi (Arkadia)*. *Obv.* Similar. R. Large AX monogram, ΛΟΥ beneath; all within laurel-wreath.   *Clerk* 183/1   ..   ..   £75

2998 — — of *Antigoneia*, formerly *Mantineia (Arkadia)*. Laur. hd. of Zeus r. R. Large AX monogram between A — N; below, EY; all within laurel-wreath. *B.M.C. 10.* 100-01. *Clerk* 192/1 ..   ..   £30

2999 — — of *Megalopolis (Arkadia)*. Similar, but with K — Δ either side of AX monogram, pedum above, and M below.   *Clerk* 204/1   ..   ..   £32

3000 — — — Similar, but with B above AX monogram, E — Λ on either side, M and syrinx below.   *B.M.C. 10.* 114.   *Clerk* 206/3 ..   ..   £30

3001 — — of *Pallantion (Arkadia)*. Similar, but with Π — A — Λ to l., above and to r. of AX monogram, and with trident and EY monogram below.   *B.M.C. 10.* 124-6.   *Clerk* 219/3   ..   ..   £30

3002 — — of *Pheneos (Arkadia)*. Similar, but with E — Y either side of AX monogram, and caduceus below.   *Clerk* 221/1   ..   ..   £35

3003 — — of *Tegea (Arkadia)*. Laur. hd. of Zeus r. R. Large AX monogram between T — E; all within laurel-wreath.   *B.M.C. 10.* 127-8.   *Clerk* 223/1   ..   ..   £30

3004 *Bronze Coinage*. Late 3rd Cent. B.C. Æ 14. Laur. hd. of Zeus r. R. Large AX monogram within laurel-wreath.   *B.M.C. 10.* 2.   *Clerk* 4/1   ..   ..   ..   £15

3005 196-146 B.C. (the Second Century bronze coinage of the Achaean League is of particular interest as the mint names are given in full, a feature not found on the silver hemidrachms. The diameter is normally between 19 and 21 mm., and the *obv.* and *rev.* types are constant for all mints — *Obv.* Zeus stg. l., holding Nike and sceptre. R. Achaia seated l., holding wreath and sceptre. Only the variable magistrates' names or monograms (on *obv.*) and mint names (on *rev.*) are given in the following lists). *Aigeira (Achaia)*. ΛΥΣΑΝ. R. ΑΧΑΙΩΝ ΑΙΓΙΡΑΤΑΝ.   *B.M.C. 10.* 137.   *Clerk* 5/5..   ..   ..   £12

Achaean League, (bronze) *continued*
3006 — *Aigion (Achaia).* ΤΕΛ. Ᵽ. ΑΧΑΙΩΝ ΑΙΓΙΕΩΝ. *B.M.C. 10.* 138. *Clerk* 14/6   £12
3007 — *Keryneia (Achaia).* ΚΑ monogram. Ᵽ. ΑΧΑΙΩΝ ΚΑΡΥΝΕΩΝ. *Clerk* 15/1..   £14
3008 — *Dyme (Achaia).* No *obv.* legend. Ᵽ. ΑΧΑΙΩΝ ΔΥΜΑΙΩΝ. *Clerk* 16/1 ..   £14

3009   3012
3009 — *Pellene (Achaia).* ΑΘΑΝΙΠΠΟΣ. Ᵽ. ΑΧΑΙΩΝ ΠΕΛΛΑΝΕΩΝ. *B.M.C. 10.* 143-4. *Clerk* 18/1 .. .. £13
3010 — *Megara.* ΔΗΜΗΤΡΙ. Ᵽ. ΑΧΑΙΩΝ ΜΕΓΑΡΕΩΝ. *Clerk* 35/2 .. .. .. £14
3011 — *Pagai (Megaris).* ΧΑΡΜΙΔΑΣ. Ᵽ. ΑΧΑΙΩΝ ΠΑΓΑΙΩΝ. *B.M.C. 10.* 135. *Clerk* 33/2 £14
3012 — *Corinth.* ΕΡΜΟΚΡΑΤΗΣ. Ᵽ. ΑΧΑΙΩΝ ΚΟΡΙΝΘΙΩΝ. *B.M.C. 10.* 139. *Clerk* 29/1 £12
3013 — *Sikyon.* ΑΝΤ monogram. Ᵽ. ΑΧΑΙΩΝ ΣΙΚΥΩΝΙΩΝ. *B.M.C. 10.* 148-9. *Clerk* 21/2 £12
3014 — *Phlius.* ΠΑΣΩΝ. Ᵽ. ΑΧΑΙΩΝ ΦΛΕΙΑΣΙΩΝ. *B.M.C. 10.* 145-6. *Clerk* 27/1 £14

3015   3017
3015 — *Argos.* No *obv.* legend. Ᵽ. ΑΧΑΙΩΝ ΑΡΓΕΙΩΝ and ΦΑΗΝΟC. *B.M.C. 10.* 155. *Clerk* 38/1 .. .. £12
3016 — — ΑΡΓΕΙΩΝ and ΝΙΚ monogram. Ᵽ. ΑΧΑΙΩΝ ΦΑΗΝΟΣ. *B.M.C. 10.* 156. *Clerk* 39/2 £13
3017 — *Kleonai (Argolis).* ΑΓΑΙΟΣ. Ᵽ. ΑΧΑΙΩΝ ΚΛΕΩΝΑΙΩΝ. *B.M.C. 10.* 157. *Clerk* 44/1 £14
3018 — *Epidauros (Argolis).* ΑΧΑΙΩΝ. Ᵽ. ΑΡΙΣΤΟΛΑΣ ΕΠΙΔΑΥΡΙΩΝ. *Clerk* 45/1 .. £14
3019 — *Hermione (Argolis).* No *obv.* legend. Ᵽ. ΑΧΑΙΩΝ ΕΡΜΙΟΝΕΩΝ. *Clerk* 48/1 £15

3020   3027
3020 — *Messene.* ΔΕΞΙΑΣ. Ᵽ. ΑΧΑΙΩΝ ΜΕΣΣΑΝΙΩΝ. *B.M.C. 10.* 154. *Clerk* 108/1 £13
3021 — *Asine (Messenia).* ΤΙΜΟΚΡΑΤ. Ᵽ. ΑΧΑΙΩΝ ΑΣΙΝΑΙΩΝ. *B.M.C. 10.* 152-3. *Clerk* 105/1 .. .. £14
3022 — *Korone (Messenia).* ΧΛΕΑΡΧ. Ᵽ. ΑΧΑΙΩΝ ΚΟΡΟΝΑΙΩΝ. *Clerk* 107/2 .. £14
3023 — *Elis.* ΔΑΜΟΝΟΣ. Ᵽ. ΑΧΑΙΩΝ ΑΛΕΙΩΝ. *Clerk* 101/3 .. .. .. £14
3024 — *Hypana (Elis).* ΘΡΑΣΥΜΑΧΟΣ. Ᵽ. ΑΧΑΙΩΝ ΥΠΑΝΩΝ. *B.M.C. 10.* 151. *Clerk* 104/1 £14

3025 — *Alea (Arkadia)*. ΙΕΡΟΣ. ℞. ΑΧΑΙΩΝ ΑΛΕΑΤΑΝ. *Clerk* 51/3 .. .. £15

3026 — *Alipheira (Arkadia)*. ΛΥΣΙΜΑΧΟΣ. ℞. ΑΧΑΙΩΝ ΑΛΙΦΕΙΡΕΩΝ. *B.M.C. 10.* 159.
Clerk 53/1 .. .. £14

3027 — *Asea (Arkadia)*. ΞΕΝΙΑΣ. ℞. ΑΧΑΙΩΝ ΑΣΕΑΤΑΝ. *B.M.C. 10.* 161. *Clerk* 54/1 £14

3028 — *Kallista (Arkadia)*. ΑΝΤΑΝΔΡΟΣ. ℞. ΑΧΑΙΩΝ ΚΑΛΛΙΣΤΑΤΑΝ. *Clerk* 57/1 £15

3029 — *Kaphyai (Arkadia)*. ΠΕΛΑΝΗΑΣ. ℞. ΑΧΑΙΩΝ ΚΑΦΥΕΩΝ. *Clerk* 58/1 .. £14

3030 — *Kleitor (Arkadia)*. ΙΚΙΑΣ. ℞. ΑΧΑΙΩΝ ΚΛΕΙΤΟΡΙΩΝ. *Clerk* 62/1 .. .. £14

3031 — *Dipaia (Arkadia)*. ΛΑΣΙΑΣ. ℞. ΑΧΑΙΩΝ ΔΙΠΑΙΕΩΝ. *Clerk* 63/1 .. .. £16

3032 — *Elisphasii (Arkadia)*. ΚΑ monogram. ℞. ΑΧΑΙΩΝ ΕΛΙΣΦΑΣΙΩΝ. *B.M.C. 10.* 163.
Clerk 66/3 .. .. £15

3033 — *Gortys (Arkadia)*. No *obv.* legend. ℞. ΑΧΑΙΩΝ ΚΟΡΤΥΝΙΩΝ, and ΑΥΡ monogram.
B.M.C. 10. 162. *Clerk* 67/1 .. .. £15

3034 — *Heraia (Arkadia)*. ΘΕΟΞΕΝΟΣ. ℞. ΑΧΑΙΩΝ ΗΡΑΙΕΩΝ. *B.M.C. 10.* 164. *Clerk* 71/1
£14

3035 — *Lusi (Arkadia)*. ΑΝΤΙΜΑΧΟΣ. ℞. ΑΧΑΙΩΝ ΛΟΥΣΙΑΤΑΝ. *B.M.C. 10.* 165. *Clerk* 72/1
72/1 .. .. £15

3036 3040

3036 — *Antigoneia*, formerly *Mantineia (Arkadia)*. ΧΙ. ℞. ΑΧΑΙΩΝ ΑΝΤΙΓΟΝΕΩΝ. *B.M.C. 10.*
160. *Clerk* 73/1 £13

3037 — *Megalopolis (Arkadia)*. ΟΡΔΙΩΞΑΝΟΣ. ℞. ΑΧΑΙΩΝ ΜΕΓΑΛΟΠΟΛΙΤΩΝ. *Clerk* 78/4 £13

3038 — *Methydrion (Arkadia)*. ΑΝΔΡΕΑΣ. ℞. ΑΧΑΙΩΝ ΜΕΘΥΔΡΙΕΩΝ. *Clerk* 74/1 £15

3039 — *Pallantion (Arkadia)*. ΙΠΠΑΡΧΟΣ. ℞. ΑΧΑΙΩΝ ΠΑΛΛΑΝΤΕΩΝ. *B.M.C. 10.* 167
Clerk 79/1 .. .. £13

3040 — *Pheneos (Arkadia)*. ΝΙΚΑΙΟΣ. ℞. ΑΧΑΙΩΝ ΦΕΝΕΩΝ. *B.M.C. 10.* 168. *Clerk* 82/1
£13

3041 — *Phigaleia (Arkadia)*. ΚΛΕΟΔΙΚΟΣ. ℞. ΑΧΑΙΩΝ ΦΙΓΑΛΕΩΝ. *B.M.C. 10.* 169. *Clerk*
80/1 .. .. £14

3042 — *Stymphalos (Arkadia)*. ΠΥΘΩΝ. ℞. ΑΧΑΙΩΝ ΣΤΥΜΦΑΛΙΩΝ. *B.M.C. 10.* 170.
Clerk 86/1 .. .. £14

3043 — *Tegea (Arkadia)*. ΘΡΑΣΕΑΣ. ℞. ΑΧΑΙΩΝ ΤΕΓΕΑΤΑΝ. *B.M.C. 10.* 171. *Clerk* 89/1
£12

3044 — *Teuthis (Arkadia)*. No *obv.* legend. ℞. ΑΧΑΙΩΝ ΤΕΥΘΙΔΑΝ and ΓΝΩΣΕΑΣ. *B.M.C.*
10. 174. *Clerk* 96/1 .. .. £14

3045 — *Theisoa (Arkadia)*. ΠΟΛΥΗΡΗΣ. ℞. ΑΧΑΙΩΝ ΘΙΣΟΑΙΩΝ. *Clerk* 97/1 .. £16

3046 — *Thelpusa (Arkadia)*. ΧΑΡΑΣΜΑΧΙ. ℞. ΑΧΑΙΩΝ ΘΕΛΠΟΥΣΙΩΝ. *Clerk* 98/1 £15

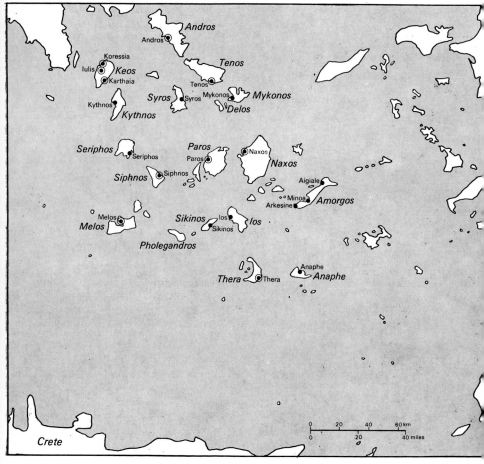

MAP 12   THE CYCLADES

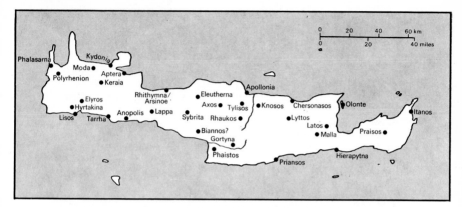

MAP 13   CRETE

THE CYCLADES AND CRETE

The Aegean islands of the Cyclades group, stretching south-east from Euboia and Attica towards Rhodes, had a considerable coinage in the archaic period, directly inspired by that of Aigina.   Their 5th Century issues were on a much smaller scale, due to Athenian imperialism. Aigina also had a strong influence on the earliest Cretan coinage, though in this island minting did not commence until the middle of the 5th Century B.C.

Archaic Period

3047   3049

3047 **ANDROS** (the most northerly of the Cyclades, Andros was famous for its wine). 525-500 B.C.   Æ *stater*.   Amphora.   Ŗ. Incuse square divided into six triangular seg- ments.   *B.M.C. 9.* (*Karthaia in Keos*) 15..   ..   ..   £2,500

3048 — Æ *obol*.   Similar.   *B.M.C. 9.* (*Karthaia*) 19   ..   ..   £150

3049 **KEOS** (a fertile island off the coast of Attica, Keos, though not large in area, possessed three towns).   **Karthaia** (situated on the south-east coast of the island).   500-480 B.C. Æ *stater*.   Amphora; to r., dolphin upwards.   Ŗ. Incuse square, of 'mill-sail' pattern, the eight triangular segments alternately raised and sunken.   *B.M.C. 9.* 17   ..   £1,750

3050 — Æ *obol*.   Similar.   *B.M.C. 9.* 22   ..   ..   £120

3051　　　　　　　　　　　　　3053

3051 **Koressia** (originally an independent town, Koressia later became merely the harbour of Keos' main settlement, Iulis). 500-480 B.C. Æ *stater*. Squid; to r., dolphin upwards. R. Incuse square, divided into eight triangular segments. *B.M.C. 9.* 48 .. £1,500

3052 — Æ *drachm*. *Obv*. Similar. R. Quadripartite incuse square. *B.M.C. 9.* 50 £650

3053 **Iulis** (the chief town of Keos, Iulis was situated in the interior of the island). 500-480 B.C. Æ *drachm*. Bunch of grapes; to r., dolphin downwards. R. Incuse square, of 'mill-sail' pattern. *B.M.C. 9.* 34 .. .. £550

3054 — Æ *obol*. Similar, but the dolphin on *obv*. is depicted upwards in field to l. *B.M.C. 9.* 36 .. .. £120

3055　　　　　　　　　　　　　3057

3055 **DELOS** (the smallest island of the Cyclades group, Delos was, nevertheless, a commercial centre of importance and became the treasury of the Greek confederacy during the Persian wars). 530-480 B.C. Æ *didrachm* (*c*. 8·2 gm.). Lyre; Δ above. R. Quadripartite incuse square, of rough form. *Weber* 4656 .. .. £4,000

3056 **MELOS** (a fertile island on the southern fringes of the group, Melos was originally colonized by Phoenicians from Byblos, and later by Dorians). 490-480 B.C. Æ *stater* (*c*. 14 gm.). Apple or quince. R. Incuse square, divided into four triangular segments by diagonal bands. *Weber* 4665 .. .. £3,500

3057 **NAXOS** (one of the largest and most important islands of the Cyclades, Naxos is situated midway between Greece and Asia Minor. In 490 B.C. it was captured by the Persians who enslaved the population). 530-490 B.C. Æ *stater*. Kantharos wreathed with ivy-leaves, a bunch of grapes suspended from each handle. R. Quadripartite incuse square. *B.M.C. 9.* 1-3 .. .. £1,500

3058 — Æ *trihemiobol*. Similar, but without bunches of grapes on *obv*. *B.M.C. 9.* 5-6 £150

3059 **PAROS** (situated immediately west of Naxos, Paros was famed for the quality of its marble, which was used extensively by the sculptors of antiquity). 530-480 B.C. Æ *stater*. Goat kneeling r., looking back; beneath, dolphin r. R. Incuse square, divided into six triangular segments. *B.M.C. 9.* 1-2 .. .. £3,000

3060 — Æ *drachm*. Goat stg. r. R. Quadripartite incuse square. *Weber* 4691 £650

3061 **SIPHNOS** (this island, situated north-east of Melos, possessed rich silver mines, though little of this wealth seems to have been used for the production of Siphnian coinage). 540-500 B.C. Æ *stater*. Eagle flying r. R. Incuse square, roughly divided into eight triangular segments. *B.M.C. 9.* 1-2 .. .. £2,750

3062   3063

3062 — Æ *hemidrachm*. Similar. *B.M.C. 9.* 3 .. .. £350

3063 **TENOS** (situated south-east of Andros, Tenos was famous for the quality of its wine, and possessed a magnificent temple of Poseidon). 530-500 B.C. Æ *hemidrachm*. Bunch of grapes formed of three pendants. R. Quadripartite incuse square. *Weber* 4727-31. *B.M.C. 9.* (*Keos*) 25 .. .. £225
    This attribution is only conjectural.

3064 **THERA** (on the southern fringes of the island group, Thera is of volcanic origin. The famous North African city of Kyrene was founded by a colony from Thera *circa* 630 B.C.). 530-500 B.C. Æ *stater*. Two dolphins, l. and r., one above the other. R. Incuse square, roughly divided into eight triangular segments. *Weber* 4739 .. .. .. £1,500

Classical and Hellenistic Periods

3065 **AMORGOS** (this narrow island, south-east of Naxos, possessed three towns which, up to the end of the 4th Cent., formed a political union issuing coins in the name of the island as a whole). Before 300 B.C. Æ 17. Star and crescent. R. AMO. Two thyrsoi crossed. *Weber* 4611 .. .. £18

3066   3068

3066 **Aigiale** (on the north-west coast of Amorgos). 3rd-2nd Cent. B.C. Æ 18. Goat-legged Pan stg. l., holding pedum. R. A — I either side of cupping-vessel; Δ beneath. *B.M.C. 9.* 2 .. .. £15

3067 — Æ 12. Turreted female hd. r. R. AIΓI. Lion's hd. l. *B.M.C. 9.* 5-6 .. £12

3068 **Arkesine** (also on the north-west coast of the island). 3rd-2nd Cent. B.C. Æ 17. Hd. of Athena r., in crested helmet. R. APK above ram stg. r. *Weber* 4617 .. £15

3069 **Minoa** (another coastal town, situated between Aigiale in the north and Arkesine in the south). 3rd-2nd Cent. B.C. Æ 15. Hd. of bearded Dionysos r., wreathed with ivy. R. M — I / N — Ω either side of kantharos; bunch of grapes above. *B.M.C. 9.* 8 £14

3070   3073

3070 **ANAPHE** (situated east of Thera, on the southern fringes of the Cyclades group, the island of Anaphe boasted a temple of Apollo Aigletes). 3rd-2nd Cent. B.C. Æ 17. Laur. hd. of Apollo three-quarter face to r. ℞. Two-handled vase; above, bee r. dividing A — N. *B.M.C. 9*. 1   ..   ..   £16

3071 **ANDROS.** 3rd-2nd Cent. B.C. Æ *didrachm* (*c.* 6·5 gm.). Hd. of young Dionysos r., wreathed with ivy. ℞. ΑΝΔΡΙΩΝ. Dionysos (?) stg. l., sacrificing over tripod and holding thyrsos. *B.M.C. 9*. 2   ..   ..   £1,000

3072 — Æ *drachm*. *Obv*. Similar; Φ behind. ℞. ΑΝΔΡΙ. Panther walking r. *B.M.C. 9*. 1
                                             £350

3073 — Æ 18. *Obv*. As 3071. ℞. ΑΝΔΡΙ. Amphora. *B.M.C. 9*. 3-5   ..   £12

3074 — — — ℞. ΑΝΔΡΙ. Thyrsos; bunch of grapes in field to l. *B.M.C. 9*. 11 ..   £12

3075 — Æ 10. Hd. of bearded Dionysos r., wreathed with ivy. ℞. ΑΝΔΡΙ. Tripod. *B.M.C. 9*. 20-22   ..   ..   £9

3076 **KEOS.** 2nd-1st Cent. B.C. Æ 18. Laur. hd. of Jupiter (or Aristaios) r. ℞. ΚΕΙ. Forepart of dog l., encircled by radiating lines (Seirios). *B.M.C. 9*. 1..   £13

3077 — Æ 12. Laur. hd. of Apollo r. ℞. As last, but without legend. *B.M.C. 9*. 12   £10
      These late issues, in the name of the island as a whole, were issued, probably, from Iulis, the principal town.

          3077   3079

3078 **Karthaia.** 480-460 B.C. Æ *stater*. Amphora, between dolphin and bunch of grapes. ℞. ΚΑΡ (retrograde) in three divisions of quadripartite incuse square. *Hist. Num.*, *p.* 483
                                           £3,000

3079 3rd-2nd Cent. B.C. Æ 19. Laur. hd. of Apollo r. ℞. ΚΑΡΘΑ above forepart of dog l.; radiating lines above and before; Σ / A behind; bee beneath. *B.M.C. 9*. 40-41   £14

3080 — — Hd. of young Dionysos r., wreathed with ivy. ℞. ΚΑΡΘΑ. Bunch of grapes; star to l. *B.M.C. 9*. 42   ..   ..   £12

3081 — Æ 14. Laur. hd. of Apollo r. ℞. ΚΑΡΘΑΙ between the rays of large star. *B.M.C. 9*. 46 ..   ..   £10

3082 **Koressia.** 480-460 B.C. Æ *stater*. Squid; to r., dolphin upwards. ℞. Incuse square, divided into four triangles by broad diagonal bands. *B.M.C. 9*. 49 ..   ..   £1,750

3083 — Æ *hemidrachm.* Similar, but with letter *koppa* in *obv.* field. *B.M.C. 9.* 52   £300

3084 — Æ *obol.* As 3082. *B.M.C. 9.* 54   ..   ..   £125

3085 — Æ *hemiobol.* Dolphin l., ꟼo beneath. ℞. Quadripartite incuse square. *B.M.C. 9.* 55
   £90

3086 3rd-2nd Cent. B.C. Æ 20. Laur. hd. of Apollo r. ℞. ΚΟΡΗ. Bee. *B.M.C. 9.* 66
   £15

3087 — Æ 18. Similar. ℞. ΚΟΡΗ. Bunch of grapes; v in field to l., bee to r. *B.M.C. 9.*
64-5 ..   ..   £13

3088   3091

3088 — Æ 13. Bearded hd. of Aristaios r. ℞. ΚΟΡΗ between rays of large star. *B.M.C. 9.* 57
   £10

3089 — Æ 11. Squid; to l., dolphin upwards. ℞. κ — o either side of bunch of grapes.
B.M.C. 9. 60   ..   ..   £11

3090 **Iulis.** 3rd-2nd Cent. B.C. Æ 17. Hd. of Artemis r. ℞. ΙΟΥΛΙΕ. Bunch of grapes.
B.M.C. 9. 75   ..   ..   £13

3091 — Æ 15. Laur. hd. of Aristaios r., bearded. ℞. ΙΟΥΛΙΕ. Bee. *B.M.C. 9.* 78   £13

3092 — Æ 13. Laur. hd. of Apollo r. ℞. ΙΟΥ. Bee. *B.M.C. 9.* 67   ..   ..   £12

3093 **KYTHNOS** (situated south of Keos, the island of Kythnos was celebrated for its cheese).
2nd-1st Cent. B.C. Æ 18. Laur. hd. of Apollo r. ℞. ΚΥΘΝ. Lyre. *B.M.C. 9.* 1   £15

3095 — Æ 15. Similar. ℞. ΚΥΘΝΙ. Rose. *B.M.C. 9.* 6..   ..   ..   ..   £13

3096 **DELOS.** 480-460 B.C. Æ *didrachm.* Lyre; Δ above. ℞. Quadripartite incuse square,
of regular form, divided by broad bands. *Weber* 4655 ..   ..   £4,000

3097 — Æ *tritartemorion* (¾ *obol*). Lyre. ℞. ΔΗΛΙ (retrograde) between spokes of wheel.
Hist. Num., p. 485 ..   ..   £200

3098 *Circa* 400 B.C. Æ *hemidrachm* (c. 1·4 gm.). Laur. hd. of Apollo l. ℞. Lyre, within
incuse square. *Weber* 4657 ..   ..   £275

3099 *Circa* 300 B.C. Æ *hemidrachm.* Similar; of later style. ℞. Lyre; Δ — H in lower field.
Grose 7254 ..   ..   £225

3100 3rd-2nd Cent. B.C. Æ 18. Laur. hd. of Apollo l. ℞. Palm-tree; Δ — H in field.
B.M.C. 9. 1 ..   ..   £17

3101   3102   3105

Delos *continued*

3101 — Æ 17. Similar. R. Lyre; Λ — H in field. *B.M.C. 9.* 4   .. .. £14

3102 — Æ 10. Similar, but hd. of Apollo r., and with cornucopiae in field to l. on *rev.*
B.M.C. 9. 9 ..   ..   £9

3103 **IOS** (midway between Naxos and Thera, Ios claimed to be the burial-place of Homer).
Circa 300 B.C. Æ *didrachm* (*c.* 6·8 gm.). OMHPOY. Bearded head of Homer r., bound
with tainia. R. IHTΩN within laurel-wreath. *Hist. Num., p.* 486   .. .. £1,750

3104 2nd Cent. B.C. Æ 20. *Obv.* Similar. R. IHTΩN. Athena advancing r., brandishing
spear and holding shield; small palm-tree before. *B.M.C. 9.* 1-3   .. .. £20
These are frequently countermarked, sometimes on both sides.

3105 — Æ 17. *Obv.* Similar, but hd. l. R. Palm-tree; I — HT in field. *B.M.C. 9.* 6   £18

3106 **MELOS** (the town was captured by the Athenians in 416 B.C., during the Peloponnesian
War, bringing its 5th Century coinage to an abrupt end). 480-450 B.C. Æ *stater.*
MAΛI (partly retrograde). Jug. R. Incuse square divided diagonally by broad bands.
Hist. Num., p. 486 ..   ..   £2,500

3107   3110

3107 450-420 B.C. Æ *stater.* MAΛI. Apple or quince. R. Incuse circle, dotted circle
within, divided into four segments by broad bands. (*British Museum*)   .. £2,000

3108 420-416 B.C. Æ *stater.* Apple or quince. R. MAΛI. Gorgoneion, surrounded by
serpents. *Grose* 7261 ..   ..   £2,000

3109 — — Similar. R. MAΛION. Hd. of Kabeiros r., wearing conical cap. *Grose* 7262
£2,000

3110 — — Similar. R. MALIO. Triskeles. *Grose* 7264 ..   ..   £1,750

3111   3113

3111 400-350 B.C. Æ *didrachm* (*c.* 7·75 gm.). Apple or quince. R. Kantharos; M — A /
Λ — I across lower field. *B.M.C. 9.* 1 ..   ..   £1,250

3112 — Æ *hemidrachm.* Similar. R. Naked archer kneeling r., discharging arrow. *B.M.C.*
9. 2 ..   ..   £300

3113 *Circa* 300 B.C. Æ *drachm* (*c.* 3·8 gm.). Hd. of Athena r. in crested Corinthian helmet.
R. MAΛIΩN, ΔEΞIKPATHΣ. Apple or quince; all within wreath. *Hist. Num., p.* 487   £350

3114 *Bronze Coinage.* 4th Cent. B.C. Æ 17. Apple or quince. R. As 3112. *B.M.C. 9.* 3
£16

3115 — Æ 13. Similar. R. Phrygian helmet l. *B.M.C. 9.* 6 .. .. .. £14

3116   3120

3116 3rd-2nd Cent. B.C. Æ 22. Similar. R. Cornucopiae between caps of the Dioskouroi; all within olive-wreath. *B.M.C. 9.* 22 .. .. £15

3117 — Æ 15. Similar. R. Amphora within linear frame. *B.M.C. 9.* 29 .. £12

3118 — Æ 11. Similar. R. Kantharos; M above. *B.M.C. 9.* 16 .. .. £8

3119 **MYKONOS** (a rocky island, east of Delos, Mykonos was noted for the propensity of its population to baldness). 4th Cent. B.C. Æ 17. Hd. of bearded Dionysos r., wreathed with ivy. R. Corn-grain and bunch of grapes; M — Y / K — O in field. *B.M.C. 9.* 1
£14

3120 — — Hd. of young Dionysos three-quarter face to r., wreathed with ivy. R. As last. *B.M.C. 9.* 3 .. .. £15

3121 — Æ 10. Hd. of Demeter r. R. As last. *B.M.C. 9.* 5-6 .. .. .. £10

3122 3rd-2nd Cent. B.C. Æ 18. Similar to 3120, but of later style and with thyrsos in *rev.* field to l. *B.M.C. 9.* 7 .. .. £14

3123 1st Cent. B.C. Æ 18. *Obv.* Similar. R. Corn-stalk with two ears; M — Y — K / O — NI / ω — N in field. *B.M.C. 9.* 10-11 .. .. £13

3124   3126

3124 **NAXOS** (this island recovered its independence in 480 B.C., after a decade of Persian rule, but for much of the remainder of the century was subject to the Athenians). 4th Cent. B.C. R *drachm* (*c.* 3·75 gm.). Hd. of bearded Dionysos r., wreathed with ivy. R. NAΞIΩN. Kantharos; ivy-leaf above. *B.M.C. 9.* 7 .. .. £350

3125 — R *trihemiobol.* Hd. of young Dionysos l., wreathed with ivy. R. NAΞIΩN. Three ivy-leaves arranged star-wise around central pellet. *Weber* 4682 .. .. £110

3126 3rd Cent. B.C. R *didrachm* (*c.* 7·75 gm.). Hd. of bearded Dionysos r., wreathed with ivy. R. Krater and thyrsos; NAΞI above, XAPO to l. (*British Museum*) .. £900

3127 *Bronze Coinage.* 4th Cent. B.C. Æ 11. *Obv.* Similar, but hd. l. R. Kantharos; bunch of grapes above; N — A in lower field. *B.M.C. 9.* 8-12 .. .. £9

3128 3rd-2nd Cent. B.C. Æ 20. Hd. of young Dionysos l., wreathed with ivy. R. Krater and thyrsos; N — A / Ξ — I in field. *B.M.C. 9.* 13 .. .. £12

3129 — Æ 17. Hd. of bearded Dionysos r., wreathed with ivy. R. Kantharos; bunch of grapes above; N — A / Ξ — I in field. *B.M.C. 9.* 18-20 .. .. £10

3130 **PAROS.** *Circa* 350 B.C. Æ *hemidrachm* (*c.* 1·9 gm.). Goat walking r. ℞. п — A
either side of corn-ear. *B.M.C. 9.* 3-4 ..   ..   £200

3131

3133

3131 — — Goat walking r., пAP above. ℞. Corn-wreath. *B.M.C. 9.* 5 ..   ..   £200
3132 3rd-2nd Cent. B.C. Æ *tetradrachm* (*c.* 15·5 gm.). Hd. of young Dionysos r., wreathed
with ivy. ℞. Demeter seated l. on cista mystica, holding corn-ears and sceptre; пAPIΩN
before, APIΣTOΔHM behind. *B.M.C. 9.* 16   ..   ..   £2,000
3133 — Æ *didrachm*. Veiled hd. of Demeter r., wreathed with corn. ℞. пAPI within ivy-
wreath. *B.M.C. 9.* 13   ..   ..   £900

3134 — — Hd. of Kore (?) r., hair bound with cord. ℞. Goat stg. r; above, ANAΞIK / пAPI.
B.M.C. 9. 11-12   ..   ..   £900
3135 — Æ *drachm*. Hd. of Demeter r., wreathed with corn. ℞. пAPI within ivy-wreath.
B.M.C. 9. 14 ..   ..   £300
3136 *Bronze Coinage.* 4th Cent. B.C. Æ 11. Goat stg. r. ℞. п—A either side of corn-ear.
B.M.C. 9. 6 ..   ..   £9
3137 3rd-2nd Cent. B.C. Æ 20. *Obv.* Similar to 3134. ℞. Goat kneeling r.; пAPI above.
B.M.C. 9. 20   ..   ..   £14
3138 — Æ 11. *Obv.* Similar to 3135. ℞. Corn-stalk with two ears; in field, п — A / P — I.
B.M.C. 9. 23   ..   ..   £10
3139 1st Cent. B.C. Æ 18. Diad. female hd. r., hair rolled. ℞. Cornucopiae; п — A / P — I
in field, monogram to l. *B.M.C. 9.* 28 ..   ..   £11
3140 **PHOLEGANDROS** (a small island, between Melos and Sikinos). 2nd Cent. B.C.
Æ 20. Hd. of Apollo (?) r. ℞. Bull butting r.; ΦΟΛE above. *B.M.C. 9.* 1 ..   £16

3140

3141

3141 **SERIPHOS** (directly north of Melos, the island of Seriphos had strong associations
with the legend of Perseus). 3rd Cent. B.C. Æ 11. Hd. of Perseus r., in winged helmet
surmounted by hd. of vulture. ℞. ΣEPI. Harpa. *B.M.C. 9.* 1   ..   ..   £14
3142 2nd Cent. B.C. Æ 17. Helmeted hd. of Perseus r. ℞. Σ — E either side of Gorgoneion;
harpa beneath. *B.M.C. 9.* 4   ..   ..   £14
3143 1st Cent. B.C. Æ 15. Gorgoneion; harpa beneath. ℞. CEPEIΦIΩN. Perseus advancing l., holding harpa. *B.M.C. 9.* 10..   ..   ..   £12

3144 **SIKINOS** (a small island between Pholegandros and Ios). 3rd Cent. B.C. Æ 19. Young male hd. r. Ŗ. ΣΙΚΙ. Bunch of grapes. *Hist. Num., p.* 491 .. .. £20

3145   3149

3145 **SIPHNOS.** 480-450 B.C. Æ *stater*. Archaic hd. of Artemis (?) r., hair bound with cord. Ŗ. ΣΙΦ (retrograde) in three corners of incuse square containing eagle flying r.; barleycorn in upper r. hand corner. *B.M.C. 9*. 4 .. .. £3,500

3146 — Æ *tetrobol* (*c.* 4 gm.). Similar. *B.M.C. 9.* 5-6 .. .. £450

3147 400-350 B.C. Æ *stater*. Diad. hd. of Artemis (?) l., hair rolled. Ŗ. Similar to 3145. *Newell* (*A hoard from Siphnos*) *p.* 3, *no.* 1 .. .. (*Unique*)

3148 — Æ *tetrobol*. *Obv.* Similar, but hd. r. Ŗ. ΣΙΦ (retrograde). Eagle flying r.; barleycorn in upper field to r. *Grose* 7287 .. .. £350

3149 — Æ 15. *Obv.* As last. Ŗ. Eagle flying r., holding serpent in beak; ΣΙ — Φ to l., either side of tail. *B.M.C. 9.* 8-10 .. .. £14

3150 **SYROS** (a fertile island near the centre of the Cyclades group). 3rd Cent. B.C. Æ *obol*. Hd. of Hermes r., in petasos. Ŗ. ΣΥΡΙ above goat stg. r. *Grose* 7290 .. .. £200

3151   3152

3151 2nd Cent. B.C. Æ *tetradrachm*. Hd. of Demeter r., wreathed with corn. Ŗ. ΘΕΩΝ ΚΑΒΕΙΡΩΝ ΣΥΡΙΩΝ. The two Kabeiroi stg. facing, each holding spear; all within olive-wreath. *Hist. Num., p.* 492 .. .. £2,500

3152 *Bronze Coinage.* 3rd Cent. B.C. Æ 18. Hd. of bearded Pan r., with goat's horn, hair bound with tainia. Ŗ. Goat stg. l.; ΣΥΡΙ above; corn-ear before. *B.M.C. 9.* 1 £14

3153 2nd-1st Cent. B.C. Æ 17. Hd. of Demeter r., wreathed with corn. Ŗ. The two Kabeiroi stg. facing; Σ — Υ — P in field. *B.M.C. 9.* 19.. .. .. .. £14

3154 — Æ 13. Bee. Ŗ. Σ — Υ either side of pileos surmounted by star. *B.M.C. 9.* 16 £9

3155 — Æ 10. Two pileoi, each surmounted by star. Ŗ. Panther springing r.; ΣΥΡΙ above, monogram below. *B.M.C. 9.* 14 .. .. £8

3155   3156

3156 **TENOS.** *Circa* 330 B.C. Æ *tetradrachm*. Laur. hd. of Zeus Ammon r., bearded. Ŗ. Poseidon enthroned l., holding dolphin and trident; T — H in field. *B.M.C. 9.* 1 £3,500

Tenos *continued*

3157 — Æ *drachm.* *Obv.* Similar. ℞. Bunch of grapes; T — H in field.   *B.M.C. 9.* 2   £400

3158   3159

3158 *Circa* 300 B.C. Æ *didrachm* (*c.* 7 gm.). Beardless hd. of Zeus Ammon r., laur. ℞. Poseidon stg. l., holding dolphin and trident; bunch of grapes in field to l., ΤΗΝΙΩΝ to r. *B.M.C. 9.* 7 .. .. £900

3159 — Æ *tetrobol.* *Obv.* Similar. ℞. Bunch of grapes; T — H / N — I in field.   *B.M.C. 9.* 8 £250

3160 *Bronze Coinage.* 4th Cent. B.C. Æ 15. *Obv.* As 3156. ℞. Trident-head; T — H in field. *B.M.C. 9.* 5 .. .. £14

3161 — Æ 10. Similar. ℞. Bunch of grapes; T — H in field. *B.M.C. 9.* 3 .. £10

3162 3rd-2nd Cent. B.C. Æ 19. Laur. hd. of Poseidon r. ℞. Ornamental trident-head; T — H / N — I in field; rose to l. *B.M.C. 9.* 20 .. .. £10

3163   3168

3163 — Æ 17. *Obv.* As 3158. ℞. Bunch of grapes; N — I / T — H in field; trident to l. *B.M.C. 9.* 10-12 .. .. £12

3164 — Æ 18. Similar. ℞. Poseidon stg. l., holding trident; ΤΗΝΙΩΝ to r., rose to l. *B.M.C. 9.* 27 .. .. £13

3165 — Æ 21. Poseidon stg. l., holding trident with dolphin at base; to r., ΤΗΝΙΩΝ. ℞. Dionysos stg. facing, looking l., holding thyrsos; altar at feet to l., dolphin in field to r. *B.M.C. 9.* 33-4 .. .. £14

3166 — Æ 10. Hd. of Poseidon r., trident at shoulder. ℞. Dolphin r.; T — H / N — I in field. *B.M.C. 9.* 39-40 .. .. £8

3167 **THERA.** 4th-3rd Cent. B.C. Æ 18. Hd. of Apollo three-quarter face to l. ℞. ΘΗ. Bull butting r.; two dolphins in ex. *B.M.C. 9.* 1 .. .. £18

3168 — Æ 13. Laur. hd. of Apollo r. ℞. ΘΗ. Lyre. *B.M.C. 9.* 3 .. .. £12

3169 **CRETE** (the Cretans had close associations with the maritime state of Aigina, and the Aiginetan coinage supplied the currency needs of the island until the middle of the 5th Century B.C. Even after the commencement of Cretan issues the types of the new coinage were frequently overstruck on the flans of obsolete staters of Aigina. The tradition of overstriking old coins with new types was maintained in Crete until the beginning of the Hellenistic age, when more plentiful supplies of bullion became available.) **Gortyna** (the second city of Crete, after Knosos, Gortyna and its close neighbour, Phaistos, were the first places in the island to issue a native coinage). 450-425 B.C. Æ *stater.* Europa seated on bull r. ℞. ΛΟΡΤVΝΟΜ ΤΟ ϹΑꟅΜΑ (retrograde) around linear square containing lion's scalp facing; all within incuse square. *Svoronos* (*Numismatique de la Crète Ancienne*), *pl. XII,* 21 .. .. £2,500

3170   3171

3170 — Æ *drachm*. Bull seated r., looking back; above, ΛΟΡΤΥΝ (retrograde). R. Similar to last. *Svoronos, pl. XII*, 27. *B.M.C. 9*. 1 .. .. £1,000

3171 425-380 B.C. Æ *stater*. Europa seated on bull r.; dolphin below. R. Lion's scalp facing within double linear frame, divided into numerous square compartments; all within incuse square. *Svoronos, pl. XII, 22, var.* £2,000

3172 380-360 B.C. Æ *stater*. *Obv*. Similar, but of more advanced style. R. Hd. of Hermes r., in winged petasos; before, caduceus and ΛΟΡΤΥΝ (retrograde). *Le Rider (Monnaies Crétoises du Veau Ier Siècle av. J.-C.), pl. XI*, 10. (*British Museum*) £3,500

3173 — — *Obv*. As last. R. Lion's scalp facing, ΓΟΡΤΥΝΙΟΝ beneath; all within incuse square. *Le Rider, pl. XI*, 11. *Svoronos, pl. XII*, 35 .. .. £1,750

3174   3175

3174 360-322 B.C. Æ *stater*. Europa (?) seated r. amid the branches of a tree, her hd. lowered and resting on her l. hand. R. Bull stg. r., looking back; ΛΟΡΤΥΝΙΟΝ (retrograde) beneath. *Le Rider, pl. XII*, 5. *B.M.C. 9*. 7 .. .. £750

3175 — Æ *drachm*. Hd. and neck of bull r. R. Hd. of Europa (?) r., wearing sphendone; ΛΟΡ (retrograde) before. *Le Rider, pl. XIX*, 12. *B.M.C. 9*. 33 .. .. £450

3176 322-300 B.C. Æ *stater*. Similar to 3174, but with large hd. of eagle l. in front of trunk of tree on *obv*.; no legend on *rev*. *Le Rider, pl. XVIII*, 14. *B.M.C. 9*. 11 .. £800

3177 — Æ *drachm*. Hd. of Europa (?) r., wearing sphendone. R. Hd. and neck of bull r. *Le Rider, pl. XX*, 13-14 .. .. £400

3178   3180

3178 300-270 B.C. Æ *stater*. Europa (?) seated facing amid branches of leafless tree; eagle, with outstretched wings, before her. R. Bull stg. l., looking back. *Le Rider, pl. XVIII*, 22. *B.M.C. 9*. 27 .. .. £850

3179 — Æ *drachm*. Female hd. r., wearing earrings and necklace, and crowned with reeds. R. Bull stg. r., looking back at raised r. hind-hoof. *Le Rider, pl. XX*, 16. (*British Museum*) £400

3180 3rd Cent. B.C. Æ *trihemidrachm*? (*c*. 6·4 gm.). Europa (?) seated r., hd. facing, amid branches of tree; eagle perched on branch behind her. R. ΓΟΡΤΥ above bull stg. l., looking back. *Svoronos* 106. *B.M.C. 9*. 40 .. .. £450

Gortyna *continued*

3181 2nd-1st Cent. (before 67 B.C.). *N stater* (*c.* 8·6 gm.). Laur. hd. of Zeus r. R.
ΓΟΡΤΥΝΙΩΝ. Bull stg. l., looking back. *Svoronos, pl. XV,* 21 .. .. (*Unique ?*)

3182   3183

3182 — R *tetradrachm.* Diad. hd. of Zeus (or Minos) l., Δ beneath. R. Athena stg. l.,
holding Nike and resting on shield, serpent at feet; ΓΟΡΤΥΝΙΩΝ behind, ΘΙΒΟΣ before;
all within olive-wreath. *Svoronos, pl. XVI,* 14. *B.M.C. 9.* 48 .. .. £1,250

3183 — — Hd. of Athena Parthenos r., wearing richly ornamented triple-crested helmet.
R. Owl stg. r., hd. facing, on prostrate amphora; Γ — ΟΡ / ΤΥ — ΝΙ / Ω / Ν in field; to r.,
bull butting r.; all within olive-wreath. *Svoronos, pl. XVI,* 23. *B.M.C. 9.* 47   £750
This issue is imitated from the contemporary 'New Style' coinage of Athens.

3184 — R *octobol ?* (*c.* 4·9 gm.). Laur. hd. of Zeus r. R. ΓΟΡΤΥΝΙΩΝ. Europa seated on
bull galloping r., veil billowing out behind her hd. *Svoronos, pl. XV,* 22. *B.M.C. 9.* 57
£250

3185 — R *drachm* (*c.* 4 gm.). Diad. hd. of Zeus (or Minos) r. R. ΓΟΡΤΥΝΙΩΝ. Apollo (?)
seated l. on rock, hd. facing, r. hand resting on knee, holding bow and arrow in l.; Β in field
to r. *Svoronos, pl. XVI,* 16. *B.M.C. 9.* 49 .. .. £140

3186   3187

3186 — — *Obv.* Similar, but hd. l. R. ΓΟΡΤΥΝΙΩΝ. Naked male figure (Gortys ?) advancing
to front, r. hand on shield, holding spear in l.; wreath in field to l.; border of rays. *Svoronos, pl. XVI,* 9. *B.M.C. 9.* 54 .. .. £140

3187 — R *drachm* (reduced weight, *c.* 3 gm.). Similar to 3185, but with Δ in *rev.* field to r.
B.M.C. 9. 52 .. .. £90

3188 — — — *Obv.* As 3185. R. Similar to 3186, but with Θ in field to l. *B.M.C. 9.* 55
£90

3189 — R *hemidrachm.* Hd. of Helios (?) three-quarter face to r., hair floating loosely.
R. Γ — Ο either side of eagle stg. l., attacking serpent; border of rays. *Svoronos, pl. XVI,*
3. *B.M.C. 9.* 58 .. .. £125

3190 *Circa* 66 B.C. R *tetradrachm.* Hd. of Roma r., in winged and crested helmet; ΡΩΜΑΣ
behind, ΚΑ monogram before. R. Cultus-statue of Ephesian Artemis; bee and elephant's
hd. in upper field to l. and to r.; ΓΟ — Ρ — Τ — ΥΝ across central field; all within laurel-
wreath. *Svoronos, pl. XVI,* 29 .. .. £4,500
This piece commemorates the Roman conquest of Crete by Q. Caecilius Metellus in 67 B.C.

3191   3192

3191 *Bronze Coinage.* 3rd Cent. B.C. Æ 18. ΓOP. Europa (?) seated r. amid branches of
tree, eagle perched behind her; border of rays. ℞. ΓOPTYNIΩN. Europa seated on bull
galloping l.; all within wreath. *B.M.C. 9.* 41-6 ..   ..   £14

3192 2nd-1st Cent. B.C. Æ 24. Laur. hd. of Zeus r. ℞. ΓOPTYNIΩN beneath bull galloping
l., carrying Europa whose veil billows out; border of rays. *Svoronos, pl. XV,* 26. *B.M.C.
9.* 66 ..   ..   £15

3193 — Æ 20. Diad. hd. of Zeus (or Minos) r. ℞. Athena stg. l., holding serpent and spear,
shield at feet; ΓOPTY / NI — ΩN across field. *B.M.C. 9.* 60   ..   ..   ..   £13

3194 — Æ 15. Laur. hd. of Apollo r. ℞. Bull butting r.; ΓOP above, TYNI in ex. *B.M.C. 9.*
69   ..   ..   £9

3195   3198

3195 **Phaistos** (west of Gortyna and close to the sea, Phaistos was a town of great antiquity and
had close associations with Herakles.   Its coinage commences about the same time as its
more powerful neighbour, and with similar types). 450-425 B.C. Æ *stater.* Europa
seated on bull l.   ℞. CA ϻ MT ϻ ON TO CA ϻ MA (retrograde) around linear square containing
lion's scalp facing; all within incuse square. *Svoronos, pl. XXII,* 34. *B.M.C. 9.* 1
£3,000

3196 425-380 B.C. Æ *stater.* Similar, but without legend on *rev. Le Rider, pl. XX,* 19
£2,500

3197 380-360 B.C. Æ *stater. Obv.* Similar. ℞. Incuse square, containing large lion's scalp
facing. *Le Rider, pl. XX,* 24. *Weber* 4545   ..   ..   £2,250

3198 360-330 B.C. Æ *stater.* CASMTSON (retrograde). Europa seated l. on rock, her r.
hand outstretched towards forepart of bull r. before her. ℞. Hermes seated l. on tree-
trunk, holding caduceus. *Svoronos, pl. XXII,* 35. *B.M.C. 9.* 2   ..   ..   £2,000

3199 — — Hd. of Europa r., wearing sphendone. ℞. Forepart of bull r. *Le Rider, pl. XXI,*
6. (*British Museum*) £2,500

3200 330-322 B.C. Æ *stater.* Herakles, naked, standing facing, hd. r., holding club and bow;
lion's skin in field to l., barleycorn to r.; four globules in field. ℞. Bull stg. l., hobbled;
all within laurel-wreath. *B.M.C. 9.* 6   ..   ..   £650

Phaistos *continued*

3201 — Æ *hemidrachm.* Youthful hd. of Herakles r., hair short. ℞. Bull's hd. facing.
      Le Rider, pl. XXII, 11.   *B.M.C. 9.* 25   ..   ..   £200

3202 — Æ *obol.* Similar.   *Le Rider, pl. XXII,* 18.   (*British Museum*) £110

3203   3204

3203 322-300 B.C. Æ *stater.* ΦΑΙΣΤΙΟΝ. Youthful Herakles, naked, seated three-quarter
      face to l. on lion's skin, hd. facing, holding club resting on ground before him; to l.,
      bow and quiver beside tree; to r., amphora. ℞. Bull walking r., hd. lowered. *Le Rider,*
      pl. XXII, 26.   *B.M.C. 9.* 14   ..   ..   £2,000

3204 — — Herakles, naked, back turned towards spectator, striding l., wielding club to attack
      the Hydra which rears up before him; crab between his legs. ℞. ΦΑΙΣΤΙΩΝ above bull
      stg. r.   *B.M.C. 9.* 12   ..   ..   £1,750

3205 — Æ *drachm.* Youthful hd. of Herakles l., hair short; ΦΑΙΣ behind. ℞. Bull's hd.
      facing within laurel-wreath.   *B.M.C. 9.* 21   ..   ..   £350

3206 — Æ *hemidrachm.* *Obv.* Similar, but legend retrograde and before hd. of Herakles.
      ℞. Bull's hd. facing.   *B.M.C. 9.* 22   ..   ..   £150

3207   3209

3207 300-270 B.C. Æ *stater.* Naked male figure (Talos), winged, advancing to front, holding
      stone in each hand, the r. one raised; τ — ΑΛ — ΩΝ across lower field. ℞. ΦΑΙΣΤΙΩΝ
      above bull butting r.   *B.M.C. 9.* 20   ..   ..   £1,500

3208 — Æ 18. *Obv.* Similar, but Talos advancing r., and without legend. ℞. ΦΑΙΣ / ΤΙΩΝ
      above and below hound r., on the scent.   *B.M.C. 9.* 27-8   ..   ..   ..   £15

3209 **Knosos** (situated close to the northern coast of the island, the famous city of Knosos,
      capital of King Minos, commenced issuing coins a little later than the southern cities of
      Gortyna and Phaistos).   425-360 B.C. Æ *stater.* The Minotaur running r., hd. facing,
      l. hand raised, holding stone in r. ℞. Labyrinth-pattern, with five pellets at centre; deep
      incuse square, containing pellet, at each corner; all within incuse square. *B.M.C. 9.* 1
                                                                              £3,250

3210 — — *Obv.* Similar, but the stone is held in Minotaur's raised l. hand; ΚΝΩΜΙ (retrograde)
      behind. ℞. As last, but with star-device at centre of Labyrinth. *Le Rider, pl. XXV,* 1.
      (*British Museum*) £3,500

3211   3214

3211 — — *Obv.* Similar to 3209, but Minotaur's hd. is turned to l. ℞. Hd. of Ariadne r. within linear-square, surrounded by maeander-pattern representing the Labyrinth; all within incuse square. *Svoronos, pl. IV*, 31. *B.M.C. 9*. 2 ..   ..   ..   £3,750

3212 — Æ *drachm.* The Minotaur running r., hd. facing, holding stone in raised l. hand. ℞. Double linear square, with pellets between, enclosing star-device; all within incuse square. *Le Rider, pl. XXV*, 4 ..   ..   £1,250

3213 — Æ *hemidrachm.* Similar. *Le Rider, pl. XXV*, 8. *Grose* 7051 ..   ..   £400

3214 360-320 B.C. Æ *stater.* Hd. of Demeter l., wreathed with corn. ℞. ΚΝΟΣΙΟΝ (retrograde). Bull's hd. facing, within frame of maeander-pattern representing the Labyrinth. *Svoronos, pl. V*, 1. *B.M.C. 9*. 10 ..   ..   £1,500

3215 — — ΚΝΩΣΙΟΝ behind hd. of Demeter r., wreathed with corn; all within frame of maeander-pattern representing the Labyrinth. ℞. Minos enthroned l., holding sceptre surmounted by flower; ΜΙΝΩΣ in field to l. *Svoronos, pl. IV*, 34   ..   ..   £2,000

3216 320-300 B.C. Æ *stater.* Hd. of Demeter r., wreathed with corn. ℞. Labyrinth of swastika-pattern; star at centre. *B.M.C. 9*. 5 ..   ..   £500

3217   3219

3217 300-270 B.C. Æ *stater.* Hd. of Hera l., wearing stephanos adorned with floral ornaments. ℞. Square Labyrinth; spear-head and Α to l., thunderbolt and Ρ to r., ΚΝΩΣΙΩΝ below. *B.M.C. 9*. 24-5 ..   ..   £1,750

3218 — Æ *drachm.* Laur. hd. of Apollo l. ℞. ΚΝΩΣΙΩΝ behind Minos seated l. on square Labyrinth, holding Nike and sceptre; monogram in field to l., ΑΓΕΙ beneath. *Svoronos, pl. VI*, 15 ..   ..   £1,000

3219 — Æ *hemidrachm. Obv.* Similar. ℞. Square Labyrinth; ΑΓΕΙ to l., thunderbolt to r., ΚΝΩ beneath. *B.M.C. 9*. 29 ..   ..   £325

Knosos *continued*

3220 2nd-1st Cent. (before 67 B.C.). Æ *tetradrachm.* Hd. of Athena Parthenos r., wearing richly ornamented triple-crested helmet. ℞. Owl stg. r., hd. facing, on prostrate amphora; κ — ΝΩ / ΣΙ — ΩΝ in upper field; square Labyrinth to r.; all within olive-wreath. *B.M.C. 9.* 40   ..   ..   £1,000
> *This issue is imitated from the contemporary 'New Style' coinage of Athens.*

3221 — — Laur. hd. of Apollo l.; ΠΟΛ — ΧΟΣ in lower field. ℞. ΚΝΩ / Σ — Ι / ΩΝ above, either side, and beneath circular Labyrinth. *B.M.C. 9.* 41   ..   ..   ..   £1,750

3222   3224

3222 — — Diademed hd. of Zeus (or Minos) r.; Α beneath. ℞. As last, but square Labyrinth. *B.M.C. 9.* 42   ..   ..   £1,500

3223 — Æ *drachm.* Bearded hd. of Zeus Ammon l. ℞. As last. *B.M.C. 9.* 45 ..   £500

3224 *Bronze Coinage.* 4th Cent. B.C. Æ 14. Laur. hd. of Apollo r.; ΚΝΩ behind. ℞. Hd. of Artemis r., wearing stephane, hair tied in top-knot; ΚΝΩ behind. *Svoronos, pl. VI,* 10. *B.M.C. 9.* 19   ..   ..   £14

3225 — Æ 9. Female hd. r., hair rolled. ℞. Hd. of Zeus r. *Svoronos, pl. VI,* 13   £10

3226 3rd Cent. B.C. Æ 14. Laur. hd. of Apollo l. ℞. Square Labyrinth; ΚΝΩ beneath. *B.M.C. 9.* 31   ..   ..   £12

3227 — Æ 11. Large star. ℞. Square Labyrinth. *B.M.C. 9.* 34   ..   ..   £11

3228   3229

3228 *Circa* 220 B.C. Æ 18. Europa seated on bull prancing l., her veil billowing out behind; two dolphins beneath; border of rays. ℞. ΚΝ — Ω — ΣΙ — ΩΝ around square Labyrinth; star above. *B.M.C. 9.* 36 ..   ..   £16
> *This type records an alliance between Knosos and Gortyna.*

3229 2nd-1st Cent. B.C. Æ 27. Laur. hd. of Zeus r.; half-thunderbolt before. ℞. Eagle stg. r., wings spread; Κ — Υ / Λ — Α / Σ in field. *B.M.C. 9.* 57 ..   ..   ..   £18

3230 — Æ 23. Laur. hd. of Zeus r. R. ΚΝΩ / Σ — I / ΩΝ above, either side, and beneath square Labyrinth. *B.M.C. 9.* 46 ..   ..   £14

3231   3234

3231 — Æ 19. Hd. of Artemis r., quiver at shoulder. R. Quiver and bow; Κ — ΝΩ / ΣΙ — ΩΝ in field. *B.M.C. 9.* 69   ..   ..   £10

3232 — Æ 15. *Obv.* Similar. R. Winged caduceus; Κ — Ν / Ω — ΣΙ / Ω — Ν in field. *B.M.C. 9.* 70 ..   ..   £8

3233 **Lyttos** (about twelve miles south-east of Knosos, Lyttos was one of the four Cretan mints which commenced striking in the 5th Cent. B.C. The town was destroyed by the Knosians in 220 B.C.). 425-400 B.C. Æ *stater*. Eagle alighting r. R. ΛVTΣΟΝ (retrograde). Boar's hd. r.; all within incuse square. *Svoronos, pl. XXI*, 1, 2   ..   £1,500

3234 — Æ *drachm. Obv.* Similar. R. ΓVΚΤΣΟΝ. Boar's hd. r.; all in linear square contained within incuse square. *B.M.C. 9.* 5   ..   ..   £600

3235 400-380 B.C. Æ *stater*. Eagle flying l. R. Forepart of boar l., within dotted square; ΛVT — Τ — ΣΟ — Ν on surrounding frame; all within incuse square. *Le Rider, pl. XXV*, 13   ..   ..   £1,250

3236   3240

3236 380-320 B.C. Æ *stater*. Eagle flying r. R. ΓVΤΤSΘΝ. Boar's hd. r.; all in dotted square contained within incuse square. *B.M.C. 9.* 1   ..   ..   ..   £750

3237 — Æ *drachm*. Similar, but eagle flying l. *B.M.C. 9.* 7   ..   ..   ..   £450

3238 — Æ *hemidrachm*. As last, but with legend ΓVΤΤSΘS. *Svoronos, pl. XXI*, 18   £300

3239 — Æ *obol*. Eagle flying r. R. Boar's hd. r., in dotted square contained within incuse square. *Svoronos, pl. XXI*, 21   ..   ..   £120

3240 320-270 B.C. Æ *stater*. Eagle flying l. R. ΛVΤΤΙ / ΟΝ (partly retrograde) above boar's hd. l.; all in dotted square contained within incuse square. *B.M.C. 9.* 10   ..   £600

3241 — Æ *drachm*. Similar, but on *rev.* boar's hd. r., and with inscription ΛV / Τ (retrograde). *B.M.C. 9.* 15   ..   ..   £400

3242 — Æ *hemidrachm*. As last, but with inscription ΛVΤΙΟΝ (retrograde). *B.M.C. 9.* 17   £250

Lyttos *continued*

3243 270-220 B.C. Æ *drachm* (*c.* 3·6 gm.). Boar's hd. r. ℞. ΛΥΤΤΙΩΝ. Eagle stg. r., wings spread. *B.M.C. 9.* 20 .. .. £225

3244   3247

3244 — Æ 17. Laur. hd. of Zeus r., monogram before. ℞. ΛΥΤΤΙΩΝ. Eagle stg. r., wings spread; boar's hd. r. in field to r., monogram between eagle's legs. *B.M.C. 9.* 23-5 £12

3245 — Æ 14. Eagle flying r. ℞. ΛΥΤ / ΤΙΩΝ above and below boar's hd. l. *B.M.C. 9.* 29-30 £11

3246 — Æ 13. Helmeted hd. of Athena r. ℞. ΛΥΤ above prow of galley r. *B.M.C. 9.* 21-2 £9

3247 **Kydonia** (a coastal city of some importance, in the north-west of the island, Kydonia was colonized from Aigina and may have been the first Cretan mint. Silver coins of Aiginetan type, though with the addition of a crescent in *obv.* or *rev.* field, have been found on Crete and are conjecturally attributed to Kydonia). 5th-4th Cent. B.C. Æ *triobol.* Tortoise; the segments of its shell represented by large pellets. ℞. Incuse square of 'skew' pattern; crescent in one of the depressions. *Le Rider, pl. XXVIII,* 8 .. £350

3248 — Æ *obol.* Similar, but the 'skew' pattern more formalized, with the two principal lines of division crossing at right angles; no crescent on *rev. Le Rider, pl. XXVIII,* 10 £150

3249 320-270 B.C. Æ *stater.* Hd. of nymph r., hair rolled and wreathed with vine; monogram behind. ℞. ΚΥΔΩΝ behind naked figure of Kydon stg. l., stringing bow; hound at his feet. *B.M.C. 9.* 1 .. .. £1,400

3250   3251

3250 — — Hd. of young Dionysos (?) l., wreathed with ivy. ℞. Hound stg. l., suckling infant Kydon; ΚΥΔΩΝ in ex. *B.M.C. 9.* 7 .. .. £1,750

3251 — Æ *drachm.* Hd. of Athena r., in crested Corinthian helmet. ℞. As last, but with star in field above. *B.M.C. 9.* 9 .. .. £600

3252 — Æ *trihemiobol. Obv.* Similar to 3250. ℞. Three crescents around κ. *B.M.C. 9.* 11 £120

3253 — Æ *obol.* Hd. of Demeter r., wreathed with corn. ℞. ΚΥΔΩ. Amphora. *B.M.C. 9.* 14 .. .. £120

3254 2nd-1st Cent. (before 67 B.C.). Æ *tetradrachm.* Hd. of Athena Parthenos r., wearing richly ornamented triple-crested helmet; ΑΙΘΩΝ before. ℞. Owl stg. r., hd. facing, on prostrate amphora; κ — ΥΔ / Ω — ΝΙΑ in upper field; hound r., suckling infant, in field to r.; all within olive-wreath. *B.M.C. 9.* 21 .. .. £1,250

This issue is imitated from the contemporary 'New Style' coinage of Athens.

3255

3257

3255 — — Hd. of Artemis / Diktynna r., bow and quiver at shoulder; Π — A / Σ — I / Ω — N in field. ℞. Artemis / Diktynna stg. facing, hd. l., holding long torch, hound at her feet; KY — ΔΩ / NIA — TA / N in field; all within laurel-wreath. *B.M.C. 9.* 22 .. £2,000

3256 — *Æ drachm?* (*c.* 2·8 gm.). Laur. hd. of Apollo r., quiver at shoulder. ℞. ΚΥΔΩΝΙΑΤΑΝ. Hound stg. r., suckling infant Kydon; thunderbolt above. *Svoronos, pl. X,* 2 £300

3257 *Bronze Coinage.* 4th-3rd Cent. B.C. Æ 11. Hd. of Pan (?) r., horned. ℞. ΚΥΔΩ. Hound seated r. *B.M.C. 9.* 16 .. .. £11

3258 2nd-1st Cent. B.C. Æ 17. Hd. of young Dionysos r., wreathed with ivy. ℞. ΚΥ / ΔΩ above and below crescent. *B.M.C. 9.* 30 .. .. £10

3259 — Æ 15. Owl stg. r., hd. facing; A — P in field. ℞. As last, but star within crescent. *B.M.C. 9.* 25 .. .. £9

3260 — Æ 13. Diad. hd. of Artemis r. ℞. Bunch of grapes; K — Y / Δ — Ω in field. *B.M.C. 9.* 29 .. .. £7

3261

3265

3261 **Allaria** (a coastal town of western Crete). 330-270 B.C. *Æ drachm.* Hd. of Athena r., in crested Corinthian helmet. ℞. ΑΛΛΑΡΙΩΤΑΝ (retrograde) to r. of naked Herakles stg. facing, resting on club and holding lion's skin. *B.M.C. 9.* 2 .. .. .. £800

3262 **Anopolis** (on the southern coast of western Crete). 2nd-1st Cent. B.C. Æ 23. Crude hd. of Apollo (?) r. ℞. A͞N / Ω and palm-branch within circle of pellets. *Svoronos, pl. I,* 6 .. .. £22

3263 — Æ 12. Large A͞N. ℞. Large Ω. *Svoronos, pl. I,* 4.. .. .. .. £15

3264 **Apollonia** (site not certainly known, perhaps near Knosos). 3rd Cent. B.C. Æ 13. Hd. of Apollo r. ℞. ΑΠΟΛ. Stern of ship, with aplustre. *Hist. Num., p.* 458. (*British Museum*) £18

3265 **Aptera** (on the north coast of western Crete, a few miles east of Kydonia). 330-270 B.C. *Æ stater.* Hd. of Artemis r., hair rolled and wearing stephane; ΑΠΤΕΡΑΙΩΝ before. ℞. ΠΤΟΛΙΟΙΚΟΣ. Armed warrior stg. l., holding spear and shield, r. hand raised towards sacred tree before him; monogram in field to l. *B.M.C. 9.* 3 .. .. £1,400

Aptera *continued*

3266 — Æ *hemidrachm.* Hd. of Artemis r., hair rolled. ℞. AΠΤ / APA above and below strung bow. *B.M.C. 9.* 4 .. .. £250

3267 2nd-1st Cent. (before 67 B.C.). Æ *stater.* Laur. hd. of Apollo r. ℞. AΠΤΑΡΑΙΩΝ to l. of naked warrior stg. facing, holding spear and shield. *Svoronos, pl. II*, 1 .. £1,100

3268   3271

3268 — Æ *hemidrachm.* Hd. of Artemis r., hair rolled and bound with cord. ℞. AΠΤΑΡΑΙΩΝ. Apollo seated l. on rock, holding patera and resting l. arm on lyre. *B.M.C. 9.* 9 £200

3269 — — Laur. hd. of Zeus r. ℞. AΠΤΑΡΑΙΩΝ. Hermes stg. l., holding caduceus. *B.M.C. 9.* 10 .. .. £200

3270 *Bronze Coinage.* 4th-3rd Cent. B.C. Æ 13. Hd. of Artemis r., hair rolled. ℞. Similar to 3266. *B.M.C. 9.* 6-7 .. .. £12

3271 2nd-1st Cent. B.C. Æ 19. Hd. of Artemis l., wearing stephane. ℞. AΠΤΑΡΑΙΩΝ. Race-torch. *B.M.C. 9.* 12 .. .. £13

3272 — Æ 15. *Obv.* Similar, but hd. r. ℞. Warrior advancing l., holding spear and shield; in field, A — Π / T — A / P — AI / ΩN. *B.M.C. 9.* 20-22 .. .. £10

3273 — Æ 14. Hd. of Artemis r., hair bound with cord. ℞. Bee; in field, AΠ — TA / P — AI / Ω — N. *B.M.C. 9.* 16 .. .. £11

3274   3277

3274 **The Arkades** (a people of central Crete, occupying territory to the north-east of Priansos). 330-270 B.C. Æ *drachm.* Hd. of Zeus Ammon r. ℞. APKAΔΩN. Athena stg. facing, hd. r., holding spear and resting on shield. *B.M.C. 9.* 1-2 .. .. .. £600

3275 — Æ 16. *Obv.* Similar. ℞. APK monogram within laurel-wreath. *Svoronos, pl. II,* 19 £16

3276 **Arsinoe** (the name given to the north-coast city of Rhithymna in honour of Arsinoe III of Egypt). After 222 B.C. Æ 15. Hd. of Athena r., in crested Corinthian helmet. ℞. APΣI between two dolphins. *B.M.C. 9.* 5 .. .. £14

3277 **Axos** (situated between Mt. Ida and the northern coast of Crete). 380-330 B.C. Æ *stater.* Laur. hd. of Apollo r. ℞. Tripod; to l., AKEΞON (retrograde) preceded by digamma. *B.M.C. 9., p.* 59, 1 (*mis-attributed to Naxos*) £1,750

3278 — Æ *drachm.* Similar, but without inscription on *rev. B.M.C. 9., p.* 59, 2 (*mis-attributed to Naxos*) £650

3279 320-270 B.C. Æ *stater.* Laur. hd. of Apollo r. ℞. Tripod; A — Ξ / Ω — I / N between legs; thunderbolt in field to l. *Svoronos, pl. III,* 1 .. .. £2,000

3280 — Æ *drachm.* *Obv.* Similar. ℞. FAΞ / IΩN either side of tripod. *Svoronos, pl. III,* 2 £800

3281 — Æ *obol.* Similar. *B.M.C. 9.* 1 .. .. £150

3281   3282

3282 3rd-2nd Cent. B.C. Æ 19. Laur. hd. of Zeus r. ℞. CAΞI / ΩN either side of tripod;
monograms beneath and in field to r. *B.M.C. 9.* 3-4 ..   ..   £12

3283 — — *Obv.* Similar. ℞. A — Ξ either side of thunderbolt. *B.M.C. 9.* 12 ..   £13

3284 **Biannos** (a few miles east of Priansos). 2nd Cent. B.C. Æ 15. Hd. of Artemis (?) r.
℞. BIANI (retrograde). Rose. *Svoronos, pl. III,* 15 ..   ..   £17

3285 **Keraia** (in the interior of western Crete, south-west of Kydonia and Aptera). Before
270 B.C. Æ *drachm.* Hd. of Artemis l., wearing head-dress composed of horns of Cretan
goats; quiver at shoulder. ℞. KEPAITAN between arrow-head and spear-head; all within
wreath. *Svoronos, pl. IV,* 16 ..   ..   £1,000

3286 — Æ 18. Laur. hd. of Apollo r. ℞. Spear-head and arrow-head; K — Є in field.
Svoronos, pl. IV, 18..   ..   ..   £18

3287   3290

3287 **Chersonasos** (situated on the coast of central Crete, north of Lyttos, Chersonasos
possessed a temple dedicated to Britomartis, a Cretan goddess who became equated with
Artemis). 330-270 B.C. Æ *stater.* Laur. hd. of Britomartis r., hair tied in top-knot.
℞. Apollo seated r. on omphalos, holding plectrum and lyre; XEPΣONAΣION behind and
above, thymiaterion before. *B.M.C. 9.* 1 ..   ..   £1,400

3288 — — *Obv.* Similar, but hd. l. ℞. XEPΣONAΣIΩN. Naked Herakles striding l., wielding
club, lion's skin over l. arm. *B.M.C. 9.* 3 ..   ..   £1,200

3289 3rd-2nd Cent. B.C. Æ 18. Hd. of Athena r., in crested Corinthian helmet. ℞. XEP
above prow l. *B.M.C. 9.* 7 ..   ..   £14

3290 — Æ 15. Large XEP monogram. ℞. Eagle stg. l., wings open. *B.M.C. 9.* 12-13   £12

3291 **Eleutherna** (an important inland town of central Crete, a few miles north-east of
Sybrita). *Circa* 350 B.C. Æ *stater.* Naked Apollo advancing l., holding stone and bow,
hound at feet; before and behind, tree. ℞. EΛEVΘEP (retrograde) behind Artemis advancing
r., discharging arrow from bow, hound at feet; all within dotted square. *Svoronos, pl. XI,*
..   ..   £1,750

Eleutherna *continued*

3292 330-300 B.C. Æ *stater*. Laur. hd. of Apollo r., of poor style. R. ΕΛΕVΘΕΝΝΑΙΟΝ (retrograde). Naked Apollo stg. facing, hd. l., holding bow and stone (?); all in dotted square within incuse square. *B.M.C. 9.* 1 .. .. £1,000

3293 — Æ *drachm*. Bust of Apollo r. within laurel-wreath. R. Similar to last, but with legend ΕΛΕ in field to l. *B.M.C. 9.* 4 .. .. £400

3294 — Æ *hemidrachm*. Similar. *Svoronos, pl. XI,* 11 .. .. £200

3295 — Æ *trihemiobol*. Hd. of Apollo (?) r., of crude style. R. ΕΛΕV monogram. *B.M.C. 9.* 5 .. .. £140

3296 300-270 B.C. Æ *stater*. Laur. hd. of Zeus r. R. Naked Apollo stg. l., holding stone and bow; to l., ΕΛΕV — ΘΕ. *B.M.C. 9.* 3 .. .. £900

3297 — Æ *drachm*. Laur. hd. of Apollo r. R. ΕΛΕV — ΘΕΡ / ΝΑΙΩΝ either side of naked Apollo stg. facing, hd. l., holding stone and bow. *Svoronos, pl. XII,* 2 .. .. £400

3298 — Æ *obol*. Hd. of Apollo (?) r., of crude style. R. Naked Apollo stg. facing, holding bow and stone in uplifted l. hand. *B.M.C. 9.* 6 .. .. £110

3299   3301

3299 3rd-2nd Cent. B.C. Æ 18. Laur. hd. of Apollo r.; border of rays. R. ΕΛΕVΘΕΡΝΑΙΩΝ Apollo seated l. on omphalos, holding stone, lyre at side; monogram in field to l. *B.M.C. 9.* 13-17 .. .. £14

3300 — Æ 11. Laur. hd. of Apollo r. R. ΕΛΕVΘΕΡΝΑΙ. Lyre. *Svoronos, pl. XII,* 6 £11

3301 **Elyros** (an inland town of some importance in the south-west of the island). 330-270 B.C. Æ *drachm*. Goat's hd. r., arrow-head l. beneath; in field, ΕΛ — Y / PIO — N. R. Bee; rose in field to l. *B.M.C. 9.* 1 .. .. £650

3302 — — Goat stg. r., r. forefoot raised and resting on tree; in ex., ΕΛΥΡΙΟΝ. R. Bee; M — I in field. *Svoronos, pl. XII,* 13 .. .. £750

3303 3rd-2nd Cent. B.C. Æ 12. Forepart of goat r., looking back; H — Λ in field. R. Bee; H — Λ in field. *Svoronos, pl. XII,* 14-17 .. .. £15

3304 **Hierapytna** (in eastern Crete, Hierapytna was situated on the southern coast and appears to have been a place of considerable commercial importance in late Hellenistic times). 330-270 B.C. Æ *stater*. Laur. hd. of Zeus r. R. Date-palm at foot of which, to r., eagle stg. r., looking back; IEPA in field to l. *B.M.C. 9.* 1 .. .. .. £1,400

3305 — Æ *obol*. Similar. *Svoronos, pl. XVII*, 8 .. .. £125

3306 2nd-1st Cent. (before 67 B.C.). Æ *tetradrachm*. Hd. of Athena Parthenos r., wearing richly ornamented triple-crested helmet. R. Owl stg. r., hd. facing, on prostrate amphora; I — E / P — AΠ / Y / Z — HNO / ΦI in field; eagle to r.; all within olive-wreath. *Svoronos, pl. XVIII*, 1.. .. .. £1,250

This issue is imitated from the contemporary 'New Style' coinage of Athens.

3307 — — Turreted hd. of City-goddess r. R. Date-palm at foot of which, to r., eagle stg. l.; IEPAΠY / TNIΩN to r.; ΦAY / OΣ and monogram to l. *B.M.C. 9.* 2 .. .. £1,250

3308 — Æ *didrachm*. *Obv*. Similar. R. Date-palm at foot of which, to l., eagle stg. r.; APIΣT / AΓOPA / Σ to r.; IEPAΠY below; all within laurel-wreath. *B.M.C. 9.* 3 .. £400

3309   3313

3309 — Æ *drachm*. Similar, but with IMEP / AIOΣ in *rev*. field to r. *B.M.C. 9.* 9 £275

3310 *Bronze Coinage*. 3rd Cent. B.C. Æ 14. Laur. hd. of Zeus l. R. Date-palm; to l., monogram of IEPAΠY; to r., aplustre. *B.M.C. 9., p.* 75, 1 (*mis-attributed to Pyranthus*)

£14

3311 2nd-1st Cent. (before 67 B.C.). Æ 20. Turreted hd. of City-goddess r. R. Date-palm; to l., monogram of IEPAΠY; to r., eagle stg. l. *Svoronos, pl. XVII*, 21 .. £15

3312 — Æ 17. Star. R. Date-palm; IE — PA / ΦA — MA in field. *Svoronos, pl. XVII*, 22-3 .. .. £14

3313 **Hyrtakina** (an inland town of western Crete, a short distance south-west of Elyros). 330-270 B.C. Æ *drachm*. YPTAKINIΩN. Goat's hd. r.; arrow-head behind. R. Bee; rose in field to r. *B.M.C. 9.* 1 .. .. £750

3314   3318

3314 **Itanos** (situated in the extreme north-east of the island). 380-320 B.C. Æ *stater*. Triton r., striking downwards with trident and holding fish. R. Stellate pattern in linear square; all within incuse square. *B.M.C. 9.* 1 .. .. £1,750

3315 — — *Obv.* Similar. R. Two sea-monsters face to face. *Svoronos, pl. XVIII,* 37 £2,000

3316 — Æ *hemidrachm.* As last, but the *rev.* type is enclosed in linear square within incuse square. *B.M.C. 9.* 7 .. .. £300

3317 — Æ *obol. Obv.* Similar. R. Large star. *B.M.C. 9.* 10 .. .. .. £120

3318 320-270 B.C. Æ *stater.* Triton r., striking downwards at fish with trident held in r. hand, l. hand raised. R. ITANION between two sea-monsters face to face. *B.M.C. 9.* 5 £1,500

3319 — — Hd. of Athena l., wearing crested Athenian helmet. R. Eagle stg. l., looking back; to l., ITANIΩN; to r., Triton; all within incuse square. *Svoronos, pl. XIX,* 17 £750

3320   3322

3320 — Æ *drachm.* Similar. *B.M.C. 9.* 13 .. .. £350

3321 — Æ *hemidrachm.* Hd. of Athena r., wearing crested Athenian helmet. R. Eagle stg. l., looking back; to r., ITANIΩN; all within incuse square. *B.M.C. 9.* 17-18 .. £200

3322 — Æ *obol. Obv.* As 3319. R. Large star. *B.M.C. 9.* 19 .. .. .. £100

3323 — Æ 14. Similar, but the star on *rev.* is enclosed by circle, thus forming a wheel. *Svoronos, pl. XIX,* 27 .. .. £15

3324 **Lappa** (situated south-west of Rhithymna, in the interior of western Crete). 330-270 B.C. Æ *stater.* Hd. of Artemis r., ΛAΠΠAION (retrograde) before. R. Apollo seated r., r. hand resting on globe at side, holding lyre in l.; AΠOΛΛON behind. *Boston Museum Catalogue* 1282 .. .. (*Unique*)

3325 — Æ *drachm.* Female hd. r., hair rolled. R. Bull's hd. facing, its r. horn curled downwards. *Svoronos, pl. XIX,* 30 .. .. £750

3326 — Æ *obol.* Bull's hd. facing, its l. horn curled downwards. R. Large Λ. *Svoronos, pl. XIX,* 33 .. .. £125

3327   3330

3327 2nd-1st Cent. (before 67 B.C.). Æ *drachm* (*c.* 3-3·5 gm.). Laur. hd. of Apollo r. ℞.
Naked Apollo stg. r., holding plectrum and lyre; to l., ΛΛΠΠΑΙ; to r., ΣΥΛΩ; ΚΟΣ in ex.
B.M.C. 9. 2 ..   ..   £200

3328 *Bronze Coinage.* 3rd Cent. B.C. Æ 13. *Obv.* As 3326. ℞. Female hd. r. *Svoronos,*
pl. XIX, 31 ..   ..   £14

3329 2nd-1st Cent. (before 67 B.C.). Æ 27. Hd. of Poseidon r. ℞. ΛΛΠΠΑΙΩΝ. Trident-
head, with two dolphins between the prongs. *Svoronos, pl. XX,* 1 ..   ..   £17

3330 — Æ 22. Laur. hd. of Apollo r. ℞. ΛΛΠΠΑΙΩΝ. Lyre. *B.M.C. 9.* 3   ..   £16

3331 — Æ 14. Hd. of Artemis r. ℞. Λ — Λ either side of tripod. *Svoronos, pl. XX,* 3 £12

3332   3334

3332 **Latos** (a coastal town of eastern Crete, on the shores of the Bay of Mirabello. Another
town, of the same name, was situated a short distance inland). 2nd-1st Cent. (before
67 B.C.). Æ 14. Hd. of Artemis l., hair tied in top-knot. ℞. Hermes advancing r.,
holding caduceus; ΛΑΤΙΩΝ behind. *B.M.C. 9.* 1 ..   ..   £15

3333 — Æ 10. *Obv.* Similar. ℞. Bust of Hermes l., wearing petasos; Λ — Λ in field; all
within incuse square. *Svoronos, pl. XX,* 21   ..   ..   £13

3334 **Lisos** (a coastal town in the extreme south-west of the island, a close neighbour of both
Hyrtakina and Elyros). 4th Cent. B.C. Æ *obol* (*c.* 1·03 gm.). Dove flying r., ΙΛ above;
border of rays. ℞. ΑΛΕΞΑΝΔΡΟΥ. Dove flying r. *Svoronos, pl. XX,* 33. (*British
Museum*) £600

3335 3rd Cent. B.C. Æ 13. Goat's hd. r.; Λ — Ι in field. ℞. Bee; Λ — Ι in field. *Svoronos,*
pl. XX, 35 ..   ..   £15

3336 2nd-1st Cent. (before 67 B.C.). Æ 20. Caps of the Dioskouroi. ℞. Bow and quiver;
ΛΙΣΙ to l. *Svoronos, pl. XX,* 37 ..   ..   £16

3337 — Æ 18. Hd. of Artemis r. ℞. ΛΙΣ / ΙΩΝ (partly retrograde) above and below dolphin r.
Svoronos, pl. XX, 28   ..   ..   £15

3338 **Malla** (an inland town of eastern Crete, about twelve miles north-west of Hierapytna).
2nd-1st Cent. (before 67 B.C.). Æ 15. Laur. hd. of Zeus l. ℞. Eagle stg. r.; ΜΑΛ
above. *Svoronos, pl. XXII,* 19   ..   ..   £16

3339 **Moda** (in the far west of the island, in the vicinity of Polyrhenion). 330-270 B.C. Æ
stater. Hd. of Zeus r. ℞. ΜΩΔΑΙΩΝ. Bull's hd. facing. *Svoronos, pl. XXII,* 20 £2,500

3340 **Olonte** (an important town of eastern Crete, Olonte possessed a sanctuary of the goddess Britomartis). 330-270 B.C. Æ *stater.* Hd. of Britomartis l., hair bound with tainia and wreath, quiver at shoulder. R. Zeus enthroned l., holding eagle and sceptre; ΟΛΟΝΤΙΩΝ behind, monogram before. *B.M.C. 9.* 1 .. .. £1,750
　　The reverse type is inspired by the silver coinage of Alexander the Great.

3341 — Æ *hemidrachm. Obv.* Similar. R Λ / Ο within laurel-wreath. *Svoronos, pl. XXII,* 24 £300

3342 — Æ *trihemiobol. Obv.* Similar. R. ΟΛΟΝΤ / ΙΟΝ (partly retrograde) either side of tripod. *Svoronos, pl. XXII,* 25 .. .. £150

3343 — Æ *obol. Obv.* Similar. R. Large star. *Svoronos, pl. XXII,* 26 .. .. £120

3344 3rd Cent. B.C. Æ 11. Hd. of Artemis r., hair tied in top-knot. R. Dolphin r., Ο — Λ / Ο — Ν above; all within incuse square. *B.M.C. 9.* 2 .. .. £13

3344　　　　　　　　　　　　　　　3345

3345 **Phalasarna** (a coastal town in the extreme north-west of the island). 330-270 B.C. Æ *stater.* Hd. of Artemis Diktynna r., hair bound with cord. R. Φ — Α between the prongs of trident-head. *B.M.C. 9.* 1 .. .. £1,000

3346 — Æ *drachm.* Hd. of Artemis Diktynna r., hair rolled. R. As last. *B.M.C. 9.* 4 £400

3347 — Æ *hemidrachm.* Similar. *B.M.C. 9.* 6 .. .. £225

3348 3rd Cent. B.C. Æ 23. Large Φ enclosing Λ — Α. R. As 3345. *Svoronos, pl. XXV,* 13 £17

3349 — Æ 12. Large Φ. R. Dolphin r. *B.M.C. 9.* 7 .. .. £10

3350　　　　　　　　　　　　　　　3351

3350 **Polyrhenion** (an important city in the far west of Crete, a few miles south-east of Phalasarna). 330-270 B.C. Æ *stater.* Laur. hd. of Zeus r. R. ΠΟΛ — ΥΡΗΝ — ΙΟΝ to l., above and to r. of bull's hd. facing, bound with fillet; arrow-head r. beneath; ΧΑΡΙΣΘ — ΕΝΗΣ above and to r. *B.M.C. 9.* 4, 6-7 .. .. £1,250

3351 — Æ *drachm.* ΠΟ — ΛΥΡΗΝΙ — ΟΝ to l., above and to r. of bull's hd. facing, bound with fillet. R. ΠΟΛΥ / ΡΗΝΙ either side of spear-head. *B.M.C. 9.* 9.. .. .. £350

3352 — Æ *hemidrachm.* Hd. of Artemis Diktynna l., hair rolled; before, ΠΥΘΟΛΩΡΟΥ. R. Bull's hd. facing, bound with fillet. *B.M.C. 9.* 1-2 .. .. £225

3353   3357

3353 2nd-1st Cent. (before 67 B.C.). Æ *tetradrachm.* Young male hd. r., bound with tainia,
bow and quiver at shoulder. R. ΠΟΛΥΡΗ / ΝΙΩΝ behind and before female figure seated
l., holding Nike; thunderbolt beneath. *B.M.C. 9.* 18 .. .. £1,750

3354 — Æ *hemidrachm.* Dr. bust of Artemis Diktynna three-quarter face to r., bow and
quiver at shoulder. R. ΠΟΛΥΡΗ / ΝΙΩΝ either side of naked Apollo stg. l., holding arrow
and bow. *B.M.C. 9.* 20-22 .. .. £175

3355 *Bronze Coinage.* 3rd Cent. B.C. Æ 16. Shield, of Boeotian type. R. Goat's hd. r.,
arrow-head behind; in field, ΠΟ — ΛΥ / Ρ — Η. *Svoronos, pl. XXV,* 33 .. £16

3356 — Æ 18. Bull's hd. facing. R. ΠΟΛ / ΥΡΗ either side of spear-head. *B.M.C. 9.* 14
£15

3357 — Æ 12. Circular shield, ornamented with bull's hd. R. Arrow-head, upwards;
Π — Ο / Λ — Υ in field. *B.M.C. 9.* 17 .. .. £13

3358 2nd-1st Cent. (before 67 B.C.). Æ 13. Hd. of Athena r., in Corinthian helmet. R.
Owl stg. r. on amphora; Π — Ο / Λ — Υ in field; all within wreath. *Svoronos, pl. XXVI,* 28
£12

3359 — Æ 10. Dr. bust of Hermes r., wearing petasos. R. Caduceus; Π — Ο / Λ — Υ in
field. *Svoronos, pl. XXVI,* 29 .. .. £10

3360   3363

3360 **Praisos** (the most important city of eastern Crete, Praisos was destroyed by Hierapytna
about the middle of the 2nd Cent. B.C.). 350-325 B.C. Æ *stater.* Naked Herakles
kneeling r., firing arrow from bow. R. Eagle alighting r., ΠΡΑΙ Ϟ below; all in linear square
within incuse square. *B.M.C. 9.* 2 .. .. £1,800

3361 — Æ *hemidrachm.* Similar, but the *rev.* legend Π — Ρ — Α — Ι is in the four corners of
the linear square. *Svoronos, pl. XXVII,* 5 .. .. £350

3362 325-270 B.C. Æ *stater.* Female hd. r., wearing stephanos. R. ΠΡΑΙΣΙΟΝ above bull
butting l. *Weber* 4581 .. .. (*Unique* ?)

3363 — — Zeus Diktaios enthroned l., hd. facing, holding eagle and sceptre. R. Forepart of
goat l., looking back. *B.M.C. 9.* 6 .. .. £1,600

3364   3368

Praisos *continued*

3364 — — Laur. hd. of Apollo l. R. As last, but also with arrow-head behind and ΠΡΑΙΙΣ above. *B.M.C. 9*. 7   ..   ..   £2,000

3365 — Æ *drachm*. Laur. hd. of Apollo r. R. Naked Herakles stg. r., brandishing club and holding bow; ΠΡΑΙΣΙΩΝ before. *Svoronos, pl. XXVIII,* 7   ..   ..   ..   £750

3366 — Æ *hemidrachm*. Hd. of Demeter l., wreathed with corn. R. ΠΡΑΙΣΙ. Bee; rose in field to l. *B.M.C. 9. 13* £275

3367 — Æ *obol*. Female hd. r. R. Bull's hd. facing, ΠΡΑΙ above. *Svoronos, pl. XXVII,* 16   £120

3368 Before *circa* 148 B.C. Æ 18. Laur. hd. of Apollo r. R. ΠΡΑΙ / ϹΙΩΝ above and below thunderbolt; ϰ in field above. *B.M.C. 9. 16* £16

3369 **Priansos** (an inland town of central Crete, about eighteen miles east of Gortyna). 330-270 B.C. Æ *stater*. Persephone (?) seated l., hd. facing, caressing serpent which rears before her; to r., date-palm. R. ΠΡΙΑΝΣΙΕΩΝ. Poseidon stg. l., holding trident; dolphin above outstretched r. hand. *B.M.C. 9. 1* £1,750

3370   3371

3370 — Æ *drachm*. Hd. of Artemis (?) r., hair rolled. R. ΠΡΙΑΝΣΙΕΩΝ. Date-palm between dolphin and rudder. *B.M.C. 9. 5* £550

3371 2nd-1st Cent. (before 67 B.C.). Æ *tetradrachm*. Hd. of Athena Parthenos r., wearing richly ornamented triple-crested helmet. R. Owl stg. r., hd. facing, on prostrate amphora; Π — ΡΙ / ΑΝ — ΣΙ / ΠΥ — ΡΓΙ / Α — Σ / Κ — Λ in field; date-palm to r.; all within olive-wreath. *B.M.C. 9. 10* £1,250
    This issue is imitated from the contemporary 'New Style' coinage of Athens.

3372 *Bronze Coinage*. 3rd-2nd Cent. B.C. Æ 15. Hd. of Artemis (?) r., hair rolled. R. ΠΡ — Ι either side of date-palm. *B.M.C. 9. 9* £14

3373 — Æ 17. *Obv*. Similar. R. ΠΡΙΑΝ. Poseidon striding l., brandishing trident. *B.M.C. 9. 11* £14

3374 3375

3374 **Rhaukos** (situated near the centre of the island, between Knosos and Gortyna, Rhaukos was eventually attacked and destroyed by these two cities, *circa* 166 B.C.). 350-330 B.C. *Æ stater.* Naked Poseidon stg. facing, hd. r., holding trident; his horse stg. r. in background. R. PAYK / ION (retrograde) either side of trident-head; all within incuse square. *B.M.C. 9.* 1 ..   ..   £800

3375 330-270 B.C. *Æ stater.* Similar, but of more advanced style; monogram in field to r. on *obv.*, and *rev.* legend is divided PAY / KION (no incuse square). *B.M.C. 9.* 5 ..   £850

3376 — *Æ drachm.* Hd. of Poseidon r. R. PAVKIΩN. Trident-head, with two dolphins between the prongs. *Svoronos, pl. XXIX,* 17 ..   ..   £450

3377 — *Æ hemidrachm.* Laur. hd. of Poseidon l., trident at shoulder, monogram before. R. PAYKION between two dolphins. *Svoronos, pl. XXIX,* 25 ..   ..   ..   £250

3378 3381

3378 — *Æ obol.* Hd. of Demeter l., wreathed with corn. R. PAY / KION either side of trident-head. *B.M.C. 9.* 6 ..   ..   £125

3379 3rd-2nd Cent. (before 166 B.C.). Æ 20. Laur. hd. of Poseidon r. R. PAYKIΩN. Trident-head between two dolphins. *B.M.C. 9.* 8 ..   ..   £15

3380 — Æ 18. PAYKIΩN. Horse's hd. r. R. Dolphin r., trident above. *B.M.C. 9.* 7   £14

3381 **Rhithymna** (on the northern coast of central Crete, Rhithymna was re-named Arsinoe in 222 B.C.). 330-270 B.C. *Æ stater.* Laur. hd. of Apollo r. R. Naked Apollo stg. facing, holding stone and bow; PI in field to l. *B.M.C. 9.* 1 ..   ..   ..   £2,000

3382 — *Æ drachm.* Hd. of Athena r., in Corinthian helmet. R. Trident-head between two dolphins; P — I in field. *Svoronos, p.* 310, 4 ..   ..   £450

3383 — *Æ hemidrachm.* *Obv.* Similar. R. P — I (retrograde) between the prongs of trident-head. *B.M.C. 9.* 2 ..   ..   £200

3384 Before 222 B.C. Æ 14. *Obv.* Similar. R. Two dolphins, upwards; P — I — Θ in field. *B.M.C. 9.* 3 ..   ..   £14

For a later coin of Rhithymna, under the name of Arsinoe, see no. 3276.

3385 Sybrita (an inland town of central Crete, south-west of Eleutherna). *Circa* 380 B.C.
Æ *stater*. Naked Hermes seated three-quarter face to r. on rock, holding caduceus.
R. MVNDSTSΘN (retrograde). Winged hippocamp r.; all within incuse square. *Le Rider,*
pl. XXXIV, 19. (*British Museum*)   ..   ..   (*Unique ?*)

3386 360-330 B.C. Æ *stater*. Europa seated l. amid the branches of a tree, her hd. lowered
and resting on her r. hand. R. Bull seated l., looking back; above, MVNDS (retrograde).
Le Rider, pl. XXVII, 7   ..   ..   £2,500

3387 — Æ *drachm*. Hd. of Europa l. R. Bull's hd. three-quarter face to r., MV before.
Le Rider, pl. XXVII, 18   ..   ..   £450

3388 — Æ *hemidrachm*. Similar. *Le Rider, pl. XXVII,* 19. (*British Museum*)..   £250

3389 320-270 B.C. Æ *stater*. Young Dionysos, holding thyrsos, seated on panther springing
l. R. ΣYBPITIΩN. Hermes l., resting his r. foot on rock and stooping to tie his sandal;
caduceus to l. *B.M.C. 9.* 1   ..   ..   £3,500

3390   3392

3390 — — Bearded hd. of Dionysos r., wreathed with ivy; bunch of grapes before. R.
ΣYBPITIΩN. Hd. of Hermes r., wearing petasos; caduceus before. *Svoronos, pl. XXX,*
15-16   ..   ..   £3,500

3391 — Æ *drachm*. Apollo (?) seated l. on rock, examining bow. R. ΣYBPI. Hd. of Hermes
l., petasos suspended behind neck. *Svoronos, pl. XXX,* 19   ..   ..   ..   £1,250

3392 3rd-2nd Cent. B.C. Æ 13. Hd. of Hermes r., wearing petasos, caduceus at shoulder.
R. Jawbone of animal, ΣYBPITIΩN below. *B.M.C. 9.* 3-4   ..   ..   ..   £13

3393   3395

3393 Tarrha (on the south coast of western Crete). 330-270 B.C. Æ *drachm*. Goat's hd.
r.; arrow-head beneath, pellet behind; T — A / P in field. R. Bee. *Weber* 4597   £850

3394 — Æ 12. Goat's hd. r. R. Bee; TA monogram beneath. *Svoronos, pl. XXX,* 28   £14

3395 Tylisos (an inland city of central Crete, a few miles north of Rhaukos). 330-270 B.C.
Æ *stater*. Hd. of Hera r., wearing stephanos ornamented with floral devices. R.
TYΛIΣIΩN (retrograde). Naked Apollo stg. l., holding goat's hd. and bow; arrow-head in
field to l. *B.M.C. 9.* 1   ..   ..   £1,750

INDEX

This alphabetical listing includes geographical names (countries, districts, towns, tribes, etc.) as well as the personal names of rulers and die-engravers. The second category are shown in italic type for ease of recognition. Names of gods and goddesses, also in italics, are included; the page references in this case being to the detailed notes on deities at the beginning of the Catalogue, not to their appearances on the listed coins.

Where more than one page reference is given the entries are further differentiated thus:
(A) following a page number indicates the separate listing of *Archaic* issues for that mint.

(Æ) indicates the separate listing of *bronze* issues for that mint (for Italy and Sicily).

A page reference in italic type refers to the *map* on which the exact position of the town may be located.

is. = island.

GRAMMES-GRAINS CONVERSION TABLE

GRAMMES	GRAINS	GRAMMES	GRAINS	GRAMMES	GRAINS
·06	1	2·00	31	7	108
·13	2	2·25	35	8	123
·19	3	2·50	39	9	139
·26	4	2·75	42	10	154
·32	5	3·00	46	12	185
·39	6	3·25	50	15	231
·45	7	3·50	54	20	309
·52	8	3·75	58	25	386
·58	9	4·00	62	30	463
·65	10	4·25	66	40	617
·78	12	4·50	70	50	772
·90	14	4·75	73	60	926
1·00	15	5·00	77	70	1081
1·25	19	5·25	81	80	1234
1·50	23	5·50	85	90	1388
1·75	27	5·75	89	100	1543
		6·00	93		

INCHES-MILLIMETRES CONVERSION TABLE

INCHES	MM.	INCHES	MM.	INCHES	MM.
0·3	8	0·85	22	1·4	36
0·35	9	0·9	23	1·45	37
0·4	10	0·95	24	1·5	38
0·45	11	1·0	26	1·55	40
0·5	13	1·05	27	1·6	41
0·55	14	1·1	28	1·65	42
0·6	15	1·15	29	1·7	43
0·65	17	1·2	31	1·75	44
0·7	18	1·25	32	1·8	46
0·75	19	1·3	33	1·85	47
0·8	20	1·35	34	1·9	48